Race, Ethnicity, and Economic Statistics for the 21st Century

NATIONAL BUREAU *of* ECONOMIC RESEARCH

Studies in Income and Wealth
Volume 84

NBER
NATIONAL BUREAU *of* ECONOMIC RESEARCH

Race, Ethnicity, and Economic Statistics for the 21st Century

Edited by **Randall Akee, Lawrence F. Katz, and Mark A. Loewenstein**

The University of Chicago Press

Chicago and London

The University of Chicago Press, Chicago 60637
The University of Chicago Press, Ltd., London

Published 2026
Printed in the United States of America

35 34 33 32 31 30 29 28 27 26 1 2 3 4 5

ISBN-13: 978-0-226-84378-0 (cloth)
ISBN-13: 978-0-226-84379-7 (ebook)
DOI: https://doi.org/10.7208/chicago/9780226843797.001.0001

Library of Congress Cataloging-in-Publication Data

Names: Conference on Research in Income and Wealth (2024 : Alexandria, Va.) creator | Akee, Randall K. Q. (Randall Kekoa Quinones) editor | Katz, Lawrence F. editor | Loewenstein, Mark A. editor
Title: Race, ethnicity, and economic statistics for the 21st century / edited by Randall Akee, Lawrence F. Katz, and Mark A. Loewenstein.
Other titles: Studies in income and wealth v. 84.
Description: Chicago : The University of Chicago Press, 2026. | Series: Studies in income and wealth ; volume 84 | "this volume contains revised versions of the papers presented at the Conference on Research in Income and Wealth titled "Race, Ethnicity, and Economic Statistics for the 21st Century," held in Alexandria, VA, on March 14–15, 2024."—Prefatory note. | Includes bibliographical references and index.
Identifiers: LCCN 2025025155 | ISBN 9780226843780 cloth | ISBN 9780226843797 ebook
Subjects: LCSH: Ethnicity—United States—Statistics—Congresses | Race—Demographic aspects—United States—Statistics—Congresses | Economics—Statistical methods—Congresses | United States—Economic conditions—Statistics—Congresses | United States—Population—Statistics—Congresses | LCGFT: Conference papers and proceedings
Classification: LCC HC103 .C737 2026 | DDC 330.973/00112—dc23/eng/20250820
LC record available at https://lccn.loc.gov/2025025155

⊗ This paper meets the requirements of ANSI/NISO Z39.48-1992 (Permanence of Paper).

Authorized Representative for EU General Product Safety Regulation (GPSR) queries: **Easy Access System Europe**—Mustamäe tee 50, 10621 Tallinn, Estonia, gpsr.requests@easproject.com
Any other queries: https://press.uchicago.edu/press/contact.html

Relation of the Directors to the Work and Publications of the NBER

1. The object of the NBER is to ascertain and present to the economics profession, and to the public more generally, important economic facts and their interpretation in a scientific manner without policy recommendations. The Board of Directors is charged with the responsibility of ensuring that the work of the NBER is carried on in strict conformity with this object.

2. The President shall establish an internal review process to ensure that book manuscripts proposed for publication DO NOT contain policy recommendations. This shall apply both to the proceedings of conferences and to manuscripts by a single author or by one or more coauthors but shall not apply to authors of comments at NBER conferences who are not NBER affiliates.

3. No book manuscript reporting research shall be published by the NBER until the President has sent to each member of the Board a notice that a manuscript is recommended for publication and that in the President's opinion it is suitable for publication in accordance with the above principles of the NBER. Such notification will include a table of contents and an abstract or summary of the manuscript's content, a list of contributors if applicable, and a response form for use by Directors who desire a copy of the manuscript for review. Each manuscript shall contain a summary drawing attention to the nature and treatment of the problem studied and the main conclusions reached.

4. No volume shall be published until forty-five days have elapsed from the above notification of intention to publish it. During this period a copy shall be sent to any Director requesting it, and if any Director objects to publication on the grounds that the manuscript contains policy recommendations, the objection will be presented to the author(s) or editor(s). In case of dispute, all members of the Board shall be notified, and the President shall appoint an ad hoc committee of the Board to decide the matter; thirty days additional shall be granted for this purpose.

5. The President shall present annually to the Board a report describing the internal manuscript review process, any objections made by Directors before publication or by anyone after publication, any disputes about such matters, and how they were handled.

6. Publications of the NBER issued for informational purposes concerning the work of the Bureau, or issued to inform the public of the activities at the Bureau, including but not limited to the NBER Digest and Reporter, shall be consistent with the object stated in paragraph 1. They shall contain a specific disclaimer noting that they have not passed through the review procedures required in this resolution. The Executive Committee of the Board is charged with the review of all such publications from time to time.

7. NBER working papers and manuscripts distributed on the Bureau's web site are not deemed to be publications for the purpose of this resolution, but they shall be consistent with the object stated in paragraph 1. Working papers shall contain a specific disclaimer noting that they have not passed through the review procedures required in this resolution. The NBER's web site shall contain a similar disclaimer. The President shall establish an internal review process to ensure that the working papers and the web site do not contain policy recommendations, and shall report annually to the Board on this process and any concerns raised in connection with it.

8. Unless otherwise determined by the Board or exempted by the terms of paragraphs 6 and 7, a copy of this resolution shall be printed in each NBER publication as described in paragraph 2 above.

Contents

Prefatory Note

This volume contains revised versions of the papers presented at the Conference on Research in Income and Wealth titled "Race, Ethnicity, and Economic Statistics for the 21st Century," held in Alexandria, VA, on March 14–15, 2024.

We are grateful for support for this project from the U.S. Census Bureau through an award to Reveal Global Consulting. Support for the general activities of the Conference on Research in Income and Wealth is provided by the following agencies: Bureau of Economic Analysis, Bureau of Labor Statistics, the Census Bureau, the Board of Governors of the Federal Reserve System, the Statistics of Income/Internal Revenue Service, and Statistics Canada.

We thank Randall Akee, Lawrence F. Katz, and Mark Loewenstein, who served as conference organizers and as editors of the volume.

Introduction

Randall Akee, Lawrence F. Katz,
and Mark A. Loewenstein

The findings from the 2020 US Census of Population in comparison to those of the 2010 Census illustrate the increasing racial and ethnic diversity of the population in the United States, as well as a rise in the number of people who identify as multiracial (Jensen et al. 2023). The US Census Bureau has developed a series of innovative reports and interactive data visualizations to help the public explore and analyze various measures of racial and ethnic composition and diversity measures, such as the diversity index, prevalence maps, prevalence rankings, and diffusion scores.[1]

As a result of the increasing racial and ethnic diversity of the population, race and ethnicity categories and definitions may need to be updated if the demographic statistics on which government officials, business decision-makers, and private citizens rely are to clearly present the changing US population. This conference volume explores the production of meaningful and innovative economic statistics by race and ethnicity that accurately depict the complex racial and ethnic diversity of the US population in the 21st century. Papers in this volume examine the consequences for economic analyses of different measurement choices concerning race and ethnicity, introduce new datasets with richer demographic information, compare mea-

Randall Akee is a professor in the Department of Public Policy and American Indian Studies and Chair of the America Indian Studies Interdepartmental Program at the University of California, Los Angeles, and a research associate of the National Bureau of Economic Research.

Lawrence F. Katz is the Elisabeth Allison Professor of Economics at Harvard University and a research associate of the National Bureau of Economic Research.

Mark A. Loewenstein is division chief of Employment Research and Program Development at the Bureau of Labor Statistics.

1. https://www.census.gov/newsroom/blogs/random-samplings/2021/08/measuring-racial-ethnic-diversity-2020-census.html.

sures of race and ethnicity in administrative vs. survey datasets, and apply the existing data in creative ways to better characterize the changing US workforce and illuminate important policy questions.

Accurate indicators of race and ethnicity in individual-level microdatasets are necessary to measure and understand the sources of group differences in economic and social outcomes including racial and ethnic disparities in earnings, employment, educational attainment, intergenerational mobility, and safety net program participation. Such indicators are also essential to measure the extent of racial and ethnic segregation by residential neighborhoods, occupations and firms, and schools. Comparable measures of race and ethnicity over time are needed to accurately track historical changes in group differences in economic and social outcomes and changes in racial and ethnic segregation. A key trade-off in the collection of race and ethnicity in economic statistics for the changing US population (highlighted in the papers in this volume) concerns that of using the same questions and categories over time to maintain historical consistency vs. modifying questions to better reflect contemporaneous views of racial and ethnic identity and to provide more accurate measures at a point in time.

US federal statistical agencies follow the standards on race and ethnicity set by the US Office of Management and Budget (OMB). These standards, previously revised in 1997, have guided how the federal government collects and presents data on race and ethnicity. State and local governments, school districts, and many social service organizations also often use race and ethnicity questions that follow the federal government guidelines. The 1997 OMB standards[2] identified five minimum categories: White, Black or African American, American Indian or Alaska Native, Asian, and Native Hawaiian or Other Pacific Islander. The Census Bureau has been required by Congress to include a sixth category, Some Other Race, for people who do not identify with any of the OMB race categories. Other agencies also have allowed respondents to indicate Some Other Race. For ethnicity, the 1997 OMB standards classified individuals in one of two categories: "Hispanic or Latino" or "Not Hispanic or Latino." Two separate questions, a first one on ethnicity (Hispanic or Not Hispanic) and a second one on race, typically have been used by federal agencies to implement the approach indicated by the 1997 OMB standards.

On March 29, 2024 OMB provided their final decisions on the revision of Statistical Policy Directive (SPD) No.15[3] that governs standards for the classification of federal data on race and ethnicity (US Office of Management and Budget 2024). The SPD had undergone an extensive period for comments by stakeholders and government officials. The revised standards

2. https://www.govinfo.gov/content/pkg/FR-1997-10-30/pdf/97-28653.pdf.

3. https://www.federalregister.gov/documents/2024/03/29/2024-06469/revisions-to-ombs-statistical-policy-directive-no-15-standards-for-maintaining-collecting-and.

now advise that federal statistics agencies collect race and ethnicity in a single combined question; add the new category of Middle Eastern and North African to the list of race categories; collect detailed race and ethnicity data by default; and update certain terms or definitions of race and ethnicity categories. Several chapters of this volume provide background on the demographic trends and methodological innovations that motivated the updated federal approach to collecting data on race and ethnicity, and others analyze the implications of the revisions for consistently tracking changes in US economic outcomes by race and ethnicity.

I. Background Facts

Changes in the US Racial and Ethnic Composition over US Censuses

After a long period of relative stability in the White population share from 1860 to 1970, the racial and ethnic composition of the US population changed dramatically over the past five decades, as seen in figure I.1. This figure is based on decennial US Census data from 1860 onward; we show new and expanded race and/or ethnic categories as they have been added to the US Census over the years. The proportion of the population self-reporting (or having another household member report) a race other than White has greatly increased since 1970. There also has been a large increase in the share of the population that identifies as Hispanic, reaching almost 20 percent in the 2020 US Census. These changes in measured US racial and ethnic composition have been driven by high rates of immigration and large shifts in the mix of countries of origin of immigrants away from traditional European source countries and toward the Americas and Asia since the major reform of US immigration policy in 1965 (figure I.2). They also reflect changes in US Census enumeration methods and in the societal norms that impact how individuals self-identify along race and ethnic categories.

Changes in the Country of Origin for US Immigrants Over Time

Changes in the immigrant country of origin arising from both economic and political considerations here and abroad (Abramitzky and Boustan 2017, 2022) are one important determinant of changes in the racial and ethnic composition of the United States. In figure I.2, the immigrant flows over time are represented in different shadings depending upon their origin region: Europe, Americas, Asia, Africa, Middle East, and Other regions. In the mid-19th century, immigration to the United States was drawn primarily from European countries (especially Ireland and Germany). Country-of-origin quotas in US immigration law in the 1920s in response to increased immigration from Southern and Eastern Europe and the earlier Chinese Exclusion Act of 1882 tried to cement in the earlier 19th-century pattern of source countries for immigration and to reduce overall immigration rates.

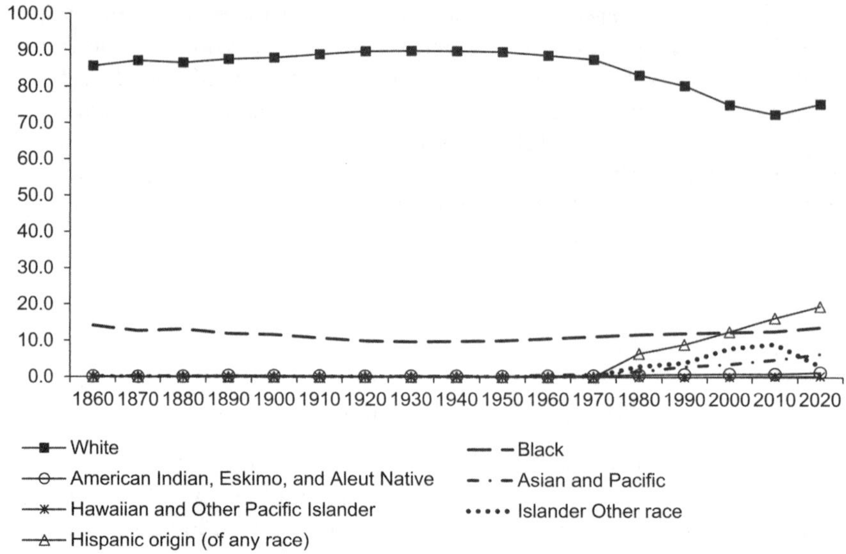

Fig. I.1 US population race and ethnic percentage shares since 1860

Source: Historical Census Statistics on Population Totals by Race, 1790 to 1990, and by Hispanic Origin, 1790 to 1990, for the United States, Regions, Divisions, and States. C. Gibson and K. Jung. Washington, DC: US Census Bureau. (2002).

Overview of race and Hispanic origin: 2010. Karen Humes, Nicholas A. Jones, and Roberto R. Ramirez. US Department of Commerce, Economics and Statistics Administration, US Census Bureau (2011).

Overview of race and Hispanic origin: 2000. Elizabeth M. Grieco and Rachel C. Cassidy. US Department of Commerce, Economics and Statistics Administration, US Census Bureau (2001).

US Census Bureau, Quick Facts, 2020 US Census Data.

(https://www.census.gov/quickfacts/fact/table/US/PST045221).

Note: Race categories total to 100 percent; Hispanic origin is reported as separate percentage for individuals of any race category. Native Hawaiian and Other Pacific Islander is a separate category from Asian starting in 2000 US Census onward.

Subsequently, after major changes in US immigration laws including the elimination of country-of-origin quotas starting in 1965, there has been an upward trend in immigration flows from the Americas (including a large influx from Mexico) and Asia, greatly altering US racial and ethnic composition.

The changes in source countries of US immigrants over the past 60 years have motivated the inclusion of expanded and novel race and ethnic categories (and their various combinations) to more accurately describe the US population. Increasingly, it has become important to be able to distinguish among new arrivals from similar race or ethnic populations in the United States, as there may be significant differences in their social and economic conditions. Race or ethnic category aggregation may obscure significant

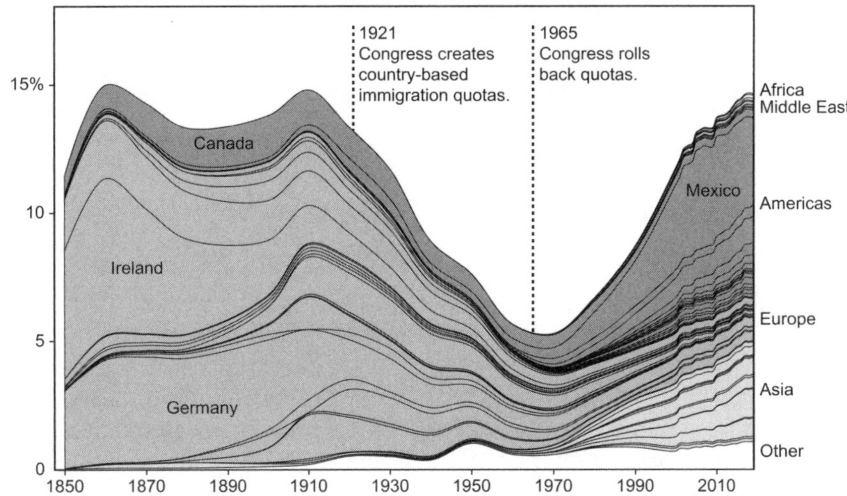

Fig. I.2 Share of the US population that was born abroad
Sources: Ran Abramitzky, Leah Boustan, based on IPUMS data.

heterogeneity in certain groups such as Asians, Hispanics, and the African American/Black population, for example, as shown in chapters in this volume.

Racial and Ethnic Differences in Median Earnings

Data collection by governmental agencies has facilitated our ability to measure differences and changes in economic and social outcomes across race and ethnic groups and to explore within group variation in outcomes. Measured racial and ethnic group disparities in key outcomes or access to programs from governmental sources are often an input into policy advocacy and policy formulation and may help to identify a novel or persistent problem in a particular population. Substantial racial and ethnic differences are apparent today for many economic outcomes (such as earnings, employment, and income) although the relative contributions of different sources (e.g., current discrimination vs. inequality of opportunity due to premarket conditions or historical discrimination) remain contentious. When consistent data are available over an extended time period, researchers may also be able to conduct credible program evaluations. We illustrate in the table below the persistence of group differences in US labor market outcomes through a straightforward comparison of contemporaneous differences by race and ethnicity in the median weekly earnings of US full-time wage and salary workers between the ages 25 to 54 (from the second quarter of 2024). Black men earn 80 percent of what White men earn, Hispanic men earn 74 percent, and Asian men earn 129 percent. Comparing the weekly median earnings for

Table I.1 **Contemporary group differences in wages**

	Median weekly earnings of US full-time wage and salary workers, 25 to 54, 2024 Q2	
	Male	Female
White	1,361	1,113
Black	1,093	937
Hispanic	1,003	885
Asian	1,756	1,465

Source: BLS, "Usual Weekly Earnings of Wage & Salary Workers," https://www.bls.gov/news.release/wkyeng.t03.htm.

different race or ethnic groups relative to White women, we find that Black women earn 84 percent of what White women earn, Hispanic women earn 67 percent, and Asian women earn 132 percent of that amount.

II. Measuring Race and Ethnicity in the Federal Statistical System

The four chapters in the first part of the book illustrate (i) the ongoing challenges to measuring race and ethnicity in the federal statistical system of a large, changing, and diverse nation; and (ii) the implications of changes in official methods of collecting race and ethnicity for consistently tracking racial and ethnic group changes in labor market outcomes. Official definitions of existing race and ethnic groups are not necessarily widely agreed upon at a point in time. And over time some agreed-upon definitions may change based on political, legal, and social changes. Thus, it is not surprising that the questions and methods for measuring race and ethnicity have changed through the history of the US decennial censuses and the federal statistical system.

In chapter 1, "Measuring the Racial and Ethnic Composition and Diversity of the United States Population: Historical Challenges and Contemporary Opportunities," Nicholas Jones, Eric Jensen, Karen Battle, and Rachel Marks provide a historical review of race questions contained in the US decennial censuses starting with the first one in 1790. They document the larger changes made over the years to accommodate changing norms and modes of racial and ethnic identification. The paper provides a useful backdrop to understanding the current topics and issues related to the collection, comparison, and analysis of race and ethnic categories across time and surveys, serving as a foundation for the rest of the volume. The authors highlight US Census Bureau's efforts to communicate findings on racial and ethnic diversity from the 2020 Census results. They also summarize the work undertaken by the federal statistical system to review and revise the guidelines for federal data on race and ethnicity with the goal of improving future data on US race and ethnicity. These guidelines are contained in the 2024 revision of OMB SPD No. 15 which proposes a combined race and ethnicity question because prior research has shown such an approach improves the accuracy of results and reduces respondent burden. The authors further discuss the advances made to address and account for the changes in race and ethnicity measures over time including "adjustment" factors to help data users bridge from earlier to updated OMB race/ethnicity categories. Another contribution is a comparison with approaches to the measures of race and ethnicity used by Canada and Australia.

In chapter 2, "Data Collection Without Definitions," William Darity and Stephan Lefebvre challenge the need for providing explicit definitions for the existing federal race and ethnicity categories. Their central thesis focuses on the inconsistencies and ambiguity embedded in the existing definitions and categories. They note that the definitions themselves may create unnecessary ambiguity and confusion for respondents. The authors detail that the definitions contain circular logic, are inconsistent across categories, and lack comprehensiveness; often the categories conflate race with related concepts such as ancestry and nationality. The implication is that formal definitions are likely to do little to assist respondents and instead may unnecessarily constrain the identity choices of individuals and groups. The authors analyze a proposal to dispense with definitions for the race and ethnic categories altogether. They argue that eliminating definitions for race and ethnicity categories would eliminate the frequent need to update definitions and might increase data comparability over time.

In chapter 3, "Measuring Potential Effects of Introducing the 2024 Race and Ethnicity Standards into the Current Population Survey," Mark Loewenstein, David Piccone, and Anne Polivka explore the potential effect of changes to federal race and ethnicity definitions using a nationally representative dataset. The Current Population Survey (CPS) currently follows the 1997 OMB standards, which prescribes race and Hispanic ethnicity be asked in separate questions. Under this approach, Hispanics can be of any race, everyone is identified as being Hispanic or not, and every race group has a Hispanic, non-Hispanic designation associated with it. In 2024, OMB updated the standards to stipulate that race and ethnicity be asked in one question and that a distinct category be added for Middle Eastern and North African. Loewenstein, Piccone, and Polivka examine the CPS microdata to assess the effects that the 2024 standards might have on CPS time series estimates. Their estimates imply that individuals who indicate they are Middle Eastern or North African will likely be among those who previously would have indicated that they are White, however the proportion is small. In contrast, Hispanics make up a large proportion of the population. "Other Race" responses in the CPS provide a lower bound estimate of the number of individuals who will identify as Hispanic in a combined question while responses to the ethnicity question provide an upper bound. Results from the Census

Bureau's National Content test suggest that the upper bound estimate is likely to be closer to the mark. Loewenstein, Piccone, and Polivka calculate the labor force estimates corresponding to the lower and upper bounds. The authors provide suggestions on how to construct an experimental series that may be more comparable across time. They also note, given the CPS rotation pattern, that administering a combined question to all respondents (rather than just to the usual one quarter of the sample who are new entrants or reentrants) the month that the combined question is introduced to the CPS could provide an approach to obtaining tighter estimates of the effect of change in standards.

In a similar vein, Kevin McKinney and John Abowd explore in chapter 4, "Estimating the Potential Impact of Combined Race and Ethnicity Reporting on Long-Term Earnings Statistics," how combining the race and ethnicity questions into a single question may affect the reporting on long-term earnings by subgroups. They attempt to disentangle the differences in long-term real earnings associated with self-reported racial and ethnic identities as distinct from country of origin with a focus on foreign-born persons from countries that are majority Hispanic and from countries in the Middle East and North Africa (MENA). The authors combine individual-level earnings data from the Longitudinal Employer-Household Dynamics data (based on state-level unemployment insurance earnings records), race and ethnicity information from the 2010 Census, and place of birth information from Social Security Administration data. Their findings show that there are nuanced differences in estimates of long-term earnings (spanning 2010–2015) across the various race and ethnicity combinations within countries of origin. Their results indicate that, relative to the two separate questions, the single-question format will lose some detailed information for certain immigrant groups, although the effects vary across immigrant subgroups and are not uniform in nature. For example, the authors note that some respondents may only answer Hispanic in the updated single race/ethnicity question and not indicate one of the past racial categories making it increasingly difficult to identify Afro-Latinos in the data and their distinctive experiences. Similar concerns arise for other smaller MENA populations. Their findings suggest that providing country of birth data for the foreign born may enhance historical comparability.

In summary, the first section of the book explores the ongoing challenges to measuring race and ethnicity inherent in a large country with a diverse and changing population. The chapters in this section provide evidence that our conclusions on socioeconomic outcomes by demographic groups may differ depending upon how the definitions of racial and ethnic groups are worded and on how racial and ethnic questions are ordered. The work may be of particular interest to academics and policymakers who use Census and other standard datasets to understand policy interventions and programs aimed at reducing disparity among economic and racial groups.

III. Implications of Mismeasured and Imputed Race and Ethnicity

The next set of chapters in the volume focus on the problems that occur when race and ethnic categories are mismeasured or need to be imputed in important domains including criminal justice, child welfare, and employment. The authors propose new approaches to improve measurement or account for systematic mismeasurement of race and ethnicity in administrative, survey, and online social network datasets. All levels of government and researchers rely on these data to assess progress (or the lack of) in various social and economic characteristics in certain populations over time and across space. When the questions and category definitions are poorly understood by the respondents or when those recording race and ethnicity information face little incentive for accurate reporting, the data collected and imputed may contain serious measurement errors harming assessments of program effectiveness or the identification of racial or ethnic group disparities (and whether measured disparities are "warranted" or represent bias or discrimination).

In chapter 5, "Race and Ethnicity (Mis)measurement in the US Criminal Justice System," Keith Finlay, Elizabeth Luh, and Michael Mueller-Smith examine how systematic mismeasurement of race and ethnicity in administrative data may lead to an underestimate of racial and ethnic disparities in criminal justice outcomes. Their analysis focuses on how race and ethnicity are recorded by administrative agents in the US criminal justice system, how operational concerns limit corrections to misreported race and ethnicity, and the implications for measures of racial disparities in criminal justice outcomes from administrative data sources. They quantify mismeasurement of race and ethnicity in the criminal justice system using novel linkages of administrative microdata from the Criminal Justice Administrative Record System (CJARS) to race and ethnicity composites from US Census Bureau data mostly based on self-reported or family-reported race and ethnicity. Finlay, Luh, and Mueller-Smith find substantial inconsistencies between agency-recorded race/ethnicity labels and Census Bureau composites—the agency label is not consistent with the composite measure for 17 percent of criminal defendants and 10 percent of prison inmates. Criminal justice agencies appear to be particularly poor at measuring the race/ethnicity of individuals identified in Census Bureau data as Hispanic, Asian, Pacific Islander, or American Indian and Alaska Native (AIAN). Using estimated correspondences between agency reported and Census Bureau composite race and ethnicity, the authors find that federal series on incarceration rates that use small survey samples to impute racial and ethnic prison population shares, appear to have substantially underestimated the incarceration rates of Blacks, Whites, and AIANs. Research on US crime and justice topics increasingly use administrative data. Finlay, Luh, and Mueller-Smith's analysis indicates that the underestimate of racial and ethnic disparities in criminal justice outcomes can potentially be improved by individual-level microdata linkages of multiple administrative and Census data sources as in CJARS.

E. Jason Baron, Joseph Doyle, Natalia Emanuel, Peter Hull and Joseph Ryan explore another case of race and ethnic mismeasurement in chapter 6, "Unwarranted Disparity in High-Stakes Decisions: Race Measurement and Policy Responses." Their analysis focuses on racial discrimination in child protective services (ChPS) and how racial misclassification in administrative ChPS data may affect measures of overall and unwarranted racial disparities in foster care placement and other ChPS case outcomes. They build on earlier work by Baron et al. (2024) who exploit the quasi-random allocation of calls to ChPS screeners and then investigators in Michigan, and who find that even among children with the same potential for maltreatment at home, calls with maltreatment allegations are much more likely to result in foster care placement for Black children than for White children. The new work in this volume by Baron et al. assesses racial misclassification in administrative ChPS data by linking the Michigan ChPS administrative data to public school records containing a "self-reported" measure of the child's race reported by the child or child's guardian. They find that ChPS investigators misclassify 8 to 9 percent of Black and White children relative to their self-reported race, and that racial misclassification leads to an understatement by about 24 percent of unwarranted racial disparity in foster care decisions. Baron et al. further extend their analysis to examine unwarranted disparities in multi-stage systems, such as initial call screening to determine whether an investigation is warranted plus the investigation itself in the ChPS setting, to assess how taking account discrimination in an earlier stage (screening) should impact algorithmic recommendations at a later stage (investigation to determine whether foster care placement is warranted).

In chapter 7, "Quantifying the Uncertainty of Imputed Demographic Disparity Estimates: The Dual-Bootstrap," Benjamin Lu, Jia Wan, Jacob Goldin, Daniel E. Ho, and Derek Ouyang investigate how imputing race or ethnicity can affect the uncertainty (standard errors) of estimates of average differences in an outcome by racial or ethnic groups. The authors focus on a common problem where survey or administrative data contain important outcomes of interest but where race or ethnicity data is not collected or has low response rates. Their approach accounts for the sampling uncertainty inherent in standard analyses but also explicitly incorporates the measurement uncertainty associated with the imputation that is required to address non-response or non-collection of race or ethnicity measures in the primary survey of interest. The authors develop a dual-bootstrap approach with an application in a BISG (Bayesian Improved Surname Geocoding) setting and find that BISG race imputation does not appear to significantly increase estimation uncertainty. Lu et al. show in an example analyzing health outcomes that the widths of the dual-bootstrap and single-bootstrap confidence intervals for the estimates are essentially the same for the race groups Asian and Pacific Islander, Black, Hispanic, and White populations; these results indicate that imputation does not necessarily result in estimates with larger variances. On the other hand, they also find that that imputations for small populations which are less represented in training data may result in larger estimated variances. The authors conclude that bias in estimates of group difference rather than imprecision of such estimates is likely the predominant worry from BISG race imputation.

Alexander Berry, Elizabeth Maloney, and David Neumark examine alternative methods to identify or infer race and/or ethnic identity for firms using publicly (or approximately public) available datasets in chapter 8, "The Missing Link? Using LinkedIn Data to Measure Race, Ethnic, and Gender Differences in Employment Outcomes at Individual Companies." The analysis in the chapter is motivated by the fact that the data necessary to detect racial, ethnic, and gender discrimination at the firm level is not always publicly available. Berry, Maloney, and Neumark's exploratory analysis attempts to use information extracted from LinkedIn data to measure the racial, ethnic, and gender composition of individual company workforces. The authors use readily available tools to predict individuals' race, ethnicity, and gender based on their names and LinkedIn profile pictures and then compare their estimates from scraped LinkedIn data to those from two alternative sources: the American Community Survey (ACS) and company diversity (or EEO-1) reports. After demonstrating that their estimates are reasonable, Berry, Maloney, and Neumark apply their methodology to analyze the race, ethnic, and gender composition of hires and mass layoffs at two large companies. They also explore the use of the LinkedIn data to analyze race, ethnic, and gender differences in promotions. The authors conclude that LinkedIn data have the potential to be useful for assisting in the enforcement of anti-discrimination laws and could prove a valuable research tool to study worker mobility within and across firms and how worker mobility patterns differ by race, gender, and ethnicity.

In summary, the papers in this section aim to identify whether misclassification of race and ethnicity affects estimates of important outcomes. Two of the papers find that misclassification of race and ethnicity in administrative data is widespread and leads to underestimates of the degree of incarceration and incidence of discrimination. However, one paper finds that, even though imperfect, racial and ethnic classification available from commercially available data may be good enough to identify within firm instances of discrimination. We also learn that race imputation may come at the cost of accuracy (larger standard errors) for relatively small populations in existing datasets. These papers highlight the potential costs to researchers and policymakers of having misclassified, missing or erroneous measures of race and ethnicity.

IV. Applications

The final four chapters provide different examples of the ways in which innovative data collection, data linkages, and data disaggregation can facilitate novel research focusing on racial and ethnic populations and their social and economic progress. Bruce Meyer, Nikolas Mittag, and Derek Wu motivate chapter 9, “Race, Ethnicity, and Measurement Error,” by observing that the accuracy of analyses of racial and ethnic disparities of economic outcomes and access to the safety net based on survey data depends on survey accuracy not varying by race and ethnicity. They review the evidence provided by eighteen empirical studies that link various Census survey datasets to administrative data to assess the accuracy of individuals’ responses about the receipt of safety net and retirement programs (SNAP, Social Security, Unemployment Insurance, TANF, Medicaid, Medicare, and private pensions) and how reporting accuracy varies by race and ethnicity. Meyer, Mittag, and Wu find that Blacks and Hispanics are consistently more likely to fail to report program receipt than Whites. In most studies, false reports of program receipt are also higher for Blacks and Hispanics, but underreporting is typically the dominant error. Furthermore, this pattern persists when one controls for other covariates besides race and ethnicity. The authors conclude that measurement error in the major US Census survey datasets tends to systematically understate safety net program receipt by Blacks and Hispanics relative to Whites.

Francisca Antman and Brian Duncan hypothesize in chapter 10, “Ethnic Identity and Anti-Immigrant Sentiment: Evidence from Proposition,” that racial and ethnic tensions may affect individuals’ responses to survey questions about their racial and ethnic identity. They test for such a phenomenon by examining how survey responses to the Census and the CPS were affected by local support for California’s Proposition 187, a 1994 ballot initiative that was designed to deny social services to undocumented immigrants. Antman and Duncan anticipate that individuals’ willingness to identify as Mexican was affected by local support for Proposition 187 since much of the anger behind Proposition 187 was directed at Mexicans. The authors predict that individuals who might be more likely to be perceived as Mexican because of a last name or direct paternal lineage would be less likely to identify as Mexican. In contrast, individuals who were less likely to be viewed as Mexican and faced fewer adverse consequences might be more likely to identify as Mexican as the result of their increased ethnic awareness. Antman and Duncan’s empirical test involves estimating an equation using pre- and post-Proposition 187 data and interacting a post-Proposition 187 indicator with the share of the county vote share in favor of Proposition 187. Separate equations are estimated for individuals with varying strengths of Mexican ancestry. The estimation results are in accord with the authors’ hypotheses.

In chapter 11, “Granular Income Inequality and Mobility Using IDDA:

Exploring Patterns Across Race and Ethnicity," Natalie Gubbay, Brandon Hawkins, Illenin Kondo, Kevin Rinz, John Voorheis, and Abigail Wozniak illustrate how the creation of a rich public use dataset based on linking restricted-access US government administrative data may improve our ability to track economic outcomes by demographic groups across geographic areas and be a useful input into policy analyses. They link the universe of household 1040 tax filings from 2008 to 2019 and the universe of individual W-2 filings to construct a novel dataset called Income Distributions and Dynamics in America (IDDA). The IDDA is very large, allowing granular analysis for many US demographic groups, for geographic areas below the national level, and for intersections of demography and sub-national geography. Using this dataset, the authors explore the evolution of income inequality and mobility for subnational race and ethnic groups, and they compare IDDA estimates with those in the CPS (and with the ACS in an appendix). Kondo et al. find broadly similar aggregate patterns in the estimates from the tax data and the public survey data. For example, 75–25 percentile income gap estimates align well between IDDA and the CPS. However, there are stark differences at a more granular level: the CPS is not well suited for producing distributional estimates for many racial and ethnic groups at the state level. The authors conclude by looking at a couple of applications of the IDDA. In the first, they show that in contrast to other racial and gender groups, the labor earnings of Blacks in the upper half of the income distribution have fallen relative to Whites since the Great Recession. In the second, they show that since the Great Recession the earnings of Native people living inside Native areas have fallen relative to that of Native people living outside Native areas.

Randall Akee, Sonya Porter, and Emilia Simeonova also demonstrate the benefits of linking administrative datasets to increase the sample size for smaller and hard-to-count race and ethnic groups. In chapter 12, "Earnings Inequality and Immobility for Hispanics and Asians: An Examination of Variation Across Subgroups," Akee, Porter, and Simeonova examine earnings inequality and earnings immobility within US Hispanic and Asian ethnic and racial groups over the period of 2005–2015 using confidential-use data linked from the ACS to Internal Revenue Service W-2 and 1099 forms. Because of the large sample size of their administrative data sources, the authors are able to disaggregate the Hispanic and Asian categories into their subgroups and distinguish between individuals who are long-term residents or native-born Hispanics and Asians and those who are recent (post-2005) immigrants to the United States. The disaggregation of data into these smaller subpopulations is often impossible in standard datasets given sample size limitations in survey datasets or lack of information on immigrant arrival status or labor force attachment. The results show that for the Asian and Hispanic population aged 18–45, earnings inequality is constant or slightly decreasing for the long-term legal resident and native-born populations over the 2005–2015 period. The addition of new labor market entrants appears to be a driving force for observed increases in earnings inequality over time for some relatively small populations. New Asian and/or Hispanic immigrants to the United States contribute significantly to the earnings inequality within these groups at both the aggregate and disaggregated levels. The authors also show that there are significant differences across the various subgroups in their average earnings, inequality measures, and share of the top and bottom 10 percent of earnings. Akee, Porter, and Simeonova's analysis highlights that our existing race and ethnicity measures for broad categories obscure significant variation across subgroups and that these different subgroups have significantly different experiences, earnings and outcomes.

In summary, this final section provides novel directions for research where more complete and well-specified data may exist for race and ethnic groups. We learn that political influences and prevailing sentiment may play a role in shaping how individuals self-identify. We also learn that response rates for certain survey questions (such as program receipt) may differ across race and ethnic groups and that these differences may play a role in leading to an underestimate of program use and provision for certain groups. Finally, we see in the last two chapters that administrative data can help us identify socioeconomic characteristics and outcome for smaller race and ethnic groups. Linked longitudinal Census and administrative data may play an important role in future research examining dynamic and intergenerational outcomes by race and ethnicity.

V. Closing Thoughts

The papers in this volume illuminate the challenges in accurately measuring the race and ethnicity of the US population and how systematic mismeasurement impacts our understanding of levels and trends in economic and social outcomes by race and ethnicity. They also illustrate how new data, linkages between large representative administrative and survey datasets and innovative methods can improve the accuracy of race and ethnicity measurement and yield novel insights into racial and ethnic group disparities in multiple areas including the labor market, health care, criminal justice system, and social safety net programs.

For acknowledgments, sources of research support, and disclosure of the authors' material financial relationships, if any, please see https://www.nber.org/books-and-chapters/race-ethnicity-and-economic-statistics-21st-century/introduction-race-ethnicity-and-economic-statistics-21st-century.

References

Abramitzky, Ran, and Leah Boustan. 2017. "Immigration in American Economic History." *Journal of Economic Literature* 55(4): 1311–45.

Abramitzky, Ran, and Leah Boustan. 2022. *Streets of Gold: America's Untold Story of Immigrant Success*. New York: Public Affairs.

Baron, Jason, Joseph Doyle, Natalia Emanuel, Peter Hull, and Joseph Ryan. 2024. "Discrimination in Multi-Phase Systems: Evidence from Child Protection." *Quarterly Journal of Economics* 139(3): 1611–64.

Jensen, Eric, Nicholas Jones, Megan Rabe, Beverly Pratt, Lauren Medina, Kimberly Orozco and Lindsay Spell. 2023. "2020 US Population More Racially and Ethnically Diverse Than Measured in 2010." US Census Bureau, America Counts: Stories. https://www.census.gov/library/stories/2021/08/2020-united-states-population-more-racially-ethnically-diverse-than-2010.html.

US Office of Management and Budget. 2024. "The 2024 Statistical Policy Directive No. 15." Resource Website. https://spd15revision.gov/content/spd15revision/en/2024-spd15.html.

I

Measuring Race and Ethnicity in the Federal Statistical System

1

Measuring the Racial and Ethnic Composition and Diversity of the US Population
Historical Challenges and Contemporary Opportunities

Nicholas Jones, Eric Jensen, Karen Battle, and Rachel Marks

1.1 Introduction

Every decennial census in the United States, since the very first in 1790, has included a question on race. However, the design of the race question has always been different, in some shape or form (US Census Bureau 2021; Pratt et al. 2015). The history of measuring race in the US decennial census reflects over two centuries of social, political, and economic change in the United States (Humes and Hogan 2009). The history of the race question—asked in various ways—follows the trajectory of our nation, encapsulating the era of slavery and emancipation, the incorporation of American Indians into the general US population, the annexation of parts of Mexico, immigration from Asia and Latin America, the admittance of Alaska and Hawaii as the 49th and 50th states, the Civil Rights movement, the growth of the foreign-born population, and the increase of the Multiracial/ethnic population.

The first federal standards for race and ethnicity data were established in 1977 by the US Office of Management and Budget's (OMB) Statistical Policy Directive No. 15 (OMB 1977). The original standards were established by OMB in the late 1970s, in cooperation with federal agencies, to provide consistent data on race and ethnicity (when aggregated to the minimum reporting categories) throughout the federal government, including the decennial census, household surveys, and federal administrative forms

Nicholas Jones is the Director of Race/Ethnicity Research and Outreach in the Population Division of the US Census Bureau.

Eric Jensen is the Senior Research Scientist for Population Estimates and Coverage Measurement in the Population Division of the US Census Bureau.

Karen Battle is the chief of the Population Division of the US Census Bureau.

Rachel Marks is the chief of the Racial Statistics Branch in the Population Division of the US Census Bureau.

(e.g., benefit application forms). Initial development of this data standard stemmed in large part from federal responsibilities to enforce civil rights laws. The goals of SPD 15 are to ensure the comparability of race and ethnicity across federal datasets and to maximize the quality of that data by ensuring that the format, language, and procedures for collecting the data are consistent and based on rigorous evidence. To achieve these goals, SPD 15 provides a minimum set of categories that all federal agencies must use if they intend to collect information on race and ethnicity, regardless of the collection mechanism (OMB 2024a).

Prior to 1980, the decennial census and other federal data collections had varying categories for race, ethnicity, and color. For example, a race category for "Mexican" was included in the 1930 Census, and the 1970 Census included a question about Hispanic origin on the long-form sample questionnaire. Following the establishment of the original SPD 15 in 1977, a separate question on Hispanic origin first appeared on the full decennial census in 1980, and continued through the 2020 Census. Throughout this period, the question underwent changes with each decade.

The original 1977 SPD 15 was reviewed in the 1990s, and OMB issued a revision in 1997 with the *Standards for Maintaining, Collecting, and Presenting Federal Data on Race and Ethnicity*.

Since the 1997 revision to SPD 15, there have been large societal, political, economic, and demographic shifts in the United States, including increasing racial and ethnic diversity, a growing number of people who identify as more than one race or ethnicity, and changing immigration and migration patterns. Recognizing the many calls for revisions to SPD 15, OMB announced a formal review of SPD 15 in June 2022 with the goal of updating SPD 15 to better reflect the diversity of the nation (Orvis 2022).

All federal information collections that collect information on race and ethnicity must adhere to SPD 15. The frequent modification to the race and ethnicity questions reflects the difficulty inherent with measuring these characteristics in the US population. In this paper, we review the historical challenges and contemporary opportunities with accurately measuring the racial and ethnic composition and diversity of the US population using the decennial census. Specifically, we provide an overview of the evolution of the race and ethnicity questions from the 1790 Census to the 2020 Census, review the Census Bureau's efforts to measure racial and ethnic diversity, and discuss potential plans for improving the measurement of these characteristics in data collections moving forward.

This paper addresses two of the issues of interest listed for the CRIW Conference. These include (1) "Current and historical collection of race and ethnicity data" and (2) "The future of terminology and communication of measures, such as retiring the constructs of *minority* and *majority* and introducing more informative measures and concepts, such as the *diversity index*."

We organize the paper in three sections. Section 1.1 discusses the history of measuring race and ethnicity in the United States through the lens of the US decennial census, and the social context of the surrounding time periods. Section 1.2 describes work undertaken by the US Census Bureau to measure and communicate analyses of racial and ethnic diversity with the 2020 Census results. Section 1.3 presents future opportunities for measuring race and ethnicity, with a discussion of the work that was undertaken in the federal statistical system to review and revise SPD 15, and the resulting updated standards which were published in early 2024 with the goal of improving future data on race/ethnicity in the United States.

1.2 Measuring Race and Ethnicity Throughout the History of the US Decennial Census

The evolution of measuring race and ethnicity in the decennial census reflects changes in US population and the methods used to collect the census data over more than two centuries. The original 1790 Census included three response categories: "Free White Females and Males," "All Other Free Persons," and "Slaves." Fast forward to the 2020 Census and there were six categories for race (White, Black or African American, American Indian or Alaska Native, Asian, Native Hawaiian or Other Pacific Islander, and Some Other Race) and two categories for ethnicity (Hispanic or Latino; Not Hispanic or Latino). Because the 2020 Census included the option for respondents to select more than one race category, there were 63 possible combinations of the race categories.

For much of US decennial census history, the primary method for taking the census was to have US marshals, and later Census Bureau enumerators, collect the census information (Anderson 2015). The traditional census approach, where the census is administered to respondents, usually relied on the personal observations of the enumerator when measuring race (Gauthier 2002). The 1960 Census was the first to use a "mail-out" approach where self-response was the primary method for collecting the census data. This effectively instituted self-identification as the conceptual framework for reporting information about racial and ethnic identity, as people were asked to report their responses to the questions that were posed on the form.

Today, the Census Bureau values and prioritizes the concept of "self-identification" when collecting data on race and ethnicity. After SPD 15 was revised in 1997, beginning with Census 2000, respondents could select more than one category in the *race* question. This allowed the Census Bureau to produce statistics on the racial distribution of the US population for both single race groups ("race alone" concept), multiple race groups ("in combination" or "multiracial" concept), and the maximum number of people reporting one or more race groups for each category ("race alone or in combination" concept).

The design of the race and ethnicity questions for the 2020 Census provided an opportunity for individuals from all communities, for the very first time, to "write-in" more detailed information for every one of the race and ethnicity categories, which allowed us to code the maximum amount of information on race for each respondent and all communities in the United States (Marks and Rios-Vargas 2021). These changes to measuring race have been critical for allowing respondents to fully self-identify their racial identity and not limit their response to one racial category. Subsequently, the 2010 Census and 2020 Census have both allowed respondents to select more than one race category, and the Multiracial population has grown with each census (Jones et al. 2021).

1.2.1 History of Race and Ethnicity Categories in the US Census

There are several excellent resources that discuss how the race and Hispanic origin questions on the decennial census have changed over time (Anderson 2015; Humes and Hogan 2009; Pratt et al. 2015). For example, Humes and Hogan (2009) outline five distinct historical periods in the measurement of race and ethnicity in the decennial census. Pratt et al. (2015) produced an infographic showing the specific race categories in each census from 1790 to 2010. Both use a timeline approach that shows the evolution of the race and Hispanic origin questions over time. For this analysis, we focus on each of the current racial and ethnic groups other than White and highlight the key changes to the collection and tabulation for that group (table 1.1).

The history of collecting information about the Black or African American population on the decennial census goes back to the first census in 1790, although these terms were not used. The census used the phrase "three-fifths of all other Persons," but it was clear to everyone that this refereed to the slave population (Humes and Hogan 2009). In 1820, the category "Free Colored People" was added to reflect the growth of the free-Black population. In 1850, blood quantum was introduced with the "Mulatto" category as an attempt to denote people with mixed heritage. This was expanded in 1890 to include the categories "Quadroon" and "Octoroon," which sought to quantify the percentage of Black blood a person had. These categories were dropped after one census because the data collected were not considered very accurate (Humes and Hogan 2009). However, "Mulatto" was added back as a category for the 1910 Census and the "one-drop" rule was added to enumerator instructions for the 1930 Census. The term "Negro" was first used on the census in 1900 and remained on the census questionnaire until 2010 (Pratt et al. 2015). It was not until 2000 that "African American" was included as a category descriptor on the census.

The Asian category on the decennial census in many ways mirrors the historical trajectory of Asian immigration to the United States over the past two centuries. "Chinese" was added as a category to the 1870 Census following several decades of immigration from China (Humes and Hogan 2009).

Table 1.1 **Notable milestones for the decennial census by race and ethnicity category**

Race and Ethnicity	Census Year	Notable Milestones
Black or African American	1790	Slaves counted as "three-fifths of all other Persons"
	1820	"Free Colored Persons" added as a race category
	1850	Blood quantum introduced with the "Mulatto" category
	1890	"Quadroon" and "Octoroon" included as categories
	1900	The term Negro was used for the first time
	1910	"Mulatto" added back as a category
	1930	"One-drop" rule added to enumerator instructions
	2000	"African American" added as a category descriptor
	2020	"Negro" is removed from the race question
Asian	1870	"Chinese" added as a race category
	1890	"Japanese" added as a race category
	1920	"Filipino," "Hindu," and "Korean" added as race categories
	1950	"Hindu" and "Korean" dropped as race categories
	1970	"Korean" added back as a race category
	1980	"Asian Indian" and "Vietnamese" added as race categories and 6 detailed checkboxes added for the largest Asian categories
	1990	Data tabulated as Asian or Pacific Islander
	2000	Data tabulated as Asian after 1997 OMB Directive 15
American Indian and Alaska Native	1860	Data collected on "Indians" who are taxed
	1890	First attempt to enumerate all American Indians
	1900	Blood quantum used to approximate assimilation
	1960	"American Indian" replaces "Indian" as a category; "Eskimo" and "Aleut" added after Alaska became a state
	2000	Data tabulated as American Indian or Alaska Native
Hispanic	1930	"Mexican" added as a race category
	1970	Hispanic self-identification question asked to a sample
	1980	Hispanic origin question asked to everyone and categories were added for specific Hispanic categories (Mexican, Puerto Rican, and Cuban)
Native Hawaiian or Other Pacific Islander	1960	"Hawaiian" and "Part-Hawaiian" added after Hawaii became a state
	1990	"Other Asian Pacific Islander" added as a category
	2000	New minimum category for Native Hawaiian or Other Pacific Islander; use of 3 detailed Pacific Islander checkboxes
Multiracial Population	2000	Census allows respondents to select more than one race
	2020	Expanded write-in and improved coding allows respondents to better report their complete heritages
Some Other Race	1790–1840	"All Other Free Persons"
	1910–1990	"Other", "etc.?" and "Other Race"
	2005	"Some Other Race" is mandated by Congress

Source: Adapted from Humes and Hogan (2009) and Pratt et al. (2015).

"Japanese" was added in 1890 after immigration from Japan increased when the US government enacted laws restricting immigration from China (table 1.1). For the 1920 Census, "Filipino," "Hindu," and "Korean" were added as race categories. "Hindu" and "Korean" were then dropped from the 1950 Census form, but "Korean" was added back on the form in 1970. "Asian Indian" and "Vietnamese" were added as race categories for the 1980 Census, the latter being added after the Vietnam War. Also in 1980, there were six detailed checkboxes added for the largest Asian categories ("Japanese," "Chinese," "Filipino," "Korean," "Vietnamese," and "Asian Indian).

The 1980 Census was the first time that the different nationalities from Asia were combined to form the Asian category. The tabulations from the 1970 Census reported "White," "Negro," and "Other Race," which included "Indian," "Japanese," Chinese," "Filipino," and "All Other." The 1980 Census tabulated the Asian and Pacific Islander population, while still asking about the different Asian nationality groups on the form. It should be noted that the Census Bureau was following the then recently issued 1977 OMB Standards on Race and Ethnicity. Similarly, the Asian category was split out from the Pacific Islander group for the 2000 Census, again following the newly revised 1997 OMB Standards on Race and Ethnicity.

American Indians were not explicitly counted in the decennial census until 1860 when a category was added for "Indians" who are taxed (table 1.1). The 1890 Census marked the first attempt to enumerate all American Indians (Humes and Hogan 2009). Blood quantum was dropped for the Black population in the 1900 Census but was still used on the American Indian questionnaire (Snipp 2000). With Alaska becoming a state in 1959, two new categories for "Eskimo" and "Aleut" were added to the 1960 Census form. Additionally, the term "American Indian" replaced "Indian" in 1960. Starting with the 2000 Census, the data for this population were tabulated as American Indian or Alaska Native.

In 1848, the Treaty of Guadalupe-Hidalgo was signed, and the United States annexed territory from Mexico that would become states in the current Southwest and West regions. Despite this change to the US population, "Mexican" was not added to the census until 1930 when it became one of the race categories. A Hispanic self-identification question was added to the 1970 Census, but this was only one of the long-form items that were sent to a sample of households. Hispanic origin was included on the short-form of the 1980 Census. Also in 1980, categories were added for specific Hispanic categories: Mexican, Puerto Rican, and Cuban.

The categories "Hawaiian" and "Part-Hawaiian" were added to the 1960 Census after Hawaii became a state in 1959. "Other Asian Pacific Islander" was added as a category to the 1990 Census. At this time, the Native Hawaiian or Other Pacific Islander data were tabulated in the Asian Pacific Islander category. For the 2000 Census, Native Hawaiian and Other Pacific Islander became their own separate race category from Asian. Additionally, in 2000, three detailed Pacific Islander checkboxes for "Native Hawaiian," "Guamanian or Chamorro," and "Samoan" were added to the race question.

As noted above, the decennial census has a long and checkered history with collecting data on people with multiple racial identities. It seems that the underling purpose of asking about multiple racial identities for the Black population was exclusion, while the purpose for asking similar questions for American Indians was to measure assimilation and ultimately erase the population. The 2000 Census allowed respondents to select more than one race category and the Census Bureau tabulated the data as "alone or in combination" and "Two or more Races" categories. In contrast to past attempts to measure the Multiracial population, the goal of the new approach was to be inclusive of the growing number of people who identified and celebrated more than one race. The 2020 Census expanded the write-in categories and improved coding of the race responses, which allowed respondents to better report their complete heritages.

From 1790 to 1840, people who did not fit into the listed race groups were put into the "All Other Free Persons" category. For six decades there was not an "Other" category on the census. From 1910 to 1990, the category was labeled as "Other," "etc.?" and "Other Race." The 1997 OMB standards discouraged federal agencies from collecting an "Other" race category. However, Congress passed the 2005 Omnibus Appropriation Bill, which mandated that the Census Bureau include "Some Other Race" (SOR) as a category when collecting census data. The reasoning behind requiring the Some Other Race category was to provide a response category for Hispanics who may not see themselves in the official OMB race categories (Humes and Hogan 2009). In the 2020 Census, the Some Other Race population was the second largest alone or in combination race group in the United States—behind only the White population—making up 15.1 percent of the population (Jones et al. 2021).

1.2.2 Comparative Approaches

The changing approaches to measuring race and ethnicity in the census is not unique to the United States. Canada and Australia have followed similar historical paths to the United States regarding how race and ethnicity have been categorized in the census data. However, in recent rounds of censuses the three countries take very different approaches (Stevens et al. 2015).

The United States, Canada, and Australia share similar historical, political, and social trajectories including their origins as British colonies, their status as immigrant receiving countries, and their large indigenous populations (Stevens et al. 2015). As former British colonies, the earliest collections of data on race and ethnicity focused mainly on establishing the size of the White population relative to all other groups.

This focus on the White population was evident in the immigration policies enacted by each country in the 19th and early 20th centuries. From

1882 to 1910, the United States enacted several laws that prohibited Chinese immigrants and their families from immigrating and becoming permanent residents (Calavita 2000). Canada adopted similar restrictive policies for Chinese immigrants (Holland 2007). Australian immigration policy long favored immigrants from the United Kingdom under a policy called "White Australia" that prevented immigration from other regions (Stevens and Fozdar 2021). After World War II, these countries adopted new policies that allowed immigration from all over the world, which greatly increased the racial and ethnic diversity in each country.

A final similarity between these three countries is that they have large indigenous populations that were living in the territory at the time of contact and later became part of the country's population. For example, the United States did not include "Indian" as a category on the census until 1870, but since that time there has been a race category for the indigenous population on each subsequent census (Pratt et al. 2015). Canada's first census in 1871 included questions about "origins"; however, enumerators often faced resistance from the indigenous population when trying to conduct the census (Hamilton 2007; Kwan-Lafond and Winterstein 2020). Since Australia became an independent country in 1901, the aboriginal and Torres Straight Islander populations were included in the census, but they were not part of the official population totals until 1971 (Markham and Biddle 2018).

Despite these shared historical trajectories, today the United States, Canada, and Australia have significantly different approaches to measuring race and ethnicity in the census. The United States focuses on self-identified race and ethnicity, for which respondents can choose between different options and write in detailed information about their racial and ethnic identity. Since the 1996 Census, Canada has used an approach to measuring race called the "visible minority" where respondents are asked "is this person . . ." and then given a series of response categories including White, South Asian, Chinese, Black, Filipino, Arab, Latin American, Southeast Asian, West Asian, Korean, Japanese, and Other (Statistics Canada 2022a). The responses are then categorized into visible minority status, which consists of "persons, other than Aboriginal peoples, who are non-Caucasian in race or non-White in color" (Statistics Canada 2022a). A separate question is used for indigenous status where people can identify as Inuit, First Nations, or Metis (Statistics Canada 2022b). Metis is a category that was originally used to identify the population in the Red River area of present-day Manitoba who had both indigenous and European ancestry, but the term has been used more broadly in recent decades by people who identify as multiracial, including indigenous origins (Kwan-Lafond and Winterstein 2020).

After the 1976 Census, Australia stopped including a race or racial origins question on their census; however, they still include variables such as religion, birthplace, parental place of birth, year of arrival, language spoken, indigenous status, and ancestry (Stevens et al. 2015). Public sentiment about the concept of "race" was the biggest factor in the decision to stop using a race question on the census, but the various indicators of social and cultural origins in Australia are still used as proxies for identifying different population groups.

1.2.3 Broader Limitations to the Census Approach to Measuring Race and Ethnicity

The US Census Bureau's current focus on using self-identified race and ethnicity may have some limitations for measuring the impact of race/ethnicity on different socioeconomic outcomes. For example, research focusing on phenotype characteristics has found that wages, educational attainment, health outcomes, and other socioeconomic characteristics vary by skin tone (Dixon and Telles 2017; Goldsmith et al. 2006; Keith et al. 2017; Monk 2014). The empirical research shows a consistent pattern where lighter-skinned people have better outcomes than darker-skinned people.

Many of these studies focus on *within* group variation in phenotype characteristics. For example, Monk (2021) argues that skin tone stratification within the Black or African American race group can sometimes be more pronounced than differences between the Black and White race categories. Studies have pointed to the variation in outcomes based on phenotype characteristics within a race group as an indicator of increased discrimination faced by people with darker skin tones (Keith et al. 2017). There can also be variation *between* race groups in phenotype characteristics that leads to increased discrimination, especially for the Hispanic or Latino population (Dixon and Telles 2017; Golash-Bonza and Darity 2008).

Some scholars have cautioned that measuring race and ethnicity using only self-identified categories may show different outcomes from methods that focus on phenotype characteristics (López et al. 2018; Telles 2018). One novel method to overcome this problem combines the phenotypical approach and broad category approach by asking Hispanic or Latino respondents to not only report how they self-identify but also "how do you think others see your race" (López et al. 2018). This research has found that the multidimensional approach to measuring race and ethnicity exposes more heterogeneity in health outcomes within the Hispanic or Latino population than just using a self-identified race and ethnicity question.

While it is unlikely that the US Census Bureau will include questions about skin tone or perceived race on the decennial census or in large demographic surveys, these other approaches may offer means for exploring and understanding additional dimensions of stratification within race/ethnicity groups that cannot currently be captured solely with self-identification measures.

1.2.4 Using Administrative Records

With declining response rates to household surveys, organizations that collect data are increasingly using administrative records to populate race and ethnicity information for non-responding households (Ennis et al. 2018; Rastogi et al. 2014). The Census Bureau has conducted considerable research on this topic and even used administrative records to impute race and Hispanic origin information for non-responding households in the 2020 Census (Cantwell 2021). However, for this approach to provide valid data, the administrative records need to have accurate detail on race and ethnicity, which can be difficult because administrative data for these variables may be limited, outdated, or nonexistent.

Research looking at the correlation between self-reported race and race in administrative data has often found that the agreement varies across different race groups (Kressin et al. 2003; Ennis et al. 2018; Jarrín et al. 2020). Using data from the US Department of Veterans Affairs, Kressin et al. (2003) found that there was the least agreement between administrative data and self-reported race for Native American, Asian, and Pacific Islander patients. Ennis et al. (2018) found that Hispanics were more likely to have non-matching race and ethnicity responses between administrative records and third-party data and their 2010 Census response. An analysis comparing race and ethnicity codes in Medicare administrative data to self-reported race found that the highest agreement was for the Black population and the lowest agreement was for the AIAN population (Jarrín et al. 2020).

Some administrative data sources do not include information about race and ethnicity, but researchers have developed methods for assigning these variables based largely on surname and geographic residence (Filice and Joynt 2017). For example, Elliot et al. (2008) developed a Bayesian approach to estimate race and ethnicity using surname and geocoded residential addresses that they compared to self-reported responses. The model—the Bayesian Surname and Geocoding (BSG) method—was more efficient than a non-Bayesian method for predicting the individual's response and developing population-level statistics. Later research expanded this approach to develop the Bayesian Improved Surname Geocoding (BISG) method that uses additional information such as first and middle name to predict race in administrative data (Imai et al. 2022).

The US Census Bureau has developed a hybrid approach where administrative data are linked to self-responses from a prior census or survey using probabilistic matching. The probabilistic matching process assigns a unique identifier called a Personal Identification Key (PIK) to individuals using the Social Security Administration Numerical Identification file (SSA Numident) as a reference file (Wagner and Layne 2014). The PIK is the foundation of the administrative records work being done by the US Census Bureau.

The administrative records linked to past census or ACS responses were

Table 1.2 **National usage of past census and administrative records during characteristic imputation processing: 2020 Census**

Characteristic	Percent of 331.4 million assigned from Past Census or ACS Response	 Other Administrative Records
Race	3.2%	1.5%
Hispanic Origin	3.2%	0.9%
Age	2.6%	1.4%
Sex	2.6%	1.2%

Source: US Census Bureau, CBDRB-FY22–172.

used for the first time in the 2020 Census for item-nonresponse and the administrative records modeling portion of the non-response follow-up operation (Cantwell 2021). Table 1.2 shows that of the 331.4 million people in the 2020 Census, approximately 3.2 percent had their race and Hispanic origin response carried over from a past census or ACS response as part of the administrative records enumeration (Mule 2022). This was slightly higher than the age and sex characteristics where 2.6 percent of responses came from a past census or ACS response. When a past census or ACS response was not available, we used information from other administrative records (table 1.2). However, the information from other administrative records accounted for a relatively small proportion of the total demographic characteristics tabulated in the 2020 Census.

There are several concerns with this approach. First, if the PIK is not assigned correctly, the race response from a past census or survey response will not be valid. Even though research has shown that the false match rate for PIK assignment is relatively low (Layne et al. 2014), there is still a risk that the census or survey response is coming from another individual. Second, a person may change how they identify their race or Hispanic origin over time.

Liebler et al. (2017) looked at matched Census 2000 and 2010 results and found that a non-trivial number of individuals changed their race and/or ethnicity response in the later census. Using administrative data linked to past census or survey responses will not capture potential changes in an individual's racial or ethnic identity.

Finally, the race and ethnicity data on the past census or survey will only be available in the format in which they were originally collected. This could be problematic if there are large changes to the way that data on race and ethnicity are collected on a future census or survey. For example, the past census and survey data linked to administrative records that were used for 2020 Census operations had race and ethnicity in the separate question format and may not align well with the data from a combined question approach.

However, there could be resources developed to help map race and ethnicity data collected using different formats (see section on race bridging).

1.3 Measuring Racial and Ethnic Diversity

Over the years, the Census Bureau has used different approaches to describe changes in the racial and ethnic composition of the US population. Beginning in 2008, we started using the majority/minority framework to describe geographic places where the non-Hispanic White population fell below 50 percent of the total population. This framework was applied to decennial census results, population estimates, and population projections. In particular, the Population Projections program received considerable attention for releasing their forecasts of when the "majority-minority crossover" would occur for the total US population (Colby and Ortman 2015). However, this way of conceptualizing the changing composition of race and ethnicity was met with criticism by some race scholars (Alba 2018).

Changes to the racial and ethnic composition of the US population are driven by subtle differences in demographic processes across groups. As birth rates decline for some groups and remain high for others, the racial and ethnic composition of the youngest cohorts will be different from older generations. Mortality can impact the racial and ethnic composition through differential mortality rates as well as the age structure of the population. For example, the oldest-aged population, who are most at risk of dying, tend to be less racially and ethnically diverse than younger ages and therefore population decline from mortality will impact certain groups more than others. Immigration can also affect racial and ethnic composition. In recent decades, there has been substantial immigration from Latin America and Asia that has shifted the color line beyond the historical Black/White divide (Lee and Bean 2010).

Social scientists use different frameworks to describe the changing racial and ethnic composition of a population. These include the diversity index, segregation measures, and methods based on the percentage distribution of different groups (Johnson and Lichter 2010; Iceland and Weinberg 2002; Massey, Rothwell, and Domina 2009; Meyer and McIntosh 1992). Each of these approaches highlights a different way to conceptualize and operationalize changes in the racial and ethnic composition of a population.

The diversity index is a probability-based measure of racial and ethnic diversity in a population (Meyer and McIntosh 1992). Conceptually, the diversity index measures how similar or different the racial characteristics of two people would be that are randomly selected from the population. The diversity index ranges from 0 to 1, with a 0-value indicating that the two people randomly selected from the population will have similar racial and ethnic characteristics, while a value of 1 indicates that two people randomly selected will have different characteristics. Additionally, there are other indexes for measuring racial and ethnic diversity, such as the Entropy Index.

Racial and ethnic segregation measures quantify the degree to which groups are concentrated or dispersed across different categories. Residential segregation focuses on where members of different racial and ethnic groups live within a specific geography (e.g., Metropolitan Statistical Area or county). Similar methods are used to measure occupational segregation where racial or ethnic groups are concentrated in a particular occupation or industry. Segregation is measured along different dimensions including evenness, isolation, clustering, centralization, and concentration (Massey and Denton 1988). Segregation measures highlight the amount of potential interaction between different race and ethnic groups within a specific geographic area.

As the Census Bureau released the results of the 2020 Census, it was important that the results present information on race and ethnicity in ways that accurately reflect the characteristics of the population, use statistically appropriate methods, and show respect to census and survey respondents who trust the Census Bureau with their information. In 2019, the Population Division of the Census Bureau formed the *Disseminating Diversity Working Group* to provide recommendations about how to present information on race and ethnic diversity in the 2020 Census data products and beyond. The Working Group is made up of subject matter experts in the areas of race and ethnicity, applied demography, statistical measurement, and data visualization.

One of the key issues that the Working Group discussed and deliberated on was the Census Bureau's past and future uses of the majority/minority framework. The Working Group came to a consensus that the agency should not use the majority/minority framework moving forward. This approach has several conceptual and practical challenges that limit its ability to illustrate the complex racial and ethnic diversity of the US population. For example, while some researchers and datasets classify individuals who identify with multiple population groups as part of the majority population (such as Hispanic and White; White and Black or African American; and White and Asian), other researchers and datasets classify them as part of the minority population. The dual identities of these groups and their inclusion or exclusion in various approaches for data highlight the social, political, and economic complexities of race and ethnicity in 21st-century US society.

The inclusion of certain groups as part of the "majority" or "minority" has also become more complex and contested in recent decades, especially as many people may not identify with certain population groups even if that is how they are classified and tabulated per SPD 15. The majority-minority approach is ambiguous, and it is further complicated by complex demographic and social realities.

To overcome these limitations, Census Bureau researchers focused on alternative racial and ethnic diversity measures to illustrate the complex racial and ethnic composition of the population in the 2020 Census results. In August 2021, based on the Working Group's analyses and data visualiza-

Table 1.3 **Ten states with the highest diversity index: 2020 and 2010**

State	Diversity Index 2010	Diversity Index 2020	Percentage Point Difference
Hawaii	75.1	76.0	0.9
California	67.7	69.7	2.0
Nevada	62.5	68.8	6.3
Maryland	60.7	67.3	6.6
District of Columbia	61.9	67.2	5.3
Texas	63.8	67.0	3.2
New Jersey	59.4	65.8	6.4
New York	60.2	65.8	5.5
Georgia	58.8	64.1	5.3
Florida	59.1	64.1	5.1

Source: US Census Bureau, 2010 Census Redistricting Data (Public Law 94–171) Summary File. 2020 Census Redistricting Data (Public Law 94–171) Summary File.

Note: Demographic changes, as well as improvements to the ways in which race and ethnicity data are collected and processed, reveal the US population is more racially and ethnically diverse than measured in 2010. States were selected using 2020 data and may not include the 10 states with the highest diversity index in 2010.

Percentage Point Difference based on unrounded values.

Information on confidentiality protection, nonsampling error, and definitions is available at https://www.census.gov/programs-surveys/decennial-census/technical-documentation/complete-technical-documents.html#redistricting.

tions, the Census Bureau released several measures to describe the racial and ethnic diversity of the US population in the 2020 Census. These included the diversity index (as described above), prevalence ranking tables and graphs, and prevalence maps (Jensen et al. 2021a, 2021b).

1.3.1 Diversity Index

Table 1.3 presents results for the states with the highest diversity index in the 2020 Census and the diversity index for these states in 2010. The probability statistics were converted into percentages to make the results easier for the public to interpret. For example, in 2020, there was a 76 percent chance that two people chosen at random in the state of Hawaii had a different race and ethnicity, which was a slight increase from 2010. Maryland was the state with the largest increase in the diversity index between 2010 and 2020, with a 6.6 percentage point increase.

1.3.2 Prevalence Rankings

Prevalence rankings show the percent of the population that falls into the first-largest, second-largest, or third-largest racial or ethnic groups. In the 2020 Census, the most prevalent racial or ethnic group for the United States was the White alone non-Hispanic population at 57.8 percent. The group's prevalence decreased from 63.7 percent in 2010. The Hispanic or

Latino population was the second-largest racial or ethnic group, comprising 18.7 percent of the total population. The Black or African American alone non-Hispanic population was the third-largest group at 12.1 percent.

Census Bureau researchers also calculated a diffusion score, which measures the combined percentage of all racial and ethnic groups that are not in the first-largest, second-largest, or third-largest racial and ethnic group. This calculation illustrates how diverse and "diffused" the population is relative to the largest groups. The higher the score, the less concentrated the population is in the three largest race and ethnic groups. In 2020, the remaining racial and ethnic groups combined to make up 11.4 percent of the total population, representing the diffusion score.

1.3.3 Prevalence Maps

Prevalence maps provide an additional measure of diversity, showing how the largest racial and ethnic groups are geographically distributed across geographic areas. Figure 1.1a shows the counties where the White alone non-Hispanic population was the most prevalent racial or ethnic group. In the 2020 Census, White alone non-Hispanic was the most prevalent group for 90.8 percent of counties. Figure 1.1b shows counties where the Black or

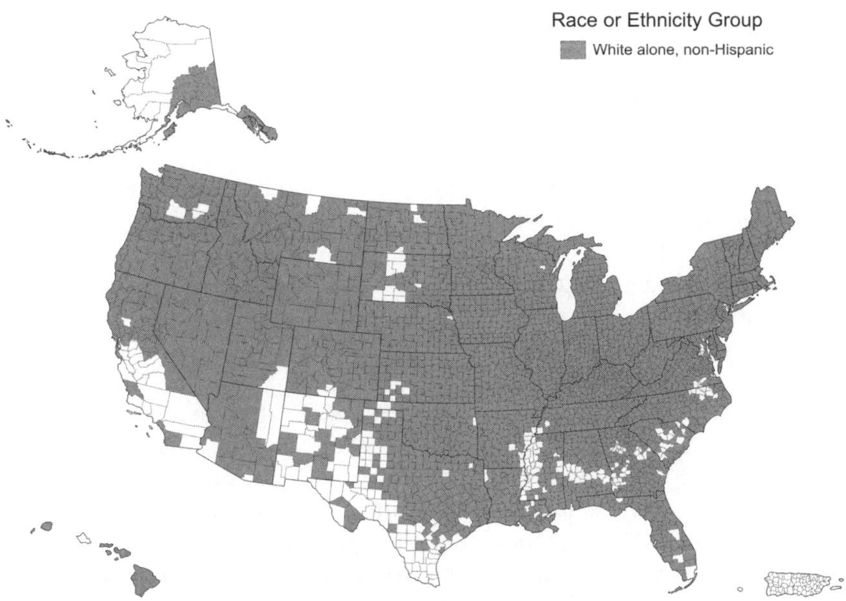

Fig. 1.1a Most prevalent race or ethnicity group by county: 2020

Source: Public US Census Bureau, 2020 Census Redistricting Data (Public Law 94-171) Summary File.

Note: Native Hawaiian and Other Pacific Islander alone, non-Hispanic, Some Other Race alone, non-Hispanic, and Two or More Races, non-Hispanic were not the most prevalent group in any county.

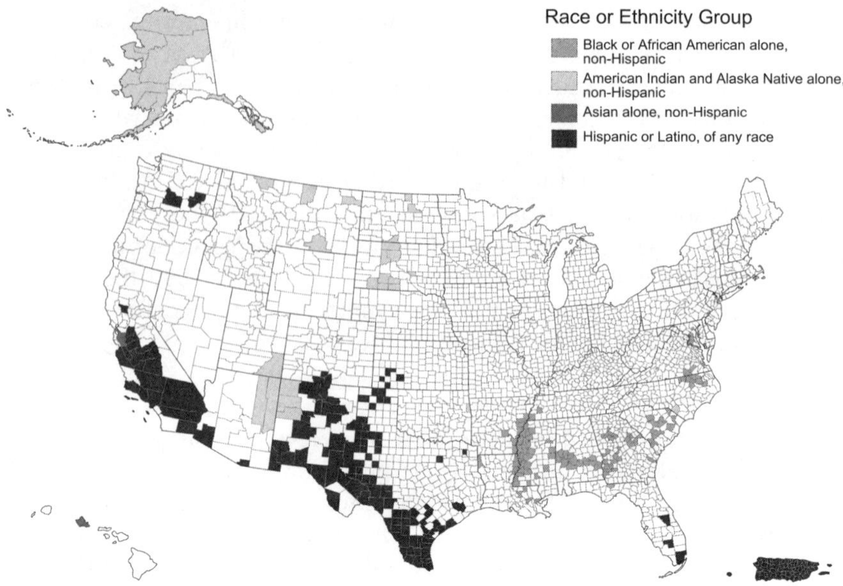

Fig. 1.1b Most prevalent race or ethnicity group by county: 2020

Source: Public US Census Bureau, 2020 Census Redistricting Data (Public Law 94-171) Summary File.

Note: Native Hawaiian and Other Pacific Islander alone, non-Hispanic, Some Other Race alone, non-Hispanic, and Two or More Races, non-Hispanic were not the most prevalent group in any county.

African American alone non-Hispanic, American Indian and Alaska Native alone non-Hispanic, Asian alone non-Hispanic, and Hispanic or Latino populations were the most prevalent. The most prevalent counties for these racial and ethnic groups tended to be clustered regionally.

For example, counties where the Black or African American alone non-Hispanic population was the most prevalent group were in the South, especially along the Mississippi Delta. Counties where the Hispanic or Latino population was the most prevalent racial or ethnic group were in the Southwest, California, and Central Washington. The American Indian and Alaska Native alone non-Hispanic population was the most prevalent group in some counties in the Great Plains, the Four Corners area of the Southwest, and in Alaska. Finally, the Asian alone non-Hispanic population was the most prevalent racial or ethnic group in a few counties in California and Hawaii (figure 1.1b).

There is considerably more variation in the second-most prevalent race or ethnicity group by county across the United States. Large numbers of counties where the Hispanic or Latino population was the second-most prevalent group are found in every region, spanning the continental United

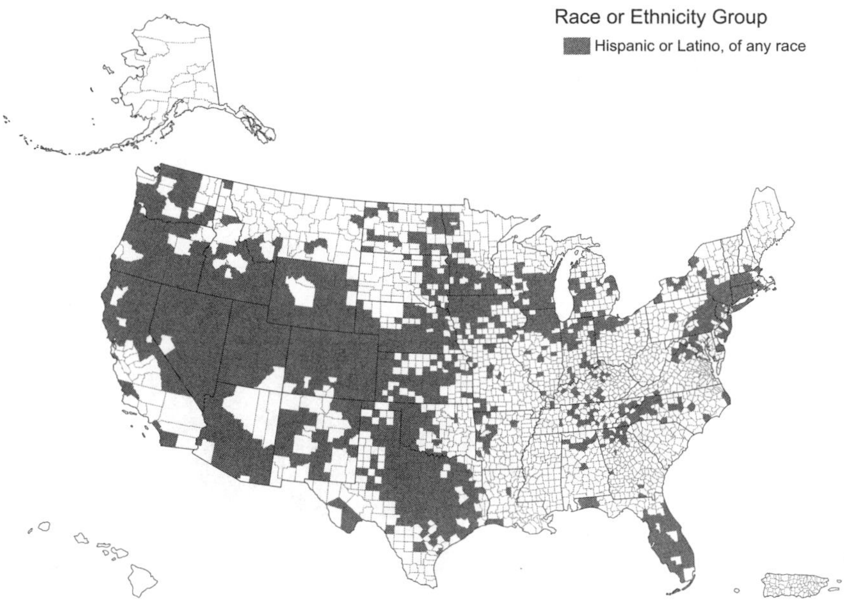

Fig. 1.2a Second-most prevalent race or ethnicity group by county: 2020

Source: US Census Bureau, 2020 Census Redistricting Data (Public Law 94-171) Summary File.

Note: Native Hawaiian and Other Pacific Islander alone, non-Hispanic, and Some Other Race alone, non-Hispanic were not the second-most prevalent group in any county.

States (figure 1.2a). The Black or African American non-Hispanic population was the second-most prevalent racial or ethnic group in many of the counties in the South (figure 1.2b). The Multiracial non-Hispanic population was the second-most prevalent group in counties in the Midwest, along the country's northern border, and in Hawaii (figure 1.2c). Often, these patterns in the second-most prevalent group maps show an inverse relationship to the most prevalent group maps.

Over the years, the US Census Bureau has used different approaches to measure racial and ethnic diversity. For the 2020 Census results, Census Bureau researchers expanded beyond limited approaches such as the majority/minority framework and focused on statistical methods that highlight the complexity of racial and ethnic diversity in the United States. The chosen measures—diversity index, prevalence rankings, prevalence maps, and diffusion scores—allow researchers, data users, and the public to explore the full array of race/ethnicity groups in a particular geographic area and not just through the limited singular perspective of a dichotomous framework.

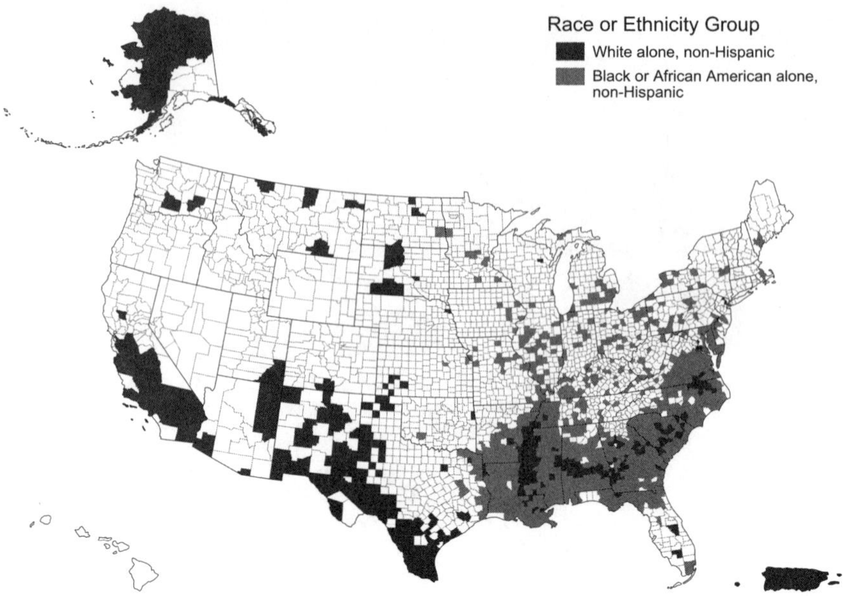

Fig. 1.2b Second-most prevalent race or ethnicity group by county: 2020

Source: US Census Bureau, 2020 Census Redistricting Data (Public Law 94-171) Summary File.

Note: Native Hawaiian and Other Pacific Islander alone, non-Hispanic, and Some Other Race alone, non-Hispanic were not the second-most prevalent group in any county.

1.4 Future Opportunities for Race and Ethnicity

1.4.1 Background: Previous Census Bureau Research on Race and Ethnicity

The Census Bureau has made revisions and improvements to the race and ethnicity questions for the decennial census and demographic surveys since 1980 based on evidence from empirical qualitative and quantitative research, as well as consultation and engagement with stakeholders, advisors, and the public, and adhering to OMB's SPD 15 for collecting and reporting race and ethnicity (OMB 2017). Future improvements to the measurement of race and ethnicity, and the design of a question or questions to do so, will be guided by these three factors—empirical research, public engagement, and federal standards.

In 2015, the Census Bureau conducted the National Content Test (NCT) in preparation for the 2020 Census. The NCT included a combined race and Hispanic origin question to test if this format created less burden and provided better data than the two separate questions approach. The results showed that using a combined question format—with multiple detailed

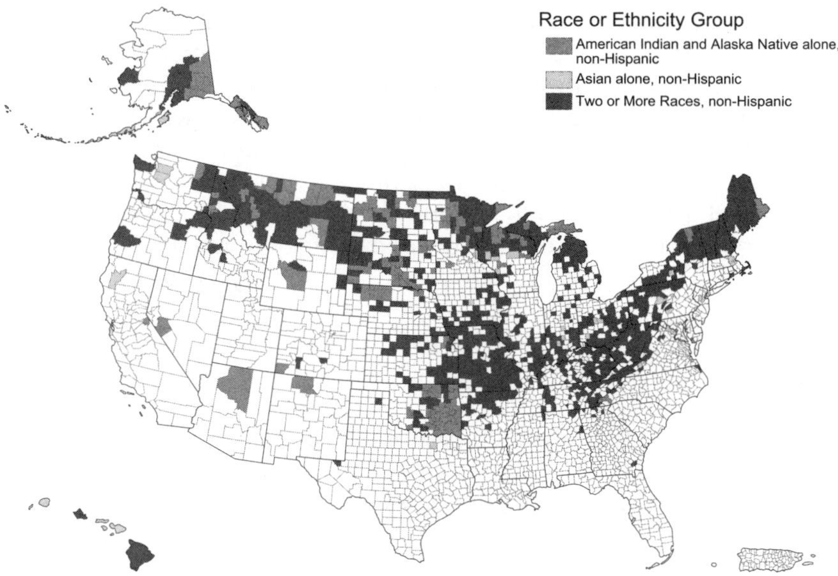

Fig. 1.2c Second-most prevalent race or ethnicity group by county: 2020

Source: US Census Bureau, 2020 Census Redistricting Data (Public Law 94-171) Summary File.

Note: Native Hawaiian and Other Pacific Islander alone, non-Hispanic, and Some Other Race alone, non-Hispanic were not the second-most prevalent group in any county.

checkboxes, write-in fields, and a dedicated option for Middle Eastern or North African (MENA) respondents—reduced respondent burden and improved the accuracy of the results, especially for the Hispanic or Latino population and the Multiracial/ethnic population (Matthews et al. 2017).

Another key finding from the NCT was that using the combined question format greatly reduced the number of people identifying as SOR. SOR was intended to be a relatively small category but was the third-largest race group in both the 2000 Census and 2010 Census (Humes et al. 2011) and has since grown to be the second-largest race alone or in combination category in the 2020 Census, at 50 million people (Jones et al. 2021). SOR is often selected by Hispanic or Latino respondents who do not see their racial identity reflected in the SPD 15 race categories. While not all Hispanic or Latino respondents identify as SOR, nearly all SOR responses are Hispanic or Latino, and reducing the size of the SOR race group was an improvement to the data collected in the 2015 NCT.

Ultimately, the greatest factor in changing the design of the race and ethnicity question(s) is federal standards issued by OMB with SPD 15. The original 1977 SPD 15 was revised in 1997 in part to respond to concerns that it did not adequately allow for self-identification, especially for people of multiracial heritage, or reflect the increasing diversity of the US population.

The US Census Bureau has a long history of conducting research to improve questions and data on race and ethnicity and inform federal standards. Since the 1970s, the Census Bureau has conducted content tests to research and improve the design and function of different questions, including questions on race and ethnicity. Over the past decade and a half, the Census Bureau conducted extensive research and outreach, including two groundbreaking national studies, on how to improve race and ethnicity question(s) so that these statistics better measure our nation's population, and to inform explorations of how Americans identify as our society continues to grow more diverse and more complex.

The Census Bureau's research last decade identified that a combined race and ethnicity question with multiple detailed checkboxes and a dedicated Middle Eastern or North African category is the optimal design for improving race and ethnicity data, in comparison with designs which use two separate questions (figure 1.3). This approach was strongly supported by myriad stakeholders and organizations during OMB's review of potential revisions to 1997 SPD 15.

However, the Census Bureau does not make a unilateral decision on the content of the census.

In fact, determining the content for a census is an extensive undertaking with a three-pronged approach involving empirical research, outreach, and engagement with stakeholders, and ultimately the review and approval from the US Office of Management and Budget and the US Congress.

1.4.2 Race and Ethnicity in the 2020 Census

In the 2020 Census, the Census Bureau collected race and ethnicity data in accordance with the 1997 OMB standards on race and ethnicity, and responses to these questions are based on self-identification. The Census Bureau, along with other federal statistical agencies, must follow SPD 15, which require two separate questions when collecting data on race and ethnicity. The decennial census race question, for the first time in 2020, collected detailed responses for the White population and for the Black or African American population (figure 1.4).

Our research and public feedback over the past decade illuminated strong interest from respondents to be able to self-identify their detailed racial/ethnic background, such as German, Lebanese, Mexican, Jamaican, Nigerian, Chinese, Navajo, Samoan, etc. SPD 15 encourages this collection of detailed responses, and to address this, new examples and write-in areas were added to the 2020 Census ethnicity question and race question to give respondents from all backgrounds the opportunity to self-identify their racial/ethnic identities in the 2020 Census.

For the 2020 Census, we collected detailed responses for all major categories (Hispanic, White, Black or African American, Asian, American Indian or Alaska Native, Native Hawaiian or Other Pacific Islander, and Some Other Race). In turn, this provided the ability to produce detailed tabula-

8. What is Person 1's race or ethnicity?
*Mark all boxes that apply **AND** print ethnicities in the spaces below. Note, you may report more than one group.*

☐ **WHITE** – *Provide details below.*

☐ German ☐ Irish ☐ English
☐ Italian ☐ Polish ☐ French

Print, for example, Scottish, Norwegian, Dutch, etc.

☐ **HISPANIC, LATINO, OR SPANISH** – *Provide details below.*

☐ Mexican or Mexican American ☐ Puerto Rican ☐ Cuban
☐ Salvadoran ☐ Dominican ☐ Colombian

Print, for example, Guatemalan, Spaniard, Ecuadorian, etc.

☐ **BLACK OR AFRICAN AMERICAN** – *Provide details below.*

☐ African American ☐ Jamaican ☐ Haitian
☐ Nigerian ☐ Ethiopian ☐ Somali

Print, for example, Ghanaian, South African, Barbadian, etc.

☐ **ASIAN** – *Provide details below.*

☐ Chinese ☐ Filipino ☐ Asian Indian
☐ Vietnamese ☐ Korean ☐ Japanese

Print, for example, Pakistani, Cambodian, Hmong, etc.

☐ **AMERICAN INDIAN OR ALASKA NATIVE** – *Print, for example, Navajo Nation, Blackfeet Tribe, Mayan, Aztec, Native Village of Barrow Inupiat Traditional Government, Tlingit, etc.*

☐ **MIDDLE EASTERN OR NORTH AFRICAN** – *Provide details below.*

☐ Lebanese ☐ Iranian ☐ Egyptian
☐ Syrian ☐ Moroccan ☐ Israeli

Print, for example, Algerian, Iraqi, Kurdish, etc.

☐ **NATIVE HAWAIIAN OR OTHER PACIFIC ISLANDER** – *Provide details below.*

☐ Native Hawaiian ☐ Samoan ☐ Chamorro
☐ Tongan ☐ Fijian ☐ Marshallese

Print, for example, Palauan, Tahitian, Chuukese, etc.

☐ **SOME OTHER RACE OR ETHNICITY** – *Print details.*

Fig. 1.3 Optimal design from research last decade

→ **NOTE: Please answer BOTH Question 6 about Hispanic origin and Question 7 about race. For this census, Hispanic origins are not races.**

6. Is this person of Hispanic, Latino, or Spanish origin?

- ☐ **No,** not of Hispanic, Latino, or Spanish origin
- ☐ Yes, Mexican, Mexican Am., Chicano
- ☐ Yes, Puerto Rican
- ☐ Yes, Cuban
- ☐ Yes, another Hispanic, Latino, or Spanish origin – *Print, for example, Salvadoran, Dominican, Colombian, Guatemalan, Spaniard, Ecuadorian, etc.*

Fig. 1.4a 2020 Census separate question on ethnicity (Hispanic origin)

tions for myriad population groups in the United States, such as German, Lebanese, Mexican, Jamaican, Nigerian, Chinese, Navajo, Samoan, Brazilian, etc.

Building upon our research over the past decade, the Census Bureau improved the two separate questions design and updated our data processing and coding procedures for the 2020 Census. This work began in 2015 and was centered on findings from our National Content Test, with the new designs implemented in the 2018 Census Test. The improvements and changes enabled a more thorough and accurate depiction of how people self-identify, yielding a more accurate portrait of how people report their Hispanic origin and race within the context of a two-question format. These changes revealed that the US population is much more multiracial and diverse than what was measured in the past.

However, results from the 2020 Census also showed the persisting problems with two separate questions on race and ethnicity. We are confident that differences in the overall racial distributions are largely due to improvements in the design of the two separate questions, as well as some demographic changes over the past 10 years. We are also confident, as shown in our research over the past decade, that using a single combined question for race and ethnicity in the decennial census would ultimately yield an even more accurate portrait of how the US population self-identifies, especially for people who self-identify as multiracial or multiethnic.

1.4.3 OMB Review of Race Ethnicity Standards (SPD 15)

OMB announced their formal review of SPD 15 in June 2022, with the goal of ensuring that the standards better reflect the diversity of the nation.

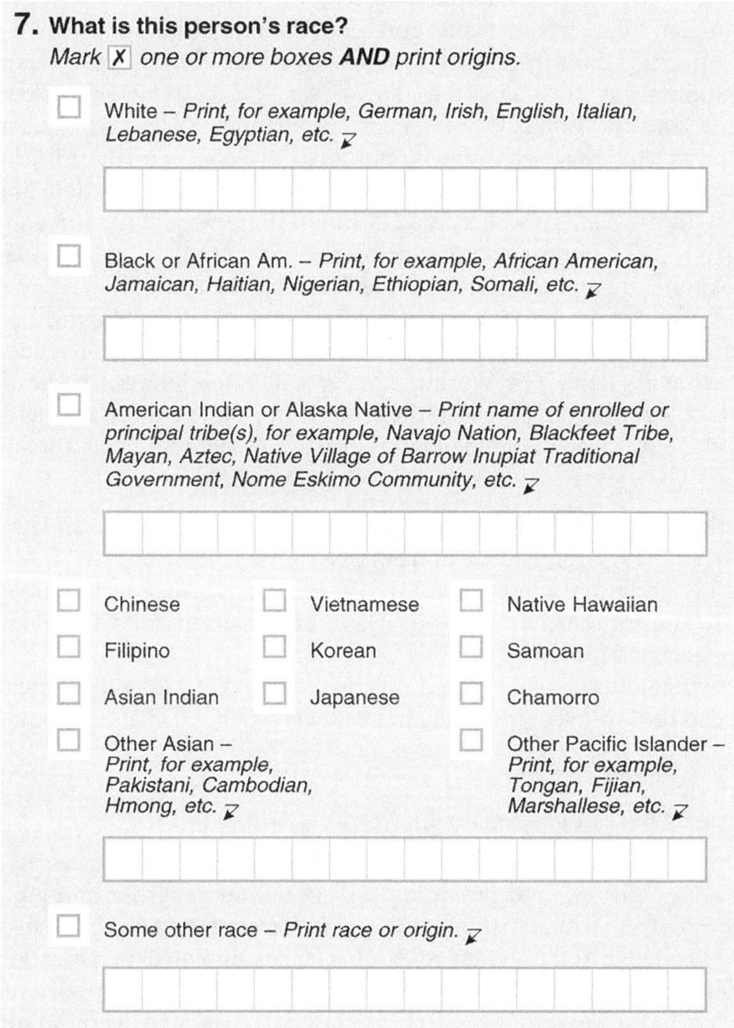

7. What is this person's race?
Mark [X] *one or more boxes* ***AND*** *print origins.*

☐ White – *Print, for example, German, Irish, English, Italian, Lebanese, Egyptian, etc.*

☐ Black or African Am. – *Print, for example, African American, Jamaican, Haitian, Nigerian, Ethiopian, Somali, etc.*

☐ American Indian or Alaska Native – *Print name of enrolled or principal tribe(s), for example, Navajo Nation, Blackfeet Tribe, Mayan, Aztec, Native Village of Barrow Inupiat Traditional Government, Nome Eskimo Community, etc.*

☐ Chinese ☐ Vietnamese ☐ Native Hawaiian

☐ Filipino ☐ Korean ☐ Samoan

☐ Asian Indian ☐ Japanese ☐ Chamorro

☐ Other Asian – *Print, for example, Pakistani, Cambodian, Hmong, etc.*

☐ Other Pacific Islander – *Print, for example, Tongan, Fijian, Marshallese, etc.*

☐ Some other race – *Print race or origin.*

Fig. 1.4b 2020 Census separate question on race

The chief statistician of the United States, Dr. Karin Orvis, and her staff organized the Federal Interagency Technical Working Group[1] (referred to as Working Group). OMB and the Working Group undertook a revision process similar to those used for the development and revision of other trusted statistical standards, which helps ensure the rigor, validity, objectivity, and impartiality of the resulting recommended revisions.

1. Source: Information about OMB's Interagency Technical Working Group on Race and Ethnicity Standards, https://spd15revision.gov/content/spd15revision/en/about.html.

Consistent with OMB's established process, the working group was composed of federal career staff who represent programs that collect or use race and ethnicity data from over 20 agencies across the federal government, including statistical agencies, almost every Chief Financial Officers Act agency, and the Equal Employment Opportunity Commission. The agencies on the Interagency Council on Statistical Policy, i.e., the 13 Principal Statistical Agencies,[2] and the 24 agencies enumerated by the Chief Financial Officers Act,[3] as well as the US Equal Employment Opportunity Commission—selected for its reliance on race and ethnicity data—were invited to nominate representatives to the Working Group.

The Working Group undertook the important work of developing a set of recommendations for improving the quality and usefulness of federal race and ethnicity data. The Working Group evaluated relevant research, engaged in a meaningful way with the American public and all impacted agencies, and developed recommendations on topics including, but not limited to:

- Whether the minimum reporting categories should be changed and how to best address detailed race and ethnicity groups in SPD 15;
- Whether updates should be made to the question format, terminology, and wording of the questions, as well as the instructions for respondents and associated guidance; and
- Whether guidance for the collection and reporting of race and ethnicity data can be improved, including in instances when self-identification is not possible.

1.4.4 Census Bureau Leadership for Working Group

The Census Bureau worked closely with OMB, serving as the co-chair of the Working Group, and providing subject matter expertise and guidance for each of the teams within the Working Group based on the Census Bureau's knowledge and previous research. Census Bureau experts worked with OMB and federal agency colleagues to provide technical support and expertise for the formal review of SPD 15. The goal of revising the standards was to improve the ability of the government to capture the diversity of the US population, to ensure that they are keeping pace with changes in the population and evolving needs and uses for data.

1.4.5 Development of Initial Proposals

The Working Group reviewed existing research and evidence to develop initial proposals. For example, the Working Group reviewed what was done by the previous OMB Working Group last decade when they reviewed SPD

2. For reference, a list of the 13 Principal Statistical Agencies is available online, https://nces.ed.gov/FCSM/agencies.asp.

3. For reference, a list of the 24 Chief Financial Officers Act Agencies is available online, https://www.cfo.gov/about-the-council/.

15, as they focused on many of the same issues that the current Working Group is tackling. Throughout, Census Bureau experts on race and ethnicity collaborated with fellow Working Group members and contributed to the discussions by presenting evidence from extensive research and engagement over the past decade, as well as data and experiences from the 2020 Census, and other sources.

The initial proposals[4] were released in January 2023 for public comment, and are summarized below:

- **Initial Proposal 1:** Collect race and ethnicity information using one combined question.
- **Initial Proposal 2:** Add "Middle Eastern or North African" (MENA) as a new minimum category.
- **Initial Proposal 3:** Require the collection of detailed race and ethnicity categories by default.
- **Initial Proposal 4:** Update Terminology in SPD 15.
- **Initial Proposal 5:** Guidance is necessary to implement SPD 15 revisions on federal information collections.

1.4.6 OMB Publishes Updated SPD 15

On March 28, 2024, the US Office of Management and Budget published the results[5] of its review of Statistical Policy Directive No. 15 (SPD 15) and issued updated standards[6] for maintaining, collecting and presenting race/ethnicity data across federal agencies.[7]

The most notable updates for the new standards are the requirement to use a combined race/ethnicity question; the addition of a new "Middle Eastern and North African" minimum reporting category; and the requirement to collect detailed race/ethnicity responses.

The Census Bureau's findings over the past decade resonate with many of the SPD 15 updates.[8] We know from our extensive research and engage-

4. For more information on the Initial Proposals for Updating OMB's Race and Ethnicity Statistical Standards, please visit https://www.federalregister.gov/documents/2023/01/27/2023-01635/initial-proposals-for-updating-ombs-race-and-ethnicity-statistical-standards (January 27, 2023). Note: These proposals were preliminary and noted that they did not reflect the settled opinions of the Working Group, the position of OMB, or the positions of the agencies participating on the Working Group. The Working Group was expected to continue to deliberate, assess evidence, and take into consideration comments received from the public before making final recommendations for OMB's consideration.

5. https://www.whitehouse.gov/omb/briefing-room/2024/03/28/omb-publishes-revisions-to-statistical-policy-directive-no-15-standards-for-maintaining-collecting-and-presenting-federal-data-on-race-and-ethnicity/.

6. https://www.federalregister.gov/public-inspection/2024-06469/statistical-policy-directive-no-15-standards-for-maintaining-collecting-and-presenting-federal-data.

7. Source: To access OMB's Updated Race and Ethnicity Statistical Standards, please visit https://spd15revision.gov/content/spd15revision/en.html (March 28, 2024).

8. This section of the paper draws from a 2024 Census Bureau blog written by the authors titled "What Updates to OMB's Race/Ethnicity Standards Mean for the Census Bureau." Source: https://www.census.gov/newsroom/blogs/random-samplings/2024/04/updates-race-ethnicity-standards.html.

ment with myriad communities, organizations, scholars, researchers, and data users across the country that a combined race/ethnicity question with a dedicated Middle Eastern or North African response category and an emphasis on the collection of detailed identities for all communities will produce more accurate race/ethnicity data for our nation's population.

The updates to SPD 15 were informed by robust empirical research, extensive engagement with experts, scholars, organization leaders, and communities across the country, and the successful and meaningful collaboration among federal agency leaders and experts on the Interagency Technical Working Group on Race and Ethnicity Standards.[9] Census Bureau leaders are confident that the updated standards will improve data on race/ethnicity across US Census Bureau programs, and that these new data will better represent the US population's rich racial/ethnic diversity and detailed identities.

Combined Race/Ethnicity Question. The updated SPD 15 requires a combined race/ethnicity question for self-response and proxy reporting. Within this approach, respondents may report one category or report multiple categories to indicate their racial/ethnic identity. In the updated standards, a single response, such as Hispanic or Latino, is considered a complete response.

New "Middle Eastern or North African" Category. The updated SPD 15 adds a new, dedicated "Middle Eastern or North African" (MENA) category, separate and distinct from all other minimum categories. As evidenced from extensive engagement[10] with the Middle Eastern or North African community in the United States, there is strong support for a MENA category and demonstrated need for demographic and socioeconomic statistics about the MENA population. New data will help inform policy decisions, health research, civil rights monitoring and enforcement, and address many other needs.

Required Collection of Detailed Race/Ethnicity Data. The updated SPD 15 requires the collection of detailed race/ethnicity data beyond the minimum categories for most situations.

The combined question with multiple detailed checkboxes and write-in response areas will improve the question design to facilitate the reporting of detailed race/ethnicity responses and increase the availability of disaggregated race/ethnicity data for *all* communities.

Question Stem and Instructions. The updated SPD 15 guidance to use the question stem, "What is your race and/or ethnicity?" aligns with Census Bureau research that found it is optimal to use the "race/ethnicity" terminology, rather than alternatives such as "race/origin" or "categories," for a combined question. The updated SPD 15 provides instructions to make clear

9. https://spd15revision.gov/content/spd15revision/en/about.html.

10. https://www.census.gov/library/working-papers/2015/demo/2015-MENA-Experts.html.

that respondents may select multiple race/ethnicity groups: “Select all that apply and enter additional details in the spaces below.” This approach aligns with Census Bureau research that found the instructions “Mark all that apply” (for paper data collections) and “Select all that apply” (for Internet data collections) performed as well, or in some instances better than, other variations.

Question Design. The updated SPD 15 envisions that agencies, whenever possible, will collect race/ethnicity data with a question format that includes the required minimum categories disaggregated by the required detailed categories with multiple detailed checkboxes and dedicated write-in response areas, as illustrated in figure 1.5. Additional question designs from the updated are shown as figure 1.6 (Combined Race/Ethnicity Question with Minimum Categories and Inclusion of Detailed Example Groups) and figure 1.7 (Combined Race/Ethnicity Question with Minimum Categories Only).

When an agency receives an OMB exemption from collecting detailed data using the approach with figure 1.5, it may use a format that includes only the minimum categories (e.g., figure 1.6 or figure 1.7). When using the minimum categories only, the updated SPD 15 guidance advises that the quality of the data and consistency with other datasets may be improved by providing the respondent with examples as shown in figure 1.6, and agencies should provide these examples when feasible over the example in figure 1.7 without examples.

For the 2024 SPD 15 decisions, OMB concurred with the Working Group’s determination that there is not sufficient evidence at this time to justify requiring a specific ordering for presentation of the minimum categories, and thus the updated SPD 15 will continue to provide agencies flexibility on how to order the response categories on information collections so that future research can inform the optimal approach to ordering response options. Although the minimum race/ethnicity reporting categories are displayed alphabetically in the updated SPD 15 example question design, the Census Bureau has historically ordered the categories by population size on its questionnaires. The updated SPD 15 allows for both formats to be used.

Terminology, Definitions, and Concepts. In terms of defining race and ethnicity, for the purposes of the SPD 15, the race and ethnicity categories set forth by OMB are noted to be sociopolitical constructs and not an attempt to define race and ethnicity biologically or genetically. The updated standards also aim to provide balance across the race/ethnicity definitions and to remove any outdated and offensive terminology.

The 2024 SPD 15 provides a conceptual framework of “Race and/or Ethnicity” and requires all race and/or ethnicity categories to be treated *equally* in collection and tabulation. The standards advise that respondents may select as many race and/or ethnicity options that correspond to how they identify and require agencies to treat the categories equally and report them as “race and/or ethnicity” categories.

What is your race and/or ethnicity?

Select all that apply and enter additional details in the spaces below.

☐ **American Indian or Alaska Native** – *Enter, for example, Navajo Nation, Blackfeet Tribe of the Blackfeet Indian Reservation of Montana, Native Village of Barrow Inupiat Traditional Government, Nome Eskimo Community, Aztec, Maya, etc.*

☐ **Asian** – *Provide details below.*

☐ Chinese ☐ Asian Indian ☐ Filipino
☐ Vietnamese ☐ Korean ☐ Japanese

Enter, for example, Pakistani, Hmong, Afghan, etc.

☐ **Black or African American** – *Provide details below.*

☐ African American ☐ Jamaican ☐ Haitian
☐ Nigerian ☐ Ethiopian ☐ Somali

Enter, for example, Trinidadian and Tobagonian, Ghanaian, Congolese, etc.

☐ **Hispanic or Latino** – *Provide details below.*

☐ Mexican ☐ Puerto Rican ☐ Salvadoran
☐ Cuban ☐ Dominican ☐ Guatemalan

Enter, for example, Colombian, Honduran, Spaniard, etc.

☐ **Middle Eastern or North African** – *Provide details below.*

☐ Lebanese ☐ Iranian ☐ Egyptian
☐ Syrian ☐ Iraqi ☐ Israeli

Enter, for example, Moroccan, Yemeni, Kurdish, etc.

☐ **Native Hawaiian or Pacific Islander** – *Provide details below.*

☐ Native Hawaiian ☐ Samoan ☐ Chamorro
☐ Tongan ☐ Fijian ☐ Marshallese

Enter, for example, Chuukese, Palauan, Tahitian, etc.

☐ **White** – *Provide details below.*

☐ English ☐ German ☐ Irish
☐ Italian ☐ Polish ☐ Scottish

Enter, for example, French, Swedish, Norwegian, etc.

Fig. 1.5 Updated 2024 SPD 15 combined race/ethnicity question with minimum categories, multiple detailed checkboxes, and write-in response areas with example groups

What is your race and/or ethnicity?
Select all that apply.

☐ **American Indian or Alaska Native**
For example, Navajo Nation, Blackfeet Tribe of the Blackfeet Indian Reservation of Montana, Native Village of Barrow Inupiat Traditional Government, Nome Eskimo Community, Aztec, Maya, etc.

☐ **Asian**
For example, Chinese, Asian Indian, Filipino, Vietnamese, Korean, Japanese, etc.

☐ **Black or African American**
For example, African American, Jamaican, Haitian, Nigerian, Ethiopian, Somali, etc.

☐ **Hispanic or Latino**
For example, Mexican, Puerto Rican, Salvadoran, Cuban, Dominican, Guatemalan, etc.

☐ **Middle Eastern or North African**
For example, Lebanese, Iranian, Egyptian, Syrian, Iraqi, Israeli, etc.

☐ **Native Hawaiian or Pacific Islander**
For example, Native Hawaiian, Samoan, Chamorro, Tongan, Fijian, Marshallese, etc.

☐ **White**
For example, English, German, Irish, Italian, Polish, Scottish, etc.

Fig. 1.6 Updated 2024 SPD 15 combined race/ethnicity question with minimum categories and inclusion of detailed example groups

What is your race and/or ethnicity?
Select all that apply.

☐ **American Indian or Alaska Native**

☐ **Asian**

☐ **Black or African American**

☐ **Hispanic or Latino**

☐ **Middle Eastern or North African**

☐ **Native Hawaiian or Pacific Islander**

☐ **White**

Fig. 1.7 Updated 2024 SPD 15 combined race/ethnicity question with minimum categories only

OMB's decision on this recommendation reflects the strong evidence that a combined question format results in higher quality and more useful data and provides a format that is clearer and more concise for respondents while still allowing them to select as many race and/or ethnicity options that correspond to how they identify.

The new, minimum race and/or ethnicity categories with the updated SPD 15 are:

- American Indian or Alaska Native
- Asian
- Black or African American
- Hispanic or Latino
- Middle Eastern or North African
- Native Hawaiian or Pacific Islander
- White

OMB advises that with respect to collection, the seven minimum race/ethnicity categories shall be treated *co-equally* except if a program or collection effort focuses on a specific racial or ethnic group, and only as approved by OMB. Further, collection forms may not indicate to respondents that they should interpret some categories as ethnicities and others as races, or otherwise indicate conceptual differences among the minimum categories.

The revised category definitions list six example groups reflecting the largest population groups in the United States according to the 2020 Census. These revisions bring the terminology in SPD 15 more up to date and greatly increase the consistency and clarity of the minimum category definitions. While the minimum category definitions and detailed categories rely heavily on the concept of nationality, in the updated standards OMB acknowledges that nationality is one of several components that contribute to racial and ethnic identity. The updated standards are intended to facilitate individual identity to the greatest extent possible while still enabling the creation of consistent and comparable data. Table 1.4 presents the updated definitions for each of the minimum race/ethnicity categories as delineated in the 2024 SPD 15.

As discussed previously in the paper, it is important to note that the Census Bureau is also required by the US Congress[11] to offer the category "Some Other Race" in the American Community Survey and decennial census. Extensive Census Bureau research has shown that the use of a combined race/ethnicity question reduces the reporting of "Some Other Race" as respondents are able to find a category or multiple categories to report their racial/ethnic identity.

Tabulation Guidance. Since Census 2000, when respondents were first permitted to self-identify and select more than one race response, the Cen-

11. https://www.congress.gov/109/plaws/publ108/PLAW-109publ108.pdf.

Table 1.4 Updated 2024 SPD 15 definitions for minimum race/ethnicity categories

Minimum Race/ Ethnicity Category	Definition
American Indian or Alaska Native	Individuals with origins in any of the original peoples of North, Central, and South America, including, for example, Navajo Nation, Blackfeet Tribe of the Blackfeet Indian Reservation of Montana, Native Village of Barrow Inupiat Traditional Government, Nome Eskimo Community, Aztec, and Maya.
Asian	Individuals with origins in any of the original peoples of Central or East Asia, Southeast Asia, or South Asia, including, for example, Chinese, Asian Indian, Filipino, Vietnamese, Korean, and Japanese.
Black or African American	Individuals with origins in any of the Black racial groups of Africa, including, for example, African American, Jamaican, Haitian, Nigerian, Ethiopian, and Somali.
Hispanic or Latino	Includes individuals of Mexican, Puerto Rican, Salvadoran, Cuban, Dominican, Guatemalan, and other Central or South American or Spanish culture or origin.
Middle Eastern or North African	Individuals with origins in any of the original peoples of the Middle East or North Africa, including, for example, Lebanese, Iranian, Egyptian, Syrian, Iraqi, and Israeli.
Native Hawaiian or Pacific Islander	Individuals with origins in any of the original peoples of Hawaii, Guam, Samoa, or other Pacific Islands, including, for example, Native Hawaiian, Samoan, Chamorro, Tongan, Fijian, and Marshallese.
White	Individuals with origins in any of the original peoples of Europe, including, for example, English, German, Irish, Italian, Polish, and Scottish.

sus Bureau has published data for the "race alone," "race in combination," and "race alone or in combination" populations to frame the discussion of racial composition. These concepts have been central to understanding our country's changing demographics.[12] The updated standards encourage the reporting of as much information on race/ethnicity as possible in data tabulations, and we will continue to emphasize these important approaches for data tabulations, analyses, and discussions following the guidance of the updated standards.

1.4.7 Bridging Guidance

As the standards for collecting data on race and ethnicity have changed over time, there is a need for resources to harmonize categories from one

12. https://www.census.gov/library/stories/2021/08/improved-race-ethnicity-measures-reveal-united-states-population-much-more-multiracial.html.

format to another. When the original 1977 standards were revised in 1997, this necessitated the need for bridging the two formats. The 1977 OMB race standards included four categories: American Indian or Alaska Native, Asian or Pacific Islander, Black, and White. In 1997, SPD 15 was revised with two major changes: (1) Pacific Islander became a separate category from Asian and (2) people could select more than one race category.

In Census 2000, for the first time, respondents were allowed to report multiple race categories. While this led to more accurate information and nuanced data about the complexity of people's racial identity and the composition of the US population, having multiple race responses did not map on the race data collected by other state and federal agencies, many of whom were still using the 1977 OMB standards.

In 2003, the National Center for Health Statistics (NCHS) developed a series of adjustment factors that allowed data users to "bridge" from the 1977 OMB categories with only four single-race categories to the 1997 OMB stands that included a possibility of 31 race categories (5 single-race and 26 multiracial categories).

To develop the bridging factors, researchers at NCHS pooled data from the 1997 to 2000 National Health Interview Survey, which first asked respondents their race in the 1997 categories and then asked them to identify a "primary race" from the 1977 categories (Ingram et al. 2003). Next, they used logistic regression models to create the bridging factors from the 1997 to the 1977 categories. The models included covariates for demographic characteristics at the person level and contextual variables at the county level (Ingram et al. 2003; Liebler and Halpern-Manners 2008). The bridging had the biggest impact on the data for the AIAN and NHPI populations, which are the two groups with the largest proportion of multiracial individuals (Humes et al. 2011). The NCHS bridging factors have been widely used by researchers to harmonize race data from the 1997 to the 1977 OMB standards. Additionally, researchers also need to convert data from the 1977 to the 1997 OMB standards, which the US Census Bureau does using a process called "reverse bridging" (Sink and Colby 2014).

As part of the release of the updated SPD 15, OMB and the Working Group developed and published a technical report and resources for bridging the 1997 SPD 15 and the 2024 SPD 15.[13] An initial, basic bridging program was released for general use on all federal data used by federal agencies and public data users. The tools developed by the Working Group are intended to help federal agencies estimate and compare race/ethnicity specific statistics over time. OMB advised that agencies are not required to use these tools and may choose to use their own program data to replace or supplement the bridging tools provided here.

13. Source: To access OMB's Bridging Data Tools" resource website, please visit https://spd15revision.gov/content/spd15revision/en/data-tools.html (March 28, 2024).

Complementary research and the development of more robust methodologies in the future are expected to be developed by the Federal Committee for SPD 15, which OMB established in the summer of 2024. It is expected that bridging will be one of the key topics undertaken to provide agencies with information and guidance to assist with implementation of the updated standards. In the future, as additional data are collected under the 2024 SPD 15, the race/ethnicity bridging programs, user guides, and test datasets will be updated with insights from research and feedback on their utility.

1.5 Conclusion and Next Steps

This paper contributes to the theme of the 2024 NBER Conference on Research in Income and Wealth titled "Race, Ethnicity, and Economic Statistics for the 21st Century" in several ways. First, the paper provides historical context for how race and ethnicity have been measured in the decennial census. This history is not only about the population groups that were included on the decennial census form but also the groups that were not. Historical decisions on which groups to include or exclude were essentially about visibility, representation, and power.

The paper also provides an overview of the federal government's recent review of SPD 15 and the decision-making process completed by OMB that helped determine how federal agencies will collect, tabulate, and report information on race and ethnicity in the coming years, including the 2030 Census, following the updated 2024 race/ethnicity standards.

The US Census Bureau's race/ethnicity research team is thoroughly reviewing the SPD 15 updates and collaborating with colleagues across the Census Bureau to begin the development of an agency action plan to implement the updated standards within the OMB's required five-year period. The Census Bureau has communicated publicly that updates will be made as expeditiously as possible for Census Bureau data collections that include race and ethnicity, such as the American Community Survey and the 2030 Census. Throughout this process, Census Bureau leaders will engage with stakeholders and keep them posted as the Census Bureau develops implementation plans. The Census Bureau will partner with the public, stakeholders, and data users as the updated race/ethnicity standards are implemented in an effort to provide the most accurate, reliable, and relevant data possible about our changing and diversifying nation.

The collaboration, research, and engagement undertaken by the Working Group, federal agencies, and OMB are another milestone in the long history of race and ethnicity in the United States as described in this paper. This ambitious endeavor to improve standards for measuring, collecting, and tabulating data on race/ethnicity has been no small undertaking, in any sense. The potential positive impacts of the updated race/ethnicity standards will go far and wide to improve data and our understanding of the complex demographic makeup and the socioeconomic characteristics of our country's population and our myriad diverse communities.

Disclaimer

This presentation is released to inform parties of ongoing research and to encourage discussion in progress. Any opinions and conclusions expressed herein are those of the authors and do not reflect the views of the US Census Bureau. For acknowledgments, sources of research support, and disclosure of the authors' material financial relationships, if any, please see https://www.nber.org/books-and-chapters/race-ethnicity-and-economic-statistics-21st-century/measuring-racial-and-ethnic-composition-and-diversity-united-states-population-historical-challenges.

References

Alba, Richard. 2018. "What Majority-Minority Society? A Critical Analysis of the Census Bureau's Projections of America's Demographic Future." *Socius* 4.

Anderson, Margo J. 2015. *The American Census: A Social History*. Yale University Press.

Calavita, Kitty. 2000. "The Paradoxes of Race, Class, Identity, and 'Passing': Enforcing the Chinese Exclusion Acts, 1882–1910." *Law & Social Inquiry* 25(1): 1–40.

Cantwell, Pat. 2021. "How We Complete the census When Households or Group Quarters Don't Respond." Random Samplings Census Blogs.

Colby, Sandra L., and Jennifer M. Ortman. 2015. "Projections of the Size and Composition of the US Population: 2014 to 2060." Population Estimates and Projections. Current Population Reports. P25–1143. US Census Bureau.

Dixon, Angela R., and Edward E. Telles. 2017. "Skin Color and Colorism: Global Research, Concepts, and Measurement." *Annual Review of Sociology* 43: 405–24.

Elliott, Marc N., Allen Fremont, Peter A. Morrison, Philip Pantoja, and Nicole Lurie. 2008. "A New Method for Estimating Race/Ethnicity and Associated Disparities Where Administrative Records Lack Self-Reported Race/Ethnicity." *Health Services Research* 43(5p1): 1722–1736.

Ennis, Sharon, Sonya Porter, James Noon, Ellen Zapata. 2018. "When Race and Hispanic Origin Reporting Are Discrepant Across Administrative Records and Third Party Sources: Exploring Methods to Assign Responses." *Statistical Journal of the IAOS* 34(2): 179–189.

Filice, Clara, and Karen Joynt. 2017. "Examining Race and Ethnicity Information in Medicare Administrative Data." *Medical Care* 55(12): e170–e176.

Gauthier, Jason G. 2002. *Measuring America: The Decennial Censuses from 1790 to 2000*. US Department of Commerce, Economics and Statistics Administration, US Census Bureau.

Golash-Boza, Tanya, and William Darity Jr. 2008. "Latino Racial Choices: The Effects of Skin Colour and Discrimination on Latinos' and Latinas' Racial Self-Identifications." *Ethnic and Racial Studies* 31(5): 899–934.

Goldsmith, Arthur H., Darrick Hamilton, and William Darity Jr. 2006. "Shades of Discrimination: Skin Tone and Wages." *American Economic Review* 96(2): 242–45.

Hamilton, Michelle A. 2007. "'Anyone Not on the List Might As Well Be Dead':

Aboriginal Peoples and the Censuses of Canada, 1851–1916." *Journal of the Canadian Historical Association* 18(1): 57–79.

Holland, Kenneth M. 2007. "A History of Chinese Immigration in the United States and Canada." *American Review of Canadian Studies* 37(2): 150.

Humes, Karen, and Howard Hogan. 2009. "Measurement of Race and Ethnicity in a Changing, Multicultural America." *Race and Social Problems* 1: 111–13.

Humes, Karen, Nicholas A. Jones, and Roberto R. Ramirez. 2011. "Overview of Race and Hispanic Origin: 2010." US Census Bureau.

Iceland, John, and Daniel H. Weinberg. 2002. *Racial and Ethnic Residential Segregation in the United States 1980–2000*. Bureau of Census.

Imai, Kosuke, Santiago Olivella, and Evan T. R. Rosenman. 2022. "Addressing Census Data Problems in Race Imputation via Fully Bayesian Improved Surname Geocoding and Name Supplements." *Science Advances* 8(49): eadc9824.

Ingram, Deborah D., Jennifer D. Parker, Nathaniel Schenker, James A. Weed, Brady E. Hamilton, Elizabeth Arias, and Jennifer H. Madans. 2003. "United States Census 2000 Population with Bridged Race Categories." National Center for Health Statistics. Vital Health Stat 2(135). Available from: http://www.cdc.gov/nchs/data/series/sr_02/sr02_135.pdf.

Jarrín, Olga F., Abner N. Nyandege, Irina B. Grafova, XinQi Dong, and Haiqun Lin. 2020. "Validity of Race and Ethnicity Codes in Medicare Administrative Data Compared to Gold-Standard Self-Reported Race Collected during Routine Home Health Care Visits." *Medical Care* 58(1): e1.

Jensen, Eric, Nicholas Jones, Kimberly Orozco, Lauren Medina, Marc Perry, Ben Bolender, and Karen Battle. 2021a. "Measuring Racial and Ethnic Diversity for the 2020 Census." US Census Bureau.

Jensen, Eric, Nicholas Jones, Megan Rabe, Beverly Pratt, Lauren Medina, Kimberly Orozco, and Lindsay Spell. 2021b. "2020 US Population More Racially and Ethnically Diverse Than Measured in 2010." *Census Bureau* 12.

Johnson, Kenneth M., and Daniel T. Lichter. 2010. "Growing Diversity among America's Children and Youth: Spatial and Temporal Dimensions." *Population and Development Review* 36(1): 151–76.

Jones, Nicholas, Rachel Marks, Roberto Ramirez, and Merarys Ríos-Vargas. 2021. "Improved Race and Ethnicity Measures Reveal US Population is Much More Multiracial." US Census Bureau, August 12.

Keith, Verna M., Ann W. Nguyen, Robert Joseph Taylor, Dawne M. Mouzon, and Linda M. Chatters. 2017. "Microaggressions, Discrimination, and Phenotype among African Americans: A Latent Class Analysis of the Impact of Skin Tone and BMI." *Sociological Inquiry* 87(2): 233–55.

Kressin, Nancy R., Bei-Hung Chang, Ann Hendricks, and Lewis E. Kazis. 2003. "Agreement between Administrative Data and Patients' Self-Reports of Race/Ethnicity." *American Journal of Public Health* 93(10): 1734–1739.

Kwan-Lafond, Danielle, and Shannon Winterstein. 2020. "The Canadian Census and Mixed Race: Tracking Mixed Race through Ancestry, Visible Minority Status, and Métis Population Groups in Canada." *The Palgrave International Handbook of Mixed Racial and Ethnic Classification* (2020): 75–94.

Layne, Mary, Deborah Wagner, and Cynthia Rothhaas. 2014. "Estimating Record Linkage False Match Rate for the Person Identification Validation System." Center for Administrative Records Research and Applications Working Paper 2.

Lee, Jennifer, and Frank D. Bean. 2010. *The Diversity Paradox: Immigration and the Color Line in Twenty-First-Century America*. Russell Sage Foundation.

Liebler, Carolyn A., and Andrew Halpern-Manners. 2008. "A Practical Approach to Using Multiple-Race Response Data: A Bridging Method for Public Use Microdata." *Demography* 45: 143–55.

Liebler, Carolyn A., Sonya R. Porter, Leticia E. Fernandez, James M. Noon, and

Sharon R. Ennis. 2017. "America's Churning Races: Race and Ethnicity Response Changes between Census 2000 and the 2010 Census." *Demography* 54(1): 259–84.

López, Nancy, Edward Vargas, Melina Juarez, Lisa Cacari-Stone, and Sonia Bettez. 2018. "What's Your 'Street Race'? Leveraging Multidimensional Measures of Race and Intersectionality for Examining Physical and Mental Health Status among Latinxs." *Sociology of Race and Ethnicity* 4(1): 49–66.

Markham, Francis, and Nicholas Biddle. 2018. "Recent Changes to the Indigenous Population Geography of Australia: Evidence from the 2016 Census." *Australian Population Studies* 2(1): 1–13.

Marks, Rachel, and Merarys Rios-Vargas. 2021. "Improvements to the 2020 Census Race and Hispanic Origin Question Designs, Data Processing, and Coding Procedures." US Census Bureau, August 3.

Marks, Rachel, Nicholas Jones, and Karen Battle. 2024. "What Updates to OMB's Race/Ethnicity Standards Mean for the Census Bureau." US Census Bureau, April 8. https://www.census.gov/newsroom/blogs/random-samplings/2024/04/updates-race-ethnicity-standards.html.

Massey, Douglas S., and Nancy A. Denton. 1988. "The Dimensions of Residential Segregation." *Social Forces* 67(2): 281–315.

Massey, Douglas S., Jonathan Rothwell, and Thurston Domina. 2009. "The Changing Bases of Segregation in the United States." *The Annals of the American Academy of Political and Social Science* 626(1): 74–90.

Matthews, Kelly, Jessica Phelan, Nicholas A. Jones, Sarah Konya, Rachel Marks, Beverly Pratt, Julia Coombs, and Michael Bentley. 2017. "2015 National Content Test: Race and Ethnicity Analysis Report." US Census Bureau.

Meyer, Philip, and Shawn McIntosh. 1992. "The USA Today Index of Ethnic Diversity." *International Journal of Public Opinion Research* 4(1): 51–58.

Monk Jr, Ellis P. 2014. "Skin Tone Stratification Among Black Americans, 2001–2003." *Social Forces* 92(4): 1313–1337.

Monk Jr, Ellis P. 2015. "The Cost of Color: Skin Color, Discrimination, and Health among African-Americans." *American Journal of Sociology* 121(2): 396–444.

Monk Jr, Ellis P. 2021. "The Unceasing Significance of Colorism: Skin Tone Stratification in the United States." *Daedalus* 150(2): 76–90.

Mule, Thomas. 2022. "Quality of the Administrative Record Data Used in the 2020 Census." Presentation at the meetings of the Census Bureau's National Advisory Committee. May 6.

Orvis, Karin. 2022. Reviewing and Revising Standards for Maintaining, Collecting, and Presenting Federal Data on Race and Ethnicity, The White House. https://www.whitehouse.gov/omb/briefing-room/2022/06/15/reviewing-and-revising-standards-for-maintaining-collecting-and-presenting-federal-data-on-race-and-ethnicity/.

Orvis, Karin. 2023. "Initial Proposals for Revising the Federal Race and Ethnicity Standards." US Office of Management and Budget.

Pratt, Beverly, Lindsay Hixson, and Nicholas Jones. 2015. "Measuring Race and Ethnicity Across the Decades: 1790–2010." Washington, DC: US Census Bureau. https://www.census.gov/data-tools/demo/race/MREAD_1790_2010.html.

Rastogi, Sonya, Leticia Fernandez, James M. Noon, Ellen Zapata, and Renuka Bhaskar. 2014. "Exploring Administrative Records Use for Race and Hispanic Origin Item Non-Response." Center for Administrative Records Research and Applications Working Paper 2014–16). Washington, DC: US Census Bureau. Retrieved from https://www.census.gov/srd/carra/16_Exploring_Admin_Recs_for_Race_and_Hispanic_Origin_Item_NR.pdf.

Snipp, C. M. 2000. "American Indians and Alaska Natives." In *Encyclopedia of the US Census*, edited by M. J. Anderson, 28–31. Washington, DC: CQ Press.

Statistics Canada. 2022a. "Visible Minority and Population Group Reference Guide." Census of Population.

Statistics Canada. 2022b. "Indigenous Peoples Reference Guide." Census of Population.

Stevens, Catriona, and Farida Fozdar. 2021. "Ethnicity, Race or Nation? Census Classifications as Barriers to the Measurement of Mixedness in Australia." *Australian Population Studies* 5(1): 49–55.

Stevens, Gillian, Hiromi Ishizawa, and Douglas Grbic. 2015. "Measuring Race and Ethnicity in the Censuses of Australia, Canada, and the United States: Parallels and Paradoxes." *Canadian Studies in Population [ARCHIVES]* 42(1–2): 13–34.

Sink, Larry D., and Sandra L. Colby. 2014. "Race Bridging: An Evaluation of the Census Bureau's Current Method for Converting NCHS Data into OMB 1997 Categories." Paper presented at the 2014 Southern Demographic Association. Memphis, TN.

Telles, Edward. 2018. "Latinos, Race, and the US Census." *The ANNALS of the American Academy of Political and Social Science* 677(1): 153–64.

US Census Bureau. 2021. "US Decennial Census Measurement of Race and Ethnicity Across the Decades: 1790–2020." Data Visualization. https://www.census.gov/library/visualizations/interactive/decennial-census-measurement-of-race-and-ethnicity-across-the-decades-1790–2020.html.

US Office of Management and Budget. 1977. *Statistical Policy Directive No. 15*—Race and Ethnic Standards for Federal Statistics and Administrative Reporting. https://www2.census.gov/about/ombraceethnicityitwg/1978-statistical-policy-handbook.pdf.

US Office of Management and Budget. 1997. "Standards for Maintaining, Collecting, and Presenting Federal Data on Race and Ethnicity." Statistical Policy Directive No. 15.

US Office of Management and Budget. 2023a. "Initial Proposals for Updating OMB's Race and Ethnicity Statistical Standards." *88 Fed. Reg.* 18, 5375–84.

US Office of Management and Budget. 2023b. "Initial Proposals." Resource Website. https://spd15revision.gov/content/spd15revision/en/proposals.html.

US Office of Management and Budget. 2024a. *History of Statistical Policy Directive No. 15*. https://spd15revision.gov/content/spd15revision/en/history.html.

US Office of Management and Budget. 2024b. "The 2024 Statistical Policy Directive No. 15." Resource Website. https://spd15revision.gov/content/spd15revision/en/2024-spd15.html.

Wagner, Deborah, and Mary Lane. 2014. *The Person Identification Validation System (PVS): Applying the Center for Administrative Records Research and Applications'(CARRA) Record Linkage Software*. No. 2014–01. Center for Economic Studies, US Census Bureau.

2

Data Collection Without Definitions

William A. Darity Jr. and Stephan Lefebvre

2.1 Introduction

Since at least 1977, the US government has recognized the need for a coordinated federal minimum standard for the collection and reporting of data by race and has promulgated these standards through the Office of Management and Budget's Statistical Directive No. 15 (OMB 1978; OMB 1997; OMB 2024). Notwithstanding numerous benefits pursuant upon Directive 15, it includes a set of unworkable definitions for each of the racial and/or ethnic categories that unnecessarily constrain individual identification options, dilute a focus on race-based civil rights that was the Directive's impetus, and involve the federal government in a process of legitimation of racial hierarchy (Swartz 1997). Building on previous critiques, we find that the Directive's definitions are inconsistent, circular, incomplete, and they inappropriately conflate race with concepts such as nationality and the geographical origin of hereditary ancestors.

In light of these problems, we analyze a novel proposal: dispense with the definitions altogether. We find that getting rid of the definitions for each of the racial and/or ethnic categories would have few negative consequences, it would overcome the problems of ill-defined racial groups, it would facilitate improved data collection and analysis by eliminating sources of confusion and inconsistency, and it would significantly lessen the federal government's role in ascribing characteristics to racial groups and racialized individuals. To vet the policy, we anticipate various counterarguments, finding, as a practical matter, the proposed change will not endanger data validity, nor

William A. Darity Jr. is the Samuel DuBois Cook Distinguished Professor of Public Policy at Duke University.

Stephan Lefebvre is an assistant professor of economics at Bucknell University.

comparability across time, nor data interpretability, but rather enhance data quality. In practice, the definitions are rarely included in surveys and they do not seem to be considered by most respondents to government questionnaires. Thus, there seems to be little to lose and much to gain. If implemented, this proposal would contribute to the federal government and the public's legitimate interests in monitoring outcomes by race.

Directive 15 specifies a minimum set of seven racial and ethnic categories and provides definitions that characterize membership for each group. The seven categories are: American Indian or Alaska Native, Asian, Black or African American, Hispanic or Latino, Middle Eastern or North African, Native Hawaiian or Pacific Islander, and White. Prior to the March 2024 update (see table 2.1), there were five racial categories and the two ethnic categories, Hispanic or Latino and Not Hispanic or Latino.

As of March 2024, there is no longer a distinction between race and ethnic categories; the new scheme is one question for which individuals may indicate membership in multiple groups, with the possibility of checkboxes for detailed subcategories (e.g., Mexican, Puerto Rican, Cuban for Hispanic or Latino) and/or space for write-in responses.

Directive 15 provides additional guidance on working with federal race data. It specifies, for example, that racial groups be treated as "social-political constructs" (OMB 2024, 22191), it recommends self-identification of race whenever possible, and it provides an example of specific wording for the race and ethnicity question. More detailed information can be collected so long as the data can be aggregated into the main seven categories listed in the Directive. These standards are designed to be used in all federally sponsored data collection or reporting that includes race or ethnicity, general federal program administrative and grant reporting, and civil rights and other compliance reporting.

The definitions have a number of problems. Table 2.1 reproduces the full text of the original 1977 definitions alongside the revisions made in 1997 and 2024. For an example of inconsistency across the categories and circularity within the definitions, consider the category Black or African American. The definition reads, in part, "Individuals with origins in any of the Black racial groups of Africa," making it the only category that specifies a color in the definition.

For an example of lack of comprehensiveness, which we interpret to mean that some potential respondents do not have at least one category that is appropriate for them, consider the "American Indian or Alaska Native" category which, in the 1977 version, did not include indigenous people from South America. The definition was changed in 1997 to include descendants of "the original peoples of . . . South America," but the condition that individuals "maintain[ ] tribal affiliation or community attachment" was added.

This addition reflects the specific legal and citizenship implications of tribal affiliation in the United States. This change shows how problems with comprehensiveness were only partially addressed since it is not clear that such criteria should apply to all indigenous groups in the Americas. The latest revision dispenses with the "tribal affiliation or community attachment" requirement and instead lists examples of groups, some of which are federally recognized tribes in the United States. This is significant and creates yet more problems, because each tribal nation has latitude in determining criteria for membership that may or may not align with the Directive 15 definition.

Our critique of the definitions is not based on the idea that racial group membership is so amorphous or subjective that it inherently presents problems for defining terms or quantifying dimensions of racial hierarchy. Rather, we argue that the current definitions are unworkable and that any similar attempt to define membership in broad racial groups for uniform application as a minimum standard by the federal government and by industries with significant ties to the federal government (the stated purpose of Directive 15) is likely to fail.

The social operation of race cannot be reduced to definitions for the expansive purposes of Directive 15. The proposal to remove the definitions is limited in scope and does not constitute a comprehensive plan for revising the Directive. It is possible to support the proposed change as a move toward better data collection regardless of one's position on a number of other issues related to Directive 15. Removing the definitions is not a sign that we should throw up our hands and conclude quantitative data on race is uniquely difficult.

The general problem of collecting information about an individual's race is complex. Race is a multidimensional concept (Roth 2016). Some of these dimensions are phenotype, self-identity, social identity, legal standards (which ultimately are "community standards") and family history. Any of these dimensions may be geographically and temporally contingent, and they may have extensive and intensive margins.

The specific problem of designing and implementing federal minimum standards is of even greater complexity. "Federal" means that the standards need to be designed with a full appreciation of both the country's diversity and the diverse needs of hundreds of federal agencies. The standards should be designed considering every conceivable person who may find themselves filling out a federal government form or survey. "Minimum" means the standards need to be designed with the full complexity of race in mind, while pairing down the guidance to its most succinct and economical form, leaving as much flexibility as possible for different use cases.

The main contribution of this paper is to analyze a novel policy proposal. The latest revision of Directive 15 involved a sprawling interagency process that leveraged the Census's extensive 2015 National Content Test (Mathews et al. 2017) and involved "[collecting] over 20,000 comments . . . , 94 separate

Table 2.1 **OMB Statistical Directive No. 15 definitions: original 1977 policy and updates made in 1997 and 2024**

Category	Definition 1977	Category	Definition 1997	Category	Definition 2024
American Indian or Alaskan Native	A person having origins in any of the original peoples of North America, and who maintains cultural identification through tribal affiliation or community recognition.	No change	A person having origins in any of the original peoples of North and South America (including Central America), and who maintains tribal affiliation or community attachment.	No change	Individuals with origins in any of the original peoples of North, Central, and South America, including, for example, Navajo Nation, Blackfeet Tribe of the Blackfeet Indian Reservation of Montana, Native Village of Barrow Inupiat Traditional Government, Nome Eskimo Community, Aztec, and Maya.
Asian or Pacific Islander	A person having origins in any of the original peoples of the Far East, Southeast Asian, the Indian subcontinent, or the Pacific Islands. This area includes, for example, China, India, Japan, Korea, the Philippine Islands, and Samoa.	Asian	A person having origins in any of the original peoples of the Far East, Southeast Asia, or the Indian subcontinent including, for example, Cambodia, China, India, Japan, Korea, Malaysia, Pakistan, the Philippine Islands, Thailand, and Vietnam.	No change	Individuals with origins in any of the original peoples of Central or East Asia, Southeast Asia, or South Asia, including, for example, Chinese, Asian Indian, Filipino, Vietnamese, Korean, and Japanese.
Black	A person having origins in any of the black racial groups of Africa.	Black or African American	A person having origins in any of the black racial groups of Africa. Terms such as "Haitian" or "Negro" can be used in addition to "Black or African American."	No change	Individuals with origins in any of the Black racial groups of Africa, including, for example, African American, Jamaican, Haitian, Nigerian, Ethiopian, and Somali.

Hispanic	A person of Mexican, Puerto Rican, Cuban, Central or South American or other Spanish culture or origin, regardless of race.	Hispanic or Latino	A person of Cuban, Mexican, Puerto Rican, Cuban, South or Central American, or other Spanish culture or origin, regardless of race. The term "Spanish origin," can be used in addition to "Hispanic or Latino."	No change	Includes individuals of Mexican, Puerto Rican, Salvadoran, Cuban, Dominican, Guatemalan, and other Central or South American or Spanish culture or origin.
White	A person having origins in any of the original peoples of Europe, North Africa, or the Middle East.	No change	A person having origins in any of the original peoples of Europe, the Middle East, or North Africa.	No change	Individuals with origins in any of the original peoples of Europe, including, for example, English, German, Irish, Italian, Polish, and Scottish.
		Native Hawaiian or Other Pacific Islander	A person having origins in any of the original peoples of Hawaii, Guam, Samoa, or other Pacific Islands.	Native Hawaiian or Pacific Islander	Individuals with origins in any of the original peoples of Hawaii, Guam, Samoa, or other Pacific Islands, including, for example, Native Hawaiian, Samoan, Chamorro, Tongan, Fijian, and Marshallese.
				Middle Eastern or North African	Individuals with origins in any of the original peoples of the Middle East or North Africa, including, for example, Lebanese, Iranian, Egyptian, Syrian, Iraqi, and Israeli.

30-minute listening sessions, and" virtual town halls where "3,350 people joined [and] where over 200 people spoke" (OMB 2024, 22184). This paper's scope is limited to the definitions included in Directive 15 and considers a proposal, to the best of our knowledge, that has not been considered in the studies above or elsewhere.

Our paper is also distinct in that it combines theories of racialization with research on the practical realities of policy change around Directive 15 specifically and survey methodology more broadly. Other researchers have critiqued the categories and definitions of Directive 15 (Tamayo Lott 1997), particularly in the realms of law (Toro 1995) and health (Wallman, Evinger, and Schechter 2000). However, these works do not analyze alternatives. There is little academic work analyzing practical policy changes to address the problems we echo in this paper. For example, Hernández (1998, 167) contains a critique of the definitions and an interesting example of how to elicit individual race identity in a survey (a lengthy prompt to "invite[ ] responses about personal identity"), but it is presented as "a vehicle for initiating . . . discussion . . . rather than being a concrete model for statistical data collection."

Gimenez (1989) argues that "any standardized terminology" for racial groups "is unavoidably flawed and conducive to the development of racist . . . analysis of the data thus produced," but her proposal for a new question only discusses Latinxs. Gimenez's proposed solution to disaggregate Latinxs into six[1] categories is not qualitatively dissimilar to the current standards and echoes other calls for data disaggregation or, similarly, abandoning the pan-ethnic category "Hispanic or Latino."

The proposal we analyze is consistent with many different levels of (dis)aggregation, and we express no preference or analysis for how many groups or which groups should be present in Directive 15. The proposal's limited scope reflects our interest in practicality for implementation. As Skerry (2000, 43) reminds us, this does not imply that the seemingly small change lacks importance because "the most contentious boundaries that the Census Bureau has to deal with are those concerning race and ethnicity."

In section 2.2, we present an overview of Directive 15's contents, its policy history, as well as its reach and lack of enforcement mechanism. In section 2.3, we argue that the definitions for the racial groups used in the Directive are inconsistent, circular, incomplete, unhelpful because they conflate race with other demographic concepts, and also involve the federal government in unintentionally and authoritatively assigning particular racial groups with characteristics that are not accepted by all members of that group. Section 2.4 contains details of the proposal, and section 2.5 provides an analysis of its benefits, potential drawbacks, and implications.

1. The six groups proposed in Gimenez (1989) are Mexicans, Puerto Ricans, Cubans, Central American refugees, Central American immigrants, and South American immigrants.

2.2 Contents of OMB Directive 15

Directive 15 (OMB 2024) defines seven race and ethnic categories and prescribes these as minimum categories for data collection by the federal government. The categories are: American Indian or Alaska Native, Asian, Black or African American, Hispanic or Latino, Middle Eastern or North African, Native Hawaiian or Pacific Islander, and White. As of the 1997 version, the standards require that respondents be able to select more than one racial category. In addition to setting the number and names of the minimum categories, Directive 15 defines each of the categories. Table 2.1 reproduces definitions from the original 1977 standards, the first revision made in 1997, and the second and latest Directive 15 text issued in March 2024.

Successive changes to Directive 15, namely increasing the number of categories, highlight the contradictions of using a scheme that was intended for use in race-based civil rights but which currently erases distinctions between groups that are racialized differently in the United States and abroad (e.g., Palestinians and Israelis, Indians and Chinese, Turks and Kurds). The standards do not preclude collecting data with finer gradations, but they require any such collection be done in such a way as to allow the aggregation of individuals into one or more of the seven official categories.

Directive 15 states its purpose for "Federal statistics, program administrative reporting, and civil rights compliance reporting" (OMB 2024, 22191) but does not specify the circumstances under which the definitions are to be used. For example, it is not clear whether the definitions should be provided to survey respondents; if provided, it is not clear whether they should be visible alongside the category options, included as a footnote, linked to as an online reference, or something else. To our knowledge, no major national survey provides the definitions from Directive 15 alongside the questions on race and ethnicity.

On the rare occasions that the definitions do appear outside of direct commentary on Directive 15, they are reproduced as supplemental background information and provided alongside reported statistics after the fact, not in connection with the survey instrument. In some cases, the data are aggregated from surveys that ask more detailed questions on race and so the definitions were likely not used in data collection, raising questions about the appropriateness of applying the definitions.

Directive 15 provides additional guidance around the nature of race, different question formats, and which body is authorized to provide exceptions to the standards. Since 1977, the standards contain similar language that: (1) the categories are "sociopolitical constructs" that "are not an attempt to define race and ethnicity biologically or genetically" (OMB 2024, 22183); (2) the categories "are not to be used as determinants of eligibility for participation in any Federal program" (OMB 2024, 22183); and (3) any deviation from the standards requires specific authorization by the Office of Management and Budget. The latest standards establish that (4) race and ethnicity should be collected in a one question format and that (5) "the seven minimum race and ethnicity categories shall be treated co-equally. . . . collection forms may not indicate to respondents that they should interpret some categories as ethnicities and others as races, or otherwise indicate conceptual differences among the minimum categories" (OMB 2024, 22195). The last item presents a change from previous Directive 15 standards that emphasized a conceptual difference between Hispanics or Latinos, who could be of any race and were defined by reference to "Spanish culture or origin."

2.2.1 Policy History

Statistical Directive 15, first issued in 1977, came in response to a growing need for data on race and ethnicity for civil rights monitoring and enforcement (Federal Interagency Committee on Education 1975). Agencies within the federal government collect data as part of their mission or due to legal mandates. For example, both the Civil Rights Act of 1964 and the Voting Rights Act of 1965 require specific agencies to collect data on race and ethnicity. The 1977 standards created a new scheme for collecting racial data that required, at minimum, four categories or the ability to aggregate more detailed data into the four broad categories, which were American Indian or Alaska Native, Asian or Pacific Islander, Black, and White.

The 1977 Directive 15 implemented the previous year's Public Law 94-311, which required the federal government to collect information to make Hispanics as a group identifiable in the nation's statistical reports (94th Congress 1976). This mandate led to a two-part question, whereby respondents are asked to identify as Hispanic or non-Hispanic in one question and asked to identify their race in a second question. Public Law 94-311 was proposed and passed in Congress largely due to the efforts of Representative Edward Roybal of California and the newly formed Congressional Hispanic Caucus (Robbin 2000).

The first interagency process for updating and revising Directive 15 began in 1993 (Citro 1997). Official reports and statements from government officials frequently cite the need to "reflect[ ] the increasing diversity of our Nation's population that has resulted primarily from growth in immigration and interracial marriages" (Wallman 1998, 31). The 1997 update to Directive 15 (1) split the "Asian or Pacific Islander" group into "Asian" and "Native Hawaiian or Other Pacific Islander," thus establishing five racial categories as opposed to four; (2) allowed individuals to select (or be assigned to) more than one racial group; (3) edited the definitions to include indigenous peoples from South and Central America in the Native American category; and (4) changed the category names and definitions for some of the groups, altering the list of country examples in the Asian group and adding the term *Latino* to the Hispanic category. As with Public Law 94-311, the separation of Native Hawaiians from Asians and from Native Americans was achieved in part through the advocacy of a particular congressman, Senator Daniel Akaka of Hawaii. The original 1977 and the revised 1997 version of Directive 15 both represent the outcome of intergroup and intragroup cooperation and competition, a complex interagency process, and numerous compromises with uneven representation of expertise. For example, no experts in American Indian affairs, or community or political representatives, were involved in drafting the original Directive 15 (Forbes 1992).

The US Census Bureau is subject to Directive 15. Therefore, the millennial census operated under the then three-year-old, revised Directive 15 with one high-profile exception that allows us to illustrate how the standards work in practice. The standards allow for significant flexibility, including the selection of more than one category and including any number of detailed categories for race and ethnicity, so long as it is possible to aggregate up to the broad Directive 15 categories.

The Census Bureau requested and was granted an exemption to this requirement in order to add a sixth category, "Some other race."[2] This category is problematic under Directive 15 because those indicating "Some other race" with no other racial category could not be aggregated into one or even multiple of the five official racial categories. In the 2000 Census, 97 percent of those who indicated Some other race also identified as Hispanic or Latino. As census officials indicate, the Bureau has as an explicit goal "to reduce reporting of 'Other race' by Hispanics in the race item" (Martin, Demaio, and Campanelli 1990, 551). Although beyond the scope of this paper, we note that the Census Bureau has spent the past 35 years struggling to collect race data on Hispanics.

Since 1997, the most contentious issues involve (1) allowing an explicit "Multiracial" category to "directly promote a distinct multiracial identity" (Hernández 1998, 100); (2) combining the race and ethnicity question, which reverses decades-long messaging that Hispanics are not a race but a panethnic category incorporating people of any race; (3) accurately reflecting the identities of American Indian and Native Hawaiians; and (4) creating a Middle East and North Africa category that includes individuals who, in the past, would have fallen under the definitional category of White (see table 2.1).

The latest revision of Directive 15 is only the second in nearly 50 years. It was led by the Federal Interagency Technical Working Group on Race and Ethnicity Standards, a combination of the 13 Principle Statistical Agencies along with 25 additional agencies selected for their reliance on race and ethnicity data (OMB 2023). This 2024 revision added a new category, Middle Eastern or North African, edited each of the category definitions, removed

2. The residual category "Other" has been in use by the Census since 1910.

the word "Other" from the category name Native Hawaiian or Other Pacific Islander, and contained several other changes in guidance discussed later in this paper.

The revision processes have not been construed narrowly, signaling a need to refocus on the purpose and effects of Directive 15. In particular, the process has increasingly focused on reflecting the nation's "diversity," though diversity of what is not well defined. In public comment and instrument testing, the focus on ethnic or cultural identities has not explicitly tied to the civil rights monitoring or other of Directive 15's original purposes discussed below. These observations are made not to suggest that these other topics are not important in many contexts, but to suggest that they may be of only minor relevance for a minimum standard for all race data collection undertaken by the federal government.

Data are generally more comparable over time if changes to statistical standards are infrequent and modest. Standards have changed only twice since their adoption, despite generally recognized problems with the definitions, in part due to the costliness and contentiousness of the revision process.

2.2.2 Stated Purpose, Reach, and Enforcement

In this section, we review the purpose, reach, and enforcement mechanisms of Directive 15. Both the original and the revised Directive 15 contain language about its intended use: the minimum categories are to be used "by all agencies . . . for civil rights compliance reporting and equal employment reporting for both the public and private sectors and for all levels of government" and for all "federally sponsored statistical data collection where race and/or ethnicity is required" (OMB 1978).

The federal minimum standards around race and ethnicity set forth in Directive 15 provide a number of benefits. They help to encourage similar practices around data across the federal government and related bodies, which facilitates sharing and comparing data across official statistical reports. The standards contribute to government functioning through increased efficiency: while each department and agency is charged with planning and executing its own strategies around data, the guidance, particularly around this contentious and contested issue, reduces duplication of efforts.

The standards do not preclude data collection that goes beyond Directive 15's broad racial and ethnic categories, and they do not limit studies of racial and ethnic inequality to particular multiple choice questions or survey methods. Agencies are free to experiment or to pursue research that is based on qualitative approaches or alternative quantitative methodologies. Directive 15 is intended to provide *minimum standards* for regular agency functions.

Whether intended or not, comprehensive use of these standards by the federal government has a trickle-down effect. Directive 15 influences the operations of organizations and institutions with significant contact with the federal government. OMB recognizes this in official communications: "Even where it is not required, Directive No. 15 standards are often used in State and business record systems and by markets as a matter of convenience and to facilitate comparisons with other data sets" (OMB 1995, 44676).

Insofar as Directive 15 shapes administrative practices throughout the country, nearly everyone in the country fills out a form or survey where they are asked to fit their identity into its categories. The far-reaching nature of Directive 15 is a key consideration for any proposed changes: "Any changes in Directive No. 15 will be imposed on tens of thousands of State and local agencies such as law enforcement agencies (through the Uniform Crime Reporting system), school districts, the business community, and others required to use the Directive in reporting these data to the Federal government" (OMB 1995, 44680).

In section 2.5, we will argue that removing the definitions would not have negative consequences even when taking an expansive view of its reach and influence. While Directive 15 has a number of important benefits, none of these depend on the definitions. Part of the reason that the proposed change would not be disruptive has to do with which aspects of Directive 15 are the most influential on practices within the agencies, institutions, and organizations listed above.

The influence of Directive 15 is most directly seen in which racial and ethnic categories are available in surveys. The current standards require that individuals can be aggregated into one or more of seven specific race and/or ethnic categories. Surveys in compliance with Directive 15 provide these categories or they provide additional options that are clearly subcategories. There is little evidence that the definitions provided in Directive 15 are used in practice as they are rarely cited or reproduced and rarely if ever included in surveys for respondents to refer to as they make their selections.

The first update to Directive 15 required setting forth guiding principles for the revision process. There were 12 principles, including "Respect for individual dignity" (OMB 1994). Interestingly, the principles, originally published in 1994, were reissued in 1995 with small changes that reveal some of the thinking or intended purpose of Directive 15. For example, the later version reproduces Principle 5, "Foremost consideration should be given to data aggregations by race and ethnicity that are useful for statistical analysis, program administration and assessment, and enforcement of existing laws and judicial decisions," but removes reference to "enforcement of existing laws and judicial decisions."

Similar changes were made to limit the scope of Principle 6, "While Federal data needs for racial and ethnic data are of primary importance, consideration should also be given to needs at the State and local government levels, including American Indian tribal and Alaska Native village governments," which was edited to more clearly subordinate non-federal data needs.

Directive 15 is far reaching, both by explicit intention and in practical effect. Any critique of proposed changes to Directive 15 should account for the fact that the purpose of Directive 15 is not to define racial groups for individuals or to provide guidance for researchers doing work on race apart from the design of federal government surveys, administrative forms, and reports.

There is no clear enforcement mechanism for Directive 15. In our exploration we found no evidence of active enforcement efforts. The Directive does not specify when race and ethnicity data should be collected. It specifies the category names and definitions but does not provide any explanation regarding how the definitions are to be used.

The effect of Directive 15 is to promote a lower limit of data comparability and collaboration between agencies. This does not guarantee data on race and ethnicity are easily comparable across federal statistical agencies. One study, though not at the federal level, illustrates the current landscape. It found that data on race were not comparable across states or even within a state across different survey modalities. The State Health Access Data Assistance Center at the University of Minnesota (2021) found large discrepancies from state to state and within states between online and paper versions of enrollment forms for Medicaid applications. Of the states in their sample, 14 offered more racial category options online, 9 offered more on the paper version, and 10 offered the same number on both forms.

Policy guidance outside of Directive 15 significantly affects how the standards function in practice. For example, an OMB Bulletin from March 2000 states that "Responses that combine one minority race and white are allocated to the minority race" (Lew 2000). That is, statistical practices arguably consistent with Directive 15 can follow rules of hypodescent in which Whiteness is treated as "pure" so that children with both White and non-White parents are assigned their non-White parent's race. This is significant in several ways (Myers 1997), but for our argument the key point is this: the definitions provided in the text of Directive 15 are not the only or even the most important way in which the federal government provides guidance about how to work with data on race. In other instances, the Census recoded respondents who indicated Hispanic into the "Some other race" group (Schuster 2021) and recoded individuals to Native American when they include particular write-in tribal categories (e.g., Cherokee), even when the survey respondent did not check the box for Native American (Eschbach and Taylor, in press).

In other words, Directive 15 is not the superseding or sole source of information for understanding what race categories mean; the categories are defined implicitly by recommended and implemented practices such as the rule of hypodescent, though these may contradict the definitions. This means that removing the definitions has the potential to end the problems associated with them. We know of no alternative definitions or way of writing alternative definitions that meet the necessary criteria for Directive 15.

The problem at issue in this paper does not involve questions about how the US government should ideally or usually collect data on race. Those questions do not recognize that Directive 15 only specifies *minimum* standards. As is acknowledged in the text setting out the revision principles, "The agencies recognize that these principles may in some cases represent competing goals for the standard. . . . Through the review process, it will be necessary to balance statistical issues, needs for data, and social concerns" (OMB 1994, 29834). In section 2.5 we discuss our findings that the proposed change would bring Directive 15 closer to fulfilling multiple of the latest revision principles, with little to no downside in terms of the other principles.

2.3 Problems with the Federal Government's Definitions

In this section, we identify several major problems with the definitions for racial groups as they are written in the latest Directive 15 text. The problems we raise are not new to the literature; many have been advanced as critiques of racial classification schemes without reference to Directive 15, others have been levied against Directive 15 specifically, and many have been discussed in official government reports as part of various revision processes. Our argument is unique because we only deal with the definitions for racial groups as part of a set of minimum standards for statistical practices and because we evaluate a practical solution that we have determined would immediately resolve all of the problems discussed in this section, could feasibly be implemented, and is compatible with many other modifications to the Directive.

As part of the 1997 revision process, the US government acknowledged that "the categories in Directive No. 15 confuse some respondents because they are inconsistent, too broad for some purposes, and the concepts of race, Hispanic origin, and ancestry overlap" (OMB 1995, 44677). Despite this admission, table 2.1 shows that only modest changes were made in each revision and that many of the problems remain.

The original categories from the 1977 Directive 15, largely unchanged in the 1997 revision, were presented using a great deal of research and administrative jargon, but they clearly conform to anthropologically discredited ideas of "the ethno-racial pentagon" (Hollinger 2000). Under different names, the five categories would be familiar to educated Americans of the 19th century: white (European), black (African), red (Native American), brown (South American), and yellow (East Asian). It seems to be impossible to craft definitions for these specific categories that (1) fulfill the stated purposes of Directive 15; (2) provide sufficient uniformity for their countless federal applications; (3) capture the real-world asymmetries in how racial groups function; and (4) respect individual and group identity choice. Here, we discuss problems with the current definitions.

2.3.1 Inconsistent, Circular, and Noncomprehensive

The definitions provided in Directive 15 are inconsistent, noncomprehensive, and, in some cases, weak due to circularity. Among the many inconsistencies, consider the following three examples.

First, if black is a skin color, it is only referenced for the Black or African American group. This group is also the only racial category that does not contain the phrase "any of the original peoples of" in reference to a geographical origin which, given the diversity and intensity of centuries-old colonial projects in Africa, functions to deemphasize African claims to particular land and resources.

Second, the category American Indian or Alaska Native was the only category requiring specific cultural and political practices ("maintains tribal affiliation or community attachment"), though this qualifier was officially removed in the latest revision. The added burden to identification included for American Indian or Alaska Natives in Directive 15 functionally served to reduce the size of this group, consistent with the project of settler colonialism.[3]

There is not yet enough evidence to reach conclusions about the March 2024 formulation. Again, we do not argue that the qualification "maintains tribal affiliation or community attachment" is never appropriate or that removing that qualification by itself would improve the definitions. Our argument is that the definitions are flawed and unnecessary for achieving Directive 15's intended purpose. The last and certainly the most humorous of the inconsistencies was the typographical error in the 1997 version wherein the term "Cubans" appears twice in the definition of Hispanic or Latino, corrected in the latest revision.

Consider the definition of the category Black or African American, "Individuals with origins in any of the Black racial groups of Africa." No independent definition of what it means to be Black is offered. Anyone who has origins in a non-Black (also undefined, since "Black" itself is undefined) racial group of Africa is presumed to have origins in some other continent or place. Indeed, the definitions are silent about any racial groups in Africa other than "Black racial groups."

Unlike most of the other racial groups in the classification scheme, the inclusion of the phrase "any of the Black racial groups" shifts this racial category from being exclusively based upon geographic origin (see table 2.1). Oddly enough, the definition of White does not include the qualifier that individuals with European ancestry must have origins in any of the White racial groups, and this was true even when the White category included those from the Middle East and North Africa.

3. Forbes (1992, 63) writes, "One reason for the directive's treatment of Native Americans was to reduce the numbers of persons qualifying for federal services as Indians."

Even if parallelism were achieved—even if the wording of each definition were edited to be more consistent—that would not mean the categories would be more accurate or the meanings would be similar, given the different historical contexts relevant for each group. Historically, African Americans as a group have been subject to campaigns intended to suppress African culture and Afrocentric identities and to devalue links with Africa.

Some self-identified Blacks who have been in the United States for generations have no record of where in Africa their ancestors were born and do not wish to be called "African Americans." In short, there are reasons why many Blacks in the United States might or might not want to emphasize a connection with Africa. Removing the problematic definition would not preclude any self- and group-identification choices but would eliminate the symbolic imposition of a unified definition through government statistics.

Not only are the definitions inconsistent but they are inconsistent without reason or rationale unsupportive of 19th-century constructs of race. Reference to the "Black racial groups of Africa" with no similar reference to the "White racial groups of Europe" in the White category definition does not conform, to the best of our knowledge, to any substantive current sociopolitical and scientific understanding of race (for current conceptualizations of race, see American Anthropological Association 1998; American Association of Biological Anthropologists 1996).

Though we argue that the definitions are inconsistent, we recognize that hierarchy and unequal power are inherent in characterizing racial groups in all societies in which they have been studied. The way race functions since European colonization of North America has been to create hierarchies, and, correspondingly, conventional definitions of who is White, Black, non-White, or non-Black do not function symmetrically.

This operates at every level, including the social rules that characterize membership in racial groups. As Fields (1982, 149) writes, there is "a well-known anomaly of American racial convention that considers a white woman capable of giving birth to a black child but denies that a black woman can give birth to a white child."

The process of collecting survey information can create a false appearance of similarity or parallelism. Any individual may have one or more racial identities in the United States, but race is not only, or even primarily, an individual characteristic. Rather, it is a sociopolitical, economic, and ideological phenomenon that has evolved over time with geospatial variation.

Racial groups have specific histories, such as the relationship between Whites and Blacks during and in the wake of chattel capitalism or the relationship between Whites and American Indians during and in the wake of the genocidal intent of the nation's settler colonial project. The historical and hierarchical characteristics of race as a social group phenomenon mean that creating a comprehensive list of definitions for individual membership is beside the point; definitions are not necessary to ensure meaningful data collection or any of the other goals of Directive 15.

Another inconsistency with respect to the Directive 15 definitions involves the legal meanings and implications of race for US jurisprudence. For the first 89 years of the nation's existence an individual's race determined whether one was considered property or capable of owning other humans. Today, an individual's race is central for anti-discrimination case law (Desautels-Stein 2012).

The court system typically considers a number of criteria when seeking to understand an individual's race, including "physical characteristics, documentary evidence, community perception, and expressive self-identification" (Yang 2005, 406). In anti-discrimination cases, a suspect's perception of a person is a major consideration, and the "truth" of that person's heritage or other ancestral characteristics is largely irrelevant.

So, the federal government defines membership in racial groups narrowly and specifically based on whether an individual has "origins in any of the original peoples" of various geographically defined regions (with notable exceptions that we have discussed), but for the purposes of applying the nation's laws, a variety of other standards is used (Ford 1994).

The distinction is not just that the law is more nuanced, which would be an expected difference between the use of a concept in civil or criminal case law as opposed to questions on a survey or administrative form. Instead, the concepts contained in the Directive 15 definitions carry virtually no weight legally, and, conversely, little of the sociopolitical definition of race is captured by geographically based category definitions.

Interestingly, there is a new, recursive type of circularity in the definitions that was not present for the original Directive 15 that arises because the standards are nearly five decades old. The goal of the category names and definitions is to reflect social practice, to give people options that are close to how they might identify if given an open-ended response option, but social practice itself has been shaped by Directive 15.

Revisions to Directive 15 can account for changes in the social meaning of racial groups while preserving data comparability over time. However, *those revisions also have shaped how people think of themselves*. The categories and their associated meanings, if not the precise definitions, take on a legitimacy and authority of their own. They influence social change through a feedback loop.

Consider the Hispanic ethnicity category, introduced into federal data collection in Census 1970. For many today, it would be sensible to refer to Brazilians as Latinos/Latinas/Latinxs (Margolis 1995). The particular recognition given to Spanish speakers that arose from a specific political climate reified them as an ethnic group through the administrative practices of the US government (Fears 2003).

Today, defining Latinidad in the United States, a former colony and current colonial power, through reference to another colonial power, Spain, is not something that all Latinxs embrace (Rosa and Flores 2017).

Public Law 94-311 was part of a flurry of activity following the 1964 Civil Rights Act. Seeing the legislative successes of the Black community, various Latino groups interested in consolidating power realized that by joining the Mexican American community of the west and Southwest, the Puerto Rican community in New York, and the Cuban American community in South Florida, their numbers could be compared to that of African Americans.

The outcome of these efforts is a reified understanding of Latinos in the United States conceptually distinct from blackness despite the groups' interconnected histories of racism and slavery throughout the Americas. Therefore, reciprocally, revisions to the categories in Directive 15 are influenced by social phenomena that are themselves affected by Directive 15's definitions.

Furthermore, categories are not complete. Where does one racially situate individuals whose ancestors are Australian aborigines or New Zealand Maoris or any of the more than 40 indigenous Arctic zone communities (Walter and Anderson 2013)? Given that much of the list is organized by countries, what specific countries constitute North Africa for the purposes of distinguishing the Middle Eastern or North African from the Black or African American category? Is the concept of "Black racial groups of Africa" an accepted construct from the perspective of immigrants from the African continent whose families arrived after the 1960s when they find themselves in the United States filling out a form?

The definitions are based on the false premise that a particular set of racial meanings, however familiar they may be in the United States, is appropriate for application through the federal government's minimum standards for race and ethnicity statistics. Although the revision process involves dozens of agencies, costly survey instrument testing, focus groups, and contentious consultations, anyone with access to a map and an internet search browser can find problems with the exhaustiveness of the definitions.

The categories are also incomplete when it comes to accounting for racialization as Chicano/Chicana/Chicanx (Martinez 1997; Toro 1995). Sociological evidence shows that many Latinxs think of themselves as *racially* Latino (Hitlin, Brown, and Elder 2007), and for good reason.

There are histories of racial epithets, discriminatory policies and practices, lynchings and other extrajudicial killings directed against Americans with Mexican and Central American heritage (Mirandé 2019; Shadowen 2018). Latinxs are frequently racialized as "slightly tan, with dark hair and eyes" in media (see Rodríguez 1997 for a book-length elaboration of the visual language around Latinidad), and there is a two-way racialization of "looking Latinx" and "sounding Latinx" involving speaking Spanish or Spanish-accented English (Rosa 2019).

Yet, not all Latinxs are racialized as "brown." Collapsing Latinidad into a single-race group privileges phenotypically white Latinxs. A specific proposal for collecting race information on Latinidad must confront the highly successful campaign, of which the 1977 Directive 15 was a major part, to create a new social panethnicity called Hispanic (Mora 2014). Such an analysis is beyond the scope of the current paper, but the significance of this issue for this type of proposal emphasizes problems with the current definitions and recognizes that various ways of better collecting information on Latinxs' racialization would be consistent with removing definitions from Directive 15.

For example, it would be possible to list race as a sociopolitical concept on surveys and within the Directive, while asking questions about identity or what López and Hogan (2021, 1) term "street-race," the typical category others assign you to "if you were walking down the street." Their proposed survey question includes the category "brown" as an option and, crucially, *does not provide definitions for the individual categories*.

The OMB has stated, "In line with the subjective nature of the concept, research shows people change how they classify themselves with respect to race and ethnicity" over time (OMB 1995, 44677). This is not entirely accurate. Race is a multidimensional concept and some dimensions are more "subjective" than others; certainly, group-based phenomena such as the realities of race-based slavery and its aftermath are not completely "subjective."

The critiques we discuss in this section demonstrate how difficult it will be to fix the definitions in Directive 15 through edits. Given its wide-ranging intended purpose, no set of definitions we can conceive would not be subject to the critiques we raise. Still, our critique must not be taken as a proposal to eliminate federal race categories altogether. We have written extensively in favor of race-conscious policies, including reparations for US descendants of slavery, and we have detailed the identity and ancestry requirements that could accompany such a policy (Darity and Mullen 2020). Continuing the use of categories modified in accordance with changing social standards and eliminating official definitions of the categories could be an effective way to address the criticisms.

2.3.2 Conflating Race with Related Concepts

In this section, we review problems with the definitions stemming from how Directive 15 unhelpfully conflates race with related concepts such as geographical origin by region (usually continents), nationality, ancestry, tribal affiliation, and ethnic identity.

Reading the definitions, one is struck by a repeated use of the phrase "Individuals with origins in any of the original peoples of . . . ," which appears in five of the seven category definitions. An implicit power law is operative when accounting for generations in human lineages. Assuming each individual has two parents and counting back by generations, we obtain four grandparents, eight great-grandparents, then 16, 32, 64, and 128 in still earlier generations. Going back to the year 1619, approximately 13 generations ago, we would be tracking the "origins" (not the location) of 8,192 individuals.

Taken literally, this is patently unworkable. It is also not how people think about their racial identity. What does it mean for a person to "have origins" in an "original peoples" of a broad, ill-defined, contested geographical area? There are no sensible answers to these questions, so any group definitions constructed in this way are likely to be inaccurate, misleading, and imprecise.

Although the original framing of Directive 15 and the 1997 revision insist that race is a sociopolitical concept, the definitions do not reflect this. The definitions in Directive 15 are ahistorical in two ways. First, they do not allow for changes in the meaning of racial categories over time. Instead they refer to fixed geographical referents consistent with 19th-century hierarchies of "race." Second, they do not conform to the historical and contemporary ways in which race functions socially. The definitions support the myth of a biological (consanguine) construction of race. They draw on historically and anthropologically inaccurate assumptions about different groups as having discrete origins in fixed geographical areas.

The definitions and discussions around the revision process work to naturalize the idea of racial groups originating in discrete continents (Africa, Europe, North and South America) and seem to take for granted that individuals with a presumed ancestry from the same country share the same race. Or, incorporating logic implied by the phrase "original peoples," if we go back far enough, all the peoples in a given country's territory would be identified in the same "race" today. This is a fiction. It is zombie anthropology: disavowed by physical anthropologists today but difficult to extricate from our cultural and governmental administrative practices (Fuentes et al. 2019).

There are many examples that illustrate the error in this framework. Filipinos are categorized as Asians under Directive 15, but the earliest known evidence of human inhabitants in the Philippines were people from Africa. These are the ancestors of various (typically) dark-skinned, contemporary Filipino ethnic groups (Larena et al. 2021).[4] To state the obvious, the original peoples of Asia and elsewhere likely came from Africa because *Homo sapiens* first evolved in what we call present-day Africa. Skin did not lighten immediately upon crossing into Europe 50,000 years ago. Evidence indicates that lighter skin might have emerged later than previously thought, perhaps only 8,000 years ago (Mathieson et al. 2015).

There is a link between our critique of the definitions, which point to consanguinity (ancestry) as an important determinant of race, and critiques

4. This is not to suggest that some dark-skinned Filipino ethnic groups are not Asian, but that there are problems with the fundamental concepts used in the Directive 15 definitions.

of race as a biological concept. In a biomedical research context, A. M. Johnson Jr. (2008) writes, "It is not their race that predisposes [African Americans] to hypertension, but their discriminatory treatment that is predicated on their grosser morphological traits. I cannot believe that there is anything in their genetic makeup that predisposes 'blacks' to have a higher rate of hypertension, because there is no identifiable genetic definition of a black person, only a societally constructed, morphologically based definition." Indeed, race is not primarily an individual characteristic. We support calls for more analysis of racialized organizations (Ray 2019), institutions, systems, and phenomena based on data that are not limited to individual reports on race.

The problem of mixing concepts of race with geographical regions is apparent in the contentious issue, yet only partially resolved, of adding a separate Middle Eastern and North African (MENA) designation. Prior to March 2024, individuals "having origins in any of the original peoples of . . . the Middle East or North Africa" were classified as white. There is now a MENA category, notwithstanding disagreement among individuals who might be located in this group about this term. A common refrain asks, for example, middle of or east of what?[5] There is no agreement about the boundaries for this region.

Lack of a consistent understanding is found between international bodies, different official publications of the US government, and among individuals who potentially might identify with this group.

It seems futile to attempt to resolve this disagreement for the purposes of federal minimum standards around race and ethnicity data. For our purposes, it is not necessary to rehearse the historically fraught colonial project of defining boundaries and characterizing the Middle East distinct from other parts of the Asian continent or the separation of North Africa from Africa south of the Sahara. Indeed, the treatment of the globe as consistent of seven distinct continents is a construction arising out of the needs of the imperialist project (Kaplan 2024).

What is clear is that even if we were to resolve what countries constitute the Middle East and North Africa, defining a racial category in this way for the purposes of Directive 15 would still face the criticism that racialization is not primarily about geographical origin.

Discussions around adding a MENA category, perhaps alongside others that allow respondents to select Black or African American, White, or something else in addition to MENA, reveal a similar dynamic as the Hispanic group. People are racialized as Arab/Muslim or as Hispanic/Mexican/Latino based on phenotype, cultural markers, language use, and local context, but

5. An alternative that has been adopted by some in the community is SWANA or South West Asia and North Africa.

the definitions do not correspond to the ways in which individuals locate themselves across the categories, instead focusing on having "origins" in the "original peoples" of various ambiguously defined geographical regions.

These definitions simply are not necessary. Each of our critiques taken individually seems to suggest the possibility of an alternative definition that is not subject to the critique. For example, in this case we could rewrite the definitions to remove or deemphasize references to "original peoples" from various continents.

But, taken together, the critiques imply that it is not possible to generate usable, practical definitions for the intended purposes of Directive 15, much less move these forward given the political and administrative realities that are documented in the record of the inter-agency deliberation and public consultation for the 1977 drafting and the 1997 and 2024 revisions. The fact that the standards were written originally and revised with many of these problems acknowledged indicates that the political process of achieving consensus between different civil society constituencies and stakeholders within the federal government is difficult, costly, and always results in compromise.

To be clear, what makes the Directive 15 definitions wrong is not just that they are built on debunked racial science but that they function to naturalize a social phenomenon. Critical Black thought in the United States has, since the beginnings of White supremacy (Robinson and Kelley 2000), recognized that what separates Whites from Blacks in the United States is not "having origins in the original peoples of" different regions but group-based differences in power.

Race is invented, and racism is maintained, challenged, and circumvented through historical struggle. Racism endures because it accomplishes instrumental aims, namely, material and psychological benefits to members of the dominant group at the expense of members of the marginalized group (Mason 2023). Racial groups do not need to be "defined" for this system to operate.

Toro (1995, 1244) articulates a widely accepted view in the social sciences applied specifically to Directive 15:

> The drafters of Directive No. 15 did not attend to this crucial distinction between the fiction of race and the reality of racism. Instead, they assumed that a person can be said to belong to a race, and that racism occurs when someone falsely attributes other characteristics to a person that are dependent on the physical, racial appearance of that person.

Efforts to denaturalize racial difference interrupt the operation of symbolic violence (Swartz 1997), the process by which social group-based inequality is justified and becomes part of dominant, hegemonic understandings of the world. Removing the definitions from Directive 15 constitutes one more step toward denaturalizing racial categories.

2.3.3 Constraining Identity

Directive 15 has taken on a life of its own, beyond the scope of its stated purpose. The administrative practices of the nation-state influence peoples' identities and the realities of group-based inequality. Initially designed to collect data, Directive 15 has played a role in how Americans view themselves.

As we contemplate updates to Directive 15 in the future, we must reckon with the Directive's role in reifying particular understandings of racial identities. Walter and Anderson (2013, 8) write from the standpoint of indigenous scholarship: "As we invest ourselves and our communities in their categories, we increasingly use statistics to help us tell *ourselves* who we are." Or, as the late Pierre Bourdieu (2009, 224) wrote, "[*R*]*epresentations* . . . can give rise in reality, by specific effectiveness of evocation, to the very thing they represent."

The categories and definitions in Directive 15 are meant to reflect social reality, but they have the effect of reflexively affecting our social reality. To the extent that the definitions reflect dominant ideas about race, they may shape social reality in ways that maintain or deepen racial hierarchies rather than challenge them.

The current definitions ascribe attributes to groups that may not be embraced by all persons who identify with the group, and they can omit attributes that some members would find indispensable to their understanding of their identity. These distortions need to be balanced with the potential benefits that can come from federally sponsored data collection. We find that, in light of the proposed change to Directive 15, this balance can be better achieved by providing category names without definitions.

There are many examples of constraints on identity choices that would not be present absent the definitions. Persons choosing the Black category, particularly if they are descendants of persons enslaved in the United States, may self-identify as Black without the definition of their status referring to an African country of origin, particularly if they do not necessarily want to do so.

With respect to ethnic identification, these individuals may see themselves as descendants of American Freedmen, in contrast with a smaller share of the self-reported Black population comprised of more recent immigrants to the United States or the much smaller share who are descendants of the American Indian Freedmen emancipated from the "Five Civilized Tribes." Only the second group may possess a primary sense of "origin" in and identification with countries in Africa or Africa writ large.

Under the current system, in principle, anyone with any known White ancestry should identify as White. People routinely ignore this, which is both a reflection of historical hypodecendency but also a personal choice to identify with a different community. These choices can be strategic, reflecting individual utility maximization (Darity et al. 2006), they may be ethical positions, the result of sociocultural phenomena, or some combination.

In either case, including the definitions in Directive 15 injects needless confusion into the effectiveness of identification choices: individuals are free to believe what they like under the current standards, but they are limited in their ability to express carefully considered positions for the purposes of government and nongovernment statistics.

2.4 Proposal to Delete Racial Group Definitions in Directive 15

The benefits of federal minimum standards for the collection and reporting of data on race and ethnicity are substantial. We find that this proposal for deleting the definitions is compatible with many different future revisions, and it will better enable achievement of Directive 15's aims. In many cases, this proposal would not result in any change in actual practice because the definitions are rarely used explicitly, but it does represent a profound symbolic change and it resolves contradictions in how the policy works in practice.

Under the proposed change, the federal government would set out a minimum set of categories and provide other guidance around data collection and reporting. Individuals might be asked if they identify as or are part of one of the groups, say, White, but this term would not be defined. In practice, surveys rarely provide the definitions from Directive 15, so this would imply little change in most cases.

Asking individuals to identify with categories while not providing a definition is a common practice. This is typically how questions are asked concerning gender. As with race, there are many different ways to solicit this information, and the number and meaning of categories can vary from survey to survey.

The number of categories and which specific ones to include is a key matter of debate in each round of revision of the standards. The original 1977 policy had four racial categories, the revised 1997 version had five racial categories, and the latest issued in March 2024 has seven race and/or ethnicity categories.

Individuals with strong preferences about adding particular categories can support the proposed change, since it would increase the freedom of individuals and groups to define and implicitly assign characteristics to categories. The possibility of deleting categories also always will be available. The proposal does not require or preclude changes to the number or arrangement of the minimum standard categories.

The proposal under consideration will eliminate the use of definitions in the required minimum standards. Each round of revision is accompanied by an extensive consultation period with stakeholders both outside and within the federal government, including other organizations that share data with the federal government, community groups, and advocates. While it would be tempting to write from scratch our preferred Directive 15 text, we value the democratic potential of deliberation that is part of the revision process and also the specialized knowledge that federal administrators have around the costs of implementing changes to Directive 15 in terms of survey length, data processing and storage, and redesigning surveys. The proposal is narrowly tailored and consistent with these considerations for the administrative process of revising Directive 15.

2.5 Policy Evaluation and Discussion

2.5.1 Evaluating the Proposal

In this section, we evaluate the proposal to remove the Directive 15 definitions that define membership in racial groups. Obviously, all the problems discussed in section 2.3 of this paper are resolved immediately, eradicating (1) the inconsistency, noncomprehensiveness, and circularity of definitions; (2) the problems with defining race in a way that conflates race with other factors such as nationality or refers to the so-called "original peoples" of various continents; and (3) the difficulties with the federal government defining membership and characteristics of racial groups.

Eliminating the definitions from the minimum standards also removes a significant piece of controversy around the federal handling of data on race, while yet preserving comparability and flexibility in how data are collected and reported.

Another justification for eliminating the definitions concerns White people's understanding of their own racial identity as key to fostering a commitment to take anti-racist action (Wingfield 2015). That is, individuals interrogating how their own race affects their life is consciousness raising, and, for White Americans, this has little to do with having "origins in any of the original peoples of Europe," per se. The definitions in Directive 15 constitute an act of official messaging by the federal government defining the boundaries and characterizing the broad racial groups to which, presumably, we all belong. Even if the benefits from the proposed change are "merely" symbolic, race operates significantly on the level of representation and has been used to unfairly allocate material resources and life chances.

The proposed change to Directive 15 is also justified with reference to the modern understanding of race as a sociopolitical construct that has the appearance of being an individual quality but is more accurately understood as primarily a group-based phenomenon. Some people experience their racial identity as context-specific and multifaceted, and they often experience conflict between self-identity and outward perceptions.

The federal definitions give the appearance of creating a straightforward criterion for racial identity, but the contradictions of race are not and cannot be resolved in the way that Directive 15 approaches racial definitions. Racism as a system is resistant to change not because of its coherence but, in some ways, because of its contradictions. M. Omi (1985, 21) writes:

> Among scholars there is a continuous temptation to think of race as an essence, as something fixed, concrete and objective. There is also an opposite temptation: to imagine race as a mere illusion, a purely ideological construct which masks some other more fundamental division, such as class.

As M. Omi (1985) argues, both of these approaches are inadequate.

Data on race are important primarily because they are necessary for quantifying how hierarchy predicated on social identity groups manifests in society and for understanding how we may better pursue change toward greater racial justice and liberation. We can balance the benefits of data collection, which provides a powerful way of understanding the reality of racial hierarchy as a produced sociopolitical phenomenon, with the symbolic violence of asking people to reduce this complexity to a choice made from a list of pre-populated categories by having the federal government not dictate how the groups are characterized.

2.5.2 Practical Considerations

How would this proposed change work in practice? In this section, we discuss what we imagine statistical practices would look like if definitions were removed from Directive 15. If the proposal were implemented, the government would collect data on surveys, administrative forms, or other methods much as it currently does. Neither the phrasing of the questions on a Census or American Community Survey nor the categories offered would necessarily change under this proposal.

The existing definitions provide a false sense of objectivity and knowledge. They appear to tell us, definitively, what it means when someone selects a particular racial group (i.e., that they have "origins in any of the original peoples . . ." of a particular continent), but this is in fact inadequate for understanding an individual's selection(s). It may be beside the point.

Removal of the definitions would mean that revisiting Directive 15 in the future would not require revising the definitions. It would require potentially revising the categories themselves for consistency with extant social usage, but this makes complete sense, since the meaning of race is socially constructed and changing over time.

In summary, the proposed change would end the regular need to update definitions and the regular political fights about the definitions. It would also end ongoing symbolic violence associated with the definitions.

2.5.3 Clarifying What the Proposal Is Not

There are political efforts aimed at curtailing critical attention to racial inequality, and one of their manifestations is advocacy around statistical data collection. Many different proposals have been structured with the instrumental intent of reducing critical attention to racial hierarchies (Prewitt 2016). M. Omi (2001, 248) cites one example, writing, "House Speaker Newt Gingrich . . . used the issue of multiraciality to illustrate the indeterminacy of racial categories and to vigorously advocate for their abolition in government data collection, much as advocates of color-blindness do."

In contrast, this proposed change is consistent with more accurate collection and reporting around race. It is consistent with calls for more disaggregated data and calls for attention to the multidimensional nature of race, including more data collected on skin shade and other phenotypical characteristics that may dictate social identification of an individual's race (Diette et al. 2015; Goldsmith et al. 2006; Goldsmith et al. 2007; Hamilton et al. 2009; Jones 2000).

Going further, some have argued that we should pursue a strategy that minimizes or eliminates any explicit mention of race as a precondition of anti-subordination (Johnson 1996) or that multiracial identities have the potential to destabilize racial hierarchies. We disagree. As Kimberlé Crenshaw (1988, 1336) writes, "History has shown that the most valuable political asset of the Black community has been its ability to assert a collective identity and to name its collective political reality."

Regardless, removing the definitions from Directive 15 does not require or incentivize the government to collect less (or more) data on race and ethnicity, and such a proposal could draw support from those who believe that anti-racism requires abandoning racial identity as well as those who believe that anti-racism requires continued political organization along racial identity lines.

2.5.4 Comparability of Data on Race over Time

Finally, a comment about comparability of data over time. At the level of data collection, holding aside immigration, demographics, and related issues, the identity of any particular racial group obtained through surveys changes over time due to two factors: (1) changes in the social meaning attached to different groups or terms; and (2) changes in survey methodology.

For example, individuals with both White and Black parentage changed their behavior in surveys coincident with the election and visibility of President Barack Obama, who identified strongly as someone with both Black and White heritage (Mason 2017). This form of change over time reflects the fundamentally social nature of race. As another example, "Prior to the late 1960s . . . there were no people who identified as 'Asian American'" because that category did not exist (Espiritu 1993, 17).

But there are also changes in the data that come from purely methodological decisions. The composition of Asian or Pacific Islander changed when the group's definition changed in 1997 with a separate category for Native Hawaiians and Other Pacific Islanders.

The meaning of race as reflected in datasets changes over time, and the proposal in question would eliminate one source of variation: changes to the definitions. The problem of keeping up with social categories remains. This problem has additional complexity in the context of the federal government because, "as racial categories change, so do racial hierarchies" (Bashi 1998). Visible decisions around statistical practices by the federal government, including Directive 15 and the decennial Census, have the power to affect social reality even when their primary intended purpose is to facilitate quantitative measurement of social reality.

Seen in this light, perhaps the observation that "no single set of racial categories has been used in more than two censuses, and most were only used once" (Martin et al. 1990, 553) is rather hopeful, compared to the rigidity of the definitions of Directive 15 which have remained largely unchanged since 1977.

2.6 Conclusion

The race categories identified by Census and OMB have powerful social meaning. Self-reported race correlates strongly with a wide range of social outcomes. But self-reported race is not selected based on the official definitions.

Given the inadequacy of the definitions and the fact they do not seem to inform the choices made by respondents to federal surveys, we conclude that dispensing with the definitions altogether could have substantial advantages over the status quo routine of intermittently trying to update specific definitions for race and ethnicity categories. Independent research and opportunities to receive public comments and recommendations can ensure the Office of Management and Budget and the US Census Bureau are making use of an appropriate list of categories that are popularly understood and socially meaningful.

For acknowledgments, sources of research support, and disclosure of the authors' material financial relationships, if any, please see https://www.nber.org/books-and-chapters/race-ethnicity-and-economic-statistics-21st-century/data-collection-without-definitions.

References

94th Congress. 1976. Joint Resolution Relating to the Publication of Economic and Social Statistics for Americans of Spanish Origin or Descent. June.

American Anthropological Association. 1998. AAA Statement on Race. https://americananthro.org/about/policies/statement-on-race.

American Association of Biological Anthropologists. 1996. AABA Statement on Race. https://bioanth.org/about/aaba-statement-on-race.

Bashi, V. 1998. "Racial Categories Matter Because Racial Hierarchies Matter: A Commentary." *Ethnic and Racial Studies* 21(5): 959–68. DOI: 10.1080/014198798329748.

Bourdieu, P. 2009. *Language and Symbolic Power*, translated by J. B. Thompson and G. Raymond. Cambridge: Polity Press.

Citro, C. F. 1997. "Window on Washington: Recognizing Diversity: Recommendations to OMB on Standards for Data on Race and Ethnicity. *CHANCE* 10(4): 26–31. DOI: 10.1080/09332480.1997.10542059.

Crenshaw, K. W. 1988. "Race, Reform, and Retrenchment: Transformation and Legitimation in Antidiscrimination Law." *Harvard Law Review* 101(7): 1331–1387.

Darity, W. A., P. L. Mason, and J. B. Stewart. 2006. "The Economics of Identity: The Origin and Persistence of Racial Identity Norms." *Journal of Economic Behavior & Organization* 60(3): 283–305. DOI: 10.1016/j.jebo.2004.09.005.

Darity, W. A., and A. K. Mullen. 2020. *From Here to Equality: Reparations for Black Americans in the Twenty-First Century*. Chapel Hill: University of North Carolina Press.

Desautels-Stein, J. 2012. "Race as a Legal Concept." *Columbia Journal of Race and Law* 2(1): 1–74.

Diette, T. M., A. H. Goldsmith, D. Hamilton, and W. Darity. 2015. "Skin Shade Stratification and the Psychological Cost of Unemployment: Is there a Gradient for Black Females?" *Review of Black Political Economy* 42(1–2): 155–77. DOI: 10.1007/s12114-014-9192-z.

Eschbach, K., and J. Taylor. "The Explosion of the 2020 Census 'Indian' Population and Its Implications for Tribal Policymaking." Forthcoming in *Beyond Blood Quantum: Refusal to Disappear*, edited by N. Hill, K. Ratteree, M. Hill, and D. Hill. Fulcrum Publishing.

Espiritu, Y. 1993. *Asian American Panethnicity: Bridging Institutions and Identities*. Philadelphia: Temple University Press.

Fears, D. 2003. "The Roots of 'Hispanic'; 1975 Committee of Bureaucrats Produced Designation." *Washington Post*, October 15.

Federal Interagency Committee on Education. 1975. Report of the Ad Hoc Committee on Racial and Ethnic Definitions, April.

Fields, B. J. 1982. "Ideology and Race in American History." In *Region, Race and Reconstruction: Essays in Honor of C. Vann Woodward*, edited by J. M. Kousser and J. M. McPherson, 143–77. New York: Oxford University Press.

Forbes, J. D. 1992. "The Hispanic Spin: Party Politics and Governmental Manipulation of Ethnic Identity." *Latin American Perspectives* 19(4): 59–78. DOI: 10.1177/0094582X9201900406.

Ford, C. A. 1994. "Administering Identity: The Determination of 'Race' in Race-Conscious Law." *California Law Review* 82(5): 1231. DOI: 10.2307/3480910.

Fuentes, A., R. R. Ackermann, S. Athreya, D. Bolnick, T. Lasisi, S.-H. Lee, . . . and R. Nelson. 2019. "AAPA Statement on Race and Racism." *American Journal of Physical Anthropology* 169(3): 400–402. DOI: 10.1002/ajpa.23882.

Gimenez, M. E. 1989. "Latino/'Hispanic'—Who Needs a Name? The Case against a Standardized Terminology." *International Journal of Health Services* 19(3): 557–71. DOI: 10.2190/HN6N-P1TH-8CHL-KW5X.
Goldsmith, A. H., D. Hamilton, and W. Darity. 2006. "Shades of Discrimination: Skin Tone and Wages." *American Economic Review* 96(2): 242–45. DOI: 10.1257/000282806777212152.
Goldsmith, A. H., D. Hamilton, and W. A. Darity Jr. 2007. "From Dark to Light: Skin Color and Wages Among African-Americans." *Journal of Human Resources* XLII(4): 701–38. DOI: 10.3368/jhr.XLII.4.701.
Hamilton, D., A. H. Goldsmith, and W. Darity. 2009. "Shedding 'Light' on Marriage: The Influence of Skin Shade on Marriage for Black Females." *Journal of Economic Behavior & Organization* 72(1): 30–50. DOI: 10.1016/j.jebo.2009.05.024.
Hernández, T. K. 1998. "Multiracial Discourse: Racial Classifications in an Era of Color-blind Jurisprudence." *Maryland Law Review* 57: 97–173.
Hitlin, S., J. S. Brown, and G. H. Elder Jr. 2007. "Measuring Latinos: Racial vs. Ethnic Classification and Self-Understandings." *Social Forces* 86(2): 587–611. DOI: 10.1093/ sf/86.2.587.
Hollinger, D. A. 2000. *Postethnic America: Beyond Multiculturalism*. New York: Basic Books.
Johnson, A. M., Jr. 1996. "Destabilizing Racial Classifications Based on Insights Gleaned from Trademark Law." *California Law Review* 84(4): 887–952. California Law Review, Inc.DOI: 10.2307/3480986.
Johnson, A. M., Jr. 2008. "The Re-Emergence of Race as a Biological Category: The Societal Implications—Reaffirmation of Race." *Iowa Law Review* 94: 1547–1585.
Jones, T. 2000. "Shades of Brown: The Law of Skin Color." *Duke Law Journal* 49.
Kaplan, J. 2024. "Race and Racialized Populations: Ascriptions, Power, and Identity." *Argumenta*, 1–13.
Larena, M., F. Sanchez-Quinto, P. Sjödin, J. McKenna, C. Ebeo, R. Reyes, . . . and M. Jakobsson. 2021. "Multiple Migrations to the Philippines During the Last 50,000 Years." *Proceedings of the National Academy of Sciences* 118(13): e2026132118. March. DOI: 10.1073/pnas.2026132118.
Lew, J. J. 2000. Guidance on Aggregation and Allocation of Data on Race for Use in Civil Rights Monitoring and Enforcement. Office of Management and Budget. March.
López, N., and H. Hogan. 2021. "What's Your Street Race? The Urgency of Critical Race Theory and Intersectionality as Lenses for Revising the US Office of Management and Budget Guidelines, Census and Administrative Data in Latinx Communities and Beyond." *Genealogy* 5(3): 75. DOI: 10.3390/genealogy5030075.
Margolis, M. 1995. "Brazilians and the 1990 United States Census: Immigrants, Ethnicity, and the Undercount." *Human Organization* 54(1): 52–59. DOI: 10.17730/ humo.54.1.5487w18130176194.
Martin, E., T. J. Demaio, and P. C. Campanelli. 1990. "Context Effects for Census Measures of Race and Hispanic Origin." *Public Opinion Quarterly* 54(4): 551. DOI: 10.1086/269227.
Martinez, G. A. 1997. "The Legal Construction of Race: Mexican-Americans and Whiteness." *Harvard Latino Law Review* 2: 321–47.
Mason, P. L. 2017. "Not Black-Alone: The 2008 Presidential Election and Racial Self- Identification among African Americans." *Review of Black Political Economy* 44(1–2): 55–76. DOI: 10.1007/s12114–017–9247-z.
Mason, P. L. 2023. *The Economics of Structural Racism*. Cambridge, United Kingdom; New York, NY: Cambridge University Press.
Mathews, K., J. Phelan, N. A. Jones, S. Konya, R. Marks, B. M. Pratt, . . . and

M. Bentley. 2017. 2015 National Content Test: Race and Ethnicity Analysis Report: A New Design for the 21st Century. February.

Mathieson, I., I. Lazaridis, N. Rohland, S. Mallick, B. Llamas, J. Pickrell, . . . and D. Reich. 2015. "Eight Thousand Years of Natural Selection in Europe." bioRxiv, March. (Pages: 016477 Section: New Results) DOI: 10.1101/016477.

Mirandé, A., ed. 2019. *Gringo Injustice: Insider Perspectives on Police, Gangs, and Law*. New York: Routledge.

Mora, G. C. 2014. *Making Hispanics: How Activists, Bureaucrats, and Media Constructed a New American*. Chicago: University of Chicago Press.

Myers, S. L., Jr. 1997. "The Error of the Third Type." In *Double Exposure: Poverty and Race in America*, edited by C. W. Hartman. New York: Routledge. DOI: 10.4324/9781315479378.

Office of Management and Budget. 1978. Transfer of Responsibility for Certain Statistical Standards from OMB to Commerce. *Fed. Reg.* 43(87). May.

Office of Management and Budget. 1994. Standards for the Classification of Federal Data on Race and Ethnicity. *Fed. Reg.* 59(110). June.

Office of Management and Budget. 1995. Standards for the Classification of Federal Data on Race and Ethnicity. *Fed. Reg.* 60(166). August.

Office of Management and Budget. 1997. Revisions to the Standards for the Classification. *Fed. Reg.* 62(210). October.

Office of Management and Budget. 2023. Initial Proposals for Updating OMB's Race and Ethnicity Statistical Standards. January.

Office of Management and Budget. 2024. Revisions to OMB's Statistical Policy Directive No. 15: Standards for Maintaining, Collecting, and Presenting Federal Data on Race and Ethnicity. *Fed. Reg.* 89(62). March.

Omi, M. 1985. "Racial Identity and the State: The Dilemmas of Classification." *Minnesota Journal of Law & Inequality* 15(1).

Omi, M. 2001. "The Changing Meaning of Race." In *America Becoming: Racial Trends and Their Consequences*, vol. 1, edited by N. J. Smelser, W. J. Wilson, and F. Mitchell, 243–63. Washington, DC: National Academies Press. DOI: 10.17226/9599.

Prewitt, K. 2016. *What Is "Your" Race? The Census and Our Flawed Efforts to Classify Americans*. Princeton, NJ: Princeton University Press.

Ray, V. 2019. "A Theory of Racialized Organizations." *American Sociological Review* 84(1): 28.

Robbin, A. 2000. "The Politics of Representation in the US National Statistical System: Origins of Minority Population Interest Group Participation." *Journal of Government Information* 27(4): 431–53. DOI: 10.1016/S1352–0237(00)00178–7.

Robinson, C. J., and R. D. G. Kelley. 2000. *Black Marxism: The Making of the Black Radical Tradition*. Chapel Hill, NC: University of North Carolina Press.

Rodríguez, C. E. 1997. *Latin Looks: Images of Latinas and Latinos in the US Media*. Boulder, CO: Routledge.

Rosa, J. 2019. *Looking Like a Language, Sounding Like a Race*. Oxford University Press.

Rosa, J., and N. Flores. 2017. "Unsettling Race and Language: Toward a Raciolinguistic Perspective." *Language in Society* 46(5): 621–47. DOI: 10.1017/S0047404517000562.

Roth, W. D. 2016. "The Multiple Dimensions of Race." *Ethnic and Racial Studies* 39(8): 1310–1338. DOI: 10.1080/01419870.2016.1140793.

Schuster, L. 2021. "We're Reporting Census Data All Wrong." *Boston Indicators*, December. Retrieved February 27, 2024 from https://www.bostonindicators.org/article-pages/2021/december/census reporting.

Shadowen, S. D. 2018. "US Border Patrol's Policy of Extrajudicial Killing." *Berkeley La Raza Law Journal* 28(1).

Skerry, P. 2000. *Counting on the Census? Race, Group Identity, and the Evasion of Politics*. Washington, DC: Brookings Institution Press.

State Health Access Data Assistance Center at the University of Minnesota. 2021. Collection of Race, Ethnicity, Language (REL) Data in Medicaid Applications: A 50-state Review of the Current Landscape. May.

Swartz, D. 1997. *Culture and Power: The Sociology of Pierre Bourdieu*. University of Chicago Press.

Tamayo Lott, J. 1997. *The Limitations of Directive 15. In Double Exposure: Poverty and Race in America*. New York: Routledge. DOI: 10.4324/9781315479378.

Toro, L. A. 1995. "A People Distinct from Others: Race and Identity in Federal Indian Law and the Hispanic Classifications in OMB Directive No. 15." *Texas Law Review* 26(4): 1219–1274.

Wallman, K. K. 1998. "Data on Race and Ethnicity: Revising the Federal Standard." *American Statistician* 52(1): 31–33. DOI: 10.1080/00031305.1998.10480533.

Wallman, K. K., S. Evinger, and S. Schechter. 2000. "Measuring Our Nation's Diversity: Developing a Common Language for Data on Race/Ethnicity." *American Journal of Public Health* 90(11): 1704–1708.

Walter, M., and C. Anderson. 2013. *Indigenous Statistics: A Quantitative Research Methodology*. Walnut Creek, CA: Left Coast Press.

Wingfield, A. H. 2015. "Color Blindness Is Counterproductive." *Atlantic*, September. Retrieved March 5, 2024, from https://www.theatlantic.com/politics/archive/2015/09/color-blindness-is-counterproductive/405037/.

Yang, T. 2005. "Choice and Fraud in Racial Identification: The Dilemma of Policing Race in Affirmative Action, the Census, and a Color-Blind Society." *Michigan Journal of Race & Law* 11.

3

Measuring Potential Effects of Introducing the 2024 Race and Ethnicity Standards into the Current Population Survey

Mark A. Loewenstein, David S. Piccone Jr., and Anne E. Polivka

3.1 Introduction

The Census Bureau and other agencies have long attempted to obtain information on individuals' race and ethnicity. In 1980, Census began asking individuals whether they were of Hispanic ethnicity. Prior to the 2024 update, the race and ethnicity standards were last revised in 1997. At that time, the Office of Management and Budget (OMB) mandated five different race groups: White; Black or African American; American Indian or Alaskan Native; Asian; and Native Hawaiian or Pacific Islander. The 1997 OMB standards also allowed individuals to select more than one of the five different race groups. Hispanic was explicitly treated as an ethnicity, not as a race, and was to be obtained from a separate question.

Prior to the 2024 update, there was interest in revising the race and ethnicity standards for several reasons. The proportion of the population identifying as Hispanic has been growing over time: As noted by Jones et al. (2021), the proportion of the population that is Hispanic as measured by the Decennial Census increased from 16.3 percent in 2010 to 18.7 percent in 2020. A large proportion of Hispanics viewed themselves as "Hispanic or Latino" and selected the "Some Other Race" category rather than one of the five OMB race categories in the decennial census. In addition, the 1997 standards did not include a Middle Eastern and North African category, but rather defined "White" as individuals having origins in any of the original

Mark A. Loewenstein is division chief of Employment Research and Program Development at the Bureau of Labor Statistics.

David S. Piccone Jr. is a statistician in Employment Research and Program Development at the Bureau of Labor Statistics.

Anne E. Polivka is research chief of Employment Research and Program Development Staff at the Bureau of Labor Statistics.

peoples of Europe, the Middle East, or North Africa. There had been an increased advocacy to allow individuals to identify as Middle Eastern or North African since these individuals often do not identify with any of the existing race categories and because it was felt that there is a need for data about this group.[1]

The "Some Other Race" (SOR) classification was initially intended to be a small residual category. However, in the 2020 Decennial Census, about 8.4 percent of respondents identified as SOR alone. This represented an increase from the 2010 Census, in which 6.2 percent of respondents classified themselves as SOR alone. In addition, SOR was "the second-largest alone or in combination race group" in the 2020 Census. The high percentage of respondents identifying as SOR was primarily due to reporting by Hispanic respondents. About 93.9 percent of the individuals who were classified as SOR alone were of Hispanic origin (Jones et al. 2021).

OMB announced a new set of race and ethnicity standards in March 2024. There will no longer be an attempt to distinguish between race and ethnicity. Instead, OMB is mandating a combined race and ethnicity question with the following categories: White; Hispanic or Latino; Black or African American; Asian; American Indian or Alaskan Native; Middle Eastern or North African; and Native Hawaiian or Pacific Islander. Furthermore, individuals may select more than one category (i.e., they may identify as multiracial/multiethnic).

A general issue arises whenever one modifies questions and corresponding categorizations in long-standing surveys because of the potential to disrupt time series. There is inevitably a tension between choosing questions that may seem to be best today and the loss of information about time trends. One should be cognizant of the likely effects of methodological changes on time series and ascertain whether whatever improvements the new methodology may offer justify the loss of time series information. If possible, one should try to bridge the old and new series to minimize this loss.

In obtaining information on individuals' race and ethnicity, the Current Population Survey (CPS) currently follows the 1997 OMB standards. The effects that switching to the 2024 OMB combined Race and Ethnicity standards has on time series estimates will depend on the estimates that BLS and data users are currently generating and on how the pieces of information collected using the 2024 standards are combined to form new estimates.

In this paper, we examine the CPS micro data in an attempt to tease out these potential effects. Questions that we ask are: How will the introduction of the combined racial/ethnicity question that includes Hispanic and Middle Eastern or North African as distinct categories affect racial and ethnicity distributions? How will key labor force estimates for various groups, such

1. For example, in 2013, the Arab American Institute sent a letter to the Census Bureau and OMB requesting a distinct category on the racial or ethnic questions for people of Middle Eastern or North African origin. The letter was co-signed by 26 different organizations and scholars (US Census Bureau 2017).

as unemployment rates, employment-to-population ratios, labor force participation ratios, and earnings, be affected?

The proportion of the population that identifies as Hispanic has been increasing because of the large number of immigrants from Mexico and Central and South America. The higher fertility rate of Hispanics compared to non-Hispanics has also played a role.[2] An ongoing question is how the children of Hispanic immigrants who were born in the United States will view themselves. After all, racial/ethnic identification is at its root a subjective concept. We therefore look at the tendency of individuals to identify as Hispanic: because they were either born in a Hispanic country or were born in the United States but have one or two Hispanic parents. In turn, we speculate how this identification might affect race and ethnicity distributions when comparing estimates generated using the 1997 OMB standards versus the 2024 OMB standards.

The remainder of the paper is organized as follows. In section 3.2, we provide a detailed look at the current CPS race and ethnicity questions. In section 3.3, we discuss likely effects on published estimates along with other estimates frequently derived using CPS data. Section 3.4 describes our methods for ascertaining the possible effects of the new race/ethnicity standards. We present our estimates in section 3.5. Section 3.6 looks more closely at individuals who identify as Hispanic. Section 3.7 discusses issues associated with generating comparable estimates across time. Concluding remarks can be found in section 3.8.

3.2 A Detailed Look at the CPS Race and Ethnicity Question Using the 1997 Standards

Respondents are asked their and other household members' race and ethnicity the first time they are interviewed, and sometimes during the fifth interview. Field Representatives are also instructed to collect race and ethnicity for people who have been added to households (i.e., those who have moved into the household since a previous interview) and for replacement households (i.e., households that have replaced the previous household that has moved out).[3] When individuals are asked about their race and ethnicity they are first asked about their Hispanic ethnicity. Box 3.1 below shows the exact wording of the CPS Hispanic ethnicity question.

After being asked about their ethnicity, respondents are asked about their race. Interviews may be by phone or in person. The wording of the question differs slightly depending on whether it is asked in an in-person interview or by phone. Most initial and fifth interviews are done in person, where respon-

2. See "Hispanics and the Future of America," section 3 (National Research Council [US] Panel on Hispanics in the United States 2006).

3. The CPS uses a rotating panel design where households are interviewed for four consecutive months, are not interviewed for the next eight months, and are then interviewed for four consecutive months.

Box 3.1 Hispanic ethnicity question in the CPS using the 1997 standards

(Are you/Is NAME) of Hispanic, Latino, or Spanish origin?

VALID ENTRIES

1 Yes
2 No

Box 3.2 Race telephone question in the CPS using the 1997 standards

I'm going to read a list of race categories. You may choose one or more races. For this survey, Hispanic origin is not a race. (Are/Is) (you/name): White; Black or African American; American Indian or Alaska Native; Asian; OR Native Hawaiian or Other Pacific Islander?

DO NOT PROBE-Unless response is Hispanic or is a Hispanic origin.

Valid Entries

1. White
2. Black
3. American Indian or Alaska Native
4. Asian
5. Native Hawaiian or Other Pacific Islander
6. Other -DO NOT READ

dents are shown a flash card with the race categories. Beginning in 2012, respondents are explicitly told that Hispanic origin is not a race. For ease of explication, the telephone version of the question is presented in box 3.2.

Respondents not choosing one of the five race categories are put in the "Other Race" category. An imputation is made to place "Other Race" respondents in one of the five allowable race categories for the published estimates. This is done by first looking at the respondent's previous answers to the CPS race questions. If there is no previous race information, a relational approach is used to assign missing race data based on relatives within the household. If a person's mother is in the household and has a race, the person is assigned a race based on the mother's race. If the mother is not in the household, race is assigned to the individual based on the most appropriate relative in the household. If there is no potential donor within the household, a hot-deck imputation is used. Because people can choose more than one of the five race categories, the race imputation in CPS is handled as a grouped allocation, so that the donor's responses for all five race categories are imputed at once. This means that if a relative or donor is multiracial, the person to whom a race is allocated will also have more than one race assigned.

Box 3.3 presents a combined race and ethnicity question. The language in this box comes from the 2024 standards and does not necessarily reflect the exact wording the CPS will adopt.[4]

Box 3.3 Combined race and ethnicity question in line with 2024 standards

What is your race and/or ethnicity?
Select all that apply.

Valid Entries

1. American Indian or Alaska Native
2. Asian
3. Black or African American
4. Hispanic or Latino
5. Middle Eastern or North Africa
6. Native Hawaiian or Pacific Islander
7. White

3.3 Explanation of Possible Effects on Estimates

In subsequent sections, we estimate the possible effects that switching to the 2024 OMB combined Race and Ethnicity standards may have on CPS time series estimates. Prior to exploring these effects in the data, it may be helpful to outline the information collected under each of the standards and discuss likely effects on the estimates. As discussed below, these effects will depend on what estimates are being calculated and how the various pieces of information collected using the 1997 and 2024 standards are combined.

Recall that under the 1997 standards, respondents are first asked a ques-

4. The new standards can be found in the Federal Register: 2024 OMB Standard Link (Federal Register 2024) https://www.federalregister.gov/documents/2024/03/29/2024-06469/revisions-to-ombs-statistical-policy-directive-no-15-standards-for-maintaining-collecting-and. The standards permit flexibility in the wording of the question and the order of response categories.

tion to determine whether they are Hispanic or not. In a subsequent question, they are asked to identify their race. People can identify as only one race, or they can say that they are any combination of several races. For example, people might identify as White Alone, Black Alone, Asian Alone, or two or more races (i.e., White/Black or White/Black/Asian).[5] This structure means that everyone is identified as Hispanic or non-Hispanic regardless of their race and that everyone who is Hispanic has a race. It also means that each race group can be divided into Hispanic or non-Hispanic. For example, those who are White Alone will be either White Alone Hispanic or White Alone non-Hispanic.

Under the 2024 combined race/ethnicity standards, respondents are only asked a single question in which Hispanic is an option. Individuals can identify with a single group or a combination of groups. For example, among other possibilities, individuals might identify as White Alone, Black Alone, Asian Alone, Hispanic Alone or White/Hispanic, Black/Hispanic or Asian/Hispanic. As with the 1997 standard, this structure means that everyone will be identified as Hispanic or non-Hispanic, but this is done through only one question. People who are Hispanic will be identified by selecting responses that indicate they are Hispanic—specifically by saying they are Hispanic Alone or Hispanic in combination with one of the other groups (e.g., White/Hispanic). Individuals who are non-Hispanic will be identified by selecting one or more race groups that are not Hispanic. For instance, White Alone non-Hispanics will be those who only identify as White Alone. Furthermore, unlike the 1997 structure, not all people who are Hispanic will have another race associated with them when the 2024 standards are used.

The BLS monthly Employment Situation news release currently contains estimates for individuals who are White Alone, Black Alone and Asian Alone. These "Alone" race categories currently include individuals who are Hispanic and who are non-Hispanic. However, under the 2024 standards using a combined Race/Ethnicity question, the Race Alone categories will not include those who identify as Hispanic (either Hispanic alone or with another group). Therefore, the Race Alone categories will be smaller under the 2024 standards than under the 1997 standards. One can, of course, get closer to the estimate under the 1997 standards by combining the new Alone race group and Hispanics of the same race group, but this number will still be smaller because of the new Hispanic Alone group. For example, combining individuals who are White Alone and White/Hispanic will leave out those who indicate that they are Hispanic Alone, but would have identified as Hispanic and White under the 1997 standards when everyone who was Hispanic was also asked to identify a race.

Another common way to present the race data is to split the race categories by whether a person is Hispanic or non-Hispanic. Typically, in these pre-

5. Under the 1997 standards in the CPS, individuals who only identify as "Other Race" are allocated a race using the five specified race categories.

sentations, race estimates are disaggregated by Hispanic and non-Hispanic for the single Race Alone categories (multiracial is not disaggregated) and often non-Hispanic estimates are only presented for those who are White. For example, Census uses data from the CPS Annual Social and Economic Supplement (ASEC) to publish poverty estimates for those who are White Alone non-Hispanic and Hispanic (of any race).

Theoretically estimates for non-Hispanics by race groups should be the same under both the 1997 and the 2024 standards (abstracting, of course, from the new MENA category). For example, under the 2024 standards, individuals will be counted as White Alone non-Hispanic if they indicate that they are White Alone and do not also indicate that they are Hispanic. Under the 1997 standards, these people are identified as White Alone non-Hispanic if they explicitly indicate that they are non-Hispanic when asked about their ethnicity and indicate they are White Alone when asked about race. However, the actual comparability of estimates for data collected under the two standards will be completely dependent on how people identify themselves under the two paradigms. It is plausible that some individuals identified as White and Hispanic when asked two separate questions will identify as just White when answering a combined race and ethnicity question as prescribed by the 2024 standards. This would make the estimate of White non-Hispanics larger when collected using the combined question than when data are collected using two separate questions. Correspondingly the estimate of Hispanics would be smaller using the combined question than when data are collected using two questions under this scenario. In contrast, while perhaps unlikely, if more people identify as Hispanic using the combined race and ethnicity question than when asked the two separate questions (for example those who were a mixture of Hispanic and non-Hispanic are more likely to identify their Hispanic origin in a combined question), the estimate of non-Hispanics by race groups would be smaller and the estimate of Hispanics would be larger than estimates generated using the 1997 standards.[6] The estimate of Hispanics will also be influenced by whether people who identify as Hispanic and one of the other race groups prescribed under the 2024 standards are considered Hispanic or are considered multiracial, multiethnic.

6. Comparisons between estimates obtained asking two separate questions as opposed to a single combined question also will depend on the how the separate question about being Hispanic is presented. The Census's 2015 National Content Test found a slightly larger percentage of people identified as Hispanic in a combined question as opposed to those who were asked two separate questions. However, to be counted as Hispanic in the National Content Test, people who were asked the two separate questions had to indicate "yes they are Hispanic" by selecting response categories that were combinations of both yes and a Hispanic subgroup. (For example, people whose parents were born in Mexico would have to select "Yes, Mexican, Mexican Am, Chicano" to indicate they were Hispanic.) In contrast, in the CPS people are first asked a simple yes/no question as to whether they are Hispanic, and identification of Hispanic subgroups is obtained in a follow-up question. It is likely that the CPS question would obtain a higher proportion of people responding that they are Hispanic than the National Content Test. We contend that it is unlikely more people will identify as Hispanic using a combined question than when asked the CPS direct question.

While adoption of the 2024 standards could disrupt estimates regardless of how the data are presented, the disruption will almost certainly be larger for estimates, such as those published in BLS's monthly Employment Situation that do not disaggregate the 1997 standards race groups by ethnicity. This is because individuals who identify as Hispanic Alone in the combined race and ethnicity question will have no other race group associated with them. In the work that follows we try to estimate the number of people who will identify as Hispanic Alone using a combined question and the effect this will have on the proportion of the population in the 1997 standards racial groups and the corresponding labor force and earnings estimates. Because the 2024 standards call for Middle Eastern North African (MENA) to be a separate race category, as part of this comparison, we also estimate the number of people we expect to identify as MENA alone and the effect this separate racial group will have on population and labor force estimates for the existing 1997 racial groups.

3.4 Methodology

As noted above, the 2024 OMB standards are a combined race and ethnicity question with the following seven categories: American Indian or Alaskan Native; Asian; Black or African American; Hispanic or Latino; Middle Eastern or North African; Native Hawaiian or Pacific Islander; and White, with respondents able to choose more than one category. Based on responses to the existing CPS race and ethnicity questions, we would like to obtain estimates for the proportion of individuals who likely will be classified as Hispanics Alone under the 2024 standards.

In the collection process using the 1997 standard, individuals who select "Other Race" are asked a follow-up question to identify what the other race is at the time the data are collected. The "Other Race" follow-up question has 40 response categories. We have identified eight of these possible responses as Hispanic: Hispanic, Chicano, Cuban or Cuban American, Latin American, Latino, Mexican or Mexican American, and Spanish.

It seems a safe bet that individuals who indicate that they are an Other Race for their first race in the unedited data and then select one of the Hispanic "Other Race" categories would classify themselves as only Hispanic when responding to the new question. As a **lower bound Hispanic Alone estimate**, we count individuals as Hispanic Alone if (a) their first race was coded as "Other Race"; and (b) they selected one of the eight "Other Race" categories that we have identified as Hispanic.[7]

7. We exclude individuals who selected one of the five prespecified race categories as their first race and select "Other Race" as a subsequent race. This situation is extremely rare, occurring in only about 0.3 percent of the individuals who select one of the five prespecified race categories as their first race.

It also seems likely that a high proportion of individuals who indicate they are Hispanic when they are asked about their ethnicity before being asked about their race would indicate only Hispanic when responding to the new combined race and ethnicity questions. As an **upper bound Hispanic Alone estimate**, we therefore count individuals as only Hispanic if they indicated they were Hispanic in response to the ethnicity question.

As discussed above, the 2024 race and ethnicity standards call for a new Middle Eastern and North African (MENA) category. We obtain rough estimates of the MENA population from the information on individuals' country of origin as well as their "Other Race" responses. Specifically, we classify an individual as MENA if they indicate that they are "Other Race" Arab or if they or either of their parents were born in one of the following countries: Algeria, Bahrain, Egypt, Iran, Iraq, Israel, Kuwait, Lebanon, Libya, Oman, Qatar, Saudi Arabia, Syria, Tunisia, Turkey, United Arab Emirates, and Yemen.[8]

3.5 Estimates

We now look at the actual CPS data. Our estimates are based on annual averages generated using a combination of edited and unedited monthly CPS data, for individuals in the civilian non-institutional population who are 16 years and older. The unedited data enable us to see individuals whose answers were recorded as "Other Race" prior to their answers being allocated to a race. We utilize 17 years of data from 2007 to 2023. The CPS race and ethnicity questions were changed significantly in 2003. Estimates before and after 2007 are not comparable. The "Other Race" estimates from 2007 on are much higher than those that are pre-2007, likely due to the Census Bureau switching to the programming language Blaise for their data collection instruments. This, among other things, affected the layout of the question on an interviewer's screen. We therefore exclude the years before 2007 from our analysis. Population and Labor Force estimates are generated using composite weights.[9] Earnings estimates use outgoing rotation weights.[10] Unlike the published BLS estimates, we generate an hourly wage

8. Where people and their parents are born is identified in a separate series of questions about nativity and citizenship.

9. Composite weights are constructed to reduce variability in monthly labor force estimates. Their construction involves two steps. First, composite estimates are calculated as a weighted average of the composite estimate from the previous month, an estimate of change from the proceeding to the current month, and a component that captures the difference between incoming and continuing parts of the current month's sample. A series of adjustments are then made to the micro data weights to bring them into agreement with the composite estimates.

10. Outgoing rotation weights are assigned to individuals in the outgoing rotation groups (ORG), which consist of individuals who have completed their fourth and eighth interviews. These weights ensure that the ORG is representative of the entire population. Earnings and hours information are only collected from those who are in the ORG.

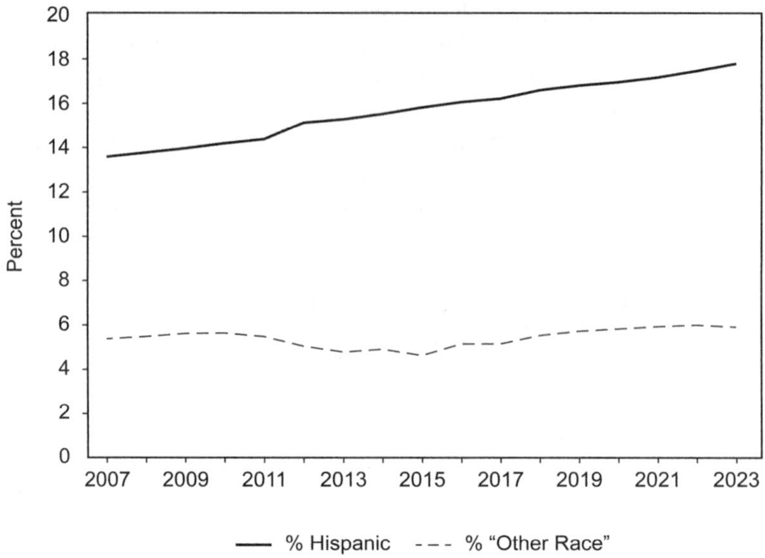

Fig. 3.1 Percent Hispanic and "Other Race"

for everyone who is employed.[11] Standard errors are generated using replicate weights.[12] Throughout the discussion, when we refer to a race category on its own, such as White, we are referring to the Alone category, such as White Alone.

3.5.1 Population, Unemployment Rate, and Earnings Estimates by Race and Ethnicity

Figure 3.1 shows how the proportion of individuals who are Hispanic and the proportion who indicate they are "Other Race" have changed over time. The proportion of individuals who indicate that they are of Hispanic ethnicity increased steadily from 13.5 percent in 2007 to 17.8 percent in 2023. In contrast, the proportion of individuals in the CPS who indicate that they are "Other Race" increased only marginally from 5.4 percent in 2007 to 5.9 percent in 2023.[13] Furthermore, this trend has not been mono-

11. BLS publishes usual weekly earnings for full-time workers and hourly earnings for people identified as hourly workers. To obtain a more complete picture we generate an hourly estimate for everyone who is employed. For respondents who do not provide an hourly wage directly, we obtain an estimate of it by dividing weekly earnings by weekly hours worked. For respondents who have no reported weekly hours, we impute weekly hours using a regression approach. All hourly wage estimates are aged to June 2023, using the CPI-U.

12. Replicate weights are used in the calculation of CPS variance estimates. They fractionally assign individuals to 160 subpopulations and are constructed using a successive difference replication method.

13. The lower percentage of people who are "Other Race" alone in the CPS compared to the Decennial Census illustrates the influence of CPS interviewers on the collection of the data and the effect of not having "Other" as an explicit option.

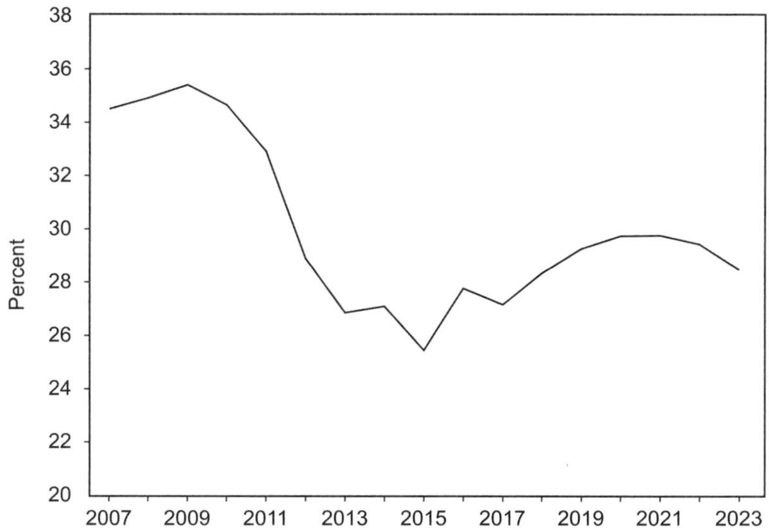

Fig.3.2 Percent Hispanic who are "Other Race"

tonic, falling somewhat in 2012 and then increasing again a few years later. The reason for the dip in "Other Race" in 2012 becomes evident in the next figure.

Figure 3.2 shows the proportion of individuals of Hispanic ethnicity who are also "Other Race." This proportion was 34.5 percent in 2007. The proportion of Hispanics who are "Other Race" fell to 28.9 percent in 2012 and then a few years later increased to nearly 30 percent. Various factors could have caused this percentage to oscillate over time. One worth noting is that beginning in 2012, respondents were explicitly told that Hispanic is not a race.

The proportion of non-Hispanics who are "Other Race" is not shown in the figure but is quite small, ranging between 0.8 percent and 1.0 percent over the period. Not surprisingly then, most individuals who are "Other Race" fall into one of the subgroups that we have identified as Hispanic. As figure 3.3 shows, the proportion of individuals who are "Other Race" that are in a Hispanic subgroup ranged between 82.8 percent and 87.8 percent over the 2007–2023 period.

Table 3.1 presents population, unemployment rate, and earnings estimates by race and ethnicity for 2023, using what respondents report is their first race. The five race categories and "Other Race" are decomposed into their Hispanic and non-Hispanic components. In table 3.2, the non-Hispanic groups are further divided into MENA and non-MENA components. Note that 0.9 percent of Whites fall into our constructed MENA category and

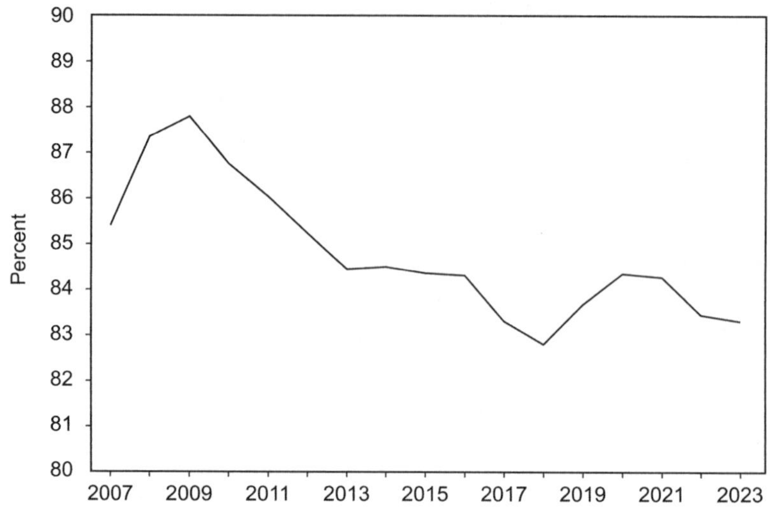

Fig. 3.3 Percent "Other Race" found in Hispanics subgroup

0.8 percent of the Asian population is MENA.[14] The percentage of individuals in the other race groups who are MENA is 0.2 percent or less. In contrast, the corresponding percentage for "Other Race" is 3.1 percent.[15]

Hispanic Whites had a higher unemployment rate than non-Hispanic Whites—4.3 percent compared to 3 percent. Hispanic Whites also had a lower median hourly wage than non-Hispanic Whites—$20.12 versus $26.75.[16] In contrast, Hispanic Blacks and non-Hispanic Blacks had unemployment rates (5.9 percent versus 5.7 percent) and hourly earnings ($20.39 versus $21.00) that were not significantly different. It should be noted, however, that the Hispanic Black portion of the sample is relatively small, containing only 2,888 individuals.[17]

When comparing MENA to non-MENA groups, we see that MENA generally had higher unemployment rates and higher median hourly wages in 2023 than non-MENA across the race groups. Due to the small number of

14. Per the 1997 standards, MENA is supposed to be part of the White category, but some individuals we classify as MENA are identified with other racial categories. Of those we identified as MENA, 88 percent identified as White, 4 percent identified as Black, and 7 percent identified as Asian.

15. The proportion of Hispanics who are MENA is negligible and is left out of the table to avoid unnecessary clutter.

16. As noted above, an hourly wage was constructed for all employed people.

17. The population and labor force estimates use all rotations of the CPS sample. The earnings estimates use only outgoing rotations, since these are the only rotations in which respondents are asked about earnings. The sample of outgoing rotations is about a quarter of the sample found in all rotations. For example, there were only 2,888 Hispanic Blacks underlying the 2023 population and labor force estimates and about a quarter of that number underlying the earnings estimates for Black Hispanics.

Table 3.1 **2023 race by Hispanic ethnicity estimates**

Race Category	Percent of Population	Hispanic Ethnicity	Percent of Race Population	Unemployment Rate	Median Hourly Wage
White	73.6%	Hispanic	16.0%	4.3% (0.1%)	$20.12 ($0.10)
		Non-Hispanic	84.0%	3.0% (0.0%)	$26.75 ($0.12)
Black	12.6%	Hispanic	3.8%	5.9% (0.8%)	$20.39 ($1.01)
		Non-Hispanic	96.2%	5.7% (0.2%)	$21.00 ($0.22)
American Indian/ Alaskan Native	1.0%	Hispanic	25.8%	7.5% (1.4%)	$20.26 ($0.94)
		Non-Hispanic	74.2%	6.8% (0.6%)	$20.31 ($0.54)
Asian	6.4%	Hispanic	1.0%	7.2% (2.3%)	$25.27 ($2.66)
		Non-Hispanic	99.0%	3.0% (0.1%)	$32.41 ($0.53)
Hawaiian Native/ Pacific Islander	0.4%	Hispanic	9.1%	4.9% (2.1%)	$23.97 ($2.45)
		Non-Hispanic	90.9%	4.3% (0.8%)	$21.12 ($0.83)
Other Race	6.0%	Hispanic	85.7%	5.1% (0.2%)	$19.83 ($0.33)
		Non-Hispanic	14.3%	3.2% (0.4%)	$23.46 ($0.81)

Table 3.2 **2023 race by non-Hispanic MENA category estimates**

Race Category	Non-Hispanic MENA Category	Percent of Race Population	Unemployment Rate	Median Hourly Wage
White	MENA	0.9%	3.6% (0.5%)	$30.17 ($1.08)
	Non-MENA	83.1%	2.9% (0.0%)	$26.73 ($0.15)
Black	MENA	0.2%	4.0% (2.4%)	$26.57 ($9.62)
	Non-MENA	96.0%	5.7% (0.2%)	$21.00 ($0.21)
American Indian/ Alaskan Native	MENA	–	–	–
	Non-MENA	74.1%	6.8% (0.6%)	$20.31 ($0.56)
Asian	MENA	0.8%	3.4% (1.5%)	$32.69 ($6.40)
	Non-MENA	98.2%	3.0% (0.1%)	$32.40 ($0.54)
Hawaiian Native/ Pacific Islander	MENA	–	–	–
	Non-MENA	90.9%	4.3% (0.8%)	$21.12 ($0.83)
Other Race	MENA	3.1%	3.7% (1.1%)	$23.80 ($1.89)
	Non-MENA	11.2%	3.1% (0.4%)	$23.43 ($0.91)

people we have classified as MENA and the low overall unemployment rates in 2023, these differences were generally not statistically different. In particular, MENA Whites had a higher unemployment rate than non-MENA Whites—3.6 percent compared to 2.9 percent—but the differential in unemployment rates was not statistically significant. MENA Whites also had a higher median hourly wage than non-MENA Whites—$30.17 compared to $26.73, and this difference was statistically significant. Due to the small number of people identifying as MENA among Blacks, Asians, and the

Table 3.3 **2010 and 2023 unemployment rates by race and Hispanic MENA category**

Race Category	Hispanic MENA Category	2010 Unemployment Rate	2023 Unemployment Rate
White	Hispanic	11.8% (0.3%)	4.3% (0.1%)
	Non-Hispanic	8.1% (0.1%)	3.0% (0.0%)
	MENA	*11.0% (1.1%)*	*3.6% (0.5%)*
	Non-MENA	*8.1% (0.1%)*	*2.9% (0.0%)*
Black	Hispanic	18.9% (1.9%)	5.9% (0.8%)
	Non-Hispanic	16.0% (0.3%)	5.7% (0.2%)
	MENA	*21.8% (9.1%)*	*4.0% (2.4%)*
	Non-MENA	*16.0% (0.3%)*	*5.7% (0.2%)*
American Indian/ Alaskan Native	Hispanic	17.6% (2.4%)	7.5% (1.4%)
	Non-Hispanic	14.2% (1.0%)	6.8% (0.6%)
	MENA	–	–
	Non-MENA	*14.2% (1.0%)*	*6.8% (0.6%)*
Asian	Hispanic	9.2% (3.0%)	7.2% (2.3%)
	Non-Hispanic	7.5% (0.3%)	3.0% (0.1%)
	MENA	*9.0% (3.9%)*	*3.4% (1.5%)*
	Non-MENA	*7.5% (0.3%)*	*3.0% (0.1%)*
Hawaiian Native/ Pacific Islander	Hispanic	18.8% (4.4%)	4.9% (2.1%)
	Non-Hispanic	12.0% (1.2%)	4.3% (0.8%)
	MENA	–	–
	Non-MENA	*12.0% (1.2%)*	*4.3% (0.8%)*
Other Race	Hispanic	13.4% (0.4%)	5.1% (0.2%)
	Non-Hispanic	9.7% (0.7%)	3.2% (0.4%)
	MENA	*11.4% (1.8%)*	*3.7% (1.1%)*
	Non-MENA	*9.3% (0.7%)*	*3.1% (0.4%)*

other race groups, the differences between those who were MENA and those who were not in these race groups were not statistically different. Although more people who were MENA identified as "Other Race," the estimates for MENA and non-MENA among those identified as "Other Race" also were relatively similar and not statistically different.

Unemployment rates were relatively low in 2023. Table 3.3 presents unemployment rate estimates by race and ethnicity for 2023 and 2010, the latter being a year with relatively high unemployment rates. As in 2023, White Hispanics had a higher unemployment rate than White non-Hispanics, but the difference was substantially larger in 2010. In both years, the White Hispanic unemployment rate was almost one and a half times the White non-Hispanic rate. In 2010, the difference between Black Hispanic and Black non-Hispanic unemployment rates also was substantial, but again as in 2023 the difference was not statistically significant. The large 7.9 percent differential between the Black and White unemployment rates for non-Hispanics in

Table 3.4 **2023 Hispanic ethnicity by race estimates**

Hispanic Ethnicity	Race Category	Unemployment Rate	Median Hourly Wage
Hispanic	Not-Other Race	4.5% (0.1%)	$20.12 ($0.13)
	Other Race	5.1% (0.2%)	$19.83 ($0.33)
	Other Race Hispanic Subgroup	5.1% (0.2%)	$19.81 ($0.37)
Non-Hispanic	Not-Other Race	3.4% (0.0%)	$25.84 ($0.07)
	Other Race	3.2% (0.4%)	$23.46 ($0.81)
	Other Race Hispanic Subgroup	3.8% (1.2%)	$21.42 ($1.32)

Note: All wages are adjusted using the CPI-U to be in June 2023 dollars

2010 is mirrored by a statistically significant 7.1 percent differential between the Black and White unemployment rates for Hispanics.

Comparing MENA and non-MENA unemployment rates in 2010 and 2023, we see that the gap between the MENA White and non-MENA White unemployment rate was larger in 2010 and, in fact, was statistically significant.

Table 3.4 presents unemployment rate and earnings estimates for 2023 by ethnicity and "Other Race" versus "Not-Other Race." As mentioned above, nearly 30 percent of individuals of Hispanic ethnicity are in the "Other Race" category. Individuals of Hispanic ethnicity who say "Other Race" had a higher unemployment rate than individuals of Hispanic ethnicity who did not say "Other Race"—5.1 percent compared to 4.5 percent. Individuals of Hispanic ethnicity who say "Other Race" also had a lower median wage than that for individuals of Hispanic ethnicity who did not say "Other Race"—$19.83 compared to $20.12.

3.5.2 How Might the 2024 Race and Ethnicity Standards Affect CPS Population Estimates?

With the preceding estimates in mind, we are now ready to examine possible effects that changing to the 2024 race and ethnicity standards has on CPS population, unemployment rate, employment-to-population, labor force participation rate, and earnings estimates. Because BLS currently publishes these estimates for the racial groups without distinguishing between Hispanic and non-Hispanics, in this discussion we are only considering the effect on the current race estimates where no distinction is made by ethnicity. Specifically, we examine the effects on the current estimates of White Alone, Black Alone, and Asian Alone.

Table 3.5 shows how the 2024 race and ethnicity standards might have affected the population estimates in 2023. Recall that our lower bound estimate counts individuals as Hispanic Alone if (a) their race was only coded as "Other Race," and (b) they selected one of the eight "Other Race" categories that we have identified as Hispanic. Our upper bound estimate counts individuals as Hispanic Alone if they indicated they were Hispanic in response

Table 3.5 **2023 population percentage estimates, 1997 vs. 2024 standards**

	Percent of the Population		
Race Category	1997 Race/Ethnicity Standards	2024 Race/Ethnicity Standards Lower Bound	2024 Race/Ethnicity Standards Upper Bound
White Only	76.6% (0.01%)	71.7% (0.08%)	60.1% (0.04%)
Black Only	13.0% (0.01%)	12.6% (0.02%)	12.1% (0.03%)
American Indian/Alaskan Native Only	1.1% (0.05%)	1.0% (0.04%)	0.7% (0.04%)
Asian Only	6.6% (0.03%)	6.4% (0.03%)	6.3% (0.03%)
Hawaiian/Pacific Islander Only	0.4% (0.02%)	0.4% (0.02%)	0.3% (0.02%)
Hispanic Only	–	4.8% (0.07%)	17.8% (0.01%)
MENA Only	–	0.9% (0.03%)	0.9% (0.03%)
Multiple Race	2.3% (0.04%)	2.1% (0.04%)	1.7% (0.03%)

Note 1: Lower bound estimates of Hispanic Alone consist of those who said "Other Race" and selected one of the eight "Other Race" categories we have identified as Hispanic.

Note 2: Upper bound estimates consist of those who said they were Hispanic in the Ethnicity question.

to the ethnicity question. Whether one uses the lower bound estimate or the upper bound estimate, most Hispanics who are reclassified are originally in the White racial group.[18] Consequently, the population estimate for Whites is most affected by the 2024 standards. The proportion of the population that is White is 76.6 percent with the current race and ethnicity questions. Under the 2024 standards, this falls to 71.7 percent according to our lower bound estimate and 60.1 percent according to our upper bound estimate. The effect on the Black population estimate is non-trivial, although much smaller, falling from 13 percent of the population to either 12.6 percent or 12.1 percent depending on whether the lower bound or upper bound is used. Our lower bound and upper bound estimates give us a large range for the proportion of the population that would be classified as Hispanic Alone. This proportion ranges from 4.8 percent according to our lower bound estimate to 17.9 percent according to our upper bound estimate. Our suspicion is that the actual outcome would be closer to the upper bound estimate, since our intuition is that many of the respondents who currently indicate that they are of Hispanic ethnicity would only choose Hispanic when answering the new questions. Support for this is provided by the 2015 National Content Test which tested among other items a combined race/ethnicity question, with Hispanic and Middle Eastern being categories people could select. When presented with a combined race/ethnicity question only 30 percent of those identified as Hispanic selected Hispanic in combination with another race/

18. The majority of "Other Race" Hispanics being White under the lower bound reflects that the majority of "Other Race" Hispanics are allocated a race of White in the imputation process. The majority of Hispanics being White using the upper bound is primarily due to those who identify as Hispanic choosing White when asked to identify a race separately.

Table 3.6 **2010 and 2023 unemployment rate estimates, 1997 vs. 2024 standards**

		Unemployment Rate		
Year	Race Category	1997 Race/Ethnicity Standards	2024 Race/Ethnicity Standards Lower Bound	2024 Race/Ethnicity Standards Upper Bound
2010	White Only	8.7% (0.1%)	8.4% (0.1%)	8.0% (0.1%)
	Black Only	16.0% (0.2%)	16.0% (0.3%)	16.0% (0.3%)
	American Indian/Alaskan Native Only	15.1% (0.9%)	14.5% (0.9%)	13.8% (1.0%)
	Asian Only	7.5% (0.3%)	7.4% (0.3%)	7.4% (0.3%)
	Hawaiian/Pacific Islander Only	12.0% (1.3%)	12.2% (1.4%)	11.8% (1.3%)
	Hispanic Only	–	13.4% (0.4%)	12.5% (0.2%)
	MENA Only	–	11.1% (0.9%)	11.1% (0.9%)
	Multiple Race	13.6% (0.6%)	13.5% (0.6%)	13.4% (0.7%)
2023	White Only	3.3% (0.0%)	3.1% (0.0%)	2.9% (0.0%)
	Black Only	5.5% (0.2%)	5.6% (0.2%)	5.6% (0.2%)
	American Indian/Alaskan Native Only	6.6% (0.5%)	6.9% (0.6%)	6.8% (0.6%)
	Asian Only	3.0% (0.1%)	3.0% (0.1%)	2.9% (0.1%)
	Hawaiian/Pacific Islander Only	4.1% (0.7%)	3.8% (0.7%)	3.9% (0.8%)
	Hispanic Only	–	5.1% (0.2%)	4.6% (0.1%)
	MENA Only	–	3.7% (0.4%)	3.6% (0.4%)
	Multiple Race	5.4% (0.4%)	5.4% (0.4%)	5.7% (0.5%)

Note 1: Lower bound estimates of Hispanic Alone consist of those who said "Other Race" and selected one of the eight "Other Race" categories we have identified as Hispanic.

Note 2: Upper bound estimates consist of those who said they were Hispanic in the Ethnicity question.

ethnicity. The vast majority of those identified as Hispanic in the Content Test selected Hispanic Alone (US Census Bureau 2017). However, given the information that is available, there is simply no way of saying for sure how many people in the CPS will identify as Hispanic Alone with a combined question.

In addition to Hispanic Only, MENA is a second new race/ethnicity category in the 2024 standards. As table 3.5 indicates, according to our rough estimate, MENA Only would constitute about 0.9 percent of the population. Most individuals who are MENA Only would be classified as White under the 1997 standards. Given the small percentage of people who we expect to identify as MENA, the effect on the 1997 race categories of removing those who identify as MENA is not shown separately from the effects of removing those identifying as Hispanic Alone. Clearly, the effect of allowing people to identify as MENA on the proportion of the population identified as White and the other 1997 race groups will be small.

Table 3.6 shows the potential effect of the 2024 race and ethnicity standards on estimates of the unemployment rate in 2010 and 2023. With our lower bound Hispanic Alone estimate, the White unemployment rate falls from 8.7 percent to 8.4 percent in 2010, reflecting the fact that Hispanics

Table 3.7 2010 and 2023 employment-to-population ratio estimates, 1997 vs. 2024 standards

		Employment-to-Population Ratio		
Year	Race Category	1997 Race/Ethnicity Standards	2024 Race/Ethnicity Standards Lower Bound	2024 Race/Ethnicity Standards Upper Bound
2010	White Only	60.2 (0.1)	60.0 (0.1)	59.2 (0.1)
	Black Only	59.6 (0.3)	59.5 (0.3)	59.4 (0.3)
	American Indian/Alaskan Native Only	55.3 (1.7)	54.4 (1.9)	52.6 (2.2)
	Asian Only	63.1 (0.4)	63.2 (0.4)	63.2 (0.4)
	Hawaiian/Pacific Islander Only	63.3 (1.8)	63.3 (1.9)	62.9 (1.9)
	Hispanic Only	–	63.8 (0.5)	63.8 (0.3)
	MENA Only	–	60.5 (1.1)	60.7 (1.1)
	Multiple Race	61.8 (0.8)	61.9 (0.8)	61.6 (0.8)
2023	White Only	59.4 (0.1)	59.5 (0.1)	59.5 (0.1)
	Black Only	52.3 (0.3)	52.2 (0.3)	52.3 (0.3)
	American Indian/Alaskan Native Only	49.0 (1.1)	48.6 (1.2)	48.3 (1.3)
	Asian Only	59.9 (0.4)	60.0 (0.4)	60.0 (0.4)
	Hawaiian/Pacific Islander Only	60.1 (1.4)	59.8 (1.4)	59.8 (1.4)
	Hispanic Only	–	59.7 (0.5)	59.0 (0.2)
	MENA Only	–	54.3 (1.2)	54.3 (1.3)
	Multiple Race	56.5 (0.7)	56.0 (0.7)	55.5 (0.8)

Note 1: Lower bound estimates of Hispanic Alone consist of those who said "Other Race" and selected one of the eight "Other Race" categories we have identified as Hispanic.

Note 2: Upper bound estimates consist of those who said they were Hispanic in the Ethnicity question.

who are currently classified as "Other Race" (the vast majority of whom are imputed a race of White) have a higher unemployment rate than Hispanics who are not "Other Race" as well as White non-Hispanics.[19] With our upper bound estimate, the White unemployment rate in 2010 falls to 8.0 percent, reflecting the fact that Whites who are of Hispanic ethnicity have a higher unemployment rate than Whites who are not of Hispanic ethnicity. In 2010, the Hispanic Alone unemployment rate is 13.4 percent according to our lower bound Hispanic estimate and 12.5 percent according to our upper bound Hispanic estimate (with the upper bound estimate being the same as the current estimate for Hispanics). The higher unemployment rate estimate corresponding to the lower bound Hispanic Alone estimate reflects the fact that individuals of Hispanic ethnicity who are "Other Race" have a higher unemployment rate than individuals of Hispanic ethnicity who are not "Other Race."

Comparing the MENA Only unemployment rate to that for other race

19. In 2023 79.8 percent of "Other Race" were allocated a Race of White, 9.4 percent were allocated a race of Black, and 4.0 percent were allocated a race of Asian. The proportion of "Other Race" within these racial groups that was Hispanic was 90.0 percent, 66.0 percent and 44.0 percent, respectively

Table 3.8 **2010 and 2023 labor force participation rate estimates, 1997 vs. 2024 standards**

		Labor Force Participation Rate		
Year	Race Category	1997 Race/Ethnicity Standards	2024 Race/Ethnicity Standards Lower Bound	2024 Race/Ethnicity Standards Upper Bound
2010	White Only	62.3 (0.1)	61.9 (0.1)	61.0 (0.1)
	Black Only	63.1 (0.3)	63.1 (0.3)	62.9 (0.3)
	American Indian/Alaskan Native Only	59.2 (2.1)	58.4 (2.3)	56.4 (2.6)
	Asian Only	65.0 (0.4)	65.1 (0.4)	65.1 (0.4)
	Hawaiian/Pacific Islander Only	66.0 (1.4)	65.8 (1.5)	65.4 (1.6)
	Hispanic Only	–	67.3 (0.5)	66.9 (0.2)
	MENA Only	–	62.8 (1.0)	63.0 (1.1)
	Multiple Race	65.3 (0.7)	65.5 (0.7)	65.3 (0.8)
2023	White Only	65.1 (0.1)	64.9 (0.1)	64.7 (0.1)
	Black Only	62.2 (0.3)	62.2 (0.3)	62.2 (0.3)
	American Indian/Alaskan Native Only	57.7 (1.1)	56.8 (1.1)	56.1 (1.3)
	Asian Only	64.7 (0.4)	64.8 (0.4)	64.8 (0.4)
	Hawaiian/Pacific Islander Only	68.4 (1.3)	68.1 (1.4)	67.9 (1.4)
	Hispanic Only	–	68.9 (0.5)	67.5 (0.2)
	MENA Only	–	61.1 (1.2)	61.1 (1.2)
	Multiple Race	65.4 (0.7)	64.8 (0.7)	64.0 (0.8)

Note 1: Lower bound estimates of Hispanic Alone consist of those who said "Other Race" and selected one of the eight "Other Race" categories we have identified as Hispanic.

Note 2: Upper bound estimates consist of those who said they were Hispanic in the Ethnicity question.

categories, one sees in 2010 the MENA Only unemployment rate of 11.1 percent exceeds the White Only rate (of 8.4 percent or 8.0 percent), which largely reflects the fact that the MENA, White unemployment rate exceeds that of the non-MENA White unemployment rate. The MENA Only unemployment rate also exceeds that of the Asian Only unemployment rate, primarily reflecting the fact that most MENA Only individuals come from the non-Hispanic White population, which has a higher unemployment rate than the Asian population. The MENA Asian unemployment rate being larger than the non-MENA Asian unemployment rate also slightly contributes (although given the small proportion of Asians who are MENA this difference is not statistically significant).

Unemployment rate patterns in 2023 are similar to those in 2010. As expected, given the smaller unemployment rate differentials between the various groups, the effects of the 2024 standards are much smaller in 2023.

Tables 3.7 and 3.8 show the effects of the 2024 race/ethnicity standards on the employment-to-population ratios and labor force participation rates of the various racial/ethnic groups in 2010 and 2023. As can be seen from the estimates in the table, the effects of the 2024 standards are quite modest.

Finally, tables 3.9 and 3.10 show the effect of the 2024 race/ethnicity stan-

Table 3.9 **2023 median hourly wage estimates, 1997 vs. 2024 standards**

Race Category	Median Hourly Wage 1997 Race/Ethnicity Standards	2024 Race/Ethnicity Standards Lower Bound	2024 Race/Ethnicity Standards Upper Bound
White Only	$24.95 ($0.10)	$25.27 ($0.07)	$26.78 ($0.08)
Black Only	$20.89 ($0.19)	$20.97 ($0.20)	$20.99 ($0.21)
American Indian/Alaskan Native Only	$20.28 ($0.32)	$20.28 ($0.46)	$20.45 ($0.53)
Asian Only	$32.24 ($0.53)	$32.40 ($0.52)	$32.50 ($0.55)
Hawaiian/Pacific Islander Only	$21.36 ($0.86)	$21.50 ($0.91)	$21.36 ($1.06)
Hispanic Only	–	$19.81 ($0.37)	$20.00 ($0.05)
MENA Only	–	$28.77 ($0.92)	$28.85 ($0.90)
Other/Multiple Race	$21.76 ($0.45)	$21.98 ($0.32)	$22.86 ($0.49)

Note 1: Lower bound estimates of Hispanic Alone consist of those who said "Other Race" and selected one of the eight "Other Race" categories we have identified as Hispanic.

Note 2: Upper bound estimates consist of those who said they were Hispanic in the Ethnicity question.

Table 3.10 **2023 median weekly earnings estimates, 1997 vs. 2024 standards**

Race Category	Median Weekly Earnings 1997 Race/Ethnicity Standards	2024 Race/Ethnicity Standards Lower Bound	2024 Race/Ethnicity Standards Upper Bound
White Only	$998.10 ($2.84)	$1,014.19 ($4.46)	$1,082.49 ($8.76)
Black Only	$835.52 ($10.55)	$840.72 ($10.15)	$842.71 ($11.20)
American Indian/Alaskan Native Only	$800.66 ($9.83)	$800.96 ($12.63)	$811.35 ($26.14)
Asian Only	$1,310.40 ($27.13)	$1,318.42 ($28.14)	$1,334.28 ($32.00)
Hawaiian/Pacific Islander Only	$843.47 ($39.23)	$843.47 ($36.97)	$843.47 ($38.25)
Hispanic Only	–	$762.53 ($6.09)	$793.03 ($6.41)
MENA Only	–	$1,166.35 ($40.60)	$1,170.21 ($41.51)
Other/Multiple Race	$823.58 ($27.12)	$840.00 ($24.12)	$875.30 ($16.36)

Note 1: Lower bound estimates of Hispanic Alone consist of those who said "Other Race" and selected one of the eight "Other Race" categories we have identified as Hispanic.

Note 2: Upper bound estimates consist of those who said they were Hispanic in the Ethnicity question.

dards on earnings estimates in 2023. Using our lower bound Hispanic estimate to generate a White Alone estimate, the median hourly wage of Whites increases from $24.95 to $25.27, reflecting the fact that Hispanics who are currently classified as "Other Race" (the vast majority of whom are imputed a race of White) have lower wages than both Hispanics who are not "Other Race" and non-Hispanic Whites. According to our upper bound Hispanic estimate, the median hourly wage of Whites increases still further to $26.78, reflecting the fact that Whites of Hispanic ethnicity have lower wages than non-Hispanic Whites. According to our lower bound Hispanic estimate, the median hourly earnings of Hispanics in 2023 are $19.81. The median hourly earnings of Hispanics increase to $20.00 when using the upper bound. The higher hourly wage corresponding to our upper bound Hispanic estimate reflects the fact that individuals of Hispanic ethnicity who are "Other Race" have lower hourly wages than individuals of Hispanic ethnicity who are not "Other Race." MENA median hourly wages are about $28.80 according to both our lower and upper bond Hispanic estimates. This is higher than that for all racial groups other than Asians.

Weekly earnings show the same pattern as hourly wages. Median usual weekly earnings of Whites increase from $998.10 to $1,014.19 according to our lower bound Hispanic estimate. According to our upper bound Hispanic estimate, median weekly earnings of Whites increase to $1,082.49. Hispanic weekly earnings are $762.53 according to our lower bound Hispanic estimate and $793.03 according to our upper bound Hispanic estimate.

3.6 A Closer Look at Individuals Who Identify as Hispanic

As discussed above, our lower bound and upper bound estimates give us a very large range for the proportion of the population that would be classified as Hispanic Alone. Our intuition, supported by the 2015 National Content test, suggests the upper bound is closer to the mark—individuals who indicated they were of Hispanic ethnicity when asked seem likely to indicate that they are Hispanic when faced with the new race-ethnicity combined question, and we suspect that many of them will only identify as Hispanic. In any case, a good argument can be made for looking more closely at the background characteristics of individuals who identify as Hispanic currently in the CPS using the 1997 standards.

One would expect that individuals from countries with large numbers of Hispanics—"Hispanic Countries"—are likely to identify as Hispanic when asked about their identity. Individuals born in the United States who have parents from a "Hispanic Country" also would seem likely to identify as Hispanic. They might also be more likely to identify as Hispanic if they have a grandparent from a "Hispanic Country," but as a general principle, the more distant a person's Hispanic ancestry, the less likely it is that they would iden-

Table 3.11 Country of origin estimates, from 2007 to 2023

Year	Percent of population born in a Hispanic country	Percent of population born in United States with two parents born in a Hispanic country	Percent of population born in United States with only one parent born in a Hispanic country
2007	7.7%	2.1%	1.2%
2008	7.5%	2.2%	1.2%
2009	7.5%	2.3%	1.2%
2010	7.6%	2.5%	1.3%
2011	7.5%	2.7%	1.3%
2012	7.5%	2.8%	1.4%
2013	7.4%	2.9%	1.5%
2014	7.4%	3.0%	1.5%
2015	7.7%	3.1%	1.5%
2016	7.8%	3.2%	1.5%
2017	7.7%	3.3%	1.5%
2018	7.8%	3.4%	1.6%
2019	7.7%	3.5%	1.6%
2020	7.6%	3.6%	1.8%
2021	7.8%	3.7%	1.7%
2022	8.1%	3.7%	1.7%
2023	8.3%	3.9%	1.8%

tify as Hispanic.[20] The CPS asks individuals where they were born and where their parents were born. As can be seen in table 3.11, the percentage of the population born in a Hispanic country increased from 7.7 percent in 2007 to 8.3 percent in 2023. There was a larger percentage increase in the population of individuals who had Hispanic parents but were born in the United States. Specifically, the percentage of the population born in the United States and having both parents born in a Hispanic country increased from 2.1 percent in 2007 to 3.9 percent in 2023. The percentage of the population born in the United States and having only one parent born in a Hispanic country increased from 1.2 percent in 2007 to 1.8 percent in 2023.

Table 3.12 shows the percentage of individuals born in a Hispanic country who indicated they were of Hispanic ethnicity in 2010 and 2023. The table also shows this percentage for individuals who were born in the United States but who had one or two parents born in Hispanic countries. In 2023, 97.5 percent of individuals born in Hispanic countries indicated that they were of Hispanic ethnicity. This percentage was virtually the same for indi-

20. We define individuals as being born in a Hispanic country if they have any of the following answers for the question asking where they were born: Puerto Rico, Spain, Mexico, Belize, Costa Rica, El Salvador, Guatemala, Honduras, Nicaragua, Panama, Central America, Cuba, Dominican Republic, Argentina, Bolivia, Chile, Colombia, Ecuador, Paraguay, Peru, Uruguay, Venezuela, South America, Baja California, Chiapas, Veracruz, and Latin America.

Table 3.12 **2010 and 2023 population percentage and Hispanics percentage for country of origin categories**

	Percent of Population		Percent Hispanic Ethnicity	
Country of Origin Category	2010	2023	2010	2023
Born outside United States in a Hispanic country	7.6%	8.3%	97.2%	97.5%
Born outside United States in a Non-Hispanic country	10.5%	12.6%	6.5%	8.6%
Born in United States with both parents born in a Hispanic country	2.0%	3.1%	96.4%	97.3%
Born in United States with only one parent born in a Hispanic country	1.1%	1.4%	84.8%	87.9%
Born in United States with no parent born in a Hispanic country	78.8%	74.7%	4.1%	5.9%

viduals who were born in the United States, but both of whose parents were born in Hispanic countries. Among individuals who were born in the United States and had only one parent born in a Hispanic country, the percentage indicating they were Hispanic fell to 87.9 percent. Clearly, as expected, the weaker their ties to a Hispanic country, the less likely individuals are to identify as being of Hispanic ethnicity. These estimates also strongly suggest that those of mixed ethnicity will be less likely to indicate they are Hispanic. Our upper bound estimate of those who will identify as Hispanic Alone is thus likewise impacted by the strength of individuals' ties to the Hispanic country from which they or their parents originated. Note also that even with a direct question asking whether someone is Hispanic, there is a divergence between any possible measure of Hispanic based on observable characteristics and a measure based on individuals' own subjective assessments. Amongst those who were themselves or had both parents from a Hispanic country, approximately 2.5 percent did not identify as Hispanic when asked a direct question. Among those with only one parent born in a Hispanic country, the percentage not identifying as Hispanic increases to 12.1 percent, a percentage that is likely to be larger if Hispanic identity is determined from a combined race ethnicity question.

A similar pattern arises for those who identify as "Other Race"-Hispanic. As is the case with ethnicity, the weaker an individual's ties to a Hispanic country, the less likely the person is to be identified as "Other Race"-Hispanic. As indicated in table 3.13, among those born in a Hispanic country, 31.2 percent identify as "Other Race"-Hispanic in 2023. The proportion is similar, 31.3 percent, for those who were born in the United States and had both parents born in a Hispanic country. In contrast, 18.1 percent of individuals who were born in the United States and had only one parent born in

Table 3.13 **2010 and 2023 "other race" Hispanic subgroup percentage for country of origin categories**

	Percent in "Other Race" Hispanic Subgroup	
Country of Origin Category	2010	2023
Born outside United States in a Hispanic country	37.3%	31.2%
Born outside United States in a Non-Hispanic country	2.5%	2.7%
Born in United States with both parents born in a Hispanic country	37.8%	31.3%
Born in United States with only one parent born in a Hispanic country	24.1%	18.1%
Born in United States with no parent born in a Hispanic country	1.0%	1.0%

Table 3.14 **2023 labor force statistics for individuals born in a Hispanic country vs. individuals born in United States with both parents born in a Hispanic country**

Labor Force Statistics	Hispanic Ethnicity	Individuals born in a Hispanic country	Individuals born in United States with two parents born in a Hispanic country
Unemployment Rate	Hispanic	4.1% (0.2%)	5.5% (0.3%)
	Non-Hispanic	2.9% (0.9%)	8.3% (2.0%)
	Overall	**4.1% (0.2%)**	**5.6% (0.3%)**
Employment-to-Population Ratio	Hispanic	64.3 (0.3)	65.6 (0.6)
	Non-Hispanic	55.2 (2.2)	51.7 (3.3)
	Overall	**64.1 (0.3)**	**65.3 (0.6)**
Labor Force Participation Rate	Hispanic	67.1 (0.3)	69.5 (0.5)
	Non-Hispanic	56.9 (2.2)	56.4 (3.2)
	Overall	**66.8 (0.3)**	**69.1 (0.5)**

a Hispanic country identify as "Other Race"-Hispanic. Given that our lower bound estimate for Hispanic Alone consists of those identified as "Other Race"-Hispanic, these estimates indicate that our lower bound estimates also will be influenced by the strength of people's ties to a Hispanic country.

Table 3.14 presents labor force estimates for individuals born in a Hispanic country and for individuals who were born in the United States and had Hispanic parents. These estimates indicate individuals who were born in a Hispanic country had a lower unemployment rate than individuals who were born in the United States but had parents who were born in a Hispanic country. In contrast, the employment-to-population ratio and labor force participation rate were slightly lower for individuals who were born in a Hispanic country than for individuals who were born in the United States and had parents born in Hispanic countries.

3.7 Generating Comparable Estimates Across Time

As can be seen from the estimates presented in this paper, the adoption of the 2024 OMB race and ethnicity standards with the inclusion of Hispanic and MENA categories in a combined race and ethnicity question could have a considerable effect on the comparison of estimates across time. This is particularly true for estimates such as those published in the BLS Monthly Employment Situation new release where estimates for racial groups are presented regardless of whether people are identified as Hispanic (racial estimates are for Hispanics and non-Hispanics combined). Using the 2024 OMB standards, individuals who identify as Hispanic Alone will not have a race associated with them and people who identify with one of the 1997 OMB race groups either alone or in combination will only be those who are non-Hispanic in these race groups. Consequently, the estimate of the number of people who are in one of the five racial groups specified in the 1997 OMB standards will be smaller when the 2024 OMB standards are used. Associated estimates, such as the labor force estimates presented in the BLS's Monthly Employment Situation, also will likely differ.

For example, in 2023 the proportion of the population identified as White (Hispanic and non-Hispanic combined) as presented in the Employment Situation using the 1997 two question standards is 76.6 percent. Depending on how many people identify as Hispanic Alone or MENA, estimates presented in this paper indicate the corresponding proportion of the population identified as White using a combined race and ethnicity question could fall to 71.7 percent or 60.1 percent. Similarly, the 2023 annual unemployment rate for Whites could decrease from 3.3 percent using the 1997 OMB two question standards to 3.1 percent or 2.9 percent when a combined race and ethnicity question is used.

Differences such as these raise the question of how to construct comparable estimates across time. As alluded to earlier, one approach would be to generate an experimental series where people were placed into definitionally equivalent non-Hispanic racial groups and into a separate Hispanic group. Specifically, the categories would be White Alone (including MENA) non-Hispanic; Black Alone non-Hispanic; Asian Alone non-Hispanic; American Indian or Alaskan Native Alone non-Hispanic; Hawaiian or Pacific Islander Alone non-Hispanic; More than one race non-Hispanic; and Hispanic.

To construct this experimental series for data collected under the 1997 OMB standards, people in the non-Hispanic race groups would be identified by combining answers to the ethnicity question and the race question. Hispanics would be identified using the ethnicity question. To construct this experimental series for data collected under the 2024 standards, people in the non-Hispanic race groups would be identified as those who answered White; Black or African American; Asian; American Indian or Alaskan Native; Hawaiian or Pacific Islander; or Middle Eastern or North African either alone or in combination with another of these racial groups who did not also identify as Hispanic. People in the Hispanic group would be identified as those who answered Hispanic either alone or in combination with another racial group. For example, using the 2024 combined race and ethnicity standards, in this experimental series people who identified as only White would be White non-Hispanics. People who answered White and Asian would be classified as multiple race non-Hispanic. People who only answered Hispanic and people who answered Hispanic and White would be identified as Hispanic. In order to construct a definitionally equivalent series, people who identified as MENA would be combined with those who identified as White. This experimental series for data collected using the 1997 OMB standards would be definitionally close to the upper bound estimates presented earlier in this paper. The only difference is the upper bound estimates also placed MENA in a separate category rather than including them in the estimates of Whites.

Such an experimental series would be definitionally consistent whether it is based on information collected under the 1997 or 2024 standards. However, it may not generate a completely comparable series across time. To be completely comparable, individuals would have to report their identities using the two-question approach exactly the same as they report their identities using the combined race and ethnicity question. It is well established in the survey methodology literature that asking questions in different ways results in different answers even when the underlying concepts are the same. These differences will generally be magnified when the underlying concept is fluid and may not be the same for self and proxy responses.

To shed light on differences in measurement introduced by asking the race and ethnicity questions in a different manner with different response options, it would be beneficial to ask the same individuals both sets of questions. One way to achieve this would be to ask the single race and ethnicity 2024 OMB standards question as a supplement to the CPS. Unfortunately, neither Census nor BLS may have funding for this. As an alternative, we suggest that all respondents receive the new question in the month that the 2024 OMB standards are implemented in CPS data collection. Given the CPS rotation pattern, three-fourths of individuals will then have the race and ethnicity questions asked using both the two question 1997 OMB standards and the single race and ethnicity question 2024 OMB standards.[21]

A comparison of answers obtained for the same individuals with each set

21. Another alternative, if funding permitted, would be to obtain more information before the 2024 standards are implemented by asking people in a continuing month-in-sample the combined race/ethnicity question and carrying over people's race and ethnicity information from the previous month that was collected using the 1997 standards for comparison. To be successful, sample sizes would need to be sufficient to detect different responses under the two sets of questions and consideration would need to be taken of how frequently people's race and ethnicity change month to month under the 1997 standards. Estimates under this alternative would continue to be generated using the information collected under the 1997 standards.

of questions would provide a way to refine and adjust the experimental series to make it more comparable across time. It also would provide information to bridge population and correspondingly published survey estimates that are generated making no distinction between those who are Hispanic and those who are not, such as the labor force estimates currently published in the Employment Situation. For example, it would provide information on what proportion of those who answered White using the two question 1997 OMB standards answered White Alone (non-Hispanic), White and Hispanic, and Hispanic Alone using the combined race and ethnicity question 2024 OMB standards. It also would provide information about the effect of the 2024 OMB standards on estimates of interest for these groups such as the unemployment rate and poverty rate. There is much to be said for generating these estimated effects from the CPS itself as opposed to trying to infer effects on the basis of population estimates from other surveys. The final 2024 OMB standards implementation plan will be jointly developed by BLS and the Census Bureau, approved by OMB, and publicly communicated prior to implementation.

3.8 Conclusion

In obtaining information on individuals' race and ethnicity, the Current Population Survey currently follows the 1997 OMB Standards. However, OMB published a new set of race and ethnicity standards in March 2024. There will no longer be an attempt to distinguish between race and ethnicity. Instead, OMB is mandating a combined race and ethnicity question with the following categories: White; Hispanic or Latino; Black or African American; Asian; American Indian or Alaskan Native; Middle Eastern or North African; and Native Hawaiian or Pacific Islander. Furthermore, individuals may select more than one category (i.e., they may identify as multiracial/multiethnic).

Racial and ethnic classification is at its root a subjective exercise. For example, nearly all individuals born in a country that one would call Hispanic indicate that they are of Hispanic ethnicity. About as many indicate that they are Hispanic if they were born in the United States but both their parents were born in a Hispanic country. This number falls markedly for individuals who were born in the United States and only had one parent who was born in a Hispanic country. Given the subjectivity of the race/ethnicity classification, the evolution of how children of immigrants identify themselves over time, and the ambiguity in the distinction between race and ethnicity, one would expect the new standards to affect the time series comparability of estimates that BLS publishes. Whatever advantages they may otherwise offer, a change to a single combined race and ethnicity question will lead to a break in time series estimates that BLS currently produces. The change to a single combined race and ethnicity question will affect both the distribution across race and ethnicity categories and key labor force estimates from the CPS. We have examined the CPS micro data in an attempt to tease out these potential effects. Our results indicate that the effects will be most notable for Whites and Hispanics.

We have generated rough estimates for the Middle Eastern and North African category from the "Other Race" responses and from responses about parents' country of origin. Most individuals who indicate they are Middle Eastern or North African will likely be those who previously would have indicated that they are White, but the proportion is small. Our estimates indicate they would constitute only about 0.9 percent of the White population.

Individuals born in a Hispanic country, born in the United States with both parents born in a Hispanic country, and born in the United States with only one parent born in a Hispanic country have been increasing since 2007 as a percentage of the overall US population. "Other Race" responses provide a lower bound estimate of the number of individuals who will identify as Hispanic, while responses to the ethnicity question provide an upper bound. The resultant range is large, but the Census 2015 National Content test suggests that upper bound estimates are closer to the mark. Results from the National Content test indicate that about 70 percent of individuals who indicate that they are Hispanic when asked a separate ethnicity question will respond that they are Hispanic alone when confronted with the combined race ethnicity question. There is insufficient information in the National Content test, however, to determine how this will affect the various CPS labor force estimates. To address this issue, we have calculated the labor force estimates corresponding to our upper and lower bounds for the Hispanic Alone category.

While we have only been able to generate effects within a fairly broad range, we do provide suggestions on how to construct an experimental series that may be more comparable across time. As we also point out, collecting data from the same individuals using the 1997 standards two-question approach and the 2024 OMB combined approach would be beneficial. Given that funding limitations may preclude conducting a supplement to the CPS, administering a combined question to everyone when the combined question is introduced to the CPS is one way of achieving this. Given the CPS rotation pattern, under this scenario in the month the combined question is introduced three-fourths of the respondents will have race and ethnicity collected using both the 1997 two-question approach and the 2024 combined question approach. This information would assist in analyzing the effects of the combined question on labor force estimates for various race groups currently published, the experimental estimates we propose, and in generating bridge estimates. There is much to be said for generating these estimated effects from the CPS itself as opposed to trying to infer effects on the basis of population estimates from other surveys.

For acknowledgments, sources of research support, and disclosure of the authors' material financial relationships, if any, please see https://www.nber.org/books-and-chapters/race-ethnicity-and-economic-statistics-21st-century/measuring-potential-effects-introducing-2024-race-and-ethnicity-standards-current-population-survey.

References

Federal Register. 2024. "Revisions to OMB's Statistical Policy Directive no. 15: Standards for Maintaining, Collecting, and Presenting Federal Data on Race and Ethnicity." Federal Register. March. https://www.federalregister.gov/documents/2024/03/29/2024-06469/revisions-to-ombs-statistical-policy-directive-no-15-standards-for-maintainingcollecting-and.

Jones, N., R. Marks, R. Ramirez, and M. Rios-Vargas. 2021. "2020 Census Illuminates Racial and Ethnic Composition of the Country." National Research Council (US) Panel on Hispanics in the United States. 2006. *Hispanics and the Future of America*. Washington, DC: National Academies Press (US). https://www.ncbi.nlm.nih.gov/books/NBK19905/.

US Census Bureau. 2017. "2015 National Content Test Report." Technical report, US Department of Commerce.

4

Estimating the Potential Impact of Combined Race and Ethnicity Reporting on Long-Term Earnings Statistics

Kevin L. McKinney and John M. Abowd

4.1 Introduction

The United States has collected race and ethnicity data on every decennial census of population since 1790. The subjugation and abuse of minorities and indigenous peoples partially enabled by those data are part of the indelible history of the nation. Since 1970, collecting information on race and ethnicity has served a different purpose: providing statistical data for the enforcement of civil rights laws passed in the 1960s including the 1965 Voting Rights Act. In support of that effort, two important principles were embodied in the regulations governing these data collections. The first principle, embodied in the 1977 Statistical Policy Directive 15 (SPD 15 hereafter), required that the respondent provide the answers to questions on race and ethnicity, what we call self-identification, ending the practice begun in 1790 of the enumerator supplying that information.[1] The second principle, embodied in the 1997 revision of SPD 15, enabled respondents to characterize their racial identities in as many of the five categories as they wished. Amendments to the 1954 Census Act that are still in force added a sixth category, Some Other Race, to the regulatory five: American Indian or Alaska Native, Asian, Black or African American, Native Hawaiian or Pacific Islander, and White.[2] In March 2024, a third principle, embodied in

Kevin L. McKinney is an economist at the US Census Bureau.

John M. Abowd is the Edmund Ezra Day Professor Emeritus of Economics, Statistics and Data Science at Cornell University and a research associate of the National Bureau of Economic Research.

1. See Office of Management and Budget (2023) for a history of Statistical Policy Directive 15 and the proposed changes.

2. In official publications of the US Census Bureau, the category "Some Other Race" is capitalized to distinguish it from responses like "one of the other categories," "none of the above," or "other." In this paper, we use the same convention. We always mean that the respondent

the 2024 revision of SPD 15, was added: the respondent may choose from any of seven categories (the five in SPD 15 plus Hispanic or Latino and Middle Eastern or North African) without any requirement to distinguish between racial and ethnic categories. The amendments to the Census Act still require the inclusion of the category Some Other Race. We call this the "single-question" format.

The 1997 revision of SPD 15 also required that information on Hispanic or Latino ethnicity be collected separately and asked before questions about race. Research in the 2010s, culminating in the 2015 National Content Test, revealed that collecting the information on race and ethnicity in a single question that included the five 1997 categories, Hispanic or Latino, and Middle Eastern or North African (MENA) and made no distinction between "racial" and "ethnic" categories provided better-quality data and virtually eliminated respondent-provided "Some Other Race" answers (Mathews et al. 2017). The 2024 revision of SPD 15 replaced the two-question format with a single-question format like the ones tested in 2015. The design also encourages respondents to enter additional national origin detail, which is often based on place of birth (POB).[3]

The 1997 regulatory definitions of racial and ethnic categories also included rules for categorizing individuals when write-in responses provided national origin data. These included: coding any race response indicating national origin from a Spanish-speaking country as "Hispanic or Latino" ethnicity then coding "Some Other Race" for the race category, and coding "White" for many MENA countries if the respondent did not indicate a different race. Other papers at the conference (Jensen and Jones 2024) deal with these issues in detail. We note here only the consequences that are salient for our research. Data from recent censuses and 1997 SPD 15 compliant surveys like the American Community Survey always appear to have a respondent-provided determination of Hispanic or Latino ethnicity and a respondent-provided set of racial categories (up to six, including Some Other Race). But no respondent was permitted to identify as Hispanic without also identifying within racial categories that excluded Hispanic and related categories. Similarly, no respondent was permitted to identify as Black (or any other race category) without also indicating whether they identified as Hispanic or Latino. Under the single-question format, multicategory responses must be entirely initiated by the respondent. Our research informs comparisons of differences in outcomes based on self-identification with those based on

selected Some Other Race in lieu of, or in addition to, any of the other choices available on the instrument. Under the 1997 SPD 15, those categories are American Indian or Alaska Native, Asian, Black or African American, Native Hawaiian or Pacific Islander, and White.

3. See Marks and Jones (2020) for a detailed explanation of the race and ethnicity coding rules for the 2010 and 2020 Censuses. See Waddell et al. (2022) for a discussion of the implications for economic measurement. Jensen and Jones (2024) consider these issues in detail.

place of birth or parent's place of birth as recorded on the individual's Social Security number application form.[4]

In this paper, we use data from three distinct sources—detailed place-of-birth data from the Social Security Administration (SSA), detailed race and ethnicity responses from decennial censuses of population, and earnings data from state Unemployment Insurance (UI) systems—to try to disentangle the differences in long-term real earnings associated with self-reported racial and ethnic identities as distinct from country of origin. To do so, we consider a cohort of foreign-born adults along with a similar cohort of US-born adults. For US-born adults we create a sub-sample of young workers, comparing outcomes for those with US-born or foreign-born parents. Place of birth is measured from Social Security Administration data collected when the person was issued a Social Security number. Racial and ethnic identities are measured by the detailed direct responses from the 2000 and 2010 Censuses with all allocated and edited responses removed. We characterize a place of birth as "Hispanic" if at least 50 percent of persons born in that country self-identify as Hispanic. We characterize a place of birth as MENA using the geographic location of the country, since there is no reliable way to measure MENA self-identification in the 1997 SPD 15 format. Using the combined data sources, we attempt to measure whether the self-identification of racial or ethnic origin of immigrants corresponds to identification based on administrative place of birth.

Our outcome measure is average annual real labor market earnings over the six-year period from 2010 to 2015, which we call long-term earnings. Family structure is established from the 2000 Census. We present statistics based on the measured and regression-adjusted long-term earnings organized by place of birth for the main sample and by the parent's place of birth for the children sample.

Section 4.2 describes our data sources and limitations. Section 4.3 describes our statistical methods. Section 4.4 presents the results. Finally, section 4.5 concludes.

4.2 Data Sources and Limitations

The empirical work in this paper is based on job-level earnings information from the Longitudinal Employer-Household Dynamics (LEHD) infrastructure files, developed and maintained by the US Census Bureau.[5]

4. It is important to note here that "Some Other Race" is not a social-political construct. The coding rules described in the text were intended to comply with the statutory obligation to include Some Other Race and the 1997 SPD 15 regulation to treat Hispanic ethnicity distinct from any racial self-identification when collecting and tabulating decennial census data. When bound only by the 1997 SPD 15, Census Bureau publications do not include Some Other Race. Those responses are recoded to one of the five categories listed above.

5. See Abowd et al. (2009) for a detailed summary of the construction of the LEHD infrastructure.

In the LEHD infrastructure, a job is the statutory employment of a worker by a statutory employer as defined by the UI system in each state. Mandated reporting of UI-covered wage and salary payments between one statutory employer and one statutory employee is governed by the state's UI system. Reporting covers private employers and state and local government. LEHD also receives earnings reports from the Office of Personnel Management (OPM), which provides coverage of a large share of the federal civilian workforce.[6] There are no self-employment earnings unless the proprietor draws a salary, which is indistinguishable from other employees in this case.[7]

The LEHD program is based on a voluntary federal-state partnership. When a state becomes a member of the partnership, current as well as all available historical data for that state are ingested into the LEHD internal database. By 2004, LEHD data represented the complete universe of statutory jobs covered by the UI system in the United States.[8] We use all jobs to construct person-year level annual real (deflated by the 2010 Personal Consumption Expenditures Index) earnings files covering the period 2010–2015. In our previous research we constructed earnings measures covering the entire complete universe 12-year period (2004–2015). However, in this paper we construct two samples using a shorter 6-year period from 2010 to 2015. The shorter 6-year time window is a potentially less robust measure of long-term earnings but allows us to identify a young cohort of second-generation workers (children of foreign-born and US-born parents) using information from the 2000 Census of Population and Housing.

We use methods we have employed before (e.g., Abowd et al. 2018) to create a longitudinal frame of persons that covers a known population of interest and has a relatively high level of confidence that the persons in that population use a consistent person identifier across time and jobs. To that end, we use the US Census Bureau's enhanced version of SSA's master Social Security number (SSN) database (the Census Numident) to create a set of "eligible" workers each year, removing annual earnings records for ineligible workers. The first eligibility condition is that the worker's SSN appears on the Numident. We call such SSNs "active" because if a person's SSN appears

6. Unemployment insurance for federal workers is administered through the former employee's state of residence, but the states do not collect wage reports or UI premiums from the federal government.

7. UI earnings are reported by the employer every quarter. Although there is some variability across states, UI earnings generally include regular hourly earnings or salary, overtime, bonuses, reported tips, and sick/vacation pay. Federal workers participate in the unemployment insurance system, but their earnings are reported to LEHD by the Office of Personnel Management. Private, state, local, and federal employers are all included in our analysis.

8. We have previously shown that by 1998 missing state data do not significantly affect measures of inequality and volatility (Abowd et al. 2018, McKinney and Abowd 2023). However, to minimize the impact of employer non-reports (false zeros) on estimates of individual long-term average earnings, we restrict our sample to the period 2010–2015, where data from all 50 states, DC, and the federal government are available.

on the Numident and they have wage and salary income in the United States, that income should appear in our data. Each year an eligible worker must also meet additional conditions: age within the range specified by our two samples, not reported dead, and active SSN. The worker also must not have more than 12 reported employers during the year; otherwise, we assume the SSN is being used by multiple persons and the annual earnings report is discarded.[9] We impose no additional annual earnings restrictions. Zero-earnings years are included as long as the worker is active in the labor market at least one quarter during the analysis period.[10]

We match the set of eligible workers active in UI covered jobs during 2010–2015 to information on reported detailed race and ethnicity from the 2010 Census of Population and Housing. For Sample 1, a worker must have complete data for date of birth, place of birth, and sex on the Census Numident, be between the ages of 25 and 55 (inclusive) in 2010, be "eligible" all six years as defined above, and have reported race and ethnicity on the 2010 Census.[11] These rules produce an analysis Sample 1 of 87.97 million workers.[12] Sample 2 is a subset of Sample 1 consisting of workers born in the United States, age 25 to 28 (inclusive) in 2010, who have at least one reported biological parent in the home on the 2000 Census. For Sample 2, we use the Census Numident place of birth information for the reported biological parent(s) as indicated on the 2000 Census household roster to determine whether the worker was a second-generation immigrant (child of at least one foreign-born parent) or a third- (or higher) generation immigrant (child of two parents born in the United States if two are available or child of one parent born in the United States if only one is available). These rules produce an analysis Sample 2 consisting of 7.196 million workers.

9. Abowd et al. (2018) provide detailed evidence that the use of the same SSN with 12 or more employers in a year very likely means that there are multiple users of the same SSN.

10. Zero-earnings years are not directly reported in the LEHD data; a zero-earnings year is inferred based on the absence of reported earnings. Zero-earnings years are a core part of the long-term average earnings analysis, and restricting our sample to the complete-data time period 2010–2015 ensures that each worker has a consistent, small probability each year of a non-report.

11. We use the detailed race and ethnicity data from the 2010 and 2000 Censuses. These include all checkboxes and write-ins that were captured in the data processing. We use only reported responses, excluding all allocations and edits.

12. Our analysis samples only use UI earnings records with a Protected Identification Key (PIK) found on the Census Numident. Only PIKs from the Census Numident are assigned to records on the 2010 Census by the Census Bureau's Personal Identification Validation System (Wagner and Layne 2014). An eligible worker in the LEHD data may not match to the 2010 Census if the respondent refused to take the survey (and consequently has entirely imputed data), the respondent took the survey but did not report some demographic data (and consequently received a PIK not in the LEHD data), or the respondent record was not assigned a PIK. In addition, an eligible worker in the LEHD data may link to the 2010 Census but be deleted from our analysis because that person's 2010 Census race or ethnicity data were edited or allocated. About 10 percent of the eligible workers in LEHD do not link to the 2010 Census, and an additional 10 percent did not have respondent-provided race and ethnicity data. We made no adjustments for these deletions in our statistical analyses.

4.3 Statistical Methods

We create a single long-term average annual earnings measure consisting of real annual earnings, w_i, summed across all years and all UI-covered employers and divided by 6:

$$w_i = \frac{1}{6}\sum_{t=2010}^{2015}\sum_{j} e_{ijt},$$

where e_{ijt} is the real earnings of individual i at employer j in year t.[13] Nominal earnings were converted to real using the Personal Consumption Expenditures Price Index (2010 = 100). We use w_i to explore the differences in long-term average real annual earnings across sex, place of birth, ethnicity, and race categories. Our race variable consists of the following eight categories: White, Black, American Indian or Alaska Native, Asian, Native Hawaiian or Pacific Islander, Some Other Race, 2+ Races (not SOR), and 2+ Races (SOR). The notation 2+ Races (SOR) means that one of the coded race categories is Some Other Race, and 2+ Races (not SOR) means that none of the coded race categories is Some Other Race. The ethnicity variable is binary: Hispanic or Latino, Not Hispanic or Latino.

Our universe of Hispanic-origin countries was created by tabulating the percentage of individuals who self-identified as Hispanic or Latino on the 2010 Census for every country of birth in Sample 1. We classify a place of birth as Hispanic when at least 50 percent of the immigrants from that country self-identify as Hispanic.[14] No similar exercise works for MENA countries. Instead, we coded all place-of-birth countries from Morocco on the west along the Mediterranean Sea to Syria on the north, then eastward to Iran and southward to Yemen.[15]

To better understand how the detailed race and ethnicity information contained in the 2010 Census checkbox and write-in responses relates to

13. We make no use of employer identifiers. Thus, to keep the notation simple, j is an arbitrary index that ranges over the available earnings records for individual i in year t.

14. Some Hispanic places of birth failed the minimum population criterion (1,000) for inclusion in our tables: Guinea-Bissau, Mayotte, and New Caledonia. These countries are included in "all other foreign born."

15. This definition excludes Turkey, which would also be excluded if we applied the same rule used for Hispanic-origin countries using the results in the 2015 National Content Test (Mathews et al. 2017, Table 22) because less than 50 percent of persons who self-identified as Turkish also self-identified as MENA when given the opportunity to do so, because the respondent must have written in a MENA response and also checked another race response to be in the content test tables (this also produces an overwhelmingly White content test MENA category). On the other hand, our definition includes Israel, even though less than 50 percent of self-identified Israelis also self-identified as MENA on the 2015 National Content Test. There is no clean way to define MENA-origin entities comparable to our method of defining Hispanic-origin countries unless place of birth and self-identification data are available for the same person. Some MENA entities failed the minimum population criterion (1,000) for inclusion in our tabulation: Oman, Qatar, United Arab Emirates, Gaza, and West Bank. These birth entities are included in "all other foreign born."

place of birth, we created a variable that records whether the country of birth from the Census Numident matches the country reported in the checkbox or write-in response from the 2010 Census. The country of birth on the Census Numident comes from the application for a Social Security number, whereas the 2010 Census origin countries are self-identified. When the reported country in the checkbox or write-in responses on the 2010 Census matches the place of birth on the Census Numident, we code the individual as "Census detail/SSA POB Match."[16] We interact this variable with our 16 ethnicity by race categories to create a 32-category Hispanic ethnicity by race by Census detail/SSA POB match analysis variable, which we use to stratify both analysis samples. We do not report results for all 32 categories. Instead, we focus on the top *X* reported responses, where $X \leq 10$, for each Census Numident place of birth. Fewer than 10 categories are listed when the sample for that category is too small to permit meaningful summaries.[17] In the tables we label rows with a three-character tag. The first position is H for Hispanic ethnicity, N for Not Hispanic; the second position is the numbers 1, . . . , 8 for White, Black, American Indian/Alaska Native, Asian, Native Hawaiian/Pacific Islander, Some Other Race, 2+ Races (not SOR), and 2+ Races (SOR) in that order; and the third position is P for place-of-birth match, N for no place-of-birth match. We also label panels in the tables with a mnemonic that allows us to refer to the group in that panel (e.g., FBH for Foreign-Born Hispanic) along with the sub-groups in that panel (e.g., H1P for Hispanic, White, POB match). In the text, we cross-reference numerical data from the tables using these panel and row labels.

In addition to studying long-term-average real annual earnings, we also study regression-adjusted earnings, using personal characteristics (education, age, and years living in the United States), labor force attachment (number of years with any earnings), and hours of work. Previous work indicates that these are important predictors of long-term average real annual earnings. The regression adjustment models are run separately for each POB country.

Although information on hours of work and education are not available for the entire population, we assume the data are missing at random in the sense of Little and Rubin (2002) and impute the missing values conditional on all observed data. We imputed missing hours using information from the small subset of states (Minnesota, Oregon, Rhode Island, and Wash-

16. The 2010 Census detailed race and ethnicity variables have a corresponding country code for every Hispanic country, but some MENA source countries either did not have a response or were not coded. The following MENA country codes are not available on the 2010 Census: Algeria, Bahrain, Jordan, Kuwait, Libya, Saudi Arabia, Tunisia, and Yemen.

17. Rows in the results tables are ordered from largest to smallest of these 32 categories based on the sum of the number of females and males in the row for that POB panel. Starting from the largest row, rows are included if the cumulative proportion of the within POB total is ≤ 0.99 and the sample size of the row is ≥ 100. Any remaining rows are collated into a single "All Other Responses" category. No POB panel may have more than 10 rows.

ington) for which hours data are reported. We estimated a least-squares regression model of log annual work hours at a given job as a function of a log earnings quartic, age quartic, race indicators, a foreign-born indicator, and NAICS 2017 industry sector indicators. If the worker has multiple jobs during the year, then the sum of earnings at all other jobs is included as an additional covariate. We estimated the imputation regression model separately for workers with different quarterly work patterns, dominant jobs, coincident jobs, and sex.[18]

Education is observed for respondents in the 2000 Census and all available years of the American Community Survey; approximately 20 percent of individuals have reported education. We imputed missing education using information about a person's observed characteristics (sex, place of birth, age, race, and ethnicity) as well as the characteristics of a person's job history such as the average earnings, modal industry, and characteristics of a person's co-workers and co-residents. The characteristics are used to form homogeneous cells of a minimum size within which the distribution of observed education values is used to impute missing education values.[19]

It is important to keep in mind that our methods are designed to isolate differences in adjusted long-term earnings *within recorded place of birth* between our 32-category classification of self-identified ethnicity, race, and POB match. That is, we are looking for differences in the measured outcomes that are associated with differences in the way individuals self-identify, not differences related to their place of birth. We focus on these differences related to self-identification because they are at the heart of understanding meaningful changes in the way statistics about race and ethnicity may be reported and studied when the statistical standards for those classifications change under the 2024 revision of SPD 15.

Table 4.1 presents summary statistics for both samples and all variables used in our analyses. The statistics are reported for the four main classifications we use: Foreign-Born Hispanic, Born in the Middle East and North Africa, Other Foreign Born, and Born in the United States (excluding Puerto Rico).[20] In addition, for Sample 2, the table reports Foreign-Born Parents From More Than One Group. For Sample 2, the categories refer to the place of birth of the biological parent with whom the person in Sample 2 was

18. Hahn et al. (2021) used a similar hours of work imputation methodology. That paper contains a detailed evaluation of the imputation and a comparison to hours statistics found in other data sources.

19. McKinney et al. (2021) show that the conditional missing at random assumption, given the observed data, holds for education and that this method of imputation is reliable. Margins of error are not meaningfully inflated for sample sizes comparable to those in this paper.

20. We call out the exclusion of Puerto Rico explicitly because the LEHD and 2010 Census data include records for persons living in Puerto Rico, but we deleted them from our universe. Note that individuals born in Puerto Rico and living in the United States are included in the Foreign-Born Hispanic category.

Table 4.1 **Summary statistics for samples 1 and 2**

	Sample 1		Sample 2	
	Females	Males	Females	Males
Total Sample Size	44,640,000	43,320,000	3,614,000	3,582,000
Foreign-Born Hispanic				
Median Average Annual Earnings	16,970	28,640	22,960	27,360
Mean Log Average Annual Earnings	9.35	9.93	9.69	9.90
Mean Hours Paid	1,364	1,676	1,438	1,593
Mean Full Years Worked	3.92	4.21	4.18	4.23
Mean Partial Years Worked	0.99	0.93	1.01	1.03
Mean Inactive Years	1.09	0.86	0.82	0.74
Mean Age (2010)	40.42	40.68	26.42	26.43
Mean Years in United States (2010)	18.96	19.81		
Less than High School	0.44	0.49	0.23	0.24
High School	0.21	0.21	0.28	0.30
Some College	0.21	0.18	0.33	0.32
Bachelor or Higher	0.14	0.12	0.17	0.13
Sample Size	2,610,000	2,777,000	189,000	190,000
Born in the Middle East and North Africa				
Median Average Annual Earnings	19,220	34,390	29,980	33,840
Mean Log Average Annual Earnings	9.54	10.21	9.97	10.11
Mean Hours Paid	1,312	1,594	1,426	1,547
Mean Full Years Worked	3.77	4.10	4.05	4.02
Mean Partial Years Worked	0.95	0.90	1.04	1.04
Mean Inactive Years	1.27	1.00	0.92	0.95
Mean Age (2010)	40.25	40.84	26.37	26.40
Mean Years in United States (2010)	17.62	17.95		
Less than High School	0.11	0.11	0.09	0.11
High School	0.16	0.15	0.21	0.23
Some College	0.25	0.23	0.31	0.31
Bachelor or Higher	0.48	0.51	0.40	0.34
Sample Size	208,000	302,000	15,000	16,000
Other Foreign Born				
Median Average Annual Earnings	28,250	43,930	30,260	33,370
Mean Log Average Annual Earnings	9.93	10.44	10.01	10.12
Mean Hours Paid	1,526	1,729	1,485	1,593
Mean Full Years Worked	4.29	4.48	4.32	4.31
Mean Partial Years Worked	0.79	0.74	0.93	0.95
Mean Inactive Years	0.92	0.78	0.75	0.74
Mean Age (2010)	40.22	40.25	26.43	26.45
Mean Years in United States (2010)	17.82	18.04		
Less than High School	0.12	0.12	0.12	0.13
High School	0.18	0.17	0.24	0.26
Some College	0.27	0.24	0.31	0.31
Bachelor or Higher	0.43	0.47	0.33	0.29
Sample Size	4,256,000	4,015,000	256,000	256,000

(continued)

Table 4.1 (cont.)

	Sample 1		Sample 2	
	Females	Males	Females	Males
Born in the United States (excluding Puerto Rico)				
Median Average Annual Earnings	26,730	40,160	23,570	30,490
Mean Log Average Annual Earnings	9.81	10.26	9.70	10.00
Mean Hours Paid	1,404	1,626	1,367	1,558
Mean Full Years Worked	4.39	4.49	4.22	4.33
Mean Partial Years Worked	0.80	0.79	0.96	0.96
Mean Inactive Years	0.81	0.72	0.82	0.71
Mean Age (2010)	39.97	39.93	26.42	26.46
Mean Years in United States (2010)				
Less than High School	0.08	0.11	0.13	0.15
High School	0.26	0.30	0.28	0.32
Some College	0.35	0.32	0.34	0.32
Bachelor or Higher	0.30	0.27	0.26	0.22
Sample Size	37,570,000	36,230,000	3,148,000	3,115,000
Foreign-Born Parents from More Than One Group				
Median Average Annual Earnings			30,090	31,230
Mean Log Average Annual Earnings			9.99	10.06
Mean Hours Paid			1,506	1,584
Mean Full Years Worked			4.26	4.15
Mean Partial Years Worked			0.96	1.02
Mean Inactive Years			0.78	0.83
Mean Age (2010)			26.40	26.41
Mean Years in United States (2010)				
Less than High School			0.14	0.15
High School			0.24	0.25
Some College			0.31	0.31
Bachelor or Higher			0.31	0.27
Sample Size			5,900	5,900

Notes: Sample 1 consists of 87.97 million workers and Sample 2 consists of 7.196 million workers. Workers in both samples have at least one year with positive earnings during the six-year period from 2010 to 2015. Zero-earnings years are included in the earnings measures. Sample 1 includes both foreign- and native-born workers age 25 to 55 (inclusive) in 2010, while Sample 2 includes only native-born workers age 25 to 28 (inclusive). Place of birth is determined using the Census Numident. For Sample 2, the place of birth group is assigned using the parent's place of birth. The Hispanic place of birth group is the set of countries where at least 50 percent of foreign-born persons in Sample 1 report Hispanic on the 2010 Census. The full list of Hispanic and MENA countries can be found in table 4.3.

living when the 2000 Census was collected. All Sample 2 individuals were born in the United States.

Because the individuals in Sample 1 are much older than those in Sample 2 and because long-term average annual earnings in table 4.1 are not adjusted for differences in observable characteristics, comparisons across the samples must be done with care. Our measure of average annual earnings w_i does not control for labor supply during the six-year eligible worker period, although we recognize that labor supply likely differs across groups. To address this, we incorporate years and hours worked measures into our analysis as right-hand side covariates. By controlling for labor supply as a covariate and not directly, we are able to estimate median average annual earnings for each group, either accounting for or not accounting for labor supply differences.

As expected, mean hours paid during the year and the average number of years with positive reported earnings are higher for males than for females. For example, female workers born in Hispanic countries are paid on average for 1,364 hours during an active year and are inactive on average over the six-year period for 1.09 years, compared with 1,676 hours and 0.86 years for foreign-born Hispanic males. Hispanic-born women work about one full-time week per year less than native-born female workers (1,364 compared with 1,404 hours paid per year) when active and are also more likely to spend a full year inactive (1.09 compared with 0.81 inactive years). Overall, workers born in MENA countries have somewhat less attachment to the labor force than workers born in Hispanic countries, although the differences are not large.

In addition to the labor supply differences across groups, some education patterns are worth mentioning. A very large percentage of those born in Hispanic countries have less than a high school education (44 percent of females and 49 percent of males) as compared with the much lower percentages for those born in the United States (8 percent of females and 11 percent of males) even though the samples have essentially the same average age (about 40 years old in 2010). A greater percentage of the US-born children of Hispanic-born parents also have less than a high school education (23 percent for females and 24 percent for males) as compared to the children of US-born parents (13 percent for females and 15 percent for males) even though both samples are essentially the same age (26 years old). The narrowing of the gap between the first-generation immigrants (parents) and second generation (children of foreign-born parents) is a common feature of intergenerational data.

A greater percentage of MENA-born persons in Sample 1 have at least a bachelor's degree (48 percent of females and 51 percent of males) as compared to the percentages for US-born persons (30 percent for females and 27 percent for males). This larger differential in higher education persists for the children of MENA-born parents (40 percent for females and 34 percent for males) as compared to the children of US-born parents (26 percent for females and 22 percent for males).

4.4 Results

The results in table 4.2 show how adjusted long-term average earnings change for Sample 1 workers as we sequentially add regression controls for person characteristics (PC), workplace characteristics (PCW), and hours

Table 4.2 **Mean log long-term average annual earnings by sex, place of birth of parent(s), ethnicity, race, and Census Detail/SSA place of birth match**

				Females				Males			
Row Label	Ethnicity—Race—SSA Census Detail/SSA POB Match	Proportion	Cumulative Proportion	Mean Log Earnings	Adjusted Log Earn PC	Adjusted Log Earn PCW	Adjusted Log Earn PCWH	Mean Log Earnings	Adjusted Log Earn PC	Adjusted Log Earn PCW	Adjusted Log Earn PCWH
FBH	Foreign-Born Hispanic | Sample Size = 5,386,000 | Hispanic = 0.979 | Census Detail and SSA POB Match = 0.932										
H1P	Hispanic, White, Census Detail/SSA POB Match	0.516	0.516	9.360	0.000	0.000	0.000	9.951	0.000	0.000	0.000
H6P	Hispanic, Some Other Race, Census Detail/SSA POB Match	0.347	0.863	–0.046	0.015	–0.046	–0.043	–0.036	0.001	–0.055	–0.052
H8P	Hispanic, 2+ Races (SOR), Census Detail/SSA POB Match	0.035	0.898	–0.058	–0.019	–0.049	–0.048	–0.058	–0.036	–0.054	–0.052
H1N	Hispanic, White	0.023	0.921	0.076	0.057	0.037	0.014	–0.067	–0.078	0.003	0.015
H2P	Hispanic, Black, Census Detail/SSA POB Match	0.021	0.942	–0.062	–0.144	–0.039	–0.138	–0.401	–0.423	–0.105	–0.138
H6N	Hispanic, Some Other Race	0.020	0.962	–0.062	–0.011	–0.028	–0.043	–0.185	–0.156	–0.071	–0.052
N1N	Not-Hispanic, White	0.016	0.978	0.407	0.161	0.105	0.181	0.407	0.270	0.166	0.249
XXX	All Other Responses	0.009	0.987	0.239	0.169	0.087	0.047	0.053	0.010	0.014	0.040
H3P	Hispanic, AIAN, Census Detail/SSA POB Match	0.009	0.995	–0.061	–0.007	–0.053	–0.068	–0.084	–0.055	–0.071	–0.073
H7P	Hispanic, 2+ Races (not SOR), Census Detail/SSA POB Match	0.003	0.998	0.196	0.158	0.055	–0.014	0.125	0.105	0.030	–0.002
N2N	Not-Hispanic, Black	0.002	1.000	0.494	0.299	0.086	0.005	–0.082	–0.150	–0.105	–0.010
MENA	Middle East and North Africa | Sample Size = 510,000 | Hispanic = 0.007 | Census Detail and SSA POB Match = 0.247										
N1N	Not-Hispanic, White	0.460	0.460	9.601	0.000	0.000	0.000	10.380	0.000	0.000	0.000
N6N	Not-Hispanic, Some Other Race	0.217	0.678	–0.305	–0.200	–0.144	–0.072	–0.536	–0.400	–0.209	–0.123
N6P	Not-Hispanic, Some Other Race, Census Detail/SSA POB Match	0.196	0.874	0.028	0.109	0.006	–0.009	–0.145	–0.066	–0.071	–0.062
N8P	Not-Hispanic, 2+ Races (SOR), Census Detail/SSA POB Match	0.051	0.925	0.045	0.143	0.037	–0.019	–0.068	–0.024	–0.058	–0.071
N8N	Not-Hispanic, 2+ Races (SOR)	0.030	0.955	–0.402	–0.281	–0.176	–0.121	–0.533	–0.408	–0.206	–0.155
N4N	Not-Hispanic, Asian	0.023	0.978	0.300	0.356	0.105	–0.003	0.067	0.123	–0.046	–0.065
N2N	Not-Hispanic, Black	0.011	0.988	0.067	0.132	–0.111	–0.243	–0.503	–0.330	–0.271	–0.304
XXX	All Other Responses	0.007	0.996	–0.082	–0.074	–0.162	–0.174	–0.478	–0.380	–0.276	–0.225
H1N	Hispanic, White	0.004	1.000	0.266	0.208	0.031	–0.146	–0.047	–0.043	–0.085	–0.153

OFB		Other Foreign Born | Sample Size = 8,272,000 | Hispanic = 0.012									
N4N	Not-Hispanic, Asian	0.477	0.477	9.974	0.000	0.000	0.000	10.530	0.000	0.000	0.000
N1N	Not-Hispanic, White	0.296	0.773	–0.085	–0.095	–0.044	0.029	0.024	0.070	0.124	0.128
N2N	Not-Hispanic, Black	0.131	0.904	–0.002	0.113	–0.086	–0.198	–0.455	–0.248	–0.169	–0.217
N6N	Not-Hispanic, Some Other Race	0.039	0.943	–0.272	–0.117	–0.154	–0.156	–0.560	–0.331	–0.159	–0.147
N7N	Not-Hispanic, 2+ Races (not SOR)	0.022	0.966	–0.130	–0.179	–0.100	–0.059	–0.256	–0.197	–0.101	–0.062
N8N	Not-Hispanic, 2+ Races (SOR)	0.013	0.979	–0.204	–0.141	–0.108	–0.081	–0.257	–0.152	–0.065	–0.054
N5N	Not Hispanic, Hawaiian/Pacific Islander	0.008	0.987	–0.560	–0.495	–0.264	–0.122	–0.681	–0.460	–0.271	–0.126
XXX	All Other Responses	0.007	0.994	–0.288	–0.276	–0.177	–0.198	–0.505	–0.347	–0.168	–0.183
H1N	Hispanic, White	0.006	1.000	–0.211	–0.227	–0.114	–0.134	–0.248	–0.129	–0.035	–0.089
USA		USA Born | Sample Size = 73,800,000 | Hispanic = 0.068									
N1N	Not-Hispanic, White	0.779	0.779	9.849	0.000	0.000	0.000	10.380	0.000	0.000	0.000
N2N	Not-Hispanic, Black	0.119	0.898	–0.225	–0.076	–0.076	–0.176	–0.835	–0.664	–0.270	–0.198
H1N	Hispanic, White	0.042	0.941	–0.077	0.065	–0.004	–0.137	–0.262	–0.112	–0.087	–0.160
H5N	Hispanic, Some Other Race	0.018	0.959	–0.238	–0.021	–0.067	–0.191	–0.434	–0.203	–0.147	–0.211
N7N	Not-Hispanic, 2+ Races (not SOR)	0.010	0.969	–0.223	–0.139	0.009	–0.051	–0.354	–0.271	–0.084	–0.071
N4N	Not-Hispanic, Asian	0.010	0.979	0.560	0.530	0.299	0.111	0.256	0.231	0.136	0.044
XXX	All Other Responses	0.009	0.988	–0.289	–0.124	–0.029	–0.171	–0.532	–0.360	–0.146	–0.182
N3N	Not-Hispanic, American Indian/Alaska Native	0.008	0.995	–0.534	–0.371	–0.100	–0.096	–0.825	–0.655	–0.240	–0.102
N6N	Not-Hispanic, Some Other Race	0.005	1.000	–0.324	–0.244	–0.051	–0.058	–0.453	–0.384	–0.101	–0.056

Notes: This table uses Sample 1, which consists of 87.97 million workers age 25 to 55 (inclusive) in 2010. All workers must have at least one year with positive earnings during the six-year period from 2010 to 2015. Zero-earnings years are included in the earnings measures. Place of birth is determined using the Census Numident. The Hispanic place of birth group consists of the set of countries where at least 50 percent of foreign-born persons in Sample 1 report Hispanic on the 2010 Census. The full list of Hispanic and MENA countries can be found in table 4.3. The race measure consists of eight categories collated from the 2010 Census: White, Black, American Indian/Alaska Native (AIAN), Asian, Native Hawaiian/Pacific Islander, Some Other Race (SOR), 2+ Races (not SOR), and 2+ Races (SOR). The ethnicity variable is binary; Hispanic/Latino or Not Hispanic/Latino. A "Census Detail/SSA POB Match" occurs when the 2010 Census respondent reported their Census Numident POB on the 2010 Race or Ethnicity questions using the detailed coding (the detailed Decennial POB coding is not available for eight MENA countries as shown in table 4.3). For both females and males we report four measures of mean log real long-term earnings. The first row of the Mean Log Earnings column for each POB group shows the mean log earnings of the largest Ethnicity-Race-Census Detail/SSA POB Match category, while the other rows report the difference in mean log earnings relative to the largest category. The next three columns show adjusted log real long-term earnings from linear regression models controlling for various person and job characteristics. The PC model includes controls for education and quadratic functions of age and years in the United States in 2010. The PCW model adds controls for the dominant industry/region and the number of full and partial years worked. The PCWH model adds a quadratic function of average annual hours worked. Standard errors have not been released yet for this table. Some sub-groups have fewer than 1,000 persons. Even for small sub-groups, standard errors for adjusted log earnings differentials rarely exceed 0.025 log points.

worked (PCWH). They also provide a comparison group for Sample 2 workers. Tables 4.2, 4.3, and 4.4 follow a similar layout. The rows are organized into groups based on the respondent's own place of birth (tables 4.2 and 4.3) or the place of birth of their parent(s) (table 4.4). We reference statistics in these tables using the Row Label column.

In table 4.2 we show four different, mutually exclusive groups based on the respondent's place of birth: Foreign-Born Hispanic, Middle East and North Africa, Other Foreign Born, and US-born. The first row within each POB group contains the largest population (females plus males) ethnicity by race by Census Detail/SSA POB match sub-group. The remaining rows are in decreasing size order, where the size is determined by the proportion of the total panel population in that row. For the earnings results, the largest population, or first row, in each POB group is the reference sub-group. The Mean Log Earnings column shows average log long-term real earnings for workers in the largest sub-group. For every other row the table displays the difference relative to the largest sub-group. For example, female foreign-born Hispanic average log long-term real earnings is 9.360 for the Hispanic, White, Census Detail/SSA POB Match (FBH H1P) reference sub-group, and the next largest sub-group Hispanic, Some Other Race, Census Detail/SSA POB Match (FBH H6P) has long-term average earnings –0.046 log points relative to the reference sub-group. The results for males are presented in a similar format using the same reference sub-group as females.

For both females and males, we estimate separate earnings regressions within each POB group, controlling for three sets of characteristics, with each regression model building on the previous model as you move to the right in the table. In table 4.2 only, we present the PC and PCW models to better understand the relative impact of the different sets of characteristics. The PC model includes controls for education and quadratic functions of age and years in the United States in 2010. The PCW model adds controls for the dominant industry and region and the number of full and partial years worked. The PCWH model adds a quadratic function of average annual hours worked.

In our first adjusted model, PC, we control only for person characteristics. Including person characteristics generally reduces the difference in earnings relative to the reference category although the impacts are uneven and vary by POB group, ethnicity, and race category. For example, the unadjusted difference in mean log earnings for Not Hispanic, White, females in the Other Foreign-Born group relative to the reference sub-group is –0.085 log points (OFB N1N), while the difference controlling for person characteristics (PC) is –0.095 log points (OFB N1N). Including controls for the type of workplace and the number of years worked (PCW) reduces the gap from –0.095 in the PC model to –0.044 log points in the PCW model (OFB N1N). Including controls for hours worked reduces the gap further from –0.044 log points in the PCW model to 0.029 log points in the PCWH model (OFB N1N).

When interpreting the results, the PC and PCW model estimates typically move in predictable ways, however in many cases when controlling for hours of work (PCWH), the model estimates may be counterintuitive. For example, consider the estimates for the Foreign-Born Hispanic females in the Hispanic, Black, Census Detail/SSA POB Match (FBH H2P) sub-group, the earnings gap actually increases from –0.039 log points to –0.138 log points when we control for hours worked. This result implies that for this ethnicity, race, POB-match sub-group, individuals work substantially more hours than the reference sub-group, and once we control for this difference in the PCWH model, the earnings gap increases. Although the PCWH model is our preferred specification, there are notable differences between the PCW and the PCWH model results. A case can also be made for using the PCW model results, especially if both earnings differences and hours worked are driven by similar underlying processes, for example, discriminatory practices in the labor market.[21]

Table 4.3 reports the detailed results for long-term earnings differentials for Sample 1 individuals with and without adjustment by sex for each place of birth country with at least 1,000 persons. We discuss the results for the largest immigrant birth countries in the Hispanic and MENA categories.

Mexico is the largest Hispanic immigrant source country in our data by a substantial margin. Essentially all immigrants in Sample 1 born in Mexico self-identify as Hispanic (MEX 99.3 percent).[22] Similarly, nearly all Mexican-born immigrants (MEX, 96.6 percent) self-declared Mexico as a checkbox or write-in response on the 2010 Census. Our reference subgroup (MEX H1P, 50.0 percent) self-identified as Hispanic and White in addition to indicating Mexico on either the race or ethnicity question in the 2010 Census. Compared to this reference sub-group, the sub-group that self-identified as Hispanic and Some Other Race (MEX H6P, 42.2 percent)

21. In these analyses we consider median real average annual earnings, the logarithm of real average annual earnings, mean hours paid, mean full years worked, mean partial years worked, and mean inactive years. In earlier work (McKinney et al. 2022) we performed quantile regression to assess the distributional differences in the relationship of covariates to long-term annual earnings. That work distinguished native and foreign-born workers and used the same race and ethnicity categories considered in this paper. We found substantial differences in the effect of labor-force attachment in the quantiles below the median. Our conclusion was "[a]t the bottom of the earnings distribution, differences in earnings across groups are largely due to observable characteristics suggesting that workers at the bottom of the earnings distribution may have the clearest path to improving their position. Increasing hours paid, changing employers, and attaining additional education, while difficult in many cases, are some of the standard pathways to higher real earnings. For workers above the median, differences in the return to characteristics is the dominant component. The pathway to reducing differences in the returns to observable characteristics across demographic groups is less clear. (p. 1924)." See also tables 2A and 2B therein. Because the differences in labor force attachment (measured as either average annual hours or years of zero employment) are substantial in the lower tail of the distribution by race and ethnicity but not at the median, we don't further analyze those effects in this paper.

22. In reporting results for tables 4.3 and 4.4 we use the panel label (in this case MEX) and the row label (for the reference row in the Mexican panel H1P) to help readers find the results we are discussing.

Table 4.3 **Mean log long-term average annual earnings by sex, detailed place of birth, ethnicity, race, and Census Detail/SSA place of birth match**

				Females		Males	
Row Label	Ethnicity—Race—SSA Census Detail/SSA POB Match	Proportion	Cumulative Proportion	Mean Log Earnings	Adjusted Log Earnings PCWH	Mean Log Earnings	Adjusted Log Earnings PCWH
ARG	Argentina | Sample Size = 56,500 | Hispanic = 0.903 | Census Detail/SSA POB Match = 0.858						
H1P	Hispanic, White, Census Detail/SSA POB Match	0.762	0.762	9.759	0.000	10.410	0.000
N1N	Not Hispanic, White	0.080	0.842	0.169	0.083	0.124	0.091
H6P	Hispanic, Some Other Race, Census Detail/SSA POB Match	0.069	0.911	–0.207	–0.105	–0.459	–0.153
H1N	Hispanic, White	0.034	0.945	–0.093	–0.010	–0.228	–0.047
H8P	Hispanic, 2+ Races (SOR), Census Detail/SSA POB Match	0.015	0.960	–0.222	–0.039	–0.468	–0.127
N6N	Not Hispanic, Some Other Race	0.012	0.972	0.081	–0.045	–0.682	–0.072
N4N	Not Hispanic, Asian	0.010	0.981	0.347	0.088	0.200	0.023
H6N	Hispanic, Some Other Race	0.008	0.989	–0.360	–0.106	–0.537	–0.168
XXX	All Other Responses	0.008	0.997	–0.032	–0.022	–0.357	–0.178
H4P	Hispanic, Asian, Census Detail/SSA POB Match	0.003	1.000	–0.049	–0.033	–0.193	–0.036
BOL	Bolivia | Sample Size = 23,500 | Hispanic = 0.936 | Census Detail/SSA POB Match = 0.851						
H1P	Hispanic, White, Census Detail/SSA POB Match	0.543	0.543	9.603	0.000	10.180	0.000
H6P	Hispanic, Some Other Race, Census Detail/SSA POB Match	0.243	0.787	–0.084	–0.036	–0.124	–0.052
N1N	Not Hispanic, White	0.052	0.839	0.309	0.156	0.285	0.160
H8P	Hispanic, 2+ Races (SOR), Census Detail/SSA POB Match	0.048	0.887	–0.040	–0.060	–0.173	–0.052
H1N	Hispanic, White	0.043	0.930	0.012	–0.012	–0.098	0.041
H6N	Hispanic, Some Other Race	0.024	0.954	0.102	–0.054	–0.237	–0.057
XXX	All Other Responses	0.017	0.972	0.116	0.001	–0.182	–0.086
H3P	Hispanic, AIAN, Census Detail/SSA POB Match	0.013	0.985	0.075	–0.005	–0.135	–0.051
N4N	Not Hispanic, Asian	0.009	0.993	0.158	0.149	0.152	0.134
H7P	Hispanic, 2+ Races (not SOR), Census Detail/SSA POB Match	0.007	1.000	0.421	–0.002	0.033	–0.057
CHI	Chile | Sample Size = 27,000 | Hispanic = 0.926 | Census Detail/SSA POB Match = 0.852						
H1P	Hispanic, White, Census Detail/SSA POB Match	0.653	0.653	9.627	0.000	10.260	0.000
H6P	Hispanic, Some Other Race, Census Detail/SSA POB Match	0.160	0.813	–0.154	–0.058	–0.272	–0.105
N1N	Not Hispanic, White	0.052	0.866	0.161	0.113	0.314	0.193

H1N	Hispanic, White	0.041	0.907	–0.056	0.030	–0.157	–0.029
H8P	Hispanic, 2+ Races (SOR), Census Detail/SSA POB Match	0.032	0.938	–0.145	–0.070	–0.260	–0.088
N4N	Not Hispanic, Asian	0.024	0.963	0.570	0.249	0.391	0.224
H6N	Hispanic, Some Other Race	0.021	0.983	–0.196	–0.098	–0.383	–0.116
XXX	All Other Responses	0.013	0.996	–0.002	–0.125	–0.404	–0.052
H7P	Hispanic, 2+ Races (not SOR), Census Detail/SSA POB Match	0.004	1.000	0.161	–0.117	–0.010	–0.128
COL	Colombia | Sample Size = 243,000 | Hispanic = 0.979 | Census Detail/SSA POB Match = 0.926						
H1P	Hispanic, White, Census Detail/SSA POB Match	0.692	0.692	9.528	0.000	10.130	0.000
H6P	Hispanic, Some Other Race, Census Detail/SSA POB Match	0.181	0.873	–0.039	–0.048	–0.087	–0.071
H1N	Hispanic, White	0.034	0.907	–0.056	0.006	–0.110	–0.003
H8P	Hispanic, 2+ Races (SOR), Census Detail/SSA POB Match	0.034	0.941	–0.082	–0.056	–0.110	–0.066
N1N	Not Hispanic, White	0.015	0.956	0.298	0.142	0.344	0.179
H2P	Hispanic, Black, Census Detail/SSA POB Match	0.014	0.970	–0.017	–0.159	–0.175	–0.158
H6N	Hispanic, Some Other Race	0.014	0.984	–0.098	–0.046	–0.204	–0.073
XXX	All Other Responses	0.010	0.994	–0.008	–0.020	–0.167	–0.056
H3P	Hispanic, AIAN, Census Detail/SSA POB Match	0.004	0.997	–0.113	–0.060	–0.347	–0.104
N4N	Not Hispanic, Asian	0.003	1.000	0.596	0.071	0.326	0.106
COS	Costa Rica | Sample Size = 27,000 | Hispanic = 0.926 | Census Detail/SSA POB Match = 0.833						
H1P	Hispanic, White, Census Detail/SSA POB Match	0.556	0.556	9.469	0.000	10.100	0.000
H6P	Hispanic, Some Other Race, Census Detail/SSA POB Match	0.185	0.741	–0.121	–0.062	–0.180	–0.093
N1N	Not Hispanic, White	0.059	0.800	0.282	0.153	0.367	0.202
H1N	Hispanic, White	0.052	0.852	0.018	–0.018	–0.200	0.012
H2P	Hispanic, Black, Census Detail/SSA POB Match	0.048	0.900	0.673	–0.063	0.160	–0.136
H8P	Hispanic, 2+ Races (SOR), Census Detail/SSA POB Match	0.041	0.941	–0.013	–0.062	–0.176	–0.087
H6N	Hispanic, Some Other Race	0.024	0.965	–0.115	–0.074	–0.342	–0.093
XXX	All Other Responses	0.019	0.983	0.289	–0.020	–0.340	–0.042
N2N	Not Hispanic, Black	0.011	0.994	0.577	0.029	–0.221	–0.150
N4N	Not Hispanic, Asian	0.006	1.000	0.960	0.258	0.736	0.295
CUB	Cuba | Sample Size = 348,000 | Hispanic = 0.989 | Census Detail/SSA POB Match = 0.974						
H1P	Hispanic, White, Census Detail/SSA POB Match	0.871	0.871	9.498	0.000	9.788	0.000
H6P	Hispanic, Some Other Race, Census Detail/SSA POB Match	0.050	0.921	–0.142	–0.049	–0.225	–0.068

(continued)

Table 4.3 **(cont.)**

Row Label	Ethnicity—Race—SSA Census Detail/SSA POB Match	Proportion	Cumulative Proportion	Females: Mean Log Earnings	Females: Adjusted Log Earnings PCWH	Males: Mean Log Earnings	Males: Adjusted Log Earnings PCWH
H2P	Hispanic, Black, Census Detail/SSA POB Match	0.036	0.957	–0.234	–0.162	–0.413	–0.144
H8P	Hispanic, 2+ Races (SOR), Census Detail/SSA POB Match	0.013	0.970	–0.166	–0.063	–0.310	–0.078
H1N	Hispanic, White	0.010	0.980	0.136	0.025	–0.148	–0.004
N1N	Not Hispanic, White	0.010	0.991	0.392	0.097	0.487	0.092
XXX	All Other Responses	0.009	1.000	0.151	–0.002	–0.139	–0.038
DR	Dominican Republic | Sample Size = 305,000 | Hispanic = 0.990 | Census Detail/SSA POB Match = 0.928						
H6P	Hispanic, Some Other Race, Census Detail/SSA POB Match	0.439	0.439	9.327	0.000	9.726	0.000
H1P	Hispanic, White, Census Detail/SSA POB Match	0.285	0.725	0.071	0.045	0.125	0.048
H2P	Hispanic, Black, Census Detail/SSA POB Match	0.116	0.841	0.065	–0.077	0.047	–0.055
H8P	Hispanic, 2+ Races (SOR), Census Detail/SSA POB Match	0.071	0.912	–0.020	–0.018	–0.020	–0.009
H6N	Hispanic, Some Other Race	0.025	0.937	–0.047	–0.008	–0.102	0.014
H1N	Hispanic, White	0.025	0.962	0.052	0.041	–0.044	0.032
XXX	All Other Responses	0.013	0.975	0.013	0.044	–0.004	0.017
H3P	Hispanic, AIAN, Census Detail/SSA POB Match	0.012	0.987	–0.123	–0.037	–0.199	–0.010
H2N	Hispanic, Black	0.007	0.993	0.005	–0.074	0.033	–0.050
N1N	Not Hispanic, White	0.004	0.997	0.191	0.214	0.410	0.213
N2N	Not Hispanic, Black	0.003	1.000	0.494	0.094	0.198	0.077
ECU	Ecuador | Sample Size = 114,000 | Hispanic = 0.991 | Census Detail/SSA POB Match = 0.921						
H1P	Hispanic, White, Census Detail/SSA POB Match	0.505	0.505	9.542	0.000	10.100	0.000
H6P	Hispanic, Some Other Race, Census Detail/SSA POB Match	0.334	0.838	–0.091	–0.037	–0.112	–0.045
H8P	Hispanic, 2+ Races (SOR), Census Detail/SSA POB Match	0.058	0.896	–0.150	–0.045	–0.134	–0.050
H1N	Hispanic, White	0.037	0.933	0.020	0.005	–0.090	–0.014
H6N	Hispanic, Some Other Race	0.027	0.960	–0.101	–0.037	–0.069	–0.055
N1N	Not Hispanic, White	0.011	0.972	0.300	0.149	0.284	0.166
H3P	Hispanic, AIAN, Census Detail/SSA POB Match	0.009	0.981	0.077	–0.063	–0.266	–0.087
XXX	All Other Responses	0.007	0.988	0.073	–0.011	–0.075	0.019
H2P	Hispanic, Black, Census Detail/SSA POB Match	0.005	0.993	–0.165	–0.143	–0.273	–0.153

H7P	Hispanic, 2+ Races (not SOR), Census Detail/SSA POB Match	0.004	0.997	0.209	0.022	0.124	–0.001
H8N	Hispanic, 2+ Races (SOR)	0.003	1.000	–0.173	–0.037	–0.056	–0.056
ELS	El Salvador | Sample Size = 435,000 | Hispanic = 0.993 | Census Detail/SSA POB Match = 0.887						
H6P	Hispanic, Some Other Race, Census Detail/SSA POB Match	0.465	0.465	9.423	0.000	9.927	0.000
H1P	Hispanic, White, Census Detail/SSA POB Match	0.350	0.815	0.032	0.026	0.053	0.025
H8P	Hispanic, 2+ Races (SOR), Census Detail/SSA POB Match	0.056	0.871	–0.050	–0.004	0.005	0.001
H6N	Hispanic, Some Other Race	0.055	0.926	–0.070	0.000	–0.120	–0.004
H1N	Hispanic, White	0.045	0.971	–0.010	0.021	–0.130	0.015
H3P	Hispanic, AIAN, Census Detail/SSA POB Match	0.009	0.980	0.056	–0.017	0.057	–0.003
XXX	All Other Responses	0.009	0.989	0.059	0.018	–0.057	0.012
N1N	Not Hispanic, White	0.004	0.993	0.117	0.170	–0.013	0.170
H8N	Hispanic, 2+ Races (SOR)	0.004	0.997	–0.082	–0.002	–0.174	0.000
H2P	Hispanic, Black, Census Detail/SSA POB Match	0.003	1.000	0.021	–0.084	–0.025	–0.082
GUA	Guatemala | Sample Size = 159,000 | Hispanic = 0.981 | Census Detail/SSA POB Match = 0.862						
H6P	Hispanic, Some Other Race, Census Detail/SSA POB Match	0.417	0.417	9.297	0.000	9.881	0.000
H1P	Hispanic, White, Census Detail/SSA POB Match	0.355	0.772	0.097	0.027	0.079	0.042
H6N	Hispanic, Some Other Race	0.061	0.833	–0.078	–0.006	–0.175	–0.011
H8P	Hispanic, 2+ Races (SOR), Census Detail/SSA POB Match	0.054	0.887	–0.017	–0.011	–0.053	0.013
H1N	Hispanic, White	0.049	0.936	0.036	0.016	–0.138	0.013
H3P	Hispanic, AIAN, Census Detail/SSA POB Match	0.019	0.956	–0.007	–0.016	–0.064	–0.025
XXX	All Other Responses	0.019	0.975	0.113	0.017	–0.049	0.010
N1N	Not Hispanic, White	0.010	0.985	0.400	0.191	0.362	0.273
H7P	Hispanic, 2+ Races (not SOR), Census Detail/SSA POB Match	0.005	0.990	0.121	0.013	0.162	0.022
H2P	Hispanic, Black, Census Detail/SSA POB Match	0.005	0.995	0.239	–0.145	0.060	–0.091
H8N	Hispanic, 2+ Races (SOR)	0.005	1.000	0.023	0.002	–0.168	–0.008
HON	Honduras | Sample Size = 118,000 | Hispanic = 0.975 | Census Detail/SSA POB Match = 0.873						
H1P	Hispanic, White, Census Detail/SSA POB Match	0.394	0.394	9.274	0.000	9.778	0.000
H6P	Hispanic, Some Other Race, Census Detail/SSA POB Match	0.356	0.750	–0.012	–0.036	–0.012	–0.039
H8P	Hispanic, 2+ Races (SOR), Census Detail/SSA POB Match	0.062	0.812	–0.060	–0.051	–0.014	–0.031
H6N	Hispanic, Some Other Race	0.049	0.861	–0.095	–0.046	–0.141	–0.056
H1N	Hispanic, White	0.045	0.906	–0.017	0.000	–0.060	–0.015

(continued)

Table 4.3 (cont.)

Row Label	Ethnicity—Race—SSA Census Detail/SSA POB Match	Proportion	Cumulative Proportion	Females		Males	
				Mean Log Earnings	Adjusted Log Earnings PCWH	Mean Log Earnings	Adjusted Log Earnings PCWH
H2P	Hispanic, Black, Census Detail/SSA POB Match	0.035	0.941	0.339	–0.125	0.267	–0.105
XXX	All Other Responses	0.019	0.959	0.292	0.023	0.164	0.051
H3P	Hispanic, AIAN, Census Detail/SSA POB Match	0.014	0.973	0.102	–0.062	0.046	–0.042
N1N	Not Hispanic, White	0.014	0.986	0.393	0.189	0.544	0.285
H7P	Hispanic, 2+ Races (not SOR), Census Detail/SSA POB Match	0.007	0.993	0.143	–0.097	0.167	0.001
N2N	Not Hispanic, Black	0.007	1.000	0.485	–0.013	0.220	–0.007
MEX	Mexico | Sample Size = 2,582,000 | Hispanic = 0.993 | Census Detail/SSA POB Match = 0.966						
H1P	Hispanic, White, Census Detail/SSA POB Match	0.500	0.500	9.266	0.000	10.020	0.000
H6P	Hispanic, Some Other Race, Census Detail/SSA POB Match	0.422	0.922	–0.002	–0.026	–0.063	–0.033
H8P	Hispanic, 2+ Races (SOR), Census Detail/SSA POB Match	0.028	0.950	–0.072	–0.024	–0.047	–0.035
H6N	Hispanic, Some Other Race	0.013	0.962	–0.071	–0.033	–0.183	–0.041
H1N	Hispanic, White	0.013	0.975	–0.071	–0.009	–0.168	–0.005
H3P	Hispanic, AIAN, Census Detail/SSA POB Match	0.010	0.985	0.021	–0.051	–0.064	–0.048
XXX	All Other Responses	0.009	0.994	0.075	–0.026	–0.078	–0.032
N1N	Not Hispanic, White	0.006	1.000	0.114	0.161	0.075	0.219
NIC	Nicaragua | Sample Size = 93,000 | Hispanic = 0.984 | Census Detail/SSA POB Match = 0.903						
H1P	Hispanic, White, Census Detail/SSA POB Match	0.595	0.595	9.505	0.000	9.956	0.000
H6P	Hispanic, Some Other Race, Census Detail/SSA POB Match	0.243	0.838	–0.041	–0.038	0.002	–0.038
H1N	Hispanic, White	0.045	0.883	–0.002	–0.003	–0.063	–0.019
H8P	Hispanic, 2+ Races (SOR), Census Detail/SSA POB Match	0.043	0.926	–0.024	–0.044	–0.096	–0.038
H6N	Hispanic, Some Other Race	0.030	0.957	–0.090	–0.055	–0.176	–0.052
H2P	Hispanic, Black, Census Detail/SSA POB Match	0.013	0.970	0.256	–0.087	–0.082	–0.104
XXX	All Other Responses	0.011	0.981	0.362	0.094	0.179	0.059
N1N	Not Hispanic, White	0.007	0.988	0.227	0.172	0.336	0.191
H3P	Hispanic, AIAN, Census Detail/SSA POB Match	0.006	0.994	–0.193	–0.028	–0.112	–0.090

H7P	Hispanic, 2+ Races (not SOR), Census Detail/SSA POB Match	0.003	0.997	0.264	0.043	0.324	–0.012
H8N	Hispanic, 2+ Races (SOR)	0.003	1.000	0.028	0.064	–0.142	–0.058
PAN	Panama | Sample Size = 49,000 | Hispanic = 0.724 | Census Detail/SSA POB Match = 0.633						
H1P	Hispanic, White, Census Detail/SSA POB Match	0.213	0.213	9.641	0.000	10.350	0.000
H2P	Hispanic, Black, Census Detail/SSA POB Match	0.199	0.413	0.364	–0.156	–0.155	–0.193
N1N	Not Hispanic, White	0.195	0.608	0.211	0.109	0.089	0.101
H6P	Hispanic, Some Other Race, Census Detail/SSA POB Match	0.159	0.766	–0.063	–0.075	–0.331	–0.130
N2N	Not Hispanic, Black	0.057	0.823	0.235	–0.090	–0.465	–0.130
H1N	Hispanic, White	0.049	0.872	0.209	0.029	–0.075	–0.014
H8P	Hispanic, 2+ Races (SOR), Census Detail/SSA POB Match	0.045	0.917	–0.003	–0.128	–0.381	–0.189
XXX	All Other Responses	0.035	0.951	0.144	0.004	–0.069	0.005
H6N	Hispanic, Some Other Race	0.024	0.976	–0.241	–0.090	–0.435	–0.108
N4N	Not Hispanic, Asian	0.012	0.988	0.467	0.183	0.301	0.180
H2N	Not Hispanic, Black	0.012	1.000	–0.018	–0.205	–0.433	–0.211
PER	Peru | Sample Size = 143,000 | Hispanic = 0.972 | Census Detail/SSA POB Match = 0.916						
H1P	Hispanic, White, Census Detail/SSA POB Match	0.501	0.501	9.615	0.000	10.140	0.000
H6P	Hispanic, Some Other Race, Census Detail/SSA POB Match	0.322	0.823	–0.053	–0.042	–0.094	–0.067
H8P	Hispanic, 2+ Races (SOR), Census Detail/SSA POB Match	0.050	0.873	–0.071	–0.038	–0.086	–0.054
H1N	Hispanic, White	0.032	0.905	–0.022	0.002	–0.072	0.000
H6N	Hispanic, Some Other Race	0.024	0.929	–0.121	–0.034	–0.223	–0.079
N1N	Not Hispanic, White	0.020	0.948	0.160	0.107	0.363	0.218
H3P	Hispanic, AIAN, Census Detail/SSA POB Match	0.013	0.961	–0.104	–0.066	–0.152	–0.096
XXX	All Other Responses	0.013	0.974	0.311	0.089	0.119	0.030
H7P	Hispanic, 2+ Races (not SOR), Census Detail/SSA POB Match	0.011	0.985	0.152	–0.005	0.249	0.019
H4P	Hispanic, Asian, Census Detail/SSA POB Match	0.009	0.994	0.433	0.046	0.350	0.070
H2P	Hispanic, Black, Census Detail/SSA POB Match	0.006	1.000	0.005	–0.181	–0.203	–0.155
PR	Puerto Rico | Sample Size = 530,000 | Hispanic = 0.968 | Census Detail/SSA POB Match = 0.934						
H1P	Hispanic, White, Census Detail/SSA POB Match	0.597	0.597	9.137	0.000	9.478	0.000
H6P	Hispanic, Some Other Race, Census Detail/SSA POB Match	0.238	0.834	0.100	–0.049	0.127	–0.059
H2P	Hispanic, Black, Census Detail/SSA POB Match	0.065	0.900	–0.360	–0.134	–0.438	–0.131

(continued)

Table 4.3 (cont.)

Row Label	Ethnicity—Race—SSA Census Detail/SSA POB Match	Proportion	Cumulative Proportion	Females: Mean Log Earnings	Females: Adjusted Log Earnings PCWH	Males: Mean Log Earnings	Males: Adjusted Log Earnings PCWH
H8P	Hispanic, 2+ Races (SOR), Census Detail/SSA POB Match	0.025	0.925	0.089	–0.052	0.109	–0.053
N1N	Not Hispanic, White	0.024	0.949	0.732	0.166	0.848	0.231
H1N	Hispanic, White	0.018	0.966	0.441	0.027	0.221	0.023
H6N	Hispanic, Some Other Race	0.013	0.979	0.208	–0.051	–0.119	–0.052
XXX	All Other Responses	0.008	0.987	0.287	–0.034	0.176	–0.019
H3P	Hispanic, AIAN, Census Detail/SSA POB Match	0.007	0.994	–0.111	–0.062	–0.128	–0.095
N4N	Not Hispanic, Asian	0.003	0.997	1.373	0.185	1.344	0.181
N2N	Not Hispanic, Black	0.003	1.000	0.731	–0.023	0.253	0.010
SPA	Spain | Sample Size = 44,000 | Hispanic = 0.625 | Census Detail/SSA POB Match = 0.489						
H1P	Hispanic, White, Census Detail/SSA POB Match	0.454	0.454	10.030	0.000	10.790	0.000
N1N	Not Hispanic, White	0.317	0.771	–0.143	0.058	–0.346	0.017
H1N	Hispanic, White	0.113	0.884	–0.092	–0.007	–0.223	–0.003
N2N	Not Hispanic, Black	0.027	0.912	–0.070	–0.102	–0.853	–0.159
H6P	Hispanic, Some Other Race, Census Detail/SSA POB Match	0.027	0.939	–0.176	–0.106	–0.366	–0.115
XXX	All Other Responses	0.017	0.956	–0.284	–0.113	–0.560	–0.108
H6N	Hispanic, Some Other Race	0.014	0.969	–0.256	–0.067	–0.488	–0.066
N4N	Not Hispanic, Asian	0.010	0.980	0.193	0.159	–0.162	–0.048
H8P	Hispanic, 2+ Races (SOR), Census Detail/SSA POB Match	0.010	0.990	–0.276	–0.083	–0.445	–0.216
N7N	Not Hispanic, 2+ Races (not SOR)	0.007	0.997	–0.193	0.016	–0.496	–0.012
H8N	Hispanic, 2+ Races (SOR)	0.003	1.000	–0.147	–0.081	–0.641	–0.129
URU	Uruguay | Sample Size = 11,500 | Hispanic = 0.913 | Census Detail/SSA POB Match = 0.843						
H1P	Hispanic, White, Census Detail/SSA POB Match	0.752	0.752	9.611	0.000	10.100	0.000
H6P	Hispanic, Some Other Race, Census Detail/SSA POB Match	0.075	0.827	–0.101	–0.073	–0.168	–0.098
N1N	Not Hispanic, White	0.066	0.894	0.238	0.144	0.453	0.171
H1N	Hispanic, White	0.058	0.951	0.167	0.007	–0.073	–0.006
H8P	Hispanic, 2+ Races (SOR), Census Detail/SSA POB Match	0.022	0.973	–0.202	–0.029	–0.334	–0.115

H6N	Hispanic, Some Other Race	0.013	0.987	–0.505	–0.122	–0.157	–0.100
XXX	All Other Responses	0.013	1.000	0.082	–0.023	0.097	–0.033
VEN	Venezuela | Sample Size = 78,000 | Hispanic = 0.891 | Census Detail/SSA POB Match = 0.814						
H1P	Hispanic, White, Census Detail/SSA POB Match	0.641	0.641	9.574	0.000	10.310	0.000
H6P	Hispanic, Some Other Race, Census Detail/SSA POB Match	0.126	0.766	–0.055	–0.071	–0.116	–0.112
N1N	Not Hispanic, White	0.077	0.843	0.406	0.116	0.332	0.109
H1N	Hispanic, White	0.056	0.899	0.202	0.023	0.018	0.011
H8P	Hispanic, 2+ Races (SOR), Census Detail/SSA POB Match	0.027	0.926	–0.151	–0.074	–0.171	–0.111
N4N	Not Hispanic, Asian	0.020	0.947	0.396	0.053	0.060	–0.099
H6N	Hispanic, Some Other Race	0.017	0.963	–0.013	–0.110	–0.273	–0.143
XXX	All Other Responses	0.014	0.978	0.176	–0.040	–0.012	–0.126
H2P	Hispanic, Black, Census Detail/SSA POB Match	0.013	0.990	0.060	–0.172	–0.335	–0.232
N6N	Not Hispanic, Some Other Race	0.006	0.997	–0.026	0.071	–0.366	–0.031
N2N	Not Hispanic, Black	0.003	1.000	0.322	–0.120	–0.315	–0.175
ALG	Algeria | Sample Size = 7,500 | Hispanic = 0.067						
N1N	Not Hispanic, White	0.627	0.627	9.418	0.000	10.230	0.000
N6N	Not Hispanic, Some Other Race	0.253	0.880	–0.360	–0.074	–0.366	–0.022
H1N	Hispanic, White	0.053	0.933	0.643	–0.070	0.190	0.048
N8N	Not Hispanic, 2+ Races (SOR)	0.027	0.960	0.084	–0.034	–0.118	–0.066
N2N	Not Hispanic, Black	0.020	0.980	0.325	–0.067	–0.269	–0.089
XXX	All Other Responses	0.020	1.000	0.638	–0.099	0.301	0.034
BAH	Bahrain | Sample Size = 2,800 | Hispanic = 0.014						
N4N	Not Hispanic, Asian	0.473	0.473	9.808	0.000	10.580	0.000
N1N	Not Hispanic, White	0.218	0.691	0.299	0.044	–0.028	0.024
N2N	Not Hispanic, Black	0.182	0.873	0.256	–0.156	–0.470	–0.261
XXX	All Other Responses	0.073	0.945	–0.004	–0.032	–0.193	0.012
N6N	Not Hispanic, Some Other Race	0.055	1.000	–0.302	–0.095	–0.356	–0.078
EGY	Egypt | Sample Size = 55,500 | Hispanic = 0.005 | Census Detail/SSA POB Match = 0.450						
N6P	Not Hispanic, Some Other Race, Census Detail/SSA POB Match	0.432	0.432	9.501	0.000	10.140	0.000
N1N	Not Hispanic, White	0.369	0.802	0.137	0.051	0.262	0.080

(continued)

Table 4.3 (cont.)

Row Label	Ethnicity—Race—SSA Census Detail/SSA POB Match	Proportion	Cumulative Proportion	Females: Mean Log Earnings	Females: Adjusted Log Earnings PCWH	Males: Mean Log Earnings	Males: Adjusted Log Earnings PCWH
N6N	Not Hispanic, Some Other Race	0.137	0.939	–0.061	0.046	0.095	0.058
N2N	Not Hispanic, Black	0.020	0.959	0.039	–0.111	–0.344	–0.112
N8P	Not Hispanic, 2+ Races (SOR), Census Detail/SSA POB Match	0.020	0.978	–0.217	–0.046	–0.267	–0.027
N8N	Not Hispanic, 2+ Races (SOR)	0.009	0.987	–0.085	0.049	–0.279	–0.070
N4N	Not Hispanic, Asian	0.006	0.994	0.354	0.070	0.290	0.059
XXX	All Other Responses	0.006	1.000	0.235	–0.165	–0.134	–0.145
IRN	Iran | Sample Size = 148,000 | Hispanic = 0.002 | Census Detail/SSA POB Match = 0.514						
N6P	Not Hispanic, Some Other Race, Census Detail/SSA POB Match	0.380	0.380	9.817	0.000	10.480	0.000
N1N	Not Hispanic, White	0.319	0.699	0.118	–0.014	0.115	–0.001
N8P	Not Hispanic, 2+ Races (SOR), Census Detail/SSA POB Match	0.136	0.834	–0.036	–0.030	–0.018	–0.044
N6N	Not Hispanic, Some Other Race	0.136	0.970	–0.143	–0.135	–0.626	–0.163
N8N	Not Hispanic, 2+ Races (SOR)	0.015	0.985	–0.175	–0.184	–0.614	–0.168
N4N	Not Hispanic, Asian	0.009	0.994	0.092	0.029	0.026	–0.039
XXX	All Other Responses	0.006	1.000	0.023	–0.198	–0.350	–0.245
IRQ	Iraq | Sample Size = 50,000 | Hispanic = 0.003 | Census Detail/SSA POB Match = 0.102						
N6N	Not Hispanic, Some Other Race	0.449	0.449	9.025	0.000	9.525	0.000
N1N	Not Hispanic, White	0.369	0.818	0.051	0.019	0.175	0.043
N6P	Not Hispanic, Some Other Race, Census Detail/SSA POB Match	0.068	0.886	–0.535	–0.011	–0.384	–0.040
N8N	Not Hispanic, 2+ Races (SOR)	0.056	0.942	–0.131	–0.060	–0.050	–0.050
N8P	Not Hispanic, 2+ Races (SOR), Census Detail/SSA POB Match	0.034	0.976	–0.483	–0.039	–0.080	–0.049
N4N	Not Hispanic, Asian	0.011	0.987	0.400	0.133	0.040	0.006
N7N	Not Hispanic, 2+ Races	0.009	0.996	–0.441	–0.052	0.053	–0.070
XXX	All Other Responses	0.004	1.000	–0.130	–0.136	–0.440	–0.110
ISR	Israel | Sample Size = 59,000 | Hispanic = 0.008 | Census Detail/SSA POB Match = 0.051						
N1N	Not Hispanic, White	0.796	0.796	9.616	0.000	10.440	0.000
N6N	Not Hispanic, Some Other Race	0.115	0.911	–0.508	–0.070	–0.720	–0.179

N6P	Not Hispanic, Some Other Race, Census Detail/SSA POB Match	0.044	0.955	−0.417	−0.106	−0.613	−0.119
N8N	Not Hispanic, 2+ Races (SOR)	0.020	0.975	−0.607	−0.152	−0.728	−0.225
XXX	All Other Responses	0.007	0.982	−0.226	−0.228	−0.830	−0.226
H1N	Hispanic, White	0.007	0.989	0.441	−0.067	0.044	−0.105
N4N	Not Hispanic, Asian	0.006	0.995	−0.476	−0.107	−0.590	−0.238
N8P	Not Hispanic, 2+ Races (SOR), Census Detail/SSA POB Match	0.005	1.000	−0.165	−0.176	−0.359	−0.153
JOR	Jordan | Sample Size = 30,000 | Hispanic = 0.003						
N1N	Not Hispanic, White	0.469	0.469	9.171	0.000	10.150	0.000
N6N	Not Hispanic, Some Other Race	0.419	0.888	−0.151	−0.016	−0.363	−0.052
N8N	Not Hispanic, 2+ Races (SOR)	0.090	0.978	−0.150	−0.104	−0.226	−0.083
N4N	Not Hispanic, Asian	0.013	0.992	−0.223	−0.055	−0.489	−0.074
XXX	All Other Responses	0.008	1.000	0.249	−0.060	−0.436	−0.158
KUW	Kuwait | Sample Size = 12,500 | Hispanic = 0.003						
N1N	Not Hispanic, White	0.392	0.392	9.443	0.000	10.380	0.000
N6N	Not Hispanic, Some Other Race	0.337	0.729	−0.068	−0.015	−0.304	−0.071
N4N	Not Hispanic, Asian	0.188	0.918	0.752	0.039	0.517	0.051
N8N	Not Hispanic, 2+ Races (SOR)	0.067	0.984	−0.324	−0.051	−0.132	−0.070
XXX	All Other Responses	0.016	1.000	−0.232	−0.035	−0.245	−0.166
LEB	Lebanon | Sample Size = 53,500 | Hispanic = 0.004 | Census Detail/SSA POB Match = 0.148						
N1N	Not Hispanic, White	0.583	0.583	9.647	0.000	10.620	0.000
N6N	Not Hispanic, Some Other Race	0.226	0.808	−0.065	−0.041	−0.343	−0.102
N6P	Not Hispanic, Some Other Race, Census Detail/SSA POB Match	0.117	0.925	−0.338	−0.072	−0.452	−0.123
N8P	Not Hispanic, 2+ Races (SOR), Census Detail/SSA POB Match	0.032	0.957	−0.236	−0.073	−0.247	−0.115
N8N	Not Hispanic, 2+ Races (SOR)	0.023	0.979	−0.057	−0.028	−0.269	−0.145
N4N	Not Hispanic, Asian	0.009	0.989	0.361	−0.157	−0.307	−0.321
XXX	All Other Responses	0.007	0.995	−0.140	−0.157	−0.629	−0.180
N2N	Not Hispanic, Black	0.005	1.000	0.412	−0.376	−0.400	−0.651
LIB	Libya | Sample Size = 5,400 | Hispanic = 0.019						
N1N	Not Hispanic, White	0.642	0.642	9.908	0.000	10.490	0.000
N6N	Not Hispanic, Some Other Race	0.174	0.817	−0.830	−0.029	−0.488	0.022
N4N	Not Hispanic, Asian	0.092	0.908	0.437	0.190	0.346	0.075

(continued)

Table 4.3 (cont.)

Row Label	Ethnicity—Race—SSA Census Detail/SSA POB Match	Proportion	Cumulative Proportion	Females: Mean Log Earnings	Females: Adjusted Log Earnings PCWH	Males: Mean Log Earnings	Males: Adjusted Log Earnings PCWH
N2N	Not Hispanic, Black	0.046	0.954	–0.110	–0.295	–0.336	–0.307
XXX	All Other Responses	0.046	1.000	0.128	–0.120	–0.084	–0.083
MOR	Morocco | Sample Size = 35,500 | Hispanic = 0.011 | SSA POB Match = 0.197						
N1N	Not Hispanic, White	0.536	0.536	9.453	0.000	10.160	0.000
N6N	Not Hispanic, Some Other Race	0.183	0.719	–0.328	–0.021	–0.325	–0.034
N6P	Not Hispanic, Some Other Race, Census Detail/SSA POB Match	0.181	0.900	–0.285	–0.031	–0.373	–0.064
N2N	Not Hispanic, Black	0.042	0.942	–0.141	–0.161	–0.352	–0.168
N8N	Not Hispanic, 2+ Races (SOR)	0.018	0.961	–0.147	–0.096	–0.429	–0.075
N8P	Not Hispanic, 2+ Races (SOR), Census Detail/SSA POB Match	0.016	0.976	–0.307	–0.071	–0.530	–0.128
N4N	Not Hispanic, Asian	0.008	0.984	–0.217	–0.005	–0.348	–0.079
H1N	Hispanic, White	0.008	0.993	0.498	–0.017	0.379	–0.026
XXX	All Other Responses	0.007	1.000	–0.171	–0.217	–0.258	–0.141
SAU	Saudi Arabia | Sample Size = 14,500 | Hispanic = 0.059						
N1N	Not Hispanic, White	0.486	0.486	9.853	0.000	10.660	0.000
N4N	Not Hispanic, Asian	0.162	0.648	0.096	–0.027	–0.010	–0.093
N6N	Not Hispanic, Some Other Race	0.155	0.803	–0.531	–0.023	–0.847	–0.123
N2N	Not Hispanic, Black	0.070	0.873	0.050	–0.294	–0.648	–0.414
N8N	Not Hispanic, 2+ Races (SOR)	0.042	0.915	–0.419	–0.171	–0.706	–0.085
H1N	Hispanic, White	0.032	0.947	–0.113	–0.297	–0.404	–0.321
H6N	Hispanic, Some Other Race	0.021	0.968	–0.264	–0.425	–0.620	–0.528
N7N	Not Hispanic, 2+ Races	0.021	0.989	0.082	–0.046	–0.406	–0.278
XXX	All Other Responses	0.011	1.000	–0.171	–0.275	–0.532	–0.431
SYR	Syria | Sample Size = 24,000 | Hispanic = 0.003 | Census Detail/SSA POB Match = 0.096						
N1N	Not Hispanic, White	0.561	0.561	9.319	0.000	10.520	0.000
N6N	Not Hispanic, Some Other Race	0.291	0.852	–0.059	–0.060	–0.268	–0.053

N6P	Not Hispanic, Some Other Race, Census Detail/SSA POB Match	0.067	0.919	–0.357	–0.050	–0.503	–0.107
N8N	Not Hispanic, 2+ Races (SOR)	0.037	0.956	–0.112	–0.139	–0.149	–0.045
N8P	Not Hispanic, 2+ Races (SOR), Census Detail/SSA POB Match	0.027	0.983	–0.284	–0.046	–0.343	–0.047
N4N	Not Hispanic, Asian	0.008	0.992	0.131	–0.204	–0.158	–0.070
XXX	All Other Responses	0.008	1.000	–0.005	–0.199	–0.279	–0.118
TUN	Tunisia | Sample Size = 3,400 | Hispanic = 0.006						
N1N	Not Hispanic, White	0.559	0.559	9.688	0.000	10.260	0.000
N6N	Not Hispanic, Some Other Race	0.353	0.912	–0.041	–0.008	–0.606	–0.106
XXX	All Other Responses	0.088	1.000	0.208	–0.053	–0.203	–0.171
YEM	Yemen | Sample Size = 9,500 | Hispanic = 0.004						
N6N	Not Hispanic, Some Other Race	0.561	0.561	8.160	0.000	9.396	0.000
N1N	Not Hispanic, White	0.212	0.772	0.324	0.106	0.218	0.032
N8N	Not Hispanic, 2+ Races (SOR)	0.148	0.921	–0.210	0.038	0.118	–0.029
N4N	Not Hispanic, Asian	0.058	0.979	1.262	0.048	0.318	0.048
XXX	All Other Responses	0.021	1.000	1.154	–0.135	0.052	–0.029

Notes: This table uses Sample 1, which consists of 87.97 million workers age 25 to 55 (inclusive) in 2010. All workers must have at least one year with positive earnings during the six-year period from 2010 to 2015. Zero-earnings years are included in the earnings measures. Place of birth is determined using the Census Numident. The race measure consists of eight categories collated from the 2010 Census: White, Black, American Indian/Alaska Native (AIAN), Asian, Native Hawaiian/Pacific Islander, Some Other Race (SOR), 2+ Races (not SOR), and 2+ Races (SOR). The ethnicity variable is binary; Hispanic/Latino or Not Hispanic/Latino. A "Census Detail/SSA POB Match" occurs when the 2010 Census respondent reported their Census Numident POB on the 2010 Race or Ethnicity questions using the detailed coding (the detailed Decennial POB coding is not available for 8 MENA countries). For both females and males we report four measures of mean log real long-term earnings. The first row of the Mean Log Earnings column for each POB group shows the mean log earnings of the largest Ethnicity-Race-Census Detail/SSA POB Match category, while the other rows report the difference in mean log earnings relative to the largest category. The next three columns show adjusted earnings from linear regression models controlling for various person and job characteristics. The "PC" model includes controls for education and quadratic functions of age and years in the United States in 2010. The "PCW" model adds controls for the dominant industry/region and the number of full and partial years worked. The "PCWH" model adds a quadratic function of average annual hours worked. Standard errors have not been released yet for this table. Some sub-groups have fewer than 1,000 persons. Even for small sub-groups, standard errors for adjusted log earnings differentials rarely exceed 0.025 log points.

and the sub-group that self-identified as 2+ Races (SOR), i.e., including Some Other Race (MEX H8P, 2.8 percent), have slightly lower adjusted log earnings for both females and males. Notice also that the sub-group that self-identifies as Hispanic and White but does not check or write-in Mexico on the 2010 Census (MEX H1N, 1.3 percent) is indistinguishable from the reference sub-group (less than 0.01 log point difference in adjusted log earnings for females and males). Similarly, the sub-group that self-identifies as Hispanic and Some Other Race but does not select or write-in Mexico on the 2010 Census (MEX H6N, 1.3 percent) is indistinguishable from those that self-identified as Hispanic, Some Other Race, and did check or write-in Mexico (again, less than –0.01 log point difference in adjusted earnings).

Prior research strongly suggests that all five of the top sub-groups (MEX H1P-H1N)—97.5 percent of all Mexican immigrants—will self-identify as Hispanic or Hispanic and White, and probably select the Mexican checkbox on the proposed single-question SPD 15 (Mathews et al. 2017, table 5). About half of persons who self-identified as Hispanic can be expected to self-identify as Hispanic alone in the single-question format. Only a negligible percentage can be expected to self-identify as Hispanic and Some Other Race. If so, then the race and ethnicity information on Mexican immigrants from the single-question format will lose some granularity—the difference between those who self-identify Hispanic and White versus Hispanic and Some Other Race in the two-question format.[23] Our results suggest the magnitude of this heterogeneity is not large for Mexican-born immigrants. For Mexican-born females who self-identify as Hispanic, Some Other Race, the adjusted difference is –0.033 log points (MEX H6N) compared to the unadjusted difference of –0.583 log points between Hispanic, White, Mexican-born females and Not Hispanic, White US-born females (Table 4.3 MEX H1P—Table 4.2 USA N1N). For Mexican-born males who self-identify as Hispanic, Some Other Race, the adjusted difference is –0.041 log points (MEX H6N) compared to the unadjusted difference of –0.360 log points between Hispanic, White, Mexican-born and Not Hispanic, White US-born males (Table 4.3 MEX H1P—Table 4.2 USA N1N).

The second most populous group of foreign-born Hispanics in Sample 1 is those born in Puerto Rico. Before discussing these results, we remind the reader that all persons living in the Commonwealth of Puerto Rico

23. We remind the reader that there is no social-political construct behind the category Some Other Race. We call out the distinction here because the choice "Hispanic, Some Other Race" is allowed under both the 1997 and 2024 revisions of SPD 15, but the 1997 requirement to answer a separate question about Hispanic ethnicity has been eliminated in the 2024 revision. Most published historical tables embody the coding rules discussed in the introduction. While we did not use those coding rules, we did tabulate results for individuals who complied with the 1997 format and separately answered Some Other Race. Mathews et al. 2017 shows that virtually no one who selects Hispanic in the single-question format will also select Some Other Race. Hence, a recoding of historical data might eliminate the Some Other Race response for these individuals.

are eligible for US Social Security numbers; however, only those living in the United States are included in our universe. (We did not use the recently added Puerto Rican data in the LEHD infrastructure files.)

Essentially all Puerto Rican-born US residents self-identify as Hispanic (PR, 96.8 percent). The largest sub-group, hence, our reference sub-group, self-identify as Hispanic, White, and checked or wrote-in Puerto Rico in the race or ethnicity responses on the 2010 Census (PR H1P, 59.7 percent). In terms of adjusted log earnings differentials, there is more heterogeneity among the Puerto Rican-born immigrants in our Sample 1. First, note that a substantial percentage self-identify as Hispanic, Black, and check or write-in Puerto Rico (PR H2P, 6.5 percent). This group has substantially lower adjusted log earnings (PR H2P, –0.134 log points for females and –0.131 log points for males) than the reference sub-group (PR H1P). Second, the second largest sub-group—those who self-identify as Hispanic, Some Other Race, and checked or wrote-in Puerto Rico (PR H6P, 23.8 percent); and the fourth largest sub-group—those who self-identified as Hispanic, 2+ Races including Some Other Race, and checked or wrote-in Puerto Rico (PR H8P, 2.5 percent); and the seventh largest sub-group—those who self-identify as Hispanic, Some Other Race, but did not check or write-in Puerto Rico (PR H6N, 1.3 percent)—have at least –0.049 log point lower adjusted long-term earnings for females and males than the reference sub-group (PR H1P). Finally, we note that Puerto Rican-born immigrants who self-identified as Hispanic and White but who did not check or write-in Puerto Rico (PR H1N, 1.8 percent) have slightly larger adjusted log earnings than the reference group (0.027 log points for females and 0.023 log points for males compared to PR H1P).

Because Puerto Ricans who self-identify as Hispanic and Black have substantially different long-term real earnings than Puerto Ricans who self-identify as Hispanic and White, Some Other Race or 2+ Races (SOR), the likely consequences of using the single-question format are more difficult to predict. If most of the Puerto Rican-born persons who self-identified as Hispanic and Black in the two-question format continue to do so in the single-question format, then future analysts will be able to study their distinct labor market outcomes. But if most elect to self-identify as Hispanic alone, then decompositions like the ones we do in this paper will no longer be possible. Previous research has shown that approximately the same percentage of those who self-identify as Hispanic will also self-identify as Hispanic and Black in either the single-question or two-question format (Mathews et al. 2017, table 7). Essentially no Hispanics self-identify as Hispanic and Some Other Race in the single-question format (ibid., table 7).

The third most populous group of foreign-born Hispanics in Sample 1 was born in El Salvador (ELS). Within this group the largest sub-group and, hence, our reference sub-group is persons who self-identify as Hispanic, Some Other Race, and either checked or wrote in El Salvador on the 2010 Census (ELS H6P, 46.5 percent). Only two sub-groups within El Salvador have markedly different adjusted long-term earnings differentials. As we saw for Puerto Rican–born persons, El Salvadorian immigrants who self-identify as Hispanic, Black, and checked or wrote in El Salvador (ELS H2P) had lower adjusted log earnings than the reference group (–0.084 log points for females and –0.082 log points for males). Those who self-identify as Not Hispanic, White, and did not check or write-in El Salvador (ELS N1N) have adjusted differentials of 0.170 log points for both females and males, indicating that they closely resemble US-born persons who identify as Not Hispanic and White.

The expected consequences of switching from the two-question to the single-question format for El Salvadorian immigrants are similar to the consequences for Puerto Ricans. We expect those who self-identified as Not Hispanic and White would continue to do so. The uncertainty surrounds those who would self-identify as Hispanic and Black or White vs. Hispanic alone.

The fourth most populous group of foreign-born Hispanics in Sample 1 was born in Cuba (CUB). Within this group the largest sub-group and, hence, our reference sub-group self-identified as Hispanic, White, and checked or wrote in Cuba (CUB H1P, 87.7 percent). The heterogeneity of adjusted long-term earnings is much stronger within the Cuban immigrants. Those who self-identified as Hispanic, Black, and checked or wrote in Cuba have lower adjusted earnings (CUB H2P, –0.162 log points for females and –0.144 log points for males). Those who self-identified as Not Hispanic, White, and did not check or write in Cuba had higher adjusted earnings but not as high as in most other immigrant groups (CUB N1N, 0.097 log points for females and 0.092 log points for males).

The expected consequences of switching to the single-question format are again similar to Puerto Rico, but potentially more pronounced. More heterogeneity is masked for individuals who self-identify as Hispanic alone.

Immigrants from all countries classified as Hispanic in this paper who self-identified as Not Hispanic and White rarely listed their birth country, as recorded on their Social Security number applications, as one of the detailed checkbox or write-in responses on the 2010 Census. Immigrants from the Hispanic source countries used in this paper who self-identified as Not Hispanic, White, and checked or wrote in the same country as their SSA place of birth are therefore in the "All Other Responses" category of our tables because of this paucity of data. We do show data for immigrants from Hispanic countries who self-identified as Not Hispanic and White but did not include their birth country in either the checkboxes or write-ins on the 2010 Census for the larger origin-country populations. Except for those born in Spain, immigrants born in the countries we labeled Hispanic who self-identified as Not Hispanic and White had unadjusted and adjusted long-term earnings differences compared to those who self-identified as Hispanic and White or Hispanic and Some Other Race that were similar to those of US-born persons who self-identified as Not Hispanic and White compared to US-born persons who self-identified as Hispanic and White. With respect to characterizing labor market outcomes for immigrants, therefore, there is some information in the self-declaration Not Hispanic and White for those born in countries we classified as Hispanic. Although the data are sparser, a similar pattern holds for those born in Hispanic countries who self-identify as Not Hispanic and Asian. The pattern is less clear for those born in these countries who self-identify as Not Hispanic and Black. Our results suggest that these differences would still be estimable under the single-question format.

Summarizing the results for MENA immigrants is not as complicated by comparisons of the single-question and two-questions formats because in the current two-question format self-identifying as MENA requires using a checkbox or write-in within one of the five official race categories or Some Other Race. That said, the same estimated percentage of persons self-identify as MENA alone in either format (Mathews et al. 2017, table 5). Only limited information was published about the combinations of MENA and other race groups in the results of the 2015 National Content Test that we have been citing. Very few MENA immigrants self-identify as Hispanic. The largest proportion of MENA-born persons self-identifying as Hispanic immigrated from Algeria (ALG, 6.7 percent) and the smallest from Iran (IRN, 0.2 percent). Only in Algeria, Israel, Morocco, and Saudi Arabia did any sub-groups including self-identified Hispanics meet the population threshold for inclusion in our tables. Consequently, the discussion of results for MENA-born immigrants focuses exclusively on those who self-identified as Not Hispanic.

The largest MENA-born immigrant group in Sample 1 was born in Iran. Among Iranian immigrants, the largest sub-group and, hence, our reference sub-group, self-identifies as Not Hispanic, Some Other Race, and checked or wrote in Iran on the 2010 Census (IRN N6P, 38.0 percent). The second largest sub-group self-identifies as Not Hispanic, White, and did not check or write in Iran (IRN N1N, 31.9 percent). The differences in adjusted long-term earnings between these first two sub-groups are small (–0.014 for females and –0.001 for males). The next largest sub-group self-identified as Not Hispanic, 2+ Races (SOR), and either checked or wrote in Iran (IRN N8P, 13.6 percent). The differences in adjusted long-term earnings relative to the reference sub-group may be larger for this sub-group (–0.030 log points for females and –0.044 log points for males). The fourth largest sub-group self-identifies as Not Hispanic, Some Other Race, and did not check or write in Iran (IRN N6N, 13.6 percent). For this sub-group the differences in adjusted long-term earnings are pronounced (–0.135 log points for females and –0.163 for males). Similarly, the next largest sub-group, which identifies as Not Hispanic, 2+ Races (SOR), and did not check or write in Iran (IRN N8N 1.5 percent), also has large differences in adjusted long-term earnings (–0.184 for females and –0.168 for males).

Since MENA self-identifications can only occur via checkboxes and write-ins in the current two-question format, the striking difference in sub-groups noted for Iranian immigrants is likely to present some challenges in the proposed single-question format for the style of comparisons used in this paper. When there is no explicit MENA category (as in the current two-question format), 80.7 percent of Iranians self-identify as White, 13.8 percent as Some Other Race, with the balance in one of the other current categories (Black, American Indian/Alaska Native, Asian, or Native Hawaiian/Pacific Islander) (Mathews et al. 2017, table 22). Conversely, when there is a MENA category (as in the proposed single-question format), only 14.7 percent of Iranians self-identify as White, while 85.0 percent self-identify as MENA, and only 2.1 percent self-identify as Some Other Race (ibid. table 22). The marked differences in adjusted long-term earnings that we find between Iranian immigrants who self-identified as White or Some Other Race *and indicated Iran in the checkboxes or write-ins*, compared to those who self-identified as Some Other Race (either alone or in combination) *and did not indicate Iran in the checkboxes or write-ins* will probably not be detectable in the single-question format without ancillary information on place of birth.

The second largest MENA-born group in Sample 1 was born in Israel. Among Israeli immigrants, the largest sub-group and, hence, our reference sub-group, self-identified as Not Hispanic, White, and did not check or write in Israel (ISR N1N, 79.6 percent). Very few Israeli-born immigrants checked or wrote in Israel (only ISR N6P, 4.4 percent, and ISR N8P, 0.5 percent). The second largest sub-group self-identified as Not Hispanic, Some Other Race, and did not check or write in Israel (SR N6N 11.5 percent). There are large differences in adjusted long-term earnings between this sub-group and the reference sub-group (–0.070 log points for females and –0.179 log points for females). We find even larger differences in adjusted long-term earnings for the other sub-groups of Israeli immigrants that self-identified as Not Hispanic and Some Other Race in any form.

The large differences in adjusted long-term earnings between Israelis who self-identify as White and those who self-identify as Some Other Race may also be difficult to detect in the proposed single-question format. When self-identified Israelis responded to the race question with no MENA category, 90.9 percent self-identified as White and 4.8 percent as Some Other Race. When there was a MENA category, only 49.6 percent self-identified as White, while 38.9 percent self-identified as MENA, and 10.6 percent self-identified as Some Other Race. (Mathews et al. 2017, table 22).

The third largest MENA-born immigrant group in Sample 1 is Egyptian. Among Egyptian immigrants the largest sub-group and, hence, our reference sub-group, self-identified as Not Hispanic, Some Other Race, and checked or wrote in Egypt (EGY N6P, 43.2 percent). The second largest sub-group self-identified as Not Hispanic, White and did not check or write in Egypt (EGY N1N, 36.9 percent). For this sub-group adjusted long-term earnings differentials were meaningful but not large (0.051 log points for females and 0.080 log points for males). Interestingly, the third largest sub-group, which self-identified as Not Hispanic, Some Other Race, and did not check or write in Egypt (EGY N6N, 13.7 percent), had adjusted long-term earnings differentials that were very similar to the White sub-group (0.046 log points for females and 0.058 log points for males). In contrast, the fourth largest sub-group, which self-identified as Not Hispanic, Black, and did not check or write-in Egypt (EGY N2N, 2.0 percent), had large, negative long-term earnings differentials (–0.111 log points for females and –0.112 log points for males).

When answering in the two-question format, 91.0 percent of self-identified Egyptians chose the White category, 2.3 percent chose Black, and 2.3 percent chose Some Other Race (Mathews et al. 2017, table 22). In the single-question format, 91.5 percent chose MENA, 8.4 percent chose White, and 2.3 percent chose Some Other Race (ibid.). If these choices carry over to the proposed single-question format, the adjusted earnings differentials between those who self-identify as White or Some Other Race and those who self-identify as Black will no longer be estimable even if immigrant country of origin information is available. Since more than half of Egyptian immigrants did not self-identify as Egyptian in their census responses, this may not be a serious limitation unless the presence of a MENA category in the single-question format results in a greater proportion of Egyptian immigrants choosing MENA alone.

The fourth largest MENA-born immigrant group is Lebanese. Among Lebanese immigrants, the largest sub-group and, hence, our reference category, self-identified as Not Hispanic, White, and did not check or write in Lebanese (LEB N1N, 58.3 percent). The second largest sub-group self-identified as Not Hispanic, Some Other Race, and did not check or write in Lebanese (LEB N6N, 22.6 percent). Long-term earnings differentials in the second sub-group are substantial for males (–0.041 log points for females and –0.102 log points for males). The third largest sub-group self-identified as Not Hispanic, Some Other Race, but did check or write in Lebanese (LEB N6P, 11.7 percent). Long-term earnings differentials for this third sub-group, which only differs from the second sub-group by self-identifying as Lebanese, were substantial (–0.072 log points for females and –0.123 log points for males). The fourth largest sub-group self-identified as Not Hispanic, 2+ Races (SOR) (LEB N8P, 3.2 percent). This sub-group is indistinguishable from the third sub-group in the magnitude of long-term earnings differentials (–0.073 log points for females and –0.115 log point for male). Finally, we note that Lebanese immigrants who self-identify as Not Hispanic, Black, and did not check or write in Lebanese are a small portion of the total (LEB N2N, 0.5 percent) but have enormous negative adjusted long-term earnings differentials (–0.376 log points for females and –0.651 log points for males).

When answering in the two-question format, 91.7 percent of self-identified Lebanese chose White, while only 1.9 percent chose Some Other Race, and too few chose Black to measure reliably (Mathews et al. 2017, table 22). In the single-question format, 34.0 percent chose White, and 69.0 percent chose MENA (ibid.). Like the Egyptian-born immigrants, most Lebanese-born immigrants do not self-identify as Lebanese in the current two-question format. Hence, it is difficult to predict the consequences of the proposed single-question format on these immigrants.

We now turn to table 4.4. Given the results discussed above for first-generation immigrants (workers born abroad), another population of interest is second-generation immigrants (workers born in the United States, with at least one parent born abroad). For second-generation workers we would like to understand how similar their responses and earnings across ethnicity-race-SSA POB Match categories are to those of first-generation immigrants from the same POB group. Another useful comparison group we also use is to the same ethnicity-race third-generation and above native-born workers.

Identifying second-generation workers is more complicated than identifying first-generation workers and requires additional information on the place of birth of the biological parents. We use responses from the parents on the 2000 Decennial Census to identify the biological parents when the sample member was 15 to 18 years old. At that point in time either one, two, or no biological parents may be present in the home. We retain in Sample 2 workers with at least one biological parent in the home. For a worker to be in the Hispanic group, the person must have had one Hispanic-born parent in the home; two parents in the home, one of whom is from a Hispanic source country; or two parents in the home, both of whom are from a Hispanic source country. The MENA and Other Foreign-Born groups are processed similarly. We have a final category that captures the remaining possibilities, where for example one parent is from the Hispanic group and another parent is from the MENA group.

Family structure at the age of the respondent in 2000 (15–18) matters for the responses received on the ethnicity and race questions. For example, workers with one foreign-born parent and one US-born parent are noticeably more likely to report Not Hispanic, White (2P1FBH N1N), the largest category for third-generation and above workers. For MENA workers with one foreign-born and one US-born parent, the percentage of workers who report in the largest category Not Hispanic, White is 80.3 percent in table 4.4 (2P1MENA N1N), while for workers with two MENA parents the equivalent percentage is 44.8 percent (2MENA N1N). We also find a relatively large difference in the proportion of self-identified Not Hispanic, White between the Other Foreign Born parent groups (2P1OFB N1N 78.1 per-

Table 4.4 **Mean log long-term average annual earnings by sex, place of birth of parent(s), ethnicity, race, and Census Detail/SSA POB match**

Row Label	Ethnicity—Race—Census Detail/SSA POB Match	Proportion	Cumulative Proportion	Females: Mean Log Earnings	Females: Adjusted Log Earnings PCWH	Males: Mean Log Earnings	Males: Adjusted Log Earnings PCWH
1FBH	Single Foreign-Born Hispanic Parent | Sample Size = 115,000 | Hispanic = 0.948 | Census Detail/SSA POB Match = 0.848						
H1P	Hispanic, White, Census Detail/SSA POB Match	0.429	0.429	9.619	0.000	9.792	0.000
H6P	Hispanic, Some Other Race, Census Detail/SSA POB Match	0.355	0.785	–0.072	–0.030	–0.027	–0.020
H1N	Hispanic, White	0.049	0.834	–0.059	0.004	–0.149	0.002
H6N	Hispanic, Some Other Race	0.040	0.874	–0.127	–0.006	–0.162	–0.023
N1N	Not Hispanic, White	0.039	0.913	–0.030	0.133	–0.035	0.123
H8P	Hispanic, 2+ Races (SOR), Census Detail/SSA POB Match	0.027	0.940	–0.073	–0.025	–0.128	–0.022
H2P	Hispanic, Black, Census Detail/SSA POB Match	0.023	0.963	0.002	–0.113	–0.199	–0.090
XXX	All Other Responses	0.016	0.980	–0.055	–0.005	–0.124	–0.026
H3P	Hispanic, AIAN, Census Detail/SSA POB Match	0.009	0.988	–0.212	–0.075	–0.169	–0.047
N2N	Not Hispanic, Black	0.008	0.996	–0.298	–0.031	–0.470	–0.037
H8N	Hispanic, 2+ Races (SOR)	0.004	1.000	–0.078	–0.014	–0.314	–0.021
2P1FBH	Two Parents, One Foreign-Born Hispanic, One Born USA | Sample Size = 97,500 | Hispanic = 0.805 | Census Detail/SSA POB Match = 0.738						
H1P	Hispanic, White, Census Detail/SSA POB Match	0.484	0.484	9.737	0.000	10.010	0.000
H6P	Hispanic, Some Other Race, Census Detail/SSA POB Match	0.190	0.674	–0.166	–0.044	–0.117	–0.048
N1N	Not Hispanic, White	0.175	0.849	0.037	0.128	–0.016	0.123
H1N	Hispanic, White	0.043	0.892	–0.133	–0.001	–0.088	–0.012
H8P	Hispanic, 2+ Races (SOR), Census Detail/SSA POB Match	0.033	0.925	–0.127	–0.018	–0.166	–0.030
H6N	Hispanic, Some Other Race	0.022	0.947	–0.286	–0.038	–0.240	–0.053
XXX	All Other Responses	0.017	0.964	–0.136	0.017	–0.277	–0.006
H2P	Hispanic, Black, Census Detail/SSA POB Match	0.012	0.976	0.062	–0.129	–0.236	–0.140
N2N	Not Hispanic, Black	0.010	0.987	–0.165	–0.037	–0.566	–0.068
H3P	Hispanic, AIAN, Census Detail/SSA POB Match	0.008	0.995	–0.225	–0.061	–0.261	–0.031
H7P	Hispanic, 2+ Races (not SOR), Census Detail/SSA POB Match	0.005	1.000	–0.088	–0.008	–0.091	–0.041

(*continued*)

Table 4.4 **(cont.)**

Row Label	Ethnicity—Race—Census Detail/SSA POB Match	Proportion	Cumulative Proportion	Females: Mean Log Earnings	Females: Adjusted Log Earnings PCWH	Males: Mean Log Earnings	Males: Adjusted Log Earnings PCWH
2FBH	Two Foreign-Born Hispanic Parents | Sample Size = 167,000 | Hispanic = 0.976 | Census Detail/SSA POB Match = 0.922						
H1P	Hispanic, White, Census Detail/SSA POB Match	0.493	0.493	9.809	0.000	9.995	0.000
H6P	Hispanic, Some Other Race, Census Detail/SSA POB Match	0.388	0.880	–0.093	–0.029	–0.027	–0.018
H1N	Hispanic, White	0.029	0.909	–0.065	–0.008	–0.224	–0.014
H6N	Hispanic, Some Other Race	0.023	0.933	–0.198	–0.039	–0.204	–0.018
H8P	Hispanic, 2+ Races (SOR), Census Detail/SSA POB Match	0.021	0.954	–0.138	–0.019	–0.047	–0.009
N1N	Not Hispanic, White	0.017	0.971	–0.013	0.106	–0.147	0.086
H2P	Hispanic, Black, Census Detail/SSA POB Match	0.010	0.981	–0.084	–0.124	–0.254	–0.112
XXX	All Other Responses	0.010	0.990	–0.121	–0.004	–0.164	0.006
H3P	Hispanic, AIAN, Census Detail/SSA POB Match	0.007	0.998	–0.044	–0.056	–0.102	–0.057
H7P	Hispanic, 2+ Races (not SOR), Census Detail/SSA POB Match	0.002	1.000	0.187	–0.030	–0.150	–0.039
1MENA	Single Middle East and North Africa Parent | Sample Size = 5,800 | Hispanic = 0.026 | Census Detail/SSA POB Match = 0.172						
N1N	Not Hispanic, White	0.522	0.522	9.835	0.000	9.962	0.000
N6N	Not Hispanic, Some Other Race	0.226	0.748	–0.060	–0.042	–0.208	–0.063
N6P	Not Hispanic, Some Other Race, Census Detail/SSA POB Match	0.139	0.887	0.197	0.047	0.131	0.072
XXX	All Other Responses	0.113	1.000	0.060	–0.073	–0.168	–0.069
2P1MENA	Two Parents, One MENA, One Born United States | Sample Size = 12,500 | Hispanic = 0.036 | Census Detail/SSA POB Match = 0.072						
N1N	Not Hispanic, White	0.803	0.803	9.992	0.000	10.180	0.000
XXX	All Other Responses	0.080	0.884	–0.111	–0.120	–0.178	–0.109
N6N	Not Hispanic, Some Other Race	0.064	0.948	–0.033	–0.020	–0.148	–0.044
N6P	Not Hispanic, Some Other Race, Census Detail/SSA POB Match	0.052	1.000	–0.092	0.022	–0.024	0.008
2MENA	Two Middle East and North Africa Parents | Sample Size = 12,500 | Hispanic = 0.000 | Census Detail/SSA POB Match = 0.216						
N1N	Not Hispanic, White	0.448	0.448	10.020	0.000	10.190	0.000
N6N	Not Hispanic, Some Other Race	0.304	0.752	–0.150	–0.061	–0.205	–0.050

N6P	Not Hispanic, Some Other Race, Census Detail/SSA POB Match	0.184	0.936	0.249	0.074	0.085	0.030
XXX	All Other Responses	0.036	0.972	–0.154	–0.085	–0.075	–0.008
N8P	Not Hispanic, 2+ Races (SOR), Census Detail/SSA POB Match	0.028	1.000	0.226	–0.002	0.176	0.120
1OFB	Single Other Foreign-Born Parent | Sample Size = 100,000 | Hispanic = 0.037						
N1N	Not Hispanic, White	0.389	0.389	9.724	0.000	9.949	0.000
N4N	Not Hispanic, Asian	0.269	0.659	0.470	0.054	0.191	0.009
N2N	Not Hispanic, Black	0.195	0.853	0.028	–0.159	–0.456	–0.158
N7N	Not Hispanic, 2+ Races (not SOR)	0.060	0.913	0.116	–0.013	0.001	–0.021
N6N	Not Hispanic, Some Other Race	0.027	0.940	0.082	–0.126	–0.302	–0.103
H1N	Hispanic, White	0.016	0.956	–0.082	–0.128	–0.113	–0.131
XXX	All Other Responses	0.013	0.969	–0.110	–0.171	–0.418	–0.132
N8N	Not Hispanic, 2+ Races (SOR)	0.011	0.980	0.028	–0.015	–0.168	–0.017
N5N	Not Hispanic, Native Hawaiian/Pacific Islander	0.008	0.989	–0.291	–0.088	–0.288	–0.102
H6N	Hispanic, Some Other Race	0.007	0.996	–0.221	–0.164	–0.189	–0.139
H8N	Hispanic, 2+ Races (SOR)	0.004	1.000	–0.167	–0.164	–0.123	–0.124
2P1OFB	Two Parents, One Other Foreign Born, One Born United States | Sample Size = 237,000 | Hispanic = 0.031						
N1N	Not Hispanic, White	0.781	0.781	9.893	0.000	10.160	0.000
N7N	Not Hispanic, 2+ Races	0.084	0.865	0.058	–0.012	–0.057	–0.012
N2N	Not Hispanic, Black	0.046	0.912	–0.142	–0.168	–0.545	–0.162
N4N	Not Hispanic, Asian	0.035	0.947	0.245	0.007	0.073	–0.007
H1N	Hispanic, White	0.017	0.964	–0.081	–0.110	–0.239	–0.138
XXX	All Other Responses	0.010	0.974	–0.298	–0.151	–0.291	–0.163
N6N	Not Hispanic, Some Other Race	0.008	0.982	–0.133	–0.039	–0.272	–0.046
N8N	Not Hispanic, 2+ Races (SOR)	0.008	0.990	–0.122	–0.051	–0.300	–0.021
H6N	Hispanic, Some Other Race	0.004	0.994	–0.239	–0.166	–0.193	–0.146
N5N	Not Hispanic, Native Hawaiian/Pacific Islander	0.003	0.997	–0.257	–0.096	–0.387	–0.116
H7N	Hispanic, 2+ Races	0.003	1.000	–0.029	–0.145	–0.106	–0.130

(continued)

Table 4.4 (cont.)

Row Label	Ethnicity—Race—Census Detail/SSA POB Match	Proportion	Cumulative Proportion	Females: Mean Log Earnings	Females: Adjusted Log Earnings PCWH	Males: Mean Log Earnings	Males: Adjusted Log Earnings PCWH
2OFB	Two Other Foreign-Born Parents | Sample Size = 174,000 | Hispanic = 0.001						
N4N	Not Hispanic, Asian	0.611	0.611	10.350	0.000	10.320	0.000
N1N	Not Hispanic, White	0.211	0.823	–0.210	–0.067	–0.035	–0.014
N2N	Not Hispanic, Black	0.091	0.914	–0.312	–0.237	–0.487	–0.203
N7N	Not Hispanic, 2+ Races	0.036	0.950	–0.171	–0.040	–0.104	–0.015
N6N	Not Hispanic, Some Other Race	0.023	0.973	–0.291	–0.159	–0.356	–0.101
N5N	Not Hispanic Pacific Islander	0.010	0.983	–0.863	–0.175	–0.572	–0.105
N8N	Not Hispanic, 2+ Races (SOR)	0.010	0.993	–0.251	–0.067	–0.143	–0.027
XXX	All Other Responses	0.007	1.000	–0.453	–0.229	–0.327	–0.178
1PUS	Single US-Born Parent | Sample Size = 1,889,000 | Hispanic = 0.073						
N1N	Not Hispanic, White	0.675	0.675	9.546	0.000	9.860	0.000
N2N	Not Hispanic, Black	0.219	0.894	–0.253	–0.158	–0.733	–0.137
H1N	Hispanic, White	0.043	0.937	–0.099	–0.125	–0.151	–0.120
H6N	Hispanic, Some Other Race	0.018	0.955	–0.235	–0.159	–0.249	–0.153
N7N	Not Hispanic, 2+ Races	0.013	0.968	–0.184	–0.045	–0.303	–0.044
N3N	Not Hispanic, American Indian/Alaska Native	0.011	0.979	–0.574	–0.082	–0.729	–0.064
XXX	All Other Responses	0.008	0.988	–0.164	–0.105	–0.275	–0.083
N6N	Not Hispanic, Some Other Race	0.005	0.992	–0.340	–0.074	–0.488	–0.047
H8N	Hispanic, 2+ Races (SOR)	0.004	0.997	–0.215	–0.164	–0.301	–0.139
H2N	Hispanic, Black	0.003	1.000	–0.190	–0.250	–0.540	–0.214
2US	Two US-Born Parents | Sample Size = 4,374,000 | Hispanic = 0.037						
N1N	Not Hispanic, White	0.882	0.882	9.836	0.000	10.180	0.000
N2N	Not Hispanic, Black	0.060	0.942	–0.218	–0.185	–0.645	–0.162

H1N	Hispanic, White	0.025	0.968	–0.162	–0.138	–0.201	–0.141
N7N	Not Hispanic, 2+ Races	0.008	0.976	–0.226	–0.049	–0.287	–0.056
XXX	All Other Responses	0.008	0.984	–0.199	–0.132	–0.289	–0.122
H6N	Hispanic, Some Other Race	0.007	0.991	–0.313	–0.179	–0.287	–0.178
N3N	Not Hispanic, American Indian/Alaska Native	0.006	0.997	–0.572	–0.093	–0.612	–0.078
N6N	Not Hispanic, Some Other Race	0.003	1.000	–0.299	–0.055	–0.344	–0.031
2PDFB	Two Parents, Each Parent in a Different Foreign-Born Group | Sample Size = 12,000 | Hispanic = 0.483 | Census Detail/SSA POB Match = 0.45						
N1N	Not Hispanic, White	0.331	0.331	9.955	0.000	10.060	0.000
H1P	Hispanic, White, Census Detail/SSA POB Match	0.220	0.551	0.061	–0.157	0.067	–0.127
XXX	All Other Responses	0.102	0.653	0.050	–0.149	–0.089	–0.110
H6P	Hispanic, Some Other Race, Census Detail/SSA POB Match	0.093	0.746	–0.147	–0.218	–0.085	–0.209
N6N	Not Hispanic, Some Other Race	0.055	0.801	–0.016	–0.038	0.014	–0.042
H8P	Hispanic, 2+ Races (SOR), Census Detail/SSA POB Match	0.051	0.852	–0.014	–0.164	–0.079	–0.146
N4N	Not Hispanic, Asian	0.047	0.898	0.392	–0.004	0.275	0.025
H4P	Not Hispanic, Asian, Census Detail/SSA POB Match	0.038	0.936	0.143	–0.195	0.124	–0.150
N2N	Not Hispanic, Black	0.034	0.970	0.157	–0.194	–0.258	–0.231
H1N	Hispanic, White	0.030	1.000	0.092	–0.184	–0.152	–0.184

Notes: This table uses Sample 2, which consists of 7.196 million native born workers age 25 to 28 (inclusive) in 2010. All workers must have at least one year with positive earnings during the six-year period from 2010 to 2015. Zero-earnings years are included in the earnings measures. The worker and their parent's POB are determined using the Census Numident. The parents are identified using the family structure information on the 2000 Census. The race measure consists of eight categories collated from the 2010 Census: White, Black, American Indian/Alaska Native (AIAN), Asian, Native Hawaiian/Pacific Islander, Some Other Race (SOR), 2+ Races (not SOR), and 2+ Races (SOR). The ethnicity variable is binary; Hispanic/Latino or Not Hispanic/Latino. A Census Detail/SSA POB Match occurs when the 2010 Census respondent reported their Census Numident POB on the 2010 Race or Ethnicity questions using the detailed coding (the detailed Decennial POB coding is not available for eight MENA countries as shown in table 4.3). For both females and males we report four measures of mean log real long-term earnings. The first row of the Mean Log Earnings column for each POB group shows the mean log earnings of the largest Ethnicity-Race-Census Detail/SSA POB Match category, while the other rows report the difference in mean log earnings relative to the largest category. The next three columns show adjusted earnings from linear regression models controlling for various person and job characteristics. The PC model includes controls for education and quadratic functions of age and years in the United States in 2010. The PCW model adds controls for the dominant industry/region and the number of full and partial years worked. The PCWH model adds a quadratic function of average annual hours worked. Standard errors have not been released yet for this table. Some sub-groups have fewer than 1,000 persons. Even for small sub-groups, standard errors for adjusted log earnings differentials rarely exceed 0.025 log points.

cent vs. 2OFB N1N 21.1 percent) and between the Hispanic country parent groups (2P1FBH N1N 17.5 percent vs 2FBH N1N 1.7 percent). For the workers with only one foreign-born parent in the home the proportion Not Hispanic, White is typically larger than for workers in the same POB group with two foreign born parents, but less than those with two parents, one of whom was born in the United States.

Long-term average earnings also differ noticeably by family structure both within and across POB groups. For males, log earnings for the largest sub-group Hispanic, White, Census Detail/SSA POB Match within the Hispanic origin parent groups is highest for workers with one US-born parent (2P1FBH H1P 10.01), but this is the exception. For all other groups (females with Hispanic-origin parents, and both sexes for MENA and Other Foreign Born parent groups), workers in the largest ethnicity-race-POB Match category who have two foreign-born parents have the highest long-term average earnings. This result is similar to the earnings pattern present in most studies of immigrant assimilation where second-generation workers outperform the third generation and above.

We can also compare long-term average earnings for Hispanic second-generation male workers with two foreign-born parents to third-generation and above long-term average earning outcomes. For Hispanic White, Census Detail/SSA POB Match male workers with two foreign-born parents, log long-term average earnings is 9.995 (2FBH H1P), while for third-generation Hispanic, White male workers with two parents long-term log average annual earnings is (10.18 – 0.201 = 9.979, 2US N1N—2US H1N). Similar patterns can be found for other POB groups in table 4.4.

We focus now on comparing the results in table 4.2 for first-generation workers with second-generation workers with two foreign-born parents in table 4.4, keeping in mind that the workers in table 4.2 are significantly older on average (approximately 40 years old in 2010) than the workers in table 4.4 (approximately 26 years old in 2010). We begin with the Hispanic POB group. Although the sample composition differs, ethnicity and race reporting is about the same between the older first-generation workers and the younger second-generation workers with the same top two categories and a similar cumulative proportion for the top two categories of 0.863 (table 4.2 FBH H6P) for first-generation immigrants and 0.880 (table 4.4 2FBH H6P) for second-generation immigrants. The differences are somewhat larger for the MENA group although the top two categories are the same; the cumulative proportion is 0.678 (table 4.2 MENA N6N) for the first generation and 0.752 (table 4.4 2MENA N6N) for the second generation with most of the difference due to a higher share of second-generation workers reporting Not Hispanic, Some Other Race (table 4.4 2MENA N6N 0.304 vs table 4.2 MENA N6N 0.217). For the Other Foreign Born group, the top two ethnicity and race categories and the cumulative proportion for the top two categories are roughly similar—0.773 (Table 4.2 OFB N1N) for the first generation and 0.823 (table 4.4 2OFB N1N) for the second generation—although the share of workers in each category is noticeably different. The share of second-generation Not Hispanic, Asian workers is 0.611 (table 4.4 2OFB N4N) versus 0.477 (table 4.2 OFB N4N) for first-generation workers. It isn't entirely clear what is driving this result except perhaps changing trends in immigrant composition and the older average age for workers in Sample 1.

Long-term average earnings for second-generation workers show relatively large variability across ethnicity and race categories within POB groups, with variability at least as large and often substantially larger than for first-generation workers. For female workers in the Hispanic POB groups in tables 4.2 and 4.4, the second largest reported ethnicity and race category is Hispanic, Some Other Race, Census Detail/SSA POB Match (H6P). The difference in unadjusted long-term average earnings relative to the reference group Hispanic, White, Census Detail/SSA POB Match (H1P) is –0.046 (table 4.2 FBH H6P) for first-generation females and –0.093 (table 4.4 2FBH H6P) for second-generation females with two foreign-born Hispanic parents. It is even more important to know whether a person self-identifies White or Some Other Race for second-generation female workers than it is for first-generation female workers. For Hispanic POB males, the second-generation differences are similar across the top three ethnicity-race categories, but the unadjusted difference is very large for the Hispanic, White category; –0.067 (table 4.2 FBH H1N) for first-generation males and –0.224 (table 4.4 2FBH H1N) for second-generation males.

The pattern for Hispanic POB workers repeats itself for the MENA and the Other Foreign Born groups. Female second-generation workers tend to have larger earnings dispersion across ethnicity and race sub-groups within POB group than first-generation female workers, while the converse is true for male workers. This implies that the loss of information in the single-question format for second-generation male workers may be less than for second-generation females when, for example, a worker that would have self-identified in two race categories in the two-question format does not do so using the single-question format.

4.5 Conclusion

Changing the way a society measures its racial and ethnic diversity happens regularly. New standards for the collection and reporting of self-identified demographic data can produce statistical summaries that better reflect the current population of the United States. But these changes can also make historical comparisons more difficult. Our paper demonstrates some of these challenges. In measuring the long-term earnings of Hispanics, the proposed single-question format may complicate comparisons to analyses from the current two-question format because individuals must self-identify into White, Black, or other categories in addition to Hispanic. For individuals who volunteered self-identification as Middle Eastern or North African in the two-question format, the statistics based on the proposed single-question format may simply not be comparable to any previous analyses. Providing country of birth data for those born outside the United States may permit more comparable historical studies for immigrants.

Acknowledgments

The opinions and conclusions expressed herein are those of the authors and not those of the US Census Bureau, Cornell University, or any other research sponsor. Research presented here was authorized under project P-6000266. All results have been reviewed to ensure that no confidential information is disclosed (DRB release number CBDRB-FY23-CES-011-002). This research uses data from the Census Bureau's Longitudinal Employer-Household Dynamics Program, which was partially supported by NSF Grants SES-9978093, SES-0339191, and ITR-0427889; NIA Grant AG018854; and grants from the Sloan Foundation. For acknowledgments, sources of research support, and disclosure of the authors' material financial relationships, if any, please see https://www.nber.org/books-and-chapters/race-ethnicity-and-economic-statistics-21st-century/estimating-potential-impact-combined-race-and-ethnicity-reporting-long-term-earnings-statistics.

References

Abowd, John M., Kevin L. McKinney, and Nellie Zhao. 2018. "Earnings Inequality and Mobility Trends in the United States: Nationally Representative Estimates from Longitudinally Linked Employer-Employee Data." *Journal of Labor Economics* 36(S1): S183–S300, January. DOI: 10.1086/694104.

Abowd, John M., Bryce Stephens, Lars Vilhuber, Fredrik Andersson, Kevin L. McKinney, Marc Roemer, and Simon Woodcock. 2009. "The LEHD Infrastructure Files and the Creation of the Quarterly Workforce Indicators." In *Producer Dynamics: New Evidence from Micro Data*, edited by T. Dunne, J. B. Jensen, and M. J. Roberts, 149–230. Chicago: University of Chicago Press for the National Bureau of Economic Research.

Hahn, Joyce K., Henry R. Hyatt, and Hubert P. Janicki. 2021. "Job Ladders and Growth in Earnings, Hours, and Wages." *European Economic Review* 133: 103654. https://doi.org/10.1016/j.euroecorev.2021.103654.

Jensen, Eric, and Nicholas Jones. 2024. "Measuring the Racial and Ethnic Composition and Diversity of the U.S. Population: Historical Challenges and Contemporary Opportunities." Presented at NBER-CRIW conference on "Race, Ethnicity, and Economic Statistics for the 21st Century," March 14–15, 2024, Alexandria, VA.

Little, Roderick J. A., and Donald B. Rubin. 2002. *Statistical Analysis with Missing Data*. John Wiley & Sons, Inc. DOI:10.1002/9781119013563.

Marks, Rachel, and Nicholas Jones. 2020. *Collecting and Tabulating Ethnicity and Race Responses in the 2020 Census*. US Census Bureau, online webinar, presentation, and blog. Retrieved on March 5, 2024. https://bit.ly/2020marksjones.

Mathews, Kelly, Jessica Phelan, Nicholas A. Jones, Sarah Konya, Rachel Marks, Beverly M. Pratt, Julia Coombs, and Michael Bentley. 2017. *2015 National Content Test Race and Ethnicity Analysis Report: A New Design for the 21st Century*. Washington, DC: US Census Bureau. https://www2.census.gov/programs-surveys/decennial/2020/program-management/final-analysis-reports/2015nct-race-ethnicity-analysis.pdf.

McKinney, Kevin L., and John M. Abowd. 2023. "Male Earnings Volatility in LEHD before, during, and After the Great Recession." *Journal of Business and Economic Statistics* 41: 33–39. DOI: https://doi.org/10.1080/07350015.2022.2126479.

McKinney, Kevin L., John M. Abowd, and Hubert P. Janicki. 2022. "U.S. Long-Term Earnings Outcomes by Sex, Race, Ethnicity, and Place of Birth." *Quantitative Economics* 13(4): 1879–1945. November. DOI: https://doi.org/10.3982/QE1908.

McKinney, Kevin L., Andrew S. Green, Lars Vilhuber, and John M. Abowd. 2021. "Total Error and Variability Measures for the Quarterly Workforce Indicators and LEHD Origin-Destination Employment Statistics in OnTheMap." *Journal of Survey Statistics and Methodology* 9(5): 1146–182. (print version: November) https://doi.org/10.1093/jssam/smaa029.

Office of Management and Budget. 2023. "Initial Proposals For Updating OMB's Race and Ethnicity Statistical Standards." *Federal Register*, citation: 88 FR 5375. https://www.govinfo.gov/content/pkg/FR-2023-01-27/pdf/2023-01635.pdf.

Office of Management and Budget. 2024. "Revisions to OMB's Statistical Policy Directive No. 15: Standards for Maintaining, Collecting, and Presenting Federal Data on Race and Ethnicity." Federal Register, citation: 89 FR 22182. https://www.govinfo.gov/content/pkg/FR-2024-03-29/pdf/2024-06469.pdf.

Waddell, S. R., J. M. Abowd, C. Busette, and M. Lopez. 2022. "Measuring Race in U.S. Economic Statistics: What Do We Know?" *Business Economics* 57: 181–90. https://doi.org/10.1057/s11369-022-00274-3. Open access at: https://rdcu.be/cS0c1.

Wagner, D., and M. Layne. 2014. *The Person Identification Validation System (PVS): Applying the Center for Administrative Records Research and Applications' Record Linkage Software* (tech. rep. No. 2014–01). Retrieved September 29, 2023. Census Bureau—Center for Administrative Records Research and Applications. https://www.census.gov/content/dam/Census/library/working-papers/2014/adrm/carra-wp-2014-01.pdf.

II

Implications of Mismeasured and Imputed Race and Ethnicity

5

Race and Ethnicity (Mis)measurement in the US Criminal Justice System

Keith Finlay, Elizabeth Luh, and Michael Mueller-Smith

5.1 Introduction

Investigating the causes and consequences of racial and ethnic disparities has been one of the most important lines of criminal justice research over the last half century. For example, Blacks in the United States are five times more likely to be incarcerated compared to Whites, while Hispanics are three times as likely to be incarcerated as Whites (American Civil Liberties Union and The Sentencing Project 2022). Beyond incarceration, both qualitative and quantitative research show evidence of racial disparities in stop-and-frisks (Goel et al. 2016), charging decisions (Tuttle 2019), and sentencing outcomes (Alesina and La Ferrara 2014). Identifying these types of patterns is critically important given the well-documented broader impacts of justice involvement on individuals' lives (Pager 2003; Mueller-Smith and Schnepel 2021; Decker et al. 2014) and their family members (Rose and Clear 1998; Finlay et al. 2023).

A fundamental requirement for studying racial and ethnic disparities in criminal justice outcomes is high-quality measurement of race and ethnicity. As research increasingly relies on criminal justice administrative data or derivative series produced by statistical agencies, researchers must generally rely on the quality of race and ethnicity data originally collected for operational purposes, such as the physical identification of suspects. In contrast

Keith Finlay is an economist at the US Census Bureau.

Elizabeth Luh is a financial economist in the Office of Litigation Economics, US Securities and Exchange Commission.

Michael Mueller-Smith is an associate professor of economics at the University of Michigan and a research associate of the National Bureau of Economic Research.

to databases for public programs such as Medicaid or household surveys, where race and ethnicity may be self-reported or reported by family members, racial and ethnic information in the justice system is often determined by justice agency personnel—reflecting their perceptions of another's race and ethnicity. Thus, researchers and policymakers are dependent on the ability of officers to accurately and reliably identify race, which may be problematic if officers perceive race and ethnicity differently than does the subject. Even more troubling are cases where some police agencies have been accused of deliberately misreporting racial and ethnic information with the goal of subverting efforts to curtail racial profiling and discrimination (Webster 2021; Collister 2016; Luh 2022).

Some researchers turn to another data source: group quarters (GQ) responses in decennial censuses or the American Community Survey (e.g., Neal and Rick 2014; Bayer and Charles 2018). These data track people who reside in group living arrangements like dorms, health-care facilities, jails, or prisons. The Census Bureau increasingly relies on adult correctional facilities to electronically report facility-wide data on behalf of their residents (Belton and Durante 2021; National Academies of Sciences, Engineering, and Medicine 2023). These data are ultimately sourced from agency records systems, a practice that allows flawed data that originated in the justice system to propagate through to survey data. The American Community Survey faces the additional challenge of a two-stage sampling procedure wherein correctional facilities are first sampled and then a subset of respondents is selected within those facilities. In order to cover non-sampled facilities, full responses are imputed, drawing from the bank of observed GQ responses with weights assigned to reproduce the expected population based on the last previously observed enumeration (US Census Bureau 2022). Consequently, misreports present in justice administrative data may both directly and indirectly impact Census Bureau survey efforts to measure the incarcerated population.

As we document below, race and ethnicity data collection in the justice system is inconsistent with best practices, such as those defined at the federal level. The Office of Management and Budget (1997) revision to Statistical Policy Directive No. 15 states that "self-identification is the preferred means of obtaining information about an individual's race and ethnicity," although other means of collection are permitted when deemed more practical. An example of a permissible deviation from self-identification given in the guidelines is a coroner recording information about an autopsy where the individual in question can no longer self-report since they are deceased.

In this paper, we leverage a novel linkage between agency-recorded race and ethnicity from the Criminal Justice Administrative Records System (CJARS) and race and ethnicity composites from Census Bureau census and administrative records to quantify the accuracy of race and ethnicity information recorded in the criminal justice system.[1] There are major advantages to integrating these data systems. We can link an individual's agency-reported race and ethnicity to their race and ethnicity from census or administrative data that are primarily based on a self-report or family report; utilize paradata to exclude observations that might reflect agency perceptions (e.g., group quarters); and make these data available to researchers through the Federal Statistical Research Data Centers (FSRDCs).[2] The longitudinal structure of the CJARS data also enables us to follow individuals through the justice system (e.g., from adjudication to incarceration). Thus, we can measure the amount of racial or ethnic mismeasurement in the criminal justice system and identify the stages of the justice system where misreporting is more likely to occur. Using these linked data, we explore several related questions around the accuracy of race and ethnicity information in the criminal justice system and the implications for extant federal statistical series.

First, we document overall levels of concordance in racial and ethnic information, distinguishing between court records and state prison records. Court records typically rely on police incident reports to populate race/ethnicity fields, and these data are often not used for operational purposes. Prison systems are more likely to have intake processes that provide the inmate the opportunity to self-identify and may use that information for security and housing decisions (e.g., to prevent gang violence). Consistent with these features, we observe lower concordance rates in court data compared to prison data. Between 2000 and 2019, we find that 83 percent of felony and misdemeanor defendants and 90 percent of prison inmates have agency-recorded labels that concord with their Census Bureau race and ethnicity composites. While White and Black justice-involved individuals are typically accurately recorded by agencies as such, the justice system often struggles to accurately classify American Indians and Alaska Natives, Asians, Pacific Islanders, and Hispanics.[3]

Second, we consider how race and ethnicity data quality has evolved over time and how it varies across the United States. We find that there have been only modest changes in the accuracy of this information over the last two

1. CJARS is a longitudinal, harmonized data system of criminal justice events and a partnership between the University of Michigan and the Census Bureau (Finlay and Mueller-Smith 2022).

2. See Charles and Guryan (2011) for an excellent discussion of the important theoretical implications of self-identified versus perceived race and ethnicity, the potential mutability of racial identity, as well as a review of the relevant empirical literature grappling with the taxonomical challenge of how to measure race. Snipp (2003) reviews the history of racial data collected by the federal government, such as the changes in racial categories, and its impact on social science research.

3. Similar observations for the American Indian and Alaska Native population have also been made regarding health and mortality data (Small-Rodriguez and Akee 2021; Mays et al. 2022).

decades. There is substantial variation by geography, however. While all jurisdictions are likely to accurately label White and Black justice-involved individuals, locations with higher shares of residents who are Hispanic or American Indian and Alaska Native generally tend to more accurately identify those populations.

Finally, we apply our findings to re-estimate the imprisonment rate of racial and ethnic groups in the United States since 2000. We use data from the Bureau of Justice Statistics (BJS) National Prisoner Statistics (NPS) program together with estimated annual correspondences between agency-recorded race/ethnicity and Census Bureau race/ethnicity composites for the population of prisoners observed in CJARS to produce new aggregate counts and per capita rates that should better reflect how inmates self-identify. We find that current reporting by BJS may underestimate the size of the White and Black inmate populations in 2018 by 20 percent and 17 percent, respectively. For American Indians and Alaska Natives, the incarceration rate since 2010 may have been underestimated by 46 percent. These findings suggest that improved data linkage infrastructure can provide agencies like BJS with new opportunities to improve the accuracy of race and ethnicity measurement of prisoner populations.

The remainder of this paper is organized as follows. Section 5.2 provides background on the standards for, practices of, and sources of misreporting in race and ethnicity measurement. Section 5.3 presents our findings on the discordance between race and ethnicity recorded by criminal justice agencies relative to census and administrative data, including comparisons across stages of the justice system, across geography, and over time. Section 5.4 applies these insights to federal statistical series published by BJS to quantify how misreporting impacts the measurement of racial and ethnic disparities in the justice system. Section 5.5 concludes.

5.2 Standards, Practices, and Challenges of Collecting Race and Ethnicity Data

5.2.1 Federal Guidelines and State Practices

In 1997, the Office of Management and Budget (OMB) revised Statistical Policy Directive No. 15 (SPD15) to require that federal agencies, including the Census Bureau and the Bureau of Justice Statistics, use the following minimum categories for race: American Indian and Alaska Native (AIAN), Asian, Black or African American, Native Hawaiian or Other Pacific Islander, and White (Office of Management and Budget 1997). The same standard requires a separate identification for ethnicity, using the following minimum categories: "Hispanic or Latino" and "Not Hispanic or Latino." The OMB regulation also states that self-identification is the preferred method for measuring an individual's race and ethnicity, except where identification by an observer is more practical. The Bureau of Justice Statistics often reports a category that combines the Asian and Native Hawaiian or Other Pacific Islander categories (e.g., Harrell 2009). In 2024, the Office of Management and Budget revised SPD15 again, calling for the collection of race and ethnicity in a single question that allows multiple responses, and for the addition of Middle Eastern or North African (MENA) as a new minimum category. Our research was conducted before these revisions. Justice records management systems generally do not allow for multiple races or ethnicities to be selected, but we have found records systems that could support a new MENA category.

State and local criminal justice agencies are not obligated to collect race and ethnicity data according to OMB guidelines. Their categories may differ and change over time. Table 5.1 identifies the different race categories reported by each state's department of corrections (DOC) covered by the CJARS dataset. Of the state agencies listed, only the Michigan DOC reports race and ethnicity separately. Furthermore, there is significant heterogeneity in what race or ethnicity categories are recorded. While each state's DOC consistently reports for the White, Black, and Asian categories, Hispanic categories are not reported in 6 out of the 23 states included and AIAN categories are not reported in 5 out of the 23 states. Ten states also include an Other race/ethnicity category or race/ethnicity categories that are not included in the 1997 OMB minimum categories (e.g., Middle Eastern), while the rest do not allow for an additional Other race.

Different collection practices across states cause heterogeneity in race/ethnicity data quality across criminal justice agencies. Although the CJARS project requests race and ethnicity variables from all agencies, DOCs in Minnesota, Missouri, Montana, Ohio, and Vermont only report race and not ethnicity.[4] These states do not report any incarceration of Hispanics, which could lead to underreporting of Hispanic individuals in the justice system within those states. Since federal statistics of incarceration, such as those published by the Bureau of Justice Statistics, depend on data provided by states, non-identification of Hispanics in one state can cause underestimates of incarcerated Hispanics nationally (Carson 2021). Thus, low estimates of the incarceration of Hispanics could be driven by poor ethnicity measurement, rather than actually low incarceration rates of Hispanic individuals.

These findings are consistent with a report from the National Conference of State Legislatures that found that out of 13 states that reallocated prisoner residences during the 2020 redistricting cycle, only 1 state's department of corrections recorded race and ethnicity in a way consistent with federal guidelines (Williams 2023). The report recommended that states considering

4. We determined if a state collected ethnicity data based on whether we observed any records of Hispanic or Latino ethnicity in the raw data in the CJARS system.

Table 5.1 Race and ethnicity categories in raw CJARS data sourced from state departments of corrections

State	White	Black	Asian	Hispanic	AIAN	Other
Arizona	✓	✓	✓	✓	✓	✓
Arkansas	✓	✓	✓	✓	✓	✓
Florida	✓	✓	✓	✓	*	-
Georgia	✓	✓	✓	*	*	-
Illinois	✓	✓	✓	✓	✓	✓
Indiana	✓	✓	✓	✓	*	-
Iowa	✓	✓	✓	✓	✓	-
Kansas	✓	✓	✓	✓	✓	-
Michigan	✓	✓	✓	✓	✓	-
Minnesota	✓	✓	✓	-	✓	-
Mississippi	✓	✓	✓	✓	✓	-
Missouri	✓	✓	✓	-	✓	-
Montana	✓	✓	✓	-	✓	-
Nebraska	✓	✓	✓	✓	✓	✓
Nevada	✓	✓	✓	✓	✓	-
New Jersey	✓	✓	✓	✓	*	-
New York	✓	✓	✓	✓	✓	✓
Ohio	✓	✓	✓	-	✓	✓
Oklahoma	✓	✓	✓	✓	✓	✓
Oregon	✓	✓	✓	✓	✓	-
Pennsylvania	✓	✓	✓	✓	*	✓
Texas	✓	✓	✓	✓	✓	✓
Vermont	✓	✓	✓	-	✓	✓

Source: Authors' calculations from raw criminal justice histories using data from the CJARS 2022Q4 vintage. Calculations were made from CJARS data at the University of Michigan, not from Census Bureau data protected by 13 USC § 9(a).

Note: "✓" indicates a state DOC records that race/ethnicity category. "-" indicates that the state DOC does not record that race/ethnicity category. "*" indicates that fewer than 0.5 percent of records from this state are associated with this race/ethnicity. Only statewide DOCs that provide any race information in their incarceration data and are covered by CJARS are included in this table. Race categories are modeled off of race categories used in Bureau of Justice Statistics National Prisoners Statistics program.

reallocation adopt policies to require the federal standards, but recognized the substantial costs in recanvassing their prisoner populations.

5.2.2 Mismeasurement of Race and Ethnicity in Criminal Justice Data

Our perceptions of someone else's race or ethnicity may differ from how that person self-identifies for a number of reasons. Characteristics such as names (Gaddis 2017; Fryer and Levitt 2004; Luh 2022; Bertrand and Mullainathan 2004), clothing (Freeman et al. 2011), occupation (Freeman et al. 2011), skin tone (Monk 2021; Gyimah-Brempong and Price 2006; Naik and Farrukh 2022; Noe-Bustamante et al. 2021; Davenport 2020; Dixon and Telles 2017), and other physical features (Blair et al. 2002) can impact the perception of an individual's race or ethnicity. These physical or socioeconomic characteristics are also associated with worse criminal justice outcomes like conviction and arrest rates (Gyimah-Brempong and Price 2006; Finkeldey and Demuth 2021; King and Johnson 2016). Furthermore, the characteristics of the recorder can also impact their ability to identify an individual's race (Harris 2002). For example, Luh (2022) finds that non-White troopers are better at recording motorist race in highway searches compared to their White peers.

In addition, work by Eberhardt et al. (2004) and Bordalo et al. (2016) shows that people associate Black racial identity when primed with words associated with crime. For law enforcement officers, this may lead to over-labeling of racial minorities. While not necessarily a cause of inaccurate data, it is interesting to note that Eberhardt et al. (2004) find that causality flows in both directions, showing that seeing Black faces also primes people to detect crime-related images. These conclusions are consistent with work demonstrating statistical discrimination among employers against minorities in response to the adoption of ban-the-box policies. Agan and Starr (2018) and Doleac and Hansen (2020) find that withholding criminal records from job applications increases the Black-White gap in employment, suggesting that employers infer criminal history using race in the absence of criminal records in employment applications.

It is important to acknowledge that racial and ethnic identity need not remain static. While empirical research frequently assumes that racial identity is a fixed, mutually exclusive characteristic (Holland 2003), there is research to the contrary which shows that self-identification of racial and ethnic identity may change over an individual's lifetime (Saperstein and Penner 2012; Liebler et al. 2017; Harris and Sim 2002; Doyle and Kao 2007).[5] Seminal work by Saperstein and Penner (2012) using the National Longitudinal Survey of Youth (NLSY) showed that an individual's racial identity evolves over time. This research highlights that racial identity may not be solely based on one's parents' identities, but can be influenced by other social and environmental experiences. Other research has shown that self-identified race can also change across contexts and in response to events (Mason 2017; Telles and Paschel 2014). These findings are consistent with labeling theory, which would suggest that individuals may change their self-perceptions based on criminal justice system involvement, altering their self-identify to match beliefs about characteristics that are associated with criminality (Besemer et al. 2017). These factors may contribute to our estimates of racial and ethnic discordance and the rate of disagreement between race/ethnicity measures across censuses that we describe below, but not necessarily bias statistical reporting or research on disparities.

5. See Darity et al. (2006); Roberts (2012); Nelson (2016); Rose (2023); and Morning (2007) for additional discussion of the definition and construction of race in society. Rose (2023) provides excellent discussion of the implications of a constructivist perspective of race and ethnicity for economic theory and discrimination research.

5.2.3 The Life Cycle of Race and Ethnicity Data in the Justice System

To understand how race and ethnicity are recorded in the criminal justice system, how that information persists, and what opportunities there are to update it, we conducted qualitative research by interviewing seven personnel with knowledge of records management who have worked in multiple jurisdictions and across different stages of the justice system. To supplement these interviews, we also reviewed five publicly available procedural guidelines that document official policies and practices within state and local criminal justice agencies.[6] A summary of these sources, which cover procedures in eight states, is available in table 5.2.

Several common themes emerged from this investigation. First, information frictions arise due to the decentralization of information between agencies. Records tend to pass in one direction only, which allows potentially flawed data to propagate through multiple agencies. Second, the reliability of race and ethnicity data varies tremendously, and depends on whether agencies view this information as operationally relevant to their missions. Third, correcting misreported race and ethnicity is seen as legally or bureaucratically costly, which discourages updates. Together, these factors create an environment where flawed information may persist, which ultimately impacts the statistical reporting that relies on these data.

Figure 5.1 documents the typical flow of information and interactions in the pre-trial and adjudication phases of the criminal justice system, indicating where race and ethnicity data might be electronically recorded and where direct observation could feasibly identify misreports in the record. Based on our interviews, the police incident report (PIR) appears to be the critical point of data collection for race and ethnicity data. Typically, the information contained in the PIR reflects what the arresting officer recorded about the suspect in the field shortly after arrest, and is supplemented with victim statements and fingerprints. The PIR is then transmitted to jails, prosecutors, and courts, and tends to receive significant deference as the official record of a criminal incident and arrest.

Several sources emphasized that, even though a PIR regularly contains racial and ethnic descriptions of a suspect, officers within the court system do not view race and ethnicity information as operationally relevant to their jobs since using that information during court proceedings could be illegal and a violation of civil rights law. Since it is considered improper to use this information, these fields are not monitored for data quality issues. Consequently, race and ethnicity in court records are viewed with some degree of

6. While our conclusions in this section are drawn from a convenience sample and may not be nationally representative, the sources touched on a breadth of processes that impact race and ethnicity measurement. We could not find a systematic review of procedures to validate the findings. But see, for example, Rodriguez and Tublitz (2023) for an agency survey that measures whether Hispanic ethnicity is coded separately from race in data management systems.

Table 5.2 **Convenience sample used to study the life cycle of race and ethnicity data in criminal justice records management systems**

Source	State	Stage of the justice system	Citation
Person A	Arizona	Department of corrections	
Person B	Illinois, Michigan	State prosecutor's office, local police	
Person C	Michigan	Department of corrections, local police	
Person D	Ohio	Department of corrections	
Person E	New Jersey	Community supervision, criminal courts	
Person F	New York	Criminal courts	
Person G	New York	Criminal courts	
Guidelines A	Florida	Public defender's office	Law Offices of the Public Defender, 11th Judicial Circuit of Florida (2024)
Guidelines B	Michigan	Department of corrections	Michigan Department of Corrections (2022), Michigan Legislature (2023)
Guidelines C	Michigan	State police	Michigan State Police (2024)
Guidelines D	Texas	All stages	Texas State Legislature (2024)
Guidelines E	Texas	Criminal courts	Dallas County District Attorney's Office (2024)

Source: Authors' summary of sources consulted to study life cycle of race and ethnicity data in criminal justice records management systems.

doubt by those involved in records management. In contrast, measurement of a suspect's sex in court records is considered to be higher quality.

If misreports are identified, staff do not have an incentive to correct the record, especially for fields viewed as secondary to operational needs. For example, fixing flawed race and ethnicity information typically requires filing formal paperwork and dealing with a records management bureaucracy, work that generally would fall on top of existing job responsibilities. In addition, prosecutors and investigating officers may be hesitant to contradict information contained in the original PIR as those filings could be used by defense counsel to undermine the prosecution's case, perhaps by suggesting that law enforcement officers might have misidentified the suspect.

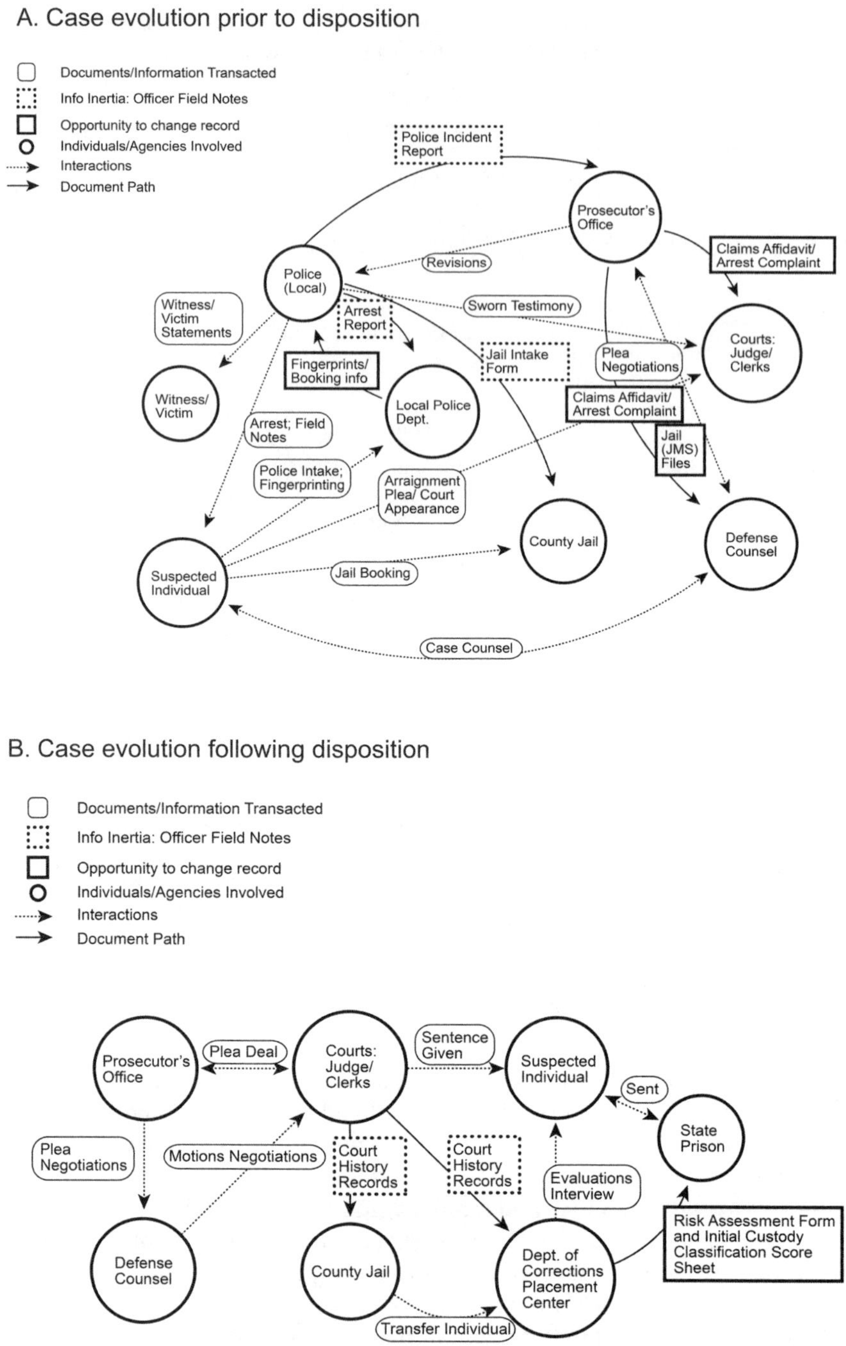

Fig. 5.1 Flow of information during criminal case adjudication

Source: Authors' summary of findings based on qualitative research. Sources consulted are enumerated in table 5.2.

If a felony defendant is convicted and sentenced to incarceration in prison, all states require an intake process to assess security risk and make housing assignments. This intake process will generally leverage some combination of the inmate's criminal history, the court documentation associated with their conviction, and a risk assessment form completed after a case manager interviews the inmate. Some court documentation may propagate into correctional records systems and thereby continue the use of any misreporting in the PIR. For example, most states that we engaged with use the Ohio Risk Assessment System (Latessa et al. 2009), which does not explicitly ask inmates about their race and ethnicity. But information on known or suspected gang affiliation, which often depends on a specific racial or ethnic identity, is taken into account by the case manager and added to the prisoner's record (York 2021). Because of the security risk associated with gang conflict, greater effort is made to accurately record and verify racial and ethnic information about inmates, since this is operationally relevant to improve safety within facilities. And because departments of corrections typically maintain their own independent data management systems, updating flawed information is significantly less burdensome on staff and does not require formal court filings.

Based on our interviews, it appears that the information recorded at the time of arrest carries significant weight in the official record. Few incentives exist to correct the official record within the adjudication phase, and this potentially flawed information may get passed onto corrections data systems. Due to the operational need and opportunity to update data management systems through the intake process at the start of an incarceration spell, race and ethnicity data within the prison context likely are of higher quality than within the arrest and adjudication phases.

5.3 Differences Between Administrative and Self-Reported Measures of Race and Ethnicity Among the Justice-Involved Population

5.3.1 Data and Methods

We identify people who have been involved in the justice system using data from the Criminal Justice Administrative Records System (CJARS), a repository of criminal history information covering all stages of the criminal justice system, including both adjudication events and incarceration spells (Finlay et al. 2022).[7] CJARS is constructed from criminal history data collected from state and local agencies, then harmonized into a unified national repository. In addition to harmonizing criminal justice event data, CJARS also collects agency-recorded race and ethnicity (Finlay and Mueller-Smith 2022). We use these administrative records to assign the most common

7. States for which CJARS has longitudinal, statewide coverage in at least one criminal justice domain constitute 66 percent of the US population.

agency-recorded race and ethnicity measures to justice-involved individuals. Importantly, we allow agency-recorded measures of race and ethnicity to vary across the stages of the justice system (e.g., adjudication, incarceration) to capture dynamics in the accuracy and persistence of information as individuals are processed through the justice system.

From the universe of available CJARS data, we focus on two common events in the criminal justice system—adjudication and incarceration events. For adjudication, we focus on defendants who were charged with misdemeanor or felony offenses in a given calendar year. Court events in the CJARS data come from Arizona, Florida, Maryland, Michigan, North Carolina, Oregon, Pennsylvania, Texas, Virginia, Wisconsin. For incarceration, we consider three measures of the incarcerated population: entry cohorts, exit cohorts, and the population of incarcerated individuals. We define an entry cohort as the population of individuals who began an incarceration spell in a given calendar year, exit cohorts as the population of individuals whose incarceration spell ends in a given calendar year, and the population as the incarcerated population as of year-end. Incarceration events in the CJARS data come from Arizona, Florida, Illinois, Indiana, Kansas, Michigan, Minnesota, Montana, Nebraska, New York, North Carolina, Oklahoma, Pennsylvania, Texas.

To construct a Census Bureau composite race/ethnicity, we use data from the 2000 and 2010 Censuses and from the Census Numident. In the 2000 and 2010 Census data, we exclude any race or ethnicity responses that were imputed or edited, and any responses from group quarters such as prisons or jails, since those may have been based on race or ethnicity measures recorded by justice personnel. The remaining race and ethnicity responses will primarily reflect self or family reports. The Census Numident is based on the Social Security Administration (SSA) Numident and serves as the backbone of record linkage at the Census Bureau. Race and ethnicity data in the Census Numident will also primarily reflect self or family reports.[8]

We link CJARS records at the person level with records from the 2000 and 2010 Censuses and the Census Numident using Protected Identification Keys (PIK), which are anonymous person identifiers assigned by the Census Bureau using the Person Identification Validation System (PVS; Wagner and Lane 2014). CJARS records without PIKs and CJARS records that could not be linked to at least one Census Bureau race/ethnicity measure were excluded from the analysis.[9]

8. The Census Numident contains SSA-collected race and ethnicity data (Scott 1999). Prior to 1980, White, Negro, and Other were the only options. In 1980, SSA began allowing White, Black, Hispanic, Asian or Pacific Islander, and American Indian and Alaska Native as options in a combined race/ethnicity field. Beginning in 1989, SSA began receiving SS-5 applications for Social Security numbers directly from hospitals at birth, but these filings often exclude race/ethnicity because it can be considered protected health data. For people born after 1989, most of these records would receive race/ethnicity data when the SSA records were updated later in life.

9. The reference files used for PVS only include people with Social Security numbers and Individual Tax Identification Numbers. Many undocumented immigrants, who are dispropor-

Table 5.3 Recoding Census Bureau race and ethnicity to BJS/CJARS race and ethnicity

BJS/CJARS race/ethnicity	Census Bureau race	Census Bureau ethnicity
White, non Hispanic	White	Not Hispanic
Black, non Hispanic	Black or African American	Not Hispanic
AIAN, non-Hispanic	American Indian, Alaska Native	Not Hispanic
Asian/Pacific Islander, non-Hispanic	Chinese, Indian, Filipino, Vietnamese, Korean, Japanese, Other Asian, Native Hawaiian, Guamanian or Chamorro, Samoan, Other Pacific Islander	Not Hispanic
Other, non-Hispanic	Some Other Race, Two or More Races/Multiracial	Not Hispanic
Hispanic	Any race	Hispanic

Source: Authors' mapping based on Finlay and Mueller-Smith (2022) and, for example, Carson (2022, 42).

Note: BJS uses the coding above in collections based on administrative records. In demographic surveys, BJS uses the separate race and ethnicity codes required by OMB (1997).

Using data from these three sources, we can construct a composite race/ethnicity that gets closer to an individual's own perception of their race and ethnicity, while covering as much of the justice-involved population as possible. Although the Census Numident data are administrative, like the census data, they will have mostly been submitted by an individual or a member of an individual's family or household. The Census Bureau composite will be much closer to the best practice in race/ethnicity measurement than those from justice sources. Future research could explore more of the survey and administrative sources of race and ethnicity available at the Census Bureau to understand how they vary for the justice-involved population.

Because of the limitations in how race and ethnicity are recorded in justice records management systems, we use the following combined race/ethnicity categories to assess the accuracy of justice-assigned labels: Hispanic, any race; White, non-Hispanic (NH); Black, NH; Asian/Pacific Islander, NH; American Indian and Alaska Native (AIAN), NH; and Some Other Race or Two or More Races/Multiracial, NH.[10] These categories, shown in detail in table 5.3, were chosen because they are mutually exclusive and align with the BJS statistics we study below.

For each justice-involved person in the CJARS data, the Census Bureau race and ethnicity sources are recoded into a single race/ethnicity. If there is a modal race/ethnicity across the three sources, that category is chosen. If there is not a single modal race/ethnicity, we use a race/ethnicity ordering

tionately Hispanic, are therefore not able to be linked and this could cause an undercount of the true share of the Hispanic population.

10. Unless otherwise noted, we use Hispanic, White, Black, Asian/PI, AIAN, and Other interchangeably with these labels.

Table 5.4 Agreement between Census Bureau race/ethnicity composites and component data sources

	Linkage rates to data sources			Among records linked to 1+ census				Among records linked to 1+ census and the Census Numident
Census Bureau race/ ethnicity composite	1–2 censuses	1 census	Census Numident	2000 Census agrees	2010 Census agrees	Either census agrees	Either census disagrees	Census Numident agrees
Felony and misdemeanor defendants, 2000–2019:								
White, not Hispanic	89%	31%	88%	98%	97%	100%	4%	99%
Black, not Hispanic	80%	39%	91%	96%	96%	99%	6%	98%
Asian/PI, not Hispanic	86%	44%	83%	78%	84%	89%	28%	80%
Hispanic	86%	41%	89%	91%	93%	97%	11%	80%
AIAN, not Hispanic	88%	49%	87%	83%	85%	93%	22%	60%
Other, not Hispanic	79%	49%	75%	76%	43%	82%	49%	29%
Ever incarcerated population, 2000–2019:								
White, not Hispanic	75%	40%	95%	98%	97%	100%	4%	99%
Black, not Hispanic	64%	41%	96%	96%	96%	98%	6%	98%
Asian/PI, not Hispanic	72%	51%	92%	71%	74%	77%	35%	70%
Hispanic	75%	46%	94%	93%	93%	96%	10%	83%
AIAN, not Hispanic	79%	54%	94%	86%	87%	92%	17%	61%
Other, not Hispanic	58%	44%	88%	81%	50%	83%	36%	23%

Source: Authors' calculations from the 2000 and 2010 Censuses, the Census Numident, and CJARS criminal histories (2022Q4 vintage). US Census Bureau, project number P-7500378, approval numbers CBDRB-FY24–0101, CBDRB-FY24–0277.

Note: Each panel reports the share of observations which meet the listed criteria, conditional on being in each row. CJARS court data come from Arizona, Florida, Maryland, Michigan, North Carolina, Oregon, Pennsylvania, Texas, Virginia, Wisconsin. CJARS prison data come from Arizona, Florida, Illinois, Indiana, Kansas, Michigan, Minnesota, Montana, Nebraska, New York, North Carolina, Oklahoma, Pennsylvania, Texas.

that prioritizes Hispanic ethnicity then less populous racial groups to resolve disagreements across the three sources. Hispanic ethnicity is selected first; then American Indian and Alaska Native, NH; then Some Other Race and Two or More Races/Multiracial, NH; then Asian/Pacific Islander, NH; then Black, NH; then White, NH. This algorithm is analogous to those used in Ennis et al. (2018) and Limburg et al. (2023).

Table 5.4 documents how the resulting Census Bureau race and ethnicity composites agree with the component data sources. Most composite values are constructed from at least one census response. For felony and misdemeanor defendants, 79 to 89 percent have one or more Decennial responses. Prison inmates have somewhat lower linkage rates (58 to 79 percent), which is expected since we exclude group quarters responses. When we observe at least one census response, there is substantial concordance between the census responses and the composite race/ethnicity. At least one of the census responses aligns with the composite in 77 to 100 percent of records. In the minority of cases where we do not have a link to a census response, we rely on the Census Numident. While we cannot validate the information in cases where we only have links to the Numident, among records with links to at least one census response and the Numident, we see very high rates of agreement for Whites and Blacks (>98 percent), with lower rates for Hispanics, Asian/PIs, and AIANs (60–83 percent).[11]

With a large set of agency-recorded race/ethnicity measures matched to high-quality race/ethnicity composites from Census Bureau data, we construct criminal justice event-by-year empirical correspondence functions that map agency-recorded to Census Bureau composite race and ethnicity over the period 2000–2019, with events defined as above (e.g., individuals with felony charges, incarcerated population). We average the correspondence tables into a single matrix by event type by taking the unweighted average across all years.

5.3.2 Concordance of Agency-Recorded Race/Ethnicity Versus Census Bureau Race/Ethnicity Composites

We consider two perspectives when trying to evaluate the quality of race and ethnicity information in criminal justice administrative records. First, we measure the percent of agency-recorded labels that are consistent with the Census Bureau race/ethnicity composites. Second, we identify the percent of Census Bureau race/ethnicity composites that concord with the racial/ethnic categories assigned by criminal justice agencies. These statistics respectively correspond to the concepts of *precision* and *recall* typically used to evaluate the performance of classifiers. While closely related, the two approaches are differentiated by who appears in the denominators—subgroups defined by Census Bureau or agency-recorded race and ethnicity. For example, precision and recall in assessing the identification of Whites would be defined as:

$$\text{precision} = \frac{\text{White in Census Bureau composite and agency data}}{\text{White in agency data}}, \text{ and}$$

$$\text{recall} = \frac{\text{White in Census Bureau composite and agency data}}{\text{White in Census Bureau composite}}.$$

Figure 5.2 presents our findings. Panel A shows that the majority of agency-recorded labels are consistent with the Census Bureau composites, meaning they generally have high precision. For example, 80–87 percent of justice-involved individuals recorded by agencies as White we also identify

11. Numident agreement rates for the Other race category are low because this option was a default category for older Numident records where White and Black were the only options and then it was removed as an option for newer records (Scott 1999).

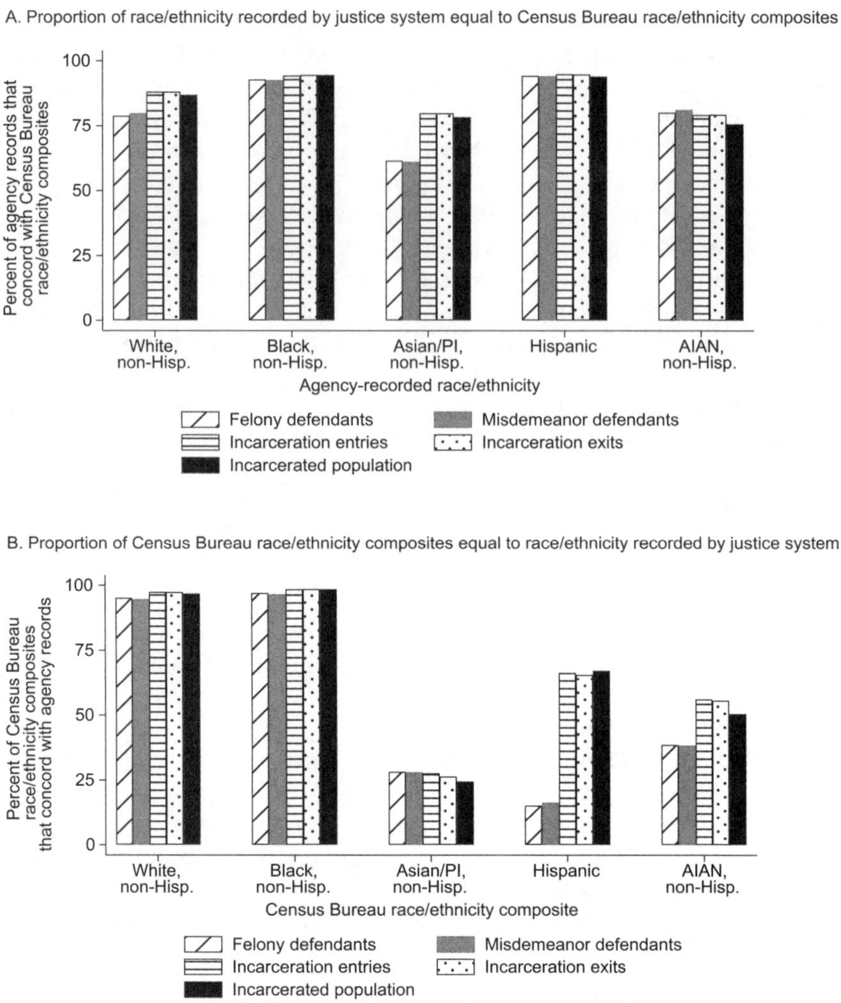

Fig. 5.2 Concordance of agency-recorded race/ethnicity versus Census Bureau race/ethnicity composite, 2000–2019, by criminal justice caseload

Source: Authors' calculations from the 2000 and 2010 Censuses, the Census Numident, and CJARS criminal histories (2022Q4 vintage). US Census Bureau, project number P-7500378, approval numbers CBDRB-FY24-0101, CBDRB-FY24-0277.

Note: CJARS court data come from Arizona, Florida, Maryland, Michigan, North Carolina, Oregon, Pennsylvania, Texas, Virginia, and Wisconsin. CJARS prison data come from Arizona, Florida, Illinois, Indiana, Kansas, Michigan, Minnesota, Montana, Nebraska, New York, North Carolina, Oklahoma, Pennsylvania, and Texas. This figure presents the concordance of agency-recorded race/ethnicity and Census Bureau race/ethnicity composites. The two panels alter the base measure/denominator. The bars represent different criminal justice caseloads. Estimates and sample sizes have been rounded according to Census Bureau DRB rules.

as White in the composite. Black and Hispanic labels fare even better with an even higher share (>92 percent, >94 percent) agreeing with the composite race/ethnicity. Two populations show relatively lower rates of precision: Asians/Pacific Islanders (61–78 percent) and American Indians and Alaska Natives (76–81 percent).

Panel B shows divergent results when examining the share of Census Bureau race/ethnicity composites that are accurately identified by agencies, a measurement concept similar to recall. White and Black populations have very high concordance, meaning that the vast majority (>94 percent, >96 percent) of those identified as White or Black are recorded as such by the justice system. Asian/Pacific Islanders, Hispanics, and AIANs, however, show substantially lower concordance. For example, whether looking at court records or prison records, slightly over one-quarter of those who self-identify as Asian/Pacific Islander are recorded as such by agencies. Hispanic individuals are rarely recorded as Hispanic by criminal court systems (15–16 percent), but have somewhat better rates within the prison context (67 percent). AIANs show a similar dynamic as Hispanics, albeit with better performance in courts (38 percent) and worse performance in prison data (50 percent).

One conclusion from these exercises is that the justice system tends to default to labeling individuals as White or Black, the largest justice-involved racial groups. As has long been recognized by the Bureau of Justice Statistics, many agencies vary in whether information on Hispanic identity is recorded in electronic records (e.g., Carson 2021, 42). We also see evidence that race and ethnicity records from prison systems tend to be higher quality than those in court data. This is consistent with what we know about how some departments of correction rely on race and ethnicity information for operational purposes, which provides an incentive for higher data standards for these fields.

This latter point regarding varying quality across procedural stages of the justice system is also shown in the full empirical correspondences shown in tables 5.5 and 5.6. These tables capture the complete set of transition probabilities for each agency recorded and Census Bureau composite pair, first for court defendants, then for prison caseloads. Overall, the concordance rate of the Census Bureau composites with agency-recorded race and ethnicity is only 83 percent in adjudication records, which increases to 90 percent in prison records. This means that 17 percent and 10 percent of these respective caseloads have some disagreement between agency-recorded and census composite labels.

It is also interesting to consider the most common types of misreports made in these systems. For example, the most common misalignment we observe in both court and prison systems is that individuals whom we identify as Hispanic in the Census Bureau composites are recorded as White in administrative records. The next most common off-diagonal pairing are individuals identified as Hispanic in the composites but labeled as Black by justice agencies. These patterns are not surprising given that some agencies do not systematically collect information about ethnicity. Three additional racial groups, AIAN, Asian/Pacific Islander, and Other, which includes Multiracial identification, also show systematic sorting to White and Black agency-recorded racial codes. While these groups constitute a smaller share of the justice-involved population overall, the misclassifications are significant enough that the majority of agency records do not reflect how individuals are identified in Census Bureau data.

The second to last rows and columns from tables 5.5 and 5.6 show the implied racial and ethnic composition of the justice system based on agency-recorded versus Census Bureau composite identity. We observe that 38 percent of inmates are identified as White, 40 percent as Black, 18 percent as Hispanic, 2 percent as American Indian and Alaska Native, and less than 1 percent identify as Asian/Pacific Islander or Other. The caseload demographics for misdemeanor and felony defendants are similar to those for prison inmates but with relatively more White defendants (48 percent) and a smaller share of Black (35 percent) and Hispanic (13 percent) defendants. While interpreting this exercise comes with the caveat that the estimates are limited to only jurisdictions contained within CJARS, Finlay et al. (2022) show that CJARS coverage is generally representative of the United States as a whole on a wide range of characteristics.

Delving further, we can disaggregate our measures of race and ethnic data quality by more detailed types of interaction with the justice system, explore how they change over time, and measure how they vary across states. Figures 5.3 and 5.4 show the annual rates of precision and recall between 2000 and 2019 for felony and misdemeanor defendants as well as incarceration entries, exits, and populations. Overall, we generally see a fair degree of stability in these quality measures over time. There is a notable increase between 2000 and 2011 in the percent of agency-recorded Asian/Pacific Islander records for misdemeanor defendants that concord with the composite race/ethnicity, but other measures tend to remain relatively constant. Since incarceration entries and exits are constructed from smaller populations, they do show higher variance year-to-year even if the running average roughly matches the more stable incarcerated population measures. Focusing on the share of Census Bureau composites accurately labeled by agencies, there do appear to be signs of improvements in data quality over time. For example, an increasing share of Hispanic inmates are labeled as such by prison systems up through 2012; unfortunately data quality on this dimension returns to the lower values from the early 2000s by the end of our statistical series in 2019.

Across states, justice agencies vary in how they code race and ethnicity. Figures 5.5 and 5.6 show the geographic variation in the share of criminal defendants and prison inmates identified in the Census Bureau composites

Table 5.5 **Concordance of agency-record race/ethnicity versus Census Bureau race/ethnicity composite, individuals charged with a felony or misdemeanor, 2000–2019, total table percents**

	Race/ethnicity recorded by justice system								
Census Bureau race/ethnicity composite	White (1)	Black (2)	AIAN (3)	Asian/PI (4)	Other (5)	Hispanic (6)	% of agency-recorded equal to composite (7)	Caseload share (8)	Row total (9)
White	45.70%	0.73%	0.05%	0.11%	1.56%	0.08%	94.76%	48.23%	737,000
Black	0.93%	33.70%	0.01%	0.03%	0.16%	0.02%	96.68%	34.85%	533,000
AIAN	0.87%	0.28%	0.76%	0.01%	0.04%	0.01%	38.39%	1.97%	30,000
Asian/PI	0.62%	0.21%	0.02%	0.38%	0.11%	0.01%	28.06%	1.35%	21,000
Other	0.16%	0.14%	0.01%	0.02%	0.02%	0.01%	4.62%	0.36%	5,000
Hispanic	9.16%	1.30%	0.09%	0.06%	0.50%	2.13%	16.10%	13.24%	202,000
% of composite equal to agency label	79.58%	92.68%	80.90%	61.15%	0.67%	94.15%	*Concordance rate* 82.69%		
Caseload share	57.44%	36.36%	0.94%	0.61%	2.39%	2.26%			
Column total	878,000	556,000	14,000	10,000	36,000	35,000			1,529,000

Source: Authors' calculations from the 2000 and 2010 Censuses, the Census Numident, and CJARS criminal histories (2022Q4 vintage). US Census Bureau, project number P-7500378, approval numbers CBDRB-FY24–0101, CBDRB-FY24–0277.

Note: CJARS court data come from Arizona, Florida, Maryland, Michigan, North Carolina, Oregon, Pennsylvania, Texas, Virginia, Wisconsin. This table presents the percent of individuals with particular combinations of agency-recorded race/ethnicity and Census Bureau race/ethnicity composites out of the total sample. For example, White, White indicates that 45.7 percent of the 1,529,000 in the sample labeled by justice agencies as White are also identified as White in the race/ethnicity composite. Race groups exclude people with Hispanic ethnicity; Hispanic includes people of all races. Estimates and sample sizes have been rounded according to Census Bureau DRB rules.

Table 5.6 **Concordance of agency-recorded race/ethnicity versus Census Bureau race/ethnicity composite, population of people in prison, 2000–2019, total table percents**

	Race/ethnicity recorded by justice system						% of agency-recorded equal to composite	Caseload share	Row total
Census Bureau race/ethnicity composite	White (1)	Black (2)	AIAN (3)	Asian/PI (4)	Other (5)	Hispanic (6)	(7)	(8)	(9)
White	37.21%	0.51%	0.15%	0.01%	0.06%	0.51%	96.78%	38.45%	190,000
Black	0.38%	39.56%	0.02%	0.00%	0.11%	0.08%	98.49%	40.15%	198,000
AIAN	0.70%	0.25%	1.04%	0.00%	0.01%	0.06%	50.46%	2.06%	10,000
Asian/PI	0.34%	0.19%	0.01%	0.20%	0.05%	0.03%	24.49%	0.82%	4,000
Other	0.10%	0.12%	0.04%	0.02%	0.02%	0.09%	5.11%	0.39%	2,000
Hispanic	4.08%	1.20%	0.12%	0.02%	0.53%	12.16%	67.19%	18.11%	89,000
% of composite equal to agency label	86.91%	94.59%	75.72%	78.37%	2.54%	93.99%	*Concordance rate* 90.2%		
Caseload share	42.81%	41.83%	1.38%	0.25%	0.78%	12.93%			
Column total	211,000	206,000	7,000	1,000	4,000	64,000			493,000

Source: Authors' calculations from the 2000 and 2010 Censuses, the Census Numident, and CJARS criminal histories (2022Q4 vintage). US Census Bureau, project number P-7500378, approval numbers CBDRB-FY24–0101, CBDRB-FY24–0277.

Note: CJARS prison data come from Arizona, Florida, Illinois, Indiana, Kansas, Michigan, Minnesota, Montana, Nebraska, New York, North Carolina, Oklahoma, Pennsylvania, Texas. This table presents the percent of individuals with particular combinations of agency-recorded race/ethnicity and Census Bureau race/ethnicity composites out of the total sample. For example, *White, White* indicates that 37.21 percent of the 493,000 in the sample labeled by justice agencies as White are also identified as White in the race/ethnicity composite. Race groups exclude people with Hispanic ethnicity; Hispanic includes people of all races. Estimates and sample sizes have been rounded according to Census Bureau DRB rules.

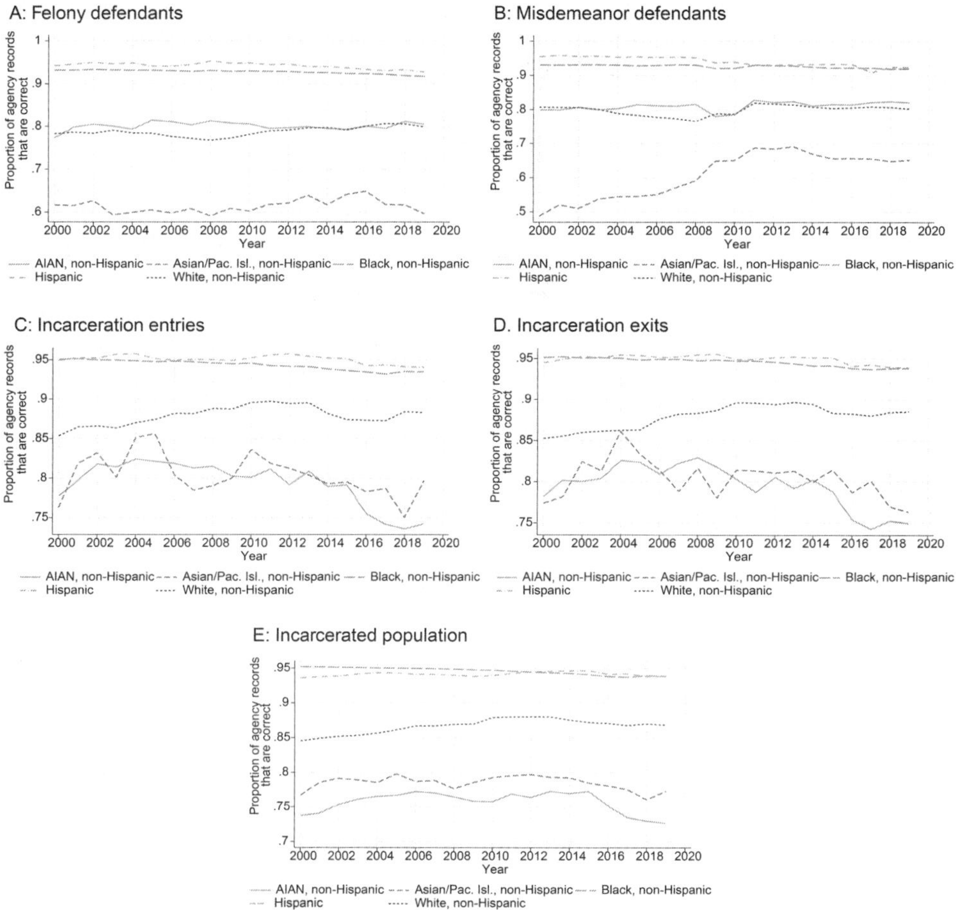

Fig. 5.3 Proportion of race/ethnicity recorded by justice system equal to Census Bureau race/ethnicity composites, 2000–2019, by criminal justice caseload and year

Source: Authors' calculations from the 2000 and 2010 Censuses, the Census Numident, and CJARS criminal histories (2022Q4 vintage). US Census Bureau, project number P-7500378, approval numbers CBDRB-FY24-0101, CBDRB-FY24-0277.

Note: CJARS court data come from Arizona, Florida, Maryland, Michigan, North Carolina, Oregon, Pennsylvania, Texas, Virginia, Wisconsin. CJARS prison data come from Arizona, Florida, Illinois, Indiana, Kansas, Michigan, Minnesota, Montana, Nebraska, New York, North Carolina, Oklahoma, Pennsylvania, Texas. These figures present the concordance of agency-recorded race/ethnicity and Census Bureau race/ethnicity composites over time. Each panel represents a different criminal justice caseload. Estimates and sample sizes have been rounded according to Census Bureau DRB rules.

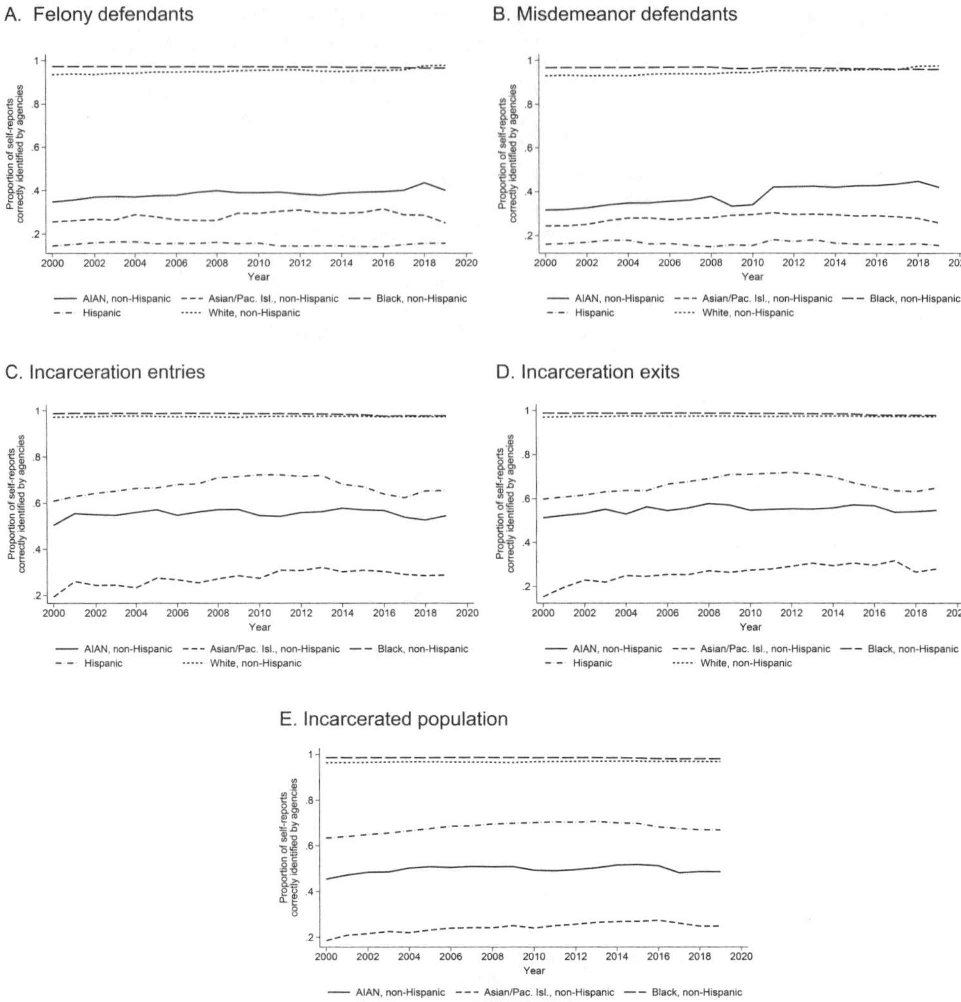

Fig. 5.4 Proportion of Census Bureau race/ethnicity composites equal to race/ethnicity recorded by justice system, 2000–2019, by criminal justice caseload and year

Source: Authors' calculations from the 2000 and 2010 Censuses, the Census Numident, and CJARS criminal histories (2022Q4 vintage). US Census Bureau, project number P-7500378, approval numbers CBDRB-FY24-0101, CBDRB-FY24-0277.

Note: CJARS court data come from Arizona, Florida, Maryland, Michigan, North Carolina, Oregon, Pennsylvania, Texas, Virginia, Wisconsin. CJARS prison data come from Arizona, Florida, Illinois, Indiana, Kansas, Michigan, Minnesota, Montana, Nebraska, New York, North Carolina, Oklahoma, Pennsylvania, Texas. These figures present the concordance of agency-recorded race/ethnicity and Census Bureau race/ethnicity composites over time. Each panel represents a different criminal justice caseload. Estimates and sample sizes have been rounded according to Census Bureau DRB rules.

Fig. 5.5 Geographic variation in the proportion of race/ethnicity recorded by justice system equal to Census Bureau race/ethnicity composites, misdemeanor and felony defendants, 2000–2019, by race/ethnicity and state

Source: Authors' calculations from the 2000 and 2010 Censuses, the Census Numident, and CJARS criminal histories (2022Q4 vintage). US Census Bureau, project number P-7500378, approval numbers CBDRB-FY24-0101, CBDRB-FY24-0277.

Note: "0"/White means that no race/ethnicity records concord across the two data sources. CJARS court data come from Arizona, Florida, Maryland, Michigan, North Carolina, Oregon, Pennsylvania, Texas, Virginia, Wisconsin. These figures present the proportion of misdemeanor and felony defendants from different subgroups accurately labeled by justice agencies, by state of criminal charge. Estimates and sample sizes have been rounded according to Census Bureau DRB rules.

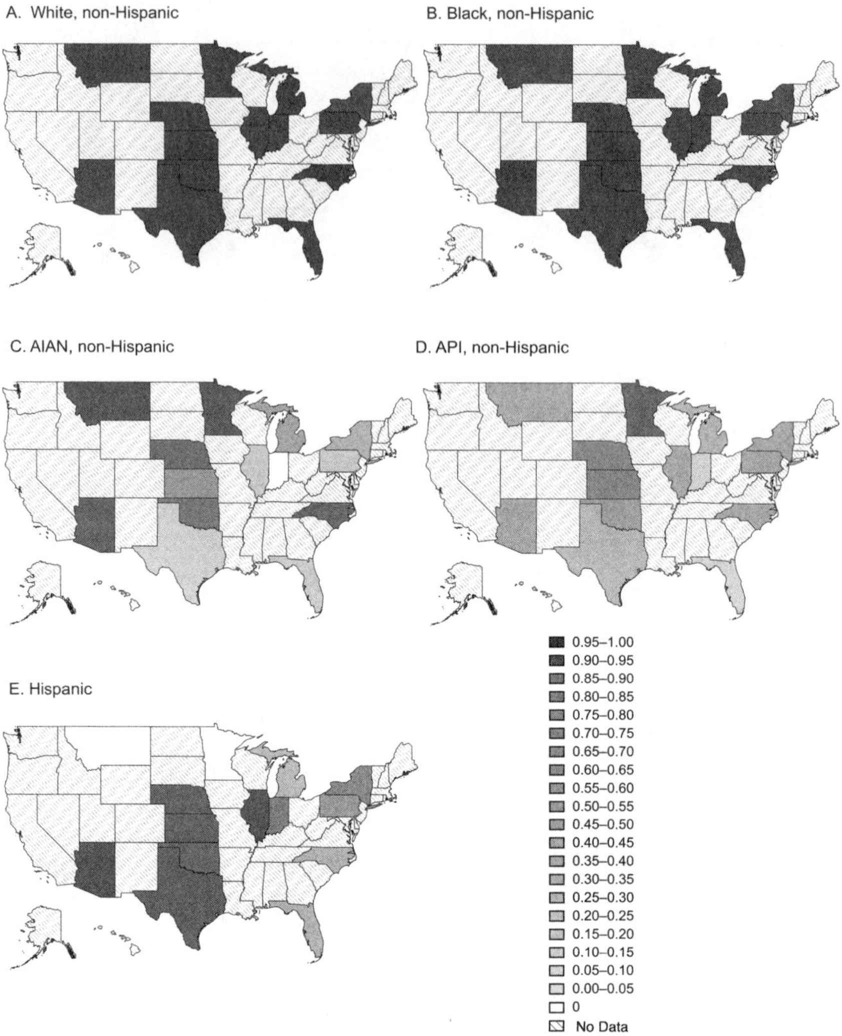

Fig. 5.6 Geographic variation in the proportion of race/ethnicity recorded by justice system equal to Census Bureau race/ethnicity composites, population of prison inmates, 2000–2019, by race/ethnicity and state

Source: Authors' calculations from the 2000 and 2010 Censuses, the Census Numident, and CJARS criminal histories (2022Q4 vintage). US Census Bureau, project number P-7500378, approval numbers CBDRB-FY24-0101, CBDRB-FY24-0277.

Note: "0"/White means that no race/ethnicity records concord across the two data sources. CJARS prison data come from Arizona, Florida, Illinois, Indiana, Kansas, Michigan, Minnesota, Montana, Nebraska, New York, North Carolina, Oklahoma, Pennsylvania, Texas. These figures present the proportion of prison inmates from different subgroups accurately labeled by justice agencies, by state of incarceration. Estimates and sample sizes have been rounded according to Census Bureau DRB rules.

in the same way as agency-recorded labels by race and ethnicity. Nationwide, the concordance for White and Black justice-involved populations is consistently high. With the exception of Maryland court records, where only 56 percent of defendants who are identified in the composite as White are recorded as White, agreement rates often are in excess of 97 percent. We find somewhat lower recall for: Black defendants in Arizona (95 percent), Oregon (90 percent), and Virginia (94 percent); White defendants in Virginia (95 percent); Black inmates in Montana (92 percent) and New York (94 percent); and White inmates in Arizona (95 percent) and New York (92 percent).

In contrast, few jurisdictions record race and ethnicity accurately for people whom we identify in Census Bureau records as American Indian and Alaska Native, Asian, Pacific Islander, or Hispanic. For AIAN and Hispanic populations, it does appear that jurisdictions with larger resident populations from these groups tend to fare better. The label agreement of AIAN justice-involved individuals is highest in Montana, Minnesota, Arizona, and Nebraska. Likewise the coverage of Hispanic inmates is highest in Arizona, Illinois, and Texas. That said, some jurisdictions break this pattern. A minority of Hispanic defendants and inmates in Florida, for example, are recorded as such by the criminal justice agencies they interact with in spite of Florida's large Hispanic population. Across the map, there is low data quality for Asian/Pacific Islander populations, perhaps related to this population's infrequent contact with the justice system in general.

5.3.3 Evaluating Alternative Hypotheses Related to Record Linkage Errors

These exercises rely on the assumption that the Census Bureau composite race/ethnicity linked with agency-recorded race/ethnicity from administrative records correspond to the same underlying person. One reason that discordance could arise between the Census Bureau composite and agency-recorded race and ethnicity is if this assumption regarding accurate record linkage fails, which may occur since the data integration relies on probabilistic record linkage. This would be even more problematic if linkage errors disproportionately affected specific minority populations.

To explore how much bias might be introduced due to record linkage errors, we explore two exercises. First, we examine the degree of concordance between agency-recorded sex and sex as recorded in the Census Numident. As discussed above, sex information in criminal justice administrative data is viewed by records administrators as high quality. Consequently, high levels of sex discordance would be a warning sign for potential flaws in the record linkage procedure that may result in an overestimate of race/ethnicity misreporting. For this exercise, we use an analogous algorithm to select a Census Bureau composite sex from the 2000 and 2010 Censuses and the Census Numident.

Figure 5.7 reports the sex concordance results. We find high agreement

Fig. 5.7 Percent of Census Bureau sex composites that concord with agency-recorded sex, 2000–2019, by criminal justice caseload

Source: Authors' calculations from the 2000 and 2010 Censuses, the Census Numident, and CJARS criminal histories (2022Q4 vintage). US Census Bureau, project number P-7500378, approval numbers CBDRB-FY240101, CBDRB-FY240277.

Note: CJARS court data come from Arizona, Florida, Maryland, Michigan, North Carolina, Oregon, Pennsylvania, Texas, Virginia, Wisconsin. CJARS prison data come from Arizona, Florida, Illinois, Indiana, Kansas, Michigan, Minnesota, Montana, Nebraska, New York, North Carolina, Oklahoma, Pennsylvania, Texas. This figure presents the concordance of agency-recorded sex and Census Bureau sex composites by criminal justice caseload. Estimates and sample sizes have been rounded according to Census Bureau DRB rules.

rates between agency-recorded and the composite sex. Over 99 percent of individuals identified as male are recorded as such by agencies. Similarly, over 98 percent of individuals identified as female are recorded that way by agencies. Sex is used as an input in the Census Bureau PVS record linkage process, whereas race and ethnicity are not, so this exercise may overstate the degree of concordance between the sex measures. Given that some minor degree of discordance may be attributable to measurement error in the Census Bureau data, differences in measurement concepts, and differences in reporting over time, these results provide evidence that record linkage is working as intended.[12]

The second exercise considers whether linked Medicaid administrative records exhibit the same degree of racial and ethnic discordance observed in criminal justice administrative records. Three factors make this a particularly interesting comparison exercise. First, the Medicaid data are compiled

12. Concordance of race and ethnicity measures may vary by sex since factors like surname change at marriage may disproportionately impact women and may influence perceptions of race and ethnicity. Understanding the intersection of these characteristics should be an important area for future research.

and linked from state agency records in a process similar to that used to harmonize the CJARS data. Second, Medicaid records should capture self-reported or family-reported race and ethnicity submitted by applicants on their enrollment paperwork. Finally, the income-targeted nature of Medicaid means the data should draw from a population more closely resembling the racial and ethnic distribution of justice-involved individuals. There are documented limitations in the quality of race and ethnicity data in Medicaid records, which might generate discordance with Census Bureau survey records in ways distinct from divergences between the composite race/ethnicity and ones based on agency perception (Limburg et al. 2023). Consequently, to the extent that Medicaid data show stronger concordance relative to the criminal justice data, this would be a lower bound on the relative impact of agency-perception.

Figure 5.8 shows the findings from the exercise. For the overall population as well as specific racial/ethnic subgroup, we show the share of Census Bureau composite labels that agree with the agency label. This is broken out for four groups: felony and misdemeanor defendants, prison inmates,

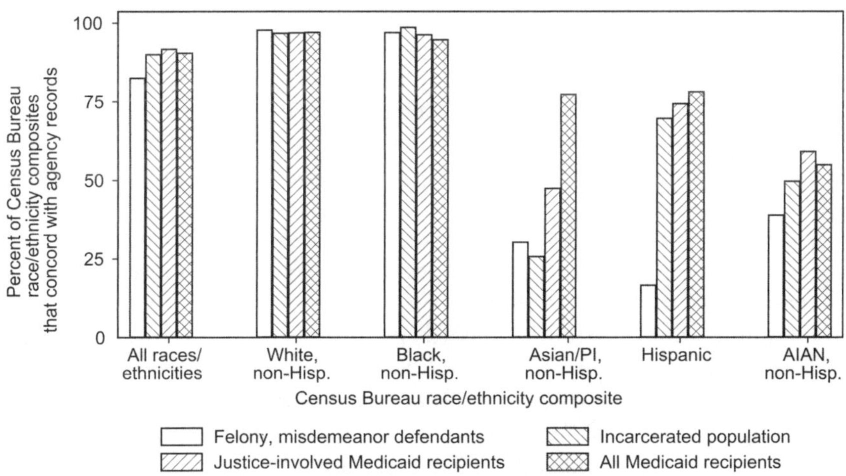

Fig. 5.8 Percent of Census Bureau race/ethnicity composites that concord with justice or Medicaid agency records, 2000–2019, by criminal justice caseload

Source: Authors' calculations from the 2000 and 2010 Censuses, the Census Numident, CJARS criminal histories (2022Q4 vintage), and CMS Medicaid Statistical Information System (MSIS)/Transformed MSIS data. US Census Bureau, project number P-7500378, approval numbers CBDRB-FY24-0101, CBDRB-FY240277.

Note: CJARS court data come from Arizona, Florida, Maryland, Michigan, North Carolina, Oregon, Pennsylvania, Texas, Virginia, Wisconsin. CJARS prison data come from Arizona, Florida, Illinois, Indiana, Kansas, Michigan, Minnesota, Montana, Nebraska, New York, North Carolina, Oklahoma, Pennsylvania, Texas. These figures present the proportion of individuals from different subgroups accurately labeled by justice agencies (in the case of the two justice populations) or state Medicaid agencies (in the case of the two Medicaid populations). Estimates and sample sizes have been rounded according to Census Bureau DRB rules.

justice-involved Medicaid recipients (either in court or prison records), and all Medicaid recipients. The first two columns reproduce results from above as a point of comparison. Overall, the Medicaid data, whether looking at justice-involved Medicaid recipients or all Medicaid recipients, have higher concordance rates (91–92 percent) than those observed in the CJARS data (83–90 percent), especially relative to the court records. Aligning with prior findings, the improvements come from better coverage of Asian, Pacific Islander, Hispanic, and American Indian and Alaska Native populations.

These two exercises show that the degree of discordance between agency-record race/ethnicity and the Census Bureau race/ethnicity composite is uniquely sizable. Sex, as measured by justice agencies, compares well with sex measured by Census Bureau sources, and race/ethnicity is measured more accurately in Medicaid data than justice data, even for the Medicaid-enrolled population that is justice involved.

5.4 Using Census Bureau Composite Race and Ethnicity Microdata to Adjust Federal Statistics on Incarceration

Since 1980, the Bureau of Justice Statistics (BJS) has published regular reports about the size and composition of state and federal prisoner populations in the United States. To do this, they rely on data from the National Prisoner Statistics (NPS) program, which solicits aggregate information on year-end prison counts from state and federal corrections agencies. Jurisdictions report back data based on information available in their records management systems.

Because not all NPS data providers record information in a manner consistent with OMB guidelines, BJS relies on supplementary survey data as a benchmark for the racial and ethnic composition of the prisoner population in the United States. For state records prior to 2016, BJS adjusted annual prisoner counts to match the distribution of self-reported race and ethnicity from the 2004 Survey of Inmates in State and Federal Correctional Facilities (SISFCF). Starting in 2016, BJS also incorporated equivalent data from the 2016 Survey of Prison Inmates (SPI) to account for potential changes in the demographic profile of inmates. Prisoner counts for prior reporting years over the preceding decade were re-released using a new set of weights that smoothed the transition between the 2004 and 2016 survey distributions. For federal prisoners, a similar process was applied using corresponding federal survey responses. Table 5.7 shows the difference between the 2004 SISFCF and 2016 SPI race distributions, and figure 5.9 shows how the weight adjustment affected the distribution of BJS-reported imprisonment per capita by race/ethnicity subgroup.

The race/ethnicity reweighting strategy employed by BJS to meet OMB guidelines creates a dependence on the accuracy of costly and therefore infrequently administered survey instruments. For example, the re-reported

Table 5.7 **Self-Reported race and ethnicity in the 2004 Survey of Inmates in State and Federal Correctional Facilities (SISFCF) and 2016 Survey of Prison Inmates (SPI)**

	2004 SISFCF		2016 SPI	
Race/ethnicity	State	Federal	State	Federal
White, non-Hispanic	36.5%	29.2%	31.9%	21.0%
	(0.7%)	(1.3%)	(1.0%)	(2.1%)
Black, non-Hispanic	40.0%	39.0%	33.8%	32.2%
	(0.7%)	(1.4%)	(1.2%)	(3.0%)
Hispanic	17.5%	24.7%	20.7%	37.1%
	(0.6%)	(1.2%)	(0.9%)	(4.2%)
American Indian/Alaska Native, non-Hispanic	1.7%	2.8%	1.4%	1.7%
	(0.2%)	(0.5%)	(0.2%)	(0.5%)
Asian/Pacific Islander, non-Hispanic	1.0%	1.7%	0.9%	1.5%
	(0.1%)	(0.4%)	(0.1%)	(0.3%)
Two or more races, non-Hispanic	3.3%	2.6%	11.3%	6.5%
	(0.3%)	(0.4%)	(0.4%)	(0.7%)
N	14,477	3,680	20,064	4,784

Source: 2004 SISFCF estimates and standard errors from authors' calculations of person-weighted proportions from publicly available survey microdata and methodology (Bureau of Justice Statistics 2019a, 2019b). 2016 SPI estimates and standard errors from Beatty and Snell (2021, 14) and Bureau of Justice Statistics (2023).

2015 prisoner estimates following the incorporation of 2016 SPI data into the reweighting methodology reduced the number of White inmates by 48,800 (9.8 percent), reduced Black inmates by 26,600 (5.1 percent), and increased Hispanic inmates by 16,400 (5.1 percent).[13] The net decline in total inmates falling into the three largest racial/ethnic categories is attributable to a high rate of respondents in the 2016 SPI reporting Two or More Races, a category for which BJS does not report prison population counts because almost no department of corrections has data to support this category. From the 2004 to 2016 survey instruments, the percent of state inmates self-reporting as Multiracial grew by 242 percent from 3.3 percent to 11.3 percent.[14]

The growth in multiracial identification is consistent with broader demographic trends in the United States. That said, it is also possible that the differences observed between these two survey waves is a by-product of the

13. Authors' calculations based on data underlying figure 5.9. In 2015, BJS reported 2015 prisoner counts for Whites, Blacks, and Hispanics as 499,400, 523,000, and 319,400. In 2022, the 2015 prisoner counts, which incorporated the 2016 SPI data, were reported as 450,600, 496,400, and 335,800.

14. The net reduction of prison inmates reported to be in one of the three largest racial and ethnic subgroups following the incorporation of the 2016 SPI is not the consequence of retroactive revisions to the number of inmates reported to BJS in the NPS; Panels D and E of figure 5.9 show that reported imprisonment rates for men and women line up perfectly across reporting years, regardless of how racial and ethnic reweighting was conducted.

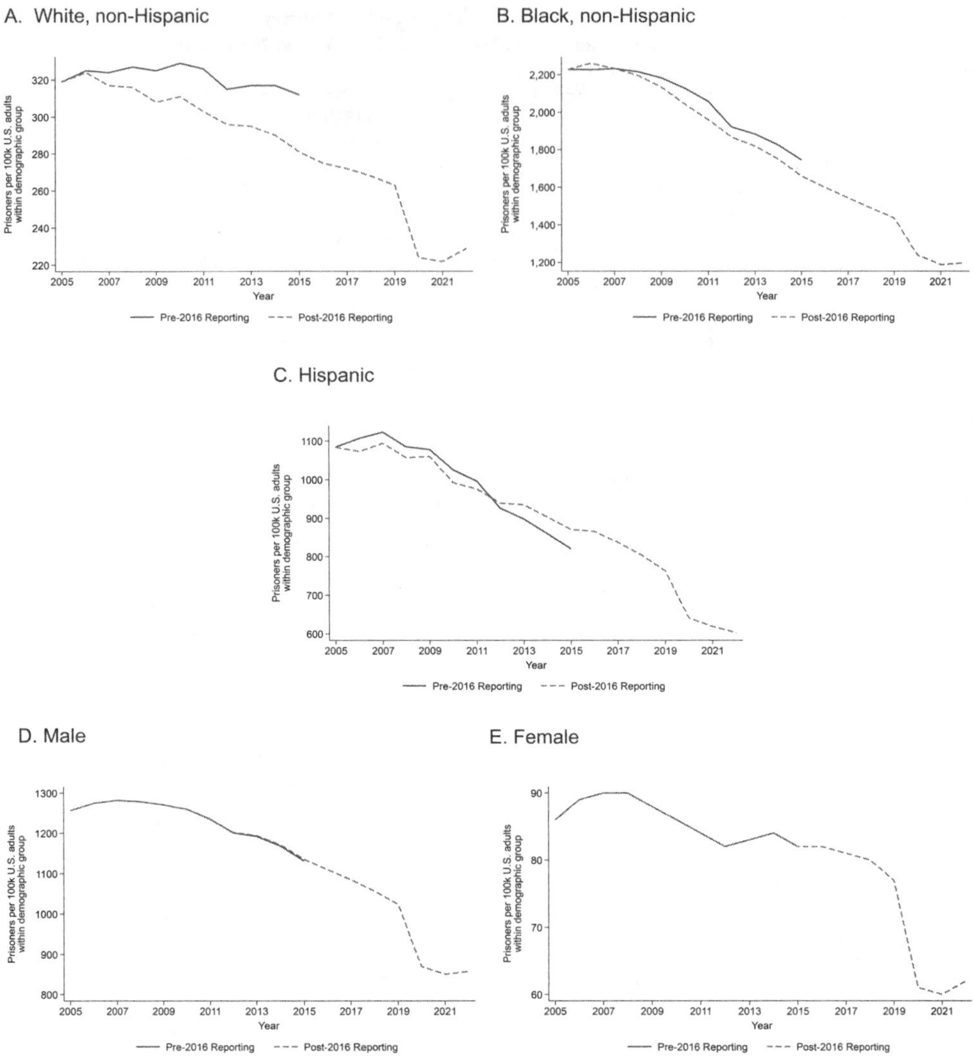

Fig. 5.9 Imprisonment rates by race/ethnicity and sex adjusted using the 2004 Survey of Inmates in State and Federal Correctional Facilities (SISFCF) and 2016 Survey of Prison Inmates (SPI)

Source: These figures report BJS published imprisonment rates by reporting method (Carson 2016, 2018; Bronson and Carson 2019; Carson 2020a, 2020b, 2021, 2022; Carson and Kluckow 2023).

Note: Pre-2016 reporting exclusively uses the 2015 BJS report and post-2016 reporting uses the latest available report as the value for each year.

surveys' stratified two-stage sample design, wherein a set of prison facilities are first sampled for inclusion in the survey (301 [364] out of 1,801 [2,001] unique facilities in the 2004 SISFCF [2016 SPI]) and then inmates within just that subset of facilities are sampled for the survey.[15] Clustered sampling strategies, while cost-effective, are known to generate higher variance in their estimates. Additionally, inmate non-response (10 percent [30 percent] in the 2004 SISFCF [2016 SPI]) may limit the representativeness of the survey estimates to the prisoner population as a whole.

With the luxury of person-level data linkages, we can take an alternative approach to reweight prison populations. We leverage the annual NPS reports by state and federal agencies of their raw, unadjusted counts by agency-recorded race/ethnicity. Those raw counts can be reweighted by our estimated year-specific concordance matrices for incarcerated populations to generate estimates that adjust for the racial and ethnic distribution of the prisoner population based on the Census Bureau race/ethnicity composite. This permits us to reallocate subpopulations within agency-recorded bins to different Census Bureau race/ethnicity composites. For example, we observe that 8 percent (4 percent) of agency-recorded White (Black) inmates in 2019 are identified in the composite measure as Hispanic. An equivalent strategy could be used with the 2004 SISFCF and 2016 SPI if those survey responses were linked to raw agency records, but the CJARS data provide a much larger sample to estimate the reweighting matrix.

There are strengths and weaknesses of this approach. On the positive side, we are able to incorporate the original NPS-reported aggregate counts by agency-recorded race and ethnicity for the entire United States. While imperfectly suited to meet OMB guidelines, this ground-truth agency data are high-quality annual information about the racial and ethnic distribution of the prisoner population. Applying a concordance matrix to these counts translates agency-recorded labels to labels closer in principle to something self reported. In the context of the population of prisoners, fewer than 10 percent of inmates on average between 2000 and 2019 are relabeled using this method. We estimate concordance matrices for these populations on an annual basis so they can adjust as the relationship between agency-record race and ethnicity and self-identification evolves over time, whether due to improvements in data quality, changes in records policies and procedures, or changes in how justice-involved people perceive their own races and ethnicities.[16]

15. In practice, only a subset of facilities is sampled at random, and randomly selected facilities are not selected with equal probability. The facilities with the largest inmate populations were "sampled" with certainty, thereby automatically entering the sample, while the remaining were stratified by census region and given a sampling probability proportional to the size of their inmate population. As a result, selected prisons are larger than non-selected prisons and selected inmates may not be nationally representative of the overall prisoner population.

16. Because of lags in data production, we apply the 2019 correspondence matrix to the 2020 and 2021 NPS counts to get CJARS-adjusted estimates in those years.

The drawback is that CJARS does not include data from all state prisons. As a result, we have to assume that the estimated concordance matrices generalize to all states. While important, we view this as an assumption that is secondary in nature since the majority of information regarding the racial and ethnic composition of the prisoner population will come from the NPS counts, which do not face the same coverage limitations as the linked CJARS microdata.

Figure 5.10 shows the results of reweighting using the CJARS/Census Bureau correspondence matrices. Results are shown separately by the five race/ethnicity groups included in BJS reporting as well as the non-reported residual category: White, Black, AIAN, Asian/Pacific Islander, Hispanic, and Other. Each panel includes the raw unadjusted NPS imprisonment rate per 100,000 adults (dot-dash line), the adjusted BJS-reported imprisonment rate using the 2004 SISFCF and 2016 SPI (dash line), and the CJARS-Census Bureau matrix-adjusted imprisonment rate (solid line). To construct the BJS-adjusted rate for the Other series, we take the total overall count of prisoners reported by BJS and subtracted the reported counts from the five major racial and ethnic groups.

Several important findings emerge. The CJARS/Census Bureau-adjusted imprisonment rates almost always exceed the BJS-adjusted statistical series. The two exceptions are the Hispanic imprisonment rate, where the two series are very close to each other, and the Other imprisonment rate, where the implied BJS-adjusted rate is significantly higher than the BJS unadjusted rate or the CJARS/Census Bureau-adjusted rate. This pattern arises because a disproportionate share of 2004 SISFCF and 2016 SPI respondents identify as multiracial compared to the agency-record race codes in the NPS or the Census Bureau composite labels linked to CJARS data.[17] These gaps become more pronounced over time between 2005 and 2016, especially for White and Black prisoners, as the BJS reweighting strategy shifts toward placing more weight on the 2016 SPI implied race and ethnicity distributions. For 2018, CJARS/Census Bureau-adjusted estimates place the imprisonment rate of White and Blacks 20 percent and 17 percent higher, respectively, compared to BJS-reported rates. In levels, this corresponds to approximately 86,000 previously unreported additional White inmates and 80,000 previously unreported additional Black inmates in 2018.[18]

If the BJS adjustments are accurate, it would imply that the imprisonment rate for Other/Multiracial individuals is the highest of any demographic

17. As can be seen in table 5.6, Column 8, only 0.39 percent of prisoners in the CJARS data between 2000 and 2019 are identified as Other/Multiracial in the Census Bureau race/ethnicity composite. This is 88 percent and 97 percent smaller than the shares reported as Multiracial in the state prison estimates from the 2004 SISFCF (3.3 percent) and the 2016 SPI (11.3 percent).

18. Authors' calculations based on data underlying figure 5.10. In 2018, the adjusted BJS prisoner counts for Whites and Blacks were 430,500 and 461,500; the equivalent prisoner counts using the CJARS/Census Bureau adjustment were 516,381 and 541,163.

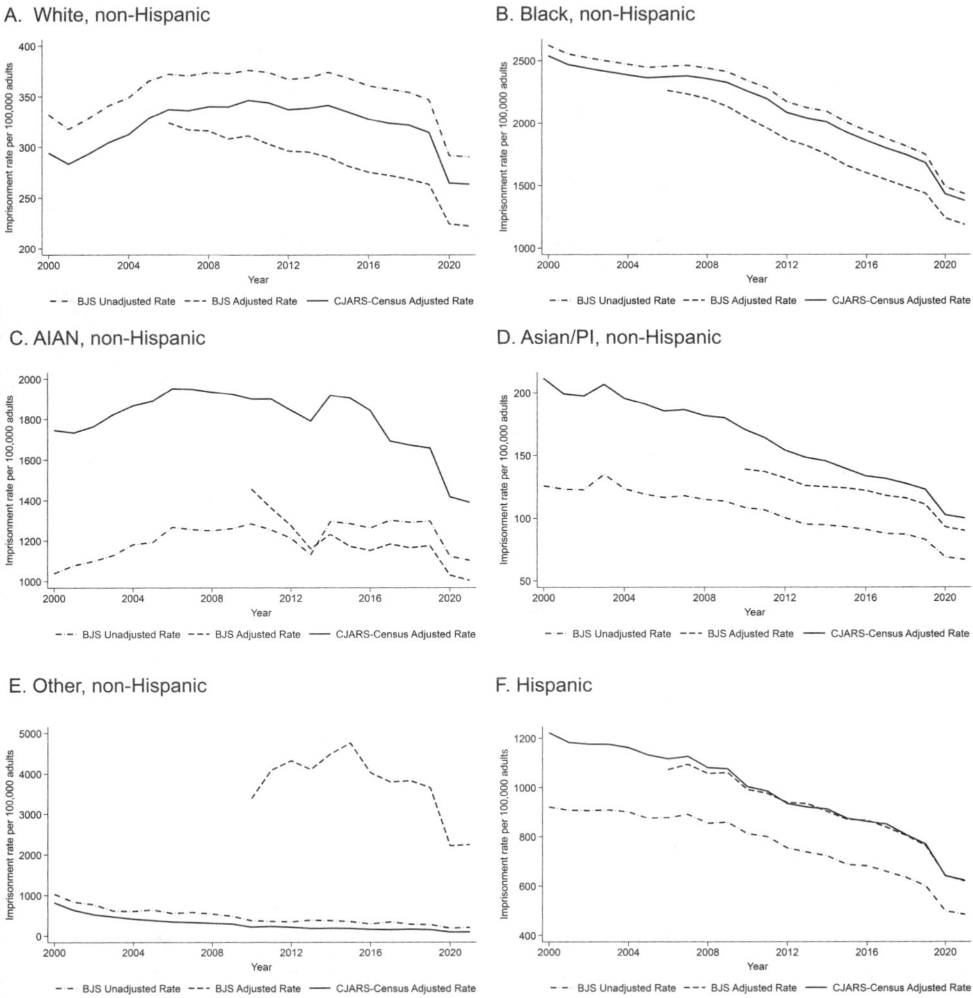

Fig. 5.10 Imprisonment rates by race/ethnicity, 2000–2021: unadjusted NPS rates, rates adjusted using BJS surveys, rates adjusted using CJARS-Census Bureau data

Source: Authors' calculations from the 2000 and 2010 Censuses, the Census Numident, CJARS criminal histories (2022Q4 vintage), and National Prisoner Statistics Program data. US Census Bureau, project number P-7500378, approval numbers CBDRB-FY24-0101, CBDRB-FY24-0277.

Note: Figures show estimated imprisonment rates for state and federal prisoners using three methods. The BJS-unadjusted rate shows the original racial and ethnic distribution reported by agencies to BJS in the NPS. The BJS-adjusted rate shows their published per capita rates which rely on imputing racial and ethnic population shares based on inmate survey data. The CJARS-Census Bureau-adjusted rate rescales the original unadjusted data reported by agencies in the NPS using year-specific versions of table 5.6. Estimates and sample sizes have been rounded according to Census Bureau DRB rules.

Table 5.8 **Socioeconomic characteristics of adults aged 18–65 years, American Community Survey, 2005–2019, by race and ethnicity**

Characteristic	White	Black	AIAN	Asian/PI	Other	Hispanic
Educational attainment						
High school graduate	0.94	0.88	0.84	0.92	0.91	0.72
	(0.0001)	(0.0002)	(0.0010)	(0.0003)	(0.0005)	(0.0003)
Some college	0.58	0.46	0.40	0.69	0.56	0.34
	(0.0001)	(0.0004)	(0.0014)	(0.0005)	(0.0009)	(0.0003)
College graduate	0.32	0.18	0.13	0.49	0.27	0.13
	(0.0001)	(0.0003)	(0.0010)	(0.0005)	(0.0008)	(0.0002)
Employment/earnings						
Unemployed	0.04	0.09	0.09	0.04	0.07	0.06
	(0.0001)	(0.0002)	(0.0008)	(0.0002)	(0.0005)	(0.0002)
Wage income	$37,857	$23,693	$20,576	$41,099	$28,994	$23,340
	(15.0)	(24.6)	(91.2)	(59.1)	(77.7)	(20.3)
Total family income	$96,807	$59,874	$59,659	$110,250	$82,007	$67,506
	(26.5)	(45.5)	(176.6)	(106.6)	(151.3)	(40.2)
Family income below federal poverty line	0.08	0.18	0.21	0.10	0.13	0.16
	(0.0001)	(0.0003)	(0.0012)	(0.0003)	(0.0006)	(0.0002)
Household structure						
Single-parent household	0.09	0.23	0.16	0.08	0.15	0.15
	(0.0001)	(0.0003)	(0.0011)	(0.0003)	(0.0007)	(0.0002)
N	19,714,757	2,925,138	249,137	1,527,804	506,110	3,837,687

Source: Authors' calculations from publicly available 2005–2019 five-year American Community Survey (ACS) IPUMS files (Ruggles et al. 2024).

Note: ACS sample is restricted to respondents aged between 18 and 65 years and stratified by the mutually exclusive race/ethnicity categories used throughout this paper. Race groups exclude people with Hispanic ethnicity; Hispanic includes people of all races. For each group, we calculate person-weighted means for each characteristic.

group in the United States, more than 200 percent higher than for Blacks. In contrast, the BJS-unadjusted and CJARS/Census Bureau-adjusted rates for the Other population place them somewhere between rates for Hispanics and Whites. Table 5.8 uses data from the American Community Survey (ACS) between 2005 and 2019 to show a variety of socioeconomic characteristics in the overall population for these racial and ethnic groups, including educational attainment, employment and earnings, and household structure.[19] On each of these measures, the Other adults appear much more similar to White and Hispanic adults, suggesting the CJARS-adjusted statistical series are more consistent with other observed population differences across racial and ethnic groups. Stated differently, it is not the case that Other adults are

19. Using publicly available 2005–2019 5-year ACS IPUMS files (Ruggles et al. 2024), we restrict to a sample of respondents aged between 18 and 65 years and stratify by the mutually exclusive race/ethnicity categories used throughout this paper. For each group, we calculate person-weighted means for the characteristics listed in table 5.8.

more economically disadvantaged than Black adults on any measure, as should be the case if the imprisonment rate in this population was more than 200 percent higher than Black adults. The treatment of the Other/Multiracial category is a potential shortcoming in the BJS imputation strategy that could be improved with the kind of record linkage used in this paper.

Another finding from figure 5.10 is that the CJARS/Census Bureau-adjusted imprisonment rate for the AIAN population is on average 45 percent larger than the BJS-adjusted imprisonment rate since 2010. In 2015, the CJARS/Census Bureau-adjusted series is 62 percent larger than the BJS-reported imprisonment rate. The increase reflected in the CJARS/Census Bureau-adjusted series is so substantial that by the latter half of the 2010s, the imprisonment rates of Blacks and AIANs are approximately equivalent. This potential major revision to our understanding of the prevalence of prison incarceration within this group reflects the challenge of accurately capturing information about less populous racial and ethnic groups with small samples from surveys like the SISFCF and the SPI.

5.5 Conclusion

In this paper, we consider the challenge of trying to analyze race and ethnicity information in the context of the US criminal justice system, where race and ethnicity data are often assigned by law enforcement officers and other justice officials. Operational priorities, limited resources, and other bureaucratic incentives limit the improvement of race and ethnicity records even when misreports have been identified.

We link agency-recorded race and ethnicity data from CJARS at the person level to a composite race and ethnicity measure constructed from 2000 and 2010 Census and Census Numident data. By being composed primarily of self- or family-reported data, the Census Bureau race/ethnicity composite better reflects best practices in race and ethnicity measurement. These matched data allow us to quantify both the degree of discordance between the justice agency-reported and Census Bureau composite sources and the types of misreports that occur in practice. Overall, we find that 17 percent of felony and misdemeanor defendants and 10 percent of prison inmates have a Census Bureau composite race/ethnicity that differs from their agency-recorded label. The most common types of discordance are where individuals are identified as Hispanic in the Census Bureau composite but are labeled by agencies as White or Black (and not Hispanic). While agency labels typically concord for the vast majority of Whites and Blacks in their caseloads, agencies are much less successful at identifying American Indians and Alaska Natives, Asians, Pacific Islanders, and Hispanics.

We apply the estimated empirical correspondences between agency-recorded and Census Bureau composite race and ethnicity to the raw, unadjusted annual National Prisoner Statistics data to re-estimate imprisonment rates by race and ethnicity. Because of concerns about the quality of race and ethnicity information reported in the NPS and its adherence to OMB guidelines, BJS's current practice is to reweight the racial and ethnic distribution of imprisonment using two national prisoner surveys from 2004 and 2016. We find large discrepancies between the BJS approach and our estimates that incorporate the original NPS data with our estimated annual correspondence matrices. For example, we find that there were approximately 85,000 additional White inmates and 80,000 Black inmates in 2018 in 2018 than BJS reported and that the imprisonment rate of AIANs was 46 percent higher on average since 2010.

These results have implications for Census Bureau collections and the downstream uses of those data to study the justice system. As decennial census and ACS group quarters responses are increasingly collected in bulk from administrators, census and ACS race and ethnicity data will more greatly reflect the limitations of justice data systems. Race/ethnicity data collected from jails are likely to be of particularly poor quality, since those data are often collocated with court data, which we find misidentify people who are not White or Black. The 2024 SPD15 revision requires federal agencies to transparently describe how race and ethnicity data have been collected (Office of Management and Budget 2024). Working with data-providing justice agencies to better document their own collection processes would allow the Census Bureau to further inform the public about any limitations of resulting census or survey data. This could be part of a broader research agenda that measures how justice data can be mapped to the collection of race and ethnicity in a single question that allows multiple responses, and for the addition of Middle Eastern or North African as a minimum category—changes required under the 2024 SPD15 revision (Office of Management and Budget 2024).

Research on crime and justice in the United States increasingly relies on administrative data with agency-recorded race and ethnicity. The race/ethnicity misreporting we measure raises questions about research that relies on agency data without further linkage or adjustments. Systematic mismeasurement may mean that existing estimates on racial and ethnic disparities in criminal justice outcomes are currently underestimated. This paper shows the value of data infrastructure efforts like CJARS that support the linkage of individual-level microdata across a range of sources. We demonstrate how leveraging the full depth of available information in integrated data environments like the Census Bureau's Data Linkage Infrastructure can strengthen our knowledge about—and meaningfully improve the monitoring of—the criminal justice system in the United States.

Acknowledgments

We are grateful to Randall Akee, Bocar Ba, Lt. Jason Barnett, Patrick Bayer, Charlie Brown, Shawn Bushway, Holly Champagne, Kerwin Charles,

Jonathan Eggleston, Jon Guryan, Larry Katz, Mark Loewenstein, Jens Ludwig, Conrad Miller, Sarah Miller, Amy O'Hara, Sgt. Julia Parr, Jordan Papp, Anne Piehl, JJ Prescott, Ebony Reid, Diana Sutton, and Hina Usman for their thoughtful and constructive comments. Arkey Barnett and James Reeves provided excellent research assistance. The Securities and Exchange Commission disclaims responsibility for any private publication or statement of any SEC employee or Commissioner. This article expresses the authors' views and does not necessarily reflect those of the Commission, the Commissioners, other members of the staff, or the Census Bureau. The Census Bureau has reviewed this data product to ensure appropriate access, use, and disclosure avoidance protection of the confidential source data (project number P-7500378, Disclosure Review Board [DRB] approval numbers CBDRB-FY24-0101, CBDRB-FY24-0277). For acknowledgments, sources of research support, and disclosure of the authors material financial relationships, if any, please see https://www.nber.org/books-and-chapters/race-ethnicity-and-economic-statistics-21st-century/race-and-ethnicity-mismeasurement-us-criminal-justice-system.

References

Agan, Amanda, and Sonja Starr. 2018. "Ban the Box, Criminal Records, and Racial Discrimination: A Field Experiment." *Quarterly Journal of Economics* 133(1): 191–235. https://doi.org/10.1093/qje/qjx028.

Alesina, Alberto, and Eliana La Ferrara. 2014. "A Test of Racial Bias in Capital Sentencing." *American Economic Review* 104(11): 3397–433. https://doi.org/10.1257/aer.104.11.3397.

American Civil Liberties Union and The Sentencing Project. 2022. "Racial Disparities in Sentencing in the United States." Shadow Report to the 107th Session of the UN Committee on the Elimination of Racial Discrimination. https://www.sentencingproject.org/app/uploads/2022/10/07-14-2022_CERD-Shadow-Report-Draft_with-endnotes.pdf.

Bayer, Patrick, and Kerwin Kofi Charles. 2018. "Divergent Paths: A New Perspective on Earnings Differences Between Black and White Men Since 1940." *Quarterly Journal of Economics* 133(3): 1459–501. https://doi.org/10.1093/qje/qjy003.

Beatty, Lauren G., and Tracy L. Snell. 2021. Profile of Prison Inmates, 2016. Bureau of Justice Statistics, NCJ 255037. https://bjs.ojp.gov/content/pub/pdf/ppi16.pdf.

Belton, Judy, and Dora Durante. 2021. 2020 Decennial Census Group Quarters Data Collection Operation. National Academies of Science. https://www.nationalacademies.org/documents/embed/link/LF2255DA3DD1C41C0A42D3BEF0989ACAECE3053A6A9B/file/D9C327E9F077C55EEBCB276E438BF7148649C4B78F4B.

Bertrand, Marianne, and Sendhil Mullainathan. 2004. "Are Emily and Greg More Employable than Lakisha and Jamal? A Field Experiment on Labor Market Discrimination." *American Economic Review* 94(4): 991–1013. https://doi.org/10.1257/0002828042002561.

Besemer, Sytske, David P. Farrington, and Catrien C. J. H. Bijleveld. 2017. "Labeling and Intergenerational Transmission of Crime: The Interaction between Criminal Justice Intervention and a Convicted Parent." *PLOS ONE* 12(3): e0172419. https://doi.org/10.1371/journal.pone.0172419.

Blair, Irene V., Charles M. Judd, Melody S. Sadler, and Christopher Jenkins. 2002. "The Role of Afrocentric Features in Person Perception: Judging by Features and Categories." *Journal of Personality and Social Psychology* 83: 5–25. https://doi.org/10.1037/0022-3514.83.1.5.

Bordalo, Pedro, Katherine Coffman, Nicola Gennaioli, and Andrei Shleifer. 2016. "Stereotypes." *Quarterly Journal of Economics* 131(4): 1753–94. https://doi.org/10.1093/qje/qjw029.

Bronson, Jennifer, and E. Ann Carson. 2019. Prisoners in 2017. Bureau of Justice Statistics, NCJ 252156. https://bjs.ojp.gov/library/publications/prisoners-2017.

Bureau of Justice Statistics. 2019a. Survey of Inmates in State and Federal Correctional Facilities, 2004. Inter-university Consortium for Political and Social Research [distributor], 2019–12–12. https://doi.org/10.3886/ICPSR04572.v6.

———. 2019b. Survey of Inmates in State and Federal Correctional Facilities, 2004: Codebook Part 1—Federal Data [Public]. Inter-university Consortium for Political and Social Research [distributor], 2019–12–12. https://doi.org/10.3886/ICPSR04572.v6.

———. 2023. 2016 SPI Data Analysis Tool (SPI DAT). Data generated on June 17, 2024. https://spi-data.bjs.ojp.gov.

Carson, E. Ann. 2016. Prisoners in 2015. Bureau of Justice Statistics, NCJ 250229. https://bjs.ojp.gov/library/publications/prisoners-2015.

———. 2018. Prisoners in 2016. Bureau of Justice Statistics, NCJ 251149. https://bjs.ojp.gov/library/publications/prisoners-2016.

Carson, E. Ann. 2020a. Prisoners in 2018. Bureau of Justice Statistics, NCJ 253516. https://bjs.ojp.gov/library/publications/prisoners-2018.

———. 2020b. Prisoners in 2019. Bureau of Justice Statistics, NCJ 255115. https://bjs.ojp.gov/library/publications/prisoners-2019.

———. 2021. Prisoners in 2020—Statistical Tables. Bureau of Justice Statistics, NCJ 302776. https://bjs.ojp.gov/library/publications/prisoners-2020-statistical-tables.

———. 2022. Prisoners in 2021. Bureau of Justice Statistics, NCJ 305125. https://bjs.ojp.gov/library/publications/prisoners-2021-statistical-tables.

Carson, E. Ann, and Rich Kluckow. 2023. Prisoners in 2022. Bureau of Justice Statistics, NCJ 307149. https://bjs.ojp.gov/library/publications/prisoners-2022-statistical-tables.

Charles, Kerwin Kofi, and Jonathan Guryan. 2011. "Studying Discrimination: Fundamental Challenges and Recent Progress." *Annual Review of Economics* 3(1): 479–511. https://doi.org/10.1146/annurev.economics.102308.124448.

Collister, Brian. 2016. Finding Errors in Texas Data. Investigative Reporters & Editors, Accessed February 16, 2024. https://www.ire.org/finding-errors-in-texas-data.

Dallas County District Attorney's Office. 2024. The Criminal Justice Process: What Happens after an Arrest? Accessed on 2/17/2024. https://www.dallascounty.org/government/district-attorney/cj-process.php.

Darity, William A., Patrick L. Mason, and James B. Stewart. 2006. "The Economics of Identity: The Origin and Persistence of Racial Identity Norms." *Journal of Economic Behavior & Organization* 60(3): 283–305. https://doi.org/10.1016/j.jebo.2004.09.005.

Davenport, Lauren. 2020. "The Fluidity of Racial Classifications." *Annual Review of Political Science* 23(1): 221–40. https://doi.org/10.1146/annurev-polisci-060418-042801.

Decker, Scott, Cassia Spohn, Natalie Ortiz, and Eric Hedberg. 2014. "Criminal Stigma, Race, Gender and Employment: An Expanded Assessment of the Consequences of Imprisonment for Employment." National Institute of Justice, NCJ 244756. https://nij.ojp.gov/library/publications/criminal-stigma-race-gender-and-employment-expanded-assessment-consequences.

Dixon, Angela R., and Edward E. Telles. 2017. "Skin Color and Colorism: Global Research, Concepts, and Measurement." *Annual Review of Sociology* 43(1): 405–24. https://doi.org/10.1146/annurev-soc-060116-053315.

Doleac, Jennifer L., and Benjamin Hansen. 2020. "The Unintended Consequences of 'Ban the Box': Statistical Discrimination and Employment Outcomes when Criminal Histories Are Hidden." *Journal of Labor Economics* 38(2): 321–74. https://doi.org/10.1086/705880.

Doyle, Jamie Mihoko, and Grace Kao. 2007. "Are Racial Identities of Multiracials Stable? Changing Self-Identification among Single and Multiple Race Individuals." *Social Psychology Quarterly* 70(4): 405–23. https://doi.org/10.1177/019027250707000409.

Eberhardt, Jennifer L., Phillip Atiba Goff, Valerie J. Purdie, and Paul G. Davies. 2004. "Seeing Black: Race, Crime, and Visual Processing." *Journal of Personality and Social Psychology* 87(6): 876–93. https://doi.org/10.1037/0022-3514.87.6.876.

Ennis, Sharon R., Sonya R. Porter, James M. Noon, and Ellen Zapata. 2018. "When Race and Hispanic Origin Reporting are Discrepant across Administrative Records and Third Party Sources: Exploring Methods to Assign Responses." *Statistical Journal of the IAOS* 34(2): 179–89. https://doi.org/10.3233/sji-170374.

Finkeldey, Jessica G., and Stephen Demuth. 2021. "Race/Ethnicity, Perceived Skin Color, and the Likelihood of Adult Arrest." *Race and Justice* 11(4): 567–91. https://doi.org/10.1177/2153368719826269.

Finlay, Keith, and Michael Mueller-Smith. 2022. Criminal Justice Administrative Records System (CJARS) [dataset]. Ann Arbor, MI: University of Michigan. https://cjars.org.

Finlay, Keith, Michael Mueller-Smith, and Jordan Papp. 2022. "The Criminal Justice Administrative Records System: A Next-Generation Research Data Platform." *Scientific Data* 9(1): 562. https://doi.org/10.1038/s41597-022-01620-y.

Finlay, Keith, Michael Mueller-Smith, and Brittany Street. 2023. "Children's Indirect Exposure to the U.S. Justice System: Evidence from Longitudinal Links between Survey and Administrative Data." *Quarterly Journal of Economics* 138(4): 2181–224. https://doi.org/10.1093/qje/qjad021.

Freeman, Jonathan B., Andrew M. Penner, Aliya Saperstein, Matthias Scheutz, and Nalini Ambady. 2011. "Looking the Part: Social Status Cues Shape Race Perception." *PLOS ONE* 6(9): e25107. https://doi.org/10.1371/journal.pone.0025107.

Fryer, Roland G., and Steven D. Levitt. 2004. "The Causes and Consequences of Distinctively Black Names." *Quarterly Journal of Economics* 119(3): 767–805. https://doi.org/10.1162/0033553041502180.

Gaddis, S. Michael. 2017. "How Black Are Lakisha and Jamal? Racial Perceptions from Names Used in Correspondence Audit Studies." *Sociological Science* 4: 469–89. https://doi.org/10.15195/v4.a19.

Goel, Sharad, Justin M. Rao, and Ravi Shroff. 2016. "Precinct or Prejudice? Understanding Racial Disparities in New York City's Stop-and-Frisk Policy." *Annals of Applied Statistics* 10(1): 365–94. https://doi.org/10.1214/15-aoas897.

Gyimah-Brempong, Kwabena, and Gregory N Price. 2006. "Crime and Punishment: And Skin Hue Too?" *American Economic Review* 96(2): 246–50. https://doi.org/10.1257/000282806777212530.

Harrell, Erika. 2009. Asian, Native Hawaiian, and Pacific Islander Victims of Crime. Bureau of Justice Statistics, NCJ 225037. https://www.ojp.gov/library/publications/asian-native-hawaiian-and-pacific-islander-victims-crime.

Harris, David R. 2002. "In the Eye of the Beholder: Observed Race and Observer

Characteristics." PSC Research Report 02–522. https://web.archive.org/web/20220121011923/, https://psc. isr.umich.edu/pubs/pdf/rr02-522.pdf.

Harris, David R., and Jeremiah Joseph Sim. 2002. "Who is Multiracial? Assessing the Complexity of Lived Race." *American Sociological Review* 67(4): 614–27. https://doi.org/10.2307/3088948.

Holland, Paul W. 2003. "Causation and Race." *ETS Research Report Series* 2003 (1): i–21. https://doi.org/10.1002/j.2333-8504.2003.tb01895.x.

King, Ryan D., and Brian D. Johnson. 2016. "A Punishing Look: Skin Tone and Afrocentric Features in the Halls of Justice." *American Journal of Sociology* 122(1): 90–124. https://doi.org/10.1086/686941.

Latessa, Edward, Paula Smith, Richard Lemke, Matthew Makarios, and Christopher Lowenkamp. 2009. Creation and Validation of the Ohio Risk Assessment System: Final Report. Center for Criminal Justice Research, School of Criminal Justice, University of Cincinnati. https://www.uc.edu/content/dam/uc/ccjr/docs/reports/project_reports/ORAS_Final_Report.pdf.

Law Offices of the Public Defender, 11th Judicial Circuit of Florida. 2024. Adult Case Process: Frequently Asked Questions. Accessed 2/17/2024. https://www.pdmiami.com/public-defender/client-information/adult-case-process.page.

Liebler, Carolyn A., Sonya R. Porter, Leticia E. Fernandez, James M. Noon, and Sharon R. Ennis. 2017. "America's Churning Races: Race and Ethnic Response Changes between Census 2000 and the 2010 Census." *Demography* 54(1): 259–84. https://doi.org/10.1007/s13524-016-0544-0.

Limburg, Aubrey, Adam Kurczewski, and Victoria Udalova. 2023. "Enhancing Race and Ethnicity Information in Medicaid Data: The Role of Census Bureau Data." Census Bureau SEHSD Working Paper 2023–05. https://www.census.gov/library/working-papers/2023/demo/SEHSD-WP2023-05.html.

Luh, Elizabeth. 2022. "Not So Black and White: Uncovering Racial Bias from Systematically Misreported Trooper Reports." SSRN Working Paper 3357063. http://dx.doi.org/10.2139/ssrn.3357063.

Mason, Patrick. 2017. "Not Black-Alone: The 2008 Presidential Election and Racial Self-Identification among African Americans." *Review of Black Political Economy* 44(1–2): 55–76. https://doi.org/10.1007/s12114-017-9247-z.

Mays, Vickie M., Abigail Echo-Hawk, Susan D. Cochran, and Randall Akee. 2022. "Data Equity in American Indian/Alaska Native Populations: Respecting Sovereign Nations' Right to Meaningful and Usable COVID-19 Data." *American Journal of Public Health* 112(10): 1416–20.

Michigan Department of Corrections. 2022. Policy Directive: Pre-Sentence Investigation and Report. Accessed 2/17/2024. https://www.michigan.gov/corrections/-/media/Project/Websites/corrections/Files/Policy-Directives/PDs-06-Field-Operations/PD-06-01-General-Provisions/06–01–140-Pre-Sentence-Investigation-and-Report-effective-01-17-22.pdf?rev=32a8e45c295f405f9e92f0760c26b97b.

Michigan Legislature. 2023. The Code of Criminal Procedure (Excerpt): Act 175 Of 1927. Accessed 2/17/2024. http://www.legislature.mi.gov/(S(0iahpxqxedowy4kxh1hd5wyp))/mileg.aspx?page=GetObject&objectname=mcl-771-14.

Michigan State Police. 2024. Traffic Stop Data. Accessed 2/17/2024. https://www.michigan.gov/msp/public-information/transparency/accordion/reports/traffic-stop-data-main.

Monk, Ellis P. 2021. "The Unceasing Significance of Colorism: Skin Tone Stratification in the United States." *Daedalus* 150(2): 76–90. https://doi.org/10.1162/daed_a_01847.

Morning, Ann. 2007. "'Everyone Knows It's a Social Construct': Contemporary

Science and the Nature of Race." *Sociological Focus* 40(4): 436–54. https://doi.org/10.1080/00380237.2007.10571319.

Mueller-Smith, Michael, and Kevin T. Schnepel. 2021. "Diversion in the Criminal Justice System." *Review of Economic Studies* 88(2): 883–936. https://doi.org/10.1093/restud/rdaa030.

Naik, Piyu Parth, and Syed Nadir Farrukh. 2022. "Influence of Ethnicities and Skin Color Variations in Different Populations: A Review." *Skin Pharmacology and Physiology* 35(2): 65–76. https://doi.org/10.1159/000518826.

National Academies of Sciences, Engineering, and Medicine. 2023. *Assessing the 2020 Census: Final Report*, edited by Teresa A. Sullivan and Daniel L. Cork. Washington, DC: The National Academies Press. https://nap.nationalacademies.org/catalog/27150/assessing-the-2020-census-final-report.

Neal, Derek, and Armin Rick. 2014. "The Prison Boom and the Lack of Black Progress after Smith and Welch." NBER Working Paper No. 20283. Cambridge, MA: National Bureau of Economic Research. http://www.nber.org/papers/w20283.

Nelson, Alondra. 2016. *The Social Life of DNA: Race, Reparations, and Reconciliation After the Genome.* Boston: Beacon Press. https://www.penguinrandomhouse.com/books/250539/the-social-life-of-dna-by-alondra-nelson.

Noe-Bustamante, Luis, Ana Gonzalez-Barrera, Khadijah Edwards, Lauren Mora, and Mark Hugo Lopez. 2021. "Majority of Latinos Say Skin Color Impacts Opportunity in America and Shapes Daily Life." Pew Research Center Hispanic Trends Project. https://www.pewresearch.org/hispanic/2021/11/04/majority-of-latinos-say-skin-color-impacts-opportunity-in-america-and-shapes-daily-life.

Office of Management and Budget. 1997. Revisions to the Standards for the Classification of Federal Data on Race and Ethnicity. *Federal Register* 62(210): 58782–90. https://www.federalregister.gov/documents/1997/10/30/97-28653/revisions-to-the-standards-for-the-classification-of-federal-data-on-race-and-ethnicity.

———. 2024. Revisions to OMB's Statistical Policy Directive No. 15: Standards for Maintaining, Collecting, and Presenting Federal Data on Race and Ethnicity. *Federal Register* 89(62): 22182–96. https://www.federalregister.gov/documents/2024/03/29/2024-06469/revisions-to-ombs-statistical-policy-directive-no-15-standards-for-maintaining-collecting-and.

Pager, Devah. 2003. "The Mark of a Criminal Record." *American Journal of Sociology* 108(5): 937–75. https://doi.org/doi/10.1086/374403.

Roberts, Dorothy. 2012. *Fatal Invention.* New York: New Press. https://thenewpress.com/books/fatal-invention.

Rodriguez, Nancy, and Rebecca Tublitz. 2023. "Exploring Latino/a Representation in Local Criminal Justice Systems: A Review of Data Collection Practices and Systems-Involvement." UCI School of Social Ecology. https://socialecology.uci.edu/sites/default/files/users/mkcruz/sjc_latinos_in_cjs_march_2023.pdf.

Rose, Dina R., and Todd R. Clear. 1998. "Incarceration, Social Capital, and Crime: Implications for Social Disorganization Theory." *Criminology* 36(3): 441–80. https://doi.org/10.1111/j.1745-9125.1998.tb01255.x.

Rose, Evan K. 2023. "A Constructivist Perspective on Empirical Discrimination Research." *Journal of Economic Literature* 61(3): 906–23. https://doi.org/10.1257/jel.20221705.

Ruggles, Steven, Sarah Flood, Matthew Sobek, Daniel Backman, Annie Chen, Grace Cooper, Stephanie Richards, Renae Rogers, and Megan Schouweiler. 2024. IPUMS USA: Version 15.0 [dataset]. Minneapolis, MN: IPUMS. https://doi.org/10.18128/d010.v15.0.

Saperstein, Aliya, and Andrew M. Penner. 2012. "Racial Fluidity and Inequality in the United States." *American Journal of Sociology* 118(3): 676–727. https://doi.org/10.1086/667722.

Scott, Charles G. 1999. "Identifying the Race and Ethnicity of SSI Recipients." *Social Security Bulletin* 62(4): 9–20. https://www.ssa.gov/policy/docs/ssb/v62n4/v62n4p9.pdf.

Small-Rodriguez, Desi, and Randall Akee. 2021. "Identifying Disparities in Health Outcomes and Mortality for American Indian and Alaska Native Populations Using Tribally Disaggregated Vital Statistics and Health Survey Data." *American Journal of Public Health* 111(S2): S126–S132. https://doi.org/10.2105/AJPH.2021.306427.

Snipp, C. Matthew. 2003. "Racial Measurement in the American Census: Past Practices and Implications for the Future." *Annual Review of Sociology* 29(1): 563–88. https://doi.org/10.1146/annurev.soc.29.010202.100006.

Telles, Edward, and Tianna Paschel. 2014. "Who Is Black, White, or Mixed Race? How Skin Color, Status, and Nation Shape Racial Classification in Latin America." *American Journal of Sociology* 120(3): 864–907. https://doi.org/10.1086/679252.

Texas State Legislature. 2024. Code of Criminal Procedure. Accessed 2/17/2024. https://statutes.capitol.texas.gov/docs/sdocs/codeofcriminalprocedure.pdf.

Tuttle, Cody. 2019. "Racial Disparities in Federal Sentencing: Evidence from Drug Mandatory Minimums." SSRN Working Paper 3080463. https://doi.org/10.2139/ssrn.3080463.

US Census Bureau. 2022. American Community Survey and Puerto Rico Community Survey Design and Methodology: Version 3.0. Washington, DC: US Census Bureau. https://www2.census.gov/programs-surveys/acs/methodology/design_and_methodology/2022/acs_design_methodology_report_2022.pdf.

Wagner, Deborah, and Mary Lane. 2014. "The Person Identification Validation System (PVS): Applying the Center for Administrative Records Research and Applications' (CARRA) Record Linkage Software." Census Bureau CARRA Working Paper 2014-01. https://www.census.gov/library/working-papers/2014/adrm/carra-wp-2014-01.html.

Webster, Richard A. 2021. "'If Everybody's White, There Can't Be Any Racial Bias': The Disappearance of Hispanic Drivers From Traffic Records." *ProPublica*, November 22, 2021. https://www.propublica.org/article/if-everybodys-white-there-cant-be-any-racial-bias-the-disappearance-of-hispanic-drivers-from-traffic-records.

Williams, Ben. 2023. Inmate Data Reallocation in the 2020 Redistricting Cycle. Washington, DC: National Conference of State Legislatures. https://www.ncsl.org/redistricting-and-census/inmate-data-reallocation-in-the-2020-redistricting-cycle.

York, Gary. 2021. "Identifying Incarcerated Gang Members is Critical in Corrections." Corrections1.com, February 24, 2021. https://www.corrections1.com/prison-gangs/articles/identifying-incarcerated-gang-members-is-critical-in-corrections-XyBFxjEhDs2lleFg.

6

Unwarranted Disparity in High-Stakes Decisions
Race Measurement and Policy Responses

E. Jason Baron, Joseph J. Doyle Jr., Natalia Emanuel, Peter Hull, and Joseph Ryan

6.1 Introduction

There are widespread concerns about racial discrimination in many high-stakes settings, from criminal justice to employment, lending, health care, and child protection. Quantifying discrimination in such settings can be challenging, however, since observed racial disparities may reflect omitted variables bias (OVB) as well as discrimination. For example, in the child protection setting, widely documented racial disparities in foster care placement rates might signal the kind of discrimination that both the United Nations and the American Bar Association have recently called on US policymakers to address.[1] But these racial disparities might also capture underlying differences in the need for intervention—specifically, differences in the risk of future abuse or neglect among Black and White children referred to child protective services (CPS). Accounting for such unobservables is essential

E. Jason Baron is an assistant professor of economics at Duke University and a faculty research fellow of the National Bureau of Economic Research.

Joseph J. Doyle Jr. is the Erwin H. Schell Professor of Management and Applied Economics at the MIT Sloan School of Management and a research associate of the National Bureau of Economic Research.

Natalia Emanuel is a research economist at the Federal Reserve Bank of New York.

Peter Hull is a professor of economics at Brown University and a research associate of the National Bureau of Economic Research.

Joseph Ryan is a professor of social work at the University of Michigan.

1. See Kelly (2022), *UN Committee Suggests the US Change or Repeal Major Child Welfare Policies*, The Imprint. Accessed at: https://imprintnews.org/subscriber-content/un-committee-suggests-to-american-child-welfare-policy/173176 (5/6/2023); White and Persson (2022), *Racial Discrimination in Child Welfare Is a Human Rights Violation–Let's Talk About It That Way*, American Bar Association. Accessed at: https://www.americanbar.org/groups/litigation/committees/childrens-rights/articles/2022/fall2022-racial-discrimination-in-child-welfare-is-a-human-rights-violation/ (5/6/2023).

for measuring unwarranted racial disparities and for forming appropriate policy responses.

A recent literature develops and applies quasi-experimental tools for addressing this OVB challenge in various contexts, like pretrial release (Arnold et al. 2022) and child protection (Baron et al. 2024). In contrast to conventional experimental studies of direct discrimination (e.g., audit or correspondence studies), which address OVB by conditioning on all observable non-race characteristics, these quasi-experimental studies condition on a latent measure of an individual's need for intervention. Baron et al. (2024), for example, use quasi-random caseworker assignment to estimate unwarranted disparities (UDs) in foster care placement rates that condition on a child's potential for future at-home maltreatment. Such an approach yields broader measures of discrimination, which can account for indirect drivers that conventional studies typically condition on. Indeed, Baron et al. (2024) show how UDs arise and perpetuate across the multi-stage CPS system from initial call screeners and subsequent investigators, and how analyses that condition on the call-screening phase miss a meaningful share of discrimination. These kinds of analyses follow a growing interest in understanding how popular direct discrimination measures can obscure various forms of indirect or "systemic" discrimination (e.g., Bohren et al. 2025).

This study develops further quasi-experimental tools to quantify the role of indirect drivers of discrimination that conventional studies often condition on. As in Baron et al. (2024), we apply these tools to the CPS setting. The foster care setting is particularly important as CPS involvement is both widespread and disparate in the United States. By the time they reach the age of 18, 37 percent of US children become the subject of formal CPS investigations due to alleged abuse or neglect. Additionally, 5 percent of children are placed in foster care at some point during their childhood as a result of these investigations. Contact with CPS is significantly more prevalent among Black children, with over half being investigated and up to 9 percent entering foster care by age 18 (Yi et al. 2020; Kim et al. 2017). Given the large documented impacts of foster care placement on later-in-life outcomes like earnings, educational attainment, and contact with the criminal justice system (Bald et al. 2022), there is significant interest in these racial disparities and the extent to which they may reflect discrimination.

We conduct two main analyses in this setting. First, we consider the role of race or ethnicity misclassification in the administrative datasets often underlying discrimination studies. In CPS systems, investigators typically record a child's race after conducting interviews with the child and family. Researchers like Baron et al. (2024) use this investigator-coded race to study discrimination, often discarding certain racial codes from their analysis (e.g., dropping individuals who are not classified as either Black or White). A concern with these sorts of studies is that conditioning on such "endogenous" racial classification decisions might obscure the level of true discrimination

(Luh 2022; Finlay et al. 2024). One could imagine, for example, investigators either consciously or subconsciously coding riskier Black children as another race or as multiracial—causing them to be discarded from analyses like Baron et al. (2024) and potentially affecting their measures of unwarranted disparity.

We study the impact of racial misclassification on unwarranted disparity measures by linking the Baron et al. (2024) administrative data to public school records, which contain a measure of the child's race as reported by either the child or the child's guardians. We refer to this measure as "self-reported" race throughout. Relative to self-reported race, we find evidence that CPS investigators misclassify the race of investigated children: around 8 percent of self-reported White children and 9 percent of self-reported Black children are classified as multiracial, Hispanic, Asian, American Indian, or missing in the CPS data; interestingly, these misclassified children appear to be less at risk of future maltreatment. To estimate the impact of this misclassification on conventional UD measures, we then develop an extension of the Baron et al. (2024) methodology that leverages quasi-random investigator assignment. We find that racial misclassification obscures around 24 percent of unwarranted racial disparity in foster care placement decisions. Thus, while the majority of UD is revealed by investigator-coded race, discrimination analyses that condition on this measure meaningfully *understate* the true level of discrimination in investigator decisions.[2]

Our second analysis considers potential policy responses to the finding of unwarranted racial disparity, and how these responses might be shaped by systemic biases in multi-stage decisions. Specifically, we study the scope for mitigating discrimination in foster care placement decisions by incorporating algorithmic guidance at the investigation stage—both with and without an awareness of previous discrimination in CPS call screening. Algorithmic predictions of underlying risk are increasingly found in CPS settings, often with the explicit goal of reducing racial disparities (Samant et al. 2021). Here, building on Arnold et al. (2021), we extend the quasi-experimental approach of Baron et al. (2024) to design algorithmic recommendations that eliminate UD at the investigation phase and compare this policy to algorithmic recommendations that eliminate UD in the multi-phase CPS system overall.

This analysis shows that unwarranted racial disparity at the CPS investigation phase can be eliminated by an algorithmic policy that reduces the predicted risk threshold for foster care placement among White children by around 4 percent. However this policy leaves significant UD in the CPS sys-

2. We use the term *misclassification* throughout to denote discrepancies between self-reported race and race as recorded by CPS. It is important to note that this term does not presuppose intentional misclassification. Instead it could, for example, capture scenarios where the investigator's perception of the child's race differs from the child's self-perception or how the parents perceive their child's race.

tem as a whole because of the unwarranted disparity in initial call screening. An alternative policy that lowers the White risk threshold by an additional 2 percent addresses this initial discrimination and eliminates unwarranted disparity among all incoming calls. Thus, as in our first analysis, we find that policy responses to unwarranted racial disparity are meaningfully affected by factors that conventional analyses typically hold fixed.

This paper connects to three distinct literatures. First, we add to a literature studying ways in which racial misclassification or miscoding may affect studies of racial inequity (Conrick et al. 2023; Finlay et al. 2024; Luh 2022; Rose 2023; Smith et al. 2010).[3] We study this question by combining a measure of self-reported race with administrative data on decision-maker-coded race, and by leveraging the quasi-random assignment of decision-makers to address OVB. Importantly, this analysis is not premised on the idea that self-reported race is the "ground truth" or even that race is a static or objective concept (Agadjanian 2022; DeFina and Hannon 2016; Telles and Paschel 2014; Roth 2012). Instead, our approach shows how researchers can study the effect of different racial classifications on measures of unwarranted disparity that take one or more racial classifications as given.

Second, we add to a literature studying how predictive algorithms might reduce inequity in high-stakes decision-making (Agan et al. 2023; Arnold et al. 2021; Grimon and Mills 2022; Kleinberg et al. 2018b; Rittenhouse et al. 2022; Albright 2023). We focus on the question of designing such algorithms in multi-phase systems like CPS, where an appropriate algorithmic policy response might need to account for discrimination at both phases. Our analysis is most closely related to the proposal in Rambachan et al. (2021), by setting race-specific thresholds on algorithmic predictions of maltreatment potential to eliminate unwarranted disparity.

Finally, as noted above, we add to a recent literature using quasi-experimental variation to estimate various notions of bias and discrimination in high-stakes decisions, such as pretrial release (e.g., Arnold et al. 2018; Hull 2021; Arnold et al. 2022; Rambachan 2022; Canay et al. 2022), traffic stops (e.g., Goncalves and Mello 2021; Feigenberg and Miller 2022), and lending (e.g., Dobbie et al. 2021). The quasi-experimental tools we develop may also prove useful in these and other settings, where race is often coded by decision-makers and decisions are often made in multiple phases.

The remainder of this paper is organized as follows. Section 6.2 summarizes the CPS context and the earlier methods and findings of Baron et al. (2024). Section 6.3 discusses racial classification by CPS investigators, documents misclassification relative to self-reported race, and studies the impact of such misclassification on measures of unwarranted disparity. Section

3. As Luh (2022) notes, these studies relate to a broader literature examining impacts of evaluations on the strategic behavior of evaluated agents (Dee et al. 2019; Dinerstein and Opper 2022; Jacob and Levitt 2003).

6.4 explores algorithmic counterfactuals designed to eliminate unwarranted disparity both at the investigation phase and in the CPS system overall. Section 6.5 concludes.

6.2 Background

This section first outlines the Michigan CPS setting, the context of Baron et al. (2024). We then review the methods that Baron et al. (2024) use to estimate unwarranted racial disparity, as well as their main findings. This review sets the stage for our extended analysis of the role of racial misclassification and algorithmic policy responses.

6.2.1 The CPS Setting

Our analysis uses administrative data from the Michigan CPS system. The CPS process in Michigan, as in most states, typically begins when someone contacts the state's centralized child maltreatment hotline with an allegation of child abuse or neglect. While reports can be submitted by anyone, the most common sources are mandated reporters such as teachers, doctors, and police officers (Benson et al. 2022). Incoming calls enter a queue, with the hotline system routing each call to the available screener who has been waiting the longest since their last call. After approximately a 15-minute call, the screener determines whether to "screen-in" the call, triggering a formal CPS investigation, or to "screen-out" the call which officially concludes CPS involvement.

Screened-in cases are assigned to a regional office based on the location of the alleged child victim. Cases are promptly assigned to investigators through a rotational system: incoming cases are assigned to the investigator at the top of the queue, and that investigator then moves to the end of the queue. Investigators examine the allegations and provide a recommendation regarding whether the child should be removed from their home and placed in foster care. Investigations can take up to 30 days and children who are removed from home spend around 17 months in foster care on average.[4]

Two features of the CPS setting are worth highlighting for our analysis. First, CPS guidelines set a clear mandate for the high-stakes decision of removing a child from home. Investigators are instructed to place a child in foster care only if the child is in "imminent risk" of maltreatment in the home and to otherwise keep the child with their family.[5] This mandate

4. Regardless of the placement decision, investigators can formally open a CPS case and recommend "targeted services" to support the family in cases that have been substantiated. These services are typically preventative referrals and range from substance abuse to parenting classes, though parents are not typically compelled to use them. Anecdotally, takeup of such service recommendations is very low; Baron et al. (2024) show that there is correspondingly little scope for these services causing exclusion restriction violations in their analysis.

5. For example, the Michigan CPS *Children's Protective Services Policy Manual* instructs investigators to initiate foster care placement "in situations where the child is unsafe, or when

yields a natural measure of unwarranted racial disparity: disparities in foster care placement rates among White and Black children with the same potential future at-home maltreatment. In practice, we follow Baron et al. (2024) and much of the child welfare literature (e.g., Antle et al. 2009; Putnam-Hornstein et al. 2021; Baron et al. 2025) by proxying for future maltreatment potential with a child's potential for CPS re-investigation within six months of the focal investigation.[6]

Second, call screeners and investigators are both quasi-randomly assigned in the Michigan CPS system. This assignment in turn yields quasi-experimental variation in screen-in rates and placement decisions which can be used to estimate unwarranted disparities, as discussed next.[7]

6.2.2 Baron et al. (2024) Methods

Baron et al. (2024) estimate unwarranted racial disparities as differences in foster care placement rates by race, conditional on subsequent at-home maltreatment potential. This measure aligns with economic notions of discrimination, the legal theory of disparate impact, and notions of algorithmic discrimination from the computer science literature (Arnold et al. 2022). Importantly, unwarranted disparity can arise from both "direct" discrimination on the basis of race itself (including canonical sources of racial bias and statistical discrimination) and "indirect" discrimination through other characteristics that are correlated with race.

To formalize these UD measures, consider a population of cases indexed by i that involve either a Black or a White child, $R_i \in \{b,w\}$. Each child has a potential for future maltreatment $Y_i^* \in \{0,1\}$, with $Y_i^* = 1$ indicating that the child would experience subsequent maltreatment when not removed from home.

Each case is initially handled by a hotline call screener who decides whether or not to screen-in the case and advance it to investigation. Conditional on the call being screened-in, a CPS investigator then decides whether to place the child into foster care. For children who are either screened-out or screened-in but not removed from home, maltreatment potential is realized and observable via their subsequent maltreatment outcomes. Otherwise, Y_i^* is not realized and hence unobservable.

there is resistance to, or failure to benefit from, CPS intervention and that resistance/failure is causing an imminent risk of harm to the child" (p.5). Similar instructions are given to CPS call screeners.

6. See Section IV.A of Baron et al. (2024) for a discussion of this proxy for future maltreatment potential. They also show that their primary findings are robust to a wide range of alternative proxies, including re-investigation over different horizons and other forms of subsequent contact with CPS.

7. See Section II of Baron et al. (2024) for a discussion of screener and investigator assignment processes. They also show assignment is empirically balanced on a wide range of observable characteristics.

To develop the UD measures, first suppose that cases are handled by a single representative hotline screener and, if screened-in, a single representative investigator. Let $S_i \in \{0,1\}$ indicate whether case *i* is screened-in by the screener and (if screened-in) let $D_i \in \{0,1\}$ indicate whether the investigator places the child in foster care. The product, $P_i = S_i D_i$, then indicates whether case *i* ultimately results in foster care placement.

We first consider a disparity in the screener's decision to screen-in a call or not among Black and White children without future maltreatment potential:

(1) $$\Delta_0^S = E[S_i \mid R_i = b, Y_i^* = 0] - E[S_i \mid R_i = w, Y_i^* = 0]$$

and a corresponding disparity among children with future maltreatment potential:

(2) $$\Delta_1^S = E[S_i \mid R_i = b, Y_i^* = 1] - E[S_i \mid R_i = w, Y_i^* = 1].$$

A measure of overall screener UD is given by averaging these conditional disparities:

(3) $$\Delta^S = \Delta_0^S(1 - \bar{\mu}) + \Delta_1^S \bar{\mu},$$

with weights $\bar{\mu} = E[Y_i^*]$, which measure the average future maltreatment risk in the population of all calls. Here, Δ^S measures the expected level of UD when the screener encounters a representative pool of cases with unknown future maltreatment potential.

We next define UDs in the investigator's decision to place screened-in children in foster care:

(4) $$\Delta_0^D = E[D_i \mid R_i = b, Y_i^* = 0, S_i = 1] - E[D_i \mid R_i = w, Y_i^* = 0, S_i = 1]$$

(5) $$\Delta_1^D = E[D_i \mid R_i = b, Y_i^* = 1, S_i = 1] - E[D_i \mid R_i = w, Y_i^* = 1, S_i = 1].$$

Here, Δ_0^D measures the investigator's placement rate disparity among screened-in cases without future maltreatment potential and Δ_1^D measures the corresponding disparity among screened-in cases with future maltreatment potential. We again measure the overall UD in the investigator's decisions by averaging these two disparities: $\Delta^D = \Delta_0^D(1 - \bar{\mu}^{S=1}) + \Delta_1^D \bar{\mu}^{S=1}$, where the $\bar{\mu}^{S=1} = E[Y_i^* \mid S_i = 1]$ weights now represent average maltreatment risk among the subpopulation of screened-in cases.

Finally, we define unwarranted disparities in placement rates among all cases referred to CPS:

(6) $$\Delta_0^P = E[P_i \mid R_i = b, Y_i^* = 0] - E[P_i \mid R_i = w, Y_i^* = 0]$$

(7) $$\Delta_1^P = E[P_i \mid R_i = b, Y_i^* = 1] - E[P_i \mid R_i = w, Y_i^* = 1],$$

with overall placement UD given by the average: $\Delta^P = \Delta_0^P(1 - \bar{\mu}) + \Delta_1^P \bar{\mu}$. Intuitively, these measures capture unwarranted disparity from both screener and investigator decisions.

A decomposition can be used to quantify the relative importance of screener and investigator UDs in shaping eventual UDs in placement rates. Specifically, since $P_i = S_i D_i$, we have:

$$(8) \quad \underbrace{\Delta_y^P}_{\text{Placement UD}} = E[S_i | R_i = b, Y_i^* = y] E[D_i | S_i = 1, R_i = b, Y_i^* = y] - E[S_i | R_i = w, Y_i^* = y] E[D_i | S_i = 1, R_i = w, Y_i^* = y] = \underbrace{\Delta_y^S \tilde{\omega}_y^S}_{\text{Screener component}} + \underbrace{\Delta_y^D \tilde{\omega}_y^D}_{\text{Investigator component}},$$

for $y \in \{0,1\}$, where $\tilde{\omega}_y^S = E[D_i | R_i = b, Y_i^* = y, S_i = 1]$ and $\tilde{\omega}_y^D = E[S_i | R_i = w, Y_i^* = y]$.

Equation (8) decomposes eventual placement UD into two components: one involving UD in screener decisions to screen-in a call (Δ_y^S) and the other involving UD in investigator decisions to place screened-in children in foster care (Δ_y^D). These UDs are weighted by $\tilde{\omega}_y^S$ (the placement rate of screened-in Black children, with $Y_i^* = y$) and $\tilde{\omega}_y^D$ (the screened-in rate of White children, with $Y_i^* = y$), respectively.[8]

The fundamental challenge in bringing each of these UD measures to data is the fact that maltreatment potential is only selectively observed. Among children who are not placed into foster care, their maltreatment potential is directly revealed by their subsequent maltreatment outcomes. However, since future maltreatment in the home is unobserved among those who are placed in foster care, one cannot directly condition on it to estimate Equations (1)–(8).

Baron et al. (2024) show how this identification challenge can be overcome with quasi-experimental variation. Namely, they first show how the different UD measures and the decomposition can be written in terms of directly estimable moments and a set of key mean risk parameters which are obscured by the selective observability of Y_i^*. They then show how these key parameters (and therefore each of the Equations [1] –[8]) can be estimated by leveraging the assignment of cases to screeners and investigators, using an "identification at infinity" approach that builds on Arnold et al. (2021, 2022) (see appendix A.1 for details). This strategy relies on the as-good-as-random assignment of screeners and investigations as well as exclusion restrictions which Baron et al. (2024) test extensively in the Michigan CPS setting. The strategy benefits from the fact that foster care placement rates are low for both Black and White children, with some quasi-randomly assigned screeners and investigators revealing nearly the full distribution of Y_i^* by leaving nearly all children in the home.

8. This equation is derived similarly to a Kitagawa–Oaxaca-Blinder (KOB) decomposition, by adding and subtracting $E[D_i | R_i = b, Y_i^* = y, S_i = 1] E[S_i = 1 | R_i = w, Y_i^* = y]$ to the first line of (8) and rearranging terms. As is the case with KOB decompositions, an alternate version of Equation (8) can be obtained by changing the "order" of the decomposition.

6.2.3 Baron et al. (2024) Findings

Baron et al. (2024) present three main findings from this approach. First, they estimate significant UD in the decisions of CPS screeners and investigators. On average, hotline calls involving Black children are found to be screened-in at a 5 percentage point (8 percent) higher rate than calls involving White children, conditional on subsequent at-home maltreatment potential. Specifically, Baron et al. (2024) estimate an average Δ^S across screeners of 0.050 (with a standard error of 0.001). Subsequent investigators inherit these initial disparities and amplify them; Baron et al. (2024) find that investigators place screened-in Black children in foster care at a 1.7 percentage point (50 percent) higher rate than screened-in White children with identical maltreatment potential. That is, they estimate an average Δ^D across investigators of 0.017 (with a standard error of 0.002).

Second, Baron et al. (2024) use the Equation (8) decomposition to link screener and investigator UDs and estimate significant overall UD in foster care placement decisions. Specifically, they find that hotline calls involving Black children are around 1.1 percentage points (55 percent) more likely to end up in foster care relative to calls involving White children with identical maltreatment potential (i.e., they estimate an average Δ^P of 0.011, with a standard error of 0.001). Screener decisions account for between 13 percent and 19 percent of this overall placement UD, with investigator decisions driving the remainder.

Third, Baron et al. (2024) show that the placement disparity is concentrated among children with subsequent maltreatment potential (i.e., driven by Δ_1^P rather than Δ_0^P). This finding adds nuance to ongoing discussions surrounding the potential "over-placement" of Black children in foster care, as it suggests that a higher placement rate may offer relative protection to Black children. This is particularly the case in light of recent work in our context, which finds that foster care placement leads to improvements in safety and other welfare-relevant outcomes for children at the margin of placement (Baron and Gross 2022; Gross and Baron 2022).

Taken together, the Baron et al. (2024) analysis shows that there is significant unwarranted racial disparity in Michigan CPS foster care decisions, and that this UD comes primarily from CPS investigators decisions among cases with future maltreatment potential. We correspondingly focus our analysis on this subpopulation.

6.3 Race Measurement and Misclassification

This section first details the measurement of race and ethnicity in the administrative data used in Baron et al. (2024). We then examine potential racial misclassification in these records by linking the CPS data to public education records, where race is self-reported. Finally, we develop and apply an empirical framework for quantifying the role of racial misclassification in estimates of investigator UDs.

6.3.1 Race Measurement in CPS Data

The primary dataset in Baron et al. (2024) comes from the Michigan Department of Health and Human Services (MDHHS). This dataset spans 2008 to 2019 and contains information on CPS hotline calls and subsequent investigations in Michigan. Overall, the data contain the details of each call, including the nature of the allegation (e.g., physical abuse versus neglect), the relationship of the alleged perpetrator to the child (e.g., a parent or uncle), the age and gender of the child, and the identity of the screener and (if screened-in) investigator assigned to the case.

The MDHHS dataset also contains the child's race both for screened-out and screened-in calls. Hotline screeners in Michigan do not directly request information about the alleged victim's race; there are two primary methods by which they learn about the race of children. First, for children with prior interactions with CPS, the race recorded previously will be available to the call screener. For children without any prior CPS involvement, screeners can observe race through a state-wide database called MIBridges. This database contains detailed information—including self-reported race—of families who have received various state benefits. These benefits encompass programs such as Medicaid coverage, food assistance, cash assistance (including the Family Independence Program, Refugee Cash Assistance, and TANF), child development and care, and state emergency relief.[9] If race information for the child is missing in the CPS system, the system will populate the race field with race information from MIBridges. Since the vast majority of children reported to the hotline have prior interactions with either CPS or MIBridges, hotline screeners can determine the child's race in most cases.[10]

Among screeened-in calls, the coding of a child's race by screeners may be updated by investigators at any point in the investigation process. These updates, and any disagreements in the investigators' coding versus the administrative MIBridges coding, are not observable in the MDHHS data, which reports a single racial code for each child.

A potential concern is that investigators could systematically reclassify White or Black children in a way that affects a researcher's estimates of unwarranted racial disparity in placement decisions. Such non-random reclassification might reflect that the beliefs of the investigator differ from

9. Unfortunately, we do not have access to MIBridges—preventing us from assessing racial misclassification within this dataset.

10. Race information is missing in fewer than 10 percent of all calls. The state believes that the majority of these instances involve Native American children, for whom the screener does not input further race details once their Native American status is established due to concerns related to jurisdiction.

self-reported race, or could be intentional—for example, if investigators deliberately code Black children in risky home environments as multiracial or "other" race in order to obscure potentially discriminatory foster care placement decisions. Evidence of such intentional misclassification has previously been documented in the criminal justice system (Luh 2022; Finlay et al. 2024). Of course, misclassification might also be idiosyncratic or otherwise inconsequential for UD calculations. We next investigate this issue with additional data.

6.3.2 Racial Misclassification

6.3.2.1 Descriptive Statistics

To study the extent and impact of racial misclassification, we use an administrative link between children appearing in the CPS data from 2008 to 2017 and public school records from the state. These records include a variable for the child's race as self-reported by their family. Specifically, whenever a student first enrolls in a school, their parents (or custodial caregivers) complete a form from the school district which includes a question about the child's race and ethnicity. We use this question to identify children with a self-reported race of either White or Black.[11]

We focus this analysis on screened-in children, for two reasons. First, this allows us to compare self-reported race with race classified by investigators in the CPS system; as noted above, our measure of race for screened-out calls often comes from state databases where race was self-reported. Second, as noted in section 6.2.3, Baron et al. (2024) find that most of the unwarranted racial disparity in foster care placement arises at the investigation stage.[12] We thus construct a dataset of Michigan CPS investigations from 2008 to 2017 following the main sample restrictions in Baron et al. (2024).[13] Using

11. In contrast to our CPS data, which contain a single value for the child's race (e.g., only White, only Black, or multiracial), the self-reported race in the public education data encompasses all the values identified by parents. For instance, if a parent records that a child is both White and Black, both variables are retained separately rather than summarizing the child's race as multiracial. To ensure comparability across the two datasets, we classify a child in the education data as White or Black only if the child's family specifically identifies them as White or Black without listing any other race.

12. A related concern regarding the analysis in Baron et al. (2024) is the potential for selection by race into initial allegations of maltreatment. This concern is especially relevant in light of evidence from other fields indicating that Black children may be more frequently reported compared to their White counterparts in similar situations (Lane et al. 2002). Addressing this issue is difficult, since it requires observing children who could have been reported to the hotline but were not. To explore this issue, table I in Baron et al. (2024) shows that the distribution of mandated and non-mandated reporters is similar across racial groups. Furthermore, their table A16 shows that estimates of investigator unwarranted disparity are similar across different types of reporters.

13. As in Baron et al. (2024), we drop (i) cases assigned to investigators with fewer than 200 investigations in our sample; (ii) children for whom we cannot observe outcomes for at least six months; (iii) repeat cases and cases involving sexual abuse; and (iv) cases with a missing child zip code.

Table 6.1 Racial misclassification analysis: summary statistics

		Well-Classified by CPS		Misclassified by CPS	
	All Children (1)	White (2)	Black (3)	White (4)	Black (5)
Panel A: Child characteristics					
Female	0.480	0.479	0.480	0.471	0.470
Age at investigation	7.230	7.371	6.953	8.248	7.673
Had a previous investigation	0.480	0.494	0.481	0.365	0.424
No. of previous investigations	1.115	1.171	1.030	0.971	1.059
Panel B: Investigation characteristics					
Physical abuse allegation	0.287	0.280	0.302	0.293	0.296
Alleged parent perpetrator	0.913	0.913	0.908	0.927	0.912
Alleged other relative perpetrator	0.051	0.045	0.061	0.057	0.063
Panel C: Treatment rates					
Foster care placement	0.028	0.025	0.037	0.026	0.032
Panel D: Maltreatment outcome, if not placed					
Re-investigated within six months	0.164	0.175	0.143	0.144	0.138
Observations	220,832	118,583	46,382	9,993	4,631

Note: Column 1 of this table summarizes the sample for the racial misclassification analysis, consisting of children investigated by Michigan CPS in 2008–2017 who can be matched to a public school record, including those who are not classified as Black or White. Columns 2–5 summarize children who are either self-identified as White or Black in the education data. Columns 2–3 summarize children whose race in the education data is correctly classified in the CPS data, while columns 4–5 summarize children whose race in the education data is misclassified in the CPS data as either multiracial or "other," which includes Hispanics, Asians, American Indians, and children with missing race.

a crosswalk created for the analysis in Gross and Baron (2022) and Baron and Gross (2022), we are able to match around 96 percent of this sample to a public school record and thus to a measure of self-reported race.[14]

The resulting analysis sample consists of 220,832 investigations involving 178,372 children. Column 1 in table 6.1 summarizes the sample, which includes children with any racial classification. Female children make up 48 percent of the sample and the average child is roughly 7.2 years old. About 48 percent of children in the sample experienced a formal CPS investigation prior to the focal one. Roughly 29 percent of investigations in the sample include a physical abuse allegation, and in 91 percent of investi-

14. Because the datasets do not contain a common numeric identifier, the records were linked using a probabilistic algorithm based on the child's first name, last name, date of birth, and gender. As explained in Gross and Baron (2022), the match rate is not expected to be 100 percent since some investigated children may be homeschooled or may move out of the state after an investigation. See Online Appendix D in Gross and Baron (2022) for additional details regarding the match.

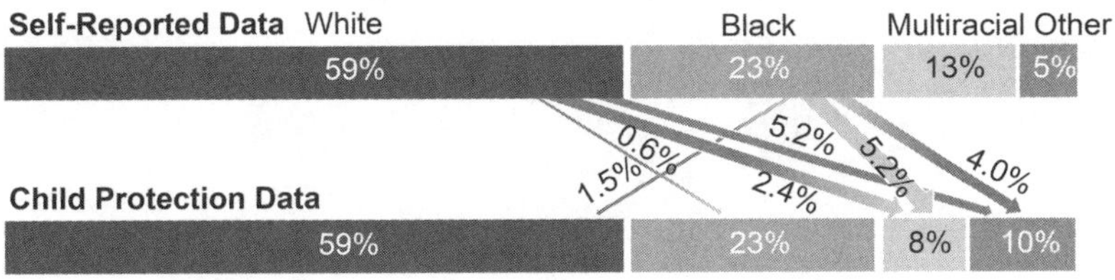

Fig. 6.1 Racial misclassification in CPS data

Note: This figure shows the distribution of child race in our analysis sample according to the self-reported racial classification from the education data (in the top row) and the racial classification by investigators from the CPS data (in the bottom row). The "other" categories consist of children whose race is either missing or categorized as Hispanic, Asian, or American Indian. The percentages indicate the share of self-reported White or Black children who are categorized differently by an investigator. Of individuals who self-report as White, 91 percent are categorized correctly. Of individuals who self-report as Black, 89 percent are categorized correctly.

gations the alleged perpetrator is the parent or stepparent. In the sample, 2.8 percent of children are placed in foster care and 16.4 percent of children experience another investigation for maltreatment in the home within six months if not placed in foster care.

Figure 6.1 illustrates the distributions of self-reported race from the education data and investigator-coded race from the CPS data. Overall, the proportion of White and Black children (reported inside the bars) is very similar across the two classifications. In both classifications, 59 percent of children are identified as White and 23 percent of children are categorized as Black. However, differences emerge in the datasets concerning the proportion of children coded as multiracial. In the self-reported classification, 13 percent of children are multiracial compared to 8.4 percent according to the CPS classification. The remaining children with "other" race consist of those whose race is categorized as Hispanic, Asian, American Indian, or have a missing race.

While most White and Black children are consistently classified across both datasets, many self-reported White and Black children are misclassified by CPS investigators. Specifically, 8 percent of the children who self-identify as White in the education data are classified as either multiracial or "other" in the CPS data. Similarly, 9 percent of those self-identified as Black in the education data are classified as either multiracial or "other" in the CPS data.

The arrows in figure 6.1 report the shares of self-reported White or Black children who are classified as another race in the CPS data. These show that most of the misclassification by CPS investigators occurs from children being coded as multiracial or the "other" category. Only 0.6 percent of self-reported White children and 1.5 percent of self-reported Black children are classified as Black and White, respectively. In contrast, the share of self-reported White (Black) children coded as multiracial by CPS investigators is

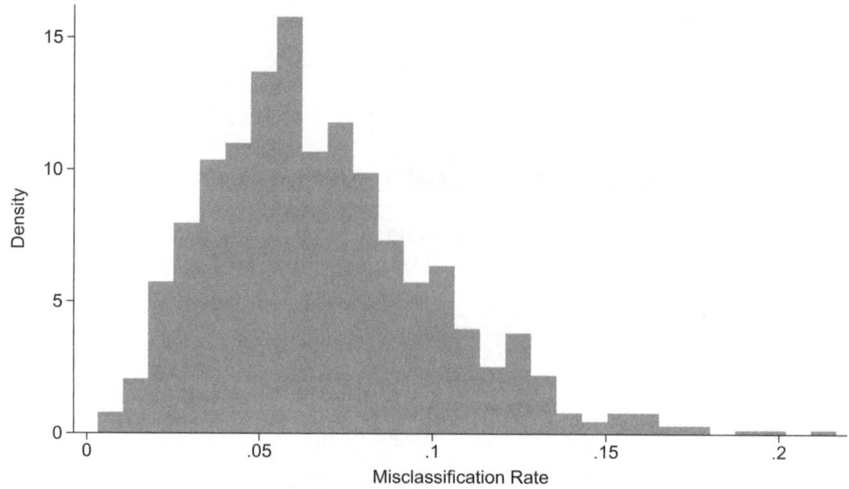

Fig. 6.2 Distribution of racial misclassification across investigators

Note: This figure plots the distribution of racial misclassification rates across the 699 investigators in our sample for whom we have demographic information. Misclassified children are those in Columns 4 and 5 in table 6.1. The denominator for the misclassification rates includes all children in Column 1 of table 6.1.

2.4 percent (5.2 percent) and the corresponding share for the other category is 5.2 percent (4.0 percent).

Columns 2–5 of table 6.1 compare the observable characteristics of self-reported White and Black children who are either well classified by CPS—in the sense of also being coded as White or Black, respectively—or who are misclassified with a different racial coding. Specifically, we consider a child to be misclassified if their CPS racial categorization is multiracial, Hispanic, Asian, American Indian, or missing but their self-reported race is White or Black.

Misclassified children tend to be older and have less prior experience with the CPS system, as captured by a lower number of previous investigations. While investigation characteristics are broadly similar between the two groups, foster care placement rates differ, with misclassified Black children being 0.5 percentage points less likely to be removed from home than well-classified Black children. Moreover, rates of re-investigation within six months among the children not removed from home are significantly lower for misclassified children: by 3.1 percentage points for misclassified White children and by 0.5 percentage points for misclassified Black children.

Figure 6.2 plots the distribution of investigators' racial misclassification rates in our sample, showing significant variation. While the average misclassification rate is roughly 6 percent, the 5th percentile of the misclassification rate is 2.3 percent, and the 95th percentile is 13 percent. Table 6.2 examines heterogeneity in the misclassification rate by investigators' observable char-

Table 6.2 **Regressions of investigator misclassification rates on investigator characteristics**

	(1)	(2)	(3)	(4)	(5)	(6)
Black investigator	0.001					
	(0.003)					
Other race	0.003					
	(0.006)					
Female investigator		0.002				
		(0.002)				
New investigator			0.018***			
			(0.002)			
Urban county				–0.005**		
				(0.002)		
High share of Black children					–0.006***	
					(0.002)	
Low placement rate						0.008***
						(0.002)
Control Mean	0.064	0.063	0.053	0.067	0.067	0.061
Observations	699	699	699	699	699	699

Note: This table reports OLS estimates of investigators' racial misclassification rates on investigator characteristics. The "control mean" refers to the average value of dependent variable, weighted by the number of investigations assigned to each investigator, for the omitted category. The omitted category in Column 1 is an indicator variable for whether the investigator is White. In our sample, 86 percent of investigators are White, 12 percent are Black, and 2 percent are another race, such as Hispanic or Asian. New investigators are defined as those hired during our estimation period. There are 457 new investigators in our sample. Investigators with a high share of Black children are those whose caseloads have an above-median share of Black children. Low placement rate investigators are those with a placement rate below the sample median. All specifications are weighted by the number of investigations assigned to the specific investigator. Robust standard errors are reported in parentheses.

acteristics. There is no difference in the racial misclassification rates of White and Black investigators. However, new and more lenient investigators are significantly more likely to misclassify. In contrast, investigators in urban counties and those who handle a relatively higher share of cases involving Black children are less likely to misclassify.

Taken together, these results provide evidence of misclassification by CPS relative to self-reported race. The patterns in table 6.1 are, however, at odds with the simple story of investigators deliberately misclassifying risky Black children as another race to hide discriminatory behavior—if anything, the misclassified Black children appear less risky. An alternative story is that the child's level of risk may affect the investigator's perception of the child's race. For example, it could be that investigators are more likely to perceive lower-risk Black children as multiracial (instead of Black) and lower-risk White children as White (instead of multiracial). While this theory can explain the patterns in table 6.1 for Black children, it is not consistent with the patterns for White children.

To understand the potential for systematic misclassification to affect discrimination measures, we next use these data to extend the Baron et al. (2024) analysis.

6.3.2.2 *Quantifying the impact of racial misclassification*

Building on the framework in section 6.2.2, we next introduce a decomposition of UD by self-reported race into a component that is revealed by the racial coding of CPS investigators and a component that is obscured by racial misclassification in CPS records. As with the main decomposition in Baron et al. (2024), this decomposition arises as a special case of the general framework in Bohren et al. (2025)—developed for disentangling discrimination from direct and systemic factors—and can be applied by leveraging quasi-random investigator assignment.

We formalize this approach by letting $R_i^* \in \{b, w\}$ be the self-reported race of child i (either Black or White) and again letting R_i be race recorded by a CPS investigator. Relative to the section 6.2.2 framework, we allow racial misclassification in CPS: $R_i \neq R_i^*$. Specifically, we let $R_i \in \{b, w, m\}$ where $R_i = m$ denotes that child i (who is either self-reported Black or White) is coded as multiracial or as "other" race in the CPS data. Since the share of children misclassified as being Black or White is very small, we focus on these other forms of misclassification.

Consider a population of screened-in cases, dropping the $S_i = 1$ conditioning from section 6.2.2 only for notational ease. Following the Baron et al. (2024) findings, we consider a measure of unwarranted disparity among children with the potential for future at-home maltreatment ($Y_i^* = 1$), now explicitly considering children who self-identify as Black or White:

$$\Delta_1^{D*} = E[D_i \mid R_i^* = b, Y_i^* = 1] - E[D_i \mid R_i^* = w, Y_i^* = 1]. \tag{9}$$

A researcher who only has access to the investigator-recorded race R_i may estimate a biased measure of such unwarranted disparity. In Baron et al. (2024), for example, unwarranted disparity is measured by comparing children with $R_i = b$ vs. $R_i = w$, discarding those coded as multiracial or another race ($R_i = m$). How does such miscoding affect estimates of Δ_1^{D*}?

Appendix A.2 derives a general decomposition of Δ_1^{D*} into two terms. The first term arises from unwarranted disparities by self-reported race among children coded as the same race r by investigators,

$$E[D_i \mid R_i^* = b, R_i = r, Y_i^* = 1] - E[D_i \mid R_i^* = w, R_i = r, Y_i^* = 1].$$

The second term arises from unwarranted disparities in investigator race-coding itself, $\Pr(R_i = r \mid R_i^* = b, Y_i^* = 1) - \Pr(R_i = r \mid R_i^* = w, Y_i^* = 1)$.[15] The

15. The first term captures what Bohren et al. (2025) call "average direct discrimination," where R_i is taken as a signal of self-reported race R_i^*. The second term captures what they call indirect or "systemic" discrimination, arising from unwarranted disparities in the signal distribution.

appendix further shows that when—as we find in figure 6.1—racial miscodings almost always occur through multiracial or other-race codings (i.e., when $\Pr(R_i = b \mid R_i^* = w) \approx 0$ and $\Pr(R_i = w \mid R_i^* = b) \approx 0$), this decomposition takes an intuitive approximate form:

$$(10) \quad \Delta_1^{D*} \approx \underbrace{E[D_i \mid R_i^* = b, R_i = b, Y_i^* = 1] - E[D_i \mid R_i^* = w, R_i = w, Y_i^* = 1]}_{\text{Revealed discriminination}} \omega_1^{Revealed}$$

$$+ \underbrace{E[D_i \mid R_i^* = b, R_i = m, Y_i^* = 1] - E[D_i \mid R_i^* = w, R_i = m, Y_i^* = 1]}_{\text{Obscured discriminination}} \omega_1^{Obscured}$$

for some non-negative weights $\omega_1^{Revealed}$ and $\omega_1^{Obscured}$.

Equation (10) shows that unwarranted disparity by self-reported race R_i^* can be approximated as the sum of two terms. The first *revealed discrimination* term captures unwarranted disparities among children whose coded race R_i matches self-reported race. Such disparities would contribute to the discrimination measures in studies like Baron et al. (2024), which only have access to R_i. The second *obscured discrimination* term, in contrast, would not contribute to these studies: it captures unwarranted disparities among self-reported Black vs. White children who are recorded as multiracial or another race by investigators and hence are discarded in Baron et al. (2024). Intuitively, appendix A.2 shows these disparities are respectively weighted by shares of children who are well- and mis-classified by CPS investigators. The appendix also shows the decomposition involves a residual term which is small in settings where misclassification rates are similar by self-reported race (as we find in figure 6.1).

Like the main decomposition in Baron et al. (2024), each of the terms in Equation (10) can be estimated using quasi-random investigator assignment. Appendix A.2 formalizes this extension, which relies on the same identifying assumptions that Baron et al. (2024) test extensively in this setting.

Figure 6.3 shows estimates of the Equation (10) decomposition in Michigan CPS. Total unwarranted racial disparity among self-identified Black and White children with future maltreatment potential, Δ_1^{D*}, is estimated at 8.3 percentage points (with a standard error of 0.037). The decomposition shows that around 75 percent of this UD (6.2 percentage points; with a standard error of 0.036) is revealed by the racial coding of CPS investigators, while around 24 percent (2.0 percentage points; with a standard error of 0.007) is obscured by racial misclassification. The remaining 1 percent is due to the decomposition residual.

The decomposition thus shows that the majority of unwarranted racial disparity, as defined by self-reported race, is revealed by investigator-coded race. Nevertheless, a meaningful share of discrimination is obscured by CPS misclassification relative to self-reported race. Among children classified by CPS as multiracial or another race, there continues to be an unwarranted disparity across self-reported Black versus White children. Conventional

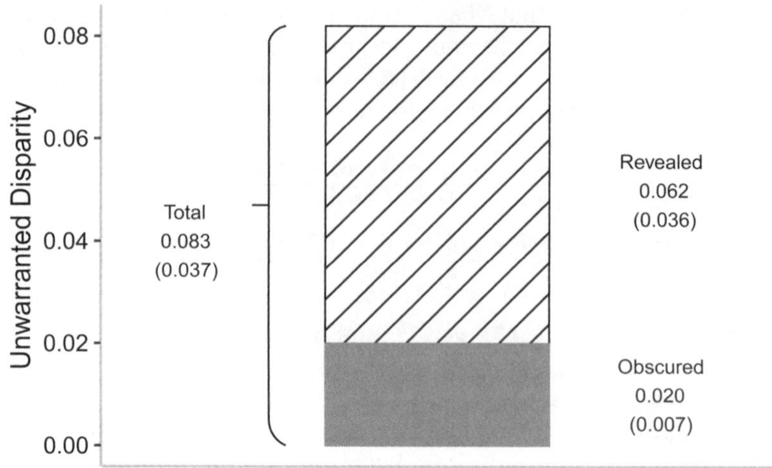

Fig. 6.3 Decomposition of unwarranted disparity in investigators' decisions (Δ_1^D)
Note: This figure shows estimates of investigator UD by self-reported race among screened-in children with maltreatment potential (Δ_1^{D*}), as well as estimates of the two terms of decomposition (10). All estimates are based on a linear extrapolation of investigator-specific placement and subsequent maltreatment rates among children left at home, as described in appendix A.2. Standard errors are two-way clustered by child and investigator and reported in parentheses.

discrimination analyses like Baron et al. (2024), which condition on the endogenous CPS classification, therefore stand to understate the full extent of racial discrimination in investigator decisions.

6.4 Algorithmic Policy Responses

This section explores potential policy responses to the finding of unwarranted disparity in foster care placement decisions, and how such policy responses might be shaped by systemic biases in the multi-phase CPS system. We focus on the scope for mitigating discrimination in foster care placement by incorporating algorithmic guidance. At least 26 states and the District of Columbia have considered using predictive analytic tools, which predict a child's potential for maltreatment from family and case characteristics, to guide CPS involvement (Samant et al. 2021).

Algorithmic tools in CPS have been piloted at both the screening phase (e.g., the Allegheny Family Screening Tool [Rittenhouse et al. 2022]) and the investigation phase (e.g., the Los Angeles County Risk Stratified Supervision Model). Given the findings in Baron et al. (2024) that the majority of unwarranted disparity in foster care placement is driven by the investigation phase (around 81 percent to 87 percent), we begin by demonstrating how a researcher or policymaker could use guidance from a race-conscious algorithm to eliminate UD during the investigation phase. We then demonstrate how this same algorithm can be used to eliminate UD in eventual foster care placement rates by offsetting disparities from initial human screening. As before, we focus on unwarranted disparity among cases where future maltreatment potential is present (i.e., Δ_1^D and Δ_1^P) which Baron et al. (2024) found to drive racial discrimination.

6.4.1 Using Algorithmic Guidance to Eliminate Δ^D

We first consider policy counterfactuals that eliminate investigator UD (Δ_1^P) when placement decisions are made by a race-conscious algorithm. In other words, we study how discrimination in algorithmic placement recommendations among screened-in children compares to existing human investigator UDs, and whether incorporating race-specific predictions and thresholds for placement can reduce or even eliminate UD at the investigation stage. For this analysis we take as fixed decisions occurring prior to the investigation; specifically, we condition on the prior screening-in decision.

We use a machine learning algorithm to predict future maltreatment potential Y_i^* as a function of case, child, and family characteristics observable to both the investigator and the econometrician, X_i. Importantly, we fit the algorithm separately for White and Black children. Denote this race-specific prediction by $m(X_i, R_i)$. Following Kleinberg et al. (2018a), we fit $m(X_i, r)$ with a gradient-boosted decision tree in the sample of screened-in children of race $R_i = r$ who were not placed in foster care, with Y_i^* indicating that the child has a subsequent maltreatment investigation in the home within six months of the focal investigation (the main maltreatment potential proxy in Baron et al. [2024]). Features in X_i include information on the reason for the CPS report (physical abuse, medical neglect, physical neglect, domestic violence, substance abuse, or improper supervision), whether the alleged perpetrator was the child's mother or father, the child's history of CPS contact (an indicator for previous contact and the number of prior investigations), the gender and age of the child, and their residing county. We tune the algorithm to select optimal parameters in the gradient boosted decision tree using a 5-fold cross-validation technique.

We then form foster care placement recommendations in the full evaluation dataset as $T_i = 1[m(X_i, R_i) > \tau(R_i)]$, where $\tau(r)$ is a risk threshold that is also allowed to depend on the child's race r. Our goal is to estimate unwarranted disparity in these algorithmic recommendations among screened-in children with maltreatment potential:

$$(11) \quad \Delta_1^T = E[T_i | S_i = 1, R_i = b, Y_i^* = 1] - E[T_i | S_i = 1, R_i = w, Y_i^* = 1].$$

Estimating discrimination in algorithmic decisions is hampered by the same fundamental selection challenge that arises when estimating discrimination in investigator decisions: data on a child's potential for subsequent maltreatment is selectively observed for individuals endogenously left at

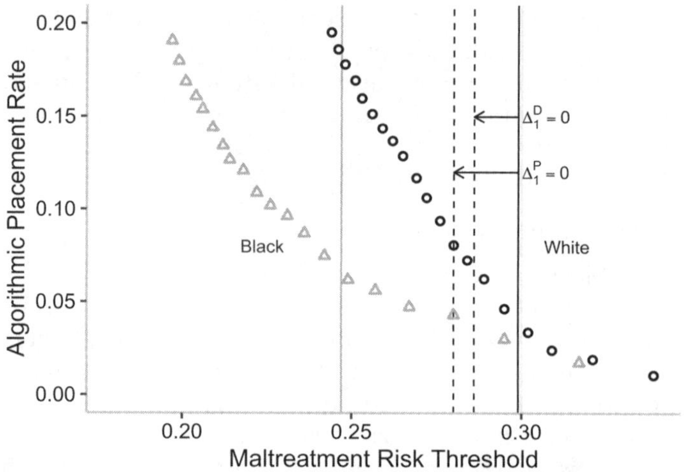

Fig. 6.4 Algorithmic placement rates at different risk thresholds

Note. The figure shows estimates of the algorithmic placement rates among screened-in children with maltreatment potential of race r as a function of various race-specific placement thresholds τ(r). The vertical lines show the thresholds that would match the placement rates by human investigators in our sample. The first dashed line (going from right to left) shows the policy change that reduces τ(w) from 29.9 percent to 28.6 percent, and would equalize placement rates among screened-in White and Black children with maltreatment potential (and thus yield a Δ_1^D equal to zero). The second dashed line shows the policy change that reduces τ(w) from 29.9 percent to 28 percent, and would equalize placement rates among the full population of calls involving White and Black children with maltreatment potential (and thus yield a Δ_1^P equal to zero).

home following an investigation. Such "selective labels problem" (Kleinberg et al. 2018a) complicates the measurement of algorithmic discrimination.

We follow the methods developed in Arnold et al. (2021) to overcome this selection challenge and estimate UD in our algorithm's placement recommendations. These methods follow the quasi-experimental approach in section 6.2.2. By varying the $\tau(w)$ and $\tau(b)$ thresholds we trace out the possibilities frontier of the race-specific placement rates among children with and without future maltreatment potential, and the corresponding disparity, Δ_1^T. Specifically, we estimate $\delta_{1r} = \Pr(T_i = 1 | S_i = 1, Y_i^* = 1, R_i = r)$ for $r \in \{w, b\}$ by combining our baseline estimates of race-specific maltreatment risk $\mu_r^{S=1} = E[Y_i^* | S_i = 1, R_i = r]$ with estimates of the conditional second moments $\rho_r = E[Y_i^* T_i | S_i = 1, R_i = r]$. The latter estimates come from a local linear extrapolation of the conditional moments $E[Y_i^* T_i | S_i = 1, R_i = r, D_{ij} = 1]$, following the logic in appendix A.1.

We bring these ideas to investigations from the analysis sample in Baron et al. (2024) from 2008 to 2017, consistent with the sample period in section 6.3 (see Baron et al. [2024] for a description of this analysis sample). Figure 6.4 shows estimates of placement rates (δ_r) for each race r that would arise from race-specific thresholds, $\tau(r)$. The vertical lines show the race-specific placement threshold $\tau(r)$ that would match the observed placement rates in our sample: predicted-risk thresholds of 29.9 percent for White children and 24.2 percent for Black children. The difference in the heights of the black and gray curves at the thresholds illustrate estimates of Δ_1^T for status quo thresholds. As we move the thresholds around, we simulate how the measures of algorithmic discrimination would change.

We find that average algorithmic discrimination among children with subsequent maltreatment potential would be around 31 percent lower than the average human investigator UD: we estimate Δ_1^T to be around 4 percentage points, vs. 5.8 percentage points for Δ_1^D (see table III in Baron et al. [2024]). Thus, incorporating algorithmic guidance in this setting meaningfully reduces unwarranted racial disparity, even while keeping average placement rates the same.

In line with our main findings in Baron et al. (2024) that White children may be "under-placed" in high-risk situations relative to Black children, we next simulate whether algorithmic discrimination during the investigation phase could be eliminated by slightly lowering the threshold for White children. Figure 6.4 shows that reducing $\tau(w)$ by 4.3 percent, from 0.299 (the solid black vertical line in the figure) to 0.286 (the dashed black vertical line) would set the placement rates for screened-in White and Black children approximately the same in cases with maltreatment potential ($\delta_{w1} \approx \delta_{b1}$), and therefore $\Delta_1^T \approx 0$.

6.4.2 Using Algorithmic Guidance to Eliminate Δ^P

The exercise above is a natural starting point for a policy response to unwarranted disparity, especially given the findings in Baron et al. (2024) that most discrimination in eventual foster care placement is driven by the investigation phase. The exercise is also policy relevant, given current efforts to use algorithmic guidance to reduce racial disparities during the investigation phase. However, in a multi-phase system such as CPS, such an exercise may leave significant unwarranted disparity on the table if discrimination exists at earlier stages in the system. Recall that Δ_1^P measures unwarranted disparities among the full set of calls to CPS, incorporating UD at both the screener and investigation stages. Per Equation (8), an algorithm designed to set $\Delta_1^D = 0$ need not set $\Delta_1^P = 0$ because $\Delta_1^S > 0$. In other words, even if disparities during the investigation stage are eliminated, unwarranted disparity in foster care placement will remain because of disparities introduced during the initial human screening. We next demonstrate how to extend the above framework to explore algorithmic counterfactuals that eliminate total discrimination.

To do so, we define a multi-phase discrimination decomposition for the algorithm-based placement rates, analogous to the Equation (8) decomposition:

$$\Delta_1^P = \Delta_1^S \tilde{\omega}_1^S + \Delta_1^D \tilde{\omega}_1^D \tag{12}$$

where, as before:

$$\Delta_1^S = E[S_i \mid R_i = b, Y_i^* = 1] - E[S_i \mid R_i = w, Y_i^* = 1] \tag{13}$$

and

$$\tilde{\omega}_1^D = E[S_i \mid R_i = w, Y_i^* = 1], \tag{14}$$

but now:

$$\Delta_1^D = E[T_i \mid R_i = b, Y_i^* = 1, S_i = 1] - E[T_i \mid R_i = w, Y_i^* = 1, S_i = 1] \tag{15}$$

and

$$\tilde{\omega}_1^S = E[T_i \mid R_i = b, Y_i^* = 1, S_i = 1], \tag{16}$$

where the algorithmic placement decisions T_i are implicitly tied to given thresholds $\tau(b)$ and $\tau(w)$. A policymaker may now, for example, wish to find the value of $\tau(w)$ that sets Δ_1^P to zero, holding fixed the value of $\tau(b)$ at the solid gray vertical line in figure 6.4.

From the findings in Baron et al. (2024) we obtain estimates of $\Delta_1^S = 0.038$ and $\tilde{\omega}_1^D = 0.595$ (see their table III and table A.VIII). We can also infer the value of $\tilde{\omega}_1^S = E[T_i \mid R_i = b, Y_i^* = 1, S_i = 1]$ for $\tau(b)$ such that $E[T_i \mid R_i = b] = E[D_i \mid R_i = b]$. This value is given by the intersection of the triangles and the solid vertical line in figure 6.4, and it is equal to 0.07.

From Equation (12), setting $\Delta_1^P = 0$ requires:

$$\Delta_1^D = -\frac{\Delta_1^S \tilde{\omega}_1^S}{\tilde{\omega}_1^D}. \tag{17}$$

Plugging in the above values, this condition is obtained with

$$E[T_i \mid R_i = w, Y_i^* = 1, S_i = 1] = 0.075.$$

A grid search based on the curves plotted in figure 6.4 finds that setting $\tau(w) = 0.280$ achieves this conditional placement rate for White children. Figure 6.4 illustrates this result: reducing $\tau(w)$ by an additional 2 percent (from 0.286 to 0.280—the new dashed vertical black line in the figure) would set the placement rate for White children with subsequent maltreatment potential at 7.5 percent, compared to the algorithmic placement rate for Black children of 7 percent. Intuitively, the placement rate for screened-in White children needs to be larger than the placement rate for screened-in Black children in order to mitigate unwarranted disparities in the initial screening decision of 3.8 percentage points.

These results show how researchers or policymakers can employ algorithmic guidance to mitigate unwarranted disparities in foster care placement, leveraging quasi-experimental variation as needed to address OVB. In multi-phase systems such as CPS, an analysis of discrimination that follows the framework developed in Baron et al. (2024) can furthermore be combined with algorithmic counterfactuals that counteract disparities introduced by human decision-makers at earlier points in the system. In our setting this exercise shows that policy responses to unwarranted racial disparity are meaningfully affected by the earlier decisions.

Our policy counterfactuals have focused entirely on eliminating unwarranted disparities in foster care placement, without consideration of the full welfare implications of such policies. Given the findings of Baron et al. (2024) that disparities are driven by an under-placement of White children in high-risk situations, we focused on counterfactuals that decrease the threshold for placing White children. A policy that places additional White children with maltreatment potential is likely to be welfare-improving, especially in our context, where the causal effects of foster care for marginal children are positive. However, it is important to recognize that, in practice, such a policy would impact both children with and without maltreatment potential. That is, since one cannot set maltreatment-potential-specific thresholds, such a policy could also result in additional White children without maltreatment potential being placed in foster care. Because the causal effects of foster care for these children are less clear in our context, we are unable to make conclusive welfare statements.

6.5 Conclusion

This study contributes to a growing literature that seeks to understand how conventional discrimination measures may obscure additional forms of "systemic" discrimination (Bohren et al. 2025) by conditioning on endogenous or upstream factors. We develop quasi-experimental tools to (i) quantify the impact of racial misclassification on measures of unwarranted disparity, and (ii) design policy responses that consider systemic biases in multi-stage decisions. Applying these methods to the context of foster care placement by CPS investigators, we showed that racial misclassification obscures around 24 percent of the unwarranted racial disparity in foster care placement documented in earlier work. We also illustrated the design of policy responses that could potentially mitigate unwarranted disparities in foster care placement. These responses address discrimination not only during the investigation phase but also in preceding phases leading up to the investigation.

The methods developed in this paper may be useful in future studies of unwarranted disparity. While the study's application is to the child protection context, this system shares several similarities with other high-stakes settings. Our methods for estimating the impact of racial misclassification on measures of unwarranted disparity, for example, could be applied in studies of the criminal justice system. Racial categorization in administrative datasets frequently used in estimating racial discrimination within the criminal justice system typically relies on coding by law enforcement officers or other involved decision-makers. Moreover, recent data collection efforts by the Criminal Justice Administrative Records System may enable researchers to cross-reference these records with self-reported racial and ethnic data from alternative sources, such as census data (e.g., Finlay et al. 2024).

Second, akin to child protection, the criminal justice system operates across multiple phases. For instance, consider the potential involvement of police officers and prosecutors in the charging decision. Simply implementing a policy counterfactual to eliminate discrimination in prosecutor decisions, while overlooking the possibility of prior discrimination in police officers' decisions to arrest, may leave remaining unwarranted disparity in charging rates. With the increasing availability of datasets tracking cases throughout the criminal justice system (Harrington and Shaffer 2022), our methods can be used to construct algorithmic counterfactuals that address discrimination from a "systems-based" perspective. Similar arguments can also be extended to multi-phase systems in housing, lending, and employment. Consequently, future research could integrate the methods from this paper with recent advancements in such settings, which have developed various quasi-experimental tools for estimating racial discrimination (e.g., Arnold et al. 2018; Arnold et al. 2022; Goncalves and Mello 2021; Lodermeier 2023).

Acknowledgments

We thank Randall Akee, Lawrence Katz, Elizabeth Linos, Mark Loewenstein, and other participants in the Summer 2023 CRIW Pre-Conference and Spring 2024 CRIW Conference for helpful comments. For acknowledgments, sources of research support, and disclosure of the authors' material financial relationships, if any, please see https://www.nber.org/books-and-chapters/race-ethnicity-and-economic-statistics-21st-century/unwarranted-disparity-high-stakes-decisions-race-measurement-and-policy-responses.

Econometric Appendix

A.1 Identification Strategy in Baron et al. (2024)

This appendix summarizes the quasi-experimental identification strategy in Baron et al. (2024). We begin by re-writing Equations (1)–(8) in terms of a set of directly estimable moments and a set of unknown parameters which capture the average risk of subsequent maltreatment among various populations of Black and White children. We then show how one can estimate these parameters leveraging the quasi-random assignment of screeners and investigators. We demonstrate this approach for estimating the screener UD measures here, and we then discuss how this approach can be easily extended to estimate both the investigator UD measures and the decompositions of placement UDs; Baron et al. (2024) also discuss an alternative bounding approach, which we omit here for brevity.

First, note that the screener UD measures (1)–(2) can be rewritten as:

$$E[S_i \mid R_i = r, Y_i^* = 1] = 1 - \frac{E[(1 - S_i)Y_i^* \mid R_i = r]}{E[Y_i^* \mid R_i = r]} \tag{18}$$

and

$$E[S_i \mid R_i = r, Y_i^* = 0] = 1 - \frac{E[(1 - S_i)(1 - Y_i^*) \mid R_i = r]}{1 - E[Y_i^* \mid R_i = r]}. \tag{19}$$

Screening decisions S_i are observed; since the subsequent maltreatment outcomes of screened-out children (with $S_i = 0$) directly reveal their subsequent maltreatment potential, the numerators in both expressions do not suffer from the selective observability of Y_i^*. The challenge of estimating screener UDs thus reduces to the challenge of estimating the parameters in the denominators: the average subsequent maltreatment risk of Black and White children in the full population of calls, $\mu_b = E[Y_i^* \mid R_i = b]$ and $\mu_w = E[Y_i^* \mid R_i = w]$. These parameters are not directly estimable because of the core selection challenge: Y_i^* is unobserved if child i is placed into foster care.

The approach of Baron et al. (2024) for estimating these key parameters builds on Arnold et al. (2021, 2022): they leverage variation in screener-specific maltreatment rates among children who are not placed in foster care. The intuition is as follows: consider a hypothetical screener whose calls have an eventual placement rate near zero. This could happen, for example, if this screener either screens-out all calls or if most of their screened-in calls do not result in foster care placement. If we were to randomly assign a subset of calls to this screener, the subsequent maltreatment rate among these calls would not suffer from the selection challenge. Moreover, by random assignment, the average Y_i^* among calls involving Black and White children in this subset of cases would be the same as the averages in the full population of calls.

Baron et al. (2024) approximate this idealized experiment. Absent such a hypothetical screener, they estimate μ_r by extrapolating variation in observed subsequent maltreatment rates across quasi-randomly assigned screeners with very low placement rates. Specifically, they use regression adjustment to account for the non-random variation in screener assignment and either linear, quadratic, or local linear approximation to estimate μ_r from screener- and race-specific estimates of at-home maltreatment rates. With estimates of μ_r and the screener-specific numerators in Equations (18)–(19), they estimate screener-specific UD measures Δ_{j0}^S and Δ_{j1}^S following Equations (1) and (2). They then aggregate these screener-specific measures, weighting by caseloads, to estimate average screener UDs Δ_0^S and Δ_1^S. Finally, they average these measures weighting by $\bar{\mu} = \mu_b \Pr(R_i = b) + \mu_w \Pr(R_i = w)$ to estimate overall average screener UD. They use the same approach to estimate investigator UDs, placement UDs in the full set of calls, and the UD decompositions.

This empirical strategy relies on two primary assumptions: the as-good-as-random assignment of screeners and investigators and an exclusion restriction requiring that the assignment of screeners and investigators only impact subsequent maltreatment potential through the decision to place children in foster care. Baron et al. (2024) discuss and probe these assumptions empirically, showing that they are both plausible in the Michigan CPS context.

A.2 Race Misclassification Decomposition

This appendix derives the approximate decomposition in Equation (10) from an exact decomposition based on Bohren et al. (2025) and discusses identification. For the latter, since for each $r^* \in \{b, w\}$ and $y \in \{0, 1\}$:

$$E[D_i \mid R_i^* = r^*, Y_i^* = y] = \sum_{r \in \{b,w,m\}} E[D_i \mid R_i^* = r^*, R_i = r, Y_i^* = y] \times \Pr(R_i = r \mid R_i^* = r^*, Y_i^* = y),$$

we have by adding and subtracting quantities of the form

$$E[D_i \mid R_i^* = r^*, R_i = r, Y_i^* = y] \Pr(R_i = r \mid R_i^* = r', Y_i^* = y)$$

for $r' \neq r^*$, and rearranging terms:

$$\begin{aligned}
\Delta_y^* &\equiv E[D_i \mid R_i^* = b, Y_i^* = y] - E[D_i \mid R_i^* = w, Y_i^* = y] \\
&= \sum_{r \in \{b,w,m\}} \left(E[D_i \mid R_i^* = b, R_i = r, Y_i^* = y] - E[D_i \mid R_i^* = w, R_i = r, Y_i^* = y]\right) \\
&\quad \Pr(R_i = r \mid R_i^* = w, Y_i^* = y) \\
&\quad + \sum_{r \in \{b,w,m\}} \left(\Pr(R_i = r \mid R_i^* = b, Y_i^* = y) - \Pr(R_i = r \mid R_i^* = w, Y_i^* = y)\right) \\
&\quad E[D_i \mid R_i^* = b, R_i = r, Y_i^* = y].
\end{aligned}$$

Suppose now that no child who self-reports as Black is miscoded as White and vice versa, such that $\Pr(R_i = w \mid R_i^* = b) = \Pr(R_i = b \mid R_i^* = w) = 0$. This eliminates several of the terms of the exact decomposition and yields an alternative decomposition by again adding, subtracting, and rearranging terms:

$$
\begin{aligned}
\Delta_y^* = {} & E[D_i \mid R_i^* = b, R_i = b, Y_i^* = y]\Pr(R_i = b \mid R_i^* = b, Y_i^* = y) \\
& + E[D_i \mid R_i^* = b, R_i = m, Y_i^* = y]\Pr(R_i = m \mid R_i^* = b, Y_i^* = y) \\
& - E[D_i \mid R_i^* = w, R_i = m, Y_i^* = y]\Pr(R_i = m \mid R_i^* = w, Y_i^* = y) \\
& - E[D_i \mid R_i^* = w, R_i = w, Y_i^* = y]\Pr(R_i = w \mid R_i^* = w, Y_i^* = y) \\
= {} & \big(E[D_i \mid R_i^* = b, R_i = m, Y_i^* = y] - E[D_i \mid R_i^* = w, R_i = m, Y_i^* = y]\big) \\
& \Pr(R_i = m \mid R_i^* = b, Y_i^* = y) \\
& + \big(\Pr(R_i = m \mid R_i^* = b, Y_i^* = y) - \Pr(R_i = m \mid R_i^* = w, Y_i^* = y)\big) \\
& \quad E[D_i \mid R_i^* = w, R_i = m, Y_i^* = y] \\
& + \big(\Pr(R_i = b \mid R_i^* = b, Y_i^* = y) - \Pr(R_i = w \mid R_i^* = w, Y_i^* = y)\big) \\
& \quad E[D_i \mid R_i^* = w, R_i = w, Y_i^* = y] \\
& + \big(E[D_i \mid R_i^* = b, R_i = b, Y_i^* = y] - E[D_i \mid R_i^* = w, R_i = w, Y_i^* = y]\big) \\
& \quad \Pr(R_i = b \mid R_i^* = b, Y_i^* = y) \\
= {} & \underbrace{\big(E[D_i \mid R_i^* = b, R_i = m, Y_i^* = y] - E[D_i \mid R_i^* = w, R_i = m, Y_i^* = y]\big)}_{\text{Obscured discrimination}} \\
& \Pr(R_i = m \mid R_i^* = b, Y_i^* = y) \\
& + \underbrace{\big(E[D_i \mid R_i^* = b, R_i = b, Y_i^* = y] - E[D_i \mid R_i^* = w, R_i = w, Y_i^* = y]\big)}_{\text{Revealed discrimination}} \\
& \quad \Pr(R_i = b \mid R_i^* = b, Y_i^* = y) \\
& + \underbrace{\big(\Pr(R_i = w \mid R_i^* = w, Y_i^* = y) - \Pr(R_i = b \mid R_i^* = b, Y_i^* = y)\big) \times \big(E[D_i \mid R_i^* = w, R_i = m, Y_i^* = y] - E[D_i \mid R_i^* = w, R_i = w, Y_i^* = y]\big)}_{\text{Residual}}.
\end{aligned}
$$

Equation (10) approximates this decomposition by assuming

$$\Pr(R_i = w \mid R_i^* = b) \approx 0 \text{ and } \Pr(R_i = b \mid R_i^* = w) \approx 0$$

and ignoring the final residual term. In practice we find only a small share of self-reported Black and White children are misclassified as White and Black and that misclassification rates are similar by self-reported race. These facts imply $\Pr(R_i = w \mid R_i^* = w, Y_i^* = y) \approx \Pr(R_i = b \mid R_i^* = b, Y_i^* = y)$, making the residual small.

Identification of these decompositions follow similarly to the Baron et al. (2024) strategy discussed above. Each term of either decomposition can be written:

$$E[D_i \mid R_i^* = r^*, R_i = r, Y_i^* = 1] = 1 - \frac{E[(1 - D_i)Y_i^* \mid R_i^* = r^*, R_i = r]}{E[Y_i^* \mid R_i^* = r^*, R_i = r]}$$

$$E[D_i \mid R_i^* = r^*, R_i = r, Y_i^* = 0] = 1 - \frac{E[(1 - D_i)(1 - Y_i^*) \mid R_i^* = r^*, R_i = r]}{1 - E[Y_i^* \mid R_i^* = r^*, R_i = r]}$$

$$\Pr(R_i = r \mid R_i^* = r^*, Y_i^* = 1) = E[Y_i^* \mid R_i^* = r^*, R_i = r] \frac{\Pr(R_i^* = r^*, R_i = r)}{\Pr(R_i^* = r^*, Y_i^* = 1)}$$

$$= E[Y_i^* \mid R_i^* = r^*, R_i = r] \frac{\Pr(R_i^* = r^*, R_i = r)}{E[Y_i^* \mid R_i^* = r^*] \Pr(R_i^* = r)}$$

$$= E[Y_i^* \mid R_i^* = r^*, R_i = r] \frac{\Pr(R_i = r \mid R_i^* = r)}{E[Y_i^* \mid R_i^* = r^*]}$$

$$\Pr(R_i = r \mid R_i^* = r^*, Y_i^* = 0)$$

$$= (1 - E[Y_i^* \mid R_i^* = r^*, R_i = r]) \frac{\Pr(R_i^* = r^*, R_i = r)}{\Pr(R_i^* = r^*, Y_i^* = 0)}$$

$$= (1 - E[Y_i^* \mid R_i^* = r^*, R_i = r]) \frac{\Pr(R_i^* = r^*, R_i = r)}{(1 - E[Y_i^* \mid R_i^* = r^*]) \Pr(R_i^* = r^*)}$$

$$= (1 - E[Y_i^* \mid R_i^* = r^*, R_i = r]) \frac{\Pr(R_i = r \mid R_i^* = r)}{1 - E[Y_i^* \mid R_i^* = r^*]}$$

The first two equations are of the form of the UD components Baron et al. (2024) estimate, just with a "combined" race category of $\{R_i^* = r, R_i = r^*\}$. We estimate them following the steps in appendix A.1. The second two equations depend on the mean risk parameters $E[Y_i^* \mid R_i^* = r, R_i = r^*]$ that are estimated in this procedure, directly estimable racial (mis-)categorization probabilities $\Pr(R_i = r \mid R_i^* = r)$, and additional mean risk parameters $E[Y_i^* \mid R_i^* = r]$ which can be estimated again by following the extrapolation approach in Baron et al. (2024).

References

Agadjanian, Alexander. 2022. "How Many Americans Change Their Racial Identification over Time?" *Socius* 8 23780231221098547.

Agan, Amanda Y, Diag Davenport, Jens Ludwig, and Sendhil Mullainathan. 2023. "Automating Automaticity: How the Context of Human Choice Affects the Extent of Algorithmic Bias." NBER Working Paper No. 30981. Cambridge, MA: National Bureau of Economic Research.

Albright, Alex. 2023. "The Hidden Effects of Algorithmic Recommendations." Preprint.

Antle, Becky F., Anita P. Barbee, Dana N. Christensen, and Dana J. Sullivan. 2009. "The Prevention of Child Maltreatment Recidivism Through the Solution-Based Casework Model of Child Welfare Practice." *Children and Youth Services Review* 31 (12): 1346–1351.

Arnold, David, Will Dobbie, and Peter Hull. 2021. "Measuring Racial Discrimination in Algorithms." *AEA Papers and Proceedings* 111: 49–54.

Arnold, David, Will Dobbie, and Peter Hull. 2022. "Measuring Racial Discrimination in Bail Decisions." *American Economic Review* 112(9): 2992–3038.

Arnold, David, Will Dobbie, and Crystal S Yang. 2018. "Racial Bias in Bail Decisions." *Quarterly Journal of Economics* 133(4): 1885–32.

Bald, Anthony, Joseph Doyle Jr., Max Gross, and Brian Jacob. 2022. "Economics of Foster Care." *Journal of Economic Perspectives* 36(2): 223–46.

Baron, Jason, Joseph Doyle, Natalia Emanuel, Peter Hull, and Joseph Ryan. 2024. "Discrimination in Multi-Phase Systems: Evidence from Child Protection." *Quarterly Journal of Economics* 139(3): 1611–64. https://doi.org/10.1093/qje/qjae007.

Baron, Jason, and Max Gross. 2022. "Is There a Foster Care-To-Prison Pipeline? Evidence from Quasi-Randomly Assigned Investigators." NBER Working Paper No. 29922. Cambridge, MA: National Bureau of Economic Research.

Baron, Jason, Joseph Doyle, Natalia Emanuel, and Peter Hull. 2025 "Unwarranted Racial Disparity in US Foster Care Placement." *Journal of Policy Analysis and Management*. https://doi.org/10.1002/pam.70030.

Benson, Cassandra, Maria D. Fitzpatrick, and Samuel Bondurant. 2022. "Beyond Reading, Writing, and Arithmetic: The Role of Teachers and Schools in Reporting Child Maltreatment." *Journal of Human Resources*, forthcoming.

Bohren, J. Aislinn, Peter Hull, and Alex Imas. 2025. "Systemic Discrimination: Theory and Measurement." *Quarterly Journal of Economics* 140(3): 1743–99. https://doi.org/10.1093/qje/qjaf022.

Canay, Ivan A., Magne Mogstad, and Jack Mountjoy. 2022. "On the Use of Outcome Tests for Detecting Bias in Decision Making." NBER Working Paper No. 27802. Cambridge, MA: National Bureau of Economic Research.

Conrick, Kelsey M., Brianna Mills, Astrid B. Schreuder et al. 2023. "Disparities in Misclassification of Race and Ethnicity in Electronic Medical Records Among Patients with Traumatic Injury." *Journal of Racial and Ethnic Health Disparities* 1–5.

Dee, Thomas S., Will Dobbie, Brian A. Jacob, and Jonah Rockoff. 2019. "The Causes and Consequences of Test Score Manipulation: Evidence from the New York Regents Examinations." *American Economic Journal: Applied Economics* 11(3): 382–423.

DeFina, Robert, and Lance Hannon. 2016. "Social Status Attainment and Racial Category Selection in the Contemporary United States." *Research in Social Stratification and Mobility* 44: 91–97.

Dinerstein, Michael, and Isaac M. Opper. 2022. "Screening with Multitasking: Theory and Empirical Evidence from Teacher Tenure Reform." NBER Working Paper No. 30310. Cambridge, MA: National Bureau of Economic Research.

Dobbie, Will, Andres Liberman, Daniel Paravisini, and Vikram Pathania. 2021. "Measuring Bias in Consumer Lending." *Review of Economic Studies* 88(6): 2799–2832.

Feigenberg, Benjamin, and Conrad Miller. 2022. "Would Eliminating Racial Disparities in Motor Vehicle Searches have Efficiency Costs?" *Quarterly Journal of Economics* 137(1): 49–113.

Finlay, Keith, Elizabeth Luh, and Michael Mueller-Smith. 2024. "Implications of Race and Ethnicity (Mis)Measurement in the US Criminal Justice System." Working Paper.

Goncalves, Felipe, and Steven Mello. 2021. "A Few Bad Apples? Racial Bias in Policing." *American Economic Review* 111(5): 1406–41.

Grimon, Marie-Pascale, and Christopher Mills. 2022. "The Impact of Algorithmic Tools on Child Protection: Evidence from a Randomized Controlled Trial." Job market paper.

Gross, Max, and E. Jason Baron. 2022. "Temporary Stays and Persistent Gains: The Causal Effects of Foster Care." *American Economic Journal: Applied Economics* 14(2): 170–99.

Harrington, Emma, and Hannah Shaffer. 2022. "Brokers of Bias in the Criminal Justice System: Do Prosecutors Compound or Attenuate Racial Disparities in Policing?" Working Paper.

Hull, Peter. 2021. "What Marginal Outcome Tests Can Tell Us about Racially Biased Decision-Making." NBER Working Paper No. 28503. Cambridge, MA: National Bureau of Economic Research.

Jacob, Brian A., and Steven D. Levitt. 2003. "Rotten Apples: An Investigation of the Prevalence and Predictors of Teacher Cheating." *Quarterly Journal of Economics* 118(3): 843–77.

Kim, Hyunil, Christopher Wildeman, Melissa Jonson-Reid, and Brett Drake. 2017. "Lifetime Prevalence of Investigating Child Maltreatment Among US Children." *American Journal of Public Health* 107(2): 274–80.

Kleinberg, Jon, Himabindu Lakkaraju, Jure Leskovec, Jens Ludwig, and Sendhil Mullainathan. 2018a. "Human Decisions and Machine Predictions." *Quarterly Journal of Economics* 133(1): 237–93.

Kleinberg, Jon, Jens Ludwig, Sendhil Mullainathan, and Ashesh Rambachan. 2018b. "Algorithmic Fairness." *AEA Papers and Proceedings* 108: 22–27. http://dx.doi.org/10.1257/pandp.20181018.

Lane, Wendy G., David M. Rubin, Ragin Monteith, and Cindy W. Christian. 2002. "Racial Differences in the Evaluation of Pediatric Fractures for Physical Abuse." *JAMA* 288(13): 1603–1609.

Lodermeier, Alison. 2023. "Racial Discrimination in Eviction Filing." Working paper. https://alilodermeier.github.io/PaperRepository/evict_discrimination.pdf.

Luh, Elizabeth. 2022. "Not so Black and White: Uncovering Racial Bias from Systematically Misreported Trooper Reports." Working Paper.

Putnam-Hornstein, Emily, John Prindle, and Ivy Hammond. 2021. "Engaging Families in Voluntary Prevention Services to Reduce Future Child Abuse and Neglect: A Randomized Controlled Trial." *Prevention Science* 22(7): 856–65.

Rambachan, Ashesh. 2022. "Identifying Prediction Mistakes in Observational Data." Working paper.

Rambachan, Ashesh, Jon Kleinberg, Sendhil Mullainathan, and Jens Ludwig. 2021. "An Economic Approach to Regulating Algorithms." NBER Working Paper No. 27111. Cambridge, MA: National Bureau of Economic Research.

Rittenhouse, Katherine. 2022. "Income and Child Maltreatment: Evidence from a Discontinuity in Tax Benefits." Working Paper. https://krittenh.github.io/katherine-rittenhouse.com/RittenhouseJMP_current.pdf.

Rittenhouse, Katherine, Emily Putnam-Hornstein, and Rhema Vaithianathan. 2022. "Algorithms, Humans, and Racial Disparities in Child Protective Services: Evidence from the Allegheny Family Screening Tool." Working paper.

Rose, Evan K. 2023. "A Constructivist Perspective on Empirical Discrimination Research." *Journal of Economic Literature* 61(3): 906–23.

Roth, Wendy D. 2012. *Race Migrations: Latinos and the Cultural Transformation of Race*. Stanford University Press.

Samant, Anjana, Aaron Horowitz, Sophie Beiers, and Kath Xu. 2021. "Family Surveillance by Algorithm: The Rapidly Spreading Tools Few Have Heard Of." ACLU, September 29. https://www.aclu.org/news/womens-rights/family-surveillance-by-algorithm-the-rapidly-spreading-tools-few-have-heard-of.

Smith, Ning, Rajan L. Iyer, Annette Langer-Gould et al. 2010. "Health Plan Administrative Records Versus Birth Certificate Records: Quality of Race and Ethnicity Information in Children." *BMC Health Services Research* 10(1): 1–7.

Telles, Edward, and Tianna Paschel. 2014. "Who is Black, White, or Mixed Race? How Skin Color, Status, and Nation Shape Racial Classification in Latin America." *American Journal of Sociology* 120(3): 864–907.

Yi, Youngmin, Frank R. Edwards, and Christopher Wildeman. 2020. "Cumulative Prevalence of Confirmed Maltreatment and Foster Care Placement for US Children by Race/Ethnicity, 2011–2016." *American Journal of Public Health* 110(5): 704–9.

7

Quantifying the Uncertainty of Imputed Demographic Disparity Estimates
The Dual-Bootstrap

Benjamin Lu, Jia Wan, Derek Ouyang, Jacob Goldin, and Daniel E. Ho

7.1 Introduction

Racial and ethnic disparities are a common focus of academic study, policymaking, and advocacy efforts across many domains, including criminal justice (Gelman et al. 2007; Berdejó 2018), health care (Azin et al. 2020; Mackey et al. 2021), technology (Buolamwini and Gebru 2018; Koenecke et al. 2020), and taxation (Brown 2022; Avenancio-León and Howard, 2022).[1]

Such disparities are straightforward to compute—if individual-level demographic and outcome data are available. In many settings where the measurement of racial disparities is of interest, however, race data are missing or otherwise inaccessible. For example, Regulation B of the Equal Credit Opportunity Act prohibits creditors from discriminating against an applicant on the basis of race. But monitoring and enforcing this prohibition is complicated by the fact that the very same laws also prohibit creditors from inquiring about an applicant's race at all.

Some researchers work around this problem by imputing individuals'

Benjamin Lu received his PhD in Statistics from the University of California, Berkeley.

Jia Wan is a second-year PhD student in Electrical Engineering and Computer Science (EECS) at the Massachusetts Institute of Technology.

Derek Ouyang is a senior research manager in the Regulation, Evaluation, and Governance Lab (RegLab) at Stanford University.

Jacob Goldin is the Richard M. Lipton Professor of Tax Law at the University of Chicago Law School and a research associate of the National Bureau of Economic Research.

Daniel E. Ho is the William Benjamin Scott and Luna M. Scott Professor of Law, Professor of Political Science, Professor of Computer Science (by courtesy), Senior Fellow at the Stanford Institute for Human-Centered Artificial Intelligence (HAI), Senior Fellow at the Stanford Institute for Economic Policy Research, and Director of the Regulation, Evaluation, and Governance Lab (RegLab) at Stanford University.

1. For brevity, we use *race* to refer to both race and ethnicity throughout the remainder of this paper.

races based on observable proxy features, then using those imputations to estimate the racial disparity. One of the most common imputation methods is Bayesian Improved Surname Geocoding (BISG), which imputes an individual's race based on their surname and geolocation (Elliott et al. 2009). Recent work has also investigated the potential power of machine learning for this task (Cheng et al. 2023; Xue et al. 2019; Kim et al. 2018).

But imputations are estimates, not oracles. Like any other statistic, each imputation is the output of an estimator fit on data, with its own bias and variance. This statistical uncertainty could affect the quality of the downstream racial disparity estimate. Many studies that use imputations ignore this potential error propagation, instead treating the imputation model as known with certainty (e.g., Brown et al. 2016; Zhang 2018; Yee et al. 2022). Doing so can imperil the reliability of the final estimate in different ways (e.g., Labgold et al. 2021, adjusting for imputation bias).

This paper examines one aspect of the problem: the effect of measurement uncertainty on statistical inference. It is standard practice in academic research to report the confidence interval or standard error associated with a racial disparity estimate. But typical confidence intervals and standard errors reflect only classical *sampling uncertainty*—i.e., uncertainty arising from the fact that the disparity estimate is based on only a sample of the broader population of interest. They do not reflect the *measurement uncertainty* that arises from estimating the race probability model and thus risk mischaracterizing the degree of confidence in the disparity estimate.

We make three contributions to the study of this issue. First, we offer a "dual-bootstrap" procedure that incorporates both sampling and measurement uncertainty and thus offers more accurate statistical inference. We prove that our procedure is consistent for some race probability models under standard regularity conditions.

Second, we adapt our procedure to the special case of BISG, where Census Bureau–imposed constraints on data availability raise particular challenges. The Census Bureau does not disclose the individual-level survey responses on which its popularly used American Community Survey race-by-geolocation estimates are based. This prevents researchers from directly applying the general dual-bootstrap algorithm. We propose one way to nonetheless approximate the measurement uncertainty of BISG race probability estimates using other information provided by the Census Bureau.

Third, we apply our approach to simulated and real data to investigate how much measurement uncertainty contributes to the final disparity estimate's standard error. Our findings suggest that, in many cases, the uncertainty of BISG imputations only negligibly increases standard errors because BISG is a relatively inflexible model based on large-scale data (i.e., full-scale census records); bias, not variance, is likely the predominant type of error in BISG. But we do find some exceptions: BISG measurement uncertainty, and the way it is estimated, can substantially affect the final inference when studying particular demographic or geographic groups. We also show that when race probability models more flexible than BISG are employed, properly accounting for measurement uncertainty can substantially affect the widths of resulting confidence intervals. We illustrate these findings through an analysis of racial disparities in common health outcomes in the American Family Cohort, a dataset containing the electronic health records of primary care visits by patients in the United States. Our method has also been applied in a recent working paper studying racial disparities in tax audit rates (Elzayn et al. 2025).

7.2 Related Work

To our knowledge, the role of measurement uncertainty in the specific context of race imputation has not been thoroughly studied. As mentioned in section 7.1, many studies where race is imputed simply ignore it. One exception is a concurrent working paper by Derby et al. (2024), who propose a fully Bayesian approach where a prior distribution for the conditional race probabilities is assumed, then updated based on reported Census Bureau estimates to obtain a posterior distribution from which conditional race probabilities are sampled.[2] Our proposal for BISG is similar in spirit. It can be viewed as the frequentist analog—but with the distinct advantage of constructing a sampling distribution of the conditional race probability estimates based on the uncertainty that the Census Bureau actually reports for those estimates, instead of a purely assumed prior model. This fidelity comes at some cost to flexibility; see section 7.5 for discussion.

This paper draws from a rich body of research on missing data, survey design, data combination, and causal inference. Especially relevant are two strands of work, on inverse propensity weighting (IPW) and Z-estimation. The disparity estimator we consider, analyzed by Chen et al. (2019) and described in section 7.3 below, weights individuals by their estimated probability of being of a given race. It is thus very similar in form to Hájek IPW estimators, which have been extensively studied by, for example, Miratrix et al. (2018) and Matsouaka et al. (2024). And, following some prior work on the properties of IPW estimators in the context of causal inference (Reifeis and Hudgens 2022; Shu et al. 2021), we rely on Z-estimator theory to establish the asymptotic properties of our proposed method (Kosorok 2008; Stefanski and Boos 2002).

We distinguish our subject of investigation from several other important but distinct areas of study. First, we focus solely on the variability of the imputed disparity estimator, as typically reflected in metrics like the standard

2. Imai et al. (2022) similarly impose a prior, but they focus on how doing so improves the accuracy of race predictions, not on how it can more accurately quantify the uncertainty of downstream estimates.

error or confidence intervals. Prior work has examined identification, bias, and consistency properties of the specific imputed disparity estimator on which we focus (Chen et al. 2019; Kallus et al. 2022; Elzayn et al. 2025). Others have examined the accuracy and bias of specific race imputation models that often underlie imputed disparity estimators. For example, Imai et al. (2022) propose ways of improving the accuracy of BISG by accounting for the possible migration of racial minorities to geographic areas where none resided prior to the latest census count. These issues are largely orthogonal to the challenge of accurately characterizing an imputation-based estimator's variability. In our theory and simulations, we assume that these issues have been favorably resolved.

Second, our work is distinct from multiple imputation, at least in its classical formulation. In the typical setting amenable to multiple imputation, race is observed as a categorical variable for a subset of the data to be analyzed, and the researcher seeks to impute the categorical race variable for the remaining subset of the data where it is missing; Fong and Tyler (2021) discuss some challenges of proper statistical inference in that setting that are similar to the ones we address here. But the setting we consider (described in section 7.3) is one where race is completely unobserved for the data to be analyzed, and the researcher seeks to estimate each unit's real-valued probability of being a given race, not the unit's actually realized race. Our problem setting is thus more closely related to that of measurement error models (e.g., Fuller 2009) and two- or split-sample instrumental variables (e.g., Angrist and Krueger 1992, 1995), with particular focus on uncertainty quantification for general, nonlinear measurement models. Nonetheless, some conceptual similarities to multiple imputation can be drawn. Perhaps the most salient connection is to the concept of "proper" multiple imputation, defined by Rubin (1987). As Murray (2018) summarizes it, multiple imputation generally yields valid inference only if, among other conditions, the uncertainty of the imputation model itself is accounted for. This same concept underpins our work.

7.3 Setup and Notation

Consider two datasets: a training dataset $\mathcal{T} \equiv \{Z_i, A_i\}_{i=1}^{n_\mathcal{T}}$ and a primary dataset $\mathcal{P} \equiv \{Z_j, Y_j\}_{j=1}^{n_\mathcal{P}}$, where Y denotes the outcome, A is a binary indicator of race, Z denotes observable proxies of race, and $n_\mathcal{T}$ and $n_\mathcal{P}$ are the number of units in the training and primary datasets, respectively. The training dataset is drawn i.i.d. from some population $\mathbb{T}$, and the primary dataset is drawn i.i.d. from a potentially different population $\mathbb{P}$. Our estimand is the racial disparity in outcomes in the primary population $\mathbb{P}$:

$$\delta \equiv \mathbb{E}_\mathbb{P}[Y \mid A = 1] - \mathbb{E}_\mathbb{P}[Y \mid A = 0].$$

If A were observed in the primary dataset, estimation and inference of δ would be straightforward. But it is not—so we impute A using Z based on some model class $\mathcal{F}_A$ instead. Specifically, we fit a model $f \in \mathcal{F}_A$ of A on Z using the training dataset, where (Z, A) is jointly observed. We then use that model to estimate the race probability of each unit in the primary dataset: $\widehat{\Pr}_{\mathbb{P}}(A = 1|Z = Z_j) \equiv f(Z_j)$. Finally, we estimate the racial disparity by the probabilistic weighting estimator that Chen et al. (2019) propose:

$$\hat{\delta} \equiv \frac{\sum_{j=1}^{n_P} \widehat{\Pr}_{\mathbb{P}}(A = 1|Z = Z_j)Y_j}{\sum_{j=1}^{n_P} \widehat{\Pr}_{\mathbb{P}}(A = 1|Z = Z_j)} - \frac{\sum_{j=1}^{n_P} \widehat{\Pr}_{\mathbb{P}}(A = 0|Z = Z_j)Y_j}{\sum_{j=1}^{n_P} \widehat{\Pr}_{\mathbb{P}}(A = 0|Z = Z_j)}.$$

Other imputation-based disparity estimators have been used or analyzed in past work. For example, Chen et al. (2019) discuss a thresholding estimator that estimates the mean outcome in each race by classifying individuals' races instead of using soft probabilities. And Elzayn et al. (2025) consider the slope coefficient in a linear regression of the outcomes on the estimated race probabilities, which they show can in conjunction with $\hat{\delta}$ bound the true disparity. But we focus on $\hat{\delta}$ because it is a commonly used estimator with favorable statistical properties (Chen et al. 2019; McCaffrey and Elliott 2008). We briefly outline how our framework might extend to the linear disparity estimator of Elzayn et al. (2025) in section C.2 of appendix C, but we defer a detailed examination of this and other extensions to future work.

We invoke standard assumptions so that the estimator $\hat{\delta}$ is consistent for δ. First, we assume that the probability model $\widehat{\Pr}_{\mathbb{P}}(A = 1|Z)$ is correctly specified. Since the model is fit on the training dataset $\mathcal{T}$ but used to characterize the primary population $\mathbb{P}$, this assumption typically also implies that the conditional distribution of A given Z is the same in $\mathbb{T}$ and $\mathbb{P}$ everywhere Z has positive density in P. Second, we assume that $\mathbb{E}_{\mathbb{P}}[Cov_{\mathbb{P}}(A,Y|Z)] = 0$. Chen et al. (2019) show that this condition is sufficient for $\hat{\delta}$ to be consistent when the true probabilities are given. Informally, this assumption can be analogized to requiring that the "unexplained" portion of a Kitagawa-Oaxaca-Blinder decomposition be zero (Kitagawa 1955; Oaxaca 1973; Blinder 1973): The difference in average outcomes between the two races can be entirely decomposed into (1) differences in the distribution of the observed proxies between the two races and (2) the association between the observed proxies and the outcome, with no need to account for the possibility that the latter might interact with or otherwise vary by race.[3] Since our focus is inference, not estimation, we take these assumptions for granted and refer interested readers to past work on the consistency of $\hat{\delta}$ (Chen et al. 2019; Kallus et al. 2022; Elzayn et al. 2025).

7.4 The Dual-Bootstrap

We propose a "dual-bootstrap" procedure to enable proper inference of $\hat{\delta}$ that accounts for both sampling and measurement uncertainty, as figure 7.1 illustrates. We first state the procedure in general terms, then investigate via

3. Thanks to Jonathan Roth for suggesting this analogy.

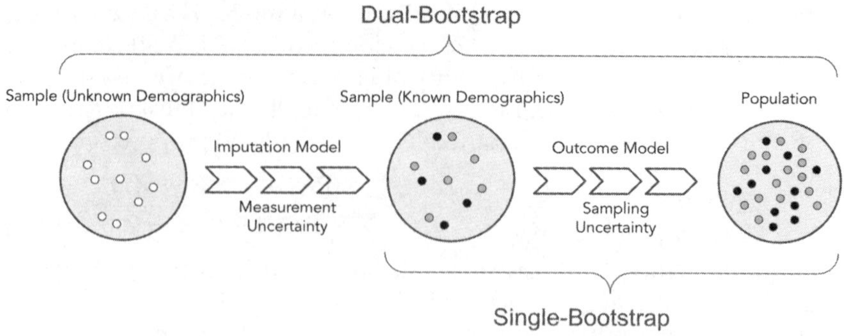

Fig. 7.1 Illustration of the uncertainties captured by the dual-bootstrap, compared to those captured by the single-bootstrap

simulation the effects of measurement uncertainty and the dual-bootstrap's ability to account for it.

7.4.1 General Procedure

Algorithm 1 states the dual-bootstrap procedure. It frames the desired output as a confidence interval estimated via the percentile bootstrap, but other uncertainty metrics can be estimated too. As Algorithm 1 shows, the dual-bootstrap is straightforward: We simply resample with replacement both the training and the primary datasets, then refit the race probability model on the resampled training dataset and apply it to estimate the racial disparity in the resampled primary dataset. The algorithm here calls for simple resampling with replacement, but other, more complex forms of resampling may be appropriate—for example, if the data are clustered (Owen 2007; Derby et al. 2024).

The key contribution of the dual-bootstrap stems from its resampling of the training dataset and refitting of the race probability model. Doing so accounts for the uncertainty of the race probability estimates themselves. This uncertainty is then propagated downstream to the bootstrap statistic $\hat{\delta}^{*b}$. As discussed above, some prior work has ignored this measurement uncertainty entirely, instead treating $\widehat{\Pr}_{\mathbb{P}}(A = 1|Z = Z_j)$ as true. This corresponds to skipping the first two lines of the for-loop in Algorithm 1.

Extreme cases can conceptually illuminate when measurement uncertainty likely is or is not substantial. When $n_{\mathcal{T}}$ is fixed and $n_{\mathcal{P}} \to \infty$, sampling uncertainty becomes negligible; only measurement uncertainty remains, so the dual-bootstrap is crucial for proper statistical inference. Conversely, when $n_{\mathcal{P}}$ is fixed and $n_{\mathcal{T}} \to \infty$, measurement uncertainty becomes negligible; only sampling uncertainty remains, so the single-bootstrap suffices. Taken together, these two extremes suggest that, in general, the greater measurement uncertainty is *relative to* sampling uncertainty, the more important the dual-bootstrap is for proper statistical inference. The concept of uncertainty amplification offers another lens through which to view this same principle: The larger the primary dataset, the more measurement uncertainty is amplified, so the more important the dual-bootstrap is for proper statistical inference. Our simulations in section 7.4.2 offer empirical evidence of this phenomenon.

We prove in section C.1 of appendix C that $\hat{\delta}$ and its dual-bootstrap analogs $\hat{\delta}^{*b}$ are asymptotically normal when the race probabilities are estimated via logistic regression and general regularity conditions hold. We limit the proof to logistic regression because doing so allows us to frame $\hat{\delta}$ as a Z-estimator—broadly, any estimator that can be expressed as the approximate zero of a data-dependent function—to which standard theoretical results can apply. The proof strategy likely applies readily to other race probability models that fall within the Z-estimation framework, albeit possibly with slight modifications to the regularity conditions. We leave such extensions to future work. It is less clear what theoretical properties the dual-bootstrap of $\hat{\delta}$ has when the race probability model does not fall within the Z-estimation framework. A closer examination of this issue might prove fruitful.

The Z-estimation theory that we apply to prove asymptotic normality also provides a closed-form expression for the variance of the limiting distribution, but this is mostly of theoretical interest. In practice, deriving the closed-form expression usually has little utility. Statistical software like the geex package in R can compute the empirical variance estimator using numerical routines, without requiring analytic derivations (Saul and Hudgens 2020). When the race probability model falls within the Z-estimation framework, using such numerical solvers can often require much less computational power than the dual-bootstrap.

7.4.2 Simulations

We demonstrate empirically that the dual-bootstrap more accurately accounts for the overall uncertainty of imputed disparity estimates. We do so through a simple simulation in which both the training and primary populations follow the same data-generating process:

- A single proxy is drawn i.i.d. from a standard normal: $Z \sim \mathcal{N}(0,1)$.
- Race is drawn i.i.d. from a Bernoulli distribution with probability logistic in Z: $A \mid Z \sim \text{Bern}[\exp(Z)/\{\exp(Z)+1\}]$.
- The outcome Y is i.i.d. normal and linear in Z: $Y \mid Z \sim \mathcal{N}(5Z,9)$.

In each simulation repetition, we draw (Z, A) tuples as the training dataset $\mathcal{T}$ and (Z, Y) tuples as the primary dataset $\mathcal{P}$. We fit a logistic regression of A on Z with $\mathcal{T}$, then apply it to $\mathcal{P}$ to obtain our point estimate $\hat{\delta}$. We then apply the dual-bootstrap with 2,000 bootstrap iterations to estimate a 95 percent confidence interval for δ. For comparison, we also estimate what we call the "single-bootstrap" standard 95 percent confidence interval, in which the race

Box 7.1

Algorithm 1: Dual-Bootstrap

Data: Training Dataset $\mathcal{T} = \{Z_i, A_i\}_{i=1}^{n_\mathcal{T}}$, Primary Dataset $\mathcal{P} = \{Z_j, Y_j\}_{j=1}^{n_\mathcal{P}}$, Model Class $\mathcal{F}_A$, Number of Bootstrap Draws $B \in \mathbb{N}$, Level $\alpha \in [0,1\}$

Result: Confidence interval for the demographic disparity estimate $\hat{\delta}$

for *b in range B* **do**

Resample $\mathcal{T}^{*b}$ by sample with replacemenet from $\mathcal{T}$

Fit $\widehat{\Pr}_{\mathbb{P}}^{*b}(A = 1|Z) \in \mathcal{F}_A$ on $\mathcal{T}^{*b}$

Resample $\mathcal{P}^{*b}$ by sampling with replacement from $\mathcal{P}$

Compute

$$\hat{\delta}^{*b} \equiv \frac{\sum_{j=1}^{n_\mathcal{P}} \widehat{\Pr}_{\mathbb{P}}^{*b}(A = 1|Z = Z_j^{*b})Y_j^{*b}}{\sum_{j=1}^{n_\mathcal{P}} \widehat{\Pr}_{\mathbb{P}}^{*b}(A = 1|Z = Z_j^{*b})} - \frac{\sum_{j=1}^{n_\mathcal{P}} \widehat{\Pr}_{\mathbb{P}}^{*b}(A = 0|Z = Z_j^{*b})Y_j^{*b}}{\sum_{j=1}^{n_\mathcal{P}} \widehat{\Pr}_{\mathbb{P}}^{*b}(A = 0|Z = Z_j^{*b})}$$

Output $(1 - \alpha)$-level percentile bootstrap confidence interval

$$\left(\hat{\delta}_B^{(\alpha/2)}, \hat{\delta}_B^{(1-\alpha/2)}\right)$$

where $\hat{\delta}_B^{(\alpha)}$ is the empirical α-percentile of the $\hat{\delta}^{*b}$

probability estimates are treated as given and only $\mathcal{P}$ is resampled. We also estimate a 95 percent confidence interval based on the empirical variance estimator implied by Z-estimation theory using the geex package.

Table 7.1 reports the resulting coverage rates of the three types of confidence intervals over 500 simulation repetitions for various sample sizes of $\mathcal{T}$ and $\mathcal{P}$. We note four trends. First, the coverage rate of the single-bootstrap is worst when $\mathcal{T}$ is small and best, though still inadequate, when it is large. This reflects the effect of measurement uncertainty on the variance of the ultimate disparity estimator in this specific simulation setup; as $\mathcal{T}$ increases, the variability of the imputations decreases and becomes less influential. Second, for any size of $\mathcal{T}$, the single-bootstrap's coverage rate decreases as $\mathcal{P}$ increases. This suggests that the importance of measurement uncertainty can amplify with the number of imputations required. One interesting consequence of this phenomenon, discussed earlier in section 7.4.1, is that the coverage rate of the single-bootstrap is lower when $n_\mathcal{T} = 1000$ and $n_\mathcal{P} = 5000$ than when they are both 100, even though the absolute sample sizes of both the training and the primary datasets are larger in the former than in the latter. Third, the dual-bootstrap provides better coverage than the

Table 7.1 **Coverage rates and widths of 95 percent confidence intervals estimated using the dual-bootstrap, the single-bootstrap, and the empirical variance estimator for varying sample sizes of $\mathcal{T}$ and $\mathcal{P}$**

		Coverage Rate			Interval Width		
$n_{\mathcal{T}}$	$n_{\mathcal{P}}$	Dual-Bootstrap	Single-Bootstrap	Empirical	Dual-Bootstrap	Single-Bootstrap	Empirical
100	100	0.91	0.81	0.92	3.8	2.2	3.7
100	1,000	0.94	0.66	0.95	3.1	0.7	3.0
100	5,000	0.94	0.54	0.94	3.0	0.3	3.0
1,000	100	0.89	0.87	0.90	2.4	2.2	2.4
1,000	1,000	0.93	0.80	0.93	1.2	0.7	1.2
1,000	5,000	0.97	0.67	0.97	1.0	0.3	1.0
5,000	100	0.87	0.86	0.87	2.2	2.2	2.2
5,000	1,000	0.88	0.84	0.88	0.8	0.7	0.8
5,000	5,000	0.94	0.83	0.94	0.5	0.3	0.5

single-bootstrap, but it requires sufficiently large sample sizes to achieve the desired 95 percent rate. This reflects the fact that the theoretical properties of the bootstrap take effect asymptotically, as we discuss in section C.1 of appendix C. Finally, the empirical variance estimator and the dual-bootstrap behave nearly identically; this is consistent with the theoretical results of section C.1 of appendix C.

7.5 Special Case: BISG

In this section, we adapt the dual-bootstrap to the BISG algorithm, which is commonly used in empirical applications as the race probability model. The key challenge to applying our dual-bootstrap approach in this setting is that the Census Bureau does not generally make publicly available the training dataset $\mathcal{T}$ on which the BISG prior probabilities are based. We suggest one way to overcome this constraint while still upholding the fundamental principle animating the generic dual-bootstrap procedure of section 7.4.1. We then apply our method to assess how prominent the uncertainty of BISG imputations are in practice. We conclude that, with some notable exceptions, the variability of BISG imputations is generally negligible in practice; bias, not variance, is likely the primary source of error in BISG.

7.5.1 BISG-Specific Procedure

BISG imputes race by naively applying Bayes' Theorem to Census Bureau estimates of the racial composition of people by surname and geolocation. In this context, A is typically categorical instead of binary, containing all race categories defined by the Census Bureau; $Z = (S, G)$, where S is a categorical variable denoting the individual's surname and G is a categorical variable denoting the individual's geolocation; and the race probability model is

$$\widehat{\Pr}_{\mathbb{P}}(A = a' \mid S = s, G = g) \equiv \frac{\widehat{\Pr}_{\mathbb{P}}(A = a' \mid G = g)\widehat{\Pr}_{\mathbb{P}}(S = s \mid A = a')}{\sum_a \widehat{\Pr}_{\mathbb{P}}(A = a \mid G = g)\widehat{\Pr}_{\mathbb{P}}(S = s \mid A = a)},$$

where the prior probabilities on the right are parameter estimates based on Census Bureau surveys. Specifically, researchers commonly use as $\widehat{\Pr}_{\mathbb{P}}(A \mid G)$ the Census Bureau's American Community Survey (ACS) estimates of the number of people of each race residing in each geolocation. And they compute $\widehat{\Pr}_{\mathbb{P}}(S \mid A)$ based on the Census Bureau's 2010 table of frequently occurring surnames. For BISG, then, the training dataset $\mathcal{T}$ is the microdata—i.e., individual-level survey responses—that the Census Bureau collects to generate the ACS and surname estimates. The standard dual-bootstrap procedure outlined in Algorithm 1 thus calls for the analyst to resample the microdata with replacement and recompute the racial composition of each geolocation and surname.[4]

The challenge, however, is that $\mathcal{T}$ is inaccessible. The Census Bureau generally does not publish microdata for privacy reasons. This is not an issue for the microdata on which the surname-race probabilities are based: Since the surname table is just a raw tabulation, we can still essentially reconstruct the microdata that produced it and resample from it.[5] But the same is not true of the microdata on which the ACS race-by-geolocation estimates are based. The ACS estimates of the racial composition of geographic areas are not raw tabulations of survey microdata; rather, they are produced by re-weighting the microdata to adjust for factors like probability of selection in an unknown and presumably complex way.[6] Thus, a solution for the race-by-geolocation probabilities is required.

The key intuition behind the solution we propose is that we seek to resample the microdata $\mathcal{T}$ and recompute the prior $\widehat{\Pr}_{\mathbb{P}}(A \mid G)$ only as a means

4. The surname table is a raw tabulation of data from the decennial census, which covers the entire population of the United States. Thus, depending on the population for which race-specific outcomes are to be estimated, resampling the data that produced the surname table might be unnecessary. Nonetheless, we outline our procedure to include resampling for two reasons. First, it could be appropriate to do so, depending on the estimand. Second, race-by-name probabilities are sometimes sourced from data that are properly characterized as a sample, rather than the entire population. For example, Imai et al. (2022) use voting records from a handful of states to estimate the race-by-name probabilities. In such cases, resampling would likely be appropriate.

5. Such a reconstruction is necessarily imprecise since the surname table aggregates all surnames held by fewer than 100 individuals into a single "Other" category. Our reconstruction of the microdata can never recover these surnames. We leave a detailed examination of the significance of this issue to future work.

6. Some ACS microdata are available, but only at levels of geographic granularity that are too low to be useful in most applications. Such microdata are also incomplete—they consist of only about two-thirds of the records used to produce the ACS estimates—and thus might not be any more amenable to direct resampling.

of, essentially, drawing from the approximate sampling distribution of $\widehat{\Pr}_{\mathbb{P}}(A|G)$. If we can approximate the sampling distribution of $\widehat{\Pr}_{\mathbb{P}}(A|G)$ in some other way, then we can just draw from it directly—no resampling or model-refitting needed. Fortunately, the Census Bureau suggests and endorses a way of estimating key parameters of the sampling distribution even without microdata. We outline the approach below, with further details available in appendix A.

As an initial matter, we center the sampling distribution of $\widehat{\Pr}_{\mathbb{P}}(A|G)$ at the published ACS estimate, which we denote by $\hat{\mu}_G$. Then, to estimate the covariance of this sampling distribution, which we denote by $\hat{\Sigma}_G$, we use the publicly available ACS variance replicates. These are 80 "pseudo-estimates" of the racial composition of each geolocation, which we denote by $\hat{\mu}_G^r$ for $r = 1, \ldots, 80$. The Census Bureau uses them to estimate variances via the successive differences replication (SDR) method. The variance replicates are not bootstrap statistics; they have "no other use [beyond calculating SDR variances] and no independent meaning" (Census Bureau 2022). So we cannot directly apply the dual-bootstrap algorithm to them. Instead, we use the variance replicates to estimate the covariance of the race-by-geolocation probability estimates based on the formula prescribed by the Census Bureau:

$$\hat{\Sigma}_G \equiv \frac{4}{80}\sum_{r=1}^{80}(\hat{\mu}_G^r - \hat{\mu}_G)(\hat{\mu}_G^r - \hat{\mu}_G)^T.$$

When ACS estimates that there are zero people of a given race in a geographic area, all associated variance replicates are zero. In such "zero-count" cases, we follow the Census Bureau's recommendation not to use the above formula; instead, we assume the estimate has zero covariance with the other estimates and essentially derive the variance from the Census Bureau's estimated margin of error (Census Bureau 2022). Section A.1 of appendix A describes the procedure in more detail. As we discuss in section 7.5.2, the choice to account for uncertainty in zero-count geolocations can be influential in specific circumstances.

Finally, we assume that the sampling distribution of $\widehat{\Pr}_{\mathbb{P}}(A|G)$ is normal, so the parameter estimates $(\hat{\mu}_G, \hat{\Sigma}_G)$ fully specify the sampling distribution as $\mathcal{N}(\hat{\mu}_G, \hat{\Sigma}_G)$. We leave generalizations of the form of the sampling distribution to future work. See section A.2 of appendix A for more discussion.

With the sampling distribution of $\widehat{\Pr}_{\mathbb{P}}(A|G)$ in hand, our modified dual-bootstrap routine can be executed. Algorithm 2 states the modified implementation. The key distinction from Algorithm 1 is that the bootstrap race-by-geolocation probability estimate $\widehat{\Pr}_{\mathbb{P}}^{*b}(A|G)$ is computed by drawing directly from the sampling distribution $\mathcal{N}(\hat{\mu}_G, \hat{\Sigma}_G)$ instead of by refitting on resampled microdata. As with Algorithm 1, the resampling steps in this algorithm use simple resampling with replacement, but more complex forms of resampling may be appropriate (Owen 2007; Derby et al. 2024).

As mentioned in section 7.2, recent work has proposed an alternative approach: setting the sampling distribution to the posterior distribution obtained by updating an assumed prior with the ACS race-by-geolocation estimates (Derby et al. 2024). We do not adopt this approach because, as discussed above, the Census Bureau offers its own account of the uncertainty of its estimates. This uncertainty is multifaceted—it includes considerations like the Census Bureau's sampling scheme and survey nonresponse, as well as adjustments the Census Bureau has made to account for them—and inscrutable to the general public. So, rather than impose our own model for this uncertainty by specifying an ultimately arbitrary prior, we prefer to use the model offered by the Census Bureau, which is best positioned to develop one.

One potential advantage to assuming a prior distribution instead of using the Census Bureau's uncertainty model is that it can accommodate a superpopulation framework for the race probability model. For example, a researcher can assume an abstract superpopulation of which each year's demographic composition is a sample. The prior distribution characterizes the superpopulation of race probabilities and is updated by a given year's observed demographic composition. To our knowledge, the Census Bureau's uncertainty model cannot accommodate such a superpopulation framework because it only models uncertainty arising from its survey sampling procedure. In our view, however, this limitation is significant only if the superpopulation parameters of the race probability model are of independent interest. In most applications—like the study of racial disparities—the race probability model is merely nuisance.

Consider, for example, the task of estimating racial disparities in tax audit rates. It is true that researchers might be interested in the racial disparity at the superpopulation level (e.g., as a parameter of an abstract data-generating process that produces the observed tax audit rates by race each year). But, to estimate such a disparity, they necessarily use observed tax audit data from certain, well-defined years. Suppose that the race of the taxpayer in each audit decision is unavailable, so the researchers impute it using BISG with ACS data from the relevant years. Quantifying the uncertainty of any individual race imputation and how it affects the uncertainty of the final disparity estimate requires only an understanding of the error of the year-specific BISG model used for that imputation; it does not require reference to any BISG (or other race probability) model at the superpopulation level.

7.5.2 BISG Simulations

We show via simulation that the uncertainty of BISG imputations generally has little effect on the variance of the resulting racial disparity estimate. For this simulation, we use the 2017–2021 ACS five-year estimates of the racial composition of each census block group and the 2010 Census Bureau surname table. We use the following data-generating process for both the training and primary populations:

Box 7.2

Algorithm 2: BISG Dual-Bootstrap

Data: ACS Estimate $\hat{\mu}$, ACS Covariance Matrix Estimate $\hat{\Sigma}$, Surname Table S, Primary Dataset $\mathcal{P} = \{S_j, G_j, Y_j\}_{j=1}^{n_\mathcal{P}}$, Number of Bootstrap Draws $B \in \mathbb{N}$, Level $\alpha \in [0,1]$, Race Groups a' and a''

Result: Confidence interval for the demographic disparity estimate $\hat{\delta}$

for *b in range B* **do**

Resample $\mathcal{S}^{*b}$ by sampling with replacement from $\mathcal{S}$ // optional; see Footnote 4

for s *in* $\{S_j\}_{j=1}^{n_\mathcal{P}}$, a *in* $supp(A)$ **do**

Compute $\widehat{\Pr}_{\mathbb{P}}^{*b}(S = s | A = a)$ from $\mathcal{S}^{*b}$ // optional; see Footnote 4

for g *in* $\{G_j\}_{j=1}^{n_\mathcal{P}}$ **do**

Sample $\widehat{\Pr}_{\mathbb{P}}^{*b}(A | G = g) \sim \mathcal{N}(\hat{\mu}_g, \hat{\Sigma}_g)$

Resample $\mathcal{P}^{*b}$ by sampling with replacement from P

for *j in range* $n_\mathcal{P}$ **do**

Compute

$$\widehat{\Pr}_{\mathbb{P}}^{*b}(A = a' | S = S_j^{*b}, G = G_j^{*b}) \equiv \frac{\widehat{\Pr}_{\mathbb{P}}^{*b}(A = a' | G = G_j^{*b}) \widehat{\Pr}_{\mathbb{P}}^{*b}(S = S_j^{*b} | A = a')}{\sum_a \widehat{\Pr}_{\mathbb{P}}^{*b}(A = a | G = G_j^{*b}) \widehat{\Pr}_{\mathbb{P}}^{*b}(S = S_j^{*b} | A = a)},$$

$$\widehat{\Pr}_{\mathbb{P}}^{*b}(A = a'' | S = S_j^{*b}, G = G_j^{*b}) \equiv \frac{\widehat{\Pr}_{\mathbb{P}}^{*b}(A = a'' | G = G_j^{*b}) \widehat{\Pr}_{\mathbb{P}}^{*b}(S = S_j^{*b} | A = a'')}{\sum_a \widehat{\Pr}_{\mathbb{P}}^{*b}(A = a | G = G_j^{*b}) \widehat{\Pr}_{\mathbb{P}}^{*b}(S = S_j^{*b} | A = a)},$$

Compute

$$\hat{\delta}^{*b} \equiv \frac{\sum_{j=1}^{n_\mathcal{P}} \widehat{\Pr}_{\mathbb{P}}^{*b}(A = a' | S = S_j^{*b}, G = G_j^{*b}) Y_j^{*b}}{\sum_{j=1}^{n_\mathcal{P}} \widehat{\Pr}_{\mathbb{P}}^{*b}(A = a' | S = S_j^{*b}, G = G_j^{*b})} - \frac{\sum_{j=1}^{n_\mathcal{P}} \widehat{\Pr}_{\mathbb{P}}^{*b}(A = a'' | S = S_j^{*b}, G = G_j^{*b}) Y_j^{*b}}{\sum_{j=1}^{n_\mathcal{P}} \widehat{\Pr}_{\mathbb{P}}^{*b}(A = a'' | S = S_j^{*b}, G = G_j^{*b})}$$

Output $(1 - \alpha)$-level percentile bootstrap confidence interval

$$\left(\hat{\delta}_B^{(\alpha/2)}, \hat{\delta}_B^{(1-\alpha/2)}\right)$$

where $\hat{\delta}_B^{(\alpha)}$ is the empirical α-percentile of the $\hat{\delta}^{*b}$

Table 7.2 **Average standard error of the estimated average outcome of each race, as estimated by the dual-bootstrap and the single-bootstrap when BISG is used for imputation**

	Average Standard Error	
Race Group	Dual-Bootstrap	Single-Bootstrap
American Indian and Alaska Native	0.11 (0.02)	0.18 (0.06)
Asian and Pacific Islander	0.11 (0.01)	0.11 (0.01)
Black	0.07 (0.00)	0.07 (0.00)
Hispanic	0.06 (0.00)	0.06 (0.00)
Multiracial	0.07 (0.01)	0.06 (0.01)
White	0.04 (0.00)	0.04 (0.00)

Note: Standard deviations over the simulation repetitions are in parentheses. The dual-bootstrap's average estimate of the standard error is the same as that of the single-bootstrap except for the American Indian and Alaska Native group, for which it is lower. We offer one explanation for this in figures 3–4 and the associated discussion below.

- The proxy tuple (G, S) is sampled i.i.d. from the marginal census block group and surname frequencies given by the ACS estimates and the Census Bureau surname table, excluding tuples where the racial composition of the surname is withheld by the Census Bureau and tuples where the surname and census block group have mutually exclusive racial compositions.
- The outcome Y is i.i.d. standard normal, independent of G, S, and A: $Y \sim N(0, 1)$.

Because the race probability model is estimated using BISG and the outcome is independent of race, no concrete race indicators need to be generated for this simulation. In each of 100 simulation repetitions, we draw 1,000 (G, S, Y) tuples as the primary dataset P. On this dataset, we estimate the average outcome $\hat{\delta}$ for each race using BISG-estimated probabilities. We then estimate the standard error using both the dual-bootstrap and the single-bootstrap.

Table 7.2 reports the results. Overall, accounting for measurement uncertainty in this setting barely affects the resulting standard errors. Our simulation results from section 7.4.2 suggest that measurement uncertainty might have a more substantial effect on the bottom line if our primary dataset $\mathcal{P}$ were larger, since it would amplify over more individuals whose races must be imputed. Future work might systematically investigate *how much* larger $\mathcal{P}$ must be for measurement uncertainty to have a substantial effect. For now, we note that Elzayn et al. (2025) also obtain only slightly larger standard errors (in absolute terms) when they apply our method to estimate the uncertainty of their BISG-based estimates of tax audit disparities by race using a primary dataset of over 100 million individual income tax returns. Figure 7.2 offers one explanation for the relative durability of this phenomenon: For

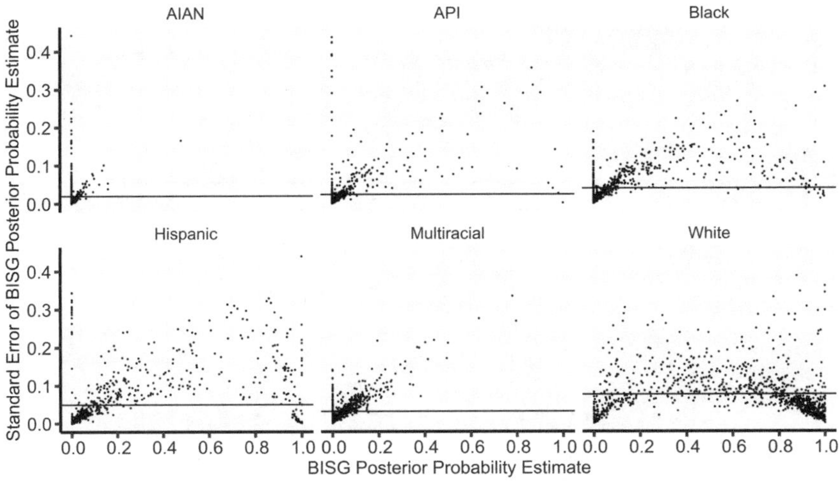

Fig. 7.2 Bootstrap standard error of the BISG-estimated probability of being a given race plotted against the BISG-estimated probability in one simulation repetition.

Note: The horizontal black line indicates the average bootstrap standard error. "AIAN" is the abbreviation for American Indian and Alaska Native, and "API" is the abbreviation for Asian and Pacific Islander.

most units, the bootstrap standard error of the posterior race probability is low, close to 0.05 on average. For comparison, the bootstrap standard errors of the race probabilities in the machine learning simulation of section 7.4.2 are about 0.23, nearly five times larger. The standard errors are much smaller here likely because the BISG model is fairly rigid, and the ACS and surname prior probabilities that parameterize it are based on millions of individual-level training points.

The notable exception in table 7.2 is the American Indian and Alaska Native group, for which the dual-bootstrap standard error is substantially less than the single-bootstrap standard error. As a theoretical matter, it might generally be possible for standard errors to decrease after properly accounting for measurement error; we do not prove so in our specific setting, but Reifeis and Hudgens (2022) show that this can occur in the closely related setting of IPW estimation of the average treatment effect on the treated. However, we believe that the specific reduction observed here is due to our handling of zero counts and our specific data-generating process, as described in more detail below.

Although measurement uncertainty appears to be of nominal significance marginally over the entire population of the United States, we find evidence that it, and the way it is modeled, can be influential in certain situations. To illustrate, we rerun the above simulations for each state—that is, we sample

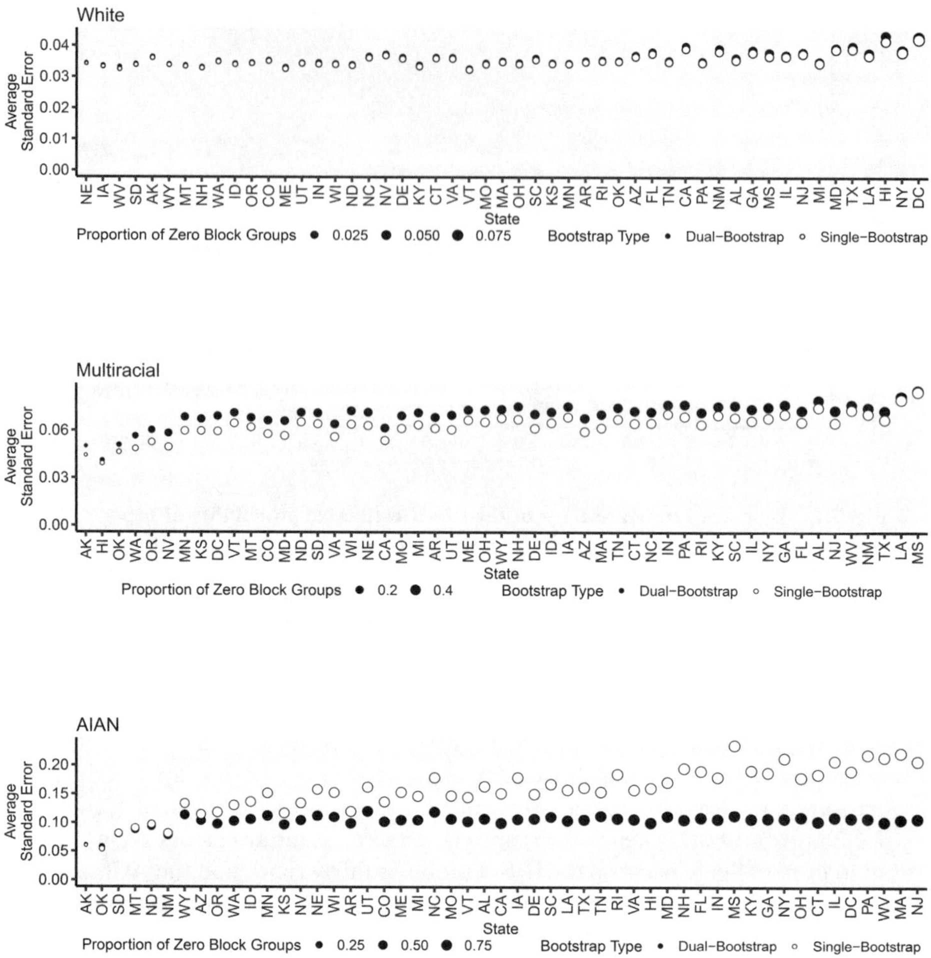

Fig. 7.3 Dual-bootstrap and single-bootstrap standard errors of the estimated average outcome for the White, Multiracial, and American Indian and Alaska Native (AIAN) race groups in each state. The states are ordered by the proportion of census block groups in which the American Community Survey estimates there are zero people of the given race.

census block groups from the marginal frequencies given by the ACS estimates within each state. Figure 7.3 shows the state-by-state results for three racial groups that we highlight here because of their particularly prominent trends; section B.1 of appendix B contains corresponding figures for other racial groups. In most states, accounting for measurement uncertainty has essentially no effect on the uncertainty of the average outcome estimate for

White people; it increases the uncertainty of the average outcome estimate for multiracial people; and it decreases the uncertainty of the average outcome estimate for American Indians and Alaska Natives.

We believe that the key to understanding these seemingly incompatible phenomena lies primarily in (1) the prevalence of each race group overall, (2) the geographic concentration of certain race groups, and (3) the distribution of the outcome among race groups. White people are much more prevalent than multiracial people overall: The 2017–2021 ACS data we use estimates that 59 percent of the population is White, while 3 percent are multiracial. Thus, ACS estimates of the proportion of White people in each census block group are more precise—in other words, have less measurement uncertainty—than estimates of the proportion of multiracial people. This explains why measurement uncertainty increases the uncertainty of the average outcome estimate for multiracial people more than it does for White people.

American Indians and Alaska Natives are even less prevalent than multiracial people overall: The 2017–2021 ACS data we use estimate that about 0.6 percent of the population is American Indian or Alaska Native. But accounting for measurement uncertainty generally *decreases* the uncertainty of the average outcome estimate in these simulations because they are a geographically concentrated minority: As figure 7.3 shows, the ACS estimates that there are zero American Indians and Alaska Natives in most census block groups in most states. As discussed in section 7.5.1, we use the ACS estimated margin of error instead of the ACS variance replicates to approximate the sampling distribution of such estimates since it is possible that American Indians and Alaska Natives in fact reside in those block groups and were simply not sampled by ACS. Accounting for measurement uncertainty in this way gives nonzero weight to people who otherwise would have none. When the outcomes of these people are informative of the average outcome of American Indians and Alaska Natives—as they are in this simulation, since all units have outcomes drawn from a standard normal distribution—giving them nonzero weight increases the effective sample size and thus decreases the standard error of the average outcome estimate. This phenomenon likely explains the overall decrease in the standard error for American Indians and Alaska Natives reported in table 7.2.

We illustrate some of these dynamics through an additional simulation focused on the American Indian and Alaska Native population in New Mexico. In this simulation, we generate synthetic states by taking ACS estimates from New Mexico and altering (1) the total prevalence of American Indian and Alaska Native people in the state and (2) the percentage of census block groups in the state in which zero American Indian and Alaska Native people are estimated to reside. Section B.2 of appendix B describes this process in detail. We then rerun the previous simulation on each synthetic state. As

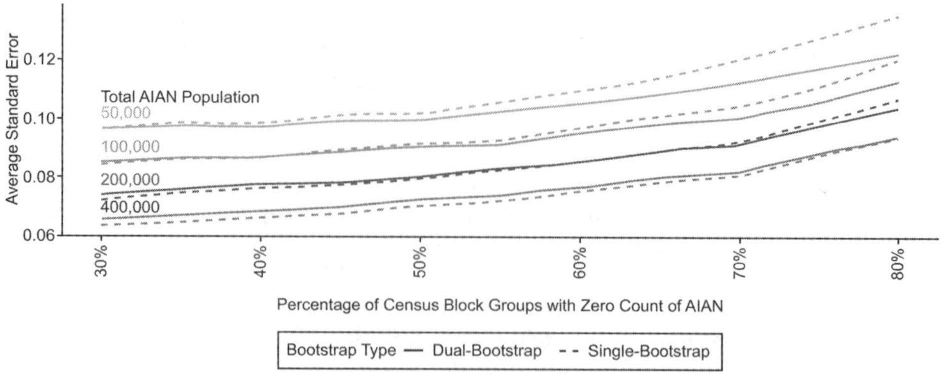

Fig. 7.4 Dual-bootstrap and single-bootstrap standard errors of the estimated average outcome for the American Indian and Alaska Native (AIAN) race group in New Mexico when American Community Survey estimates of the total counts and geographic concentrations of AIAN people in the state are artificially altered

figure 7.4 shows, accounting for measurement uncertainty decreases standard errors the less prevalent and the more concentrated the race group is.

These results for the American Indian and Alaska Native group demonstrate that a proper accounting of uncertainty in zero-count geolocations can, in specific circumstances, be influential. Our choice to take at face value the Census Bureau's margins of error when quantifying the uncertainty of the estimated average outcomes of a race group gives influence to people in geolocations where ACS estimates no people of that race group reside. This motivation to properly leverage data from zero-count geolocations also underlies some of the work of Imai et al. (2022)—though they focus on how accounting for the migration of racial minorities since the last decennial census can improve imputation accuracy, whereas we focus on how accounting for the possible nonselection of racial minorities in ACS sampling can improve uncertainty quantification of downstream estimates. We emphasize that in practice, however, properly accounting for uncertainty in zero-count geolocations might not have as drastic or counterintuitive an effect as shown here, where the outcomes of all simulated units are equally informative for all race groups. On the contrary, it might in some cases increase standard errors if the outcomes of people in zero-count geolocations are substantially different from those of the target race group. In other cases, it might have no effect on balance.

Taken together, the phenomena identified in the simulations above highlight that, although the uncertainty of BISG imputations might not be substantial in studies of the general US population, properly accounting for it in studies of particular geographic areas or demographic groups can be important to ensuring that the resulting inference is neither conservative nor anti-conservative. More generally, our finding is consistent with a broader literature on the challenges of race imputation for certain demographic groups (e.g., Imai et al. 2022).

7.6 Application

We apply the dual-bootstrap to study racial disparities in health outcomes using the American Family Cohort (AFC) dataset (Vala et al. 2023). The dataset contains electronic health records from the primary care visits of patients in the United States. Relevant features for our purposes include patient geolocation; first name; surname; self-reported race, which are provided as mapped to White, Black, Hispanic, Asian and Pacific Islander, American Indian and Alaska Native, Multiracial, and Other; and indicators for the diagnosis of asthma, obesity, and diabetes at any point during the time period covered by the dataset. We downsample the data due to computational constraints by taking a stratified random sample of 100,000 patients with the same race proportions as the full dataset. Although we do not adopt them here, general steps can be taken in practice to improve the computational efficiency of the bootstrap (e.g., Kleiner et al. 2014).

We preprocess the dataset as follows. First, we produce race proxies by converting categorical geolocation, first name, and surname data into numerical race probability estimates. Specifically, we convert the surnames into "prior probability" features by computing the probability of each of the six race categories (excluding Other) given surname based on the Census Bureau's 2010 surname table. And we convert the first names and geolocations into "update" features by computing the probability of the first name or geolocation given each of the six race categories. We use mean imputation for any missing geolocation, first name, or surname probabilities and include a binary missingness indicator for each as a separate feature. Second, we randomly split the data into a primary dataset of size 20,000 and a training dataset of size 80,000. We mask self-reported race in the primary dataset and health outcomes in the training dataset.

On the training dataset, we fit a random forest of patients' races on the processed features defined above. Although these same features could be run through BISG to output race probabilities, we choose to use a random forest because Cheng et al. (2023) find that it produces more accurate estimates in this dataset. We allow for slight tuning of the random forest hyperparameters. Specifically, we perform a grid search of the following hyperparameters using 5-fold cross-validation.

Number of Trees: 100.
Maximum Tree Splits: 20, 50, 100.
Proportion of Features per Split ($p = 21$): $\sqrt{p}$, $0.5p$, $0.75p$.
Minimum Number of Units to Initiate Split: 10, 25, 100.

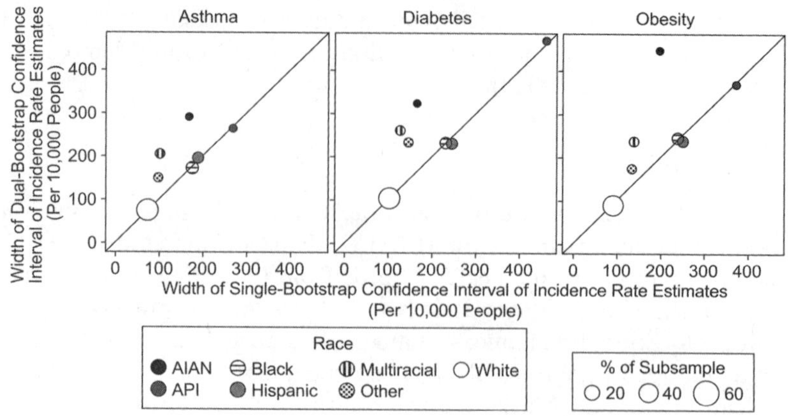

Fig. 7.5 Widths of dual-bootstrap vs. single-bootstrap confidence intervals of the estimated prevalence of certain health conditions by race. This analysis was conducted on a 100,000-unit subsample of the American Family Cohort population with the same racial composition as the full population. Points are sized by the proportion of units in the subsample that are of the given race group. AIAN is the abbreviation for American Indian and Alaska Native, and API is the abbreviation for Asian and Pacific Islander.

We then apply the random forest to the primary dataset to estimate patients' race probabilities. With those estimates in hand, we estimate the incidence rates of asthma, obesity, and diabetes for each race in the primary dataset. To compute confidence intervals for each estimate, we use both the single-bootstrap, which retains the original random forest model, and the dual-bootstrap, which refits a new random forest model on bootstrapped draws of the training dataset. We run 100 bootstrap iterations.

Figure 7.5 shows the results. In general, the single-bootstrap understates the uncertainties of the prevalence estimates compared to the dual-bootstrap. But this trend is not uniform across races. For Asian and Pacific Islander, Black, Hispanic, and White patients, the widths of the dual-bootstrap and single-bootstrap confidence intervals are essentially the same. On the other hand, the dual-bootstrap confidence intervals are substantially wider than the single-bootstrap confidence intervals for American Indian and Alaska Native, Multiracial, and Other patients—in some cases doubly so. This appears largely to be because those patients appear infrequently in the data on which the random forest model was trained, so their race probability estimates are more variable. As figure 7.6 shows, the dual-bootstrap confidence interval widths are nearly identical to the single-bootstrap ones when we alter our downsample so that all races are equally represented in the training dataset.

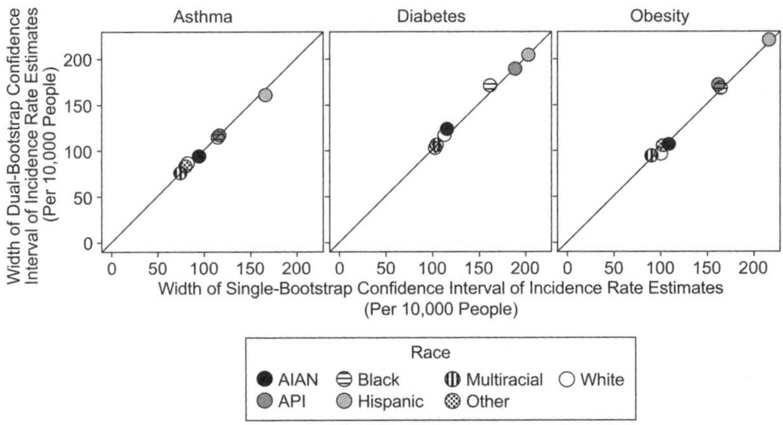

Fig. 7.6 Widths of dual-bootstrap vs. single-bootstrap confidence intervals of the estimated prevalence of certain health conditions by race. This analysis was conducted on a 100,000-unit subsample of the American Family Cohort population where each race was equally represented in the training dataset. AIAN is the abbreviation for American Indian and Alaska Native, and API is the abbreviation for Asian and Pacific Islander.

7.7 Discussion

We propose a dual-bootstrap procedure to more accurately account for the uncertainty of race imputations that are subsequently used to estimate racial disparities and other race-specific outcomes. Our method is straightforward to implement, although complications can arise when the underlying data used to train the race probability model are unavailable. We offer one way of overcoming such difficulties in the specific case of BISG, an imputation model that is often parameterized by ACS race-by-geolocation estimates that are based on undisclosed microdata. Our simulation results suggest that the measurement uncertainty of BISG generally does not impact the uncertainty of downstream estimates, likely because it is a fairly rigid model with a relatively large sample size underpinning its parameter estimates. But it can be significant for specific race groups in specific geographies, with the potential to increase or decrease the standard error of downstream estimates, as our state-by-state results show. And we emphasize that despite its overall low variability—or perhaps because of it—BISG still suffers from bias, as others have shown and sought to improve (e.g. Imai et al. 2022).

We see several opportunities for future work in this direction. Most immediately, an investigation of the theoretical properties of the dual-bootstrap when the race probability model falls outside the Z-estimator framework could be informative. On the practical side, a closer examination and improvement of some of the design choices made in our adaptation of the dual-bootstrap to BISG—such as our choice to use a normal distribution and other choices outlined in appendix A—could produce more accurate inference. Any changes or additions by the Census Bureau to the data products it publishes could help or hinder these efforts. We also see broader opportunities in this space. For example, the development of prospective heuristics for study design akin to a power analysis might prove useful to applied researchers. In some settings, researchers have a choice between analyzing a small dataset where race is observed and analyzing a larger dataset where race must be imputed. The need to account for measurement uncertainty—which, as shown in this paper, can be substantial or not—only complicates this choice. A set of heuristics that allows researchers to prospectively approximate the standard error that would result from each choice given certain parameters like the sample sizes of the datasets, the accuracy of the imputations, and the variability of the outcome might help with the decision.

Acknowledgments

We thank Stanford's Center for Population Health Sciences for data, and Randall Akee, Peng Ding, Avi Feller, Isabel Gallegos, Cameron Guage, Thomas Hertz, Melody Huang, Peter Hull, Lawrence Katz, Qiwei Lin, Mark Loewenstein, Jonathan Roth, Dan Soriano, and participants in the NBER CRIW Race, Ethnicity, and Economic Statistics for the 21st Century conference for helpful comments. This material is based upon work supported by the National Science Foundation under Grant No. 1745640. For acknowledgments, sources of research support, and disclosure of the authors' material financial relationships, if any, please see https://www.nber.org/books-and-chapters/race-ethnicity-and-economic-statistics-21st-century/quantifying-uncertainty-imputed-demographic-disparity-estimates-dual-bootstrap.

Appendices

A. Implementation Details for the BISG Adaptation of the Dual-Bootstrap

We outline our approach to a few issues that can arise when implementing our dual-bootstrap adaptation to BISG.

A.1 Zero Counts

In the ACS dataset, some geographic areas are estimated to have zero people of certain races. Intuitively, such "zero counts" are more common at the census block group level than at the ZIP code tabulation area level. In such cases, all 80 variance replicates also estimate zero people of that race, even though a full count may have revealed people of that race in that area. To nonetheless reflect this uncertainty, the Census Bureau reports a margin of error based on a different method from the successive differences replication method.

Whenever we encounter such instances of zero counts, we impute possible observed values for the 80 variance replicates from a discrete uniform distribution with minimum value 0 and maximum value determined by the margin of error. In particular, we derive the estimated variance from the reported margin of error using a formula prescribed by the Census Bureau. The variance, combined with the fact that observed counts can never be less than 0, allows us to derive the maximum possible value of the discrete uniform distribution. We sample from this distribution 80 times independently and replace the zero counts in the variance replicates with these values (and update the estimated total counts across all races in the variance replicates) for purposes of estimating the covariance matrix $\hat{\Sigma}$.

Our choice of parametric distribution here has little downstream impact since it is used only to recover the variance, which maps directly to the margin of error given by the Census Bureau. But our estimates for zero-count races in a geolocation have approximately zero covariance with the estimates for other races even though this might not be the case in reality. We leave an examination of the significance of this choice and possible improvements to it to future work.

A.2 Impermissible Sampled Probabilities

In some cases, the draws of vectors $\widehat{\Pr}_{\mathbb{P}}^{*b}(A|G = g) \sim \mathcal{N}(\hat{\mu}_g, \hat{\Sigma}_g)$ will include elements that are less than 0 or greater than 1. This arises because we assume that the sampling distribution of the conditional race-by-geolocation probability estimates is multivariate normal. In such instances, we simply round the elements to 0 or 1 accordingly. The rounding to 1 is not strictly necessary, since the normalization that occurs in Bayes' Theorem implicitly handles it; but the rounding to 0 appears to be necessary.

This problem likely can be avoided by imposing an alternative form on the sampling distribution. For example, there might exist a unique set of parameters that best fit $\hat{\mu}_g$ and $\hat{\Sigma}_g$ as a Dirichlet distribution. If so, then modeling the sampling distribution as a Dirichlet with those parameters instead would sidestep this issue. We also note here that the densities of the Dirichlet distribution and the multivariate normal distribution with the same means and covariances converge asymptotically (Ouimet 2022). This might suggest that this problem is less significant in relatively large sample sizes like the ACS, but more research is needed to be sure.

A.3 Mutually Exclusive Conditional Probabilities

In some cases, the conditional surname-by-race probabilities and the conditional race-by-geolocation probabilities are incompatible. For example, an individual might have a surname that, according to the 2010 surname table, only White people have. But he or she might live in a census block group that, according to ACS estimates, has no White people. This problem is not unique to the dual-bootstrap; it can occur in any application of BISG. But it is more likely to occur when applying the dual-bootstrap, which calls for repeated computation of BISG probabilities on resamples of the training data.

Because this problem extends beyond the dual-bootstrap, we do not propose any particular solution. For purposes of the simulations in section 7.5, however, our stopgap approach is to give primacy to the surname probabilities: If the conditional surname-by-race probabilities and the conditional race-by-geolocation probabilities are incompatible, we simply do not update the former with the latter.

B Additional Details on BISG Simulations

B.1 Additional State-by-State Results

Figure 7.7 shows the results of the state-by-state simulation in section 7.5.2 for the remaining race categories that we study. Although the trends shown here are less pronounced, we believe they can be interpreted within the framework described in section 7.5.2.

B.2 Additional Details on New Mexico Simulation

In this section, we describe in more detail the New Mexico simulation reported in section 7.5.2. We select New Mexico for illustrative purposes and focus on the effect of varying total size and census block group concentration of the American Indian and Alaska Native (AIAN) population in the state on the standard error of the average group outcome estimate. The following simulation can be conducted for any state and any race group.

The simulation follows the same general procedure as the state-by-state simulation in section 7.5.2 for just New Mexico, except we modify the 2017–2021 ACS five-year estimates of the AIAN composition of each census block group in the state. The actual estimated total population of AIAN in New Mexico is 181,021, and about 49 percent of census block groups are estimated to have zero AIAN people. We vary the proportion of census block groups with zero-count AIAN from 30 percent to 80 percent, and also vary the total population of AIAN among the values 50,000, 100,000, 200,000, and 400,000.

When modifying the proportion of census block groups with zero-count AIAN, we start with the existing distribution of AIAN counts in census block groups. We decrease the proportion of zero-count AIAN census block groups by randomly selecting zero-count AIAN census block groups (without replacement) and assigning them all the AIAN information (including ACS margins of error and variance replicate estimates) of randomly selected

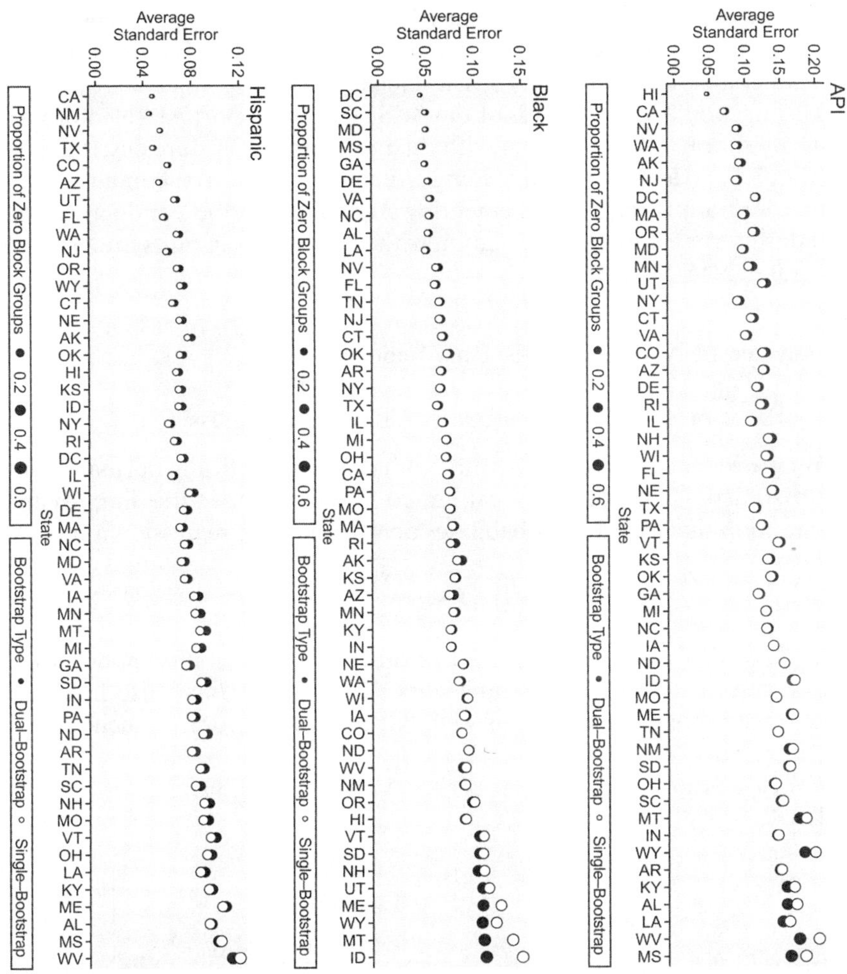

Fig. 7.7 Dual-bootstrap and single-bootstrap standard errors of the estimated average outcome for the Asian and Pacific Islander (API), Black, and Hispanic race groups in each state. The states are ordered by the proportion of census block groups in which the American Community Survey estimates there are zero people of the given race.

non-zero-count AIAN census block groups (with replacement). Similarly, we increase the proportion of zero-count AIAN census block groups by randomly selecting non-zero-count AIAN census block groups (without replacement) and assigning them the AIAN information of zero-count AIAN census block groups (with replacement). To then achieve the desired total population of AIAN, we scale all non-zero counts (and margins of error) of AIAN proportionally up or down. The result is that each synthetically generated New Mexico has different total sizes and census block group concentrations of AIAN, but a similarly shaped distribution of AIAN among non-zero-count AIAN census block groups.

Having modified the records of the ACS table that report AIAN information, we simply follow through with the rest of the procedure described in section 7.5 and appendix A, including estimating the covariance matrix with zero-count adjustments, implementing Algorithm 2, and conducting the standard error estimation simulation with 1,000 tuples in our synthetically generated New Mexico.

C Asymptotic Normality of the Dual-Bootstrap

C.1 Proof of Asymptotic Normality for Logistic Regression

We prove that the dual-bootstrap produces asymptotically normal bootstrap statistics with properly calibrated variance under the simplifying assumption that the race probabilities obey the logistic regression model

$$\text{(1)} \qquad \Pr(A = 1|Z) = \frac{\exp(\alpha^T Z)}{1 + \exp(\alpha^T Z)}.$$

The proof can be readily extended to other race probability models that fall within the Z-estimation framework. The theorem may also hold for other race probability models as well, but we leave a proof of such results to future work.

For ease of notation, let $\mu_a \equiv \mathbb{E}[Y|A = a]$ for $a \in \{0, 1\}$.

Let

$$\text{(2)} \qquad \psi_\theta(z,a,y) \equiv \begin{bmatrix} \psi_\alpha(z,a,y) \\ \psi_1(z,a,y) \\ \psi_0(z,a,y) \end{bmatrix} \equiv \begin{bmatrix} z\left\{a - \dfrac{\exp(\theta_\alpha^T z)}{1 + \exp(\theta_\alpha^T z)}\right\} \\ \dfrac{\exp(\theta_\alpha^T z)}{1 + \exp(\theta_\alpha^T z)} y - \dfrac{\exp(\theta_\alpha^T z)}{1 + \exp(\theta_\alpha^T z)} \theta_1 \\ \dfrac{1}{1 + \exp(\theta_\alpha^T z)} y - \dfrac{1}{1 + \exp(\theta_\alpha^T z)} \theta_0 \end{bmatrix}$$

and assume that $\theta \equiv [\,\theta_\alpha\ \theta_1\ \theta_0\,]^T \in \Theta \subset \mathbb{R}^p$ where Θ is open and $p < \infty$ is fixed.

Then, defining the map $\theta \mapsto \Psi(\theta) \equiv P\psi_\theta$, note that $\theta_0 \equiv [\,\alpha\ \mu_1\ \mu_0\,]^T$ satisfies $\psi(\theta_0) = 0$. We show this coordinate by coordinate. First,

$$\text{(3)} \qquad \mathbb{E}\left[Z\left\{A - \frac{\exp(\alpha^T Z)}{1 + \exp(\alpha^T Z)}\right\}\right] = \mathbb{E}[ZA] - \mathbb{E}[Z\Pr(A = 1|Z)]$$

$$\text{(4)} \qquad = \mathbb{E}[Z\Pr(A = 1|Z)] - \mathbb{E}[Z\Pr(A = 1|Z)]$$

$$\text{(5)} \qquad = 0,$$

where (4) follows from the tower property conditioning on Z and the fact that A is binary. Second,

$$(6)\quad \mathbb{E}\left[\frac{\exp(\alpha^{\intercal}Z)}{1+\exp(\alpha^{\intercal}Z)}Y - \frac{\exp(\alpha^{\intercal}Z)}{1+\exp(\alpha^{\intercal}Z)}\mu_1\right] = \mathbb{E}[\Pr(A=1 \mid Z)Y] - \mathbb{E}[\Pr(A=1 \mid Z)]\mu_1$$

$$(7)\quad = \mathbb{E}[\Pr(A=1 \mid Z)Y] - \mathbb{E}[\Pr(A=1 \mid Z)]\frac{\mathbb{E}(AY)}{\Pr(A=1)}$$

$$(8)\quad = \mathbb{E}[\Pr(A=1 \mid Z)Y] - \mathbb{E}(AY)$$

$$(9)\quad = \mathbb{E}[\Pr(A=1 \mid Z)\mathbb{E}(Y \mid Z)] - \mathbb{E}\{\mathbb{E}(AY \mid Z)\}$$

$$(10)\quad = \mathbb{E}[\mathbb{E}(A \mid Z)\mathbb{E}(Y \mid Z) - \mathbb{E}(AY \mid Z)]$$

$$(11)\quad = 0,$$

where (7), (8), and (9) follow from the law of total expectation, and (11) follows from our identifying assumption of zero covariance. The proof of the third coordinate is analogous.

Let $\hat{\theta}_n$ be an approximate zero of the estimating equation $\theta \mapsto \Psi_n(\theta) \equiv \mathbb{P}_n\psi_\theta$, and let $\hat{\theta}_n^*$ be an approximate zero of the bootstrapped estimating equation $\theta \mapsto \Psi_n^*(\theta) \equiv \mathbb{P}_n^*\psi_\theta$>. By Theorem 10.16 of Kosorok (2008),

$$(12)\quad \sqrt{n}(\hat{\theta}_n - \theta_0) \xrightarrow{d} Z \sim \mathcal{N}\left(0, V_{\theta_0}^{-1}P[\psi_{\theta_0}\psi_{\theta_0}^{\intercal}](V_{\theta_0}^{-1})^{T}\right)$$

and

$$(13)\quad \sqrt{n}(\hat{\theta}_n^* - \hat{\theta}_n) \underset{*}{\overset{P}{\rightsquigarrow}} k_0 Z$$

if five conditions hold. We verify each condition in turn. As a preliminary matter, note that Exercise 10.5.5 of Kosorok (2008) already verifies each of the five conditions for the first coordinate of $\psi\theta$. So we verify them for the remaining two coordinates, focusing without loss of generality on the first of the two.

(A) For any sequence $\{\theta_n\} \in \Theta$, $\Psi(\theta_n) \to 0$ **implies** $\theta_n - \theta_0 \to 0$.

Proof. By assumption,

$$(14)\quad \mathbb{E}\left[\frac{\exp(\theta_{\alpha n}^{T}Z)}{1+\exp(\theta_{\alpha n}^{T}Z)}Y - \frac{\exp(\theta_{\alpha n}^{T}Z)}{1+\exp(\theta_{\alpha n}^{T}Z)}\theta_{1n}\right] \to 0.$$

Distributing the expectation and dividing by both sides yields

$$(15)\quad \frac{\mathbb{E}\left[\frac{\exp(\theta_{\alpha n}^{T}Z)}{1+\exp(\theta_{\alpha n}^{T}Z)}Y\right]}{\mathbb{E}\left[\frac{\exp(\theta_{\alpha n}^{T}Z)}{1+\exp(\theta_{\alpha n}^{T}Z)}\right]} - \theta_{1n} \to 0,$$

so it suffices to show that

$$\frac{\mathbb{E}\left[\frac{\exp(\theta_{\alpha n}^{T} Z)}{1+\exp(\theta_{\alpha n}^{T} Z)} Y\right]}{\mathbb{E}\left[\frac{\exp(\theta_{\alpha n}^{T} Z)}{1+\exp(\theta_{\alpha n}^{T} Z)}\right]} \to \mu_1. \tag{16}$$

Since we know from (1) and (6) that

$$\mu_1 = \frac{\mathbb{E}\left[\frac{\exp(\alpha^{T} Z)}{1+\exp(\alpha^{T} Z)} Y\right]}{\mathbb{E}\left[\frac{\exp(\alpha^{T} Z)}{1+\exp(\alpha^{T} Z)}\right]}, \tag{17}$$

it suffices to prove that the numerator and denominator of (16) each converge to their corresponding limit. We prove the denominator first. From Example 10.5.5 of Kosorok (2008), we can take as given that $\theta_{\alpha n} \to \alpha$. Since these are constants, this implies that $\theta_{\alpha n} \xrightarrow{p} \alpha$. Moreover, it is trivially true that an i.i.d. sequence $Z_1, Z_2, \ldots$ where each Z_i is distributed as Z satisfies $Z_n \xrightarrow{d} Z$. Then Slutsky's theorem implies that $\theta_{\alpha n} Z \xrightarrow{d} \alpha Z$. The continuous mapping theorem then implies that $\theta_{\alpha n} \odot Z \xrightarrow{d} \alpha \odot Z$. Since the logistic function is bounded and continuous, convergence in distribution implies that

$$\mathbb{E}\left[\frac{\exp(\theta_{\alpha n}^{T} Z)}{1+\exp(\theta_{\alpha n}^{T} Z)}\right] \to \mathbb{E}\left[\frac{\exp(\alpha^{T} Z)}{1+\exp(\alpha^{T} Z)}\right]. \tag{18}$$

The proof for the numerator is similar but slightly more delicate. Again from Example 10.5.5 of Kosorok (2008), we can take as given that $\theta_{\alpha n} \to \alpha$. Since these are constants, this implies that $\theta_{\alpha n} \xrightarrow{p} \alpha$. Moreover, it is trivially true that an i.i.d. sequence $(Z_1, Y_1), (Z_2, Y_2), \ldots$ where each (Z_i, Y_i) is distributed as (Z, Y) satisfies $(Z_n, Y_n) \xrightarrow{d} (Z, Y)$. Since α is a constant, the portmanteau lemma implies that $(Z_n, Y_n, \theta_{\alpha n}) \xrightarrow{d} (Z, Y, \alpha)$. Then the continuous mapping theorem implies that

$$\frac{\exp(\theta_{\alpha n}^{T} Z)}{1+\exp(\theta_{\alpha n}^{T} Z)} Y \xrightarrow{d} \frac{\exp(\alpha^{T} Z)}{1+\exp(\alpha^{T} Z)} Y. \tag{19}$$

If Y has a finite second moment, then

$$\mathbb{E}\left[\left|\frac{\exp(\theta_{\alpha n}^{T} Z)}{1+\exp(\theta_{\alpha n}^{T} Z)} Y\right|^2\right] < \mathbb{E}[|Y|^2] < \infty \tag{20}$$

for all $n \in \mathbb{N}$, so

$$\frac{\exp(\theta_{\alpha n}^{T} Z)}{1+\exp(\theta_{\alpha n}^{T} Z)} Y \tag{21}$$

is uniformly integrable.[7] This, combined with convergence in distribution, implies that

7. See Uniformly Integrable Variables from Random Services, https://www.randomservices.org/random/expect/Uniform.html.

$$\mathbb{E}\left[\frac{\exp(\theta_{\alpha n}^{T} Z)}{1+\exp(\theta_{\alpha n}^{T} Z)} Y\right] \rightarrow \mathbb{E}\left[\frac{\exp(\alpha^{T} Z)}{1+\exp(\alpha^{T} Z)} Y\right]. \tag{22}$$

Thus, the proof is complete.

(B) The class $\{\psi_\theta : \theta \in \Theta\}$ is strong Glivenko-Cantelli. *Proof.* As indicated by Van der Vaart (2000), it suffices to show separately that each coordinate class is strong Glivenko-Cantelli. This can be done under several different regularity conditions. We assume two regularity conditions. First, we assume that each coordinate of (Z, A, Y) is bounded almost surely—i.e., that $(Z, A, Y) \sim P$ where P has measure zero outside a bounded subset of $\mathbb{R}^{p+2}$. Second, we assume that Θ is bounded. Then let $\mathbb{R}^{p+2} = \cup_j I_j$ be a partition in cubes of volume 1. Since each ψ_1 in the class has partial derivatives up to order $\alpha > (p + 2) / 2$ that are bounded by constants M_j on each of the cubes I_j, Example 19.9 of Van der Vaart (2000) guarantees that, for any $V \geq (p + 2) / \alpha$,

$$\log N_{[]}(\epsilon, \{\psi_\theta : \theta \in \Theta\}, L_2(P)) \leq K\left(\frac{1}{\epsilon}\right)^{V} \left(\sum_{j=1}^{\infty} (M_j^2 P(I_j))^{V/(V+2)}\right)^{(V+2)/V}. \tag{23}$$

Since P has measure zero outside a bounded subset of $\mathbb{R}^{p+2}$, the series converges for any $V \geq (p + 2) / \alpha$. Then, setting $V \in [(p + 2) / \alpha, 2)$, we see that the function class has finite bracketing integral:

$$J_{[]}(1, \{\psi_\theta : \theta \in \Theta\}, L_2(P)) \equiv \int_0^1 \sqrt{\log N_{[]}(\epsilon, \{\psi_\theta : \theta \in \Theta\}, L_2(P))}\, d\epsilon \tag{24}$$

$$\leq \int_0^1 \sqrt{K\left(\frac{1}{\epsilon}\right)^{V} \left(\sum_{j=1}^{\infty} (M_j^2 P(I_j))^{V/(V+2)}\right)^{(V+2)/V}}\, d\epsilon \tag{25}$$

$$= \sqrt{K\left(\sum_{j=1}^{\infty} (M_j^2 P(I_j))^{V/(V+2)}\right)^{(V+2)/V}} \int_0^1 \sqrt{\left(\frac{1}{\epsilon}\right)^{V}}\, d\epsilon \tag{26}$$

$$\leq C \int_0^1 \left(\frac{1}{\epsilon}\right)^{V/2} d\epsilon \tag{27}$$

$$< \infty, \tag{28}$$

where C is a constant. Thus, by Theorem 19.5 of Van der Vaart (2000), the function class is Donsker. Hence, it is strong Glivenko-Cantelli (Kosorok 2008). Note that we can probably relax the assumption that P has measure zero if we instead assume it has a certain concentration.

(C) For some $\eta > 0$, the class $\mathcal{F} \equiv \{\psi_\theta : \theta \in \Theta, \|\theta - \theta_0\| \leq \eta\}>$ is Donsker and $\mathrm{P}(\psi_\theta - \psi_{\theta_0})^2 \rightarrow 0$ as $\|\theta - \theta_0\| \rightarrow 0$.

Proof. The first statement follows immediately from our proof of (B). The second statement follows from similar logic to the proof of (A), assuming that $\mathbb{E}[|Y|^4] < \infty$. Observe that

$$P(\psi_\theta - \psi_{\theta_0})^2 = \mathbb{E}\left[\left\{\frac{\exp(\theta_\alpha^T Z)}{1+\exp(\theta_\alpha^T Z)}(Y-\theta_1) - \frac{\exp(\alpha^T Z)}{1+\exp(\alpha^T Z)}(Y-\mu_1)\right\}^2\right]. \tag{29}$$

Consider the first outer term obtained by squaring the inside:

$$\mathbb{E}\left[\left\{\frac{\exp(\theta_\alpha^T Z)}{1+\exp(\theta_\alpha^T Z)}(Y-\theta_1)\right\}^2\right] \tag{30}$$

$$= \mathbb{E}\left[\left\{\frac{\exp(\theta_\alpha^T Z)}{1+\exp(\theta_\alpha^T Z)}\right\}^2 Y^2\right] - 2\theta_1\mathbb{E}\left[\left\{\frac{\exp(\theta_\alpha^T Z)}{1+\exp(\theta_\alpha^T Z)}\right\}^2 Y\right] + \theta_1^2\mathbb{E}\left[\left\{\frac{\exp(\theta_\alpha^T Z)}{1+\exp(\theta_\alpha^T Z)}\right\}^2\right] \tag{31}$$

$$\to \mathbb{E}\left[\left\{\frac{\exp(\alpha^T Z)}{1+\exp(\alpha^T Z)}\right\}^2 Y^2\right] - 2\mu_1\mathbb{E}\left[\left\{\frac{\exp(\alpha^T Z)}{1+\exp(\alpha^T Z)}\right\}^2 Y\right] + \mu_1^2\mathbb{E}\left[\left\{\frac{\exp(\alpha^T Z)}{1+\exp(\alpha^T Z)}\right\}^2\right], \tag{32}$$

where convergence occurs by application of the continuous mapping theorem and uniform integrability (again, assuming that the fourth moment of Y is finite) to the fact that $(\theta_\alpha, \theta_1) \to (\alpha, \mu_1)$. Since this is just the second outer term obtained by squaring the inside, it suffices to show that the inner term converges to twice it. Observe that

$$\mathbb{E}\left[\left\{\frac{\exp(\theta_\alpha^T Z)}{1+\exp(\theta_\alpha^T Z)}(Y-\theta_1)\right\}\left\{\frac{\exp(\alpha^T Z)}{1+\exp(\alpha^T Z)}(Y-\mu_1)\right\}\right] \tag{33}$$

$$= \mathbb{E}\left[\frac{\exp(\theta_\alpha^T Z)}{1+\exp(\theta_\alpha^T Z)}\frac{\exp(\alpha^T Z)}{1+\exp(\alpha^T Z)}\{Y^2 - \theta_1 Y - \mu_1 Y + \theta_1\mu_1\}\right]. \tag{34}$$

Distributing and taking each term in turn, we have, by repeated application of the continuous mapping theorem,

$$\mathbb{E}\left[\frac{\exp(\theta_\alpha^T Z)}{1+\exp(\theta_\alpha^T Z)}\frac{\exp(\alpha^T Z)}{1+\exp(\alpha^T Z)}Y^2\right] \to \mathbb{E}\left[\left\{\frac{\exp(\alpha^T Z)}{1+\exp(\alpha^T Z)}\right\}^2 Y^2\right] \tag{35}$$

$$\theta_1\mathbb{E}\left[\frac{\exp(\theta_\alpha^T Z)}{1+\exp(\theta_\alpha^T Z)}\frac{\exp(\alpha^T Z)}{1+\exp(\alpha^T Z)}Y\right] \to \mu_1\mathbb{E}\left[\left\{\frac{\exp(\alpha^T Z)}{1+\exp(\alpha^T Z)}\right\}^2 Y\right] \tag{36}$$

$$\mu_1\mathbb{E}\left[\frac{\exp(\theta_\alpha^T Z)}{1+\exp(\theta_\alpha^T Z)}\frac{\exp(\alpha^T Z)}{1+\exp(\alpha^T Z)}Y\right] \to \mu_1\mathbb{E}\left[\left\{\frac{\exp(\alpha^T Z)}{1+\exp(\alpha^T Z)}\right\}^2 Y\right] \tag{37}$$

$$\theta_1\mu_1\mathbb{E}\left[\frac{\exp(\theta_\alpha^T Z)}{1+\exp(\theta_\alpha^T Z)}\frac{\exp(\alpha^T Z)}{1+\exp(\alpha^T Z)}\right] \to \mu_1^2\mathbb{E}\left[\left\{\frac{\exp(\alpha^T Z)}{1+\exp(\alpha^T Z)}\right\}^2\right]. \tag{38}$$

Combining terms completes the proof.

(D) $P\|\psi_{\theta_0}\|^2 < \infty$ and $\Psi(\theta)$ is differentiable at θ_0 with nonsingular derivative matrix V_{θ_0}. *Proof.* The first part holds for ψ_1 and ψ_0 if Y has finite second moment. To verify the second part, observe that

$$\frac{\partial}{\partial\theta_\alpha}\psi_1 = \frac{\exp(\theta_\alpha^T z)}{(1+\exp(\theta_\alpha^T z))^2}(y-\theta_1)z, \tag{39}$$

$$\frac{\partial}{\partial \theta_1}\psi_1 = \frac{\exp(\theta_\alpha^T z)}{1+\exp(\theta_\alpha^T z)}. \tag{40}$$

These continuous partial derivatives are uniformly bounded within a neighborhood of θ_0:

$$\left|\frac{\partial}{\partial \theta_\alpha}\psi_1\right| \le (|y| + |\mu_1| + \epsilon)|z|, \tag{41}$$

$$\left|\frac{\partial}{\partial \theta_1}\psi_1\right| \le 1. \tag{42}$$

Moreover, these upper bounds are integrable if we assume that $\mathbb{E}[|Y|] < \infty$, $\mathbb{E}[|Z|] < \infty$, and Z and Y have finite variances. Thus, the Leibniz integral rule (applying the dominated convergence theorem and mean value theorem) implies that

$$\frac{\partial}{\partial \theta_\alpha}\mathbb{E}[\psi_1]\,|_{\theta=\theta_0} = \mathbb{E}\left[\frac{\partial}{\partial \theta_\alpha}\psi_1\right]|_{\theta=\theta_0} = \mathbb{E}\left[\frac{\exp(\alpha^T Z)}{(1+\exp(\alpha^T Z))^2}(Y-\mu_1)Z\right], \tag{43}$$

$$\frac{\partial}{\partial \theta_1}\mathbb{E}[\psi_1]\,|_{\theta=\theta_0} = \mathbb{E}\left[\frac{\partial}{\partial \theta_1}\psi_1\right]|_{\theta=\theta_0} = \mathbb{E}\left[\frac{\exp(\alpha^T Z)}{1+\exp(\alpha^T Z)}\right]. \tag{44}$$

A similar argument holds for the partial derivatives of ψ_0. Notably, one regularity condition for the derivative matrix to be nonsingular is that the expected value of the race probabilities must be bounded away from 0 and 1.

(E) $\Psi_n(\hat\theta_n) = o_p(n^{-1/2})$ **and** $\Psi_n^\circ(\hat\theta_n^\circ) = o_p(n^{-1/2})$.

Proof. This follows for the last two coordinates of $\Psi_n(\hat\theta_n)$ because $\hat\theta_{1n}$ and $\hat\theta_{0n}$ are exact zeros of the estimating equation. The same is true of the last two coordinates of $\Psi_n^\circ(\hat\theta_n^\circ)$.

C.2 Extending the Z-Estimator Framework to Other Models

In this section, we briefly describe how the linear disparity estimator that Elzayn et al. (2025) consider might fit into the Z-estimator framework used to prove asymptotic normality of the dual-bootstrap in section C.1 of appendix C. The linear disparity estimator $\hat\delta_l$ is given by the estimated slope coefficient in the linear regression of Y on the estimated probability $\widehat{\Pr}(A=1|Z)$ plus an intercept term.

We can formulate $\hat\delta_l$ as a Z-estimator. Specifically, let

$$\psi_\theta(z,a,y) \equiv \begin{bmatrix} \psi_\alpha(z,a,y) \\ \psi_l(z,a,y) \end{bmatrix} \equiv \begin{bmatrix} z\left\{a - \dfrac{\exp(\theta_\alpha^T z)}{1+\exp(\theta_\alpha^T z)}\right\} \\ \dfrac{\exp(\theta_\alpha^T z)}{1+\exp(\theta_\alpha^T z)}\left(y - \dfrac{\exp(\theta_\alpha^T z)}{1+\exp(\theta_\alpha^T z)}\theta_l\right) \end{bmatrix} \tag{45}$$

and assume that $\theta \equiv [\ \theta_\alpha\ \ \theta_l\ ]^T \in \Theta \subset \mathbb{R}^p$ where Θ is open and $p < \infty$ is fixed. Then, defining the map $\theta \mapsto \Psi(\theta) \equiv P\psi_\theta$, we can show that $\theta_0 \equiv [\ \alpha\ \ \delta_l\ ]^T$ satisfies $\Psi(\theta_0) = 0$, where δ_l is the true disparity. If the same five conditions discussed in appendix C also hold here, then the dual-bootstrap is asymptotically normal for the linear disparity estimator as well. We leave verification of these conditions to future work.

References

Angrist, J. D., and A. B. Krueger. 1992. "The Effect of Age at School Entry on Educational Attainment: An Application of Instrumental Variables with Moments from Two Samples." *Journal of the American Statistical Association* 87(418): 328–36.

Angrist, J. D., and A. B. Krueger. 1995. "Split-Sample Instrumental Variables Estimates of the Return to Schooling." *Journal of Business & Economic Statistics* 13(2): 225–35.

Avenancio-León, C. F., and T. Howard. 2022. "The Assessment Gap: Racial Inequalities in Property Taxation." *Quarterly Journal of Economics* 137(3): 1383–1434.

Azin, A., D. H. Hirpara, S. Doshi, T. R. Chesney, F. A. Quereshy, and S. A. Chadi. 2020. "Racial Disparities in Surgery: A Cross-Specialty Matched Comparison Between Black and White Patients." *Annals of Surgery Open* 1(2): e023.

Berdejó, C. 2018. "Criminalizing Race: Racial Disparities in Plea-Bargaining." *Boston College Law Review* 59: 1187–249.

Blinder, A. S. 1973. "Wage Discrimination: Reduced Form and Structural Estimates." *Journal of Human Resources* 8(4): 436–55.

Brown, D. A. 2022. *The Whiteness of Wealth: How the Tax System Impoverishes Black Americans—And How We Can Fix It*. Crown Publishing Group.

Brown, D. P., C. Knapp, K. Baker, and M. Kaufmann. 2016. "Using Bayesian Imputation to Assess Racial and Ethnic Disparities in Pediatric Performance Measures." *Health Services Research* 51(3): 1095–1108.

Buolamwini, J., and T. Gebru. 2018. "Gender Shades: Intersectional Accuracy Disparities in Commercial Gender Classification." In *Proceedings of the 1st Conference on Fairness, Accountability and Transparency*, volume 81 of *Proceedings of Machine Learning Research*, pages 77–91. PMLR.

Census Bureau. 2022. Documentation for the 2017–2021 Variance Replicate Estimates Tables. Technical report.

Cheng, L., I. O. Gallegos, D. Ouyang, J. Goldin, and D. E. Ho. 2023. "How Redundant are Redundant Encodings? Blindness in the Wild and Racial Disparity when Race Is Unobserved." In *Proceedings of the 2023 ACM Conference on Fairness, Accountability, and Transparency*, FAccT '23, page 667–86, New York, NY, USA. Association for Computing Machinery.

Chen, J., N. Kallus, X. Mao, G. Svacha, and M. Udell. 2019. "Fairness Under Unawareness: Assessing Disparity When Protected Class Is Unobserved." In *Proceedings of the Conference on Fairness, Accountability, and Transparency*, FAT* '19, page 339–48, New York, NY, USA. Association for Computing Machinery.

Derby, E., C. Dowd, and J. Mortenson. 2024. "Constructing Confidence Intervals for BIFSG Disparity Estimates." *AEA Papers and Proceedings*, vol. 114. Nashville, TN: American Economic Association.

Elliott, M. N., P. A. Morrison, A. Fremont, D. F. McCaffrey, P. Pantoja, and N. Lurie. 2009. "Using the Census Bureau's Surname List to Improve Estimates of Race/Ethnicity and Associated Disparities." *Health Services and Outcomes Research Methodology* 9: 69–83.

Elzayn, H., E. Smith, T. Hertz, A. Ramesh, R. Fisher, D. E. Ho, and J. Goldin. 2025. "Measuring and Mitigating Racial Disparities in Tax Audits." *Quarterly Journal of Economics* 140(1): 113–63.E

Fong, C., and M. Tyler. 2021. "Machine Learning Predictions as Regression Covariates." *Political Analysis* 29(4): 467–84.

Fuller, W. A. 2009. *Measurement Error Models*. John Wiley & Sons.

Gelman, A., J. Fagan, and A. Kiss. 2007. "An Analysis of the New York City Police Department's 'Stop-and-Frisk' Policy in the Context of Claims of Racial Bias." *Journal of the American Statistical Association* 102(479): 813–23.

Imai, K., S. Olivella, and E. T. Rosenman. 2022. "Addressing Census Data Problems in Race Imputation via Fully Bayesian Improved Surname Geocoding and Name Supplements." *Science Advances* 8(49): eadc9824.

Kallus, N., X. Mao, and A. Zhou. 2022. "Assessing Algorithmic Fairness with Unobserved Protected Class Using Data Combination." *Management Science* 68(3): 1959–81.

Kim, J.-S., X. Gao, and A. Rzhetsky. 2018. "RIDDLE: Race and Ethnicity Imputation from Disease History with Deep Learning." *PLOS Computational Biology* 14(4): e1006106.

Kitagawa, E. M. 1955. "Components of a Difference Between Two Rates." *Journal of the American Statistical Association* 50(272): 1168–94.

Kleiner, A., A. Talwalkar, P. Sarkar, and M. I. Jordan. 2014. "A Scalable Bootstrap for Massive Data." *Journal of the Royal Statistical Society Series B: Statistical Methodology* 76(4): 795–816.

Koenecke, A., A. Nam, E. Lake, J. Nudell, M. Quartey, Z. Mengesha, C. Toups, J. R. Rickford, D. Jurafsky, and S. Goel. 2020. "Racial Disparities in Automated Speech Recognition." *Proceedings of the National Academy of Sciences* 117(14): 7684–7689.

Kosorok, M. R. 2008. *Introduction to Empirical Processes and Semiparametric Inference*. Springer.

Labgold, K., S. Hamid, S. Shah, N. R. Gandhi, A. Chamberlain, F. Khan, S. Khan, S. Smith, S. Williams, T. L. Lash, and L. J. Collin. 2021. "Estimating the Unknown: Greater Racial and Ethnic Disparities in COVID-19 Burden After Accounting for Missing Race/Ethnicity Data." *Epidemiology* 32(2): 157–61.

Mackey, K., C. K. Ayers, K. K. Kondo, S. Saha, S. M. Advani, S. Young, H. Spencer, M. Rusek, J. Anderson, S. Veazie, M. Smith, and D. Kansagara. 2021. "Racial and Ethnic Disparities in COVID-19-Related Infections, Hospitalizations, and Deaths: A Systematic Review." *Annals of Internal Medicine* 174(3): 362–73.

Matsouaka, R. A., Y. Liu, and Y. Zhou. 2024. "Overlap, Matching, or Entropy Weights: What Are We Weighting For?" *Communications in Statistics—Simulation and Computation* (2024): 1–20.

McCaffrey, D. F., and M. N. Elliott. 2008. "Power of Tests for a Dichotomous Independent Variable Measured with Error." *Health Services Research* 43(3): 1085–1101.

Miratrix, L. W., J. S. Sekhon, A. G. Theodoridis, and L. F. Campos. 2018. "Worth Weighting? How to Think About and Use Weights in Survey Experiments." *Political Analysis* 26(3): 275–91.

Murray, J. S. 2018. "Multiple Imputation: A Review of Practical and Theoretical Findings." *Statistical Science* 33(2): 142–59.

Oaxaca, R. 1973. "Male-Female Wage Differentials in Urban Labor Markets." *International Economic Review* 14(3): 693–709.

Ouimet, F. 2022. "A Multivariate Normal Approximation for the Dirichlet Density and Some Applications." *Stat* 11(1): e410.

Owen, A. B. 2007. "The Pigeonhole Bootstrap." *Annals of Applied Statistics* 1(2): 386–411.

Reifeis, S. A., and M. G. Hudgens. 2022. "On Variance of the Treatment Effect in the Treated When Estimated by Inverse Probability Weighting." *American Journal of Epidemiology* 191(6): 1092–1097.

Rubin, D. B. 1987. *Multiple Imputation for Nonresponse in Surveys*. John Wiley & Sons.

Saul, B. C., and M. G. Hudgens. 2020. "The Calculus of M-Estimation in R with geex." *Journal of Statistical Software* 92(2): 1–15.

Shu, D., J. G. Young, S. Toh, and R. Wang. 2021. "Variance Estimation in Inverse Probability Weighted Cox Models." *Biometrics* 77(3): 1101–117.

Stefanski, L. A., and D. D. Boos. 2002. "The Calculus of M-Estimation." *American Statistician* 56(1): 29–38.

Vala, Ayin, Shiying Hao, Isabella Chu, Robert LeRoy Phillips, and David Rehkopf. 2023. The American Family Cohort, v12.2). Stanford, CA: Redivis. https://doi.org/10.57761/jn2e-7r28.

Van der Vaart, A. W. 2000. *Asymptotic Statistics*. Cambridge University Press.

Xue, Y., O. Harel, and R. Aseltine. 2019. "Comparison of Imputation Methods for Race and Ethnic Information in Administrative Health Data." In *13th International Conference on Sampling Theory and Applications*, pages 1–4, Bordeaux, France. IEEE.

Yee, K., M. Hoopes, S. Giebultowicz, M. N. Elliott, and K. J. McConnell. 2022. "Implications of Missingness in Self-Reported Data for Estimating Racial and Ethnic Disparities in Medicaid Quality Measures." *Health Services Research* 57(6): 1370–1378.

Zhang, Y. 2018. "Assessing Fair Lending Risks Using Race/Ethnicity Proxies." *Management Science* 64(1): 178–97.

8

The Missing Link?
Using LinkedIn Data to Measure Race, Ethnic, and Gender Differences in Employment Outcomes at Individual Companies

Alexander Berry, Molly Maloney, and David Neumark

8.1 Introduction

Disparities in economic outcomes with respect to race, ethnicity, and gender are persistent in the United States. There is little doubt that labor market discrimination continues to contribute to these disparities, and that continued if not stronger enforcement of discrimination laws in the United States will help to reduce these disparities. However, the data necessary to detect possible discrimination and to act to counter it are not publicly available—in particular, data on racial, ethnic, and gender disparities within specific companies. Nor—not surprisingly—are such data readily provided by companies.

In this paper, we explore and develop methods to use information extracted from publicly available LinkedIn data to measure the racial, ethnic, and gender composition of company workforces. We use predictive tools based on both names and pictures to identify the race, ethnicity, and gender of employees. And we explore using this information, along with information from job histories on LinkedIn, to develop estimates of racial, ethnic, and gender differences in employment, layoffs, hiring, and promotions.

This paper builds on an emerging body of research that leverages data from private companies—and especially data on workers, firms, job openings, etc.—to better understand US labor markets. It also dovetails with greater efforts, via legislation, to increase transparency about labor markets, in part to increase the information workers have about jobs, to reduce labor

Alexander Berry is a consultant with Econ One Research, Inc.
Molly Maloney is an associate of The Brattle Group, Inc.
David Neumark is Distinguished Professor of Economics and Co-Director of the Center for Population, Inequality, and Policy at the University of California, Irvine, a research associate of the National Bureau of Economic Research, and a Visiting Fellow at the Hoover Institution.

market frictions and increase labor market competition, as well as to reduce discrimination.[1]

A particularly valuable application of our research is that it can be used to strengthen enforcement of discrimination laws. The strength of discrimination laws in the United States rests on class action or other "pattern and practice" lawsuits on behalf of large numbers of a company's employees. The large potential penalties/awards in these lawsuits serve both to attract resources from attorneys to pursue discrimination claims and to incentivize firms to avoid these claims. Although federal and state agencies (like the EEOC, at the federal level) can file lawsuits against companies alleged to have discriminated, most enforcement—and enforcement against the largest companies—stems from private-sector attorneys.[2] But there are three problems, all of which our research can help address.

First, only the federal government (through EEO-1 reporting) and state governments (via similar authority) obtain data on, for instance, the racial or ethnic composition of firms' workforces, or of specific occupations within those firms. These data are confidential.[3]

1. For example, New York recently passed a law that requires firms to post pay ranges in advertisements for all job positions (see "New York Becomes the Latest State to Require Salary Transparency in Job Postings" by Eli Freedberg, Thelma Akpan, and Liran Messinger, December 28, 2022, https://www.littler.com/publication-press/publication/new-york-becomes-latest-state-require-salary-transparency-job-postings), and California's recently enacted pay transparency law requires posted pay ranges by demographic group (see "Pay Transparency Laws: Your Questions Answered," *Spark* blog, ADP, Hannah Beppel, accessed December 2024, https://www.adp.com/spark/articles/2023/03/pay-transparency-laws-your-questions-answered.aspx). Further, a recent federal Executive Order (13665) prohibits federal contractors from retaliating against workers who disclose or discuss compensation information (Trotter et al. 2017). Despite expectations, some recent work suggests that pay transparency may reduce workers' bargaining power (Cullen and Pakzad-Hurson 2023), because higher wage offers can lead to more renegotiation with other workers when pay is transparent. We regard this as a still-open question requiring more research.

2. We are not aware of empirical comparisons of suits filed by the EEOC or state agencies vs. private attorneys. However, in our experience most discrimination lawsuits are filed by private attorneys. Moreover, the EEOC, for example, acknowledges that it narrowly targets cases for litigation: "The EEOC files employment discrimination lawsuits in select cases. When deciding whether to pursue litigation, the General Counsel will consider several factors, including the nature of the violation, the issues presented, and the wider impact the lawsuit could have on the EEOC's efforts to combat workplace discrimination. Because of limited resources, the EEOC cannot file a lawsuit in every case where the agency finds discrimination and the EEOC's efforts to secure voluntary compliance through the agency's conciliation process are unsuccessful" (see EEOC Litigation at the US Equal Employment Opportunity Commission website, https://www.eeoc.gov/eeoc-litigation).

3. There is some potential movement toward the Office of Federal Contract Compliance Programs (OFCCP) releasing EEO-1 reports under FOIA requests. (See, e.g., https://content.govdelivery.com/accounts/USDOLOFCCP/bulletins/3495276.) It is at this time unclear how easy it will be for companies to stop release of these data by objecting on grounds of trade secrets, financial information, etc. Of course, OFCCP data only cover federal contractors. OFCCP is reluctant to release these data, so objectors may be able to block release easily (see *Bloomberg Law*, "Labor Department Reluctant to Reveal Contractor Diversity Data" by J. Edward Moreno, October 20, 2022 https://news.bloomberglaw.com/daily-labor-report

Second, these data only measure employment (with limited information on occupational distributions). They do not measure hiring, retention, layoffs, or promotions.

Third, and most important, private attorneys—the key agents in the enforcement of discrimination laws—are severely hampered in trying to target the companies that potentially engage in discrimination. Complaints of discrimination are typically initiated by a small number of employees who may have personally experienced discrimination (or believe they have) but do not have information on statistical patterns at their employers. Plaintiffs' attorneys work on contingency fees, and hence have to decide whether to invest large sums in filing charges and commencing discovery before they can see any data on potentially discriminatory behavior. The uncertainty involved can deter them from taking on cases and reduce the efficiency of how their resources are targeted.[4]

The kinds of information we extract from LinkedIn data could potentially lead to more efficient targeting of anti-discrimination efforts. By helping attorneys identify where there is suggestive evidence of discrimination, these data could help make discrimination law more efficient, allowing attorneys to concentrate their efforts and resources on the companies where there is a higher probability that discrimination is occurring.[5] Moreover, the methods we develop could provide anti-discrimination enforcement agencies with additional tools to monitor companies and to target investigations of discriminatory behavior. While they typically obtain employment data (like EEO-1 reports to the EEOC), these reports do not cover other employment decisions—like hiring, layoffs, or promotions. These authorities can request additional data, but this process itself can be expensive and contested. Thus, the ability to better identify ex ante employers that might be discriminating can help in the targeting of public resources as well.

/labor-department-reluctant-to-reveal-contractor-diversity-data). In addition, there is a recent agreement between the EEOC and the Census Bureau to provide EEO data that can be accessed and linked to other data sources at Census Research Data Centers (see press release of September 22, 2023 from the US Equal Employment Opportunity Commission, https://www.eeoc.gov/newsroom/eeoc-signs-agreement-census-bureau-provide-secure-access-agency-data-qualified-researchers), and it is also possible that one could import the LinkedIn data we describe and match to the EEO data. There would be no ability to identify individual companies, but it might be possible to satisfy Census reporting requirements while providing some descriptive information on the correspondence between EEO data and LinkedIn data. This is a potential project for future research using the full LinkedIn dataset, in contrast to the limited extract we study in this paper.

4. This oversimplifies slightly, as state anti-discrimination agencies sometimes partner with private attorneys. But in our experience, this is rare.

5. Anecdotally, we have spoken with a handful of plaintiffs' attorneys who work on discrimination cases about the potential value of using the LinkedIn data in this way. We have confirmed that some indicated they would find it useful. One indicated they had already used the data in this way (although of course absent the kind of validation, etc., we explore in this paper). And below we cite use of LinkedIn data in a different manner in a discrimination case.

Our core research questions are: How can the LinkedIn data best be used to characterize companies' employment by race, ethnicity, and gender? How reliable are these data? And, can the LinkedIn data be used to study other company workforce decisions—in particular hiring, retention/layoffs, and promotions—and their relation to workforce demographics?

Our focus is to a large extent on the professional, scientific, and technical services sector, owing in large part to strong representation on LinkedIn. That is not to say that our methods cannot be usefully applied to other industries, although some of our conclusions about the representativeness of the LinkedIn data might not apply as strongly and future work could assess this. At the same time, jobs in this sector are significant with regard to enforcement of discrimination laws, since this sector is an important source of high-paying jobs and upward mobility.

8.2 Social Media Data vs. Scientific Samples

The LinkedIn database is not the population of workers, and is not a scientific sample. At the same time, it covers a very large number of workers and might be expected to generate quite reliable measures.[6] The evidence we report in this paper indicates that the LinkedIn data correspond reasonably well, with some exceptions, to other probability-sample estimates of workforce demographics. However, the value of what we can do with the LinkedIn data does not hinge only on the representativeness of the data being so good as to be able to claim that the estimates (e.g., of the share Black) are unbiased.

First, a growing body of research trying to study labor markets using social media data acknowledges the trade-off between probability sampling and the ability to learn from social media data what we cannot learn from other data. As examples, Schneider and Harknett (2019a, 2019b) use targeted ads on Facebook to study work schedules, based on a 1.2 percent response rate. Similarly, a number of labor economists use data on job postings or job applications to study monopsony, discrimination, minimum wages, and other topics (e.g., Azar et al. 2022; Borup and Montes Schütte 2022; Clemens et al. 2021; Marinescu and Wolthoff 2020; and Neumark et al. 2019)—in our view learning a great deal more than we could otherwise, despite data sources not being fully representative.

Second, it is critical to emphasize that the core value of the LinkedIn data for enforcement of discrimination laws is that it provides some reliability in estimates of race, ethnic, or gender differences in the outcomes the data are used to measure, to improve targeting of what would generally be more thorough investigations. As explained earlier, absent this type of information, private attorneys considering class action discrimination claims have

6. LinkedIn claims 200 million active US users.

only anecdotal evidence to rely on, and hence can be deterred from initiating lawsuits; and enforcement agencies have limited data on potential discrimination. Thus, data and estimates from LinkedIn can provide a critical complement to this limited information, and hence improve targeting of anti-discrimination efforts, even if estimated differences by race, ethnicity, and gender have some biases due to imperfect representation.

8.3 Alternative Data Sources?

This project considers the development of a data source that can fill substantial gaps in labor market data available for the United States. We have rich household and worker data, but these data contain no firm identifiers and typically do not include information on the positions people hold within companies. In principle, the data from the Longitudinal Employer-Household Dynamics program (LEHD) could be used to provide descriptive information similar to some things we can measure with the LinkedIn data. However, there are a number of limitations of the LEHD data.

First, a core limitation is that the LEHD could never be used as an enforcement tool the way we are envisioning, both because company names could never be revealed, and because those for whom this tool would be useful would never be able to access these data, to use them to study a single company. Second, the LEHD would pose severe challenges to doing this in a timely manner, both because the LEHD is updated slowly, and because securing access to the LEHD and then working with the data is a slow process.[7] Further, the LEHD data do not have any information on job titles at companies that could be used to study employees' positions within companies. In contrast, the LinkedIn data do not present these restrictions, and—importantly from both an enforcement and research perspective—are up to date and immediately accessible. Thus, although the LEHD is an extraordinarily valuable and powerful dataset that can be leveraged for the analysis of discrimination,[8] it cannot be readily used for the specific questions we will be studying with the LinkedIn data. At the same time, it is possible that our work with the LinkedIn data will prompt work with the LEHD to provide a more extensive and higher-quality characterization of employment and other dynamics one can measure with the LEHD in relation to race, ethnicity, and gender. We regard these as complementary efforts, with different strengths, weaknesses, and purposes.

The National Establishment Time Series (NETS) is a proprietary dataset in which company names are public and can be used in research (e.g., Burnes et al. 2014), but it contains no worker information aside from employment.

7. As an example, one of the most recent LEHD publications we could find on Google Scholar is a 2022 publication using LEHD data through 2016 (McKinney and Abowd 2022); and the earliest working paper version of this paper appears to be from 2020.

8. See, e.g., Barth et al. (2021), Brick et al. (2023), and Hu (2019).

(As indicated above, however, we do make some use of the NETS data in this project to select companies for our validation work.)

Aside from these datasets familiar to researchers, there is some information on the demographic composition of firms' workforces from companies that make public their "diversity reports." For example, Google releases an annual diversity report.[9] Its 2022 report provides the percentage of hires by race, ethnicity, and gender, as well as workforce representation and attrition (the only instance we have found of reporting on retention). But it says nothing about the positions different workers occupy in the company. LinkedIn's 2021 report[10] provides the race, ethnic, and gender composition of its overall, tech, and non-tech workforces, and also the composition of a vaguely defined "leadership" category (a category required in confidential EEO-1 reports). It is not difficult to find other similar reports, providing the same limited information.[11] Conversely, there is ample information on companies' resistance to providing this information,[12] and we might expect that it is supplied selectively across companies. Also, note that neither these reports, nor the EEO-1 reports, typically provide information on retention or hiring. The methods we develop and describe in this paper can provide information on the race, ethnicity, and gender dimensions of all of these aspects of firms' workforces.

Finally, a very recent paper by Kline et al. (2024) provides company-level evidence on discrimination. In particular, the authors conducted a correspondence study of discrimination based on race (distinctively Black names) at 108 companies in the Fortune 500 and report the race gaps in callbacks by company.[13] This study provides another way to garner evidence on discrimination at the company level. It has the advantage, relative to what we do, of providing more rigorous experimental evidence on hiring discrimination (Neumark 2018). It has three disadvantages, however. First, it is limited to hiring. Second, strong evidence of discrimination in callbacks does not necessarily point to companies where many workers (Blacks, in this case) are being harmed, because the companies with low callback rates for Blacks

9. For Google's 2022 Diversity Annual Report, see https://about.google/belonging/diversity-annual-report/2022/.

10. See "Our 2021 Workforce Diversity Report" published October 20, 2021, by LinkedIn at https://news.LinkedIn.com/2021/october/2021-workforce-diversity-report.

11. See, e.g., See "Our 2022 Workforce Diversity Report" published by LinkedIn on October 27, 2022, at https://news.linkedin.com/en-us/2022/october/2022-workforce-diversity-report; Apple on "Inclusion and Diversity," https://www.apple.com/diversity/.

12. See, e.g., Proxy Preview, "Data Transparency Key to Improving Diversity, Equity, and Inclusion in the Workplace," by Stephanie Rivers, March 15, 2022, https://www.proxypreview.org/2022/contributor-articles-blog/data-transparency-key-to-improving-diversity-equity-and-inclusion-in-the-workplace; Circa, EEO-1 Report and Voluntary Disclosure, https://circaworks.com/articles/eeo-1-report-and-voluntary-disclosure/.

13. They sent up to eight applications for each vacancy, or about 84,000 applications for 11,000 jobs at the 108 companies covered. Much of the focus of the paper is on how to rate companies' discriminatory behavior, given uncertainty in the estimates.

may, in reality, get few Black applicants. Third, in this study companies received a large number of artificial job applications, with as many as 1,000 applications to some firms (Table F5 in the paper). One might expect companies to respond to this inundation by implementing procedures to detect such artificial applications, rendering the method less useful. Nonetheless, such evidence—like ours—may be able to assist enforcement agencies in targeting investigations.[14]

8.4 Approach and Methods

We conduct our research using extracted, publicly available LinkedIn data offered by the company Proxycurl.[15] Given a company's LinkedIn profile, Proxycurl returns LinkedIn profile data for that company's employees with public profiles. The data reflect the publicly available LinkedIn profiles at the time they are scraped. We can query the current LinkedIn profile for each employee who has linked a company of interest as an employer, either past or current, depending on parameter selections. This means we can get information on past as well as current employment.[16] However, the data do not simply cover all employees at a single point in time. Rather, the scraping captures all individuals who have ever worked at the company, as long as they have not deleted their data. We also typically know when they were employed at the company, so we can approximate employment by year, as well as hiring, exits, etc. We extract LinkedIn profile data on all current and former employees for seven companies, the selection of which we describe below.

The information returned often includes detailed information about previous work experience (including place of employment, title, description, start date, and end date) and education (including school, field of study, degree obtained, start date, and end date). All LinkedIn data are self-reported, and voluntarily reported. These profiles may also include information about a worker's skills, activities, volunteer work, languages spoken, certifications, and recommendations, among other topics. Critically, for our purposes, it also often includes their profile picture, along with their name.

We use the DeepFace package in Python to classify workers by race, eth-

14. Moreover, in the case of audit studies, individual testers have legal standing to sue (see EEOC guidance, EEOC Notice Number 915.002, May 22, 1996: https://www.eeoc.gov/laws/guidance/enforcement-guidance-whether-testers-can-file-charges-and-litigate-claims-employment). Interestingly, case law appears to go back to an early civil rights case in which Black clergymen who were removed from segregated bus terminals were deemed to have been discriminated against even though their goal was to test the law, rather than to ride the bus. The standing of testers has been established in housing cases (*Havens Realty Corp. v. Coleman*, 455 US 363, 374 [1982]). And the EEOC, in the document referenced above, argues that the language of Title VII (covering employment discrimination) parallels that in Title VIII (covering housing discrimination).

15. See "LinkDB: A Dataset of 472,880,151 Public LinkedIn* Profiles" (https://nubela.co/proxycurl/linkdb) for more details.

16. See Proxycurl Overview (https://nubela.co/proxycurl/docs) for more details.

nicity, and gender, based on their LinkedIn profile pictures and a common training dataset ("picture classification"). We also use R packages (rethnicity, gender), which use statistical data to classify based on names ("name classification").[17] The DeepFace package is trained on the FairFace dataset for race/ethnicity identification. The gender prediction model for picture classification is trained on Wikipedia data. These both return probabilities that the worker is in each group. For details on both types of classifications, see Serengil and Ozpinar (2020, 2021). We also supplement with name classification when a picture is not available, and we combine information when both are available.[18]

We use binary classifications (Black/non-Black, Hispanic/non-Hispanic, and female/male), based on highest probabilities returned by these programs. We use names as the primary method for gender and ethnicity, and pictures as the primary method for race, based on evidence described below. Where the classification probability is missing for the primary method, the other method is used. We also change which method we use if the primary method gives a quite uncertain classification and the secondary method gives a far more certain classification, as explained in more detail below.[19]

One of our core goals in this paper is to validate our classifications against

17. There is other information that, in principle, could be used to classify people, such as other information in the images or information in LinkedIn entries on schools, locations, interests, etc. As an example, the Consumer Financial Protection Bureau (CFPB) combines information on surnames and geography to predict race and national origin to monitor compliance with fair lending laws and discrimination in the consumer credit industry. CFBP (2014) indicates that a Bayesian Improved Surname Geocoding (BISG) method works better than relying on only name or geography. Implementing something like this with the LinkedIn data would require a training sample, and the available geographic information is not as useful because it is much less detailed. Developing new classification methods is beyond the scope of this paper.

18. In our view, this kind of classification is consistent with US discrimination laws. The EEOC notes that Title VII of the Civil Rights Act does not define "race." But its guidance is based on perception—i.e., whether one is perceived as belonging to a group. In particular, "Race discrimination includes discrimination on the basis of ancestry or physical or cultural characteristics associated with a certain race, such as skin color, hair texture or styles, or certain facial features" (EEOC, "Questions and Answers about Race and Color Discrimination in Employment," https://www.eeoc.gov/laws/guidance/questions-and-answers-about-race-and-color-discrimination-employment). We would interpret this to correspond to physical characteristics or distinctly racial names. The EEOC offers similar guidance with regard to discrimination based on national origin (ethnicity): "national origin discrimination means discrimination because an individual (or his or her ancestors) is from a certain place or has the physical, cultural, or linguistic characteristics of a particular national origin group" ("EEOC Enforcement Guidance on National Origin Discrimination," https://www.eeoc.gov/laws/guidance/eeoc-enforcement-guidance-national-origin-discrimination). On the other hand, data used in discrimination lawsuits is often self-reported, and our validation exercises compare the LinkedIn data to self-reported classifications in the ACS and to EEO-1 reports or other information companies provide that is almost surely based on these reports.

19. We considered using probabilities to construct estimates of demographic shares of the workforce, etc., based on weighted averages using these probabilities. However, we found that this was not as accurate for the race and ethnicity coding, because there are other minority groups (such as Asians) that can receive some probability weight, which results in lower estimated shares Black or Hispanic than we get from using the highest probability.

Table 8.1 **Fortune 1–10 companies (by revenue) comparing 10k and Linkedin employment**

Company	10k employment (1)	LinkedIn webpage employment (2)	LinkedIn database (Proxycurl) employment (current) (3)
Walmart	2.2 million	389,386	94,192
Amazon	1.54 million	841,260	182,960
Apple	**132,000**	**289,924**	**97,927**
CVS Health	300,000	115,472	175
UnitedHealth Group	400,000	167,345	39,871
Exxon Mobil	63,000	57,735	20,939
Berkshire Hathaway	372,000 (many subsidiaries)	8,198	990
Alphabet	**190,000**	**280,107 (Google)**	**124,743**
McKesson	68,000	21,260	10,370
AmerisourceBergen	44,000	19,566	4,556

Source: https://www.zyxware.com/articles/4344/list-of-fortune-500-companies-and-their-websites and 10k reports. LinkedIn data are from July 2023.

Note: Proxycurl database employment is for those who link to company URL in their LinkedIn profile.

external data, to see how reliable the LinkedIn data are. For example, one might wonder whether particular demographic groups are under- or over-represented on LinkedIn. One approach to validating the LinkedIn data is to leverage corresponding information in two other data sources—the National Establishment Time Series (NETS) and the American Community Survey (ACS). For this validation exercise we proceed in two steps. First, we use data from the NETS, along with LinkedIn information from the LinkedIn website, to identify companies that are in a broad industry category that has good representation on LinkedIn. In particular, we focus on the professional, scientific, and technical services sector. As documented in table 8.1, which reports results for the top 10 Fortune companies, this sector (see the highlighted rows) has good representation on LinkedIn—in the sense that a large share of the companies' workers appears on the website, based on current employment (column [2]).[20]

We then use the NETS data to select companies and areas to make the ACS and LinkedIn data comparable—i.e., so that when we extract ACS

20. Column (2) captures those as reported on a company's LinkedIn page. Column (3) is current employment included in Proxycurl's database (which is also restricted to public LinkedIn profiles). The low number for CVS Health in the Proxycurl database is because of search constraints imposed when using the Proxycurl database by buying tokens for a specific number of searches, which constrains the search to workers who include company URLs in their LinkedIn profiles. Based on our investigations, non-professional workers may be less likely to do this.

data on workers by Place-of-Work PUMA (POWPUMA) and industry, we should be sampling by and large from employees of these companies in the corresponding geographic area. In particular, we identify companies in this sector that meet three criteria: (1) there is fairly negligible employment at other firms in the same industry and POWPUMA; (2) most of the company's employment in the POWPUMA is in the industry; and (3) the company has strong representation on LinkedIn. The idea behind criterion (1) is that these firms constitute most of industry employment in the POWPUMA. Thus, ACS workers in the industry and POWPUMA are likely to work for these companies. The idea behind criterion (2) is that the company's employment in the POWPUMA is concentrated in one industry. This is critical because we have an industry identifier in the ACS but not in LinkedIn. Thus, if the company had POWPUMA employment in other industries, the ACS data for a single industry might not be representative of the company's POWPUMA employment. Because these companies are largely unique in their industry-location cells, if they also have good representation on LinkedIn (criterion 3), the measures of race, ethnic, and gender composition from the two data sources should correspond. Thus, we measure the race, ethnic, and gender composition of ACS employment in those industry-location cells, and then compare to our estimates based on the LinkedIn data.

These ACS restrictions greatly limit the number of company comparators that we are able to benchmark against. We therefore also use a second validation approach, comparing the LinkedIn results to companies' DEI reports, when available, or other sources of information on the demographic composition of their workforces. This approach avoids the constraints on companies dictated by the first approach. In particular, we were able to find information in diversity reports or other information companies provided, and we use these, when available, for both the companies selected to validate against the ACS data, and other companies we selected.[21]

8.5 Companies Selected

We identified four companies that meet the criteria for the ACS validation discussed above, and that are not too large (allowing the required LinkedIn data extraction within our budget constraint). Table 8.2 reports the companies meeting the following constraints:

21. There is already some limited evidence of the reliability of the LinkedIn data. Specifically, in a large gender pay discrimination lawsuit, LinkedIn data were extracted on jobs Oracle employees held prior to coming to Oracle, as well as on their education. (See *Expert Trial Report of David Neumark in the Matter of Jewett et al. v. Oracle America, Inc.*, December 2021, redacted.) It was possible to match about 55 percent of Oracle employees in the company's data to LinkedIn observations, and to establish that the matched data were representative in one dimension; in particular, in that case the estimated gender pay gap was similar in the full company data and the subsample matched on LinkedIn.

Table 8.2 **Companies identified using National Establishment Time Series (NETS) data as having large share of total industry employment in place-of-work PUMA, large share of total company's employment in place-of-work PUMA, good representation on Linkedin, and of moderate size for initial data extraction**

NAICS (1)	Company (2)	LinkedIn webpage empl. (3)	LinkedIn webpage employment in nearby geographic "area" (4)	% of POWPUMA industry empl. at the firm (5)	% of firm empl. in industry (6)
5417	**Research Corporation of the University of Hawaii**	**286**	**229**	**82**	**100**
5413	**BWXT Technical Svcs Group Inc**	**1,928**	**722**	**81**	**100**
5415	**Chesterfield County**	**2,296**	**2,022**	**73**	**99**
5417	**Fermi Research Alliance LLC**	**2,069**	**1,771**	**96**	**100**
5415	Cognizant Tech Sltions US Corp	317,047	34,429 (US)	91	100
5417	Corning Research & Dev Corp	19,106	5,008	92	100
5417	Charles River Labs Intl Inc	14,288	1,619	86	100
5413	Tungland Corporation	215	172	76	100
5417	GlaxoSmithKline LLC	97,000	5,000	70	100

Note: LinkedIn data are from August 2023. NETS data are from 2019 (covering 2018).

1. Company's NAICS industry employment in POWPUMA vs. all NAICS industry employment in POWPUMA > 70 percent;
2. Company's NAICS industry employment in POWPUMA vs. all company employment in POWPUMA > 80 percent;
3. Firm employment > 800.

The table also shows LinkedIn employment—in this case based on ever employed, since our validation with the ACS is not based on only one year of data. Because of the per-record cost of the data, we had to constrain the choice among the companies meeting these criteria, based on number of employees. We also constrained it based on LinkedIn data showing a large share of employment in a single proximate geographic area, since otherwise we would not expect the ACS to provide a very relevant comparison. The four companies we selected for this validation exercise are shown in the shaded rows of table 8.2. The non-shaded rows are for companies that met our criteria with regard to POWPUMA, but were either very large, had low representation on LinkedIn, had low representation in the geographic area (which likely has to do with international employment not measured in the NETS), or were quite small so that we would not be able to learn that much from the data.

The additional companies selected were GlaxoSmithKline (GSK), SpaceX, and Meta. GSK made our initial list for the ACS validation; employment was not sufficiently geographically concentrated to be useful for the ACS validation, but we found other information on its workforce. Meta and SpaceX are two high-profile technology companies. And for one (Meta), we actually found EEO-1 data posted, whereas for the other (SpaceX), we found nothing reliable. Thus, we could validate the Meta data from LinkedIn against the EEO-1 data, and also illustrate the potential value of our approach for a company (SpaceX) for which neither EEO-1 nor diversity report information was available. We restricted our choices to other companies in the same sector, for comparability. Finally, we chose among these based on the ability to cover a number of companies while remaining within our data budget constraint. Clearly future work with greater funding could expand the scope of these types of analyses.

8.6 Data Extraction and Classification

For these companies, we extract publicly available data from LinkedIn from the Proxycurl LinkedIn database. To do this, we provide the company's LinkedIn URL. We request current and past employees (who can be distinguished in the database). The application then returns all data from public profiles (employment history, education, skills, etc.).

Across the seven companies for which we extracted data, we obtain 112,280 worker profiles, of which 78,639 are in the United States. The numbers and

Table 8.3 **LinkedIn worker profiles extracted**

Company	Total	U.S.
BWXT Technical Svcs Group Inc	2,187	1,705
Chesterfield County	2,104	2,093
Fermi Research Alliance LLC	4,215	3,738
GlaxoSmithKline LLC	26,636	10,761
Meta	61,265	45,274
Research Corporation of the University of Hawaii	66	65
SpaceX	15,807	15,003
Total	112,280	78,639

distributions of these observations are displayed in table 8.3. We get a sizable number of observations from all companies except Research Corporation of the University of Hawaii, and very large numbers of observations for GSK, Meta, and SpaceX. We retain only those working in the United States. We break the data for each person into separate entries for each job at each company at which they worked. Together, this results in 557,329 separate observations, although many of these are not at our companies of interest.

We then use the extracted LinkedIn data to classify workers, based on the DeepFace package in Python for picture classification, and R packages (rethnicity, gender) for name classification.[22] Before reporting our findings on demographic composition and more, there are some results about classification that are of interest, and which dictate how we use this information.

There are certainly caveats to using these methods. First, some pictures on LinkedIn make identification difficult. For example, some show multiple people, obscured images, or have bad lighting. In addition, sometimes there is no picture available. Overall, we run the DeepFace classification code for 96,651 profiles (which includes pictures from non-US profiles). Of these, 22.95 percent were missing a picture, and 1.09 percent had an image in which a face could not be detected. The distributions of these cases were roughly stable across the companies, as shown in table 8.4.

Second, we cannot always classify people by name. We run the name classification code for 75,393 names.[23] We are unable to classify gender for 9.89 percent of names, and unable to classify race/ethnicity for 4.55 percent of names. This could occur if the name recorded on an individual's LinkedIn profile does not include their first name (e.g., "Lt. Higgins") or if their name includes many non-Latin characters, for example. For predicting gender, if a name is sufficiently uncommon that it does not appear in the Social Security

22. We utilized RetinaFace for the face detection backend, and otherwise used a pre-trained neural network that comes with the package.

23. Note that this differs from the number of profiles above because we do not run the algorithm separately for repeated names as the predicted gender/race will not differ for individuals with the same name.

Table 8.4 Missing pictures or no face detected

Company	Total	Classified	Missing picture (% of classified)	No face detected (% of classified)
BWXT Technical Svcs Group Inc	1,753	1,319	29.4	11.9
Chesterfield County	1,249	952	27.8	12.1
Fermi Research Alliance LLC	3,198	2,486	26.2	9.2
GlaxoSmithKline LLC	22,985	17,106	33.2	3.4
Meta	54,256	41,855	28.7	3.1
Research Corporation of the University of Hawaii	60	48	22.9	9.1
SpaceX	13,150	9,652	32.6	11.0
Total	96,651	73,418	30.2	4.7

database used to predict gender, then no gender probability will be assigned to it. For race prediction, we do not use an individual's last name to predict race when they only provide a single initial in place of their last name (the program classifies all one-letter names as Asian).

Third, some names were problematic. For example, some first names, like "Alex," are not strongly gendered. Some last names, like "Monte," could be of Hispanic origin or another ethnicity. Some names are classified as more likely to be Black or White, without providing a strong confirmation—e.g., "Steve Fulton," with a 72 percent probability of being Black. And, of course, last name (or even first name) changes can obscure race or ethnicity. In these cases, pictures may provide more definitive information.

We use additional information on how the two programs classify people by race, ethnicity, and gender to settle on our classification "algorithm." First, as shown in figure 8.1A, the distributions of probabilities that observations are female, whether using names or pictures, are bimodal, with probabilities clustered near zero or one. This reflects the fact that names are highly gendered, as is physical appearance. There is a little more mass at the endpoints using names (about 85 percent) than using pictures (about 80 percent), which is why we use names as the first source of classification by gender.

Second, the story for ethnicity and race classification is more complicated. The charts in figure 8.1A for both ethnicity and race show large spikes at zero probability, but do not show much evidence of bimodality. Similarly, there is far less mass at the lower and upper ends of the range for Hispanic or Black classifications than for gender classifications, and correspondingly more mass between these points for Hispanic or Black classifications—and more so for Hispanic classifications. These findings reflect less definitive assignments of probabilities, potentially owing to less distinct physical differences than those by gender, or because shading of pictures can obscure race or ethnicity. Moreover, these differences are likely less pronounced for

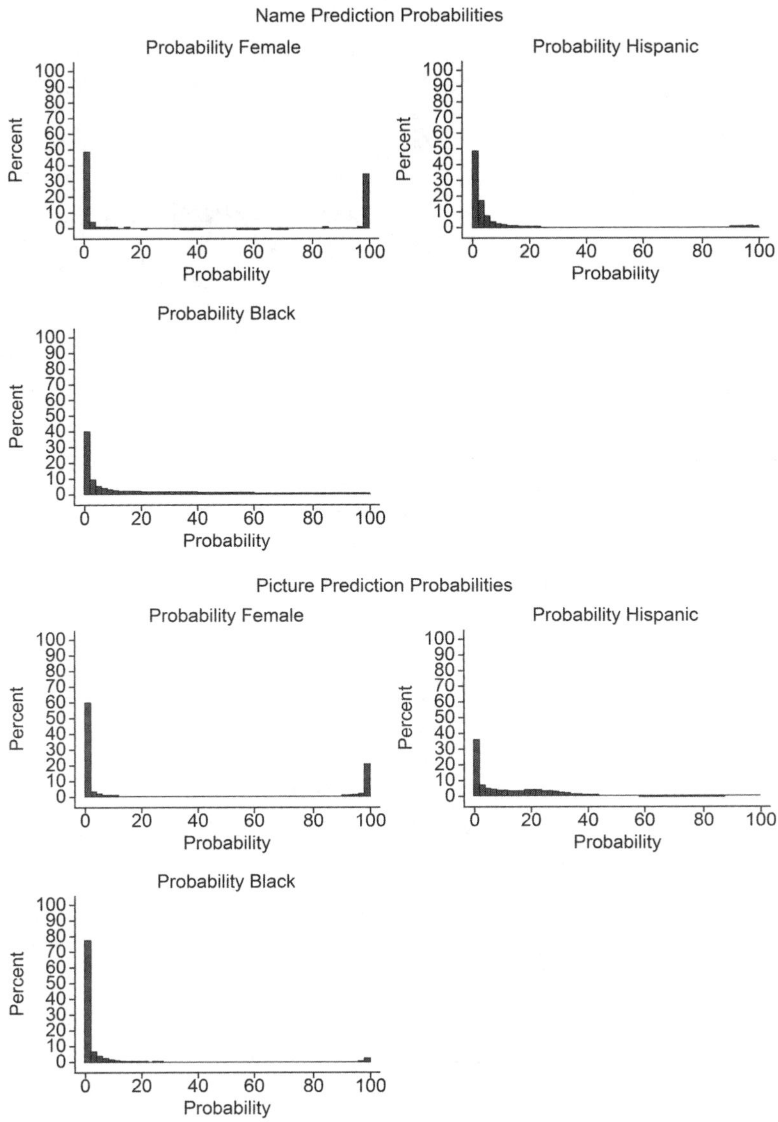

Fig. 8.1A Distributions of probabilities of gender, ethnicity, and race

Hispanics. This is consistent with the evidence in the bottom panel of figure 8.1A, indicating a good deal more mass at lower values but above zero probability for Hispanic than Black, and conversely much more mass at zero (more accurately, in the band 0–2) probability for Blacks. We learn more about what is happening at the higher probabilities from figure 8.1B, which shows more details at the higher probabilities by zooming in on the upper

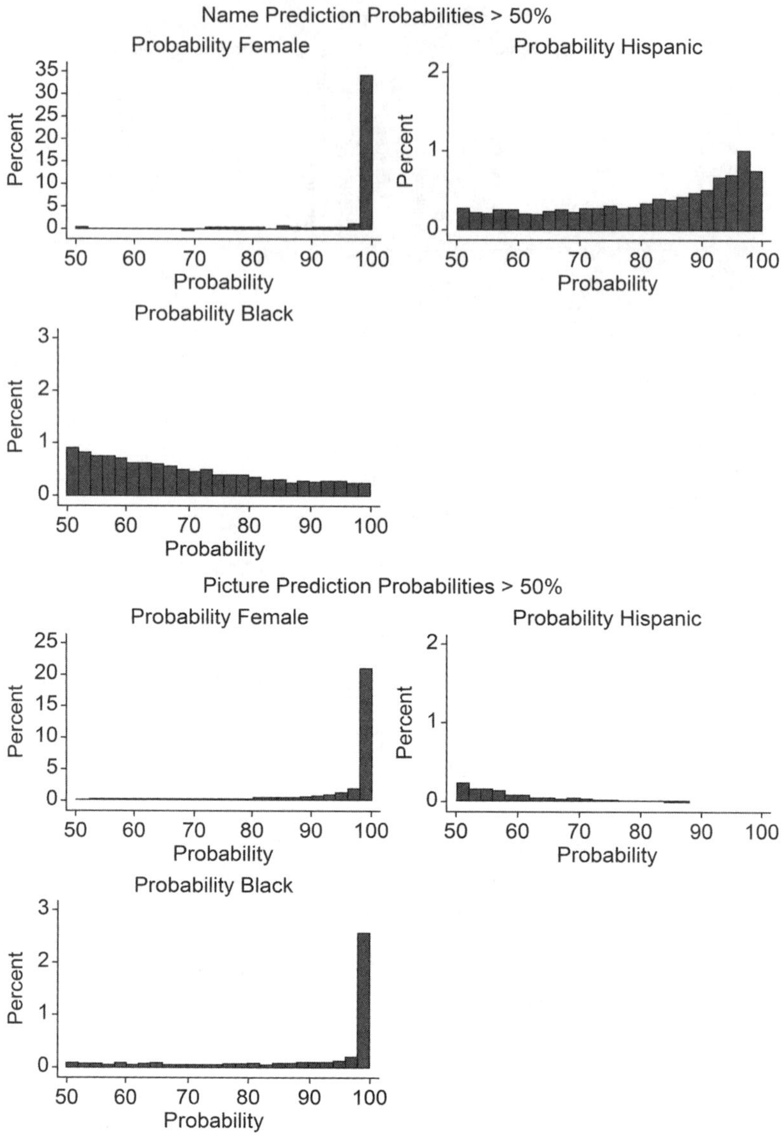

Fig. 8.1B Distributions of probabilities of gender, ethnicity, and race—upper tails

halves of the distributions.[24] We now see much more clearly that for Black classifications the distribution of probabilities based on pictures is more bimodal, with a spike at 100. We thus rely on pictures as the first source of

24. Note that in figure 8.1B the vertical scales are not the same in each graph, so that we could better highlight the details.

classification for Blacks. For Hispanic classifications, there is a much more pronounced mass of probabilities at the top of the distribution using names than using pictures, so we use names as the first source of classification for Hispanics.

As a result of these considerations, as well as the inability sometimes to classify people by gender, race, or ethnicity based on either a picture or a name, we use the following algorithm to classify people.

Race

1. If the picture probability is non-missing, we classify people as Black based on the picture if the probability Black based on picture is the highest among all "race" categories.[25]
2. If the picture probability is missing but the name probability is non-missing, we classify people as Black based on the name if the probability Black based on name is the highest among all "race" categories.
3. If both are non-missing, we rely on pictures, except when the picture classification is highly uncertain, but the name classification is not. Specifically, when no race probability based on pictures (among the six groups)[26] > 0.5, but the probability Black based on name > 0.9, we classify people as Black.[27]

Ethnicity

1. If the name probability is non-missing, we classify people as Hispanic based on the name if the probability Hispanic based on name is the highest among all "race" categories.
2. If the name probability is missing but the picture probability is non-missing, we classify people as Hispanic based on the picture if the probability Hispanic based on picture is the highest among all "race" categories.
3. If both are non-missing, we rely on names, except when the name classification is highly uncertain, but the picture classification is not. Specifically, when no race probability based on name (among the 4 groups) > 0.5, but the probability Hispanic based on picture > 0.9, we classify people as Hispanic.[28]

Gender

1. If the name probability is non-missing, we classify people as female based on the name if the probability female is higher.
2. If the name probability is missing but the picture probability is non-

25. The classification programs do not separately code race and ethnicity as commonly defined by, e.g., the US Census, but rather include these in the same overall "race" classification.

26. For pictures, these are Asian, Black, Indian, Latino/Hispanic, Middle Eastern, and White. For name, these are Asian, Black, Hispanic, and White.

27. This only results in a re-classification if the probability Black based on the picture was not the highest.

28. This only results in a re-classification if the probability Hispanic based on the name was not the highest.

missing, we classify people as female based on the picture if the probability female based on picture is higher.

We ran the classification code for all worker-company observations. After creating the race, ethnicity, and gender identifiers, we had 29,843 observations that were missing either race or gender, approximately 5.4 percent of the data. In terms of race, we have 97.44 percent coverage, and our gender variable covers 96.82 percent of the data.[29]

Table 8.5 reports on the probabilities of classification (reported as percentages) by each category based on pictures and names, including the initial classifications and the final classifications. We can see in this table some of the same results from figures 8.1A and 8.1B, and also the consequences of our final rules for classification. For example, we noted that pictures are far more reliable for classifying Black vs. non-Black than names. This is reflected in the first row, columns (1)–(8), in the higher probabilities Black for pictures at each of the percentiles reported. Note, though, that we obtain far more classifications based on name, so as a result the probabilities in columns (10)–(12), which are often based on name, are lower than in columns (2)–(4). In contrast, the probabilities Hispanic are far higher for names. For gender, the probabilities are very high in both cases, with the difference (lower probabilities based on pictures) only apparent at lower percentiles (column [2] vs. column [6]).

It is worth mentioning here that we deliberately did not tune or adjust our methodology regarding classifications to try to better match the proportions we see in the ACS or the diversity/EEO-1 reports. We are trying to demonstrate the value of these data in doing these classification exercises for other companies. Since a potential user presumably would not have any data source other than the LinkedIn data, there would be no basis for adjustments to the classifications. As a result, potential users should be most interested in the accuracy of race, ethnic, and gender classifications that use out-of-the-box algorithms (as we do), without any further fine-tuning.[30]

8.7 Classification of Companies' Workforces and Validation with ACS Data

Based on race, ethnicity, and gender classifications, we first report our results for demographic classifications of companies' workforces for the four companies for which we can perform our validation exercise with ACS data.

29. Evaluations of these methods point to fairly reliable classification. For DeepFace, see Serengil and Ozpinar (2021). As discussed in Blevins and Mullen (2015), the gender package in R assigns a probability that an individual is female based on the historical frequency at which women are observed with that name using Social Security Administration data since the 1930s.

30. At the same time, we recognize that additional exploration could help identify other code that works better, refine the existing code, or find alternative ways to use the resulting probability estimates.

Table 8.5 **Classification methods used and resulting probabilities Black, Hispanic, or female**

	Picture				Name				Final			
	N (1)	25th percentile (2)	Median (3)	75th percentile (4)	N (5)	25th percentile (6)	Median (7)	75th percentile (8)	N (9)	25th percentile (10)	Median (11)	75th percentile (12)
Black vs. non-black	2,648	62.7%	97.9%	100.0%	11,117	51.0%	60.8%	74.7%	6,289	53.8%	71.3%	95.8%
Hispanic vs. non-Hispanic	4,966	31.0%	36.2%	43.0%	7,964	61.5%	81.7%	93.4%	9,979	49.3%	72.9%	91.2%
Female vs. male	15,017	96.9%	99.8%	100.0%	24,851	99.5%	99.7%	99.9%	26,098	99.4%	99.7%	99.9%

Note: "Final" column is based on the algorithm for classification described in the text. Probabilities are expressed in percentage terms.

For these comparisons, we restrict the relevant areas in the LinkedIn data as follows: Virginia for BWXT; Hawaii for Research Corporation of the University of Hawaii; Virginia for Chesterfield County; and Illinois for Fermi Research Corporation. For the ACS comparison we limit observations to those observations with at least a portion of relevant experience at the company between 2012 and 2021 (a 10-year window). We use the LinkedIn data to construct each job spell of each person at the corresponding company, and compare the ACS data to the LinkedIn data where we measure the demographic composition of employment in each year for any spell of employment covering that year. It is the case that LinkedIn employment at each company generally trends upwards over time, which we imagine is due at least in part to increasing numbers of employees on LinkedIn. Regardless of the reason, we weight the ACS data by year to be proportional to the representation in the LinkedIn data.

These results are reported in table 8.6. The ACS numbers are weighted annual averages, based on 2012–2021 data for the same POWPUMA and four-digit NAICS code. We also show similar results for professional, technical, and managerial occupations, which are likely over-represented on LinkedIn.[31] The data are also displayed in more digestible form in figure 8.2. The results for the percent female do not indicate tight concurrence of the estimates, but there is some correspondence. For example, looking at the overall ACS numbers, the rank order across the four companies is the same for the ACS and LinkedIn data, and the LinkedIn percentages are notably higher where the ACS estimates are (for females at Research Corporation of Hawaii and for Blacks and females for Chesterfield County), and vice versa. The data for the Research Corporation of the University of Hawaii should probably be discounted, given the low representation in the LinkedIn data and the ACS data. The results for the percent Hispanic do not correspond very well. The estimates for the percent Black, excluding Research Corporation of the University of Hawaii, exhibit reasonable correspondence between the two measures, with the rank order the same in both datasets, and the values matching reasonably well. The results are very similar, generally, with the occupational restrictions, except for the decline in the percent Black at BWXT.

Of course, one issue is that the ACS samples are not very large.[32] In addition, despite our best efforts, we pick up workers at other companies in the

31. That said, the sample sizes when we restrict to these occupations are only a bit smaller, consistent with (a) most workers at these companies being in these occupations, and (b) little apparent bias from the hypothesized over-representation of these occupations on LinkedIn. A potential caveat, however, is that differences between the occupations represented on LinkedIn and overall workforces may be more marked for other industries.

32. The ACS is a 1 percent random sample for the years we use (See "What is the ACS?" from IPUMS USA, https://usa.ipums.org/usa/acs.shtml).

Table 8.6 **Validation estimates for percentages Black, Hispanic, and female in LinkedIn and American Community Survey Data**

Company	Data source	LinkedIn employment in area (N)	LinkedIn database public profiles (N)	ACS (N)	% black	% Hispanic	% female
Research Corporation of the University of Hawaii	**LinkedIn**	**229**	**15**		**12.8**	**0**	**57.1**
	ACS			67	0	8.5	45.5
	ACS, Prof/Tech Occ's			58	0	9.5	49.0
BWXT Technical Svcs Group Inc	**LinkedIn**	**722**	**390**		**16.6**	**5.6**	**23.4**
	ACS			116	9.8	0.7	18.4
	ACS, Prof/Tech Occ's			95	2.4	0.9	21.0
Chesterfield County	**LinkedIn**	**2,022**	**796**		**24.5**	**6.7**	**52.7**
	ACS			227	20.8	7.7	30.2
	ACS, Prof/Tech/Mgr Occ's			217	20.6	8.0	29.7
Fermi Research Alliance LLC	**LinkedIn**	**1,771**	**684**		**9.7**	**11.6**	**26.3**
	ACS			174	4.0	5.8	18.5
	ACS, Prof/Tech/Mgr Occ's			151	4.5	5.9	20.4

Sources/notes: LinkedIn and ACS data, 2012–2021, same POWPUMA and four-digit NAICS. The LinkedIn data in this table are restricted to the relevant areas to correspond to the ACS POWPUMA, as described in the text. We use ACS weights, and for each company also reweight by year corresponding to the representation by year in the LinkedIn data. Professional, technical, and managerial occupations excluded, based on 2018 occupation codes: Community and Social Services Occupations 2001–2060; Service Occupations 3601–4655; all occupations 6005 and higher (Farming, Fishing, and Forestry; Construction Trades; Installation, Maintenance, and Repair; Production; Transportation and Material Moving; Military). See Occupation Classification, US Census Bureau, https://www2.census.gov/programs-surveys/cps/methodology/Occupation%20Codes.pdf.

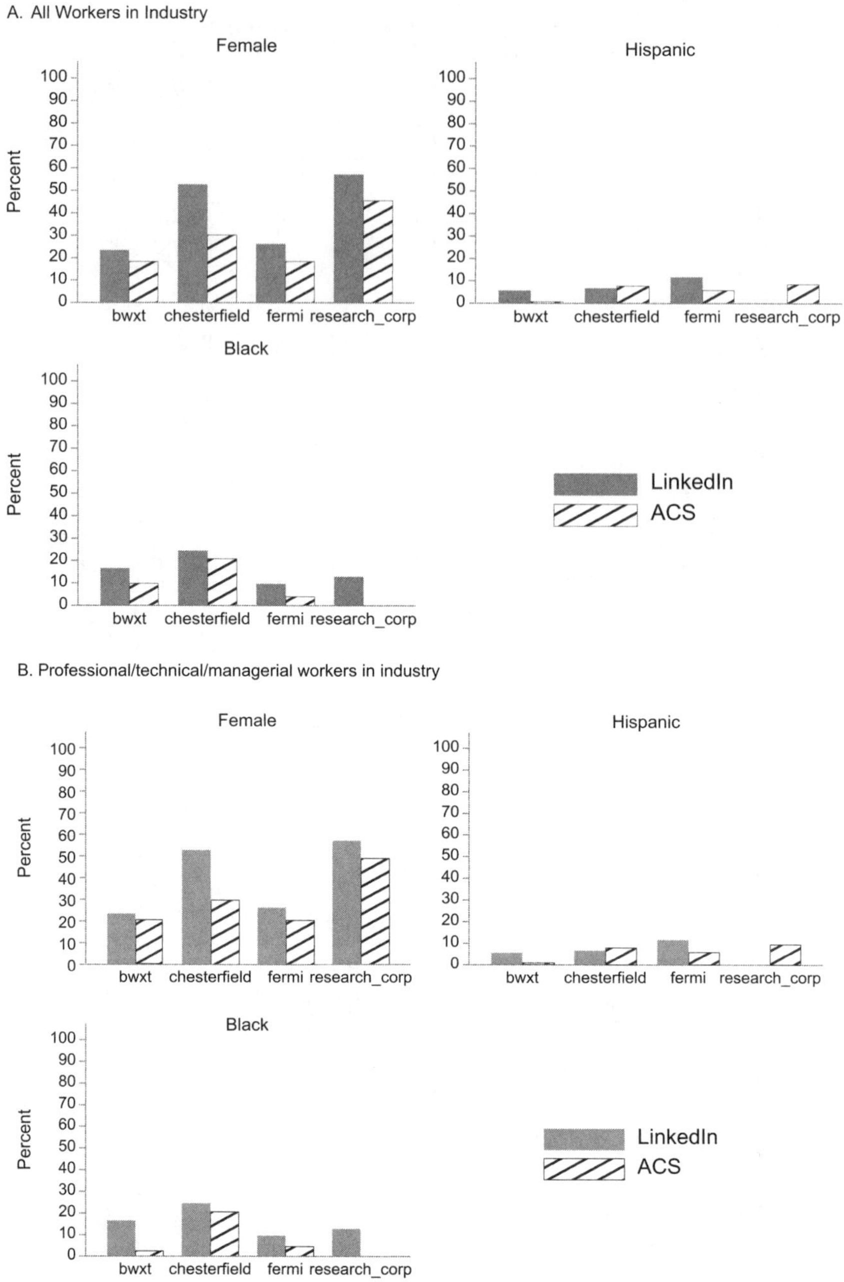

Fig. 8.2 Validation estimates for percentages Black, Hispanic, and female in Linkedin and American community survey data

Note: See note to table 8.6.

ACS data, and the geographic match is not precise.[33] We thus, in the next section, turn to comparisons between the LinkedIn data and other sources of direct measures of workforce composition at the companies in question.

8.7 Classification of Other Companies' Workforces and Other Validation Efforts

We looked for other sources of information on company demographics, including company diversity reports and other information posted on their websites. We also found that some companies post actual EEO-1 reports.[34] Table 8.7 indicates, for each company, what kind of information we could identify. The notes to the table, which also list the sources, provide details on any assumptions or computations we use to obtain comparable estimates.[35]

As the table indicates, we obtain numbers to compare, either for a single year or, in the case of Meta, many years, for three companies: Chesterfield County, Fermi Research Alliance, LLC, for which we also did the ACS validation exercise, and Meta, which fortuitously provides data from two sources, in one case (its diversity report) for many years.[36]

For the first two, the observation counts in LinkedIn are quite low, both because they are smaller companies and because we restrict to a single year. And as the table notes, for Fermi, in particular, there are so few observations that the comparison should probably be ignored. For Chesterfield County, however, there is some correspondence. In both data sources, the percent female is the highest, followed by the percent Black, and then the percent Hispanic; and the numbers roughly correspond (e.g., the percent female is much higher in both data sources), although the percent Hispanic is a good deal higher in the LinkedIn data.

The data for Meta are perhaps the most interesting, because (i) we have far more observations, and (ii) we can check some data by year. The numbers for the percent Black are close, and the pattern of increase in this percentage is similar in the two data sources, as is the amount of the increase

33. We cannot map directly to POWPUMA in the LinkedIn data for two reasons. First, the geographic information is less specific in LinkedIn (we use state). Second, the geographic information in LinkedIn is current and may not correspond to when the person worked at the company.

34. We explored with both the US EEOC and the California equivalent—the Civil Rights Division—obtaining such data. But at the company level they are confidential and could not be shared.

35. There are some SpaceX numbers available from "Zippia." It is unclear where these data come from. According to its website, Zippia gets company information from employee self-reporting, public and open data sources on the internet, and proprietary data licensed from other companies. Data sources include, but are not limited to, the BLS, company filings, H1B filings, public websites on the internet, and other public and private datasets. (See Zippia Company Profile FAQ, https://www.zippia.com/employer/zippia-faq/.) We do not regard these data as reliable and do not use them.

36. For the overlapping data—the percentages Black and Hispanic for 2021—the data are very close but do not match exactly.

Table 8.7 **Validation against other sources of data on workforce composition**

Company	Source	Statistics reported	Comparable LinkedIn data, for corresponding years
Research Corporation of the University of Hawaii	Nothing from company		
BWXT Technical Svcs Group Inc.	Nothing from company		
Chesterfield County of Virginia	EEO Utilization Report, 2020	% black: 18.9 % Hispanic: 3.7 % female: 47.7	% black: 17.2 % Hispanic: 11.2 % female: 60.3
Fermi Research Alliance, LLC	Fermilab webpage, 2023	% black: 5.6 % Hispanic: 9.3 % female: 28.1	% black: 0 % Hispanic: 0 % female: 33 Note: based on only four LinkedIn observations in 2023.
GlaxoSmithKline (GSK)	GSK website	40 percent of senior roles were held by women, up from 38 percent in 2020; 50 percent of manager roles held by women; 27.1 percent of senior leaders in the United States were "ethnically diverse" in 2021, up from 23.2 percent in 2020	Cannot compare because no way to reliably match roles, and "ethnically diverse" is vague.

SpaceX	Nothing from company		
Meta	2022 Annual Diversity Report	% black 2014: 2 2015: 2 2016: 2 2017: 3 2018: 3.5 2019: 3.8 2020: 3.9 2021: 4.4 2022: 4.9 %Hispanic 2014: 4 2015: 4 2016: 4 2017: 5 2018: 4.9 2019: 5.2 2020: 6.3 2021: 6.5 2022: 6.7	% black 2014: 4.0 2015: 4.8 2016: 5.2 2017: 5.7 2018: 6.2 2019: 6.3 2020: 6.5 2021: 7.1 2022: 7.1 %Hispanic 2014: 12.6 2015: 13.3 2016: 13.4 2017: 13.2 2018: 13.3 2019: 13.4 2020: 13.8 2021: 14.4 2022: 14.2
	2021 EEO-1 Report	Total/Professionals % black: 4.6/4.4 % Hispanic: 6.7/6.4 % female: 36.2/34.6	Total % black: 7.1 % Hispanic: 14.4 % female: 41.9

Sources/notes: **Chesterfield**, VA, EEO Utilization Report, May 3, 2023, https://www.chesterfield.gov/DocumentCenter/View/446/EEOP-DOJ-Utilization-Report-PDF. Numbers reported for six categories of jobs: Officials/Administrators; Professionals; Technicians; Protective Services (Sworn); Protective Services (Unsworn); and Administrative Support. We have assumed these include the entire workforce. **Fermi**, Demographics, https://www.fnal.gov/pub/about/demographics/. Numbers reported for six categories of jobs: Technical; Scientists; Postdocs; Mission Support; Engineers, Computing. We have assumed these include the entire workforce. Some numbers are reported as < 5 but > 0. We assume values of 2. **GSK**: https://us.gsk.com/en-us/responsibility/diversity-equity-and-inclusion/#inside-gsk. **Meta,** Annual Diversity Report, July 2022, https://about.fb.com/wp-content/uploads/2022/07/Meta_Diversity-Data-Summary-Report_2022.pdf. Percent female is also reported by year, but only globally. Percent by ethnic group is also reported for Tech, Non-Tech, and Leadership. 2021 EEO-1 Report also reports numbers for: Executive/Senior Officials & Managers; First/Mid Officials & Managers; Professionals; Technicians; Sales Workers; Administrative Support; Craft Workers; Operatives; Laborers & Helpers; and Service Workers. Professionals are the vast majority.

(2.9 percentage points in the diversity report, and 3.1 percentage points in LinkedIn). The numbers for percent Hispanic are not as close, perhaps because of how Hispanics are defined (although we find no mention of this in the Meta documents). In particular, again the share Hispanic is higher in the LinkedIn data.[37] But, again, the pattern of increase is similar, as is the amount of the increase (2.7 percentage points in the diversity report, and 1.6 percentage points in LinkedIn). The comparison with the 2021 EEO-1 report looks similar for the percentages Black and Hispanic, which is not surprising. And the percentage female is reasonably close.

What do we conclude from the validation exercises? First, there is clearly some correspondence between measures of workforce demographic composition for the LinkedIn data and other sources. For our ACS comparisons, given that we do not have an exact match, and that there is sampling error in the ACS data, we would not expect exact matches, so this is encouraging. Put differently, there is no reason to assume the ACS data are more reliable. But the rough correspondence is encouraging for using the LinkedIn data, and of course the LinkedIn data can in principle be used to study any company, whereas the ability to use the ACS to learn something about a company's workforce is highly limited to companies with a sizable share of industry employment in a POWPUMA. Second, and reassuringly for the LinkedIn data, the correspondence appears to be much tighter for large companies—although admittedly this is based on data for one company (Meta).

Recall, though, our perspective on the utility of the LinkedIn data. The data do not provide scientifically valid estimates of workforce composition with known sampling properties. Rather, they are interesting as a guide for further exploration by government agencies or attorneys seeking to enforce discrimination laws. Our take is that these data may be useful for both larger and smaller companies, although of course more reliable—and hence more useful—for larger companies. That actually meshes well with the way data are likely to be used in enforcing discrimination laws, as the class action suits that rely on statistical evidence typically are against large companies.[38]

37. There are a couple of reasons the Hispanic classifications could differ. First, EEO-1 data are based on self-reports whereas our LinkedIn classification is not, and there is research indicating potential subjectivity with which people classify themselves as Hispanic (e.g., Antman and Duncan 2026; Loewenstein et al. 2026). Second, we rely on names, which, among other things, could inflate the share Hispanic when non-Hispanics marry and change their names. There may, of course, be other reasons as well.

38. As examples, there have been fairly recent class action discrimination lawsuits against IKEA (See "Court Unseals Order Conditionally Certifying Age Discrimination Collective Action Suit Against IKEA Filed By Console Mattiacci Law," October 07, 2019 by Laura Mattiacci, https://www.consolelaw.com/court-unseals-order-conditionally-certifying-age-discrimination-collective-action-suit-against-ikea-filed-by-console-mattiacci-law/); Google ("Google Agrees to Pay $118 Million to Settle Pay Discrimination Case," by Nico Grant, *New York Times*, June 12, 2022, https://www.nytimes.com/2022/06/12/business/google-discrimination-settlement-women.html); Walmart ("Walmart Litigation," Cohen Milstein, https://www.cohenmilstein.com/case-study/wal-mart/, including a very large case two decades ago); and Twitter ("Twitter Beats Two Lawsuits Stemming from Mass Layoffs, For Now," by

Table 8.8 **LinkedIn demographic composition estimates for each company**

Company	N	% Black	% Hispanic	% Female
Research Corporation of the University of Hawaii	54	5.7	7.5	47.1
BWXT Technical Svcs Group Inc.	1,325	11.1	6.1	22.8
Chesterfield County	1,050	23.5	7.5	53.0
Fermi Research Alliance LLC	2,016	8.4	15.4	31.7
GlaxoSmithKline (GSK)	5,886	10.1	10.6	46.4
SpaceX	13,315	7.6	17.9	17.7
Meta	44,034	6.5	12.5	38.2

Notes: This table reports the demographic composition for each company, for the years 2012–2023. Observations are at the employee-firm level, and proportions are calculated based on the number of classified individuals in that company. In contrast to table 8.6, this table does not restrict to the relevant LinkedIn area to correspond to the ACS POWPUMA.

8.8 Overall Demographic Composition

Having established what we view as reasonable reliability of the *LinkedIn* data, in table 8.8 we report the overall demographic composition for each company—the shares Black, Hispanic, and female.[39] For comparability with the earlier analysis, we report this for data beginning in 2012, but we extend to the end of the data (2023). For the four companies with which we did the ACS validation, we have much larger numbers of observations for this and the following analyses. This is mainly because we no longer restrict to the geographic areas identified in *LinkedIn* to correspond to the ACS POWPUMA. In addition, we do not restrict the time period to the 10 years covered by the ACS analysis. The percent Black varies substantially, from a low of 5.7 percent at Research Corporation of the University of Hawaii to 23.5 percent at Chesterfield County. The variation in the percent Hispanic is less pronounced, but ranges from 6.1 percent at BWXT to 17.9 percent at SpaceX. In contrast, the percent female is lowest at SpaceX (17.7 percent) and highest at Chesterfield County (53.0 percent). It is also substantially higher than SpaceX at some of the other private employers, like GSK (46.4 percent) and Meta (38.2 percent). We caution, again, that any inference of discrimination would have to consider the composition of potential workers, which can vary with other factors—probably most notably geography and educational levels and fields.

Daniel Wiessner, *Reuters*, May 8, 2023, https://www.reuters.com/legal/twitter-beats-disabled-workers-lawsuit-over-layoffs-now-2023-05-08/).

39. Later we present some evidence on the intersections of minority and gender categories, although we are not able to validate these intersectional categories against the sources explored in the prior sections. In principle, other ethnic groups could be considered, although in some cases the classification models would have to be trained to identify them.

8.9 An Application to Mass Layoffs

Based on what we have learned about the reliability of the LinkedIn data, we explore using these data to study potential discrimination in mass layoffs. Given that many separations in normal times are voluntary quits,[40] from the point of view of learning about discrimination in layoffs it is more informative to look at a period of mass layoffs. That is, we refer to those "laid off," but we mean those who separated in a period of mass layoffs—when the share of layoffs in separations is much higher.

In particular, we examine layoffs at Meta, which is reported to have laid off 11,000 employees (13 percent of its workforce) in 2022, and 10,000 in 2023,[41] and at SpaceX, which is reported to have laid off about 10 percent of its workforce in 2019.[42,43] We use the LinkedIn data to measure all separations, identifying the spell of time an employee spends at the same company and inferring that an employee has separated from a company if they either stop working for at least four months or if their next employment is with a different company.[44]

As shown in table 8.9, consistent with the news stories, we see inordinately high numbers of separations from Meta in 2022 and 2023, as well as a somewhat higher share in 2021.[45] We suspect the 2023 numbers may be lower than reported layoffs because either the layoffs were not yet implemented when we extracted the data in fall of 2023, or some people do not update their profiles until they get a new job. Similarly, some of the 2022 layoffs may be

40. See, e.g., Bureau of Labor Statistics news release, "Job Openings and Labor Turnover, October 2024," https://www.bls.gov/news.release/pdf/jolts.pdf, indicating about a 2-to-1 ratio of quits vs. layoffs/discharges.

41. See "Meta Layoffs—Facebook Continues To Cut Costs By Cutting Headcount," *Forbes*, updated December 8, 2022, https://www.forbes.com/sites/qai/2022/12/07/meta-layoffsface book-continues-to-cut-costs-by-cutting-headcount/?sh=5e36a1898456; "Meta to Begin Fresh Layoffs, Cutting Heavily among Business Staff," *Washington Post*, May 23, 2023, https:// www.washingtonpost.com/technology/2023/05/23/meta-layoffs-misinformation-facebook -instagram/.

42. See "SpaceX to lay off 10 percent of its workers," *CNN*, by Jackie Wattles, January 11, 2019, https://www.cnn.com/2019/01/11/tech/spacex-layoffs/index.html; BNN Bloomberg, https://www.bnnbloomberg.ca/spacex-layoffs-include-577-positions-at-california-head quarters-1.1197570.

43. One can also confirm these layoffs and find information on layoffs at other companies from WARNtracker, https://www.warntracker.com/, which appears to be an amalgamation of announcements of large layoffs from the Worker Adjustment Training Notification (WARN) system.

44. If a spell of time at one company is entirely overlapped by a spell at another company, we drop it from our datasets. This can happen, for example, if a PhD student is employed as a teaching assistant with a university for five years but also lists a summer internship on their resume for a summer during their PhD. We would then drop the spell of time at the internship because it is completely overlapped by the teaching assistant position, rather than considering the teaching assistant as having separated from the university during the tenure of their internship. We do not drop partially overlapping positions, however.

45. Table 8.9 also exhibits the rising employment over time at these companies, as noted earlier.

Table 8.9 **Separations at Meta and SpaceX in LinkedIn data**

	Workforce	Separations	Separations/ Workforce
Meta			
2012	393	11	2.8
2013	666	20	3.0
2014	1,129	36	3.2
2015	1,776	56	3.2
2016	2,902	106	3.7
2017	5,096	189	3.7
2018	8,570	358	4.2
2019	12,837	611	4.8
2020	18,806	737	3.9
2021	**29,703**	**2,510**	**8.5**
2022	**39,632**	**9,316**	**23.5**
2023	**30,930**	**5,096**	**16.5**
Total	152,440	19,046	12.5
SpaceX			
2012	2,018	212	10.5
2013	2,791	393	14.1
2014	3,510	526	15.0
2015	4,358	668	15.3
2016	5,004	818	16.3
2017	5,691	796	14.0
2018	6,096	943	15.5
2019	**5,959**	**1,164**	**19.5**
2020	6,201	815	13.1
2021	6,856	1,043	15.2
2022	6,347	984	15.5
2023	5,558	196	3.5
Total	60,389	8,558	14.2

reflected in the 2023 data. For SpaceX, we see the highest share in 2019, again consistent with news stories.

We compare the demographic composition of those laid off against the workforce as a whole in table 8.10. To do this, we use all years of data, and estimate a linear probability model for separations for each individual in each year. We include year dummy variables, which will capture the aggregate differences in separation probabilities, including the spikes associated with mass layoffs documented in table 8.9. And we include main effects of race, ethnicity, and gender to allow for group-specific separation probabilities. We then also add interactions between dummy variables for race, ethnicity, and gender with a dummy variable for the mass layoff years. Because a higher share of separations will be involuntary in mass layoff years, the overall year dummy variables for these years will capture the higher share of involuntary

Table 8.10 **Meta and SpaceX mass layoff differentials by race, ethnicity, and gender**

	Meta	Meta	SpaceX	SpaceX
Without education and tenure controls				
Black	0.0133	0.0037	0.0039	0.0047
	(0.0035)	(0.0038)	(0.0066)	(0.0069)
Hispanic	0.0159	0.0016	–0.0292	–0.0325
	(0.0025)	(0.0026)	(0.0033)	(0.0035)
Female	0.0134	–0.0035	0.0159	0.0138
	(0.0017)	(0.0017)	(0.0036)	(0.0039)
Black x mass layoff years		0.0140		–0.0091
		(0.0064)		(0.0184)
Hispanic x mass layoff years		0.0218		0.0322
		(0.0047)		(0.0132)
Female x mass layoff years		0.0257		0.0222
		(0.0031)		(0.0154)
Year dummy variables included	Yes	Yes	Yes	Yes
Mean separation rate for non-Black/ non-Hispanic males, all years	0.1177		0.1464	
Mean separation rate for non-Black/ non-Hispanic males, mass layoff years		0.1587		0.1946
Mean separation rate for non-Black/ non-Hispanic males, non-mass layoff years		0.0397		0.1411
N	141,045	141,045	58,947	58,947
With education and tenure controls				
Black	0.0146	0.0016	0.0012	–0.0002
	(0.0038)	(0.0041)	(0.0069)	(0.0075)
Hispanic	0.0147	0.0008	–0.0169	–0.0204
	(0.0028)	(0.0029)	(0.0042)	(0.0046)
Female	0.0125	–0.0050	0.0088	0.0049
	(0.0018)	(0.0018)	(0.0043)	(0.0048)
Black x mass layoff years		0.0188		0.0146
		(0.0069)		(0.0264)
Hispanic x mass layoff years		0.0209		0.0352
		(0.0051)		(0.0181)
Female x mass layoff years		0.0266		0.0412
		(0.0033)		(0.0185)
Year dummy variables included	Yes	Yes	Yes	Yes
Mean separation rate for non-Black/non-Hispanic males, all years	0.1185		0.1656	
Mean separation rate for non-Black/non-Hispanic males, mass layoff years		0.1586		0.2082
Mean separation rate for non-Black/non-Hispanic males, non-mass layoff years		0.0402		0.1609
N	126,460	126,460	40,902	40,902

Note: Observations are employee-years, and the outcome is whether a separation occurred. Estimates are from linear probability model. Standard errors clustered at the individual level are in parentheses. "Mass layoff years" are 2021–2023 for Meta and 2019 for SpaceX. Education controls in lower panel sinclude dummy variables for high school degree, associate's degree (omitted), bachelor's degree, master's degree, or doctoral degree.

separations for non-Black, non-Hispanic males. The key variables are the race/ethnicity/gender by mass layoff interactions, which will capture the race, ethnic, or gender differences in the probabilities of a separation in the mass layoff years. We interpret the latter as reflecting the differences in layoff rates for Blacks, Hispanics, or women in the mass layoff years.

In the top panel, we use only these variables in the regression models. For Meta, the estimates in the first column indicate higher separation rates in general for Blacks, Hispanics, and women, with statistically significant differences in the range of 1.3 to 1.6 percentage points (relative to an 11.8 percent rate for the non-mass layoff years for non-Black, non-Hispanic males). These differences could reflect higher involuntary separations in non-mass layoff years, but they may reflect voluntary separations.[46] The second column reports the interactions with the dummy variable for the mass layoff years. For all three groups the separation rate is significantly higher—a 1.40 percentage point higher rate, significant at the 5 percent level, for Blacks, and 2.18 and 2.57 percentage points higher rates for Hispanics and women, significant at the 5 percent level. (These can be compared to a 15.9 percent rate for the mass layoff years for non-Black, non-Hispanic males.) Thus, there is reason to believe that Blacks, Hispanics, and women all experienced higher mass layoff rates at Meta in 2021–2023.

For SpaceX, the analysis (in the third and fourth columns) focuses on 2019 only. Here, we find a lower separation rate for Hispanics and a higher rate for women, in general. During the mass layoff years, the separation rate is significantly higher only for Hispanics (by 3.2 percentage points, relative to a separation rate of 19.5 percent for non-Black, non-Hispanic males in 2019). Thus, only for Hispanics is there evidence of a higher mass layoff rate.

To be clear, these analyses do not provide a rigorous "test" of discrimination because other factors could account for disproportionate layoffs among some groups. On the other hand, this kind of evidence could be far more helpful when trying to identify claims of systemic discrimination than anecdotal evidence one or a few plaintiffs present to a government agency or private attorney.[47] Moreover, the LinkedIn data can be used to construct

46. Enforcement agencies or private attorneys might find these differences sufficiently suggestive to undertake further efforts to obtain company data, which often contain the reason for the separation.

47. Moreover, establishing evidence of discrimination in court does not require the same level of rigor as the most cutting-edge economics research, for two reasons. First, a simple "conjecture" that unobservables could explain a difference otherwise attributable to discrimination does not constitute evidence; it has to be supported by data. Most directly, in *Bazemore v. Friday*, 478 US 385, 399–400, 403 n.14 (1986), the court rejected defendant's argument that plaintiffs' analysis was unsound because certain factors were omitted, finding that defendant "made no attempt . . . to demonstrate that when these factors were properly organized and accounted for there was no significant disparity between the salaries of Blacks and whites." Second, the standard of evidence in a civil case is a "preponderance of evidence," often interpreted as "more likely true than not." (See, e.g., Legal Information Institute, https://www.law.cornell.edu/wex/preponderance_of_the_evidence.)

some additional controls to augment the models. We have constructed controls for both highest educational degree and company tenure.

LinkedIn profiles contain self-reported education data for individuals, with fields for start and end dates, degree names, fields of study, educational institutions, and grades. Individuals can add as many education entries as they would like (e.g., a bachelor's degree and a master's degree). Since these fields are self-reported, they are not guaranteed to be accurate, but our assumption is that given the importance of education in finding employment, many individuals will choose to self-report education accurately and few individuals will omit it. We cleaned the education degree name fields for individuals in our data (beginning with 18,432 unique degree names, and standardizing these).[48] We found that 86.9 percent of employees in our data reported some information on education that could be classified as a high school, associate's, bachelor's, master's, or doctoral degree.[49] We also constructed company tenure from start and stop dates (the latter if there was more than one employment spell) of employment at the companies.[50]

The estimates with these controls are reported in the lower panel of table 8.10. Most of the estimates are very similar. The one exception is that there is now strong evidence that females at SpaceX experienced mass layoffs at a higher rate, with the probability higher by 4.2 percentage points.

The last analysis we did for layoffs considers the intersections between race and gender and ethnicity and gender. This evidence is reported in table 8.11. The one striking finding is that, at SpaceX, the probability of a mass layoff was much higher for Black females than for Black males. The differential for Black males is small and statistically insignificant, while the differential for Black females relative to Black males (which is close to the overall differential relative to white males) is 16.6 percentage points, significant at the 5 percent level.

8.9 Hires

We did similar calculations for hires. For Meta, the representation of Blacks, Hispanics, and women among hires was generally very similar to that among the workforce, as shown in table 8.12 (with some variation from year to year). For SpaceX, the comparisons suggest lower hiring of Blacks and

48. As corroborating evidence of the validity of our education coding, we found far higher percentages with doctoral degrees at Fermi, GSK, and Research Corporation of the University of Hawaii, and a far higher percentage with high school as the highest degree for Chesterfield County.

49. This latter category includes PhD, MD, JD, PharmD, and anything else with the word *doctor* in it.

50. One might also want to control for position (job). However, this is empirically challenging, given that there are very large numbers of unique/idiosyncratic job titles. Nonetheless, below we explore using job titles to identify promotions.

Table 8.11 **Meta and SpaceX mass layoff differentials by race, ethnicity, and gender, intersectional effects**

	Meta	SpaceX
Black	0.0033	–0.0044
	(0.0054)	(0.0074)
Hispanic	0.0066	–0.0183
	(0.0040)	(0.0050)
Female	–0.0031	0.0051
	(0.0020)	(0.0052)
Female x black	–0.0046	0.0261
	(0.0082)	(0.0258)
Female x Hispanic	–0.0133	–0.0114
	(0.0058)	(0.0118)
Black x mass layoff years	0.0256	–0.0081
	(0.0090)	(0.0277)
Hispanic x mass layoff years	0.0144	0.0215
	(0.0067)	(0.0195)
Female x mass layoff years	0.0258	0.0200
	(0.0037)	(0.0207)
Female x Black x mass layoff years	–0.0168	0.1662
	(0.0141)	(0.0814)
Female x Hispanic x mass layoff years	0.0144	0.0750
	(0.0102)	(0.0510)
Year dummy variables included	Yes	Yes
Tenure and education controls included	Yes	Yes
Mean separation rate for non-Black/non-Hispanic males, all years	0.1185	0.1656
Mean separation rate for non-Black/non-Hispanic males, mass layoff years	0.1586	0.2082
Mean separation rate for non-Black/non-Hispanic males, non-mass layoff years	0.0402	0.1609
N	126,460	40,902

Note: Observations are employee-years, and the outcome is whether a separation occurred. Estimates are from linear probability model. Standard errors clustered at the individual level are in parentheses. "Mass layoff years" are 2021–2023 for Meta and 2019 for SpaceX. Education controls in lower panel include dummy variables for high school degree, associate's degree (omitted), bachelor's degree, master's degree, or doctoral degree. Hispanic females make up 5.5 percent of observations (N=6,998) in the regression sample for Meta and 2.9 percent of observations (N=1,173) in the regression sample for SpaceX. Black females make up 2.4 percent of observations (N=3,045) in the regression sample for Meta and 1.08 percent of observations (N=442) in the regression sample for SpaceX.

Hispanics relative to the workforce shares, especially in more recent years, but higher hiring of women. Of course, with regard to hiring the more relevant question is the comparison of the race, ethnic, or gender composition of hires relative to applicants or the potential hiring pool. Thus, we do not report any statistical tests. Nonetheless, this table suggests that one could use

Table 8.12 Meta and SpaceX workforce and hires demographic composition

	% Black in workforce	% Black in hires	% Hispanic in workforce	% Hispanic in hires	% female in workforce	% female in hires
Meta						
2012	4.8	4.6	7.9	8.6	35.6	33.9
2013	4.7	4.2	8.7	10.2	35.1	34.2
2014	4.7	4.6	9.7	11.4	33.2	30.6
2015	4.4	4.2	11.7	14.6	33.9	34.7
2016	4.7	5.1	12.4	13.5	34.8	35.3
2017	5.2	5.8	12.3	12.4	36.6	38.3
2018	5.6	6.2	12.2	12.1	36.9	37.3
2019	5.7	5.8	12.2	12.4	36.8	36.3
2020	6.0	6.6	12.2	12.1	36.2	35.6
2021	6.5	7.3	12.5	12.9	37.2	38.7
2022	6.3	6.0	11.9	11.0	36.1	34.6
2023	6.2	6.8	11.5	12.3	35.3	31.9
SpaceX						
2012	10.0	9.5	18.4	19.4	15.6	14.9
2013	9.4	8.0	19.2	18.6	16.3	17.5
2014	9.1	8.6	19.4	17.4	16.2	17.6
2015	8.9	8.0	18.8	15.8	16.0	16.6
2016	8.2	6.8	18.6	15.8	15.9	16.2
2017	8.5	9.2	19.2	18.1	15.6	16.5
2018	8.0	6.3	19.1	16.0	15.5	17.3
2019	7.8	6.8	19.8	18.9	15.1	14.6
2020	7.5	5.5	19.8	19.7	15.6	19.6
2021	7.5	6.4	19.4	16.0	16.2	20.6
2022	7.5	4.1	19.8	18.6	16.1	23.0
2023	7.5	3.1	20.8	16.5	15.8	19.1

estimates like these, relative to "benchmark" estimates of the composition of the hiring pool sometimes used in discrimination cases, usually from the ACS, to obtain provisional evidence on discrimination in hiring.[51]

8.10 Exploring Promotions

Finally, we consider the use of LinkedIn data to measure promotions. We expect, ex ante, that measuring promotions will be more problematic. A hire

51. For an example comparing hires to such benchmarks in a discrimination case, see *Expert Report of David Neumark in the matter of Heldt et al. v. Tata Consultancy Services, Ltd.*, February 2017. For examples and discussion of EEOC guidance using benchmarks from the Decennial Census or the ACS, see "Instructions to Federal Agencies for EEO MD-715," https://www.eeoc.gov/federal-sector/management-directive/instructions-federal-agencies-eeo-md-715-1 and Amano-Patiño et al. (2022). For an example at the state level see "Equal Employment Opportunity and Minority Hiring Practices Report, Fiscal Years 2015–2016," https://www.twc.texas.gov/sites/default/files/enterprise/docs/equal-employment-opportunity-minority-hiring-practices-report-2016-twc.pdf.

or separation is relatively straightforward to measure in the LinkedIn data from the work history. But even if people report every position they hold while at a company, it is not certain that every position change is a promotion; conversely, some promotions may occur without position changes.[52] Moreover, job titles are not reported uniformly on LinkedIn. For example, in our sample of 57,097 work experiences at Meta, we observe 24,720 unique job titles, 21,460 of which only appear once. Thus, we caution that any use of the LinkedIn data to measure promotion differences by race, ethnicity, and gender must be viewed as more provisional than our other analyses, and a user of the data for these purposes will likely have to make their own assessment, based on job title transitions in the data, as to the reliability of any estimated differences across groups.[53] Reflecting this, the analysis we describe should perhaps best be viewed as exploring how one might use and assess the LinkedIn data for this purpose.

We begin by presenting evidence on the measured job title changes we see in the LinkedIn data at the companies we studied. Table 8.13 reports the 20 most common job title changes at each company. One can only assess subjectively whether most of these job title changes look like promotions or not. Our view is that most of them do for some companies, but not others. For BWXT, many transitions are not clearly promotions (e.g., Product Engineer to Design Engineer). For Chesterfield County, we think that most are (e.g., GIS Analyst to Senior GIS Analyst, and Planner to Senior Planner). For Fermi, GSK, Meta, and SpaceX, nearly all transitions look like promotions, with many including words like "senior" or "lead" or numbered levels indicating clear promotions. For Research Corporation of the University of Hawaii, some of the transitions look like promotions, but there are too few to reliably use the data anyway.[54]

Based on this assessment, it appears that we can obtain some reliable information on promotion differences by race, ethnicity, and gender for

52. Indeed, based on our experience in discrimination litigation, even with full access to a company's data the definition of promotions can sometimes be ambiguous.

53. Note that, in practice, this might be done for a specific set of jobs, like those covered in a class action claim. The same could also be true of a hiring analysis.

54. To be clear, we are not arguing that all job changes are necessarily promotions. One could conceivably select a subset of job changes for a company and study them as promotions. We have identified two studies that ask how promotions (as identified by workers) differ from other job changes. McCue (1996) studies the differences between self-reported promotions and other job changes (at the same firm) in the PSID. In her data, these are roughly equal shares. For workers with 10 or fewer years of tenure, both changes are associated with wage growth relative to no job change, with the wage growth higher for promotions. At higher tenure levels, only promotions are associated with wage growth. In a study using employer-employee data from Portugal, van der Klauw and da Silva (2011) study two kinds of promotions—clear moves up a hierarchy, or promotions as reported by firms. They report that these two measures do not overlap well, with about 40 percent of employer-reported promotions not associated with a change in job descriptions, and only about 30 percent of hierarchical step-ups are also reported as promotions by employers. Both types of "promotions" are associated with substantial wage increases.

Table 8.13 Most common job title changes at each company

BWXT Technical Svcs Group Inc.		Chesterfield County		Fermi Research Alliance LLC		GlaxoSmithKline LLC	
Job title change	#	Job title change	#	Job title change	#	Job title change	#
PRODUCT ENGINEER→ DESIGN ENGINEER	2	BUSINESS TAX ASSESSMENT SPECIALIST→ TAX COMPLIANCE AUDITOR	3	ASSOCIATE SCIENTIST→ SCIENTIST	11	PRINCIPAL SCIENTIST→ INVESTIGATOR	20
VICE PRESIDENT AND CHIEF INVESTOR RELATIONS OFFICER→ VICE PRESIDENT, CONTRACTS & PROCUREMENT	2	BATTALION CHIEF→ DIRECTOR OF COMMUNITY RELATIONS	2	SCIENTIST→ SENIOR SCIENTIST	7	SCIENTIST→ SENIOR SCIENTIST	17
QUALITY ASSURANCE ENGINEER→ QUALITY CONTROL ENGINEER	2	PLANNING TECHNICIAN→ PLANNER	2	RESEARCH ASSOCIATE→ ASSOCIATE SCIENTIST	6	ASSOCIATE SCIENTIST→ SENIOR SCIENTIST	14
SOFTWARE PROGRAMMER→ COGNIZANT AREA ENGINEER	2	GIS ANALYST→ SENIOR GIS ANALYST	2	WILSON FELLOW→ SCIENTIST	4	ASSOCIATE SCIENTIST→ SCIENTIST	9
LEAD AUDITOR→ SOFTWARE PROGRAMMER	2	LIEUTENANT→ CAPTAIN	2	ASSOCIATE SCIENTIST→ SCIENTIST I	4	INVESTIGATOR→ SCIENTIFIC LEADER	9
DESIGN ENGINEER→ PROJECT ENGINEER	2	CHIEF DEPUTY TREASURER→ TREASURER	2	ACCELERATOR OPERATOR I→ ACCELERATOR OPERATOR II	4	SENIOR SCIENTIST→ INVESTIGATOR	8
VICE PRESIDENT, INVESTOR RELATIONS AND CORPORATE PROCUREMENT→ VICE PRESIDENT AND CHIEF INVESTOR RELATIONS OFFICER	2	SENIOR CONTRACT OFFICER→ PROCUREMENT MANAGER II	2	ACCELERATOR OPERATOR→ ENGINEERING PHYSICIST	3	SENIOR SALES REPRESENTATIVE→ EXECUTIVE SALES REPRESENTATIVE	7
POLITICAL AFFAIRS MANAGER→ SENIOR MANAGER, GOVERNMENT RELATIONS	2	ADMINISTRATIVE MANAGER—PURCHASING→ SENIOR CONTRACT OFFICER	2	CHIEF INFORMATION OFFICER (CIO)→ PROJECT SCIENTIST FOR LONG BASELINE NEUTRINO EXPERIMENT	2	PHARMACEUTICAL SALES REPRESENTATIVE→ SENIOR PHARMACEUTICAL SALES REPRESENTATIVE	7
COGNIZANT AREA ENGINEER→ SMARTFORMS SME	2	EMERGENCY COMMUNICATIONS OFFICER→ ASSISTANT SHIFT SUPERVISOR	2	DISTRIBUTED COMPUTING SERVICES OPERATIONS DEPUTY DEPARTMENT HEAD→ HPC/LQCD SITE CO-MANAGER	2	SENIOR COUNSEL→ ASSISTANT GENERAL COUNSEL	7
NETWORK ENGINEER→ SR. VOIP ENGINEER	2	PLANNER→ SENIOR PLANNER	2	SCIENTIST I→ SENIOR SCIENTIST	2	ASSOCIATE BRAND MANAGER→ BRAND MANAGER	7

OPERATIONS ENGINEER→ DEVELOPMENT ENGINEER	2	MICROCOMPUTER ANALYST→ SENIOR MICROCOMPUTER ANALYST	2	JEFF METCALF INTERN→ VOLUNTEER RESEARCH ASSISTANT	2	COUNSEL→ SENIOR COUNSEL	5
QUALITY ASSURANCE→ SHIFT SUPERVISOR	1	ASSISTANT DIRECTOR, HUMAN RESOURCE MANAGEMENT→ DIRECTOR AND CHIEF LEARNING OFFICER, LEARNING & PERFORMANCE CENTER	1	CDF SPOKESPERSON→ DISTINGUISHED SCIENTIST	2	INVESTIGATOR→ SENIOR SCIENTIFIC INVESTIGATOR	4
MANAGER, SUPPLIER OVERSIGHT & SECURITY→ CORPORATE SECURITY PROGRAM MANAGER	1	SENIOR FAMILY SERVICES SPECIALIST→ LEAD FAMILY SERVICES SPECIALIST	1	SYSTEM SERVICES SPECIALIST III→ DEPUTY GROUP LEADER (SYSTEM SERVICES SPECIALIST III)	2	SENIOR SCIENTIST→ PRINCIPAL SCIENTIST	4
DIMENSIONAL INSPECTION MANAGER→ ASSEMBLY ENGINEERING MANAGER	1	STAFF AUDITOR→ SENIOR AUDITOR	1	OPERATIONS SPECIALIST→ ENGINEERING PHYSICIST	2	SALES REPRESENTATIVE→ SENIOR SALES REPRESENTATIVE	4
MATERIALS ENGINEERING TEAM LEAD→ MANAGER OF MATERIALS MANAGEMENT	1	IT SPECIALIST III→ SOLUTIONS ARCHITECT	1	RESEARCH ASSOCIATE→ COMPUTER PROFESSIONAL	2	PATENT COUNSEL→ SENIOR PATENT COUNSEL	4
INTERNAL AUDITOR→ BUSINESS ANALYST	1	CHIEF OFFICER OF ELECTIONS→ EASTERN VIRGINIA MARKET UNIT FLEET ADMINISTRATIVE ASSISTANT	1	ACCELERATOR OPERATOR II→ SENIOR ACCELERATOR OPERATOR	2	INVESTIGATOR→ PRINCIPAL INVESTIGATOR	4
MANAGER, CORPORATE DEVELOPMENT→ DIRECTOR, CORPORATE DEVELOPMENT	1	SENIOR COMPUTER ANALYST→ LEAD COMPUTER ANALYST	1	DEPUTY DIRECTOR FOR RESEARCH→ HEAD OF FERMILAB QUANTUM INSTITUTE	2	ASSISTANT SCIENTIST→ ASSOCIATE SCIENTIST	3
DIMENSIONAL INSPECTOR→ TECHNOLOGIST	1	CODE COMPLIANCE SPECIALIST→ PLANNER	1	VOLUNTEER RESEARCH ASSISTANT→ ON-CALL EMPLOYEE / RESEARCH ASSISTANT	2	SCIENTIST→ PRINCIPAL SCIENTIST	3
IT PROJECT MANAGER→ CORPORATE PROCUREMENT ANALYST	1	SR. AUTOMATION TECHNICIAN→ AUTOMATION SPECIALIST	1	DEPUTY GROUP LEADER (SYSTEM SERVICES SPECIALIST III)→ DISTRIBUTED COMPUTING SERVICES OPERATIONS DEPUTY DEPARTMENT HEAD	2	BRAND MANAGER→ SENIOR BRAND MANAGER	3
QUALITY ASSURANCE ENGINEERING SUPERVISOR→ QUALITY ASSURANCE MANAGER	1	CAPTAIN→ BATTALION CHIEF, EMERGENCY OPERATIONS DIVISION	1	PHYSICIST→ DEPUTY DIRECTOR FOR RESEARCH	2	SENIOR PHARMACEUTICAL SALES REPRESENTATIVE→ EXECUTIVE PHARMACEUTICAL SALES REPRESENTATIVE	3

(continued)

Table 8.13 (cont.)

Meta		Research Corporation of the University of Hawaii		SpaceX	
Job title change	#	Job title change	#	Job title change	#
SOFTWARE ENGINEER→ SENIOR SOFTWARE ENGINEER	210	HUMAN RESOURCES ASSOCIATE I/II→ HUMAN RESOURCES INFORMATION SYSTEMS SPECIALIST I/II/III	1	SOFTWARE ENGINEER→ SOFTWARE ENGINEER II	50
SENIOR SOFTWARE ENGINEER→ STAFF SOFTWARE ENGINEER	88	HUMAN RESOURCES INFORMATION SYSTEMS SPECIALIST I/II/III→ HRIS/IT SYSTEMS ADMINISTRATOR	1	MANUFACTURING ENGINEER→ MANUFACTURING ENGINEER II	26
SOFTWARE ENGINEER→ ENGINEERING MANAGER	84	PROGRAM MANAGER @ THE VANGUARD MAUI HIGH PERFORMANCE COMPUTING CENTER (MHPCC)→ EXECUTIVE DIRECTOR FOR THE VANGUARD MAUI HIGH PERFORMANCE COMPUTING CENTER (MHPCC)	1	MANUFACTURING ENGINEER→ LEAD MANUFACTURING ENGINEER	20
SOFTWARE ENGINEER→ SOFTWARE ENGINEERING MANAGER	68	CRAZY ANT STRIKE TEAM CREW LEAD→ CRAZY ANT STRIKE TEAM FIELD OPERATIONS COORDINATOR	1	SOFTWARE ENGINEER II→ SENIOR SOFTWARE ENGINEER	15
DATA SCIENTIST→ DATA SCIENCE MANAGER	53	HUMAN RESOURCES SUPPORT ASSOCIATE I→ HUMAN RESOURCES RECRUITMENT ASSOCIATE I	1	SOFTWARE ENGINEER→ LEAD SOFTWARE ENGINEER	14
RESEARCH SCIENTIST→ SENIOR RESEARCH SCIENTIST	49	3D PLANETARIUM OPERATOR→ 3D PLANETARIUM OPERATING INTERN	1	SENIOR SOFTWARE ENGINEER→ LEAD SOFTWARE ENGINEER	13
DATA SCIENTIST→ SENIOR DATA SCIENTIST	43			PROPULSION ENGINEER→ PROPULSION ENGINEER II	11
PRODUCT DESIGNER→ PRODUCT DESIGN MANAGER	31			STRUCTURES ENGINEER→ STRUCTURES ENGINEER II	11

CLIENT SOLUTIONS MANAGER→ CLIENT PARTNER	25			INTEGRATION AND TEST ENGINEER→ INTEGRATION AND TEST ENGINEER II	11
ROTATIONAL SOFTWARE ENGINEER→ SOFTWARE ENGINEER	24			MECHANICAL ENGINEER→ SENIOR MECHANICAL ENGINEER	11
STAFF SOFTWARE ENGINEER→ ENGINEERING MANAGER	20			SENIOR MECHANICAL ENGINEER→ MANAGER-DETECTION INFRASTRUCTURE ENGINEERING	11
TECHNICAL SOURCER→ TECHNICAL RECRUITER	17			SOFTWARE ENGINEER II→ LEAD SOFTWARE ENGINEER	10
SOFTWARE ENGINEER→ STAFF SOFTWARE ENGINEER	16			SOFTWARE ENGINEER→ SENIOR SOFTWARE ENGINEER	9
SENIOR DATA SCIENTIST→ STAFF DATA SCIENTIST	16			MANAGER-DETECTION INFRASTRUCTURE ENGINEERING→ SR. MANAGER	9
DATA ENGINEER→ DATA ENGINEERING MANAGER	16			BUILD RELIABILITY ENGINEER→ BUILD RELIABILITY ENGINEER II	8
CONTENT DESIGNER→ CONTENT DESIGN MANAGER	14			ASSOCIATE BUYER→ BUYER	8
DATA ENGINEER→ SENIOR DATA ENGINEER	12			STRUCTURES ENGINEER→ LEAD STRUCTURES ENGINEER	8
UX RESEARCHER→ SENIOR UX RESEARCHER	12			PROPULSION TECHNICIAN→ LEAD PROPULSION TECHNICIAN	8
ENGINEERING MANAGER→ SENIOR ENGINEERING MANAGER	12			MATERIAL PLANNER→ MATERIAL PLANNER II	7
MACHINE LEARNING ENGINEER→ SENIOR MACHINE LEARNING ENGINEER	12			LEAD PROPULSION ENGINEER→ MANAGER, PROPULSION ENGINEERING	6

Table 8.14 **Meta, SpaceX, GSK, and Fermi promotion rate differentials by race, ethnicity, and gender, 2012–2023**

	Meta	SpaceX	GSK	Fermi
Without education and tenure controls				
Black	0.0052	–0.0254	–0.0242	–0.0115
	(0.0032)	(0.0047)	(0.0089)	(0.0055)
Hispanic	0.0090	–0.0278	0.0180	–0.0090
	(0.0025)	(0.0032)	(0.0103)	(0.0063)
Female	0.0198	0.0195	0.0067	0.0057
	(0.0017)	(0.0043)	(0.0057)	(0.0056)
Year dummy variables included	Yes	Yes	Yes	Yes
Mean promotion rate for non-Black/ non-Hispanic males	0.0563	0.0704	0.1286	0.0296
N	141,045	58,947	24,612	8,984
With education and tenure controls				
Black	0.0054	–0.0270	–0.0224	–0.0082
	(0.0035)	(0.0066)	(0.0096)	(0.0083)
Hispanic	0.0103	–0.0152	0.0232	–0.0169
	(0.0027)	(0.0050)	(0.0108)	(0.0064)
Female	0.0194	0.0171	0.0077	0.0082
	(0.0018)	(0.0053)	(0.0060)	(0.0070)
Year dummy variables included	Yes	Yes	Yes	Yes
Mean promotion rate for non-Black/ non-Hispanic males	0.0569	0.0848	0.1324	0.0344
N	126,460	40,902	21,907	6,855

Note: Observations are employee-years, and the outcome is whether a promotion (job title change) occurred in the year. Estimates are from linear probability model. Standard errors clustered at the individual level are in parentheses. Education controls in lower panel include dummy variables for high school degree, associate's degree (omitted), bachelor's degree, master's degree, or doctoral degree.

Fermi, GSK, Meta, and SpaceX, among the seven companies we considered, by considering job title changes as promotions. As an illustration, we present estimates of promotion models for each of these companies. The analysis is similar to our earlier layoff analysis. The results are reported in table 8.14, however in this case we simply aggregate across all years and estimate promotion rate differentials by race, ethnicity, and gender, since we do not have any reference to particular years of interest as we did in the layoff analysis.

The top panel reports the more parsimonious models. At Meta, the promotion rate differentials for Blacks, Hispanics, and women are positive, and the difference for women is statistically significant (1.98 percentage points, which can be compared to a 5.6 percent promotion rate for non-Black, non-Hispanic males). The promotion rate for women is also higher at SpaceX, but the promotion rates for Blacks and Hispanics are significantly lower (2.5 and 2.8 percentage points, respectively, compared to a 7.0 percent promo-

Table 8.15 Meta and SpaceX promotion differentials by race, ethnicity, and gender, intersectional effects

	Meta	SpaceX	GSK	Fermi
Black	0.0053	–0.0233	–0.0149	–0.0016
	(0.0042)	(0.0073)	(0.0139)	(0.0102)
Hispanic	0.0102	–0.0163	0.0284	–0.0116
	(0.0034)	(0.0054)	(0.0157)	(0.0075)
Female	0.0194	0.0178	0.0102	0.0126
	(0.0020)	(0.0063)	(0.0066)	(0.0086)
Female x Black	–0.0791	–0.0817	–0.1264	–0.0389
	(0.0045)	(0.0096)	(0.0149)	(0.0133)
Female x Hispanic	–0.0860	–0.0851	–0.1671	–0.0429
	(0.0038)	(0.0080)	(0.0165)	(0.0110)
Year dummy variables included	Yes	Yes	Yes	Yes
Tenure and education controls included	Yes	Yes	Yes	Yes
Mean promotion rate for non-Black/ non-Hispanic males	0.0569	0.0848	0.1324	0.0344
N	126,460	40,902	21,907	6,855

Note: Observations are employee-years, and the outcome is whether a promotion (job title change) occurred in the year. Estimates are from linear probability model. Standard errors clustered at the individual level are in parentheses. Education controls include dummy variables for high school degree, associate's degree (omitted), bachelor's degree, master's degree, or doctoral degree. Hispanic females make up 5.5 percent of observations (N=6,998) in the regression sample for Meta, 2.9 percent (N=1,173) for SpaceX, 5.7 percent (N=1,254) for GSK, and 4.05 percent (N=279) for Fermi. Black females make up 2.4 percent of observations (N=3,045) in the regression sample for Meta, 1.08 percent (N=442) for SpaceX, 5.4 percent (N=1,191) for GSK, and 2.5 percent (N=172) for Fermi.

tion rate for non-Black, non-Hispanic males). At GSK and Fermi, the only significant differences are for Blacks, with significantly lower promotion rate differentials of 2.4 percentage points at GSK and 1.2 percentage points at Fermi. We reiterate that a particular reason the evidence on promotions should also be viewed as suggestive is because we do not necessarily measure promotions the way these companies do. Nonetheless, once again this kind of evidence could be far more helpful when trying to identify claims of systemic discrimination than anecdotal evidence one or a few plaintiffs present to a government agency or private attorney.

We did the same supplemental analyses as for layoffs. First, we add the education and tenure controls, in the lower panel of table 8.14. These generally have little impact, except that the lower promotion rate for Hispanics at Fermi more than doubles in magnitude and becomes significant at the 5 percent level. The intersectional results, in table 8.15, are striking. In every single case, Blacks or Hispanics who are also female experience far lower promotion rates, with the differential statistically significant at the 5 percent level for both Black women and Hispanic women, at each of the four companies.

Finally, we did one additional refinement, trying to identify job changes that were more clearly promotions. We matched between strings in pairs of job titles associated with positions held consecutively at a company to identify job changes that were very likely promotions, and redid the promotions analysis considering only these job changes as promotions. Specifically, we first did string matching between all pairs of job transitions at a company, using matchit in Stata. Based on this, we concluded that it was difficult to verify that pairs with a similarity score below 0.8 were promotions, while those above were more likely to be promotions. To illustrate, table 8.16 shows 10 randomly selected pairs of job titles held consecutively in the 0.7–0.8 and the 0.8–0.9 ranges of the similarity score. While some of the pairs in the top panel may be promotions, at least 6 of the 10 listed in the bottom panel appear to be (e.g., the addition of "Lead" in the first pair, or "Senior" in the second).

Based on examining these consecutive jobs pairs, we decided to code as promotions job pairs where the two job titles have a similarity score above 0.8 and the second job title contains one of the following words and the first job title does not:

- SENIOR
- SR
- II[55]
- PRINCIPAL
- LEAD
- MANAGER

In addition, we code them as promotions if the same semantic similarity criterion is met and the first job title contains one of the following and second (next) job title does not:

- ASSISTANT
- ASSOCIATE

As reflected in table 8.16, this method is likely conservative in terms of identifying promotions. Some of the transitions with similarity scores below 0.8 may also be promotions, and these rules may also fail to classify some promotions above the 0.8 threshold because they use other words to signify the promotion (e.g., the second job title has the word "Head" in it). However, all of the examples we classify as promotions do appear to be promotions.[56]

Table 8.17 reports estimates of the same specifications as in table 8.14 (the lower panel, with the additional controls), but using this narrower definition of promotions. All other job changes not classified as promotions are

55. The addition of "II" to the job title and "I" in the previous job title captured nearly all job transitions with numbers/levels that appeared to correspond to promotions.

56. As this discussion indicates, one could obviously choose somewhat different rules to classify promotions, so our analysis should be viewed as suggestive of the ability to do this and what one can learn from it, rather than as a definitive analysis of promotions.

Table 8.16 **Pairs of consecutive job titles (10 randomly selected in each range)**

Similarity score 0.7–0.8		*Promotion based on our "rules"*
DEPUTY SHERIFF RECRUIT	DEPUTY SHERIFF	No
INTERNATIONAL MARKETING MANAGER	INTEGRATED MARKETING MANAGER | WHATSAPP	No
MANUFACTURING ENGINEER II, DRAGON PROPULSION	PROPULSION ENGINEER II	No
MEDICAL CENTER REPRESENTATIVE/EXECUTIVE SALES REP	SR EXECUTIVE REPRESENTATIVE/INTERIM SALES MANAGER	No
PHARMACEUTICAL SALES REPRESENTATIVE, RESPIRATORY	PHARMACEUTICAL SALES SPECIALIST, RESPIRATORY	No
PRODUCT DEVELOPMENT SPECIALIST	PRODUCT SPECIALIST	No
PROGRAM MANAGER, BRAND	PROGRAM MANAGER, DIGITAL	No
PROGRAM MANAGER, WHATSAPP	PROGRAM MANAGER	No
SENIOR SOFTWARE ENGINEER—BUSINESS SOLUTIONS	ENGINEERING MANAGER—BUSINESS SOLUTIONS	No
TOXICOLOGIST/MANAGER, SAFETY ASSESSMENT PROJECTS	SENIOR MANAGER, SAFETY ASSESSMENT PROJECT DEVELOPMENT	No
Similarity score 0.8–0.9		
RECOVERY ENGINEER	LEAD RECOVERY ENGINEER	Yes
AI RESEARCH SCIENTIST	SENIOR MEDICAL DIRECTOR	Yes
PRODUCT MANAGEMENT LEADERSHIP RECRUITER	SENIOR MATERIAL PLANNER	Yes
CLIENT SOLUTIONS MANAGER, RETAIL & B2B	LEAD DESIGNER & SENIOR SOFTWARE ENGINEER	Yes
LEAD SPACE LASER ENGINEER	SR MANAGER, BUSINESS PRODUCT OPERATIONS	Yes
MATERIAL PLANNER II	RECRUITING MANAGER | PRODUCT DESIGN	Yes
ADMINISTRATIVE SPECIALIST—GLOBAL BUSINESS MARKETING	EXPENSE PAY FULL STACK ENGINEER (VIA K2 PARTNERING SOLUTIONS)	No
SPECIALTY ACCOUNT DIRECTOR, REGIONAL ACCOUNTS, PAYER, POLICY AND VACCINE DIVISION	GLOBAL HEAD OF SCALED REGULATORY OPERATIONS	No
MANAGER, TECHNICAL PROGRAM MANAGEMENT, LEGAL	HEAD OF LATIN AMERICA, STRATEGIC RESPONSE POLICY	No
PAYMENTS & COMMERCE PROGRAM MANAGER, PARTNERSHIP OPERATIONS	DIRECTOR SALES AND MARKETING, DERMATOLOGY (2ND LINE LEADER)	No

Table 8.17 **Meta, SpaceX, GSK, and Fermi promotion rate differentials by race, ethnicity, and gender, 2012–2023, narrower promotion definitions**

	Meta	SpaceX	GSK	Fermi
Black	–0.0020	–0.0075	–0.0021	–0.0032
	(0.0009)	(0.0028)	(0.0012)	(0.0009)
Hispanic	–0.0015	–0.0068	0.0018	–0.0025
	(0.0007)	(0.0020)	(0.0018)	(0.0013)
Female	–0.0000	–0.0007	–0.0004	–0.0018
	(0.0005)	(0.0021)	(0.0010)	(0.0014)
Year dummy variables included	Yes	Yes	Yes	Yes
Tenure and education controls included	Yes	Yes	Yes	Yes
Mean promotion rate for non-Black/ non-Hispanic males	0.0085	0.0223	0.0052	0.0039
N	126,460	40,902	21,907	6,855

Note: Observations are employee-years, and the outcome is whether a promotion (restricted job title change) occurred in the year. Estimates are from linear probability model. Standard errors clustered at the individual level are in parentheses. Education controls include dummy variables for high school degree, associate's degree (omitted), bachelor's degree, master's degree, or doctoral degree.

treated as non-promotions. Note that, as reported in the table, this results in much lower promotion rates, and the reduction relative to table 8.14 varies by company, which can be a consequence of job titles more easily identifying promotions at some companies than others.[57] The lower promotion rates are reflected in smaller estimated coefficients. The conclusions for Meta are different from table 8.14, with the models now yielding evidence of lower promotions for Blacks, and no longer indicating higher promotions for women. For SpaceX the lower promotions for Blacks and Hispanics persist, but the higher promotion rate for women is no longer evident. For GSK and Fermi the results are not qualitatively different.

As this analysis indicates, the classification of promotions from the LinkedIn data is subjective and certainly not definitive. However, in a litigation context one could choose a subset of job title changes that, for a particular company, have been identified as corresponding to promotions, although the LinkedIn job titles would not map perfectly to the job titles used at a company.

8.11 Potential Limitations

One inherent limitation of our approach is that it is more applicable (and reliable) for companies with large shares of employees on LinkedIn. We

57. Indeed, the reduction is smaller for Meta and SpaceX, for which table 8.13 suggests that job changes are more readily identifiable as promotions.

suspect that companies with large shares of lower-skilled and lower-paid jobs are less well represented on LinkedIn, and the same could be true of lower-skilled and lower-paid workers at the companies on LinkedIn. On the other hand, the composition of employment at higher-pay, higher-skilled firms, and advancement through the ranks at these companies, is critically important because these companies, and the higher-level jobs within them, are among the best jobs in the US economy. These are also the jobs at which minority groups (and women, in tech jobs) are under-represented.[58]

A second limitation is the possibility of fake profiles on LinkedIn. We have no information on how pervasive this is. We also do not know any algorithm to identify these profiles.[59] Still, this is another reason one should not interpret the type of analysis we do with the LinkedIn data—or that others could do—as definitive with respect to measuring discrimination, but rather as indicative of possible discrimination. Finally, there is some evidence that LinkedIn seems to be fairly successful at stopping fake accounts.[60]

A third limitation is that we cannot study pay (and hence pay discrimination) in the LinkedIn data. At present, we are not aware of other social media data that could be used in the same manner and that also include pay. It is not inconceivable that this could be done, however, perhaps by collecting survey data via targeted advertising like in the Schneider and Harknett (2019b) Facebook data collection on work schedules.

A fourth limitation is that we have not explored developing even better methods for classification by race, ethnicity, and gender, but instead use, by and large, "off the shelf" methods. There may be potential room for improvement, including, for example, training models based on datasets that might have more overlap with the LinkedIn data.

It is also important to clarify that the kind of evidence that can be produced with the LinkedIn data is not intended to be rigorous evidence of discrimination. Our goal is to try to use the LinkedIn data to produce estimates of race, ethnic, and gender differences in employment, hiring, separations (especially layoffs), and promotions. Our ability to look within companies can provide new descriptive evidence that is currently not available to researchers. And this evidence and methods, as we have argued, could be useful in enforcing discrimination laws. We want to be clear, however, that we are not proposing our measures based on the LinkedIn data as evidence

58. See National Center for Science and Engineering Statistics (2023).

59. Rather, "advice" on spotting them is based on reading and assessing individual profiles and does not appear very systematic (e.g., "How To Identify A Fake LinkedIn Profile In Five Minutes Or Less," by Judi Hays, *Forbes*, November 17, 2022, https://www.forbes.com/sites/forbesbusinesscouncil/2022/11/17/how-to-identify-a-fake-linkedin-profile-in-five-minutes-or-less/?sh=1421f73f1d7c; LinkedIn "Learn More about Collaborative Articles," https://www.linkedin.com/pulse/dangers-fake-profiles-how-spot-one-david-smith-cv-writer).

60. See "LinkedIn has a fake account problem it's trying to fix. Real users are part of the solution," CNBC, by Bob Violino, December 10 2022, https://www.cnbc.com/2022/12/10/not-just-twitter-linkedin-has-fake-account-problem-its-trying-to-fix.html.

of discrimination per se. Other factors can explain sorting of workers across firms, as well as differences in retention and promotion.

The intention is not that the LinkedIn data would necessarily be the data actually used to establish definitive evidence of discrimination for either legal proceedings or research. The strongest evidence would typically require richer company data, both for reliability and comprehensiveness, and to rule out other non-discriminatory explanations.[61] These data typically become available at later stages of litigation. But our findings suggest that the LinkedIn data can be used to increase the precision with which potentially discriminatory companies could be targeted for further legal exploration, including filing of discrimination claims and opening of legal discovery to access the richer data that companies have on both workforce outcomes and potential factors accounting for those differences. And, conversely, the use of these data might prevent spurious lawsuits against companies less likely to be discriminating.

8.12 Summary and Conclusions

We have shown that one can use LinkedIn data to obtain reasonably reliable measures of workforce demographic composition by race, ethnicity, and gender, based on validation exercises comparing estimates from scraped LinkedIn data to two sources—ACS data and company diversity or EEO-1 reports. To be clear though, we do this validation for a small number of companies, limited by a restriction to one industry (which we suspect is better represented on LinkedIn) and to a small number of companies dictated by our research budget. This validation is further restricted to companies that can be compared to ACS data, because they represent a high share of industry employment in a POWPUMA, and companies that make public diversity reports or EEO-1 reports. Our evidence cannot speak to the universe of industries or companies.

We emphasize that the research we present in this paper is to some extent a "proof of concept" (or more accurately an assessment of a proof of concept), exploring how well our ideas for measuring the demographic composition of companies' workforces, and the relation of other decisions of these companies to demographics, can be measured. The methods we develop and explore—which we anticipate will be improved upon by others—can potentially be used in a number of ways.

First, and most directly related to this paper, the LinkedIn data can be used by plaintiffs' attorneys or agencies charged with enforcing discrimination laws. We illustrate how this might be done by studying mass layoffs

61. On the latter point, for example, one might get information on promotions from job titles at a company and be able to test whether education and prior jobs explain any difference using LinkedIn data to supplement company data. But more rigorous evidence would likely require performance ratings, as well as perhaps a more definitive identifier of promotions.

(and hiring) at two companies for which we extracted LinkedIn data, and by exploring the measurement and analysis of promotions. We first show that the data are sufficiently comprehensive to detect mass layoffs. And we then illustrate using the data to compare the race, ethnic, and gender composition of laid off workers to the workforce as a whole. Again, we caution that the LinkedIn data are unlikely to provide the level of rigor in measuring discrimination that is required to establish a legal claim of discrimination, both because thc LinkedIn data do not provide a scientific sample (indeed, in an actual discrimination case, data on all employees covered by the case would typically be available), and because of a lack of some control variables—although it is possible to recover education and prior job history information from LinkedIn. Still, this kind of evidence may be much more convincing to attorneys or government agencies than anecdotal evidence from a handful of laid-off workers. Measuring promotions is harder because they are less directly captured in the LinkedIn data. Nonetheless, we provide evidence suggesting that one may be able to learn something about race, ethnic, and gender differences in promotions from these data.

Second, we imagine that researchers will develop other ways to use these data to measure and study the demographics of the workplace, such as the evolution of employment by race, ethnicity, and gender, overall (or at least in industries well-represented on LinkedIn), and extending to other questions like the progress women and minorities are making in reaching higher-level positions within companies. Indeed, while in this paper we only study data on a limited number of companies, the company from which we draw LinkedIn data does make available the entire public LinkedIn database. And researchers might be interested in more refined evidence on discrimination in the form of unexplained demographic differences in hiring, layoffs, promotions, etc., constructing more detailed controls from the LinkedIn data. Although this kind of evidence falls short of the level of rigor of experimental or quasi-experimental studies (Neumark 2018), the ability to provide evidence on specific firms may offer unique insights.[62]

Third, researchers could potentially delve into other dimensions of discrimination. For example, some studies examine differences in patterns suggestive of discrimination between client-facing and other jobs, to assess the role of customer discrimination (e.g., Combes et al. 2016; Neumark 2024). Other research has considered the effects of skin tone on wage differentials and other outcomes among Blacks, and relative to Whites (e.g., Goldsmith et al. 2006; Monk 2014). This kind of classification of Blacks may be feasible using the LinkedIn pictures.[63] Another line of research conducts correspon-

62. We remind the reader of the Kline et al. (2024) correspondence study approach to garnering company-specific evidence on race discrimination in hiring.

63. This would be complicated by the fact that LinkedIn photos are taken in very different lighting situations as compared to DMV or passport photos, which are fairly standardized across individuals.

dence studies of differences in outcomes based on looks, even manipulating facial symmetry in photos (Bóo et al. 2013); again, this could be pursued based on LinkedIn pictures. To be clear, though, research along these lines might be more interesting to discrimination researchers than enforcement agencies, in which case the lower rigor attainable using the LinkedIn data might be more limiting.

Finally, we think our demonstration of how we use the LinkedIn data may prompt consideration of other potential research uses one could make of these data. One can, for example, construct work histories and educational histories, as well as job titles—although the job titles are somewhat idiosyncratic and company-specific, as our promotions analysis shows. Thus, for example, the LinkedIn data could in principle be used to study the impact of education on careers, and to study career trajectories including both changes within companies and mobility across companies. This is an interesting question in its own right, and also in relation to differences by race, ethnicity, and gender. As noted earlier, the LEHD, like other linked employer-employee databases, can be used to study mobility across firms, and mobility within firms, although in both cases based more on earnings than job titles.[64] One data source that can study specific job titles is the ExecuComp data studied by Bertrand and Hallock (2001). However, this data source covers only the upper echelons of companies (the top five executives), and hence is less suited to studying mobility. Another possible source of data is targeted surveys, like Bertrand et al.'s (2010) survey research on MBAs, their careers, and the evolution of the earnings gap. A survey like this has the obvious advantage of the researchers being able to choose the questions, and the disadvantage of narrow coverage. Given these limitations, the LinkedIn data may be a unique source to study career trajectories and mobility, characterizing race, ethnic, and gender differences using the kinds of classifications we develop in this paper, providing new evidence that is complementary to what has been or can be learned from other data sources.

Acknowledgments

This paper was prepared for the NBER-CRIW Conference: Race, Ethnicity, and Economic Statistics for the 21st Century. We have received helpful comments from Anjali Adukia, Randall Akee, Keith Finlay, Lawrence Katz, Mark Lowenstein, and conference participants. The data used in this paper are proprietary, and hence we cannot produce the full dataset for other researchers to use. However, the paper fully explains how the data can be accessed for purchase. We received modest financial support for this project

64. We already noted Barth et al. (2021), which studies how the gender gap evolves as workers move across firms. For an example using Italian data, see Casarico and Lattanzio (2024).

from Econ One Research ("Econ One"). Alexander Berry is employed by Econ One and David Neumark does consulting work on discrimination cases with Econ One. Econ One had no right of review or comment on this research, and all conclusions are our own. For acknowledgments, sources of research support, and disclosure of the authors' material financial relationships, if any, please see https://www.nber.org/books-and-chapters/race-ethnicity-and-economic-statistics-21st-century/missing-link-using-linkedin-data-measure-race-ethnic-and-gender-differences-employment-outcomes.

References

Amano-Patiño, Noriko, Julian Aramburu, and Zara Contractor. 2022. "Is Affirmative Action in Employment Still Effective in the 21st Century?" US Census Bureau, Center for Economics Studies Working Paper 22–54.

Antman, Francisca M., and Brian Duncan. 2026. "Ethnic Identity and Anti-Immigrant Sentiment: Evidence from Proposition 187." In this volume.

Azar, José, Ioana Marinescu, and Marshall Steinbaum. 2022. "Labor Market Concentration." *Journal of Human Resources* 58(1): 167–99.

Barth, Erling, Sari Pekkala Kerr, and Claudia Olivetti. 2021. "The Dynamics of Gender Earnings Differentials: Evidence from Establishment Data." *European Economic Review* 134: 103713.

Bayard, Kimberly, Judith Hellerstein, David Neumark, and Kenneth Troske. 2003. "New Evidence on Sex Segregation and Sex Differences in Wages from Matched Employer-Employee Data." *Journal of Labor Economics* 21(4): 887–922.

Bertrand, Marianne, Claudia Goldin, and Lawrence F. Katz. 2010. "Dynamics of the Gender Gap for Young Professionals in the Financial and Corporate Sectors." *American Economic Journal: Applied Economics* 2(3): 228–55.

Bertrand, Marianne, and Kevin F. Hallock. 2001. "The Gender Gap in Top Corporate Jobs." *Industrial and Labor Relations Review* 55(1): 3–21.

Blevins, Cameron, and Lincoln Mullen. 2015. "Jane, John . . . Leslie? A Historical Method for Algorithmic Gender Prediction." *DHQ: Digital Humanities Quarterly* 9(3).

Bóo, Florencia López, Martín A. Rossi, and Sergio S. Urzúa. 2013. "The Labor Market Return to an Attractive Face: Evidence from a Field Experiment." *Economics Letters* 118(1): 170–2.

Borup, Daniel, and Erik Christian Montes Schütte. 2022. "In Search of a Job: Forecasting Employment Growth Using Google Trends." *Journal of Business and Economic Statistics* 40(1): 186–200.

Brick, Carmen, Daniel Schneider, and Kristen Harknett. 2023. "The Gender Wage Gap, Between-Firm Inequality, and Devaluation: Testing a New Hypothesis in the Service Sector." *Work and Occupations* 50(4): 539–77.

Burn, Ian, Patrick Button, David Neumark, and Luis Felipe Munguia Corella. 2022. "Does Ageist Language in Job Ads Predict Age Discrimination in Hiring?" *Journal of Labor Economics* 40(3): 613–67.

Burnes, Daria, David Neumark, and Michelle J. White. 2014. "Fiscal Zoning and Sales Taxes: Do Higher Sales Taxes Lead to More Retailing and Less Manufacturing?" *National Tax Journal* 67(1): 7–50.

Casarico, Alessandra, and Salvatore Lattanzio. 2024. "What Firms Do? Gender Inequality in Linked Employer-Employee Data." *Journal of Labor Economics* 42(2): 325–55.

Clemens, Jeffrey, Lisa B. Kahn, and Jonathan Meer. 2021. "Dropouts Need Not Apply? The Minimum Wage and Skill Upgrading." *Journal of Labor Economics* 39(S1): S107–49.

Combes, Pierre-Phillipe, Bruno Decreuse, Morgane Laouénan, and Alain Trannoy. 2016. "Customer Discrimination and Employment Outcomes: Theory and Evidence from the French Labor Market." *Journal of Labor Economics* 34(1, Pt. 1): 107–60.

Consumer Financial Protection Bureau. 2014. *Using Publicly Available Information to Proxy for Unidentified Race and Ethnicity.* https://files.consumerfinance.gov/f/201409_cfpb_report_proxy-methodology.pdf.

Cullen, Zoe B., and Bobak Pakzad-Hurson. 2023. "Equilibrium Effects of Pay Transparency." *Econometrica* 91(3): 765–802.

Deng, Jiankang, et al. 2019. "RetinaFace: Single-Stage Dense Face Localization in the Wild." arXiv: 1905:00641v2.

Goldsmith, Arthur H., Darrick Hamilton, and William Darity Jr. 2006. "Shades of Discrimination: Skin Tone and Wages." *American Economic* Review 96(2): 242–5.

Google. 2022. "2022 Diversity Annual Report." https://about.google/belonging/diversity-annual-report/2022/.

Hellerstein, Judith K., Mark Kutzbach, and David Neumark. 2019. "Labor Market Networks and Recovery from Mass Layoffs: Evidence from the Great Recession Period." *Journal of Urban Economics* 113: 103192.

Hellerstein, Judith, David Neumark, and Melissa McInerney. 2008. "Spatial Mismatch or Racial Mismatch?" *Journal of Urban Economics* 64(2): 464–79.

Hellerstein, Judith, Melissa McInerney, and David Neumark. 2011. "Neighbors and Co-Workers: The Importance of Residential Labor Market Networks." *Journal of Labor Economics* 29(4): 659–95.

Hellerstein, Judith, and David Neumark. 2004. "Ethnicity, Language, and Workplace Segregation: Evidence from a New Matched Employer-Employee Data Set." *Annales d'Economie et de Statistique* 71/72: 19–78.

Hellerstein, Judith K., David Neumark, and Kenneth Troske. 1999. "Wages, Productivity, and Worker Characteristics: Evidence from Plant-Level Production Functions and Wage Equations." *Journal of Labor Economics* 17(3): 409–46.

Hu, Lingqian. 2019. "Racial/Ethnic Differences in Job Accessibility Effects: Explaining Employment and Commutes in the Los Angeles Region." *Transportation Research Part D: Transport and Environment* 76: 56–71.

Kline, Patrick M., Evan K. Rose, and Christopher R. Walters. 2024. "A Discrimination Report Card." *American Economic Review* 114(8): 2472–525.

LinkedIn. 2021. "Our 2021 Workforce Diversity Report." https://news.LinkedIn.com/2021/october/2021-workforce-diversity-report.

Loewenstein, Mark, David Piccone, and Anne Polivka. 2026. "Measuring Potential Effects of Introducing the 2024 Race and Ethnicity Standards into the Current Population Survey." In this volume.

Marinescu, Ioana, and Ronald Wolthoff. 2020. "Opening the Black Box of the Matching Function: The Power of Words." *Journal of Labor Economics* 38(2): 535–68.

McCue, Kristin. 1996. "Promotions and Wage Growth." *Journal of Labor Economics* 14(2): 175–209.

McKinney, Kevin L., and John M. Abowd. 2022. "Males Earnings Volatility in

LEHD Before, During, and After the Great Recession." *Journal of Business and Economic Statistics* 41(1): 33–9.

Monk, Ellis P. 2014. "Skin Tone Stratification among Black Americans, 2001–2003." *Social Forces* 92(2): 1313–37.

National Center for Science and Engineering Statistics. 2023. *Diversity and STEM: Women, Minorities, and Persons with Disabilities*. National Science Foundation Directorate for Social, Behavioral and Economic Sciences, NSF 23–315.

Neumark, David. 2024. "Age Discrimination in Hiring: Evidence from Age-Blind vs. Non-Age-Blind Hiring Procedures." *Journal of Human Resources* 59(2): 1–34.

Neumark, David. 2018. "Experimental Research on Labor Market Discrimination." *Journal of Economic Literature* 56(3): 799–866.

Neumark, David. 2012. "Detecting Evidence of Discrimination in Audit and Correspondence Studies." *Journal of Human Resources* 47(4): 1128–57.

Neumark, David, Ian Burn, and Patrick Button. 2019. "Is It Harder for Older Workers to Find Jobs? New and Improved Evidence from a Field Experiment." *Journal of Political Economy* 127(2): 922–70.

Neumark, David. 1999. "Labor Market Information and Wage Differentials by Race and Sex." *Industrial Relations* 38(3): 414–45.

Schneider, Daniel, and Kristen Harknett. 2019a. "Consequences of Routine Work-Schedule Instability for Worker Health and Well-Being." *American Sociological Review* 84(1): 82–114.

Schneider, Daniel, and Kristen Harknett. 2019b. "What's to Like? Facebook as a Tool for Survey Data Collection." *Sociological Methods & Research* 51(1): 108–40.

Serengil, Sefik Ilkin, and Alper Ozpinar. 2020. "LightFace: A Hybrid Deep Face Recognition Framework." *2020 Innovations in Intelligent Systems and Applications Conference (ASYU)*, Istanbul, Turkey, 2020, pp. 1–5.

Serengil, Sefik Ilkin, and Alper Ozpinar. 2021. "HyperExtended LightFace: A Facial Attribute Analysis Framework." *2021 International Conference on Engineering and Emerging Technologies (ICEET)*, Istanbul, Turkey, 2021, pp. 1–4.

Trotter, Richard G., Susan Rawson Zacur, and Lisa T. Stickey. 2017. "The New Age of Pay Transparency. *Business Horizons* 60(4): 529–39.

van der Klauw, Bas, and António Dias da Silva. 2011. "Wage Dynamics and Promotions Inside and Between Firms." *Journal of Population Economics* 24: 1513–48.

Xie, Fangzhou. 2022. "Rethnicity: An R Package for Predicting Ethnicity from Names." *Software X* 17: 100965.

III

Applications

9

Race, Ethnicity, and Measurement Error

Bruce D. Meyer, Nikolas Mittag, and Derek Wu

9.1 Introduction

For decades, researchers have examined racial disparities in economic outcomes (e.g., Duncan 1968; Massey and Denton 1993; Akee et al. 2019; Chetty et al. 2020). Survey estimates from the Census Bureau, for example, show that median household incomes were 35 percent lower and the poverty rate was nearly twice as high for Black Americans in 2022 compared to White non-Hispanic Americans (Shrider and Creamer 2023; US Census Bureau 2023). A growing literature using survey data has also uncovered important differences by race and ethnicity in the receipt of government programs (e.g., Gould-Werth and Shaefer 2012; Kuka and Stuart 2021; Forsythe and Yang 2021; US GAO 2022). One group of these papers emphasizes lower receipt of transfers, particularly Unemployment Insurance, by Black and Hispanic individuals, suggesting that state laws and administrative burdens have led to disparate access to these programs. A second group of papers, focusing mostly on means-tested transfers, examines whether or not Black and Hispanic individuals are overrepresented among program recipients and the extent to which the differences can be explained by income and employment patterns (see, e.g., Moffitt and Gottschalk 2001 or the review in Currie 2006).

For such analyses that rely on survey data, it is important not only that they capture resources and program receipt well overall but also that survey

Bruce D. Meyer is the McCormick Foundation Professor at the University of Chicago Harris School of Public Policy, a research associate of the National Bureau of Economic Research, and a nonresident senior fellow at the American Enterprise Institute.

Nikolas Mittag is an associate professor at the Center for Economic Research and Graduate Education–Economics Institute (CERGE-EI).

Derek Wu is an assistant professor of public policy and economics at the University of Virginia.

accuracy does not vary by race and ethnicity. Otherwise, the racial disparities in these analyses may be confounded by differences in survey error. Survey error has long been known to be pervasive for income and program receipt. For a wide range of income sources and years, weighted totals of recipients and dollars reported in the major US household surveys have been shown to severely understate administrative aggregates (Meyer et al. 2015; Rothbaum 2015). A number of papers go beyond comparisons of aggregates and link survey and administrative microdata to show substantial survey error in the receipt of transfer programs, most commonly in the form of survey underreporting (e.g., Marquis and Moore 1990; Huynh et al. 2002; Meyer and Mittag 2019a, 2021a). Despite these high error rates, differences in distributional statistics by characteristics such as race and ethnicity could still be unbiased if these characteristics do not predict survey errors. While some studies have found that survey error varies systematically with demographics (e.g., Bollinger and David 1997; Meyer et al. 2022), the literature has paid surprisingly little attention to the question of differences in reporting and how they affect analyses of disparities between racial and ethnic subgroups. Even when race and ethnicity variables are included in these studies, the empirical evidence is generally underemphasized or ignored.

In this paper, we fill these gaps by synthesizing the evidence from 18 empirical studies on differences in survey accuracy by race and ethnicity, focusing on differences between White, Black, and Hispanic individuals (and Asian individuals when available) in existing studies that link administrative records to survey data. We then discuss the consequences of the differences we document and summarize the evidence on the biases found for commonly estimated statistics. We close by discussing paths forward for improving the accuracy of survey estimates for minority groups. Our main focus is on means-tested programs including the Supplemental Nutrition Program (SNAP, formerly Food Stamps), Temporary Assistance for Needy Families (TANF), and General Assistance (GA), as well as Unemployment Insurance (UI), government-provided health insurance (Medicaid, Medicare, and the Indian Health Service), Social Security (Old-Age, Survivors, and Disability Income or OASDI), and private pensions in three major Census Bureau surveys: the American Community Survey (ACS), the Current Population Survey Annual Social and Economic Supplement (CPS ASEC, hereafter just CPS), and the Survey of Income and Program Participation (SIPP).

We begin by discussing how misclassification of program receipt—both reports of non-receipt by true recipients (false negatives) and reports of receipt by true non-recipients (false positives)—differs by race and ethnicity. These error rates are the most frequently reported measures of error in reports of binary variables like program receipt and are of key relevance for assessing and correcting the biases from survey error. We examine differences in raw false positive and false negative rates, as well as how they differ after controlling for other demographics. Black and Hispanic individuals have consistently higher false negative rates and usually higher false positive rates. We find striking evidence that race and ethnicity strongly and reliably predict survey error, both in comparisons of raw error rates and after adjusting error rates for demographics and income. The differences are large enough to skew important conclusions. For example, OASDI receipt is roughly twice as likely to be not recorded in the survey data for minorities. These patterns are robust across multiple surveys, samples, and income sources, suggesting that the differences in survey accuracy by race and ethnicity are not limited to a particular setting but are a general phenomenon. Thus, these large surveys appear to inadequately serve racial and ethnic minorities, for whom researchers and other users of the survey data have less accurate information than for White individuals.

We then discuss implications of these pronounced and systematic differences in survey error for key statistics. We examine the biases in rates of program receipt, amounts received, and models of program receipt, before examining implications for poverty rates on the basis of the available empirical evidence. Surveys on net understate receipt rates more severely for racial and ethnic minorities than for Whites. This pattern holds both for raw measures of receipt and for the effects of minority indicators in models of receipt. For government programs where the survey already indicated higher receipt rates among minorities, the differences are amplified. For programs where the survey indicated lower receipt rates among minorities, the differences typically disappear and sometimes even change sign. Given that survey data acutely understate the resources available to minorities and the degree to which they are supported by the safety net, we also document that poverty rates are systematically overstated for minorities. To understand how survey error gives rise to these biases in common statistics, we place these findings in the context of the limited theoretical results on the consequences of nonclassical measurement error.

We conclude by discussing some paths forward. Improving the accuracy of surveys is difficult, as the fundamental causes of the differences in survey error by race and ethnicity are unclear. They could arise from differences in stigma or in trust in the government, with the latter consistent with well-documented patterns of institutional distrust among Black Americans borne out of historical traumas (e.g., Brandon et al. 2005; Bajaj and Stanford 2021). These differences could also arise from neighborhood characteristics that may affect interviewers. They may further result from the way surveys are designed and implemented, with higher error rates potentially due to minorities being assigned to interviewers who have less expertise or are more likely to be of a different race/ethnicity. Linked data can help us understand these factors better, but improving surveys in this way can be a slow and difficult process. We argue that in lieu of identifying causes, linked data can point to circumstances when errors are severe and help us devise better strategies to reduce survey error. Linked data can also help data users understand likely biases or even improve estimates. However, a key conclusion of our review is that until more accurate data (or more reliable information on the nature of errors) become available, researchers should be cautious in interpreting estimates of racial or ethnic disparities in program receipt and income from survey data alone.

9.2 Overview of Studies and Methodology

In this section, we provide an overview of the linked data studies that we examine. We review key methodological aspects and discuss potential problems for studies of race and ethnicity. The main obstacle to evaluating survey accuracy lies in obtaining measures of truth that are comparable to the survey concepts of interest. For transfer programs, comparisons to administrative aggregates clearly indicate substantial underreporting (Meyer et al. 2015). However, evaluating survey accuracy for subpopulations, including those by race or ethnicity, would at minimum require accurate aggregate statistics for each subpopulation. Such measures of truth are rarely available. Linking surveys to administrative microdata has emerged as a key tool for remedying this problem (see Meyer and Mittag 2021b for an overview of data linkage methods used to validate income information). In this paper, we focus on studies that link survey data from the Census Bureau to administrative records. This choice focuses on heavily used surveys, keeps the studies we review relatively homogeneous in terms of the survey data used, and standardizes the quality of the administrative data and the methods used for data linkage. Table 9.1 lists the studies we rely on and discusses their datasets, income sources, and samples.

9.2.1 Data Sources

All studies in this paper are based on three major US household surveys conducted by the Census Bureau: the ACS, the CPS ASEC, and the SIPP.[1] The ACS is the largest household survey in the United States, with 2.8 to 3.5 million households (0.7–0.8 million prior to 2005) selected to participate during each year we examine. The CPS is one of the most important economic surveys in the United States. The linkage studies in our review all use the Annual Social and Economic Supplement to the CPS, which is the official source of income and poverty statistics in the United States. Since 2001, the CPS ASEC has interviewed a sample of about 94,000–99,000 households, although sample sizes in earlier years were closer to 60,000–

1. One study included in our review (Brummet et al. 2018) uses the Consumer Expenditure (CE) Survey, which is conducted by the Census Bureau under contract for the Bureau of Labor Statistics (BLS). However, the CE Survey is large scale and general interest, and it can be linked to administrative records using the same probabilistic linkage system as the other census surveys we examine. We therefore include it given the high degree of comparability.

70,000. Finally, the SIPP serves as the highest-quality source of information on low-income households and the receipt of government transfers. The studies in this review primarily use the 2001, 2004, and 2008 panels of the SIPP, which sampled approximately 25,000–45,000 households intended to be surveyed for a period of approximately four years.

These three surveys are each large scale and general interest, but there are also pronounced differences in their design that affect both non-response and measurement error (Celhay et al. 2024). The ACS questionnaire is administered by mail/internet, telephone, or an in-person interview, and the CPS conducts interviews in person and by phone. While the ACS and CPS only interview one household member (i.e., the reference person), the SIPP strives to conduct in-person interviews every four months with every household member over the age of 15 (US Census Bureau 2006, 2008, 2014). In terms of reference periods, the ACS asks about income and program receipt in the 12 months prior to the interview, the CPS asks about the previous calendar year, and the SIPP asks for monthly information in the four months preceding the interview.

The linkage studies we survey vary widely in the years and samples they use. Key sample restrictions are summarized in table 9.1 and are usually based on the availability of administrative data. For linked data to provide the necessary measure of truth, the administrative records must be accurate and sufficiently detailed to exactly match the survey concept of interest. The administrative program records used in these studies are typically based on actual payments and personal information verified as part of eligibility determination. Using actual payments avoids the problem that individuals may be kept in the administrative records after they have stopped receiving payments.[2] Consequently, we consider the administrative records used in the studies below—which are sometimes also benchmarked to publicly available administrative totals—to be sufficiently accurate to provide a measure of truth.

Studies that examine federal programs and income sources often utilize administrative records covering the entire United States, with UI amounts from Internal Revenue Service (IRS) Form 1099-G, Medicare enrollment records from the Center for Medicare and Medicaid Services (CMS), Indian Health Service (IHS) receipt from IHS patient registration files, Social Security amounts from the Social Security Administration's Payment History Update System, and private pensions from IRS Form 1099-R. For programs like SNAP and TANF that are administered by individual states, administra-

2. Using monthly payment information from the administrative records also allows researchers to match the timing of receipt to the reference period exactly. While there may be discrepancies in the timing of benefits between survey reports and administrative records, these discrepancies are likely to have minimal effects on extensive margin disagreement for surveys with longer reference periods (e.g., in CPS or ACS, where receipt is measured at any time during a 12-month period).

Table 9.1 Overview of studies

Study	Survey Data	Programs	Geography	Main Sample
		Panel A: Means-Tested Transfer Programs		
Colby, Debora, and Heggeness (2016)	2010–3 SIPP	SNAP	IL, MD, VA	All individuals
Fox, Heggeness, Pacas, and Stevens (2017)	2010–6 CPS	SNAP	IL, MD, OR, VA	All individuals, no imputed benefit amounts
Shantz and Fox (2018)	2010–6 CPS	SNAP, TANF	AZ, MD, ND, TN, ID, MI, VA	All individuals, not whole imputed, no imputed benefit amounts
Stevens, Fox, and Heggeness (2018)	2010–5 CPS	SNAP	AZ, IL, MD, OR, TN, ID, VA	All individuals, no imputed benefit amounts
Celhay, Meyer, and Mittag (2021)	2008–12 ACS, 2008–13 CPS, 2007–12 SIPP	SNAP, TANF+GA	NY	All households
Rothbaum, Fox, and Shantz (2021)	2014 CPS	SNAP	AZ, ID, MD, MI, NY, ND, TN, VA	All individuals
Giefer, King, and Roth (2022)	2014–20 SIPP	SNAP	12 States	All individuals (person-months), no imputed observations
Meyer, Mittag, and Goerge (2022)	2001 ACS, 2002–5 CPS, 2001–5 SIPP	SNAP	IL, MD	All households below 2xFPL, at least one household member age ≥ 16
		Panel B: Health Insurance Programs		
Klerman, Ringel, and Roth (2005)	1990–2000 CPS	Medicaid, Welfare	CA	All CA residents aged 15–65, no imputed benefit amounts, no imputed demographic variables

Davern, Klerman, Baugh, Call, and Greenberg (2009a)	2001–2 CPS	Medicaid	USA	All individuals, no partial Medicaid benefit enrollees, no SCHIP enrollees
Bhaskar, Shattuck, and Noon (2018)	2014 ACS	IHS	USA	All individuals
Bhaskar, Noon, and O'Hara (2019)	2014 CPS	Medicare	USA	All individuals age ≥ 65
Noon, Fernandez, and Porter (2019)	2011 CPS	Medicaid	USA	All individuals age ≥ 18, no partial Medicaid benefit enrollees, no SCHIP enrollees, no imputed or edited responses
Panel C: Old-Age Income and Other Income Sources				
Bee and Mitchell (2017)	2013 CPS, 2013 ACS	OASDI, Pensions	USA	All individuals age ≥ 65
Brummet, Flanagan-Doyle, Mitchell, Voorheis, Erhard, and McBride (2018)	2013–14 CE	Retirement Income	USA	All households
Dushi and Trenkamp (2021)	2016 CPS	Income (in retirement)	USA	All individuals age ≥ 65
Meyer, Wu, Stadnicki, and Langetieg (2023)	2011 CPS, 2010 SIPP	UI	USA	All individuals age ≥ 18, not whole imputed
Meyer and Wu (2023)	2017 CPS	Retirement Income, Social Security, SSI, SNAP, Housing Assistance, TANF	USA, 23 states for SNAP, 18 states for TANF	All individuals, no whole imputed SPM units

Note: This table provides an overview of the studies surveyed in this paper, including the data used, programs examined, and key sample restrictions. The original papers provide additional detail on the samples used and key definitions, which vary between studies. FPL = Federal Poverty Level; SCHIP = State Children's Health Insurance Program; SPM = Supplemental Poverty Measure.

tive records are only available for a subset of states. While Medicaid is also administered at the state level, its administrative records are available in a centralized fashion via CMS for the vast majority of states.

9.2.2 Data Linkage

Survey data and administrative records typically do not contain common identifiers that can be used to exactly merge the two data sources. Hence, data linkage is typically probabilistic and based on algorithms that try to find records referring to the same unit in separate data sources (e.g., Winkler 2021). By virtue of restricting our review to Census Bureau surveys, the studies we review all employ the same linkage methods based on person identifiers created by the Person Identification Validation System (PVS) (Wagner and Layne 2014). In short, the PVS uses person data (such as address, name, gender, and date of birth) from the administrative records and survey data to search for a matching record in a reference file containing all transactions recorded against a Social Security number (SSN). If a matching record is found, the SSN of the record from the reference file is transformed into a Protected Identification Key (PIK)—akin to a scrambled SSN—and attached to the corresponding original record in the survey or administrative data.

In addition to the administrative data being of high quality, the linkage itself must also be sufficiently accurate for the linked administrative value to approximate a measure of truth. Linkage error can stem from missed links and wrong links, although missed links almost exclusively arise from missing PIKs in the survey data (as PIK rates are close to 100 percent in our administrative records). Contrary to most other linkage studies, those using the PVS can readily quantify and adjust for missed links.[3] For recent years, PIK rates in the survey data tend to be high (over 90 percent), although earlier survey years had lower PIK rates. Except for one (Dushi and Trenkamp 2021), all studies we consider use the linkable subsample of PIKed observations, and a number of studies also use inverse probability weighting (IPW) to adjust survey weights and restore the representativeness of the sample to its population of interest (Wooldridge 2007). Section A of the working paper appendix provides more details on the sample adjustments used by each study.

Here, we are less interested in estimates being representative of some underlying population and more in estimates being comparable between subpopulations. This may not be the case if the association between having a PIK and survey accuracy differs between Whites and minorities, although

3. This advantage arises from the fact that the PVS links both the administrative and survey records to a third data source from which common identifiers are obtained. Linking both data sources to such a population register lets the researcher distinguish cases when a record was not linked to the other source because it was not included in the data (e.g., because the household did not receive the program) from cases when the record was unlinkable.

including race and ethnicity indicators in IPW models can partially address this concern. There is some evidence that PIK rates are higher for White individuals, but the evidence is mixed (Meyer et al. 2022) and the differences are generally small enough to yield only trivial effects on the patterns we find. Differences in PIK rates are more likely to arise from the uniqueness of names and the frequency of interactions with the government than from differences in reporting behavior.

Less is known about the frequency of linkage errors—i.e., the frequency with which a survey unit is linked to the wrong record from the administrative data. Such linkage errors, if random, will tend to mute differences between subpopulations and lead our results to understate the problems we identify. Thus, the main concern is whether or not the frequency of linkage errors differs by race and ethnicity. Little is known about the prevalence of linkage errors and their causes, although one may be concerned about undocumented immigrants (many of whom are Hispanic) having more linkage errors. However, the direction of the bias is not clear. Meyer et al. (2022) conclude that linkage errors are likely to overstate false positives and understate false negatives. We find false negatives to be higher for minorities, suggesting that greater linkage error for minorities would, if anything, understate the patterns we find.

Overall, the accuracy of the administrative data, the high PIK rates, and the sophisticated linkage procedure in our reviewed studies suggest that the linked administrative variables can be considered close approximations to truth. A caveat is that the information on covariates (including race and ethnicity) is self-reported. Detailed demographic information is an invaluable aspect of survey data and is often not available in administrative records. We therefore take the accuracy of these demographic variables as given throughout, although systematic differences in their reporting could bias our estimates. Misreporting of race and ethnicity in the survey could clearly affect our results. That being said, survey reports of race and ethnicity may in fact be more appropriate than those appearing in administrative records, as the latter indicators are not used in program administration and are likely to be less accurate and scrutinized than the information on payments used to validate receipt. And until more reliable information on these demographics becomes available, researchers will continue to rely on such self-reported measures—implying that the differences identified in our review provide the relevant measures of bias.

9.3 Differences in Survey Error by Race and Ethnicity

For the programs we examine, the main source of survey error appears to be error at the extensive margin—i.e., whether or not receipt is recorded correctly (see, e.g., Meyer and Mittag 2021a). We start by summarizing the evidence on raw error rates for race and ethnicity subgroups, followed by an overview of error rates adjusted for demographic differences in the population.

9.3.1 Differences in Raw False Negative and False Positive Rates

Validation studies of program receipt typically report separate error rates for false negatives (the share of true recipients recorded as non-recipients) and false positives (the share of true non-recipients recorded as recipients). The separate focus (rather than a single focus on overall error rates) stems from the fact that over- and underreporting have been found to differ substantially. For government transfers, studies have found high rates of false negatives that sometimes exceed 50 percent (Celhay et al. 2021), while false positives are much less frequent and often lower than 1 percent. However, these patterns differ by program, with false positive rates found to be higher for reports of Social Security and Medicare (Bee and Mitchell 2017; Bhaskar et al. 2019). In our review, we are interested less in the overall levels of error and more in how error rates differ between minorities and Whites.

Table 9.2 reports false positive and false negative rates from the studies that estimate these rates separately by race and ethnicity. Many of these estimates are taken directly from published tables, while others are calculated based on the disclosed results (see section B of the working paper appendix for details on these calculations). Almost all error rates are higher for minorities, with the magnitudes of the differences being substantively important. First, we find that minorities have higher false negative rates than Whites for all income sources examined (outside of private pensions in the ACS). Most differences are large in both absolute and relative terms. In absolute terms, the differences are largest for UI, with false negative rates in the CPS being a staggering 18.4 percentage points (55 percent) higher for Hispanic individuals, 15.9 percentage points (48 percent) higher for Black individuals, and 10.1 percentage points (30 percent) higher for Asian individuals relative to Whites. The UI results from the SIPP show largely comparable patterns. For OASDI, the gaps in false negative rates are similar in relative terms: 13.6 percent, 14.3 percent, and 15.5 percent of true OASDI recipients among Black, Hispanic, and Asian individuals do not have payments recorded in the survey, more than twice as high as the rate for Whites (6.4 percent). These gaps are fractionally smaller but still pronounced for Medicare (5.3–7.9 percent for minorities vs. 3.8 percent for Whites).

For SNAP, using SIPP data for 2010–2013, Colby et al. (2016) document sizeable differences in false negative rates of 3.6 percentage points (22 percent) for Black individuals and 4.1 percentage points (26 percent) for Hispanic individuals relative to Whites. Using more recent SIPP data for 2014–2020, Giefer et al. (2022) find false negative rates for Black individuals to be only 0.5 percentage points higher than for White individuals. For Medicaid, Davern et al. (2009a) find similarly high false negative rates for all subgroups, with Black and Hispanic individuals having slightly higher

Table 9.2 **False negative and false positive rates by race and ethnicity**

Study	Program	Sample	White		Black		Hispanic		Asian	
			F. Neg (1)	*F. Pos* (2)	*F. Neg* (3)	*F. Pos* (4)	*F. Neg* (5)	*F. Pos* (6)	*F. Neg* (7)	*F. Pos* (8)
Colby et al. (2016)	SNAP	2010–13 SIPP	15.9%	1.5%	19.5%	8.0%	20.0%	4.9%	-	-
Giefer et al. (2022)	SNAP	2014–20 SIPP	24.5%	0.4%	25.1%	1.5%	-	-	-	-
Klerman et al. (2005)	Medicaid	1990–2000 CPS	-	-	29.0%	5.0%	33.0%	5.0%	-	-
	Welfare	1990–2000 CPS	-	-	42.0%	2.0%	59.0%	2.0%	-	-
Davern et al. (2009a)	Medicaid	2002 CPS	42.8%	2.3%	42.9%	5.6%	43.7%	4.5%	47.1%	2.5%
Bhaskar et al. (2018)	IHS	2014 ACS	-	-	-	-	42.9%	-	-	-
Bhaskar et al. (2019)	Medicare	2014 CPS	3.8%	54.5%	5.4%	55.9%	5.3%	41.4%	7.9%	50.8%
Bee and Mitchell (2017)	OASDI	2013 CPS	6.4%	42.9%	13.6%	45.6%	14.3%	39.6%	15.5%	34.5%
	Pensions	2013 CPS	45.5%	10.1%	46.8%	11.2%	56.2%	5.6%	61.6%	8.1%
	Pensions	2013 ACS	43.7%	9.1%	40.0%	11.7%	49.7%	7.4%	51.3%	6.2%
Meyer et al. (2023)	UI	2011 CPS	33.2%	0.3%	49.0%	0.8%	51.5%	0.7%	43.3%	0.5%
	UI	2010 SIPP	33.3%	0.9%	50.0%	1.6%	42.2%	1.3%	45.7%	1.1%

Note: This table summarizes estimates of the rate at which true recipients are recorded as non-recipients in the data (columns labeled *F. Neg*) and the rate at which true non-recipients are recorded as recipients in the survey data (columns labeled *F. Pos*) for studies that report these statistics separately for subgroups defined by race and ethnicity. See table 9.1 for details on the studies and their methodology. Error rates in Colby et al. (2016), Bee and Mitchell (2017), and Giefer et al. (2022) are reported in a different format and were converted to conform to our definition. Hispanic is mutually exclusive with other race categories in Colby et al. (2016), Giefer et al. (2022), Meyer et al. (2023), Bhaskar et al. (2019), while it may be overlapping with other race categories in Klerman et al. (2005), Davern et al. (2009a), Bhaskar et al. (2018), and Bee and Mitchell (2017). For Bee and Mitchell (2017), we bring in results for "White, not Hispanic" (rather than "White") so as to not overlap with "Hispanic (any race)."

rates (within a percentage point) and Asian individuals having meaningfully higher false negative rates by 4.3 percentage points (10 percent).[4] False negative rates for pensions are also 1–16 percentage points higher in the CPS and 6–8 percentage points higher in the ACS for minorities relative to Whites, with the only exception being that false negative rates are 3 percentage points lower in the ACS for Black individuals compared to Whites.

False positive rates are also higher for Black individuals (compared to Whites) for all income sources examined. Some differences are large in absolute terms. For example, false positive rates for SNAP in the 2010–2013 SIPP are 6.5 percentage points higher for Black than for White individuals. As baseline false positive rates tend to be much lower than false negative rates (with the exception of Medicare conditional on being elderly), the differences also tend to be smaller in absolute terms. Yet, they tend to be much larger in relative terms. In fact, false positive rates among Black individuals are more than twice as high as among White individuals in four out of nine cases in table 9.2. However, the patterns are less pronounced for Hispanic and Asian individuals, for whom false positive rates exceed those of White individuals in four out of eight cases for Hispanic and three out of seven cases for Asian individuals. Thus, table 9.2 shows a clear pattern that false negative rates tend to be higher for all minority groups examined, while false positive rates tend to be higher for Black individuals in particular.

9.3.2 Differences in Covariate-Adjusted False Negative and False Positive Rates

While the error rates above differ substantially between groups, we do not have the results of tests for the statistical significance of such differences. Therefore, we also examine covariate-adjusted error rates in the form of marginal effects of race/ethnicity indicators from regressions where the dependent variable is a binary indicator for the misreporting of program receipt. A key advantage of looking at covariate-adjusted error rates is that one can use simple *t*-tests of the marginal effects to assess whether or not the differences are statistically significant for minorities relative to Whites (the reference group). Another advantage is that they are based on models that control for demographic characteristics. Both receipt rates and the demographics associated with survey error differ substantially between racial and ethnic groups and between programs. Consequently, it is particularly useful to understand whether survey data from units with similar demographic characteristics differ systematically by race and ethnicity.

Studies typically report separate models for whether receipt is missing for true recipients (false negatives) and whether true non-recipients are recorded

4. Note that Davern et al. (2007, 2009b) also examine false negative and false positives for Medicaid by race/ethnicity, but their analyses condition on being a recipient or non-recipient based on *survey* records (rather than administrative records). Given the lack of comparability to the other estimates reviewed, we omit these two papers from our review.

as recipients in the survey (false positives). Table 9.3 provides an overview of the estimated covariate-adjusted differences in error rates in the literature, showing a clear pattern of significantly higher false positive and false negative rates for racial and ethnic minorities—even for early linkage studies with small samples.[5] We focus our discussion on the estimates in Panel A of table 9.3, which are coefficients from linear probability models or average partial effects from probit models—and are thus easy to compare and interpret. However, the logit coefficients in Panel B yield similar qualitative conclusions. For Black individuals, the false negative differences are all positive and for the most part statistically significant. The differences are large, tending to hover around 7–11 percentage points higher than the false negative rates for Whites when analyzing SNAP, TANF, and UI. Black individuals also have higher covariate-adjusted false positive rates than Whites, with the sign of all statistically significant differences being positive across all studies. In line with the raw error rates discussed above, the differences in false positive rates are smaller in absolute terms (usually up to 2 percentage points higher for minorities) but still large in relative terms.

The patterns for Hispanics are similar, as they also have more frequent instances of both types of survey error than Whites. Yet, there are some slight differences. The magnitudes of the false negative gaps (relative to Whites) appear to be smaller and less statistically significant for Hispanic than for Black individuals. However, the range of estimates is large for Hispanics, with the difference in covariate-adjusted false negative rates being as large as 12 percentage points relative to Whites for UI (in the CPS). The covariate-adjusted false positive rates for Hispanics also exceed those of White individuals for most programs, but contrary to the case of Black individuals, there are some exceptions. Hispanic individuals have lower false positive rates for cash assistance (TANF and General Assistance combined) and Medicare. The results are more sparse and noisier for the remaining minority groups, with estimates for Asian individuals available only for UI, Medicare, and Medicaid, and estimates for American Indians available only for Medicaid and the IHS. Nevertheless, false negative and false positive rates appear to be higher for these groups, consistent with the more general patterns of covariate-adjusted errors being higher for minorities.

Overall, the covariate-adjusted error rates confirm the pattern of systematically higher survey error for minorities. After conditioning on covariates, the effect sizes tend to be slightly smaller and vary less across programs. This finding suggests that some of the differences between groups and programs are explained by demographic or other economic characteristics. However, large differences remain for all programs even after conditioning on many

5. Section C of the working paper appendix provides details on the covariates included in each study. These covariates are generally based on survey-reported demographic or economic variables and include measures such as family size, family composition, education status, age, income, employment, citizenship, geographic area, and disability status.

Table 9.3 **Differences in covariate-adjusted error rates between minorities and Whites**

			Black		Hispanic		Asian		AI/AIAN	
Study	Program	Sample	*F. Neg* (1)	*F. Pos* (2)	*F. Neg* (3)	*F. Pos* (4)	*F. Neg* (5)	*F. Pos* (6)	*F. Neg* (7)	*F. Pos* (8)
		Panel A: LPM Coefficients and Probit Average Partial Effects								
Fox et al. (2017)	SNAP	2010–16 CPS	0.0680***	-	0.0390	-	–0.0420	-	-	-
Celhay et al. (2021)	SNAP	2008–12 ACS	0.0678***	0.0098***	0.0410***	0.0085***	-	-	-	-
		2008–13 CPS	0.0958***	0.0116***	0.0554***	0.0139***	-	-	-	-
		2007–12 SIPP	0.0841***	0.0137***	0.0382**	0.0044	-	-	-	-
	TANF+GA	2008–12 ACS	0.0877***	0.0005	0.0467***	–0.0028***	-	-	-	-
		2008–13 CPS	0.0683	0.0015	0.0744*	–0.0017	-	-	-	-
		2007–12 SIPP	0.0800*	0.0059***	0.0508	–0.0027*	-	-	-	-
Meyer et al. (2022)	SNAP	2001 ACS, IL	0.0897**	0.0239***	-	-	-	-	-	-
		2001 ACS, MD	0.1110***	0.0082	-	-	-	-	-	-
		2002–5 CPS, IL	0.0503	–0.0046	-	-	-	-	-	-
		2002–5 CPS, MD	0.0509	–0.0094	-	-	-	-	-	-
		2001–5 SIPP, IL+MD	0.0672*	0.0207**	-	-	-	-	-	-
Meyer et al. (2023)	UI	2011 CPS	0.0945***	0.0036***	0.1190***	0.0037***	0.1120***	0.0031**	-	-
		2010 SIPP	0.1100***	0.0023**	0.0583***	0.0015	0.0866**	0.0012	-	-

Panel B: Logistic Regression Coefficients										
Colby et al. (2016)	SNAP	2010–13 SIPP (2008 panel)	0.1480	1.5300***	0.0860	0.5770**	-	-	-	-
Klerman et al. (2005)	Medicaid	1990–2000 CPS	0.3670	0.9270	0.7070	N/A	-	-	-	-
	Welfare	1990–2000 CPS	N/A	N/A	0.3470	N/A	-	-	-	-
Bhaskar et al. (2018)	IHS	2014 ACS, AIAN only	-	-	0.4300***	-	-	-	0.0900	-
		2014 ACS, AIAN only, age>=25	-	-	0.4400**	-	-	-	0.0100	-
		2014 ACS, non-AIAN	-	-	0.1900	-	-	-	–2.1200***	-
Bhaskar et al. (2019)	Medicare	2014 CPS	0.5200**	–0.1500	0.4000*	–1.2000*	0.3900	–0.4600	-	-
Noon et al. (2019)	Medicaid	2011 CPS	0.1900**	0.3000	0.2900***	0.8300***	0.3000*	0.9600**	0.2900	0.6300

Notes: This table reports estimated effects of minority indicators from models where the binary dependent variable indicates not receiving a program in the survey conditional on being a true recipient (columns labeled *F. Neg*) and models where the dependent variable indicates receiving a program in the survey conditional on being a true non-recipient (columns labeled *F. Pos*). The models vary in the sample and covariates used; see table 9.1 and the original studies for additional details. Logistic coefficients for Colby et al. (2016), Bhaskar et al. (2018), Bhaskar et al. (2019), and Noon et al. (2019) are reported as odds ratios in the published papers and were converted to logistic regression coefficients to facilitate comparability. Hispanic is mutually exclusive with other race categories in Celhay et al. (2021), Meyer et al. (2023), Colby et al. (2016), and Bhaskar et al. (2019), while it may be overlapping with other race categories in Fox et al. (2017), Klerman et al. (2005), Bhaskar et al. (2018), and Noon et al. (2019). When reporting results from Fox et al. (2017), we include estimates for "White, not Hispanic" (rather than "White") so as to not overlap with "Hispanic (any race)." Meyer et al. (2022) report results for non-White individuals whom we classify under the "Black" race/ethnicity category. AIAN = American Indian or Alaska Native.

covariates. While some of the bias in our multivariate analyses could also stem from systematic differences in reporting error of certain covariates (such as income), this is likely to have little effect on the overall conclusions.[6] That being said, a better understanding of the importance of these additional differences in survey accuracy by race and ethnicity is beyond the scope of the present review.

It is worth noting that the marginal effects we document for the race/ethnicity indicators are large compared to those for other predictors of misreporting. For example, Celhay et al. (2021) show that the difference in the false negative rates between Black and White individuals is consistently larger than (and up to almost four times as large as) the increase in false negatives when moving from income at the poverty line to twice the poverty line. The racial and ethnic differences in survey accuracy they find vastly exceed differences by education or household structure and are of similar magnitude or larger than differences by gender or between the elderly and non-elderly.[7] Consequently, the marginal effects of the minority dummies tend to be among the strongest predictors of survey error in the models that Celhay et al. (2021) estimate, falling only short of other selected indicators of program receipt and a few demographic characteristics.[8]

In conclusion, our findings in this section paint a striking picture of lower survey accuracy among racial and ethnic minorities. Race and ethnicity reliably predict survey error, with differences large enough to skew important conclusions. These patterns hold for multiple programs, surveys, and years and also persist across different minority groups (including Black, Hispanic, and Asian individuals), suggesting that our main household surveys poorly serve minorities by providing less accurate information about their incomes and program receipt.

9.4 Consequences of Survey Error

The patterns of survey error documented in section 9.3 raise concerns about the extent to which surveys can accurately provide key statistics of interest for racial and ethnic minorities. The nature of measurement error in surveys is non-classical, given that survey error is correlated with key covariates. Only a few general results exist for the consequences of such non-classical measurement error. Therefore, most of what we know about bias stems from empirical assessments using linked data. In this section, we

6. The differences we observe are meaningful both with and without covariates, and they are also robust to different sets of covariates.

7. Researchers have long been concerned about measurement error differences in program receipt by age (e.g., Haider et al. 2003). Here, we see that differences by race and ethnicity are much larger than differences by age.

8. These variables include indicators for household income being above 10x the poverty line (which systematically exceeds race and ethnicity effects) and whether or not the household head is disabled or employed (which exceeds race and ethnicity effects in some cases).

discuss the empirical evidence on bias from survey error in common statistics such as rates of program receipt, determinants of program receipt, and poverty rates. We show that survey errors can introduce substantial biases in estimates of racial or ethnic differences.

9.4.1 Bias in Estimates of Program Receipt and Average Amounts Among True Recipients

For differences in continuous variables such as raw gaps in average dollars received, the bias in the survey estimate for a group is simply the difference between the average survey reports and administrative values for that group. If this difference in survey error between groups is known, then the relative bias is straightforward to assess. Unfortunately, only a few papers report such estimates (see, e.g., Shantz and Fox 2018; Meyer et al. 2023). For binary variables like program receipt, the bias in statistics such as receipt rates is also just the difference between average misclassification rates—equivalent to the false positive rate weighted by the share of non-recipients net of the false negative rate weighted by the share of true recipients.

Table 9.4 reports measures of program receipt by race and ethnicity, both in terms of the number of recipients and average dollars received (conditional on receipt).[9] For each subgroup, we report the statistic of interest according to the survey data and the linked administrative variable, as well as the statistical significance of the difference (if reported in the study). Due to the severe net underreporting of program receipt documented in the previous literature, receipt rates are markedly higher using the administrative values than the survey values. This finding holds for all programs, samples, and minority groups studied. In line with the higher rates of survey error we document above, the increases in receipt rates when correcting for survey error tend to be largest for Black and Hispanic individuals. SNAP and pension receipt rates approximately double for all minority groups, and TANF receipt rates increase by approximately 50 percent for Black and Hispanic individuals and about a quarter for Asian individuals. In addition, UI receipt rates are higher by around 75 percent for Black and Hispanic individuals (compared to approximately 50 percent for Asian individuals). For White individuals, the biases in receipt rates are smaller in fractional terms, with SNAP and pension receipt less than doubling and TANF and UI receipt increasing by about a third. While tables 9.2 and 9.3 showed that minority groups have larger errors in terms of both false positives and false negatives, the results here suggest that they translate to greater net underreporting of program receipt. Thereby, survey error leads us to understate both the degree to which the safety net supports minorities and its contribution to reducing inequality.

9. Section D of the working paper appendix contains additional details on the sources for these statistics.

Table 9.4 **Bias in estimates of program receipt and average amounts for true reporting recipients**

				White			Black			Hispanic			Asian		
Study	Program	Sample	Statistic	*Survey* (1)	*Admin* (2)	Δ *Sig?* (3)	*Survey* (4)	*Admin* (5)	Δ *Sig?* (6)	*Survey* (7)	*Admin* (8)	Δ *Sig?* (9)	*Survey* (10)	*Admin* (11)	Δ *Sig?* (12)
Fox et al. (2017)	SNAP	2010–6 CPS	Receipt rate	6.0%	11.0%	-	17.0%	38.0%	-	16.0%	32.0%	-	5.0%	10.0%	-
			Average amount	$3,324	$3,660	-	$3,648	$4,080	-	$3,576	$4,092	-	$3,708	$3,912	-
	SNAP	2010–6 CPS	Receipt rate	8.5%	14.6%	***	21.8%	38.8%	***	22.9%	37.7%	***	5.4%	10.1%	***
			Average amount	$3,409	$3,607	***	$3,825	$4,172	***	$3,528	$3,638		$2,803	$3,286	*
Shantz and Fox (2018)	TANF	2010–6 CPS	Receipt rate	0.9%	1.2%	***	4.6%	7.1%	***	2.0%	3.0%	***	0.4%	0.5%	
			Average amount	$2,567	$2,196	**	$3,420	$2,640	***	$3,006	$1,455	**	*S*	*S*	*S*
Meyer et al. (2023)	UI	2011 CPS	Receipt rate	4.2%	5.9%	-	4.8%	8.3%	-	3.4%	6.2%	-	2.9%	4.5%	-
			Average amount	$8,065	$8,808	-	$6,917	$7,990	-	$7,556	$8,803	-	$9,421	$10,990	-
		2010 SIPP	Receipt rate	4.7%	6.1%	-	5.1%	8.2%	-	5.8%	8.8%	-	3.7%	5.3%	-
			Average amount	$7,194	$9,301	-	$5,762	$8,573	-	$5,963	$8,562	-	$8,023	$9,664	-
Brummet et al. (2018)	Pensions	2013–4 CE	Receipt rate	40.3%	74.6%	-	31.6%	65.7%	-	23.6%	48.3%	-	21.0%	45.3%	-

Note: This table reports receipt rates and average annual amounts received for studies that provide these statistics separately for subgroups defined by race and ethnicity. For each subgroup, the first column provides the estimate according to the survey data and the second column provides the same statistic according to the linked administrative variable. The third column for each group indicates the significance level of the difference between the two estimates (* 10%, ** 5%, *** 1%, with blank indicating not significant at conventional levels) if such a test was performed and "-" otherwise. See table 9.1 for additional details on the data and samples used. *S* indicates suppressed results. Brummet et al. (2018) also report results for AIANs and Pacific Islanders that we omit in this paper. Average amounts are conditional on receiving benefits in both the survey and administrative data (i.e., being a true reporting recipient). As a result, differences in average amounts reflect errors on the intensive margin, while differences in receipt rates reflect errors on the extensive margin. Average amounts in Fox et al. (2017) were originally reported at the monthly level and we have multiplied them by 12 to represent annual levels. Rates of program receipt and average amounts from Meyer et al. (2023) are reported in a different format and were converted to conform to our definition. Hispanic is mutually exclusive with other race categories in Meyer et al. (2023), while it may be overlapping with other race categories in Fox et al. (2017), Shantz and Fox (2018), and Brummet et al. (2018). When reporting results from Fox et al. (2017) and Shantz and Fox (2018), we include estimates for "White, not Hispanic" (rather than "White") so as to not overlap with "Hispanic (any race)."

Several studies also calculate average benefit amounts among true reporting recipients (i.e., those reporting receipt in both the survey and administrative data) and find more muted evidence of these patterns. True reporting recipients have higher average amounts of SNAP and UI and lower average amounts of TANF when replacing survey values with administrative data. For all recipients, the fractional gaps in dollar biases tend to be larger for minority groups than Whites (although these biases are positive for SNAP and UI and negative for TANF). While these results could be indicative of real intensive margin differences in dollars reported, they could also reflect differential selection of survey individuals into reporting by race/ethnicity. Fewer recipients report receipt among minorities, so those who are correctly recorded as recipients in both sources may be differentially selected in terms of reporting accuracy among minorities. However, we can conclude overall that the survey data greatly understate the access of racial and ethnic minorities to the safety net, with clear differences attributable to extensive margin variation in reporting rates.

9.4.2 Bias in Racial and Ethnic Predictors of Program Receipt

The raw differences in program receipt by race and ethnicity are used in many contexts to characterize disparities across groups. However, several studies go beyond raw receipt rates and account for differences in demographic or other characteristics between individuals when analyzing differences in receipt rates by race or ethnicity. In binary choice models of program receipt differences by race or ethnicity, there is both an attenuation of estimated effects due to mismeasurement of the dependent variable and an additional bias due to correlation of the explanatory variable with the error rates. We first discuss the main patterns in past empirical results, and in the next section discuss the econometric relationships that explain the patterns and provide predictions for future analyses of racial and ethnic differences.

To examine whether the patterns for raw differences hold for estimated differences in receipt after controlling for other factors, table 9.5 reports empirical estimates of the effects of race and ethnicity indicators on program receipt from probit models. For each minority group, the table reports the average marginal effect of the respective minority indicator in two receipt models—one using survey-reported receipt and the other using administrative receipt—as well as the level at which the difference in estimates between the two models is statistically significant. A useful aspect of these models is that they include covariates for other demographic characteristics.[10]

The results for Black and Hispanic individuals are remarkably uniform across datasets and samples. As a starting point, the SNAP and TANF

10. Section E of the working paper appendix provides details on the covariates included in each study. These covariates are again generally based on survey-reported demographic or economic variables and are similar to those included in the misreporting regressions whose estimates are in table 9.3.

Table 9.5 Bias in marginal effect of minority variable in models of program receipt

			Black			Hispanic			Asian		
Study	Program	Sample	*Survey* (1)	*Admin* (2)	Δ *Sig?* (3)	*Survey* (4)	*Admin* (5)	Δ *Sig?* (6)	*Survey* (7)	*Admin* (8)	Δ *Sig?* (9)
Celhay et al. (2021)	SNAP	2008–12 ACS	0.1098***	0.1708***	***	0.0987***	0.1405***	***	-	-	-
		2008–13 CPS	0.0291*	0.1075***	***	0.0743***	0.1445***	***	-	-	-
		2007–12 SIPP	0.0759***	0.1232***	***	0.0697***	0.1096***	*	-	-	-
	TANF+GA	2008–12 ACS	0.0177***	0.0753***	***	0.0114***	0.0579***	***	-	-	-
		2008–13 CPS	0.0204**	0.0835***	***	0.0122	0.0761***	***	-	-	-
		2007–12 SIPP	0.0258***	0.0647***	***	–0.0011	0.0286***	***	-	-	-
Meyer et al. (2022)	SNAP	2001 ACS, IL	0.0380**	0.0801***	***	-	-	-	-	-	-
		2001 ACS, MD	–0.0055	0.0355	**	-	-	-	-	-	-
		2002–5 CPS, IL	0.0211	0.0762***	***	-	-	-	-	-	-
		2002–5 CPS, MD	–0.0048	0.0118		-	-	-	-	-	-
		2001–5 SIPP, IL+MD	0.0767***	0.1069***	***	-	-	-	-	-	-
Meyer et al. (2023)	UI	2011 CPS, all	0.0060	0.0280***	***	–0.0020	0.0140***	***	–0.0090	–0.0090**	
		2010 SIPP, all	–0.0030	0.0170***	***	0.0070*	0.0240***	***	–0.0200***	–0.0170***	

Notes: This table reports the estimated effects of minority indicators in models of program receipt or take-up (i.e., from models where program receipt is the dependent variable). For each minority subgroup, the first column provides the estimate using the survey measure of receipt as the dependent variable and the second column provides the same statistic using the administrative measure of receipt as the dependent variable. The third column for each group indicates the significance level of the difference between the two estimates (* 10%, ** 5%, *** 1%, with blank indicating not significant at conventional levels) if such a test was performed and "-" otherwise. Table 9.1 provides additional detail on the studies and the data and samples used. All estimates are average partial effects from probit models. Hispanic is mutually exclusive with other race categories in Celhay et al. (2021) and Meyer et al. (2023), whereas Meyer et al. (2022) report results for non-White individuals whom we classify under the "Black" race/ethnicity category.

receipt rates according to the survey data tend to be higher for Black and Hispanic individuals than for Whites, with the magnitudes varying across samples. The results are more mixed for UI, where we tend to observe survey-only receipt rates being not significantly different for Black individuals, higher and lower for Hispanic individuals, and lower for Asian individuals relative to Whites. In comparing differences between the survey and administrative data, we find that the survey data understate receipt rates among all subgroups, even holding constant other covariates. The magnitudes of these biases are large and important: the covariate-adjusted Black-White and Hispanic-White gaps in the probability of program receipt typically more than double after correcting for survey error, and these differences are statistically significant for the most part. For SNAP, the differences in receipt rates (relative to Whites) increase by 4 to 8 percentage points after replacing survey values with administrative values. The differences are of the same magnitude for cash assistance (TANF and GA combined) at 4 to 6 percentage points. They tend to be a bit smaller for UI, but still reach up to 2 percentage points.

Survey data can sometimes get the statistical significance and even the sign of the difference wrong. This is particularly true for the analyses of UI (Meyer et al. 2023), where the survey data tend to suggest that minorities are no more likely to receive UI payments than Whites. When using administrative values instead, Black individuals have covariate-adjusted receipt rates that are higher by 2.8 percentage points in the CPS and 1.7 percentage points in the SIPP, relative to White individuals. Hispanic individuals also have significantly higher UI receipt rates than Whites (1.4 percentage points in the CPS and 2.4 percentage points in the SIPP) after substituting administrative values. On the other hand, Asian individuals tend to have lower rates of UI receipt than White individuals using either survey or administrative data.

9.4.3 Bias in Poverty Rates

For poverty rates, the differential biases by race and ethnicity depend on the error patterns in a complex way, as we discuss further in section 9.5. Consequently, it is impossible to predict how patterns of survey error translate to biases in poverty rates, even for the specific samples for which we have extensive misreporting information from linkage studies. That being said, some empirical evidence exists on the implications of survey misreporting for poverty rates. Table 9.6 reports poverty rates by race and ethnicity that prior studies have calculated separately using survey data and administrative measures, as well as the percentage change when correcting for survey error.[11] We do this for the regular poverty rate and when available for the share with incomes below various multiples of the poverty line, including 50 percent, 125 percent, 150 percent, and 200 percent.

11. Section F of the working paper appendix contains additional details on the sources for these statistics.

Table 9.6 **Bias in poverty rates (%)**

Study	Program	Sample	White				Black				Hispanic				Asian			
			Svy (1)	*Admin* (2)	*% Diff* (3)	*Δ Sig?* (4)	*Svy* (5)	*Admin* (6)	*% Diff* (7)	*Δ Sig?* (8)	*Svy* (9)	*Admin* (10)	*% Diff* (11)	*Δ Sig?* (12)	*Svy* (13)	*Admin* (14)	*% Diff* (15)	*Δ Sig?* (16)
Fox et al. (2017)	SNAP	2010–6 CPS	8.6	8.3	–4%	*	18.8	17.8	–6%	*	21.4	19.7	–9%	*	12.9	12.4	–4%	*
Shantz and Fox (2018)	SNAP & TANF	2010–6 CPS	9.4	9.2	–2%	***	20.2	19.4	–4%	***	23.3	22.3	–4%	***	13.4	12.9	–4%	*
Stevens et al. (2018)	SNAP	2010–5 CPS	9.0	8.8	–2%	*	17.9	17.0	–5%	*	22.3	21.1	–6%	*	12.9	12.8	–1%	*
Rothbaum et al. (2021)	SNAP	2014 CPS	10.0	9.6	–4%	***	23.7	23.4	–1%		24.9	24.1	–3%	*	15.8	15.8	0%	
Bee and Mitchell (2017)	Various	2013 CPS	6.6	4.8	–38%	***	18.4	14.0	–31%	***	20.9	19.1	–9%		12.4	11.7	–6%	
Dushi and Trenkamp (2021)	Various	2016 CPS	7.5	6.0	–25%	-	18.4	12.9	–43%	-	17.5	16.5	–6%	-	-	-	–	-
. . . <1.25x FPL	Various	2016 CPS	12.1	9.5	–27%	-	26.1	19.5	–34%	-	25.7	24.2	–6%	-	-	-	–	-
Meyer and Wu (2023)	Various	2017 CPS	6.4	3.9	–66%	-	14.7	7.5	–96%	-	13.6	8.0	–70%	-	8.3	5.7	–46%	-
. . . <0.5x FPL	Various	2017 CPS	2.5	1.1	–122%	-	5.2	1.6	–217%	-	4.4	1.8	–140%	-	4.2	2.3	–80%	-
. . . <1.5x FPL	Various	2017 CPS	14.7	10.4	–41%	-	32.7	20.5	–59%	-	34.5	22.6	–52%	-	16.4	12.4	–32%	-
. . . <2x FPL	Various	2017 CPS	25.7	20.0	–28%	-	49.4	38.5	–28%	-	52.8	41.0	–29%	-	26.5	22.0	–20%	-

Note: This table reports estimated poverty rates from papers that estimate poverty rates (or variants of poverty rates) separately for subgroups defined by race and ethnicity. For each subgroup, the first column provides the estimate using survey measures only and the second column provides estimates after replacing survey measures of the relevant income sources with the linked administrative variables. The third column for each subgroup indicates the fractional difference between the survey and administrative estimates (using the survey value as the baseline), and the fourth column indicates the significance level of the difference between the two estimates (* 10%, ** 5%, *** 1%, with blank indicating not significant at conventional levels) if such a test was performed and "-" otherwise. Table 9.1 provides additional detail on the studies, data, and samples used. Unless specified otherwise, all poverty rates are defined as having incomes below 100% the federal poverty line. Bee and Mitchell (2017) correct earnings, Social Security, SSI, interest and dividends, and retirement income. Dushi and Trenkamp (2021) correct earnings, Social Security, SSI, and interest and dividends. Meyer and Wu (2023) correct earnings, interest and dividends, retirement income, Social Security, SSI, AGI and other cash income, tax liabilities and credits, SNAP, housing assistance, and TANF. Hispanic is mutually exclusive with other race categories in Meyer et al. (2023) and Dushi and Trenkamp (2021), while it may be overlapping with other race categories in Fox et al. (2017), Shantz and Fox (2018), Stevens et al. (2018), Rothbaum et al. (2021) and Bee and Mitchell (2017). When reporting results from Fox et al. (2017), Shantz and Fox (2018), Stevens et al. (2018), Rothbaum et al. (2021), and Bee and Mitchell (2017), we include estimates for "White, not Hispanic" (rather than "White") so as to not overlap with "Hispanic (any race)."

Poverty measures are lower for all racial and ethnic subgroups after correcting for survey error, which is not surprising given that the surveys are known to miss so much program receipt (Meyer and Mittag 2019a). In most cases, the fractional reductions are larger for Black and Hispanic individuals than for White individuals, although the patterns vary considerably. When using the administrative data to correct for misreporting of SNAP alone or SNAP and TANF together, poverty falls for Black and Hispanic individuals by 6–9 percent relative to 4 percent for Whites (Fox et al. 2017), 4 percent relative to 2 percent for Whites (Shantz and Fox 2018), and 5–6 percent relative to 2 percent for Stevens et al. (2018). The one exception is Rothbaum et al. (2021), who find reductions in poverty of 1–3 percent for Black and Hispanic individuals relative to 4 percent for Whites.

The effects are more pronounced in the studies correcting simultaneously for survey error in multiple income sources, with some papers finding poverty measures to be two or three times higher according to the survey data. Meyer and Wu (2023), for example, find that correcting for measurement error in multiple income sources leads to reductions in poverty for Black and Hispanic individuals of 70–96 percent relative to 66 percent for Whites. The larger fractional declines for Black and Hispanic subgroups persist when looking at multiples of the poverty line. Dushi and Trenkamp (2021), in bringing in multiple administrative data sources for the elderly, find that poverty rates decline by 43 percent for Black individuals relative to 25 percent for Whites. The fractional decline for Hispanics, however, is only 6 percent. Finally, Bee and Mitchell (2017) also bring in multiple sources of administrative data to correct measurement error for the elderly. They find a slightly different pattern, with poverty rates falling by 38 percent for White individuals, compared to 31 percent for Black individuals and 9 percent for Hispanics.

In summary, the percentage reductions in poverty due to the administrative records are larger for Black individuals (and to a lesser extent for Hispanic individuals) than for White individuals in most studies examined. These results are a direct implication of program receipt—and thus the poverty reduction effects of programs—being more understated for Black and Hispanic individuals. In contrast, the fractional reductions in poverty tend to be smaller for Asian individuals, for whom differences in error and receipt rates tend to be smaller, relative to White individuals in the reviewed studies. Overall, these results provide further evidence for the extent to which survey data understate how well the safety net serves racial and ethnic minorities.

9.5 Theoretical Context for Estimated Biases

In reviewing the empirical results above, we have documented clear and systematic differences in survey error across racial and ethnic subgroups. Specifically, Black and Hispanic individuals tend to have both higher false negative rates and higher false positive rates than Whites. These same groups tend to have receipt rates that are most understated (both unconditionally and adjusted for covariates) and to some degree poverty rates that are often overstated most severely. In this section, we place these findings in the context of the (scarce) theoretical results on the consequences of non-classical measurement error to understand how survey error gives rise to these biases. Better understanding the relationship between survey error and the biases in common statistics can help illuminate which of the patterns we find are likely to generalize and under which conditions researchers need to be particularly cautious.

When analyzing means like receipt rates for a particular group, the bias is relatively simple. This result occurs because false positives cause an upward bias, while false negatives cause a downward bias. Thus, biases from both overreporting and underreporting can potentially cancel out. The fact that Black and Hispanic individuals tend to have lower net receipt rates in the survey despite having higher rates of survey error in both directions shows that the bias from false negatives outweighs the bias from false positives. When analyzing receipt rates conditional on covariates, however, the determinants of the bias are more complicated.

The key result from Meyer and Mittag (2017) is that the joint presence of false positives and negatives serves to collectively attenuate (rather than mitigate) differences across subgroups. In discussing the general bias from misclassification of a binary dependent variable in modeling the determinants of program receipt or receipt, Meyer and Mittag (2017) find that the bias in the coefficient of a predictor (such as a dummy variable for non-White) is proportional to the sum of the false positive and false negative rates for the full sample. Mathematically, in the simplest case of a linear probability model with errors that are not predicted by the covariates, the formula for the bias in the slope coefficients simplifies to $-(\alpha_0 + \alpha_1)\beta_k$, where β_k is the true slope coefficient and α_0 and α_1 are the false positive and false negative rates.[12] Consequently, even if there are no differences in error rates across subgroups, the differences in receipt rates would still be biased toward zero in the presence of overall error. The reason why both false positive and false negative rates attenuate coefficients is that for $\beta_k > 0$ false positives create positive residuals when $X\beta$ is low and false negatives create negative residuals when $X\beta$ is high. Both types of error thereby push $X\hat{\beta}$ toward zero. This tendency remains when covariates predict error.

The theoretical predictions have so far assumed homogeneous survey errors between subgroups, but there are further implications when the errors differ across groups. Specifically, when the predictor is correlated with net error (e.g., when receipt rates of minorities are over- or understated more than receipt rates of Whites), that leads to further bias. This stems from the general fact that differences in net reporting rates between groups diminish

12. In non-linear models, the two sources of bias we discuss here remain the same, but the overall bias contains two additional terms.

or amplify estimated differences in receipt. If a group has a higher net reporting rate than the omitted group, then the survey data will overstate relative receipt by this group (biasing the coefficient estimate upward). Conversely, lower net reporting rates lead to negative bias. In our case, true receipt rates are higher for minorities ($\beta_k > 0$) and net reporting rates are lower for minorities. Thus, the systematic part of survey error biases estimates toward (or even across) zero. This theoretical framework helps to rationalize the empirical results we document: the differences in receipt rates between Whites and minority groups are already understated in the presence of overall error that attenuates all coefficients, but they are further understated given the more severe net underreporting by racial and ethnic minorities. One would expect this finding to generalize whenever the difference in net reporting rates between groups has the opposite sign of the difference in receipt rates.

Beyond binary choice models, survey error can also lead to measurement error in the dependent variable of multivariate linear regressions (such as continuous amounts of income). If the dependent variable is affected by measurement error that differs across subgroups, then we may obtain biased estimates of regressors corresponding to such groups (e.g., defined by race and ethnicity). More generally, it can be difficult to predict the sign and size of biases, even when analytic results and empirical evidence on the errors are available. This situation occurs because biases depend on the distribution of other variables and their relationship to the error and variable of interest. This problem is greatly amplified for statistics that depend on the mismeasured variable in nonlinear ways, including simple descriptive statistics such as poverty rates.

The case of poverty rates illustrates the problem that determining the bias can quickly become intractable. The impact of survey error on poverty rates clearly depends on the relationship between survey error and income. If misreporting is more severe close to the poverty line, then the effect on poverty rates will be larger. The relationship between income and reporting may differ by race and ethnicity, implying differences in how a given level of misreporting affects the poverty rate of each group. In addition, the effect on poverty rates depends on the distribution of income itself. The closer households are to the poverty line, the more likely survey error is to affect their poverty status. Hence the bias in *differences* in poverty rates between groups also depends on how the distribution of incomes differs between these groups. Thus, even for simple statistics such as poverty rates, we would need to know not only the levels of reporting error by group, but also how reporting errors relate to income for each group and how income differs between groups. Thus, it is not surprising that the pattern of bias is most pronounced and most clearly aligned with the error rates for covariate-adjusted receipt rates. For poverty rates, substantial biases remain, but their relation to theory and the documented error rates is complicated as they are affected by additional forces.

9.6 Discussion of Paths Forward

In this paper, we consolidate evidence from a series of data linkage studies documenting high survey error rates for income sources that significantly and substantially differ between racial and ethnic groups. While few studies explicitly discuss the differences they find by race and ethnicity, their results paint a clear picture of lower survey accuracy for minorities. These patterns hold across programs and surveys and persist even after controlling for differences in demographics and income. The errors in program receipt lead to large biases in common estimates. For simple statistics such as receipt rates, the error rates we document allow researchers to gauge the size of the bias. However, for more complicated statistics such as regression coefficients or poverty rates, determining the biases quickly becomes intractable even when information from linked data are available. These biases are sizeable and systematically distort our understanding of the well-being of racial and ethnic minorities, as well as differences between racial and ethnic groups.

While we unearth a surprising number of estimates by race and ethnicity that paint a remarkably clear picture of lower survey accuracy, our review leaves many questions open. It is important to understand to what extent the patterns we find also affect other programs and other survey variables. Our review focuses on errors in program receipt, since these variables are easier to validate than other variables such as earnings or education for which there is no readily available measure of truth.[13] Yet, to fully understand how differences in survey accuracy skew our estimates of differences between racial and ethnic groups, we also need to know whether the patterns of severe survey error extend to these variables. For example, differences in the reporting of earnings, especially in the top percentiles, may have a substantial impact on racial income gaps. There is some evidence that inaccuracies in one dimension of survey error predict inaccuracies in other dimensions, suggesting the pronounced errors we document likely extend to other variables in some form.[14] But since little is known about differences in reporting

13. We identified several studies that compare survey reports of earnings to administrative records for subgroups defined by race and ethnicity (see, e.g., Pedace and Bates 2000; Cristia and Schwabish 2007; Bricker and Engelhardt 2008; Kim and Tamborini 2012; Abowd and Stinson 2013; Kim and Tamborini 2014; Chenevert et al. 2016; Brummet et al. 2018). While these analyses reveal important discrepancies across subgroups that strongly suggest the presence of differential measurement error, no measure of truth is available for earnings. Therefore, we focus on the clearer case of programs for which measures of truth can be easily gleaned from the administrative records. Black et al. (2003) also look at measurement error in the reporting of education in surveys, but they focus on higher education for which they bring in the National Survey of College Graduates.

14. For example, item non-response has been shown to predict measurement error (Bollinger and David 2001; Celhay et al. 2021), and measurement error in one variable appears to predict future measures of the same variable and errors in other variables (Bollinger and David 2005; Celhay et al. 2021; Bollinger and Tasseva 2023).

of other variables such as earnings by race and ethnicity, the direction of the bias in statistics such as income gaps remains unclear.

The studies we review only examine the accuracy of a given sample, but to understand survey accuracy more comprehensively requires understanding how other aspects of survey accuracy like coverage and weighting adjustments differ across groups. To fully comprehend how survey accuracy differs for minorities, we also need more research into whether the effects of other predictors of survey error such as income or education differ between racial and ethnic groups. To our knowledge, no paper includes interactions of other predictors of error with race and ethnicity indicators. More evidence is also needed on joint misreporting (i.e., whether survey error is correlated across different questions), which can be crucial for further understanding the biases from survey error. While our focus in this review is on household surveys administered by the Census Bureau, these patterns likely affect survey data more generally. Several studies have documented concerning rates of misreporting of transfer receipt for other surveys, including the National Health and Nutrition Examination Survey (Kirlin and Wiseman 2014), the ACCESS study (Rosen et al. 2007), the FoodAPS Survey (Courtemanche et al. 2019; Meyer and Mittag 2019b), and the Health and Retirement Survey (Dushi et al. 2017; Dushi and Trenkamp 2021). These and similar questions are beyond the scope of this review but could be examined in future studies that make use of linked data.

Perhaps the most important question raised by our paper pertains to how we can still make progress on understanding economic disparities by race and ethnicity in the presence of pronounced differences in survey accuracy and their corresponding biases for key estimates. The ideal solution would be to improve survey accuracy, but this can be costly and difficult—especially when little is known about the causes of survey error (Bound et al. 2001; Celhay et al. 2024). Differences in survey accuracy could arise from cultural factors, given that trust in the government may be lower among minority groups or that program receipt carries more stigma (see, e.g., Brandon et al. 2005; Bajaj and Stanford 2021). While strategies exist to reduce the effects of mistrust and stigma, they may only go so far if the root causes of deep-seated inequities remain present. Differences could also arise from neighborhood characteristics or from the way the surveys are designed and implemented. Such factors may be easier to address. For example, interviewers have been found to vary substantially in their error rates (e.g., Meyer and Mittag 2019b), and the differences in survey error between minorities and Whites could either stem from interviewers with higher error rates being more likely to interview minority groups or from match effects between interviewers and respondents. Differences arising from interviewer assignment or match effects could be reduced through changes in assignment and interviewer training.

Linked data can help us better understand these causes and the extent to which they contribute to differences in survey error. For example, the evidence from linkage studies casts doubt on a large role for stigma. While stigma should lead to higher false negative rates and lower false positive rates, we find both rates to be higher for racial and ethnic minorities. Our review also shows that rates of underreporting do not seem to be systematically lower for programs where stigma is likely to be lower, such as UI and private pensions. In addition, Celhay et al. (2022) find that reporting accuracy is better in neighborhoods with higher receipt rates, suggesting that stigma may be lower and reporting better in neighborhoods with a higher fraction of minorities with high receipt rates. Yet, linked data can help survey producers to devise pragmatic strategies to reduce survey error. For example, linked data can be used to examine which neighborhood or demographic characteristics predict misreporting and help interviewers to probe more when survey error appears likely. Linked data can also be used to study the role of interviewers to examine whether systematic changes in interviewer assignment or improvements in interviewer performance can provide a practical way to substantially increase survey accuracy.

Ultimately, survey data are unlikely to become completely error-free and any improvements are likely to take time. In the short run, researchers will have to rely on error-ridden data, raising the question of how survey users can harness the available information to improve estimates of racial and ethnic disparities. Surveys are increasingly linked to administrative data, which is one way of creating more accurate data on a timely basis. However, linked data are often not accessible to external researchers or may be unavailable for a certain population of interest. Without direct access to the linked data, researchers could still apply corrections to the survey estimates based on information derived from the linked data. For example, linked survey and administrative data allow for the estimation of models of the determinants of survey errors. Making the parameters of these models available to the public would allow survey data users to correct not only unconditional statistics, but also estimates of racial and ethnic differences. Several corrections for misclassified dependent variables exist (Hausman et al. 1998) and have been found to work well when information from administrative data is incorporated (Meyer and Mittag 2017). More generally, estimates can still be improved by imputing or integrating out mismeasured variables (Blackwell et al. 2017; Mittag 2019). Such corrections may work reasonably well even when only parameters from prior years or some states are available (Mittag 2019; Meyer and Mittag 2019b). In order for the corrections to work well for minority subgroups, the models also need to include indicators for these groups of interest. However, this strategy crucially depends on data producers providing the required estimates from the linked data on a timely and systematic basis.

In the absence of any information from linked data (i.e., for estimates based on survey data alone), our overview of the literature sends a clear message of caution in interpreting racial and ethnic differences. Corrections based solely on survey data and aggregate receipt rates have been found to work reasonably well for analyses of unconditional statistics such as SNAP receipt rates (Mittag 2019) but are unlikely to improve estimates of racial and ethnic differences as these corrections tend to replicate differences recorded in surveys. Our discussion above clearly shows that the bias depends not only on the frequency and severity of survey error but also on the statistic of interest. Thus, even if researchers do not have the information required to correct estimates, linkage studies can still provide them with useful guidance about when increased caution is warranted. A better understanding of the extent and nature of survey error can help researchers judge whether or not the bias is likely to be large enough to affect their substantive conclusions. But in the presence of error rates as high as the ones we document above, biases can often be large, and our review provides a strong call for caution.

In conclusion, we find high rates of survey error for racial and ethnic minorities. Survey error differs substantially between Whites and minorities, leading to large biases in important statistics. From a methodological perspective, these results indicate that more research is needed into the sources of survey error and how survey error and its differences by group can be reduced. Such research would help to improve both the quality of survey data and the ability of researchers to work with error-ridden data. Until these problems are ameliorated or at least better understood, researchers should be cautious when analyzing survey estimates of differences between racial and ethnic groups. Substantively, our findings show that these large surveys do not serve racial and ethnic minorities adequately, as they provide less accurate information about minorities than Whites. On the positive side, correcting for differences in survey error shows that the safety net serves minorities much more favorably than the survey estimates we currently rely on suggest.

Acknowledgments

We thank Mandana Vakil and Gabriel Rogow-Patt for excellent research assistance. For helpful comments, we thank Randy Akee, Larry Katz, Mark Loewenstein, Maxim Massenkoff, Robert Moffitt, and audiences at the 2024 NBER CRIW Conference, 2024 AEA Meetings, and 2023 NBER CRIW pre-conference. We are grateful to the Alfred P. Sloan Foundation, Russell Sage Foundation, Charles Koch Foundation, Menard Family Foundation, National Institute on Aging, and American Enterprise Institute for their support of the Comprehensive Income Dataset Project. For acknowledgments, sources of research support, and disclosure of the authors' material financial relationships, if any, please see https://www.nber.org/books-and-chapters/race-ethnicity-and-economic-statistics-21st-century/race-ethnicity-and-measurement-error.

Appendix

This appendix contains additional details on the sources that our main tables draw from, and the methods used for extracting relevant statistics from these sources.

Table 9.1: Overview of Studies

Table 9.1 presents an overview of the studies discussed in this paper. The first column lists the authors of each respective paper and year of publication. The second column lists the census survey(s) used in each paper and the relevant survey years (i.e., the years in which the survey was conducted). The third column lists the program(s) being evaluated using the linked survey and administrative data. In the fourth column, we specify the geography of the sample. Finally, the "Main Sample" column reports the restrictions for the broadest sample considered in each paper. Any further restrictions for specific results are subsequently noted alongside the relevant results.

We categorize the studies examined into three groups, based on the types of programs examined. The first set of papers focuses on means-tested transfer programs—principally the Supplemental Nutrition Assistance Program (SNAP), Temporary Assistance for Needy Families (TANF), and General Assistance (GA). The second set of papers examines health insurance programs—principally Medicaid, Medicare, and the Indian Health Service (IHS), although one of the papers also reports additional results for Welfare. The third set of papers analyzes programs relevant to elderly individuals (including Social Security, pensions, and retirement income) as well as a variety of other income sources (such as Unemployment Insurance and combined income sources).

Panel A: Means-Tested Transfer Programs

Colby, Debora, and Heggeness (2016)

Colby et al. (2016) link individuals surveyed between 2010 and 2013 in the 2008 SIPP Panel to administrative state-level SNAP records for Illinois, Maryland, and Virginia. The units of analysis for the matched survey-administrative record sample for these results are individual members of households. Prior to linkage, the authors kept SNAP recipients who were interviewed in the survey for all 12 months. The sample does not exclude imputations. The authors drop all un-PIKed individuals and continue to use the original survey weights for PIKed individuals (i.e., do not reweight to account for non-PIKing). For reference on the determinants of having a PIK, table 1 on p. 16 reports the results of running a logistic regression predicting the probability of PIK assignment in the SIPP survey data.

The race/ethnicity demographic categories include "Non-Hispanic White," "Non-Hispanic Black," "Non-Hispanic Other Races," and "Hispanic," which are mutually exclusive and exhaustive groups in this study.

Fox, Heggeness, Pacas, and Stevens (2017)

Fox et al. (2017) link observations from the 2010–2016 CPS ASEC survey (reference years 2009–2015) to administrative state-level SNAP records for Illinois, Maryland, Oregon, and Virginia. The linked survey-administrative dataset in this study is a pooled individual-level sample that covers Illinois and Maryland for calendar years 2009–2015, Oregon for calendar years 2009–2014, and Virginia for calendar years 2009–2013. The authors drop all un-PIKed observations and reweight using inverse probability weighting (IPW) to account for the bias arising from non-random missing PIKs. They exclude observations with imputed SNAP values and state mismatches, which occur when the state of residency for an individual is not the same in the survey and administrative data. For more information about the excluded observations, see figure 2 on p. 20 in the original paper.

The authors include race/ethnicity categories of "White," "White, not Hispanic," "Black," "Asian," and "Hispanic (any race)." When reporting results from this paper, we include estimates for "White, not Hispanic" to exclude overlap with "Hispanic (any race)." However, the estimates for "Black" and "Asian" may be overlapping with those of "Hispanic (any race)."

Shantz and Fox (2018)

Shantz and Fox (2018) link observations from the 2010–2016 CPS ASEC survey (reference years 2009–2015) to state-level administrative SNAP and TANF records for seven states (Arizona, Idaho, Maryland, Michigan, North Dakota, Tennessee, and Virginia). The matched survey-administrative records constitute an individual-level pooled sample that covers Arizona, Maryland, North Dakota, and Tennessee for calendar years 2009–2015, Idaho and Michigan for calendar years 2010–2015, and Virginia for calendar years 2009–2013. The authors drop all un-PIKed observations and reweight using IPW. They exclude households that do not complete the ASEC, do not respond to enough of the survey for an interview, and those that do not respond to enough income questions to be included in the analysis. They also exclude households for which program (SNAP or TANF) participation or benefit amount was imputed. Lastly, they exclude state mismatches (see above for definition).

The authors include race/ethnicity categories of "White," "White, not Hispanic," "Black," "Asian," and "Hispanic (any race)." When we report results from this paper, we include estimates for "White, not Hispanic" (rather than "White") so as to not overlap with "Hispanic (any race)."

Stevens, Fox, and Heggeness (2018)

Stevens et al. (2018) link observations from the 2010–2015 CPS ASEC survey (reference years 2009–2014) to state-level administrative SNAP records for seven states (Arizona, Illinois, Maryland, Oregon, Tennessee, Idaho, and Virginia). The matched survey-administrative records cover all individuals for calendar years 2009–2014 for Arizona, Illinois, Maryland, Oregon, and Tennessee and calendar years 2009–2013 for Virginia. The authors drop all un-PIKed observations and reweight using IPW excluding observations with imputed SNAP values.

The race/ethnicity categories included in this paper are "White," "White, not Hispanic," "Black," "Asian," and "Hispanic (any race)." When we report results from this paper, we include estimates for "White, not Hispanic" (rather than "White") so as to not overlap with "Hispanic (any race)."

Celhay, Meyer, and Mittag (2021)

Celhay et al. (2021) link the 2008–12 ACS, 2008–2013 CPS ASEC, and 2007–2012 SIPP to New York State administrative records from the NY Office of Temporary and Disability Assistance (OTDA) for all SNAP and Public Assistance (PA) recipients in the state. The sample of analysis in the matched survey-administrative data is restricted to households where at least one individual is PIKed. The authors weight all results using household IPW weights adjusted for the probability of having at least one member who is PIKed. For more information about the probability of being assigned a PIK based on different demographic characteristics, see the results in table A1 on p. 55. Imputations are not excluded from this sample.

The race/ethnicity categories included in this paper are "White," "Hispanic," "Black non-Hispanic," and "Other non-Hispanic," and are mutually exclusive. All demographic characteristics pertain to the reference person for the household.

Rothbaum, Fox, and Shantz (2021)

Rothbaum et al. (2021) link individuals from the 2014 CPS ASEC to state administrative SNAP records for eight states: Arizona, Idaho, Maryland, Michigan, New York, North Dakota, Tennessee, and Virginia. The authors restrict the sample to individuals in households where the head of household is PIKed. They do not mention reweighting to account for non-representative non-PIKing.

The race/ethnicity categories included in this paper are "White," "White, not Hispanic," "Black," "Asian," and "Hispanic (any race)." When we report results from this paper, we include estimates for "White, not Hispanic" (rather than "White") so as to not overlap with "Hispanic (any race)."

Giefer, King, and Roth (2022)

Giefer et al. (2022) link 2014–2020 data from the 2014 and 2018 SIPP Panels to state-level administrative SNAP records from 12 states. The matched survey-administrative records cover Connecticut for calendar years 2013–2015, Hawaii, Idaho, Indiana, Mississippi, Nevada, New York, Tennessee, and Utah for calendar years 2013–2019, Maryland for calendar years 2013–2016, North Dakota for calendar years 2014–2018, and Oregon for calendar years 2013–2017. Only survey respondents who are observed in the survey and report their SNAP status for all 12 months are included. The sample consists of un-PIKed non-imputed individuals and estimates are unweighted. The unit of analysis is a person-month.

The race/ethnicity categories included in the paper are "Non-Hispanic White," "Non-Hispanic Black," and "Other," and are mutually exclusive. We suspect that "Other" includes Hispanics and non-Hispanic other races.

Meyer, Mittag, and Goerge (2022)

Meyer et al. (2022) link the 2001 ACS, 2002–2005 CPS ASEC, and the 2001–2005 SIPP to state-level administrative SNAP records for two states: Illinois and Maryland. The Illinois administrative records come from the Illinois Longitudinal Public Assistance Research Database (ILPARD) created by Chapin Hall from data provided by the Illinois Department of Human Services (IDHS), while the Maryland administrative records come from the Client Automated Resource and Eligibility System (CARES) of the Maryland Department of Human Resources.

The sample includes all households with income less than twice the federal poverty line with at least one household member aged 16 or older and at least one PIKed household member. Sample weights are adjusted for nonrandom missing PIKs and do not exclude imputations. The results of probit models predicting the probability of an individual having a PIK based on demographic characteristics are available in table 1 on p. 45 in the online appendix of the original paper. All demographic characteristics pertain to the reference person.

The race/ethnicity categories included in this paper are "White" and "Non-White," which are mutually exclusive.

Panel B: Health Insurance Programs

Klerman, Ringel, and Roth (2005)

Klerman et al. (2005) link the 1990–2000 CPS ASEC to MEDS (Medi-Cal Eligibility Data System) administrative data for the California Medicaid program, Medi-Cal.

The sample for this analysis is made up of all individuals aged 15 to 65 at the time of the CPS ASEC survey who are California residents. The authors drop all un-PIKed observations, any "movers" (those who were in California in the year prior to being surveyed but not at the time of the survey), and any observations with imputed responses for Medicaid or welfare enrollment or imputations for basic demographic characteristics used in matching (i.e., gender, age). They include race/ethnicity categories of "Black" and "Hispanic" in their paper, which may be overlapping groups.

Davern, Klerman, Baugh, Call, and Greenberg (2009a)

Davern et al. (2009a) link the 2002 CPS ASEC to administrative Medicaid records from the Medicaid Statistical Information System (MSIS). The sample covers all individuals in the United States. All un-PIKed observations are dropped, and the remaining observations are reweighted to align with the full CPS ASEC population. The authors drop SCHIP enrollees, duplicates, partial benefit Medicaid cases, and individuals living in institutional group quarters. They do not exclude imputations.

The demographics for which results are available include "White," "Black," "Native American," "Asian Pacific Islander," and "Hispanic." Note that "Hispanic" appears under a separate category of "Hispanic ethnicity" rather than under the "Race/ethnicity" category under which the rest of the groups are classified. This indicates that "Hispanic" likely overlaps with the other race categories.

Bhaskar, Shattuck, and Noon (2018)

Bhaskar et al. (2018) link the 2014 ACS to administrative records on the Indian Health Service (IHS) from the 2014 IHS Patient Registration file. The authors drop all un-PIKed observations and use ACS sample weights adjusted to address the probability of not being randomly assigned a PIK. They do not exclude imputations but limit the sample to records for individuals who reside within the 50 states and the District of Columbia.

The authors examine two sets of binary race/ethnicity categories: (1) Hispanic vs. non-Hispanic; (2) AIAN (American Indian or Alaska Native) ancestry vs. no AIAN ancestry (as reported in ACS). Hispanic and AIAN may be overlapping.

Bhaskar, Noon, and O'Hara (2019)

Bhaskar et al. (2019) link the 2014 CPS ASEC to administrative Medicare records from the Medicare Enrollment Database (MEDB) for the civilian noninstitutionalized population. Results are restricted to those aged 65 and older at the time of the survey with addresses within the 50 states or the District of Columbia. The authors also remove all duplicate records and individuals who have a listed date of death. They do not exclude imputations but drop all un-PIKed observations and adjust survey weights accordingly for non-random non-PIKing.

The authors include a "Race and Hispanic Origin" category with the following variables: "Non-Hispanic White alone," "Non-Hispanic Black alone," "Non-Hispanic Asian alone," "Non-Hispanic Other," and "Hispanic." The race/ethnicity groups are mutually exclusive and exhaustive.

Noon, Fernandez, and Porter (2019)

Noon et al. (2019) link the 2011 CPS ASEC to Medicaid administrative records from the MSIS submitted by states to the Centers for Medicare and Medicaid Services (CMS). The sample includes individuals aged 18 and older. The authors drop individuals living in institutional group quarters and duplicate records. They exclude partial Medicaid benefit enrollees and SCHIP enrollees. They also drop all un-PIKed observations, adjust survey weights to compensate for the observations that do not have a PIK, and exclude imputations.

The authors include distinct race and ethnicity categories. The first is a variable indicating "Hispanic origin" vs. "not Hispanic." The second is a race category, which includes "White alone," "Black alone," "American Indian or Alaska Native alone," "Asian alone," "Native Hawaiian or Pacific Islander alone," or "Two or more races." As such, the Hispanic and race categories can overlap, but the groups within the race category are mutually exclusive.

Panel C: Old-Age Income and Other Income Sources

Bee and Mitchell (2017)

Bee and Mitchell (2017) link the 2013 CPS ASEC and the 2013 ACS to administrative records comprised of Social Security Administration (SSA) and Internal Revenue Service (IRS) microdata. The administrative data include Forms W-2, 1040, and 1099-R from the IRS as well as total Social Security (OASDI) and Supplemental Security Income (SSI) benefits from the SSA, and we focus on the authors' estimates on OASDI and pensions. The sample is restricted to individuals aged 65 or older. The authors do not exclude imputations but drop un-PIKed observations and adjust weights for selection into having a PIK.

The race/ethnicity categories of "White," "White, not Hispanic," "Black," "Asian," and "Hispanic (any race)" are included in the paper. We bring in results for "White, not Hispanic" (rather than "White") so as to not overlap with "Hispanic (any race)."

Brummet, Flanagan-Doyle, Mitchell, Voorheis, Erhard, and McBride (2018)

Brummet et al. (2018) link the 2013–2014 Consumer Expenditure (CE) survey to IRS administrative records from Forms 1040, W-2, and 1099 information returns. They evaluate retirement income based on administrative data from Form 1099-Rs. The authors conduct the analysis at the household level using demographic characteristics of the individual respondents.

The race/ethnicity categories included in their analysis are "White Alone," "Black Alone," "Asian Alone," and "Other Race." Hispanic origin is a separate demographic category in this paper ("Hispanic" vs. "Not Hispanic") and can overlap with the other race/ethnicity groups.

Dushi and Trenkamp (2021)

Dushi and Trenkamp (2021) link the 2016 CPS ASEC to administrative records from the SSA and IRS. The SSA administrative records provide data on earnings, Social Security benefits, and SSI payments. The IRS administrative records provide data on retirement income.

The sample is restricted to individuals aged 65 and older and includes un-PIKed observations. The paper is concerned with measuring family income of older individuals, defining a family to be "a group of two or more individuals (one of whom is the householder) related by birth, marriage, or adoption and residing together."

The race/ethnicity categories used in this analysis are "Non-Hispanic White," "Non-Hispanic Black," "Non-Hispanic other," and "Hispanic (any race)" and are mutually exclusive and exhaustive groups.

Meyer, Wu, Stadnicki, and Langetieg (2023)

Meyer et al. (2023) link the 2011 CPS ASEC and 2010 data from the 2008 SIPP Panel to administrative records from IRS Form 1099-G containing information on Unemployment Insurance (UI) amounts. The sample is restricted to individuals above age 18. Wholly imputed observations are excluded for estimates using the CPS ASEC (but not for estimates using the SIPP), and all un-PIKed observations are dropped. The remaining observations are reweighted to be representative of the entire population.

The authors include race/ethnicity categories of "White," "Black, non-Hispanic," "Asian, non-Hispanic," "Other or multi-race, non-Hispanic," and "Hispanic" in their analyses, which are mutually exclusive and exhaustive categories.

Meyer and Wu (2023)

Meyer and Wu (2023) link the 2017 CPS ASEC to various administrative records. They exclude individuals in SPM units where anyone is wholly imputed or all members are un-PIKed and adjust survey weights for non-randomness in whole imputations and PIKing.

The race/ethnicity categories include "White (non-Hispanic)," "Black (non-Hispanic)," "Asian (non-Hispanic)," "Other (non-Hispanic)," and "Hispanic," which are mutually exclusive and exhaustive groups.

Table 9.2: False Negative and False Positive Rates by Race and Ethnicity

Table 9.2 presents the estimates of false negative rates (defined as the share of true recipients who are erroneously recorded as non-recipients in the survey data) and false positive rates (defined as the share of true non-recipients who are erroneously recorded as recipients in the survey data). Here, we provide additional details on the results from each paper, identifying the location of the originally published results, definitions used by the authors, and any necessary calculations we performed to convert published numbers to false negative and false positive rates (as defined above).

Colby et al. (2016)

Colby et al. (2016) report unweighted counts of true negatives (true non-recipients who do not report receipt in the survey), false positives, false negatives, and true positives (true recipients who report receipt in the survey) by race and ethnicity in table 3 on pp. 20–23 in the original paper. The authors do not report false positive and false negative rates scaled by the relevant populations, but we are able to calculate these rates using the published counts.

Specifically, false positive rates can be calculated as follows: (false positive counts)/(false positive counts + true negative counts). False negative rates can be calculated as follows: (false negative counts)/(false negative counts + true positive counts). We therefore obtain the following estimates:

- White False Negative Rate: (182)/(182+962)
- White False Positive Rate: (230)/(230+15,416)
- Black False Negative Rate: (294)/(294+1,217)
- Black False Positive Rate: (278)/(278+3,201)
- Hispanic False Negative Rate: (64)/(64+256)
- Hispanic False Positive Rate: (68)/(68+1,321)

A caveat of our calculations is that they are based off unweighted counts, and so reflect false positive and false negative rates for the unweighted sample rather than the population.

Giefer et al. (2022)

Giefer et al. (2022) report rates of demographic characteristics among subgroups defined by SNAP receipt concurrence (true negatives, false positives, false negatives, and true positives) in table 4 (p. 13). To calculate false positive and false negative rates, we start by backing out the overall counts of true negatives, false positives, false negatives, and true positives from the unconditional shares and sample sizes. We can then use these counts to calculate false positive rates as (false positive counts)/(false positive counts + true negative counts) and false negative rates as (false negative counts)/(false negative counts + true positive counts).

This yields the following estimates:

- White False Negative Rate: (.45*2,600)/(.45*2,600 + .48*7,500)
- White False Positive Rate: (.35*350)/(.35*350 + .73*44,000)
- Black False Negative Rate: (.27*2,600)/(.27*2,600 + .28*7,500)
- Black False Positive Rate: (.21*350)/(.21*350 + .11*44,000)

A caveat of our calculations is that they are based off unweighted shares and sample sizes (i.e., person-months), and so reflect false positive and false negative rates for the unweighted sample rather than the population.

Klerman et al. (2005)

Klerman et al. (2005) report two types of false positives and false negatives drawing a distinction between what they call the "behavioral" type (conditioning on truth using the administrative data) and the "imputational" type (conditioning on the survey response). As such, the authors define behavioral false negatives as individuals reporting "not enrolled" in the CPS given that the MEDS data reports enrollment, while behavioral false positives indicate individuals reporting "enrolled" in the CPS given that the administrative data does not indicate enrollment. On the other hand, imputational false negatives indicate being enrolled in MEDS given answering "not enrolled" in the CPS, while imputational false positives correspond to being not enrolled in the MEDS given answering "enrolled" in the CPS. For the purposes of this paper, we are only concerned with the behavioral error results from Klerman et al. (2005).

Klerman et al. (2005) calculate misreporting error rates for Medicaid (specifically Medi-Cal) and Welfare (AFDC/TANF/CalWORKs). We report the results for false negative and false positive rates (specifically, what the authors refer to as "behavioral" misreporting rates), which can be found in columns 1 and 2 of table 3.4 on p. 20 of the paper.

Davern et al. (2009a)

Davern et al. (2009a) calculate the share of true Medicaid recipients (table 2 on pp. 975–77) and true Medicaid non-recipients (table 3 on pp. 978–79) who have the following responses in the CPS: "Medicaid only," "Medicaid and something else," "some other type of health insurance coverage," and "uninsured." False negative rates can therefore be calculated as the sum of "persons coded with some other type of health insurance coverage" and "persons coded as being uninsured" among true Medicaid recipients (using table 2). False positive rates can therefore be calculated as the sum of "persons coded Medicaid only" and "persons coded Medicaid and something else" among true Medicaid non-recipients (using table 3).

This yields the following estimates:

- White False Negative Rate: 25.7 percent + 17.1 percent
- White False Positive Rate: 1.0 percent + 1.3 percent
- Black False Negative Rate: 25.1 percent + 17.8 percent
- Black False Positive Rate: 2.9 percent. 2.7 percent
- Hispanic False Negative Rate: 21.2 percent + 22.5 percent
- Hispanic False Positive Rate: 3.0 percent + 1.5 percent
- Asian False Negative Rate: 30.0 percent + 17.1 percent
- Asian False Positive Rate: 1.4 percent + 1.1 percent

Bhaskar et al. (2018)

Bhaskar et al. (2018) report false positive and false negative error rates for reports of Indian Health Service (IHS) coverage. Values for false negatives are taken from table 4 found on p. 24. However, the authors define false positives as the share of survey recipients who are not true recipients—which is inconsistent with our preferred definition. As a result, we do not include false positive values from the paper.

Bhaskar et al. (2019)

Bhaskar et al. (2019) report false negative rates (defined as the share of survey individuals aged 65+ who link to administrative Medicare records but do not report survey Medicare receipt) in table 4 on pp. 1816–1817. False positive rates (defined as the share of survey individuals aged 65+ who do not link to administrative Medicare records but do report survey Medicare receipt) are taken from table 5 on pp. 1819–1820.

Bee and Mitchell (2017)

Bee and Mitchell (2017) report unconditional rates of true negatives, false positives, false negatives, and true positives for OASDI in the 2013 CPS ASEC in table 6, Panel A on pp. 48–50, for private pension income in the 2013 CPS ASEC in table 6, Panel B on pp. 51–53, and for private pension income in the 2013 ACS in appendix table 7 on pp. 79–81. False negative rates can be calculated as (false negative rates)/(false negative rates + true positive rates) and are reported in column 7 of the respective tables. However, we calculate false positive rates ourselves as (false positive rates)/(false positive rates + true negative rates), using the numbers disclosed in these tables.

This yields the following estimates for OASDI using the CPS:

- White False Positive Rate: (.051)/(.051 + .068)
- Black False Positive Rate: (.072)/(.072 + .086)
- Hispanic False Positive Rate: (.084)/(.084 + .128)
- Asian False Positive Rate: (.118)/(.118 + .224)

This yields the following estimates for pensions using the CPS:

- White False Positive Rate: (.035)/(.035 + .310)
- Black False Positive Rate: (.050)/(.050 + .396)
- Hispanic False Positive Rate: (.035)/(.035 + .594)
- Asian False Positive Rate: (.050)/(.050 + .571)

This yields the following estimates for pensions using the ACS:

- White False Positive Rate: (.032)/(.032 + .320)
- Black False Positive Rate: (.054)/(.054 + .409)
- Hispanic False Positive Rate: (.048)/(.048 + .602)
- Asian False Positive Rate: (.040)/(.040 + .605)

Meyer et al. (2023)

Meyer et al. (2023) report false negative and false positive rates for Unemployment Insurance (UI) receipt. Values are taken from table 3 (p. 48) of the unpublished paper.

Table 9.3: Differences in Covariate-Adjusted Error Rates Between Minorities and Whites

Table 9.3 reports the effects of minority indicators from regression models where the binary dependent variables are either an indicator for being a false negative (where the sample consists of true recipients) or an indicator for being a false positive (where the sample consists of true non-recipients). Here, we provide additional details on the location of the originally published results, definitions used by the authors, and any calculations we performed to convert published numbers to an alternate format. We report results from papers that used probit models (Panel A) and logit models (Panel B). While certain papers report results from logit models as odds ratios, for ease of comparison we convert these numbers to logistic regression coefficients (more details below).

All of the covariates in these models are survey-reported variables (unless otherwise noted).

Panel A: Linear Probability Model (LPM) Coefficients and Probit Average Partial Effects

Fox et al. (2017)

Fox et al. (2017) report results estimating effects of demographic characteristics on false negative misreporting using a linear probability model (table 7 on pp. 33–36). We focus on the coefficients for “Black,” “Asian,” and “Hispanic (any race),” which are evaluated relative to the omitted “White” category.

Other key covariates include log earnings, the number of children in the household, household head type (married partner—omitted, cohabiting partners, female reference person, male reference person, unrelated individuals); nativity (no foreign-born individuals—omitted, at least one foreign-born individual); education (share of household at least 25 years old with less than high school diploma, share of household at least 25 years old with a high school diploma—omitted, share of household at least 25 years old with some college, share of household at least 25 years old with a bachelor’s degree, no one 25 years old or older); whether owning or renting (owner/mortgage—omitted, owner/no mortgage/rent free, renter); geographic area (inside principal cities—omitted, outside principal cities but within MSA [Metropolitan Statistical Area], outside MSA); health insurance (with private insurance—omitted, with public and no private insurance, not insured); work status (share with full-time year-round work—omitted, share with less than full-time year-round work, share that did not work at least one week, no one of working age 18–64 in the household); and disability (no one with a disability in the household—omitted, at least one individual with a disability in the household). The regression includes year-level and state-level fixed effects.

Celhay et al. (2021)

Celhay et al. (2021) report the determinants of false negatives and false positives for SNAP and TANF+GA (referred to as "PA" for Public Assistance in the paper), using average marginal effects from probit models for three surveys (ACS, CPS ASEC, and SIPP). The false negative estimates are reported in table 4 on p. 48 and false positive estimates are reported in table 5 on p. 49. We focus on the estimates for "Hispanic" and "Black non-Hispanic," evaluated relative to the omitted "White" category.

Other key covariates include family type (single adult with no children, single adult with children, multiple adults with children—omitted, multiple adults no children); number of children; number of adults; geographic area (non-rural—omitted, rural); gender (female—omitted, male); disability status (not disabled—omitted, disabled); age (16–29, 30–39, 40–49—omitted, 50–59, 60–69, 70+); education (less than high school, high school graduate, college graduate—omitted, complete graduate and beyond); household language (household language is English only); English proficiency (speaks English poorly); citizenship status (citizen—omitted, non-citizen); income (household income/poverty line, household income/poverty line>10); employment (anyone in household employed); whether report program receipt (housing assistance, public assistance, SNAP receipt); and a linear time trend. The paper provides details on additional sets of covariates that accompany specific regressions.

Meyer et al. (2022)

Meyer et al. (2022) report the determinants of false negatives and false positives for SNAP, using average marginal effects from probit models for three surveys (ACS, CPS ASEC, and SIPP) for two states: Illinois, and Maryland. For the ACS, the sample includes individuals in a single year and results are reported separately for Illinois and Maryland. For the CPS, the samples are pooled across the available years and are reported separately for the two states. For the SIPP, the samples are collapsed at the wave level and are pooled across states and available years.

The estimates for false negatives are reported in table 3 on pp. 1622–1625, and the estimates for false positives are reported in table 4 on pp. 1628–1630. We focus on the estimates for "White" (evaluated relative to the omitted "non-White" category). For the purposes of our paper and for ease of comparison with other studies, we reverse the sign on "White" and designate it as corresponding to "Black."

The key covariates include family type (single no children, single with children, multiple adults with children—omitted, multiple adults, no children); number of adults; number of children; number of PIKed members; age (whether aged 50 or older); gender (female—omitted, male); education (less than high school, high school graduate, some college—omitted, college graduate and beyond); employment, income (income divided by the poverty line); disability status (non-disabled—omitted, disabled); citizenship status (US citizen—omitted, non-US citizen); geographic area (rural, within-MSA—omitted); whether reported public assistance receipt; whether reported housing assistance receipt; whether food stamp receipt was imputed; and administrative TANF receipt. The paper provides details on additional sets of covariates that accompany specific regressions.

We assume all covariates are survey-level variables unless otherwise noted (i.e., administrative TANF receipt, length of food stamp receipt spell).

Meyer et al. (2023)

Meyer et al. (2023) report the results from probit models of determinants of false negatives and false positives for the CPS and the SIPP. Average partial effects from probit models for both false positives and false negatives for both surveys can be found in table A4 (pp. 61–64). We focus on the coefficient corresponding to "Black, Non-Hispanic," "Asian, Non-Hispanic," and "Hispanic" (which are evaluated relative to the omitted category of "White Non-Hispanic").

Other key covariates include Census division (New England—omitted, Middle Atlantic, East North Central, West North Central, South Atlantic, East South Central, West South Central, Mountain, Pacific); education level (less than high school, high school graduate, some college, bachelor's degree or more—omitted); family income relative to poverty line (0–1x poverty line, 1–2x poverty line, 2–3x poverty line, 3–4x poverty line, >4x poverty line—omitted); age (<25, 25–34, 35–44, 45–54, 55–64, 65+—omitted); family type (single non-elderly parent, single non-elderly childless, multiple adults with at least one child—omitted, multiple non-elderly adults childless, elderly reference person); industry type (retail, heavy industry, financial & professional services, education & health, other, not in labor force, unemployed—omitted); whether individual is the reference person; citizenship status (citizen—omitted, non-citizen); sex (female—omitted, male); geographic area (non-metropolitan—omitted, metropolitan); number of adults; number of children; whether the UI item was imputed; admin UI amount; number of weeks worked in the past year; and whether the individual was a full-time worker in the past year. The paper provides details on additional sets of covariates that accompany specific regressions.

Panel B: Logistic Regression Coefficients

Colby et al. (2016)

Colby et al. (2016) report results from logistic regressions estimating the effects of various demographic characteristics on the likelihood of being a false positive or false negative regarding SNAP receipt. The estimates can be found in table 4 on p. 24 of the original paper. The results are originally reported as odds ratios, and we converted these results to logistic regression coefficients by taking the natural logarithm of the original estimates.

This yields the following calculations:

- Black False Negative Covariate-Adjusted Error Rate: ln(1.16)
- Black False Positive Covariate-Adjusted Error Rate: ln(4.63)
- Hispanic False Negative Covariate-Adjusted Error Rate: ln(1.09)
- Hispanic False Positive Covariate-Adjusted Error Rate: ln(1.78)

Other key covariates include geographic area (metro—omitted, rural); age (0–17, 18–24—omitted, 65 and older); education (less than high school, high school—omitted, some college or more); employment (employed—omitted, not employed); nativity (US born—omitted, foreign born); language (English only—omitted, other language spoken); sex (male—omitted, female); SNAP imputation (not imputed—omitted, imputed); number of families in household; number of people in household; and family type (single with children, single no children, married with children—omitted, married no children).

Klerman et al. (2005)

Klerman et al. (2005) report coefficients from logistic regressions predicting the likelihood of being a false positive or a false negative for Medi-Cal (Medicaid in California) and welfare receipt. The results for Medicaid can be found in table B.1 on p. 58 in the original paper and the results for welfare can be found in table B.2 on p. 59 of the original paper. In both tables, we focus on the first two columns, which contain determinants of "behavioral" false positives and false negatives. The logistic regression results are unweighted.

We focus on the coefficients for "Black" and "Hispanic" individuals, evaluated against individuals from any other race/ethnicity (as the omitted category). Given sample size limitations, the authors are not able to disclose (1) "Black" estimates in the false negative and the false positive models for Welfare or (2) "Hispanic" estimates in the false positive models for either Medicaid or welfare. We note these suppressed values as "N/A" in our table.

Other key covariates include pure time effects alongside time invariant covariates as well as linear time interactions. The time invariant covariates are composed of variables for age (15–25, 26–35—omitted, 36–65, 46–65; note that these overlap); gender (female—omitted, male); education (high school dropout, at least some college which includes college graduates); poverty (income less than 0.5x the poverty line, income less than 1x the poverty line, income less than 1.5x the poverty line, income less than 2x the poverty line; note that these overlap); family structure (any children in the household, single female-headed household with children); and other health insurance (health insurance other than Medi-Cal). The paper provides details on additional sets of covariates that accompany specific regressions.

Bhaskar et al. (2018)

Bhaskar et al. (2018) report results from a logit model for IHS coverage predicting the probability of being a false positive or false negative given a set of demographic characteristics. The results for the full sample of AIANs can be found in table 5 on p. 25 of the original paper. The results for the sample of AIANs aged 25 or older can be found in table 6 on p. 26 of the original paper. The results for the sample of non-AIANs can be found in appendix table A on p. 27 in the original paper. We focus on the effects associated with "any AIAN ancestry reported" (relative to no AIAN ancestry, which is the omitted category) and any "Hispanic" (relative to not Hispanic, which is the omitted category). Since the results are reported as odds ratios, we convert them to logistic regression coefficients by taking the natural logarithm of the original estimates.

This yields the following calculations for IHS using the 2014 ACS for the AIAN only sample:

- Hispanic False Negative Covariate-Adjusted Error Rate: ln(1.54)

This yields the following calculations for IHS using the 2014 ACS for the AIAN only sample restricted to individuals aged 25 and older:

- Hispanic False Negative Covariate-Adjusted Error Rate: ln(1.56)

This yields the following calculations for IHS using the 2014 ACS for the non-AIAN sample:

- Hispanic False Negative Covariate-Adjusted Error Rate: ln(1.21)

Because the sample of analysis for the false positive regressions consists of survey-reported recipients rather than true non-recipients (i.e., not conforming to our preferred definition), we do not report results for the false positive model. Other key covariates include reported tribal affiliation; reported any AIAN ancestry; child; gender (male—omitted, female); nativity (not foreign born—omitted, foreign born); reported any health insurance coverage; disability status (no disability—omitted, has a disability); years since information was last updated with IHS; whether lives in an IHS Contract Health Service Delivery Area; geographic area (not urban area—omitted, urban area); region of residence (Northeast—omitted, Midwest, South, West); whether respondent was the householder or spouse (vs. other relative, non relative, or if unit was a group quarter); whether another individual in respondent's household reported having IHS coverage; and whether IHS coverage response in the ACS was imputed. These are all the covariates included in table 5 for the full sample of AIANs. The paper provides details on additional sets of covariates that accompany specific regressions.

Bhaskar et al. (2019)

Bhaskar et al. (2019) report results from a logit model that evaluates the characteristics associated with being a false negative or a false positive reporter with respect to Medicare receipt. We focus on the estimates associated with being "Non-Hispanic Black alone," "Non-Hispanic Asian alone," and "Hispanic" (evaluated relative to the omitted race/ethnicity category of "non-Hispanic White"). The authors report their results as odds ratios in table 6 on pp. 1821–1822 in the original paper. We convert these numbers to logistic regression coefficients by taking the natural logarithm of the original results to facilitate comparison.

This yields the following calculations:

- Black False Negative Covariate-Adjusted Error Rate: ln(1.69)
- Black False Positive Covariate-Adjusted Error Rate: ln(0.86)
- Hispanic False Negative Covariate-Adjusted Error Rate: ln(1.49)
- Hispanic False Positive Covariate-Adjusted Error Rate: ln(0.3)
- Asian False Negative Covariate-Adjusted Error Rate: ln(1.47)
- Asian False Positive Covariate-Adjusted Error Rate: ln(0.63)

Other key covariates include sex (male—omitted, female); educational attainment (no high school, high school degree—omitted, some college, bachelor's degree, graduate or professional degree); citizenship/year of entry (native—omitted, naturalized entered 10+ years ago, naturalized entered less than 10 years ago, noncitizen entered 10+ years ago, noncitizen entered less than 10 years ago); marital status (now married—omitted, widowed/separated/divorced, never married); income to poverty ratio of the health insurance unit (less than 100 percent, 100 percent–149 percent, 150 percent–199 percent, 200 percent+—omitted); labor force participation (employed—omitted, unemployed, not in labor force); disability status (no disability—omitted, has a disability); Medicare status of other household members (no others with Medicare—omitted, others in household have Medicare); private insurance (no private insurance—omitted, has private insurance); and imputation of Medicare response (not imputed—omitted, imputed).

Noon et al. (2019)

Noon et al. (2019) report results from logistic regression models evaluating the probability of being a false negative or a false positive reporter with respect to Medicaid receipt. The results can be found in table 4 on p. 41 of the original paper. We focus on the estimates associated with being "of Hispanic origin" (evaluated relative to the omitted group of "not Hispanic") and the estimates associated with "Black alone," "AIAN alone," and "Asian alone" (evaluated relative to the omitted group of "White alone." Since the results are reported as odds ratios, we convert them to logistic regression coefficients by taking the natural logarithm of the original estimates.

This yields the following calculations:

- Black False Negative Covariate-Adjusted Error Rate: ln(1.21)
- Black False Positive Covariate-Adjusted Error Rate: ln(1.35)
- Hispanic False Negative Covariate-Adjusted Error Rate: ln(1.34)
- Hispanic False Positive Covariate-Adjusted Error Rate: ln(2.30)
- Asian False Negative Covariate-Adjusted Error Rate: ln(1.35)
- Asian False Positive Covariate-Adjusted Error Rate: ln(2.60)
- AI/AIAN False Negative Covariate-Adjusted Error Rate: ln(1.34)
- AI/AIAN False Positive Covariate-Adjusted Error Rate: ln(1.87)

Other key covariates include sex (female, male—omitted); age (18–24—omitted, 25–44, 45–64, 65+); education (less than high school—omitted, high school degree, some college, bachelor's degree, graduate degree); foreign born (US born—omitted, foreign born); insurance coverage (reported Medicare coverage, reported enrolled in another insurance program, whether enrolled in Medicaid in survey year 2011); and household variables (shared coverage, logged household income). The paper provides details on additional sets of covariates that accompany specific regressions.

Table 9.4: Bias in Estimates of Program Receipt and Average Amounts for True Reporting Recipients

Table 9.4 reports estimates of program receipt rates as well as average annual benefit amounts conditional on receipt using survey versus administrative data from various papers. Unless otherwise specified, the receipt rates are calculated over the entire sample (not conditional on eligibility and so should not be interpreted as "take-up" rates) and the benefit amounts are conditional on receiving a program in both the survey and administrative data (i.e., being a true reporting recipient). Here, we provide additional details on the results from the respective papers, the sources of the original results, and any adjustments we performed.

Fox et al. (2017)

Fox et al. (2017) report SNAP receipt rates in table 3 on pp. 25–27 in the original paper and average SNAP benefit amounts in table 4 on pp. 28–30 in the original paper. We converted average monthly SNAP benefit amounts reported in table 4 to annual amounts by multiplying by 12.

Shantz and Fox (2018)

Shantz and Fox (2018) report SNAP receipt rates in table 3 on pp. 28–29 and TANF receipt rates in table 5 on pp. 33–34 of the original paper. Average annual SNAP amounts are reported in table 4 on pp. 30–32 and average annual TANF amounts are reported in table 6 on pp. 35–37 of the original paper.

Meyer et al. (2023)

Meyer et al. (2023) report receipt rates and average benefit amounts for UI in unpublished tables. Specifically, the authors have tables showing aggregate benefit dollars and recipients for each race/ethnicity subgroup, and we back out receipt rates by dividing the former by the latter. In addition, the authors have tables showing average administrative UI amounts among true reporting recipients as well as the mean net error in surveys; the average survey UI amount can be backed out by subtracting the latter from the former.

Brummet et al. (2018)

Brummet et al. (2018) report receipt rates for pensions in Column 2 (survey) and Column 3 (admin) in table 14 on p. 33 of the original paper.

Table 9.5: Bias in Marginal Effect of Minority Variable in Models of Program Receipt

Table 9.5 reports estimates of the marginal effects of minority variables in models of program receipt. We show estimates for models where receipt (as the dependent variable) is measured using survey versus administrative data. These regressions sometimes condition on some proxy of program eligibility (measured using survey or administrative data), in which case they can be interpreted as effects on take-up. Here, we describe the nature of the results from the respective papers and identify the location of the original results.

All reported estimates are average partial effects from probit models, and all the covariates in these models are survey-reported variables (unless otherwise noted).

Celhay et al. (2021)

Celhay et al. (2021) report the determinants of survey and administrative SNAP and TANF + GA (PA) receipt, using as their sample linked households with (survey-reported) income below twice the poverty line. The estimates for SNAP can be found in table 6 on p. 50 and the estimates for TANF + GA can be found in table 7 on p. 51 of the original paper. We focus on the estimates associated with "Black Non-Hispanic" and "Hispanic," which are evaluated relative to the omitted race/ethnicity category of "White Non-Hispanic."

Other key covariates include family type (single adult with no children, single adult with children, multiple adults with children—omitted, multiple adults no children); number of children; number of adults; rural status (non-rural—omitted, rural); gender (female—omitted, male); disability status (not disabled—omitted, disabled); age (16–29, 30–39, 40–49—omitted, 50–59, 60–69, 70+); education (less than high school, high school graduate, college graduate—omitted, complete graduate and beyond); household language (household language is English only); English proficiency (speaks English poorly); citizenship status (citizen—omitted, non-citizen); household income relative to the poverty line (household income/poverty line); employment (anyone in household employed); whether report housing assistance receipt; and the linear time trend. The SNAP survey and administrative data regressions from table 6 include covariates for reporting public assistance receipt. Conversely, the PA survey and administrative data regressions from table 7 include covariates for reporting public assistance receipt. The paper provides details on additional covariate restrictions that accompany specific regressions.

Meyer et al. (2022)

Meyer et al. (2022) report the determinants of survey and administrative SNAP receipt, using as their sample linked households with (survey-reported) income below twice the poverty line. The estimates can be found in table 5 on pp. 1632–1636 of the original paper. We focus on the estimates corresponding to "White" in each of these models (evaluated against the omitted category of non-White), but we reverse the sign and report the adjusted estimates as referring to "Black."

Other key covariates include family type (single no children, single with children, multiple adults with children—omitted, multiple adults, no children); number of adults; number of children; number of PIKed members; age (16–29, 30–39, 40–49—omitted, 50–59, 60–69, 70+); education (less than high school, high school graduate, some college—omitted, college graduate and beyond); employment (employed, not employed—omitted); income divided by poverty line; disability status (non-disabled—omitted, disabled); geographic area (rural, within-MSA—omitted); whether reported public assistance receipt; and whether reported housing assistance receipt. The paper provides details on additional sets of covariates that accompany specific regressions.

Meyer et al. (2023)

Meyer et al. (2023) report the determinants of survey and administrative UI receipt from three different models for both surveys (the CPS and the SIPP): one with interaction terms on race, one with no interaction terms on race, and one without controlling for family income relative to poverty line. For this paper, we focus on the results for the model with no interaction terms on race.

For the CPS and SIPP, we report results for all individuals aged 18+, rather than conditioning on some proxy for eligibility. The results for the CPS sample can be found in table A5a on p. 65 of the original paper, while the results for the SIPP sample can be found in tables A6a on p. 81. We focus on estimates associated with "Black, Non-Hispanic," "Asian, Non-Hispanic," and "Hispanic," evaluated relative to the omitted group of "White Non-Hispanic."

Key covariates include Census division (New England—omitted, Middle Atlantic, East North Central, West North Central, South Atlantic, East South Central, West South Central, Mountain, Pacific); education level (less than high school, high school graduate, some college, bachelor's degree or more—omitted); family income relative to poverty line (0–1x poverty line, 1–2x poverty line, 2–3x poverty line, 3–4x poverty line, >4x poverty line—omitted); age (<25, 25–34, 35–44, 45–54, 55–64, 65+—omitted); family type (single non-elderly parent, single non-elderly childless, multiple adults with at least one child—omitted, multiple non-elderly adults childless, elderly reference person); industry type (retail, heavy industry, financial & professional services, education & health, other); whether individual is the reference person; citizenship status (citizen—omitted, non-citizen); sex (female—omitted, male); geographic area (non-metropolitan—omitted, metropolitan); the number of adults; the number of children; the number of weeks worked in the past year; and whether the individual was a full-time worker in the past year.

Table 9.6: Bias in Poverty Rates

Table 9.6 compares poverty rates calculated according to survey records and selected administrative records from various papers. Unless otherwise noted, poverty rates are defined as the share of individuals with incomes below some multiple (usually 100 percent) of some absolute poverty line. For each race/ethnicity subgroup, we show poverty levels calculated using the survey and administrative data sources, as well as the percentage difference between the levels (using the survey value as the baseline) and an indicator for the level at which the difference is statistically significant (if reported). Here, we provide additional details on the results from the respective papers and the sources of the original estimates.

Fox et al. (2017)

Fox et al. (2017) report the number and percent of people in poverty using the Supplemental Poverty Measure (SPM) in table 8 on pp. 37–39 of the original paper. These levels are calculated using either survey data alone or survey data combined with administrative SNAP records. We calculate the percentage difference using the survey poverty estimate from column 4 and the administrative poverty estimate from column 8. Column 11 reports the statistical significance of the difference between survey and administrative estimates.

Shantz and Fox (2018)

Shantz and Fox (2018) report the percent of people in poverty according to the SPM in table 10 on pp. 41–42 of the original paper. These levels are calculated using either survey data alone or survey data combined with administrative SNAP and TANF records. We calculate the percentage difference using the survey poverty estimate from column 2 and the administrative poverty estimate from column 6. Column 8 reports the statistical significance of the difference between survey and administrative estimates.

Stevens et al. (2018)

Stevens et al. (2018) report the percent of people in poverty according to the SPM in table 5 on pp. 42–45 of the original paper. These levels are calculated using either survey data alone or survey data combined with administrative SNAP records. We calculate the percentage difference using the survey poverty estimate from column 2 and the administrative poverty estimate from column 6. Column 8 reports the statistical significance of the difference between the survey and administrative estimates.

Rothbaum et al. (2021)

Rothbaum et al. (2021) report the percent of people in poverty according to the SPM in table 2 on p. 27 of the original paper. These levels are calculated using either survey data alone or survey data combined with administrative SNAP records. We calculate the percentage difference using the survey poverty estimate from column 1 and the administrative poverty estimate from column 2. Column 4 reports the difference between the estimates along with its statistical significance.

Bee and Mitchell (2017)

Bee and Mitchell (2017) report the percent of elderly individuals in poverty according to the Official Poverty Measure (OPM) in table 3 on pp. 43–44 of the original paper. These levels are calculated using either survey data alone or survey data combined with various administrative records (covering earnings, Social Security, SSI, interest and dividends, and retirement income). We calculate the percentage difference using the survey poverty estimate from column 6 and the administrative poverty estimate from column 8. Column 10 reports the difference between the estimates along with its statistical significance.

Dushi and Trenkamp (2021)

Dushi and Trenkamp (2021) report the percent of elderly individuals in poverty according to the Official Poverty Measure (OPM) in table 6 on p. 20 of the original paper. Poverty rates are calculated in two ways: having income at or below 100 percent of the federal poverty line and having income at or below 125 percent of the federal poverty line. These levels are calculated using either survey data alone or survey data combined with administrative SSA and IRS records. We report survey poverty estimates from column 2 and administrative poverty estimates from column 4. We calculate the percentage difference using these estimates. The authors do not report the statistical significance corresponding to this difference.

Meyer and Wu (2023)

Meyer and Wu (2023) report the percent of individuals in poverty, using SPM resource units, a full-income measure that accounts for taxes and in-kind transfers, and the OPM threshold for a two-adult, two-child family multiplied by the SPM equivalence scale. These results are in unpublished tables. Poverty rates are calculated in four ways: having income at or below 100 percent of the federal poverty line, as well as below 50 percent, 150 percent, and 200 percent of the federal poverty line. These levels are calculated using either survey data alone or survey data combined with various administrative records. The authors report neither the difference not the significance between the two estimates.

References

Abowd, John M., and Martha H. Stinson. 2013. "Estimating Measurement Error in Annual Job Earnings: A Comparison of Survey and Administrative Data." *Review of Economics and Statistics* 95(5): 1451–1467.

Akee, Randall, Maggie R. Jones, and Sonya R. Porter. 2019. "Race Matters: Income Shares, Income Inequality, and Income Mobility for All US Races." *Demography* 56(3): 999–1021.

Aigner, Dennis J. 1973. "Regression with a Binary Independent Variable Subject to Errors of Observation." *Journal of Econometrics* 1: 49–60.

Bajaj, Simar Singh, and Fatima Cody Stanford. 2021. "Beyond Tuskegee—Vaccine Distrust and Everyday Racism." *New England Journal of Medicine* 384: e12.

Bee, Adam, and Joshua Mitchell. 2017. "Do Older Americans Have More Income Than We Think?" SEHSD Working Paper 2017–39. Washington, DC: US Census Bureau.

Bhaskar, Renuka, James Noon, and Brett J. O'Hara. 2019. "The Errors in Reporting Medicare Coverage: A Comparison of Survey Data and Administrative Records." *Journal of Aging and Health* 31(10): 1806–29.

Bhaskar, Renuka, Rachel Shattuck, and James Noon. 2018. "Reporting of Indian

Health Service Coverage in the American Community Survey." CARRA Working Paper 2018-04. Washington, DC: US Census Bureau.

Black, Dan, Seth Sanders, and Lowell Taylor. 2003. "Measurement of Higher Education in the Census and Current Population Survey." *Journal of the American Statistical Association* 98(463): 545–54.

Blackwell, Matthew, James Honaker, and Gary King. 2017. "A Unified Approach to Measurement Error and Missing Data: Overview and Applications." *Sociological Methods & Research* 46(3): 303–41.

Bollinger, Christopher R., and Martin H. David. 1997. "Modeling Discrete Choice with Response Error: Food Stamp Participation." *Journal of the American Statistical Association* 92(439): 827–35.

———. 2001. "Estimation with Response Error and Nonresponse: Food-Stamp Participation in the SIPP." *Journal of Business & Economic Statistics* 19(2): 129–41.

———. 2005. "I Didn't Tell, and I Won't Tell: Dynamic Response Error in the SIPP." *Journal of Applied Econometrics* 20(4): 563–69.

Bollinger, Christopher R., and Iva Valentinova Tasseva. 2023. "Income Source Confusion Using the SILC." *Public Opinion Quarterly* 87(S1): 542–74.

Bound, John, Charles Brown, and Nancy Mathiowetz. 2001. "Measurement Error in Survey Data." In *Handbook of Econometrics*, vol. 5, edited by J. J. Heckman and E. Leamer, 3705–3843. Amsterdam: Elsevier Science.

Brandon, Dwayne T., Lydia A. Isaac, and Thomas A. LaVeist. 2005. "The Legacy of Tuskegee and Trust in Medical Care: Is Tuskegee Responsible for Race Differences in Mistrust of Medical Care?" *Journal of the National Medical Association* 97(7): 951–56.

Bricker, Jesse, and Gary V. Engelhardt. 2008. "Measurement Error in Earnings Data in the Health and Retirement Study." *Journal of Economic and Social Measurement* 33(1): 39–61.

Brummet, Quentin, Denise Flanagan-Doyle, Joshua Mitchell, John Voorheis, Laura Erhard, and Brett McBride. 2018. "Investigating the Use of Administrative Records in the Consumer Expenditure Survey." CARRA Working Paper #2018-01. Washington, DC: US Census Bureau.

Celhay, Pablo, Bruce D. Meyer, and Nikolas Mittag. 2021. "Errors in Reporting and Imputation of Government Benefits and Their Implications." NBER Working Paper No. 29184. Cambridge, MA: National Bureau of Economic Research.

———. 2022. "Stigma in Welfare Programs." NBER Working Paper No. 30307. Cambridge, MA: National Bureau of Economic Research.

———. 2024. "What Leads to Measurement Error? Evidence from Reports of Program Participation in Three Surveys." *Journal of Econometrics* 238(2): 105581.

Chenevert, Rebecca L., Mark A. Klee, and Kelly R. Wilkin. 2016. "Do Imputed Earnings Earn Their Keep? Evaluating SIPP Earnings and Nonresponse with Administrative Records." SEHSD Working Paper 2016-18. Washington, DC: US Census Bureau.

Chetty, Raj, Nathaniel Hendren, Maggie R. Jones, and Sonya R. Porter. 2020. "Race and Economic Opportunity in the United States: An Intergenerational Perspective." *Quarterly Journal of Economics* 135(2): 711–83.

Colby, Sandy, Jose Debora, and Misty L. Heggeness. 2016. "How Well Do Individuals Report Supplemental Nutrition Assistance Program (SNAP) Take Up in Household Surveys?" SEHSD Working Paper 2017-03. Washington, DC: US Census Bureau.

Cristia, Julian, and Jonathan A. Schwabish. 2007. "Measurement Error in the SIPP: Evidence from Matched Administrative Records." Working Paper 2007-03. Washington, DC: Congressional Budget Office.

Currie, Janet. 2006. "The Take-Up of Social Benefits." In *Public Policy and the Income Distribution*, edited by A. Auerbach, D. Card, and J. Quigley, 80–148. New York: Russell Sage Foundation.

Courtemanche, Charles, Augustine Denteh, and Rusty Tchernis. 2019. "Estimating the Associations between SNAP and Food Insecurity, Obesity, and Food Purchases with Imperfect Administrative Measures of Participation." *Southern Economic Journal* 86(1): 202–28.

Davern, Michael, Jacob Alex Klerman, and Jeanette Ziegenfuss. 2007. "Medicaid Under-reporting in the Current Population Survey and One Approach for a Partial Correction." RAND Corporation, WR-532.

Davern, Michael, Jacob Alex Klerman, David K. Baugh, Kathleen Thiede Call, and George D. Greenberg. 2009a. "An Examination of the Medicaid Undercount in the Current Population Survey: Preliminary Results from Record Linking." *Health Services Research* 44(3): 965–87.

Davern, Michael, Jacob Klerman, Jeanette Ziegenfuss, Victoria Lynch, and George Greenberg. 2009b. "A Partially Corrected Estimate of Medicaid Enrollment and Uninsurance: Results from an Imputational Model Developed off Linked Survey and Administrative Data." *Journal of Economic and Social Measurement* 34(4): 219–40.

Duncan, Otis Dudley. 1968. "Inheritance of Power or Inheritance of Race?" In *On Understanding Poverty: Perspectives from the Social Sciences*, edited by D. Moynihan, 85–110. New York: Basic Books.

Dushi, Irena, Howard Iams, and Brad Trenkamp. 2017. "The Importance of Social Security Benefits to the Income of the Aged Population." *Social Security Bulletin* 77(2): 1–12.

Dushi, Irena, and Brad Trenkamp. 2021. "Improving the Measurement of Retirement Income of the Aged Population." ORES Working Paper No. 116. Washington, DC: Social Security Administration.

Forsythe, Eliza, and Hesong Yang. 2021. "Understanding Disparities in Unemployment Insurance Recipiency." Report to the Department of Labor.

Fox, Liana E., Misty L. Heggeness, Jose Pacas, and Kathryn Stevens. 2017. "Precision in Measurement: Using SNAP Administrative Records to Evaluate Poverty Measurement." SEHSD Working Paper 2017-49. Washington, DC: US Census Bureau.

Giefer, Katherine G., Michael D. King, and Veronica L. Roth. 2022. "SNAP Receipt in SIPP: Using Administrative Records to Evaluate Data Quality." SEHSD Working Paper 2022–22. Washington, DC: US Census Bureau.

Gould-Werth, Alix, and H. Luke Shaefer. 2012. "Unemployment Insurance Participation by Education and by Race and Ethnicity." *Monthly Labor Review* 135: 28–41.

Haider, Steven J., Alison Jacknowitz, and Robert F. Schoeni. 2003. "Food Stamps and the Elderly: Why is Participation so Low?" *Journal of Human Resources* 38(S): 1180–220.

Hausman, Jerry A., Jason Abrevaya, and Fiona M. Scott-Morton. 1998. "Misclassification of the Dependent Variable in a Discrete-Response Setting." *Journal of Econometrics* 87(2): 239–69.

Huynh, Minh, Kalman Rupp, and James Sears. 2002. "The Assessment of Survey of Income and Program Participation (SIPP) Data using Longitudinal Administrative Records." SIPP Working Paper No. 238. Washington, DC: Census Bureau.

Kim, ChangHwan, and Christopher R. Tamborini. 2012. "Do Survey Data Estimate Earnings Inequality Correctly? Measurement Errors Among Black and White Male Workers." *Social Forces* 90: 1157–181.

———. 2014. "Response Error in Earnings: An Analysis of the Survey of Income and Program Participation Matched with Administrative Data." *Sociological Methods and Research* 43(1): 39–72.

Kirlin, John A., and Michael Wiseman. 2014. "Getting It Right, or at Least Better: Improving Identification of Food Stamp Participants in the National Health and Nutrition Examination Survey." Working Paper.

Klerman, Jacob Alex, Jeanne S. Ringel, and Elizabeth Roth. 2005. Under-Reporting of Medicaid and Welfare in the Current Population Survey. RAND Working Paper WR-169-3.

Kuka, Elira, and Bryan A. Stuart. 2021. "Racial Inequality in Unemployment Insurance Receipt and Take-Up." NBER Working Paper No. 29595. Cambridge, MA: National Bureau of Economic Research.

Marquis, Kent H., and Jeffrey C. Moore. 1990. "Measurement Errors in SIPP Program Reports." In *Proceedings of the 1990 Annual Research Conference*, 721–45. Washington, DC: US Census Bureau.

Massey, Douglas S., and Nancy A. Denton. 1993. *American Apartheid: Segregation and the Making of the Underclass*. Cambridge, MA: Harvard University Press.

Meyer, Bruce D., and Nikolas Mittag. 2017. "Misclassification in Binary Choice Models." *Journal of Econometrics* 200(2): 295–311.

———. 2019a. "Using Linked Survey and Administrative Data to Better Measure Income: Implications for Poverty, Program Effectiveness, and Holes in the Safety Net." *American Economic Journal: Applied Economics* 11(2): 176–204.

———. 2019b. "Misreporting of Government Transfers: How Important are Survey Design and Geography?" *Southern Economic Journal* 86(1): 230–53.

———. 2021a. "An Empirical Total Survey Error Decomposition Using Data Combination." *Journal of Econometrics* 224(2): 286–305.

———. 2021b. "Combining Administrative and Survey Data to Improve Income Measurement." In *Administrative Records for Survey Methodology*, edited by A. Y. Chun, M. D. Larsen, G. Durrant, and J. P. Reiter, 297–322. New York: John Wiley and Sons.

Meyer, Bruce D., Nikolas Mittag, and Robert M. Goerge. 2022. "Errors in Survey Reporting and Imputation and Their Effects on Estimates of Food Stamp Program Participation." *Journal of Human Resources* 57(5): 1605–44.

Meyer, Bruce D., Nikolas Mittag, and Derek Wu. 2024. "Race, Ethnicity, and Measurement Error." NBER Working Paper No. 32860. Cambridge, MA: National Bureau of Economic Research.

Meyer, Bruce D., and Derek Wu. 2023. "Poverty in the United States." Working Paper.

Meyer, Bruce D., Derek Wu, Matthew Stadnicki, and Patrick Langetieg. 2023. "The Reporting of Unemployment Insurance and Unemployment in Survey and Administrative Sources." Working Paper.

Meyer, Bruce D., Wallace KC Mok, and James X. Sullivan. 2015. "Household Surveys in Crisis." *Journal of Economic Perspectives* 29(4): 199–226.

Mittag, Nikolas. 2019. "Correcting for Misreporting of Government Benefits." *American Economic Journal: Economic Policy* 11(2): 142–64.

Moffitt, Robert A., and Peter T. Gottschalk. 2001. "Ethnic and Racial Differences in Welfare Receipt in the United States." In *America Becoming: Racial Trends and Their Consequences*, vol. 2, ch. 7, 152–73. Washington, DC: The National Academies Press.

Noon, James M., Leticia E. Fernandez, and Sonya R. Porter. 2019. "Response Error and the Medicaid Undercount in the Current Population Survey." *Health Services Research* 54(1): 34–43.

Pedace, Roberto, and Nancy Bates. 2000. "Using Administrative Data to Assess Earnings Reporting Error in the Survey of Income and Program Participation." *Journal of Economic and Social Measurement* 26: 173–92.

Rosen, Marc I., Thomas J. McMahon, and Robert A. Rosenheck. 2007. "Homeless People Whose Self-Reported SSI/DI Status is Inconsistent with Social Security Administration Records." *Social Security Bulletin* 67(1): 53–62.

Rothbaum, Jonathan L. 2015. "Comparing Income Aggregates: How do the CPS and ACS Match the National Income and Product Accounts, 2007–2012." SEHSD Working Paper 1. Washington, DC: US Census Bureau.

Rothbaum, Jonathan, Liana Fox, and Kathryn Shantz. 2021. "Fixing Errors in a SNAP: Addressing SNAP Under-reporting to Evaluate Poverty." Working Paper. Washington, DC: US Census Bureau.

Shantz, Kathryn, and Liana E. Fox. 2018. "Precision in Measurement: Using State Level Supplemental Nutrition Assistance Program and Temporary Assistance for Needy Families Administrative Records and the Transfer Income Model (TRIM3) to Evaluate Poverty Measurement." SEHSD Working Paper 2018-30. Washington, DC: US Census Bureau.

Shrider, Emily A., and John Creamer. 2023. "Poverty in the United States: 2022." Current Population Report P60–280. Washington, DC: US Census Bureau.

Stevens, Kathryn, Liana E. Fox, and Misty L. Heggeness. 2018. "Precision in Measurement: Using SNAP Administrative Records and the Transfer Income Model (TRIM3) to Evaluate Poverty Measurement." SEHSD Working Paper 15. Washington, DC: US Census Bureau.

US Census Bureau. 2006. "Design and Methodology: Current Population Survey." Technical Paper 66, US Census Bureau.

———. 2008. "Survey of Income and Program Participation: User's Guide." Washington, DC: US Census Bureau.

———. 2014. "American Community Survey: Design and Methodology." Washington, DC: US Census Bureau.

———. 2023. "Historical Income Tables: Households; Table H-5. Race and Hispanic Origin of Householder—Households by Median and Mean Income." Washington, DC: US Census Bureau. https://www.census.gov/data/tables/time-series/demo/income-poverty/historical-income-households.html.

US Government Accountability Office (GAO). 2022. "Pandemic Unemployment Assistance: Federal Program Supported Contingent Workers Amid Historic Demand, but DOL Should Examine Racial Disparities in Benefit Receipt" Report to Congressional Committee GAO-22–104438, Washington, DC.

Wagner, Deborah, and Mary Layne. 2014. "The Person Identification Validation System (PVS): Applying the Center for Administrative Records Research and Applications' (CARRA) Record Linkage Software." CARRA Working Paper 2014-01. Washington, DC: US Census Bureau.

Winkler, William E. 2021. "Cleaning and Using Administrative Lists: Enhanced Practices and Computational Algorithms for Record Linkage and Modeling/Editing/Imputation." In *Administrative Records for Survey Methodology*, edited by A. Y. Chun, M. D. Larsen, G. Durrant, and J. P. Reiter, 297–322. New York: John Wiley and Sons.

Wooldridge, Jeffrey M. 2007. "Inverse Probability Weighted Estimation for General Missing Data Problems." *Journal of Econometrics* 141(2): 1281–1301.

10

Ethnic Identity and Anti-Immigrant Sentiment
Evidence from Proposition 187

Francisca M. Antman and Brian Duncan

"Everyone had a clear sense that this was a moment of racial threat. . . . That it was a Latino threat, not just anti-immigrant threat."
—Lisa García Bedolla, quoted in Denkmann (2019)

10.1 Introduction

In recent years, many elections have centered on stoking racial and ethnic divisions. At the same time, mounting evidence points to the fluidity of racial and ethnic identity over time and generations (Penner and Saperstein 2008; Dahis et al. 2020; Duncan and Trejo 2011). Additional research suggests individuals may change their racial identities in response to the relative costs and benefits of doing so (Cassan 2015; Francis and Tannuri-Pianto 2013; Antman and Duncan 2015; Antman and Duncan 2023).[1] This raises the possibility that individuals may change their racial and ethnic identities in response to an increasingly tense political and social climate that targets racial and ethnic groups.

However, the expected effect of anti-minority sentiment on willingness to identify as a racial or ethnic minority is not obvious. Individuals from ethnic or racial minorities might be less likely to identify with their minority groups if they fear the political discourse may have negative consequences for them, for example due to discrimination and hostility. On the other hand, individuals from minority groups may be more likely to identify as minorities if the heightened salience of race and ethnicity has raised their consciousness surrounding this aspect of their identity.

To address these questions, we use data surrounding one of the first and most well-known ballot measures widely seen to be anti-immigrant and anti-Latino, Proposition 187, which is sometimes credited for changing the

Francisca M. Antman is professor of economics at the University of Colorado Boulder.
Brian Duncan is chair and professor of economics at the University of Colorado Denver.

1. This can be considered in a larger theoretical framework of how identity shapes economic outcomes (Akerlof and Kranton 2000).

political trajectory of California. Passed by a wide margin in 1994, Proposition 187, also known as the "Save our State" initiative, called for denying public social, health, and education services to unauthorized immigrants (Martin 1995). Its provisions called on state and local officials to investigate and report anyone suspected of being in the United States in violation of immigration laws, including public school districts which would be required to verify the legal status of students and their parents/guardians (Ogilvie 2019; Martin 1995). Proposition 187 was also widely viewed to be anti-Latino (Ogilvie 2019), as its measures could plausibly discriminate against the Latino community in California, regardless of legal status. Mexican origin individuals in particular were viewed to be under threat (Martin 1995) as Mexico is the top origin country for US immigrants (Budiman 2020) and Mexicans are by far the largest Hispanic origin group in the United States (Moslimani et al. 2023). Significant opposition to Proposition 187 from the Mexican origin community was a salient feature of the social and political climate surrounding its passage (Martin 1995).

In the days leading up to the election, many protests were held, including student walkouts and school boycotts, which included many newly organized Latino students (Martin 1995; Ogilvie 2019). The measure passed by a wide margin in November 1994 but faced significant court challenges and was ultimately found to be unconstitutional. Although Proposition 187 never went into effect, its impact on increased Latino political participation and mobilization has been widely speculated (Denkmann 2019; Abrajano and García Bedolla 2020), suggesting that Proposition 187 may have indeed awakened Latino identity for a broader population, a question we pursue here. Using data from the US Census and Current Population Survey, as well as county-level vote share information on the passage of Prop 187, we ask whether individuals with documented Hispanic ancestry or parentage are more likely to identify ethnically as Hispanic/Latino or as Mexican origin in areas with higher support for the initiative after it was passed. To our knowledge, this is the first investigation into this question and the first to document a connection between political discourse, participation, and endogenous ethnic identity.

Our results suggest that anti-minority sentiment indeed plays a role in an individual's willingness to identify as an ethnic minority. Specifically, we find that individuals with stronger ancestral ties to a Mexican origin identity, who are arguably more likely to be perceived as Mexican due to a Spanish last name or direct parental lineage, are less likely to identify as Mexican in response to the anti-immigrant sentiment surrounding the passage of Proposition 187. At the same time, we find that individuals with weaker ancestral or observable ties to a Mexican origin identity, who are arguably less likely to be perceived as Mexican and thus face fewer adverse effects of anti-minority sentiment, are more likely to identify as Mexican in response to the passage of Proposition 187. These results are consistent with our predictions that anti-minority sentiment plays a role in driving ethnic identity, which varies depending on the relative costs and benefits of identifying as a racial or ethnic minority. The rest of the paper proceeds as follows. Section 10.2 discusses the data used in the analysis. Section 10.3 discusses the empirical strategy and predictions. Section 10.4 presents the results, and section 10.5 concludes.

10.2 Data

To explore the impact of anti-immigrant sentiment on ethnic identity, we link county-level vote share data showing support for Proposition 187 from the November 1994 election in California with two sources of individual-level data. We use data from the US Census to explore the impacts at the county level with the benefit of a larger sample size. The drawback is that since these data are from the decennial censuses, we only observe impacts well before (1990) or well after (2000) the passage of Proposition 187. This means that our interpretation of the Census results might be best described as measuring long-run impacts. At the same time, the long intervals between measurements of the outcomes also raises questions about whether some other variable, correlated with vote share for Proposition 187, might actually be driving the results. To address this concern, in separate analysis we use the 1994 and 1995 Current Population Survey (CPS), which enables us to measure short-run impacts of the passage of Proposition 187, thus measuring outcomes just after the vote, relative to a period immediately preceding the vote.

It should be noted that difference-in-differences analyses of the type employed here typically use data from a longer pre-treatment period to establish evidence for parallel trends between treatment and comparison groups. The analysis of pre-trends can then bolster the argument that the difference-in-differences estimates are accurately capturing causal effects. In this case, however, several features of our data and policy setting preclude that as a useful avenue of exploration. We do not use earlier waves of the Census to analyze pre-trends due to significant changes in immigration policy over the earlier period, e.g., the Immigration Reform and Control Act of 1986, which might be correlated with both our treatment and outcome variables. We do not utilize earlier waves of the CPS because 1994 is the first year in which parental place of birth is asked of respondents, and thus, for symmetry, we focus only on the 1995 CPS as the post-treatment period.[2] This effectively reduces our sample window to the survey waves immediately before and after the passage of Proposition 187. Nevertheless, we argue that the fact that the results show responses in opposite directions for ethnic

2. For more details on the Hispanic origin questions and race questions in the US Census and Current Population Survey, as well how they have changed over time, see Antman et al. (2023).

minority groups based on the strength of the group's ancestral ties serves as prima facie evidence that the results are not driven by any preexisting trends, as any unobservable variable driving these trends would likely impact all groups in the same direction.

10.2.1 Census Sample

The census sample is from the 1990 and 2000 Census 5 percent microdata drawn from IPUMS USA (Ruggles et al. 2023). The sample is limited to US-born individuals living in California in 1990 and 2000. Individuals with an allocated Hispanic origin have been dropped from the sample. Note that county is not identified in the 1990 and 2000 public-use microdata. IPUMS identifies counties from the Public Use Microdata Areas (PUMA), where possible. Since we will need to link these data to vote share information at the county level, the census sample is restricted to individuals living in 33 identifiable counties in the 1990 and 2000 Census. This accounts for approximately 95 percent of the population in California.

The analysis of the US Census sample also makes use of two distinct questions on the US Census: (1) the Hispanic origin question, which is used to measure rates of Hispanic/Latino and Mexican ethnic identification specifically,[3] and (2) the ancestry question, which is used to elicit the strength of Mexican ancestry, as measured by whether individuals list only Mexican ancestry, Mexican and non-Mexican ancestries, or no Mexican ancestry. While some may debate the difference between the two questions, Antman and Duncan (2023) review further background on the ancestry question and show that ancestry exhibits relatively limited response to external incentives. This suggests the response to the ancestry question provides a more objective indicator of ancestral heritage which is less subject to change. In contrast, the Hispanic origin question is more likely to measure ethnic self-identification that may evolve in response to various stimuli.

Table 10.1 shows rates of ethnic identification for the census sample based on the strength of Mexican ancestry in 1990 and 2000, specifically, by separating the sample into three groups: individuals with no Mexican ancestry, individuals with Mexican and non-Mexican ancestry (described as multi-ancestry Mexican), and individuals with only Mexican ancestry. Since ethnic identification may vary across the life course, and adult family members may be responding for children in the household, the table further decomposes the sample into children (panel A) and adults (panel B). Rates of identification appear roughly similar for children and adults in the group

3. Importantly, the context is a low-stakes survey environment, which is unconnected to any government benefit or consequence. Thus, we argue that the data are more likely to reflect the true ethnic identities of respondents and enable our analysis to uncover the impact of anti-immigrant sentiment on ethnic identity. While it is likely that parents are indicating their own view of the ethnic identities of their children, a parent's view of a child's ethnic identity is an important predictor of the child's own ethnic identity, and thus highly relevant for the analysis here.

Table 10.1 **Self-Reported Hispanic origin of children and adults in California in the 1990 and 2000 Census, by Mexican ancestry**

	No Mexican Ancestry	Multi-Ancestry Mexican	Only Mexican Ancestry
	Panel A: Children		
1990 Census			
Hispanic	11.32	80.99	98.55
Mexican	5.90	75.86	97.89
Other Hispanic	5.42	5.12	0.66
2000 Census			
Hispanic	17.98	86.68	98.76
Mexican	9.43	67.79	93.93
Other Hispanic	8.55	18.89	4.83
1990 Sample size	233,767	9,712	69,320
2000 Sample size	262,140	13,607	100,940
	Panel B: Adults		
1990 Census			
Hispanic	3.81	80.97	98.32
Mexican	1.77	77.77	97.76
Other Hispanic	2.03	3.20	0.56
2000 Census			
Hispanic	5.60	84.97	98.63
Mexican	2.77	72.88	93.65
Other Hispanic	2.83	12.09	4.98
1990 Sample size	654,325	6,343	57,746
2000 Sample size	655,601	8,914	75,521

Source: 1990 and 2000 Census data. The samples include US-born individuals living in identifiable counties in California in 1990 and 2000 with the indicated ancestry. Individuals with allocated Hispanic origin are excluded.

Note: All numbers are percentages. Sampling weights were used in the calculations.

of individuals with multiple Mexican and non-Mexican ancestries as well as individuals with only Mexican ancestry; however, children with no Mexican ancestry listed generally display higher rates of Mexican identification than adults in the same category. This may be related to the fact that children are not likely to be responding to the survey directly. Thus, children's ethnic identification may be reflecting, in part, the parent's view of the child's ethnic identity, which may be more distinct from the child's own view for those children with no Mexican ancestry listed. To ensure these differences are not confounding our analysis, throughout we will analyze results separately for children and adults and include age and age squared as control variables in the regression analysis below.

To address concerns that individuals in the sample may identify as Hispanic origin as opposed to Mexican origin, especially considering the census sample is restricted to US-born individuals, table 10.1 also includes statistics on Hispanic identification rates. While rates of identification to a Hispanic origin are slightly higher than rates of Mexican identification, the increase is relatively small, thus justifying our primary focus on Mexican identification as the main outcome variable throughout the analysis.

From table 10.1 it is also clear that patterns of Mexican identification vary by strength of ancestry in predictable ways, i.e., those with a stronger Mexican ancestral tie are, all else equal, more likely to identify as Mexican. However, it is important to note that the precise relationships are not entirely predictive. For example, 97.89 percent of children and 97.76 percent of adults with only Mexican ancestry identify as Mexican origin in 1990, but these rates are not 100 percent for either group. Moreover, rates of Mexican identification among those with no Mexican ancestry listed are perhaps higher than expected (5.90 percent among children and 1.77 percent among adults in 1990), but they are not 0 percent. This likely reflects the fact that some individuals with no Mexican ancestry listed actually have some ancestral link to a Mexican origin, but a connection that is not as strong as for those with some or only Mexican ancestry listed.

Finally, table 10.1 shows a pattern of increasing Mexican identification in California between 1990 and 2000, i.e., after the passage of Proposition 187, for those with no Mexican ancestry, while this pattern is reversed for those with only Mexican ancestry who demonstrate a decreased willingness to identify over time. This would be consistent with the predicted patterns described above, where individuals with stronger ties to Mexican ancestry, who are arguably more likely to be perceived as Mexican origin, decrease their willingness to identify as Mexican, whereas individuals with weaker ties to Mexican ancestry increase their willingness to identify as Mexican due to the increased salience of ethnic identity and raising of ethnic consciousness surrounding the passage of Proposition 187. Table 10.1 also shows that between 1990 and 2000, individuals with only Mexican ancestry substantially increased their identification with other Hispanic, non-Mexican identities, just as they decreased identification as Mexican origin.[4] This pattern suggests an increased willingness for individuals with only Mexican ancestry to choose a non-Mexican Hispanic identity in the wake of Proposition 187 and would be consistent with the perception of a specifically anti-Mexican sentiment associated with the measure. We will return to further discussion of this question in the regression analysis below where we link these patterns with strength of support for Proposition 187.

10.2.2 CPS Sample

The data covering the period immediately before and after the passage of Proposition 187 (1994 and 1995) come from the Current Population Sur-

4. A similar pattern is observed in descriptive statistics from the 1994 and 1995 waves of the CPS (not shown), where second-generation adults with both parents born in Mexico exhibit a greater willingness to identify with another non-Mexican Hispanic identity after the 1994 election.

Table 10.2 **Self-Reported Hispanic origin of adults in California by Mexican generation**

	Hispanic	Mexican	Other Hispanic
First-generation Mexican	99.12	98.35	0.77
Second-generation Mexican	95.38	93.20	2.18
Both parents born in Mexico	99.11	97.94	1.16
One parent born in Mexico	90.78	87.34	3.44
Only mother born in Mexico	88.03	84.82	3.21
Only father born in Mexico	93.10	89.47	3.63

Source: 1994–1995 Current Population Survey (CPS) fourth outgoing rotation group data.

Note: The samples include first- and second-generation Mexican Americans 18 and older who reside in a California county that can be identified in the CPS data. First-generation Mexican Americans are individuals who were born in Mexico. Second-generation Mexican Americans are US-born individuals who have at least one parent born in Mexico. The sample sizes are 2,540 for the first generation and 833 for the second generation. Sampling weights were used in the calculations.

vey, which is drawn from IPUMS CPS Basic Monthly data (Flood et al. 2023). Questions regarding the place of birth of the individual and their parents were added to the CPS in 1994. These questions allow us to identify first- and second-generation adults and children. For children who reside with their parents, we can also identify third-generation children. First-generation Mexican Americans are individuals who were born in Mexico. Second-generation Mexican Americans are US-born individuals who have at least one parent born in Mexico. Third-generation Mexican Americans are US-born individuals with two US-born parents and at least one grandparent born in Mexico.

The sample is limited to individuals living in an identifiable California county who were interviewed in the fourth outgoing rotation group. We do not limit the CPS sample to US-born individuals in order to exploit the information on parental place of birth available only in the CPS, which allows us to explore impacts on ethnic identification by immigrant generation. County is not identified in the CPS data, thus metropolitan areas were matched to counties, where possible, in order to link with vote share data which are reported by county. Just over 6 percent of the sample (6.1 percent) was dropped due to individuals living in metropolitan areas with populations too small to be identified.

Table 10.2 presents summary statistics on Mexican identification rates from the CPS sample of adults based on immigrant generation. Perhaps unsurprisingly, almost all of first-generation Mexican immigrant adults identify as Mexican (98.35 percent). Rates of Mexican identification are almost as high for (US-born) second-generation Mexican individuals if both parents were born in Mexico (97.94 percent). However, rates of Mexican identification drop much more dramatically for second-generation Mexican individuals if only one parent was born in Mexico (87.34 percent).

Table 10.3 Self-Reported Hispanic origin of children in California by Mexican generation

	Hispanic	Mexican	Other Hispanic
First-generation Mexican	98.15	97.79	0.35
Second-generation Mexican	96.68	94.31	2.37
Both parents born in Mexico	99.50	99.07	0.44
One parent born in Mexico	89.22	81.73	7.49
Only mother born in Mexico	86.04	83.16	2.88
Only father born in Mexico	92.82	80.11	12.71
Third-generation Mexican	72.79	68.19	4.60
Grandparent born in Mexico on:			
Mexican Both Sides	100.00	89.97	10.03
Mexican One Side	65.22	62.13	3.09
Mexico only on mother side	67.97	67.97	0.00
Mexico only on father side	62.67	56.73	5.95

Source: 1994–1995 Current Population Survey (CPS) fourth outgoing rotation group data.

Note: The samples include first- and second-, and third-generation Mexican Americans 17 and younger who are living with both parents and who reside in a California county that can be identified in the CPS data. First-generation Mexican Americans are individuals who were born in Mexico. Second-generation Mexican Americans are US-born individuals who have at least one parent born in Mexico. Third-generation Mexican Americans are US-born individuals with two US-born parents and at least one grandparent born in Mexico. The sample sizes are 275 for the first generation, 1,321 for the second generation, and 196 for the third generation. Sampling weights were used in the calculations.

These summary statistics reveal patterns of ethnic attrition, whereby individuals do not identify ethnically with their ancestral lineages. These data also highlight the link between ethnic attrition and intermarriage, which has been established in the literature (Duncan and Trejo 2011; Antman et al. 2016, 2020). Moreover, table 10.2 shows that if only the individual's mother was born in Mexico, rates of Mexican identification are even lower (84.82 percent) compared with rates of Mexican identification if only an individual's father was born in Mexico (89.47 percent). This likely reflects the importance of patrilineage and resulting naming conventions on ethnic identification.

Table 10.3 is the analogue of table 10.2, but for children who reside with their parents, so that immigrant generation can be traced to the third generation using the data on parental place of birth for the respondent. A similar pattern of falling rates of Mexican identification is observed at the second generation, which can again be traced to intermarriage and in particular matrilineal ancestral lines. For third-generation Mexican Americans, who, it is worth emphasizing, have parents who are also US born, Mexican identification rates are relatively high if the child has Mexican-born maternal and paternal grandparents (89.97 percent), but rates fall precipitously if the child has Mexican-born grandparent(s) on only one side (62.13 percent).[5]

10.2.3 County Vote Share Data

The data on county-level vote share showing support for Proposition 187 come from the November 8, 1994, General Election Statement of Vote compiled by the California secretary of state.[6] Figure 10.1 shows votes in favor of Proposition 187 and rates of self-reported Mexican origin in California in the 1990 and 2000 Census analysis samples. In it we see that in most counties in the sample, the vote share in support of Proposition 187 exceeded 50 percent. Moreover, there is significant variation in the vote share across California. The bottom two maps show the shares of Mexican identification across the two census waves, which shows growth in the share of Mexican-identifying population in many counties, especially those in Southern California and central California, over time. The spirit of the identification strategy in this paper is to link the bottom and top sets of figures to analyze the extent to which anti-immigrant sentiment, as measured by voter support for Proposition 187, is driving rates of ethnic identification. However, it is important to recognize that the patterns observed in figure 10.1 may simply reflect an increased presence of Mexican-origin individuals in those counties due to migration, as opposed to a greater willingness of the Mexican-origin population to identify as Mexican.

We begin to address this concern by splitting the census sample into three groups, based on the extent of their Mexican ancestry. Figure 10.2 shows the share of the population reporting to be of Mexican origin in California counties in the 1990 and 2000 Census, for individuals with no Mexican ancestry, individuals with Mexican and non-Mexican ancestry, as well as individuals with only Mexican ancestry. Here, the pattern appears to show increases in rates of Mexican identification for those with no Mexican ancestry between 1990 and 2000, while individuals with only Mexican ancestry appear less likely to identify as Mexican over the same time period. This pattern is consistent with the predicted effects noted above, i.e., individuals with the strongest ties to Mexican identity (those reporting only Mexican ancestry) are less likely to identify as Mexican while those individuals with the weakest ties to Mexican identity (those reporting no Mexican ancestry) are more likely to identify as Mexican, after the passage of Proposition 187. Since it is difficult to visually link county-level support for Proposition 187 from figure 10.1 with the rates of self-identification in figure 10.2, we will do this via regression analysis below. We also address the concern that migration may be driving these results by examining the period immediately before

5. The third-generation sample is especially small once we divide it up into those with Mexican-born grandparents on only the mother's side and only on the father's side, respectively, so we do not emphasize those results here.

6. Available at https://elections.cdn.sos.ca.gov/sov/1994-general/sov-complete.pdf.

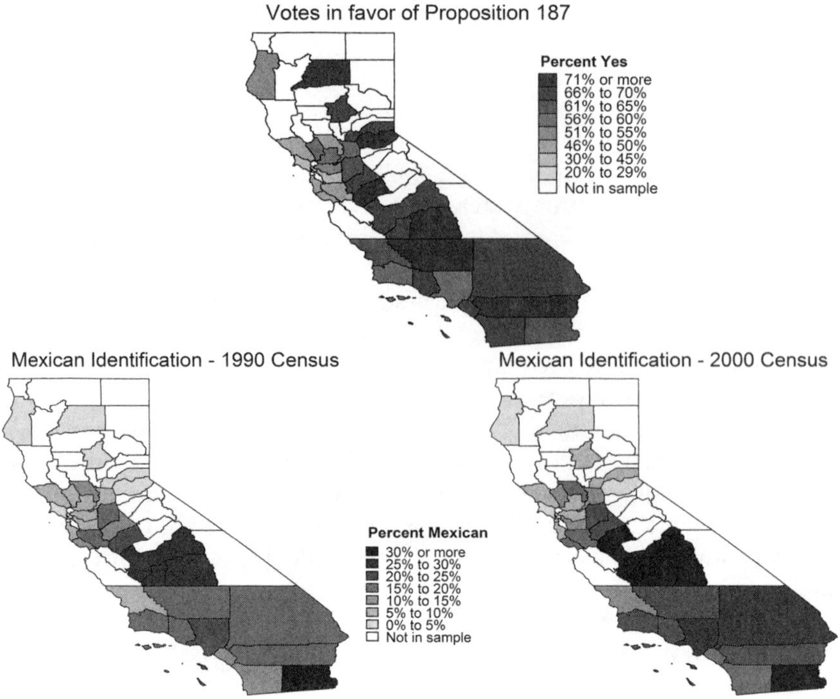

Fig. 10.1 Votes in favor of Proposition 187 and self-reported Mexican origin in California in the 1990 and 2000 Census, by county

Source: 1990 and 2000 Census Data. The samples include US-born individuals living in identifiable counties in California in 1990 and 2000.

and after the passage of Proposition 187 with CPS data from 1994 and 1995 and further decompose the sample to examine effects by immigrant generation and maternal versus paternal sources of Mexican ancestry.

10.3 Empirical Strategy

We measure the impact of anti-immigrant sentiment, as proxied by county-level vote share for Proposition 187, on the ethnic identification of individuals with the following difference-in-differences style regression model:

$$(1) \quad Mexican_{icy} = \alpha + \beta(Post\_1994_y \times Yes187_c) + \delta Post\_1994_y + \lambda_c + \mathbf{X}_{icy}\pi + \epsilon_{icy},$$

where $Mexican_{icy}$ is an indicator variable equal to one if person i in county c in year y identifies as Mexican on the Hispanic origin question. $Yes187_c$ is the percentage of votes in favor of Proposition 187 in county c (which ranges from 29.3 percent to 75.1 percent and averages 60 percent). This vote

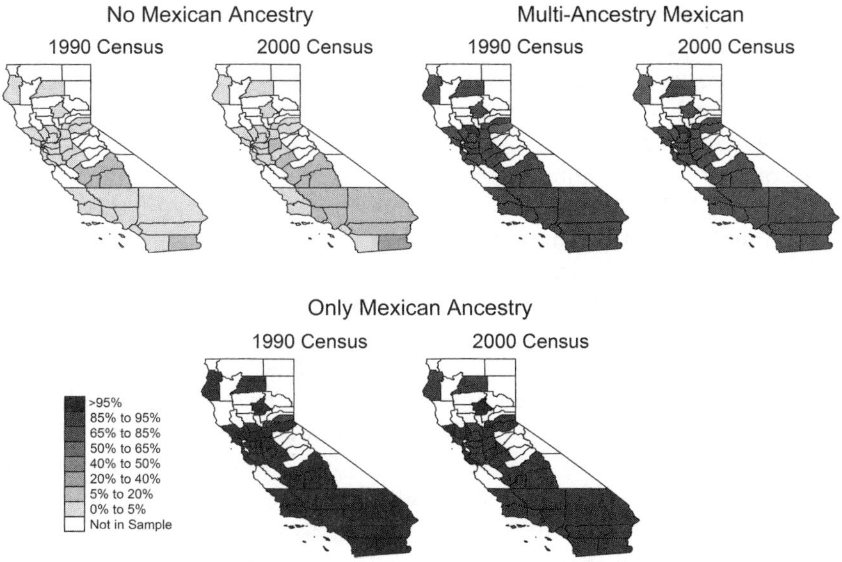

Fig. 10.2 Self-reported Mexican origin in California counties in the 1990 and 2000 Census, by Mexican ancestry

Source: 1990 and 2000 Census Data. The samples include US-born individuals living in identifiable counties in California in 1990 and 2000.

share measure is interacted with an indicator variable, $Post\_1994_y$, equal to one if the person is observed after the passage of Proposition 187, i.e., after the November 1994 California election, and zero otherwise. Since we use two survey waves from each data source, in the analysis using CPS data, $Post\_1994_y$, equals one for the 1995 survey year and zero for the 1994 survey year, while in the analysis using the census data, $Post\_1994_y$, equals one for the 2000 survey year and zero for the 1990 survey year. The coefficient of interest, β, is the estimated effect of 1 percentage-point increase in the percentage of votes in favor of Proposition 187 in the county on the probability that a person in that county will identify as Mexican. All regressions include individual level controls ($\mathbf{X}_{icy}$) for age, age squared, gender, a $Post\_1994_y$ indicator, and county fixed effects (λ_c). Sampling weights were used in the calculations and standard errors are clustered at the county level.

In principle, equation (1) could be driven by changes in the ethnic composition of the county-level population, which might change over time due to migration and be driven by variables that are correlated with support for Proposition 187 (e.g., county-level economic growth patterns), thus confounding our interpretation of the coefficient of interest (β) as the impact of Proposition 187 on ethnic identification. Thus, analyzing heterogeneity in our results by population group will be a critical component of arguing that the anti-immigrant, anti-Latino climate surrounding Proposition 187 affected individuals' willingness to identify as being of Mexican origin. As noted above, individuals with ties to a Mexican identity may be affected by the anti-immigrant sentiment exemplified by support for Proposition 187 in two opposite ways: (1) they may feel adverse impacts, like discrimination and hostility, which would reduce their willingness to identify as Mexican, and (2) they may feel greater salience of their Mexican identity which is activated in response to the heightened focus on Mexicans in the local community, thus increasing their willingness to identify as Mexican origin.

Although both effects may manifest in any individual, it is likely that they will vary based on the strength of the individual's ties to Mexican ancestry, and relatedly, the extent to which they are perceived to be Mexican. Specifically, individuals with stronger ties to Mexican ancestry may be more likely to be identified as Mexican and thus are more likely to feel threatened by adverse impacts of anti-immigrant sentiment, like discrimination or hostility, thus the net effect on their willingness to identify as Mexican may be negative. At the same time, individuals with weaker ties to Mexican ancestry, who may be less likely to be identified by others as Mexican and thus be relatively more protected from adverse impacts, may on balance feel the increased salience of their Mexican identity, and thus the net effect on their willingness to identify as Mexican may be positive.

To assess the evidence for these predictions, we exploit proxies for the strength of ties to a Mexican origin and observed Mexican ancestry available in the Census and the CPS. Specifically, in the Census, we estimate equation (1) separately for individuals with: (*i*) Any Mexican ancestry, (*ii*) no Mexican ancestry, (*iii*) Mexican ancestry along with other non-Mexican ancestry, and (*iv*) only Mexican ancestry, respectively, where categories (*ii*) through (*iv*) are mutually exclusive and exhaustive. In the CPS, we estimate equation (1) separately for individuals by immigrant generation, utilizing the CPS information on parental place of birth. We further decompose higher-order immigrant generations based on the source of the Mexican ties in their family lineage. For example, for second-generation Mexican Americans, we analyze results separately based on whether both parents were born in Mexico, or only the father was born in Mexico, or only the mother was born in Mexico. Note that the CPS does not include data on grandparental place of birth, so for third-generation Mexican Americans, our sample is limited to children living with both parents, for whom we can trace grandparental Mexican origin through data collected on the parental place of birth of the child's parents.

10.4 Results

10.4.1 Census Results

Table 10.4 shows the results of estimating equation (1) on the census sample using the full population of children and adults. In it, we see that US-

Table 10.4 Effect of a 1 percentage point increase in yes votes on Proposition 187 in county on the Hispanic identification of children and adults

	Children	Adults
Dependent Variable: Identified as Hispanic		
Percent Yes on 187 × 1{year = 2000}	.00218***	.00086***
	(.00052)	(.00030)
Mean of the dependent variable	.3745	.1399
Dependent Variable: Identified as Mexican		
Percent Yes on 187 × 1{year = 2000}	.00192***	.00056***
	(.00059)	(.00019)
Mean of the dependent variable	.3113	.1145
Dependent Variable: Identified as Other Hispanic		
Percent Yes on 187 × 1{year = 2000}	.00025	.00030**
	(.00042)	(.00011)
Mean of the dependent variable	.05611	.02105
Sample size	689,486	1,458,450

*Statistically significant at 10 percent level; **at 5 percent level; ***at 1 percent level.

Source: 1990 and 2000 Census Data.

Note: Robust standard errors clustered at the county level are shown in parentheses. Sampling weights were used in the calculations. The sample includes US-born children (ages 0–17) and adults (ages 18 and older) living in identifiable counties in California in 1990 and 2000. Individuals with allocated Hispanic origin are excluded. All regressions include controls for age, age squared, gender, a year 2000 indicator, and county fixed effects. Percent Yes on 187 is the percentage of yes votes on Proposition 187 in the county.

born children and adults in California are more likely to identify as Mexican origin in 2000 the greater the support for Proposition 187. However, as noted above, this positive association may simply reflect a positive correlation between the share of Mexican origin individuals in a given county and anti-immigrant sentiment in that location that is increasing over time, and may be driven by migration.

Table 10.5 instead focuses on the crux of the causal identification strategy by decomposing the sample into individuals based on the strength of their Mexican ancestry. The most striking results are the opposing patterns of Mexican identification between individuals with no Mexican ancestry and those with only Mexican ancestry. Specifically, a 1 percentage point increase in support for Proposition 187 results in an increase in identifying as Mexican origin of 0.117 percentage points for children with no Mexican ancestry (relative to a mean of 7.76 percent), and 0.04 percentage points for adults (relative to a mean of 2.27 percent). At the same time, the signs of the coefficient of interest are negative for those with only Mexican ancestry (–0.0003 for children and –0.00095 for adults), though only statistically significant for adults. The latter shows that a 1 percentage point increase in support for Proposition 187 results in a decrease in identifying as Mexican origin of 0.095 percentage points for adults with only Mexican ancestry (relative to a mean of 95.45 percent).[7] It is also worth noting that table 10.5 shows that adults with only Mexican ancestry are more likely to identify with another non-Mexican Hispanic identity in response to Proposition 187 (coefficient estimate 0.00082, p-value 0.005). The fact that the latter set of coefficients is similar in magnitude, but opposite in sign, suggests that individuals may be switching out of Mexican identity into a non-Mexican Hispanic identity in response to Proposition 187. All together, these results are consistent with the interpretation that anti-immigrant sentiment, and specifically anti-Mexican sentiment, as measured by the county-level support for Proposition 187, decreased the willingness to identify as Mexican origin for those most likely to be targets of hostility and discrimination, while it increased the willingness to identify as Mexican origin for those who would be relatively more protected from the adverse effects of anti-immigrant sentiment, yet more likely to be affected by the increased salience of their Mexican identity.

10.4.2 CPS Results

As mentioned above, one concern with the US Census results is that there is a large gap between the measurement of ethnic identification in the survey waves (1990 and 2000) and the passage of Proposition 187 in 1994. This raises concerns about differential migration rates over these long time periods and raises the possibility that an omitted variable, correlated with ethnic identification and support for Proposition 187, might be driving the results. To address these concerns, we use the 1994 and 1995 waves of the CPS, which also include information on parental place of birth that allow us to further explore mechanisms underlying our results.

Table 10.6 shows the CPS sample results from estimating equation (1) for adults distinguished by immigrant generation. Results show that ethnic identification of first-generation immigrants does not appear responsive to anti-immigrant sentiment as the coefficient of interest is not statistically significant. This makes sense since this group was born in Mexico and may not have an obvious choice of ethnic identity since they are likely to be perceived universally as Mexican-born. A choice of ethnic identity may thus only really be possible at higher-order immigrant generations, who are US-born, and especially those with parents who are intermarried, and thus come from different ethnic backgrounds, resulting in the possibility of a choice of ethnic identity for their children.

For second-generation adults, who are all US-born Americans, table 10.6 shows a negative impact of the passage of Proposition 187 on willingness to

7. To interpret these results in greater context, one might consider going from the 25th percentile to the 75th percentile in voter support for Proposition 187, which is a 13.2 percentage point difference. Thus, a 0.095 percentage point drop in identification for adults with only Mexican ancestry translates to a 1.3 percent decrease comparing the 25th percentile to the 75th percentile in the distribution of voter support, relative to the mean of the dependent variable (i.e., [13.2*.095]/.9545).

Table 10.5 **Effect of a 1 percentage point increase in yes votes on Proposition 187 in county on Hispanic identification of children and adults, by Mexican ancestry**

	Any Mexican Ancestry		No Mexican Ancestry		Multi-Ancestry Mexican		Only Mexican Ancestry	
	Children	Adults	Children	Adults	Children	Adults	Children	Adults
Dep. Var.: Identified as Hispanic								
Percent Yes on 187 × 1{year = 2000}	.00013	–.00019	.00145**	.00062***	.00058	–.00077	.00004	–.00013
	(.00032)	(.00020)	(.00056)	(.00018)	(.00119)	(.00089)	(.00016)	(.00014)
Mean of the dependent variable	.9691	.9689	.1483	.0470	.8428	.8328	.9867	.9850
Dep. Var.: Identified as Mexican								
Percent Yes on 187 × 1{year = 2000}	.00037	–.00067**	.00117***	.00040***	.00304*	–.00002	–.00030	–.00095***
	(.00042)	(.00026)	(.00022)	(.00011)	(.00155)	(.00094)	(.00030)	(.00022)
Mean of the dependent variable	.9257	.9329	.0776	.0227	.7118	.7494	.9556	.9545
Dep. Var.: Identified as Other Hispanic								
Percent Yes on 187 × 1{year = 2000}	–.00024	.00049*	.00029	.00022**	–.00246**	–.00075	.00034	.00082***
	(.00023)	(.00027)	(.00046)	(.00010)	(.00117)	(.00071)	(.00021)	(.00027)
Mean of the dependent variable	.04151	.0347	.06166	.01952	.1166	.06594	.03032	.02983
Sample size	193,579	148,524	495,907	1,309,926	9,163	5,635	170,260	133,267

*Statistically significant at 10 percent level; **at 5 percent level; ***at 1 percent level.

Source: 1990 and 2000 Census Data.

Note: Robust standard errors clustered at the county level are shown in parentheses. Sampling weights were used in the calculations. The sample includes US-born children (ages 0–17) and adults (ages 18 and older) living in California in 1990 and 2000. Individuals with allocated Hispanic origin are excluded. All regressions include controls for age, age squared, gender, a year 2000 indicator, and county fixed effects. Percent Yes on 187 is the percentage of yes votes on Proposition 187 in the county.

Table 10.6 **Effect of a 1 percentage point increase in yes votes on Proposition 187 in county on the Mexican identification of adults by Mexican generation**

	Mexican			
	1st-Generation	2nd-Generation		
Percent Yes on 187 × 1{year=1995}	.0008	–.0072***		
	(.0007)	(.0021)		
Mean of Dependent Variable	.9835	.932		
Sample size	2,540	833		
Second-generation Mexican:	Both parents Mexican	One parent Mexican	Only mom Mexican	Only dad Mexican
Percent Yes on 187 × 1{year=1995}	–.0024	–.0137***	–.0131*	–.0173**
	(.0023)	(.0042)	(.0066)	(.0082)
Mean of Dependent Variable	.9794	.8734	.8482	.8947
Sample size	460	373	174	199

Source: 1994–1995 Current Population Survey (CPS) fourth outgoing rotation group data.

Note: The samples include adults 18 and older who reside in a California county that can be identified in the CPS data. Robust standard errors clustered at the county level are shown in parentheses. All regressions include controls for age, age squared, gender, year fixed effects and county fixed effects. Percent yes on 187 is the percentage of yes votes on Proposition 187 in the county. Sampling weights were used in the calculations.

identify as Mexican (coefficient estimate –0.0072, p-value 0.003). Further analysis shows that this effect is driven by second-generation immigrants with only one Mexican-born parent (coefficient estimate –0.0137, p-value 0.004). Similar magnitudes are obtained if the individual has Mexican parentage on their mother's or father's side.[8]

Note that we can only trace the adult sample to the second generation using the CPS data on parental place of birth, and thus one might argue that the entire adult sample has relatively strong ties to Mexican identity, since one of their parents was born in Mexico. Thus, for the adult sample, it makes sense that we only observe negative impacts of anti-immigrant sentiment on rates of Mexican identification.

Moving to the sample of children in table 10.7, we can explore the impacts of anti-immigrant sentiment on the first, second, and third immigrant generations. As with other papers that have studied ethnic attrition, we do not

8. It should also be noted that the magnitudes of the estimates using the CPS sample are generally larger than the magnitudes of the estimates using the census sample. This may be due to the longer lag between the 1994 election and the census survey, which would be consistent with an informational effect of the vote that dissipates over time. Another possible explanation is that the CPS results report impacts on a precisely defined treatment group based on immigrant generation, whereas the Census results demonstrate impacts on groups defined by the relatively more nebulous categories of Mexican ancestry.

Table 10.7 **Effect of a 1 percentage point increase in yes votes on Proposition 187 in county on the Mexican identification of children by Mexican generation**

	Mexican			not Mexican
	1st-Gen.	2nd-Gen.	3rd-Gen.	3rd+-Gen.
Percent Yes on 187 × 1{year=1995}	.0004	–.0018	.0206**	.0007
	(.0013)	(.0024)	(.0095)	(.0012)
Mean of Dependent Variable	.9779	.9431	.6819	.08004
Sample size	275	1,321	196	2,354
Second-generation Mexican:	Both parents Mexican	One parent Mexican	Only mom Mexican	Only dad Mexican
Percent Yes on 187 × 1{year=1995}	.0010	–.0123	.0097	–.0347**
	(.0011)	(.0114)	(.0129)	(.0148)
Mean of Dependent Variable	.9907	.8173	.8316	.8011
Sample size	967	354	196	158
Third-generation Mexican:	Mexican on both sides	Mexican on one side	Mexican only on mom side	Mexican only on dad side
Percent Yes on 187 × 1{year=1995}	–.0563***	.0269**	.0906***	–.0130**
	(.0109)	(.0106)	(.0112)	(.0051)
Mean of Dependent Variable	.8997	.6213	.6797	.5673
Sample size	41	155	74	81

Source: 1994–1995 Current Population Survey (CPS) fourth outgoing rotation group data.

Note: The samples include children 17 and younger who are living with both parents and who reside in a California county that can be identified in the CPS data. Robust standard errors clustered at the county level are shown in parentheses. All regressions include controls for age, age squared, gender, year fixed effects, and county fixed effects. Percent yes on 187 is the percentage of yes votes on Proposition 187 in the county. Sampling weights were used in the calculations. Not Mexican 3rd+ generation are US-born individuals with two US-born parents and no grandparents born in Mexico.

see much evidence of an impact on second-generation children (Duncan and Trejo 2011; Antman and Duncan 2023). This may in part be due to the fact that the racial and ethnic identities of children are likely being entered into surveys by their parents. This reduces the amount of discordance we might observe between ethnic identification of second-generation children and their parents, who are first-generation Mexican immigrants and, as we have seen above, are not likely to change their ethnic identities in response to Proposition 187. This would explain why we do not find a statistically significant impact of Proposition 187 on the ethnic identification of second-generation children, though the coefficient is negative (–0.0018).

When we further decompose the sample into the source of Mexican parentage, we see a reduced willingness to identify as Mexican in the sample of children with only Mexican-born fathers (coefficient –0.0347, p-value 0.034). As this group would also likely have a Spanish surname, these results are consistent with our hypothesis that those with the strongest link to a Mexican origin, who are most likely to be perceived as Mexican by others, would reduce their willingness to identify as Mexican in response to the anti-immigrant sentiment surrounding Proposition 187.

At the third generation, we also see more nuanced responses, consistent with both predictions regarding reduced and increased motivations to identify with a Mexican-origin identity. First, we see that third-generation children with the strongest ties to Mexican ancestry, that is, children with Mexican-origin ancestors on both their mother's and father's sides, are less likely to identify as Mexican after the passage of Proposition 187 (coefficient estimate –0.0563, *p*-value 0.002). Second, we see that children with Mexican ancestry on only one side of their family are more likely to identify after the passage of Proposition 187 (coefficient estimate 0.0269, *p*-value 0.021).

Unpacking this further, we see that this positive impact is driven by third-generation children with a Mexican-origin ancestor only on their mother's side, and thus who are arguably the least likely to be perceived as Mexican since their last name is not likely to reveal their Mexican identity (coefficient estimate 0.0906, *p*-value <0.001). For third-generation children with a Mexican-origin ancestor on their father's side, and who are thus more likely to have a Spanish surname and thus more likely to be perceived outwardly as Mexican, we see a reduced willingness to identify as Mexican in response to Proposition 187 (coefficient estimate –0.0130, *p*-value 0.025). These results are consistent with our predictions that individuals with stronger ties to a Mexican-origin identity, who are arguably more likely to suffer adverse impacts related to the anti-immigrant, anti-Latino, hostility surrounding Proposition 187, will be less likely to identify as Mexican in response. At the same time, those with weaker ties to a Mexican-origin identity, who may be less likely to suffer these adverse impacts, increase their willingness to identify as Mexican due to the raising of ethnic consciousness which surrounded the passage of Proposition 187. The latter might also be described as a reaction in direct opposition to the anti-immigrant sentiment expressed by supporters of the measure.

10.5 Conclusion

To our knowledge, this paper is the first to explore the causal impacts of anti-immigrant sentiment, and political discourse more broadly, on the choice of ethnic identity. It is also the first paper to extend the research on the causal impacts of incentives to identify as a racial minority group (Antman and Duncan 2015, Antman and Duncan 2023) to an ethnic minority group and specifically, to Hispanic and Mexican identity. Thus, we bring an important causal perspective to the existing literature on ethnic attrition which has largely focused on linking intermarriage, itself a choice, with the choice of ethnic identity (Duncan and Trejo 2011; Antman et al. 2016, 2020).

Our results suggest that individuals with stronger ancestral ties to a Mexican origin identity, and those who are more likely to be perceived as Mexican due to last name or direct parentage, are less likely to identify in response to the passage of Proposition 187. At the same time, we find that individuals with weaker ancestral ties to a Mexican origin identity, who are arguably less likely to be perceived as Mexican, are more likely to identify as Mexican. The fact that these effects run in opposing directions bolsters our argument that our results are not due to some confounding variable but instead are driven by the anti-immigrant sentiment that is more prevalent after the passage of Proposition 187 and in those counties with greater support for the measure. The fact that we find evidence suggesting increased willingness to identify as non-Mexican Hispanic origin for those individuals with only Mexican ancestry also bolsters our interpretation that these changes are driven by the specific anti-Mexican sentiment associated with Proposition 187. Nevertheless, to the extent that other anti-immigrant, anti-Latino sentiments developed over this period and may also be correlated with support for Proposition 187, our estimates may be picking up those changes as well. While we have tried to address these concerns by narrowing the time window around the passage of Proposition 187, we acknowledge that it is possible that our results are driven by a multitude of factors resulting in a broader anti-immigrant climate, which is itself reflected in local support for Proposition 187. Further research should try to disentangle these effects to shed greater light on the mechanisms underlying the choice of ethnic identity. Other important avenues of exploration include interactions between ethnic identity, racial identity, and behavior that may mitigate the adverse impacts from anti-immigration sentiment, such as choice of residence, intermarriage, languages spoken, occupation, and voting behavior. Given changes in US immigration flows which now stem more substantially from other parts of Latin America, additional analyses should also link the ethnic identification of other (non-Mexican) Hispanic groups with anti-immigrant rhetoric that targets these groups, and thus give a more complete picture of evolving ethnic identity.

Acknowledgments

We thank Randall Akee, Lawrence F. Katz, Mark Loewenstein, Sergio Barrera, Stephen J. Trejo, as well as seminar and conference participants at the NBER-CRIW 2023 Pre-Conference and 2024 Conference on Race, Ethnicity, and Economic Statistics for the 21st Century, IPUMS 30 Research Conference, Pew Research Center, 2023 Southern Economic Association Conference, and Colorado Applied Workshop. For acknowledgments, sources of research support, and disclosure of the authors' material financial relationships, if any, please see https://www.nber.org/books-and-chapters/race-ethnicity-and-economic-statistics-21st-century/ethnic-identity-and-anti-immigrant-sentiment-evidence-proposition-187.

References

Abrajano, Marisa, and Lisa García Bedolla. 2020. "Latino Political Participation 25 Years After the Passage of Proposition 187: Opportunities and Continuing Challenges." *UC Davis Law Review* 53(4): 1831–1858.

Akerlof, George A., and Rachel E. Kranton. 2000. "Economics and Identity." *Quarterly Journal of Economics* 115(3): 715–53.

Antman, Francisca M., and Brian Duncan. 2015. "Incentives to Identify: Racial Identity in the Age of Affirmative Action." *Review of Economics and Statistics* 97(3): 710–13.

Antman, Francisca M., and Brian Duncan. 2023. "American Indian Casinos and Native American Self-Identification." *Journal of the European Economic Association* 21(6): 2547–2585. https://doi.org/10.1093/jeea/jvad018.

Antman, Francisca M., Brian Duncan, and Stephen J. Trejo. 2016. "Ethnic Attrition and the Observed Health of Later Generation Mexican Americans." *American Economic Review* 106(5): 467–71.

Antman, Francisca M., Brian Duncan, and Stephen J. Trejo. 2020. "Ethnic Attrition, Assimilation, and the Measured Health Outcomes of Mexican Americans." *Journal of Population Economics* 33(4): 1499–1522.

Antman, Francisca M., Brian Duncan, and Stephen J. Trejo. 2023. "Hispanic Americans in the Labor Market: Patterns over Time and across Generations." *Journal of Economic Perspectives* 37(1): 169–98. DOI: 10.1257/jep.37.1.169.

Budiman, Abby. 2020. "Key Findings About US immigrants." Pew Research Center, August 20. Accessed on June 28, 2024. https://www.pewresearch.org/short-reads/2020/08/20/key-findings-about-u-s-immigrants/.

Cassan, Guilhelm. 2015. "Identity-Based Policies and Identity Manipulation: Evidence from Colonial Punjab." *American Economic Journal: Economic Policy* 7: 103–31.

Dahis, Ricardo, Emily Nix, and Nancy Qian. 2020. "Choosing Racial Identity in the United States, 1880–1940." NBER Working Paper No. 26465. Cambridge, MA: National Bureau of Economic Research.

Denkmann, Libby. 2019. "After Prop 187 Came the Fall of California's Once-Mighty GOP, and the Rise of Latino Political Power." *LAist*, November 11. Accessed on June 28, 2024. https://laist.com/news/prop-187-political-impact-california-latino-participation-power-surges-republican-party-fading.

Duncan, Brian, and Stephen J. Trejo. 2011. "Intermarriage and the Intergenerational Transmission of Ethnic Identity and Human Capital for Mexican Americans." *Journal of Labor Economics* 29(2): 195–227.

Flood, Sarah, Miriam King, Renae Rodgers, Steven Ruggles, J. Robert Warren, Daniel Backman, Annie Chen, Grace Cooper, Stephanie Richards, Megan Schouweiler, and Michael Westberry. 2023. IPUMS CPS: Version 11.0 [dataset]. Minneapolis, MN: IPUMS, 2023. Extracted on September 6, 2023. https://doi.org/10.18128/D030.V11.0.

Francis, A. M., and M. Tannuri-Pianto. 2013. "Endogenous Race in Brazil: Affirmative Action and the Construction of Racial Identity among Young Adults." *Economic Development and Cultural Change* 61: 731–53.

Martin, Philip. 1995. "Proposition 187 in California." *International Migration Review* 29(1): 255–63.

Moslimani, Mohamad, Mark Hugo Lopez, and Luis Noe-Bustamante. 2023. "11 Facts About Hispanic Origin Groups in the US." Pew Research Center,

August 16. Downloaded June 28, 2024. https://www.pewresearch.org/short-reads/2023/08/16/11-facts-about-hispanic-origin-groups-in-the-us/.

Ogilvie, Jessica P. 2019. "Proposition 187: Why a Ballot Initiative That Passed In 1994 (And Never Went into Law) Still Matters." *LAist*, November 6. Accessed on June 28, 2024. https://laist.com/news/proposition-187-what-you-need-to-know/.

Penner, A. M., and A. Saperstein. 2008. "How Social Status Shapes Race." *PNAS Proceedings of the National Academy of Sciences of the United States of America* 105:19628–19630.

Ruggles, Steven, Sarah Flood, Matthew Sobek, Daniel Backman, Annie Chen, Grace Cooper, Stephanie Richards, Renae Rogers, and Megan Schouweiler. 2023. IPUMS USA: Version 14.0 [dataset]. Minneapolis, MN: IPUMS, 2023. Extracted on May 19, 2023. https://doi.org/10.18128/D010.V14.0

11

Granular Income Inequality and Mobility Using IDDA
Exploring Patterns Across Race and Ethnicity

Illenin Kondo, Kevin Rinz, Natalie Gubbay, Brandon Hawkins, John Voorheis, and Abigail Wozniak

11.1 Introduction

Earnings in the United States are significantly more unequal today than 50 years ago, when a multi-decade pattern of widely shared growth began to retreat. Since 1980, the pace of earnings growth has been uneven, and varying, for Americans throughout the earnings distribution. The course of widening earnings disparities has been well documented, and a number of patterns and episodes have emerged (Hoffmann et al. 2020). The highest earners have experienced consistent growth in their earnings since 1980, although since about 2000, this has slowed or become more concentrated among the very highest earners (Kopczuk et al. 2010; Blanchet et al. 2022). Relative real earnings for workers below the median have fallen and partially recovered more than once (Autor et al. 2008; Blanchet et al. 2022; Autor et al. 2023). Although these patterns are robust, important differences across demographic groups—notably between women and men—have been documented (Guvenen et al. 2022).

Illenin Kondo is a senior research economist with the Opportunity & Inclusive Growth Institute at the Federal Reserve Bank of Minneapolis.

Kevin Rinz is a senior fellow and research advisor at the Washington Center for Equitable Growth.

Natalie Gubbay was a research associate at the Opportunity and Inclusive Growth Institute of the Federal Reserve Bank of Minneapolis when this chapter was written. She was critical to its successful completion, and her coauthors are saddened by her premature death in late 2024.

Brandon Hawkins is a graduate student in the Economics Department at the University of California, Davis.

John Voorheis is a principal economist in the Center for Economic Studies at the US Census Bureau.

Abigail Wozniak is vice president of the Research Division and director of the Opportunity & Inclusive Growth Institute at the Federal Reserve Bank of Minneapolis.

A parallel literature has documented increases in inequality in broader measures of income after 1980—for instance, tax-unit-level-adjusted gross income from IRS tax data or household income reported on surveys such as the Current Population Survey (Burkhauser et al. 2012; Piketty and Saez 2003). While broad measures of inequality that are sensitive to the middle of the distribution (such as the Gini coefficient) have continued to increase at a measured pace, top income inequality (measured, for example, by the top 1 percent share of income) saw most of its increase before 2000 (Burkhauser et al. 2011). Over the period from 2000 through 2019, there has not been a clear trend in most top income inequality measures (Piketty et al. 2017; Auten and Splinter 2024).[1]

In spite of this significant body of evidence, there is still much we do not know about how earnings and income have changed for many Americans over the last five decades of stubbornly rising inequality. The open questions are particularly acute at the subnational level. For example, have US groups defined by race and ethnicity experienced the major episodes in changing income inequality in similar ways, or not? Questions about how income evolves over time for members of these groups have also been difficult to answer. Do low earners in all demographic groups move into higher earnings percentiles at the same rate? Do these patterns differ depending on the state where individuals live and work? Observing the evolution of income distributions for subnational groups like these is key for more fully understanding and, potentially, addressing US earnings and income inequality, particularly in light of the non-uniform patterns identified in the literature.

Answering these questions requires data on income distributions and income mobility at high levels of granularity. We define a data source as having this granularity if measures of income distributions and dynamics are available in three dimensions: for many demographic groups, for geographic areas below the national level, and for intersections of the previous two dimensions. Yet, the availability of such data has been limited. In this paper, we construct and use a novel data source with extensive information in the three dimensions of granularity: the Income Distributions and Dynamics in America, or IDDA, data. IDDA has been made publicly available as part of this project.

Using IDDA, we first document patterns of income inequality in the United States as a whole that differ in some important ways from patterns identified in publicly available survey sources, although the patterns are similar at a high level. Our main comparison is with the Current Population Survey (CPS). Despite broadly similar aggregate patterns, we find that the

1. Measuring inequality of broader income, particularly at the top of the distribution, is complicated by economy-wide changes in the structure of business ownership toward closely held pass-through entities, now the dominant source of income for top earners. Assumptions about how to allocate unreported and untaxed income flowing through these pass-through entities have outsized importance for inferred trends in top income inequality (Smith et al. 2019).

CPS is inadequate for producing basic distributional statistics for many race and ethnicity groups at the state level.[2] Moreover, the material differences between the distributional patterns produced by IDDA and the CPS at the national level suggest that researchers would benefit from using IDDA as a reference when studying inequality for race and ethnicity groups, and other groups, even at this highly aggregate level.

To illustrate the relevance of granular approaches to studying income and earnings inequality in US race and ethnicity groups, we extend comparisons in a key paper on earnings convergence for Black and White men (Bayer and Charles 2018) to more recent years, more top percentiles, and more granular race and ethnicity groups using IDDA. We show a unique receding pattern for Black men and Black women between 2005 and 2019, relative to White men. Across the earnings distribution, earnings for both groups fell further behind earnings for White men. The divergence begins following the Great Recession and continues through the end of the data period. Over this period, relative to White men, earnings for men in other race and ethnicity groups, for women in other race and ethnicity groups, or for White women do not consistently lose ground.

We then ask, What income dynamics patterns accompanied the development of inequality that we observed? This analysis leverages the longitudinal dimension of the administrative data underlying IDDA statistics on income mobility and income changes by demographic group. As we did with the distributional measures, we begin by documenting how changes in incomes reported in IDDA compare with income dynamics constructed using survey-based, public-use data. Do those differ across population subgroups, such as those defined by race and ethnicity, or initial income? We find that the distribution of earnings growth as estimated using public-use survey data is more spread out relative to the distribution estimated using IDDA, and survey-based estimates are substantially more variable within groups. This noise obscures differences in earnings growth across groups, but IDDA data point to consistent differences in earnings growth across groups defined by race and ethnicity. Asian and White earners typically see faster growth, while Black and American Indian or Alaska Native earners see slower growth, especially over longer horizons.

Finally, we document earnings and income patterns for individuals living in Native areas, which include American Indian reservations, trust lands, and other Native geographies as delineated by the Census Bureau. We find that since the Great Recession, earnings have fallen for Native earners living in Native areas relative to American Indian or Alaska Native earners throughout the United States. Combined, our analysis of income distributions and dynamics for US race and ethnicity groups suggests that rela-

2. Appendix material reveals similar issues with measuring some subnational distributions using the American Community Survey (ACS).

tive earnings can evolve quite differently across groups during a given time period. Moreover, this evolution can vary across locations and at different earnings percentiles.

To answer our research questions, we compiled the Income Distribution and Dynamics in America granular dataset, or IDDA, alongside this paper. IDDA is built from the universe of tax records matched to internal Census Bureau demographic information for the period 1998 to 2019. It reflects the experiences of the populations of US tax filers and W-2 employees over this period. Broadly, we tabulate statistics from individual-level tax records to describe the distribution of incomes and movements through it over time for a large set of demographic groups. More precisely, we compute statistics for groups defined by four elements: income source and unit; United States or individual states; year; and demographic groups defined by age bins, sex, race, ethnicity, birthplace (US or abroad), and intersections of the demographic groups. Within each group, we calculate two types of statistics. The first type characterizes the distribution of incomes for a group in several ways. These include percentile values ranging from the 10th percentile to the top 99.999th percentile for the group; shares of income going to top earners; and shares of the group among all top earners at a point in time. The second type characterizes the mobility of incomes in the group across income distribution bins over time, as well as the distribution of income changes experienced starting from a given initial income distribution bin.

We developed this novel resource to answer our questions because even large surveys like the American Community Survey (ACS) may capture samples that are small in absolute terms for groups that constitute small shares of the population (either nationally or in a specific place). Such samples may not support reliable estimates that describe the full distribution of income. Surveys also tend not to follow respondents over time, thereby making it difficult to use them to understand income dynamics, or they trade off cross-sectional sample size against panel duration, limiting the granularity of any income dynamics estimates that may be producible. Moreover, measuring top incomes well is critical for understanding inequality, but measures based on surveys can be distorted by both disclosure avoidance procedures (e.g., topcoding) and survey misreporting (Burkhauser et al. 2011; Bee and Mitchell 2017; Bee et al. 2023).

Such data issues are particularly important when it comes to understanding differences in income inequality and dynamics across groups defined by race and ethnicity, as these groups are unevenly distributed across space and differentially likely to be affected by measurement issues related to top incomes. It is especially important to be aware of differences in the prevalence of groups across space in this context, as state income distributions have become less similar to each other at the top in recent decades, and this phenomenon appears to be driven by the top of the White income distribution (Rinz and Voorheis 2023).

This paper and the underlying data construction contribute to a growing field in which administrative sources are leveraged to understand detailed distributional patterns in the US economy while also sharing aggregate data so that other researchers may more quickly innovate.[3] Chetty et al. (2014) analyze measures of intergenerational income mobility by location of residence for a cohort of individuals born in the early 1980s and make their data available via their Opportunity Atlas portal (Chetty et al. 2018). Blanchet et al. (2022) analyze shares of income and economic growth accruing in the most recent daily period to US earners by percentile, and they make their method available on their Realtime Inequality site. In a recent issue of *Quantitative Economics*, multiple papers explored detailed country-level inequality data constructed from administrative data from 13 countries and released as the Global Repository of Income Dynamics Repository (GRID).[4] Additionally, the Census Bureau's Mobility, Opportunity and Volatility Statistics (MOVS) and National Experimental Wellbeing Statistics (NEWS) projects will produce public data products measuring income inequality, poverty, and income mobility using linked survey, census, and administrative data.[5]

Relative to these efforts, IDDA offers several advantages for studying subnational patterns in labor market earnings and incomes for its populations of US tax filers and W-2 employees. First, our data are granular: IDDA includes a wide range of statistics for national and subnational geographic areas (states) as well as many subnational demographic populations. Second, we combine measurement of income changes and mobility with measurement of income distributions from a single source for our populations of interest. And third, the statistics that underlie our analysis are computed directly from the universe of tax information, which means we do not need to rely on modeling assumptions to link micro and macro data sources.

These features are especially important for producing granular measures characterizing experiences across income distributions and income dynamics across groups defined by place, income rank, and demographic characteristics such as gender, age, US-birth status, race and ethnicity, or their intersections. Measuring such experiences can be very demanding in terms of the number of observations required, and relying on samples generated by even large surveys like the ACS can leave some groups without estimates for most places and most groups without estimates for some places, as we will show. Even when it is possible to construct estimates of distributional features from public survey data, they are often extremely noisy. Combin-

3. We facilitate public access to IDDA through https://www.minneapolisfed.org/institute/income-distributions-and-dynamics-in-america/.

4. Visit https://mebdi.org/grid-database for the online GRID portal. See McKinney et al. (2022) for findings in the United States.

5. See MOVS (https://www.census.gov/programs-surveys/ces/data/public-use-data/mobility-opportunity-volatility-statistics.html) and NEWS (https://www.census.gov/data/experimental-data-products/national-experimental-wellbeing-statistics.html) pages on the Census website.

ing survey and administrative data, as we do in this project, substantially expands the set of groups and places that can be included, as well as the possible measures that can be produced. Akee et al. (2019) use these linkages at the US level to document differences across race and ethnicity groups in incomes, top income shares, and income mobility. Rinz and Voorheis (2023) also leverage these linkages at the subnational level for tax units to discuss large differences in income growth across race and ethnicity groups within a state, especially for top incomes. See Partridge et al. (1996), Morrill (2000), Frank (2014), and Sommeiller and Price (2014) for existing work on subnational inequality in the United States.

Our approach has many strengths, but the measures constructed for IDDA have some limitations. These stem from the specific populations and types of income observed. To answer our questions of interest, we examine the universe of US tax filers and W-2 recipients. These are certainly important groups, but they are not representative of all US workers or households, and we did not attempt to re-weight the data to reflect other important populations of interest. Also, the income from which our statistics are tabulated is limited to pre-tax and pre-transfer sources. This means it is inadequate for studying questions in which income after redistribution is a key component—for example, questions related to poverty or consumption.

This paper proceeds as follows. We describe IDDA's construction in section 11.2. In section 11.3, we use IDDA to analyze trends in earnings inequality for detailed race and ethnicity groups, and we compare these to what might be inferred from the Current Population Survey (CPS). Section 11.4 describes patterns in income mobility and conditional income changes for the same groups in IDDA. In section 11.5, we ask similar questions to those in previous sections, but we provide analysis for groups and places that are not readily available in any public sources: Native people living in Native areas. Section 11.6 concludes.

11.2 IDDA Construction

The Income Distributions and Dynamics in America (IDDA) dataset consists of novel granular statistics on the distribution of incomes, income changes, and income mobility. This dataset is generated from underlying microdata that combine select income and geographic information from the universe of individual tax returns with demographic information available from various sources through the US Census Bureau. The key features of these data are difficult to collectively replicate in other settings: for detailed US demographic groups and subnational geographies, they provide high-quality measurements of top incomes and income dynamics using statistically meaningful sample sizes and longitudinal linkage of individual observations.

A statistic $\mathcal{S}_{k,g}^{l,t}$ in IDDA is defined by four dimensions: k denotes the primary income source and income concept; t denotes the year; l denotes the geographical location, US or state; and g denotes the demographic group. Time and geography are straightforward dimensions, but we discuss income types, estimation samples, and the available demographic groups in this section.[6]

11.2.1 Primary Data Sources

IDDA statistics are generated for select income concepts derived from the universe of individual tax returns. We report IDDA statistics from two primary data sources: (i) individual-level earnings data built from the universe of Wage and Tax Statements, or Form W-2s, and (ii) address-level household income data based on the universe of Income Tax Returns, or Form 1040s.

The requirement to file an individual federal income tax statement is subject to various exemptions, including a minimum gross income filing requirement. In contrast, the US Internal Revenue Code (see US Code, Title 26, section 6051) requires employers to file a W-2 for every employee. Therefore, the primary W-2 data source spans the universe of earnings from formal employment in the United States: from the highest values to the smallest earnings for individuals with limited labor force attachment.

However, labor force attachment can vary substantially across demographic groups or over the business cycle. In order to help make earnings statistics more comparable across demographic groups and years, we define a secondary individual earnings data source restricted to prime-age workers (PAW) only: individuals ages 25–54 with annual W-2 earnings above the equivalent of earning the federal minimum hourly wages for 20 weekly hours over 13 weeks. In the absence of sub-annual employment information, we use total earnings as a proxy for labor force attachment. The longitudinal dimension of the PAW individual data also allows us to measure how many workers enter or leave this notion of labor force attachment.

11.2.2 Income Concepts and Measures from Administrative Tax Data

Form W-2 earnings. The W-2 data we use cover tax years 2005–2019 and include selected fields. IDDA contains measures for the following W-2 tax data categories: (i) individual wage and salary compensation; (ii) deferred compensation; and (iii) their sum. Wage and salary compensation is reported in Box 1 of Form W-2 and is positive for all earners included in our measurement datasets. Deferred compensation is one form of compensation recorded in Box 12 and may be positive or zero. While a worker's total compensation may include other components, such as employer-sponsored

6. More details can be found in the online documentation available on the Minneapolis Fed IDDA download page, https://www.minneapolisfed.org/-/media/assets/institute/census/data-center/idda_technical_documentation.pdf.

health care, retirement contributions, or other benefits, we only observe these two components and treat their sum as a proxy for total compensation.

From tax units to households. Even though household-level income information is commonly available in surveys, tax forms do not readily provide a household unit construct: members of a household may file their tax returns jointly or separately. According to the Census Bureau, "A household consists of all the people who occupy a housing unit" (US Census Bureau 2024). Therefore, we aggregate Form 1040 incomes from tax filing units to address-level incomes as a measure of total "household" income available to each individual member.

To construct these household incomes, we use linkages to the Census Bureau Master Address File ID (MAFID) associated with the individual people listed as primary or secondary filers on each Form 1040. We circumvent issues associated with the notion of a "household head" or the assumptions required for the apportionment of household income among its members. We do so by aggregating income values across all Form 1040s sharing a common MAFID, and assign this total to each co-residing member. The result is a concept in which each individual in the data is attached to the total income resources at their "physical address household." While, because of double counting issues, this concept does not lend itself to distributional national accounts, it allows us to preserve the rich variety of individual demographic characteristics within a household: we are able to document top household incomes and to contrast these statistics by individual race/ethnicity, age, and related intersections. In appendix B, we leverage individual-level linkages to the restricted-use CPS ASEC microdata and compare IDDA households with matched CPS households.[7]

Form 1040 household income concepts. The federal individual income tax statement data we use cover tax years 1998–2019 and include a limited number of income fields. Specifically, IDDA contains measures for three Form 1040 income categories: (i) wage and salary income (WSI); (ii) adjusted gross income (AGI); and (iii) taxable non-wage income (NWI), their difference. Each income tax category is aggregated from tax-unit-level values into a household-level total income value using the MAFID as described above. While Form 1040 wage and salary income is zero or positive, AGI may be negative because non-wage income is not necessarily positive. Taxable non-wage income encompasses numerous types of income, including, as applicable, Schedule C self-employment profit or loss, interest and dividends income, capital gains or losses, and taxable retirement income, less deductions. Unfortunately, we are not able to observe all of these individual

7. See also Guvenen and Kaplan (2017) for a discussion on income measurement units in income tax data and differences between individuals, tax-filing units, and households when it comes to top income inequality.

components separately. For a detailed description of the components of AGI, see section B of the technical documentation.

11.2.3 Demographic Groups

Individual demographic characteristics, in our primary measurement data sources, use the assignment of the Census Bureau's unique, anonymized protected identification key (PIK) to all data files we use (Wagner and Layne 2014). The PIK also facilitates longitudinal linkage, and we use the panel dimension of the data to document the distribution of income growth and mobility.[8] As in Akee et al. (2019), this allows us to link information on race, ethnicity, gender, age, foreign born status, and other demographic characteristics to individual tax records. Obtaining near-universal, high-quality administrative income data for minority racial and ethnic groups (and their intersections with gender or age) is an important feature.

Our main source for determining race and ethnicity is the Census Bureau's 2020 Best Race and Ethnicity Administrative Records Composite File, which supplements data collected via census or survey with data from a variety of sources—including records from the Department of Housing and Urban Development, the Temporary Assistance for Needy Families program, the Indian Health Service, and other agencies—to assign a single race and ethnicity (Hispanic or non-Hispanic) to individuals in the Census Bureau data system.

The large size of the IRS dataset and the quality of Census Bureau PIK/MAFID linkages allow us to disaggregate statistics for six major race and ethnicity groups: Hispanic, non-Hispanic Asian, non-Hispanic American Indian or Alaska Native (AIAN), non-Hispanic Black, non-Hispanic Native Hawaiian or other Pacific Islander (NHOPI), and non-Hispanic White. At the US level, statistics are also reported for the "non-Hispanic other or multiple-race" group.[9] Sex, place of birth, and year of birth and death (which determine age) are drawn from Social Security Administration records. State of residence is taken from Form 1040 or any available information returns.

Individuals are excluded from the cross-sectional data if we are unable to link key demographic or geographic information or if tax records indicate conflicting tax unit information. We also exclude individuals whose MAFID is shared by an unusually large number of records, defined as those

8. As discussed below, we construct income dynamics statistics conditional on initial period income. This further divides potentially small demographic cells into both base-year income brackets and final-year income brackets.

9. The non-Hispanic other or multiple race group makes up about 1.5 percent of the IDDA samples. This group is diverse, and the share of individuals identifying as multi-racial is growing. We leave a more complete measurement of incomes for multi-racial individuals for future research, since statistical guidelines and standards on reporting race/ethnicity in administrative data are actively changing. We do not report statistics for this group at the state level for this reason.

in households above the 99th percentile of household size. This restriction helps to exclude individuals living in large group settings who are unlikely to be sharing resources as a household.[10]

Once sample selection and demographic linkages are made in the cross-sectional files, we link records longitudinally over one- and five-year time horizons. Demographic information and state of residence are taken from the initial year.

11.2.4 Overall Size and Composition

The Census Bureau's Person Identification Validation System (PVS) uses personally identifiable information (PII) (e.g., name, date of birth, etc.) to uniquely map social security numbers (SSNs) and individual taxpayer identification numbers (ITINs) into PIKs.[11] As a result, datasets that contain SSNs or ITINs, such as tax records, have very high PIK assignment rates (97 percent or higher). PIK assignment rates for files that do not contain this information (such as data from the decennial census and ACS, which do not collect it) are somewhat lower (90 to 93 percent) but still high in absolute terms (Mulrow et al. 2011). False assignment rates, however, are extremely low (Layne et al. 2014). The IDDA base datasets naturally inherit these high PIK match rates, as shown in the top panel of table 11.1, for the year 2010. As a result, the primary datasets used for measuring IDDA income statistics are large, even for the minority race/ethnicity groups.

Table 11.1 also shows the demographic composition in 2010 in our primary IDDA data sources and in the CPS samples created using the IPUMS CPS dataset (see Flood et al. 2023). Overall, demographic shares are similar, even though the IDDA data derived from tax filings are not re-weighted to be representative of the overall population of filers and non-filers. The Form 1040 IDDA data source for household incomes has fewer 16-to-24-year-old individuals than the Form W-2 IDDA data source or the CPS data. This is not entirely surprising: in the Form 1040 household data source, we assign the address-level household income measure to the primary and secondary filers only. We also have fewer Hispanic, foreign-born, or non-Hispanic NHOPI shares in IDDA data sources, compared with shares in CPS samples. Non-Hispanic White and US-born shares are higher in IDDA data sources than in the CPS.

11.2.5 IDDA Modules and Availability of Granular Statistics

We use a variety of statistics to characterize income distributions within years, as well as conditional income changes and mobility across pairs of years. Table 11.2 lists these categories of statistics, which we term *modules*,

10. The 99th percentile of household size under this method has not been disclosed. For reference, in the 2010 American Community Survey, the median number of individuals aged 16 or older living in a given household was two. The 90th, 98th, and 99th percentiles of the number of individuals aged 16 or older were four, seven, and eight individuals per household, respectively.

11. See Wagner and Layne (2014) for more details.

Table 11.1 **IDDA sample sizes and composition (2010)**

	Household-1040	Individual-W2	CPS Household	CPS Individual
In Numident	182,200,000	150,400,000	–	–
Has age, gender, and state	181,000,000	146,700,000		
Has race/ethnicity	178,000,000	144,300,000		
Has valid MAFID	169,300,000	–		
Final Sample N	169,300,000	144,300,000	153,586	95,094
Demographic Composition				
Female	52.1%	49.6%	51.7%	48.0%
Male	47.9%	50.5%	48.3%	52.0%
Hispanic	11.3%	12.9%	14.7%	14.8%
Non-Hispanic AIAN	0.7%	0.9%	0.7%	0.6%
Non-Hispanic Asian	4.6%	4.6%	5.1%	5.1%
Non-Hispanic Black	10.1%	12.0%	11.5%	10.8%
Non-Hispanic NHOPI	0.1%	0.2%	0.3%	0.3%
Non-Hispanic Other	1.3%	1.5%	1.3%	1.2%
Non-Hispanic White	71.8%	68.0%	66.5%	67.1%
Foreign born	13.9%	13.2%	15.5%	15.8%
Not Foreign born	86.1%	86.8%	84.5%	84.2%
16–24	8.8%	16.4%	16.1%	13.6%
25–34	18.5%	21.2%	16.9%	21.9%
35–44	18.7%	20.2%	16.6%	21.3%
45–54	20.9%	21.9%	18.3%	22.5%
55–64	17.3%	15.3%	15.6%	15.9%
65+	15.8%	5.0%	16.5%	4.8%

Source: IDDA and IPUMS CPS. Release authorization CBDRB-FY24-0131.

Note: IDDA is built from the universe of W-2 and 1040 income tax returns merged to demographic and geographic information via the PIK. This table shows the total number of PIK-level records in this underlying dataset after successive sample restrictions, beginning with our initial merge to the Census Numident. N sizes and the sample demographic composition are reported for 2010, a year in the middle of our data series, along with the corresponding values in the CPS ASEC. We do not expect linkage to race/ethnicity information to change substantially in decennial census years, because of the prioritization of race/ethnicity data sources described above.

as well as the demographic characteristics we use to define groups. We build on Akee et al. (2019) by constructing yearly state-level statistics on income inequality by race, by race and age, and by race and gender for different types of income. These measures include group-percentile income values, top income shares within demographic groups, and the share of top income held by members of different demographic groups. We also build on the contribution of McKinney et al. (2022) in the Global Repository of Income Dynamics (GRID) project by documenting percentiles of one-year income changes and five-year income changes by initial income level, by type of income, by demographic group, and across states. For a more extensive

Table 11.2 **Summary of statistics in IDDA**

Statistics		
Income levels and income shares	Transition matrices and income change distributions	Demographic characteristics defining groups
Percentile values: p10, p25, p50, p75, p90, p95, p98, p99, p99.9, p99.99, etc., as sample size allows	**Transition matrices**: $P(B_{y+k} \mid B_y)$ for $k = \{1,5\}$ and income bins $B = \{$missing, p0p24, p25p49, p50p74, and p75p100, or p75p89 and p90p100$\}$	**Race/ethnicity**: Hispanic, Non-Hispanic Black, Non-Hispanic AIAN, Non-Hispanic Asian, Non-Hispanic NHPI, Non-Hispanic White
Top income shares (within group): of all income earned by a given group, what share was earned by the top 10%, 5%, 2%, 1%, 0.1%, 0.01%, etc. of earners, as sample size allows		**Age**: 16–24, 25–34, 35–44, 45–54, 55–64, 65+
Top income shares (across groups): of income earned by the top 10%, 5%, 2%, 1%, 0.1%, 0.01%, etc. of all earners (as sample size allows), the share earned by members of a given group	**Conditional income changes**: mean, p10, p25, p50, p75, and p90 of nominal income changes for individuals starting in each income bin B between y and y+k	**Gender**: male, female
Top income population shares: The share of the top 10%, 5%, 2%, 1%, 0.1%, 0.01%, etc. of earners (as sample size allows) belonging to a given group		**Place of birth**: US born, foreign born

Note: p# indicates percentile value. Top income percentiles used for state-level inequality statistics go up to the 98th percentile. AIAN = American Indian or Alaska Native. NHOPI = Native Hawaiian or other Pacific Islander. Top income bins in transition matrices and conditional income changes are consolidated into a single p76p100 bin for estimates at the state level. Estimates are produced nationally and at the state level within the groups listed for each demographic characteristic, as well as for two-way interactions of select demographic characteristics.

definition of the statistics included in each module of IDDA, refer to the technical documentation.

All statistics in IDDA are calculated within an income data source and income concept, a year, and a geography, and may be defined within or across demographic groups. The demographic groups included in the dataset vary across the different statistics modules and by sample and geography, in part to manage the population size underlying each statistic. While IDDA is constructed from large data, the granular information it provides can still lead to small samples, and some statistics are suppressed as a result.[12]

12. Note that each IDDA statistic is based on the universe of relevant tax records, not a randomly selected sample. It is unclear what commonly used measures of uncertainty like standard errors represent in this context. Thus, we have produced only point estimates for this analysis.

Table 11.3 **Availability of statistics by demographic group: Form 1040 data (1998–2019)**

IDDA Module	Defined	All	Age	BPL	Race	AgeXRace
US Household-1040						
Income Levels	154,176	100	100	100	90.8	83.9
Income Changes	51,300	100	100	100	100	
Transition Matrix	59,850	100	100	100	100	
State Household-1040						
Income Levels	587,928	100	100	100	94.6	
Income Changes	1,395,360	100	100	100	94.9	
Transition Matrix	1,395,360	100	100	100	92.2	

Source: IDDA.

Note: Columns provide the total number of defined statistics in each IDDA sample and geography, along with the corresponding availability rate in percentages. Each statistic is defined by a geography, sample and income concept, year(s), and demographic group. For example, the total number of transition matrix statistics defined at the state level includes all possible transitions between income quartiles, multiplied by 50 states, multiplied by the total number of income concepts, demographic groups, and pairs of years for which that statistic is computed. Availability rates for statistics that are not disaggregated by demographic group are reported in the "All" column. BPL represents place of birth (US or foreign born). Release authorization CBDRB-FY23-0277.

Tables 11.3 and 11.4 summarize the availability of statistics in each of these three categories—income levels, transition matrices, and conditional income changes—by sample and geographic level. Table 11.5 provides a more detailed analysis of availability for individual race/ethnicity subgroups. Availability is simply the percentage of all defined statistics that are available (not suppressed) given the demographic disaggregations reported in a particular sample and geography. For individual race/ethnicity groups, availability is expressed as a percentage of all defined statistics pertaining to a specific subgroup, including intersections of age and race and of race and sex. For example, statistics defined for the groups Asian Male, Asian Female, and Asian 25–34 each count as 1 in the denominator of the availability rate for the non-Hispanic Asian group.

In general, availability is lower at the intersections of age and race, which are reported in the US and state W-2 income levels, US W-2 transition matrices and income change distributions, and US 1040 income levels. Availability is quite high for cells defined over age, birthplace, and sex groups. For race and ethnicity groups, coverage falls as more intersections are included and statistics are reported further into the tail of the income distribution. Statistics are most often suppressed for the Native Hawaiian or other Pacific Islander and American Indian or Alaska Native groups within individual US states. Yet, it is rare that a group-state combination is excluded from the IDDA data entirely, and as a result, the proportion of the US working

Table 11.4 **Availability of statistics by demographic group: Form W-2 data (2005–2019)**

IDDA Module	Defined	All	Age	BPL	Race	Sex	AgeXRace	AgeXSex	RaceXSex
US Individual-W-2									
Income Levels	121,680	100	97	100	91.2	100	80.6	91.9	86.7
Income Changes	110,880	100	100	100	100	100	99.3	100	100
Transition Matrix	129,360	100	100	100	100	100	94.8	100	99.3
US PAW-W-2									
Income Levels	80,370	100	99.5	100	90.5	100	85.1	94.6	84.8
Income Changes	72,000	100	100	100	100	100	100	100	100
Transition Matrix	120,816	100	100	100	99.9	100	95.4	100	98.7
State Individual-W-2									
Income Levels	1,054,170	100	97.9	100	95.8	100	74.9	93.2	89.8
Income Changes	499,392	100	100	100	95.9	100			
Transition Matrix	499,392	100	98.8	99.6	86.2	100			

Source: IDDA.

Note: Columns provide the total number of defined statistics in each IDDA sample and geography, along with the corresponding availability rate in percentages. Each statistic is defined by a geography, sample and income concept, year(s), and demographic group. For example, the total number of transition matrix statistics defined at the state level includes all possible transitions between income quartiles, multiplied by 50 states, multiplied by the total number of income concepts, demographic groups, and pairs of years for which that statistic is computed. Availability rates for statistics that are not disaggregated by demographic group are reported in the "All" column. BPL represents place of birth (US or foreign born). Release authorization CBDRB-FY23-0277.

population that is not covered in IDDA is very small.[13] The fact that some suppression is still required emphasizes the importance of preserving population coverage of the tax data.

11.2.6 Limitations

Despite its universal underlying administrative data, IDDA income measures have important limitations. First, incomes used in IDDA are only pre-tax and taxable incomes from tax returns: IDDA incomes therefore do not reflect informal incomes or non-taxable incomes. Second, IDDA does not contain non-taxable public transfers, a very important income source for low-income households in particular. In IDDA, statistics for lower-earning individuals and households reflect income earned through formal employ-

13. For example, for 2010, percentiles of income from Form W-2 are not available for the Native Hawaiian or other Pacific Islander group in Delaware, Rhode Island, Vermont, or the District of Columbia. However, the population represented by these statistics was 0.38 percent of the total working NHOPI population. The combinations of race and age for which IDDA did not include any percentiles of income in 2010 accounted for only 0.015 percent of the total working US population. Higher in the distribution, suppression is more common, but even here, the states where statistics are suppressed represent small fractions of the total population. The 98th percentile of income was suppressed for NHOPI earners in 21 states and AIAN earners in 2 states, but those states represented only 4.57 percent of the total working NHOPI population and 0.11 percent of the total working AIAN population, per ACS estimates.

Table 11.5 **IDDA availability by race/ethnicity**

Module	Intersections	Hispanic	AIAN	Asian	Black	NHOPI	White
US-Level							
Household-1040							
Income Levels	age	91.7	76.4	89.4	88.4	68.9	95.4
Income Changes	-	100	100	100	100	100	100
Transition Matrix	-	100	100	100	100	100	100
Individual-W-2							
Income Levels	age, sex	89.9	74.1	87.7	90.6	66.4	92.3
Income Changes	age, sex	100	99.6	100	100	97.5	100
Transition Matrix	age, sex	100	95.0	99.9	100	83.5	100
PAW-W-2							
Income Levels	age, sex	93.8	77.0	90.5	93.2	70.9	94.0
Income Changes	age, sex	100	100	100	100	100	100
Transition Matrix	age, sex	100	96.2	100	99.6	87.4	100
State-Level							
Household-1040							
Income Levels	-	99.9	96.8	99.9	98.2	72.5	100
Income Changes	-	100	97.1	99.9	98.8	73.5	100
Transition Matrix	-	99.8	95.1	98.9	97.7	61.8	100
Individual-W-2							
Income Levels	age, sex	91.3	76.5	88.8	87.8	44.0	95.0
Income Changes	-	100	98.2	100	99.9	77.5	100
Transition Matrix	-	97.5	83.6	94.5	94.4	47.1	100

Source: IDDA.

Note: This table reports availability rates for individual race/ethnicity groups in IDDA. The column "intersçections" indicates whether statistics in the geography and sample are provided for the intersection of age and race, race and sex, or neither. In general, statistics are provided further into the tail of the income distribution of the US-level data than that of the state-level data. Income levels are reported up to the 98th percentile at the state level and 99.999th percentile nationally. Transition matrices and conditional income changes are calculated within quartiles of the state-level income distributions. At the US level, the top income quartile is divided into two smaller brackets (the 75th-90th percentile and above the 90th percentile). Release authorization CBDRB-FY23-0277.

ment or other non-wage taxable income sources. Researchers interested in studying poverty or income available for consumption are encouraged to use statistics from a more comprehensive source.[14] Third, IDDA does not have a breakdown of non-wage incomes by type. Given the large variety of taxable non-wage incomes and the accounting rules involved, caution should be exercised when interpreting non-wage income statistics. Fourth, IDDA is representative only of filed incomes and the population of filers, not all incomes.[15] Finally, IDDA statistics are not available for all feasible

14. These issues are discussed in detail in Corinth et al. (2022), among others, and data on the full set of income available for consumption is provided in the Comprehensive Income Dataset Project, https://cid.harris.uchicago.edu/.

15. Evidence suggests that around 90 percent of those who are required to file in our period actually do so (Erard et al. 2020). We have found no evidence on whether voluntary filing is a

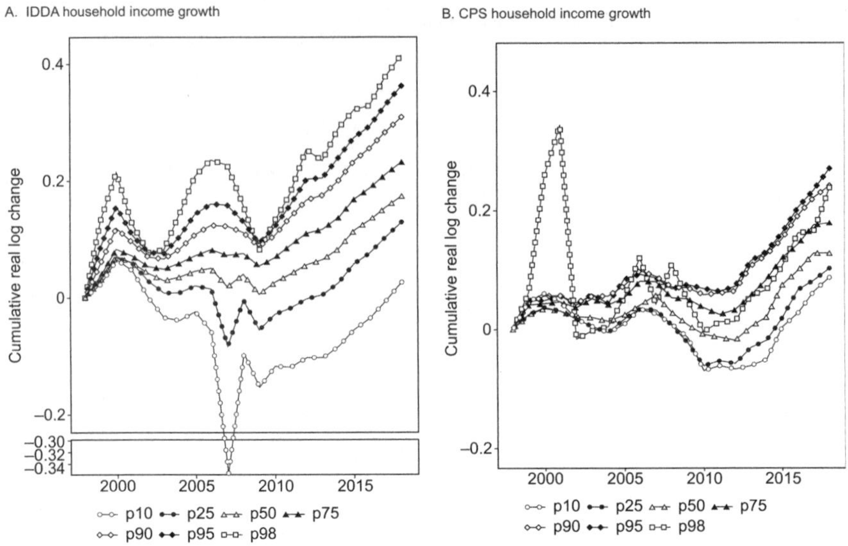

Fig. 11.1 Household income growth in IDDA vs. CPS

Source: IDDA and IPUMS CPS.

Note: CPS statistics calculated by the authors following IDDA documentation and using the sample of all ASEC respondents aged 16-plus. Data period for both sources is 1998–2018. Release authorization CBDRB-FY23-0277.

demographic groups or places, and IDDA does not contain any statistics on wealth.[16]

11.3 Income Inequality Trends for Aggregate and Granular Populations

11.3.1 Changes in Aggregate Distributional Statistics

In order to put in context the patterns of income inequality for race and ethnicity that IDDA reveals, we first plot changes in household adjusted gross income, by percentile, over time for the population of US tax filers as a whole. This provides a baseline about patterns for US earners and also allows comparisons to statistics calculated from public sources.

To begin, figure 11.1 graphs the log difference (or approximate percent change) in percentile values for real household income relative to their values in 1998. Panel (a) plots household income growth using IDDA. In Panel (b) of figure 11.1, we produce the same cumulative changes in real log household

persistent trait, but Erard et al. (2020) report a voluntary filing rate with only modest fluctuations over the three-year period they examine.

16. A key limitation of IDDA is that certain characteristics, including education and occupation, are not visible from tax data. We produce averages by demographic group for certain ACS characteristics in table 11A.1 in the appendix.

incomes using publicly available data from the Annual Social and Economic Supplement (ASEC) to the CPS; hereafter, we refer to this simply as the CPS. We use income concepts reported in IPUMS CPS that align as closely as possible with the concepts measured in our administrative data (Flood et al. 2023). For W-2 earnings, the CPS reports a close analog. For household AGI from household 1040 filings, the closest CPS income concept does not align as well.[17] We compute statistics in the public-use CPS microdata analogous to those we analyze in IDDA, imposing only the restriction that CPS state-group cells must contain at least 50 observations in order for us to include a CPS-derived statistic in our analysis.[18]

Figure 11.1 produces a familiar pattern, and at the most general level, the two sources tell a similar story: income inequality widened since the late 1990s, though more modestly than in earlier decades, with recessions slowing income growth more sharply (or even eroding income) for the lowest earners. Both series also show that income growth in recoveries has been slow to return lower earners to pre-recession levels.

However, the details suggest material differences in the patterns of income growth identified in the two sources, even at this highly aggregate level. These are most substantial at higher percentiles. Panel (a) in Figure 11.1 shows that the 90th percentile of household AGI in IDDA had risen 30 percent relative to its 1998 level by 2018, while the 25th percentile of household AGI increased by less than half that, and the 10th percentile of household AGI had not grown at all. Panel (b) shows that the CPS produces patterns that suggest it may be an unreliable measure for the highest percentiles. In the highest household income bin shown (the 98th percentile), the CPS series fluctuates widely and indicates shallower income growth for the highest percentiles. Large volatility in these top income series could reflect actual earnings changes, but they are likely also be related to changes in how the public CPS preserves confidentiality at top incomes as well as to non-random misreporting of high incomes, as is consistent with findings in Bollinger et al. (2019).[19]

The IDDA series also suggest that changes in household income percentiles among 1040 filers unfolded relatively smoothly year to year, with some notable exceptions. The sharp temporary changes at low income percentiles

17. Specifically, the corresponding variables in the CPS are HTOTVAL for household AGI and WSAL_VAL for W-2 earnings. There are several differences between the types of income included in HTOTVAL and household AGI. AGI includes capital gains and excludes non-taxable transfers. HTOTVAL excludes the former and includes the latter.

18. This is a much lower standard than that applied to IDDA statistics. For any given IDDA statistic to be reported, we require a minimum of 30 contributing observations; this threshold applies to the numerator if the statistic is a share. The CPS 50-observation threshold applies at the state-group level, not the statistic level. For shares in the CPS, we apply a higher threshold of 250 observations at the state-group level, in order to have sufficient observations in the numerator.

19. We discuss the impact of definitional differences and misreporting of income to the CPS patterns as compared with IDDA in detail in appendix B.

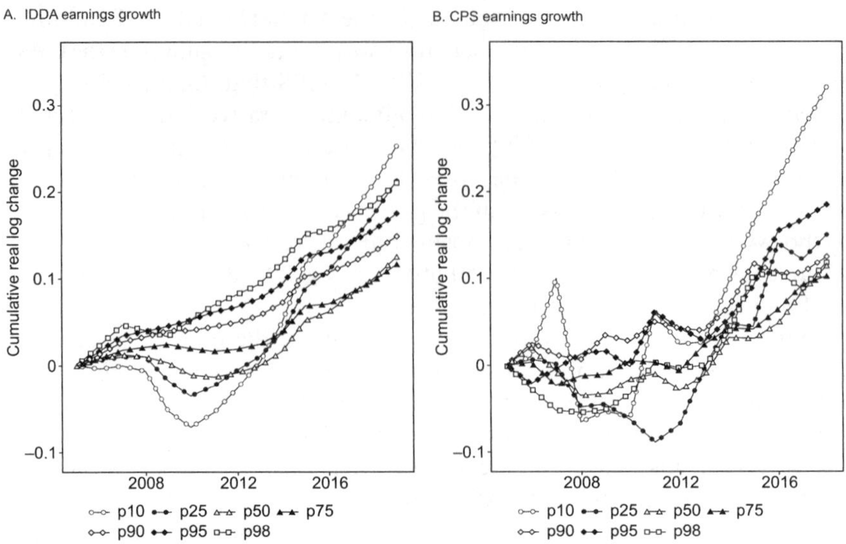

Fig. 11.2 Earnings growth in IDDA vs. CPS

Source: IDDA and IPUMS CPS.

Note: CPS statistics calculated by the authors following IDDA documentation and using the sample of ASEC respondents aged 16-plus who reported positive wage income. Data period for both sources is 2005–2018. Release authorization CBDRB-FY23-0277.

in 2007 were likely due to filing changes driven by requirements for receipt of stimulus checks.[20] Sharp changes in the value of household income at the highest percentiles—the 98th percentile, for example—also occur in the IDDA series, but these large procyclical fluctuations are probably not due to extensive margin changes in filing behavior. We use the long time series in IDDA to "look through" the filing-related fluctuations at the lowest percentiles, and we interpret fluctuations at the highest percentiles as real.

Figure 11.2 repeats the same exercise as in figure 11.1 for individual earnings from 2005 onwards. Panel (a) plots cumulative log changes in real individual W-2 earnings using IDDA. As was the case before, Panel (b) is based on the public-use CPS ASEC microdata. At a high level, the two sources again tell broadly similar stories. Both also show that the final years of recovery from the Great Recession saw greater growth in wage earnings for the lowest earners, even though this did not translate to greater income growth for the lowest-earning households.

20. A similar spike appears in 2019. In both 2007 and 2019, the data show an excess of $0 returns, consistent with temporary changes in filing related to stimulus collection (Internal Revenue Service 2009). This mechanically shifts down the household income percentile values, especially at the bottom of the distribution. We use 2018 as the end point in our analysis for this reason. The CPS also suffers from continuity issues in 2019, related to difficulties in administering the ASEC in March 2020 (IPUMS 2020).

But again, even at this aggregate level, the individual earnings series in figure 11.2 show meaningful differences across sources. First, for the lowest wage earners (at the 10th and 25th percentiles), IDDA indicates trend earnings growth beginning at the trough of the Great Recession. This growth persists through the end of the data period, albeit from a low level. By contrast, in the CPS, relative earnings growth for the lower percentiles is not clearly apparent until later in the recovery. For the highest wage earners, IDDA shows earnings were flat or modestly declined after the Great Recession, before resuming greater relative growth at higher percentiles. The CPS instead suggests that the highest earners saw some of the greatest earnings declines in the Great Recession and recovered no faster than most other groups.

These differences combine to imply some material differences between the evolution of inequality in the IDDA series as compared to the CPS. These are summarized in figures 11A.1 and 11A.2, which plot several key percentile earnings ratios. Ratios from both IDDA earnings series align well with CPS ratios for the center of the distribution, p75p25. These ratios are flat in both data sources, for both households and individuals. Differences arise when comparing the highest and lowest deciles (p90p10) in both sources or the highest household incomes with the median (p98p50). Broadly, these show more ongoing changes in inequality over the 2010s than are apparent in the CPS. In the IDDA series, individual W-2 earnings show a marked decline in inequality between the highest (p90) and lowest earners (p10) from 2010 to 2019. This decline begins earlier than in the CPS, and is larger in absolute terms, but the final level of inequality is considerably higher in IDDA. In the household statistics, IDDA shows that the extremes of the distribution became steadily more unequal, as the p90p10 and p98p50 ratios both widened. The CPS shows at most a modest change in the analogous measures. These differences suggest potentially new insights into the evolution of US inequality since the late 1990s. However, our aim in this paper is to assess IDDA as a source for patterns in earnings inequality for detailed subnational groups, so we leave these questions for future work.

Dissecting IDDA vs. CPS income differences. We further explore these notable differences between IDDA and CPS using the restricted-use CPS microdata linked at the individual level to administrative tax records (for more details, see appendix B of Kondo et al. [2024], this paper's companion NBER Working Paper). Overall, IDDA and CPS differences attenuate, but do not vanish, in the linked sample. Survey-specific limitations such as income top coding and income imputations, along with unreported incomes, help explain some of these differences.

Percentiles of individual earnings in the restricted-use CPS initially appear higher than those measured in IDDA, particularly at the bottom of the distribution. However, by linking the two samples, we find that the

IDDA W-2 data often capture small earnings values that are not reported in the CPS. This employment margin difference leads to a downward shift in the linked CPS earnings distribution, reversing the sign of CPS-IDDA differences to negative in the linked sample. We find another reversal at the highest earnings percentiles: in the linked sample, CPS earnings measures again fall below those based on IDDA, but this pattern is driven by White respondents. Black and Hispanic respondents do not exhibit top earnings in the linked CPS sample that are below their IDDA counterpart.

Differences in percentiles of household-level earnings between IDDA and the linked CPS exhibit a similar inverted U shape: CPS income percentiles of income are lower than those in IDDA in the tails of the distribution. On the other hand, we find larger CPS-IDDA gaps and different patterns for total household income measures, especially for White respondents: linked CPS household incomes are larger than IDDA AGI at the bottom and much smaller than IDDA AGI at the top.

We also examine respondent-level differences in incomes reported in the CPS and the tax data, and show that survey proxy responses, survey income imputations, and self-employment (indicated by Form 1099-MISC information returns) widen the observed mismatch, especially underreporting of incomes at the top of the distribution.

11.3.2 Changes in Granular Distributions

While examining the major earnings inequality patterns at the national level provides a helpful baseline, IDDA is designed to study these patterns in much smaller populations. How does IDDA compare with the CPS when we study changes in earnings distributions for smaller groups? We examine groups at two subnational levels: the state level and the state-by-race and ethnicity level. We compare subnational IDDA statistics with analogous measures constructed using the CPS by running a series of cross-state regressions of the state-level change in a distributional statistic as calculated using the CPS on the change in the same statistic in IDDA. (Changes in the CPS are likely measured with more noise, so regressing changes in CPS measures on changes in IDDA measures reduces attenuation bias.) This is subject to the constraint that we require a CPS subnational population to have at least 50 observations in order to compute distributional statistics for it.

The results using Form 1040 household income are presented in table 11.6. In column (1), we report the number of states or state-by-race and state-by-ethnicity cells for which the CPS contains sufficient observations to compute within-state distributional statistics used to produce the table. In columns (2)–(6), we report, for a given income percentile, the results from regressing the change log income at that percentile over 1998 to 2018 in the CPS on the same change using IDDA. Each row in table 11.6 corresponds to either state filers as a whole or to state-level race and ethnicity groups. Income percentiles are computed state-by-state for each group. Hence, each cell in the

Table 11.6 **Changes in state-level distributional statistics: CPS total household income vs. IDDA household AGI (1998–2018)**

		Estimated slope $\Delta(y)^{state}_{CPS} = \beta\Delta(y)^{state}_{IDDA} + \varepsilon^{state}$						
Group	N (1)	log(p10) (2)	log(p25) (3)	log(p50) (4)	log(p75) (5)	log(p90) (6)	p90p25 (7)	p98p50 (8)
All	51	0.628	0.780	0.806	0.780	0.710	0.634	0.214
		(0.154)	(0.066)	(0.044)	(0.032)	(0.0361)	(0.087)	(0.148)
Hispanic	33	–0.511	1.060	0.820	0.755	0.793	–0.078	–0.381
		(1.330)	(0.159)	(0.097)	(0.101)	(0.092)	(0.479)	(0.784)
AIAN	7	1.230	0.400	0.447	0.624	0.675	2.330	
		(0.725)	(0.402)	(0.165)	(0.183)	(0.416)	(2.210)	
Asian	24	1.940	0.820	0.884	0.795	0.654	0.642	–0.475
		(0.893)	(0.259)	(0.163)	(0.120)	(0.126)	(0.328)	(0.550)
Black	30	0.624	1.200	1.100	1.030	0.932	1.320	0.078
		(0.506)	(0.336)	(0.251)	(0.205)	(0.127)	(0.603)	(0.652)
NHOPI	2							
White	51	0.977	0.853	0.765	0.771	0.708	0.752	0.178
		(0.173)	(0.075)	(0.0493)	(0.040)	(0.043)	(0.134)	(0.257)

Source: IDDA and authors' calculation using IPUMS CPS.

Note: Changes are computed from 1998 to 2018 for the household-level data, with the exception of Asian and NHOPI filers, for whom CPS data are available beginning in 2002. We choose not to compare 2019, the final year in the IDDA dataset, because of changes in tax filing and an unusually low CPS response rate that resulted from the COVID-19 pandemic. We compute the 10th –90th percentiles of income for subnational populations with at least 50 observations in the CPS. We compute the 98th percentile for subnational populations with at least 250 observations in the CPS. Release authorization CBDRB-FY23-0277.

table is a coefficient on the IDDA statistic as a predictor of the CPS statistic from a separate univariate regression, with the standard error reported in parentheses. For example, the value 0.628 in column (2) in the top row is the coefficient from a state-level regression of the change in the log of 10th-percentile household income in the CPS on the change in log p10 household income in IDDA, over the 1998–2018 period. It indicates that the log household income 10th percentile in the CPS increased by about two-thirds as much as the one in IDDA, on average across states. If the corresponding state-level CPS statistics were closely related to those in IDDA, coefficients would typically be near one, with narrow standard errors. The final two columns (7 and 8) report results from the same exercise, using changes in income percentile ratios instead of changes in log incomes.

Several points are clear from table 11.6. First, sample size limitations in the CPS prevent this analysis in many cases. As shown in column (1), the exercise is possible for fewer than half the states for three race and ethnicity groups: American Indian or Alaska Native, Asian, and Native Hawaiian or other Pacific Islander. For the last of these, data are insufficient to report any results from this comparison. Second, the standard errors indicate that—for many populations—statistics as computed in the CPS bear little relationship to those in IDDA; these noisier IDDA-CPS correlations are particularly prevalent at lower household income percentiles (see p10 and p25 in columns 2 and 3) and for smaller groups.[21]

A final point is that typically, coefficient estimates of percentile-level income growth are often far from one. In table 11.6, these are often less than one; this finding is potentially related to concept differences across the sources. This means that on average, changes in household income in the CPS are smaller than the corresponding IDDA estimate at all percentiles across states, as shown in the first row of table 11.6, which reports results for state-level income distributions that pool all race and ethnicity groups. In columns (2) through (6), all estimates are less than one.

Estimates in columns (7) and (8) show that the result of these percentile-by-percentile differences is different changes in earnings inequality by the end of the period. The cross-state estimates for long changes in income percentile ratios shown are both smaller than one. In fact, for the p98p50 household income ratio in column (8), the estimated coefficient is only 0.214, with a standard error of 0.148. This illustrates a final takeaway from the table: state-level changes in inequality produced by the CPS are nearly unrelated to those measured in IDDA, particularly when comparing the highest to the more central percentiles, as in column (8).

Subsequent rows present the same analysis for state-level populations defined by race and ethnicity. As already noted, this exercise is not possible using the CPS for the AIAN and NHOPI groups, owing to small samples. In general, the conclusions of this exercise for state filers as a whole are apparent when state populations are defined by race and ethnicity.

White filers, shown in the bottom row, are the only group for which distributional statistics can be calculated for all states in the CPS. For White filers, in column (2), we see that changes in the 10th percentile of household income in IDDA and the CPS align fairly well ($\beta = 0.98$). However, above the 10th percentile, the point estimates are farther away from one, as shown in columns (3)–(6). As a result, the CPS indicates smaller increases in within-group inequality among White households than those in IDDA.

The pattern is similar for Asian filers except for the lowest income percentile, although the CPS statistics can be calculated for fewer than half of US states for this group, and the standard errors are larger. For Black and Hispanic filers, the picture is different. At the 10th percentile, the standard errors are so large that there is no statistically reliable relationship between the CPS and IDDA income changes, even though the CPS permits distributional estimates for more than half of states for these groups. In fact, the point estimate is negative for Hispanic income changes in the CPS relative to those in IDDA. Above the 10th percentile, IDDA and the CPS yield statistically similar estimates of changes in income percentiles for Black

21. Results from a sample trimmed of outliers are similar and available upon request.

Table 11.7 **Changes in state-level distributional statistics: CPS individual wage/salary income vs. IDDA W-2 earnings (2005–2018)**

		Estimated slope $\Delta(y)^{state}_{CPS} = \beta\Delta(y)^{state}_{IDDA} + \varepsilon^{state}$						
Group	N (1)	log(p10) (2)	log(p25) (3)	log(p50) (4)	log(p75) (5)	log(p90) (6)	p90p25 (7)	p98p50 (8)
All	51	1.510	1.120	1.110	1.050	0.912	0.817	0.441
		(0.116)	(0.067)	(0.068)	(0.065)	(0.061)	(0.137)	(0.418)
Hispanic	40	0.971	0.847	1.250	1.290	0.898	–0.051	1.340
		(0.258)	(0.172)	(0.141)	(0.174)	(0.204)	(0.261)	(0.854)
AIAN	4	1.060	1.260	1.250	1.090	0.844	1.250	
		(0.475)	(0.659)	(0.290)	(0.251)	(0.400)	(1.080)	
Asian	19	1.260	0.647	0.908	0.589	0.571	–0.113	
		(0.395)	(0.196)	(0.188)	(0.086)	(0.130)	(0.487)	
Black	32	1.210	0.876	1.140	0.981	1.040	0.311	0.279
		(0.187)	(0.121)	(0.203)	(0.331)	(0.232)	(0.110)	(0.309)
NHOPI	1							
White	51	1.580	1.220	1.120	1.060	0.950	1.140	0.173
		(0.128)	(0.063)	(0.062)	(0.076)	(0.074)	(0.151)	(0.438)

Source: IDDA and authors' calculation using IPUMS CPS.

Note: Changes are computed from 2005 to 2018 for individual earnings. We choose not to compare 2019, the final year in the IDDA dataset, because of changes in tax filing and an unusually low CPS response rate that resulted from the COVID-19 pandemic. We compute the 10th-90th percentiles of income for subnational populations with at least 50 observations in the CPS. We compute the 98th percentile for subnational populations with at least 250 observations in the CPS. Release authorization CBDRB-FY23-0277.

filers, and these estimates are close to one. In the final two columns, point estimates show that the CPS tends to indicate smaller increases in inequality (except for Black filers), but the standard errors show that this relationship is extremely noisy. This implies that for most states, the CPS and IDDA will give different readings on changes in inequality within groups defined by race and ethnicity.

In table 11.7, we perform the same analysis, but this time on statistics calculated from W-2 earnings. Here, the income concepts align well, so evidence of under- or overestimating changes in earnings by percentiles—that is, coefficients unequal to one—is more likely to be driven by reporting differences than concept differences. Nevertheless, most of the major patterns in table 11.6 are also apparent in table 11.7. Cell sizes in the CPS remain an issue, naturally. In other words, state-level distributional statistics either cannot be computed at all for most states (as is the case for NHOPI, AIAN, and for p98 earnings) or that the relationship between CPS-derived statistics and those from the universe of W-2 recipients in IDDA is essentially noise.

Although the coefficients are generally better centered on one, standard errors remain relatively large. Consequently, on average, percentile by percentile earnings growth across states in the CPS is not closely aligned with that in IDDA, even for state earners as a whole, as shown in the top row. As was the case with AGI, the CPS indicates smaller increases in the 90th earnings percentile than those in IDDA (see column [6]). However, differences between IDDA and the CPS reverse at lower earnings levels. Results for all race and ethnicity groups combined show that 10th-percentile earnings increased more in the CPS than in IDDA. If we look to the right, estimates show this is true for percentiles up to the median as well. The bottom rows of the table show that this pattern holds for the group of individual White earners as well.

The final two columns in table 11.7 show how changes in inequality measures in the CPS compare to IDDA when using the W-2 measures. When using the 1040 household income measures, the CPS tended to indicate smaller increases in inequality than IDDA. By contrast, in columns (7) and (8), we see that the inequality measures using W-2s show a less stable relationship between IDDA and the CPS. The CPS shows much larger declines in p90p25 inequality than IDDA for all groups (top row) but not for White earners (bottom row). However, for the p98p50 ratio, results in column (8) for the state populations as a whole show much smaller and largely noisy increases in this measure of inequality in the CPS than in IDDA. We also observe smaller and largely noisy increases in the p98p50 ratio in the CPS, compared with IDDA, for White earners and Black earners. But for Hispanic W-2 earners, this relationship reverses, with the CPS indicating larger increases in inequality (though with large standard errors).

We conclude from this analysis that the CPS is problematic for calculating distributional statistics not only at the subnational level but also, in some important cases, at the US level.[22] As is consistent with other work, we find that the CPS systematically underestimates incomes in the top percentiles and that it also diverges from administrative data at the lowest percentiles (Bollinger et al. 2019; Meyer and Mittag 2019; Bee et al. 2023). Percentiles above the 90th are not well observed in the CPS, and we view our analysis as evidence that CPS-derived statistics for race ethnicity groups at the state level are largely noise due to sample size. Moreover, IDDA is the only feasible source for subnational income distributions for AIAN and NHOPI populations.

11.3.3 Changes in Relative Earnings by Race and Ethnicity: Broadening Bayer and Charles (2018)

With over 6 million statistics, IDDA offers many possible ways for researchers to investigate earnings gaps by race and ethnicity. To demonstrate just

22. We repeat the analysis in table 11.6 and replace the CPS with the ACS for the purposes of constructing comparison statistics with a public source. The results appear in table 11A.2. The relationship between IDDA and ACS-based statistics is closer than the one between it and CPS statistics; coefficients in the cross-state regressions are closer to 1 and more often significant. But in many cases, standard errors remain large and the ACS statistics are on average 10 or more percentage points larger or smaller than those in IDDA.

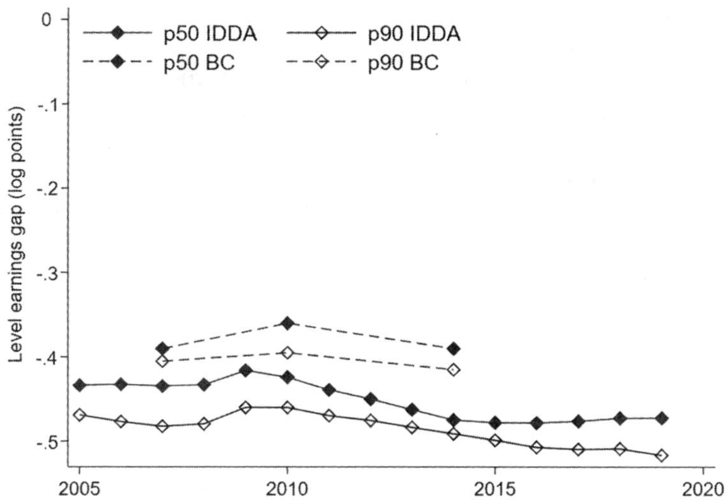

Fig. 11.3 Log earnings gaps between Black and White male earners
Source: IDDA, Bayer and Charles (2018), authors' calculations.
Note: Figure charts the earnings gap between prime-age White and Black men at the median and 90th percentile using different data sources. Gap is measured in log points. Trends in red are reproduced from Bayer and Charles (2018) figure IV using replication files. The IDDA prime-age sample includes workers aged 25–54 with earnings at least equivalent to working 20 hours a week for 13 weeks at the federal minimum wage. Ethnicity is non-Hispanic unless otherwise specified. Release authorization CBDRB-FY23-0277.

one option, we use IDDA to replicate and extend some of the analysis in Bayer and Charles (2018)—a paper that represents the current frontier of our understanding of the evolution of earnings gaps between Black and White men. The prime-age subsample of W-2 recipients in IDDA is similar to those from the Bayer and Charles (2018) sample of prime-age workers from the decennial census and the American Community Survey (ACS).[23] We use this to extend the motivating analysis in Bayer and Charles (2018).

In figure 11.3, we plot estimates of the gap in earnings for Black and White men, following Bayer and Charles (2018), expressed as differences in the log of earnings at the median and the 90th percentile of the respective distributions. Dashed lines indicate the Bayer and Charles (2018) estimates.[24] Solid lines indicate estimates of the same earnings gaps from IDDA. The figure shows that to a first approximation, earnings gaps at the median and p90 in IDDA are similar to those estimated by Bayer and Charles (2018), although gaps in IDDA are somewhat larger in all years where both mea-

23. A comparison of demographic characteristics across the prime-age subsample of W-2 recipients in IDDA and prime-age workers in the CPS is provided in table 11A.4.

24. The Bayer and Charles (2018) analysis uses decadal observations from the decennial census starting in 1940, and concludes with the first set of three-year ACS estimates post-2010. The prime-age worker subsample in IDDA overlaps with the final portion of the Bayer and Charles (2018) period, and the earnings concepts (wage and salary) align well.

sures are observed. Both series also show a modestly larger earnings gap at the 90th percentile than at the median.

The differences between the series grow after 2010, a period for which Bayer and Charles (2018) has only a single estimate. In the IDDA series, the gap at the median begins to widen. The gap at p90 also widens in the IDDA series, but in the Bayer and Charles (2018) series, it moves sideways. Overall, there is more divergence between the two series by 2014, when the Bayer and Charles (2018) analysis ends. The IDDA series shows that the earnings gap at the 90th percentile for Black men relative to White men continued to expand through the end of the series in 2019, while the gap at the median stabilized at its wider, post-2015 level.

The detail in IDDA allows us to expand the Bayer and Charles (2018) analysis along several dimensions. We first ask whether the patterns in the median and p90 earnings gaps extend to earnings gaps higher in the distribution, which are difficult to calculate credibly in the ACS. Panel (a) of figure 11.4 shows the results from plotting the Black-White earnings gaps for men at p98, in addition to the median and p90. The figure shows that moving into the tail results in substantial changes to the earnings gap. The earnings gap at p98 is almost double the gap at the median. Figure 11A.4a shows that the gap is even larger at p99 and p99.9. However, for the very highest partial percentiles, the gap narrows again, falling back closer to the gap at the median. Gaps at most percentiles also widen over time following the Great Recession. This is true for gaps at the median through p99.9. At the very highest sub-percentile, p99.999, the gap narrows more or less consistently over the period, shrinking from about 0.6 to less than 0.2 log points.

IDDA also allows investigation of earnings gaps at the state level.[25] Figure 11A.3a in the appendix shows the earnings gap at the median from figure 11.3 as a bold line along with the same gaps for all states as lighter lines. The figure shows that gaps at the median follow similar trajectories across states, but the size of the gap varies considerably, ranging from about 0.2 to 1.2 log points at the end of the period. Rinz and Voorheis (2023) report that cross-state differences in Black-White earnings disparities overall are driven largely by variation in White earnings. Data from their paper are available and can form a useful complement to IDDA in exploring these questions at the state level.[26]

Using IDDA, we can also readily extend the Bayer and Charles (2018) earnings gaps to other race and ethnicity groups. Deriving statistics from the universe of tax forms allows for credible estimates of distributional moments even for populations that are small relative to the United States as a whole (AIAN and NHOPI earners) and those that are small in a large

25. Bayer and Charles (2018) provide analysis at the region level.

26. Broadly, the data from Rinz and Voorheis (2023) contain more distributional detail but less demographic detail and do not address person-level income changes over time.

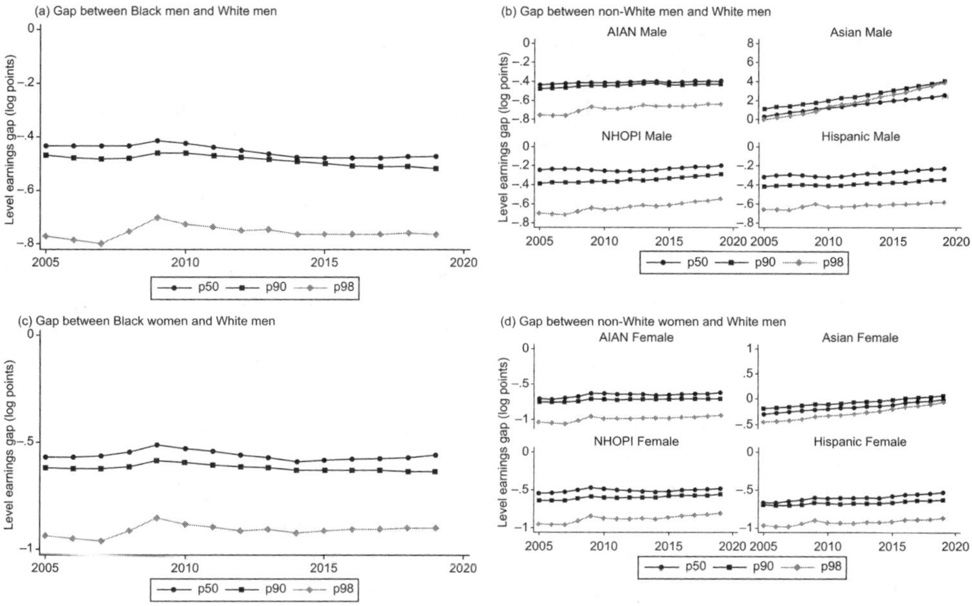

Fig. 11.4 Log earnings gaps between non-White and White earners

Source: IDDA and authors' calculations.

Note: Each panel plots the earnings gap between prime-age non-White earners and White men, in log points. Panels (a) and (c) show earnings gaps for Black men and women across several percentiles; (b) and (d) show earnings gaps at selected percentiles for other non-White groups. Includes workers aged 25–54 with earnings at least equivalent to working 20 hours a week for 13 weeks at the federal minimum wage. AIAN abbreviates American Indian or Alaska Native. NHOPI abbreviates Native Hawaiian or other Pacific Islander. Ethnicity is non-Hispanic unless otherwise specified. Release authorization CBDRB-FY23-0277.

number of states (Asian, Hispanic, and even Black earners). We show Bayer and Charles (2018)–style analyses of median and p90 earnings gaps, as well as the p98 gap, for men in these groups in panel (b) of figure 11.4. The figure shows that, relative to those for White men over the period since 2005, earnings at all three of these percentiles have grown for all other race and ethnicity groups, in contrast to relative earnings for Black men. This is true for groups where relative earnings in 2005 were below those of White men at the same percentile (AIAN, NHOPI, and Hispanic) and for Asian men, who had relative earnings in 2005 that were roughly on par with those for White men.

The divergence since the Great Recession of Black men's earnings paths from those of men in other groups identified as non-White is striking. To understand if this experience is unique to Black men, we repeat the analysis in panel (a) for Black women, reporting their earnings gaps relative to White men in panel (c). Earnings gaps for Black women at the beginning of the period were larger than for men: a little under 0.6 log points at the median, versus a little over 0.4 for men. As was the case for Black men, earnings gaps for Black women increase considerably at higher percentiles. These gaps narrowed modestly before the Great Recession, but widened again after it at most percentiles. Figure 11A.4 in the appendix shows that at the highest sub-percentiles, p99.9 through p99.999, earnings gaps with White men narrowed somewhat over the period.[27]

Earnings gaps with White men for women in other race and ethnic groups are shown in panel (d) for the same three percentiles reported for men. Hispanic women and Asian women experienced earnings gains relative to White men over the period. For Hispanic women, these gains came after 2015, and a large gap remains. For Asian women, earnings gains were steady over the period and have largely closed the earnings gap with White men at all three percentiles shown. NHOPI and AIAN women saw their earnings at these percentiles make modest gains relative to White men or hold steady.

We conclude that Black earners in the United States have experienced less earnings growth than earners from any other race and ethnicity group, relative to a comparison group of White men since the Great Recession. Black men are unique relative to other groups of men in seeing their earnings at all but the highest sub-percentiles decline relative to White men. Black women, too, saw some decline relative to White men. AIAN women and NHOPI women saw their relative earnings stagnate, but other groups of women (Hispanic and Asian) experienced earnings growth in the top half of the distribution, relative to White men. The unique divergence among Black men was undetected in Bayer and Charles (2018), in part because of their data period but also because of limited ability to explore the relative experiences of other non-White earners and earners in higher percentiles.[28]

11.4 Trends in Income Dynamics for Aggregate and Granular Populations

In addition to understanding the shape of earnings distributions, researchers would also like to know about how individuals move through them. This is a much more demanding analysis, requiring a panel dimension to the data (at a minimum) and sufficiently large samples to estimate highly variable changes (ideally). Tracking changes in cross-sectional estimates of different percentiles of the income distribution—as in the previous section's

27. Figures 11A.5 and 11A.6 in the appendix show that using White women as a reference group does not alter our conclusion that Black women's relative earnings declined while those of other women increased or held steady.

28. A challenge with IDDA, like any aggregate statistic, is accounting for differences in characteristics that may contribute to the gaps in aggregate measures. For example, is the group of Black men in the United States changing over time in a way that would reduce their earnings relative to all other groups? Perhaps the group as a whole is becoming younger or less likely to be born in the United States/ IDDA statistics cannot be re-estimated holding population characteristics constant, but researchers can use other sources to control for or test hypotheses about changing observables in the aggregate. This is left for future research.

analysis—can provide a sense of how growth varies across the distribution. However, because people do not remain at the same percentile of the income distribution over time, changes in percentile values do not necessarily align with the income growth experienced by specific people in different parts of the income distribution. The panel dimension of the data underlying IDDA permits the construction of within-person income growth statistics by initial income level, providing detail on how income growth experiences differ across the income distribution. IDDA also has sufficiently large samples to measure conditional income dynamics statistics for many demographic groups.

11.4.1 Percentiles of Income Growth over Time

A limited set of income growth measures can be constructed from publicly available sources, such as longitudinally linked Current Population Survey data, but the reliability of these estimates for smaller groups or nonstandard moments of the distribution is an open question. Attrition, item non-response, and other challenges could also influence survey-based estimates for groups of any size. As we did in the previous section, we begin by comparing basic income dynamics measures in IDDA against analogously constructed measures from the CPS. This helps illustrate the advantages of IDDA relative to other publicly available sources for studying income dynamics.[29]

Figure 11.5 plots measures of income growth based on IDDA data, as well as corresponding measures constructed from the CPS. Panels (a) and (b) show selected percentiles of the wage and salary income growth distribution, estimated using the CPS and IDDA, respectively, for people initially in the 26th through 50th percentiles of the income distribution, a group for which measurement challenges related to especially high and low incomes are less likely to be relevant. Median growth aligns reasonably well across data sources for the group initially earning in the second quartile. The differences between the two sources are much more pronounced in the tails of the growth distribution. Early in the period considered, the CPS shows 90th percentile wage and salary income growth in this quartile that is about twice as fast as that shown in IDDA, and that gap increases over time. At the other extreme, the 10th percentile of growth is consistently more than twice as negative as the 10th percentile of growth in IDDA. In summary, for people starting out in the second quartile of the income distribution, the CPS shows that the 10th percentile of growth is consistently lower than shown in IDDA, median growth is relatively comparable across data sources,

29. The Panel Study of Income Dynamics (PSID) is another publicly available data source that can be used to construct measures like those discussed in this section. The PSID, which began in 1968, features longer panels than other surveys, but its granularity is limited by small sample sizes.

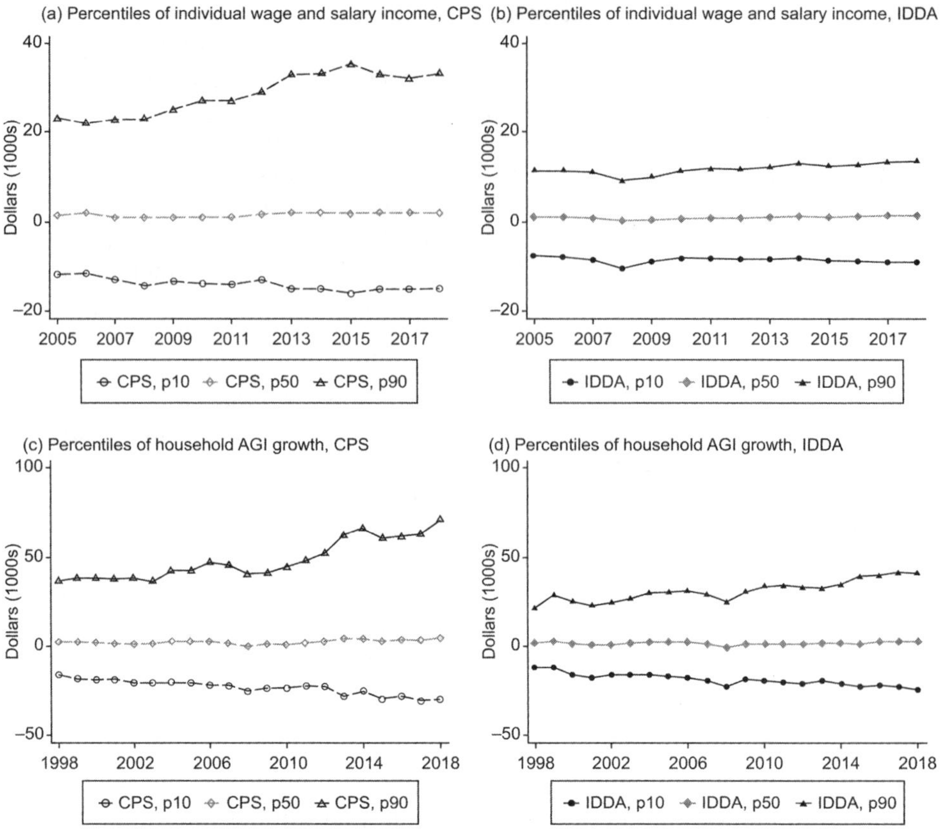

Fig. 11.5 Select income growth measures, CPS vs. IDDA

Source: CPS, IDDA and authors' calculations.

Note: Values are in nominal dollars. Adjusted gross income (AGI) in panel (d) is aggregated to the household level by summing across tax returns filed from the same address. Wage and salary income in other panels is aggregated across employers within person. Growth measures are computed at the individual level. Growth is calculated among people with income in the 26th through 50th percentiles of base year income. Release authorization CBDRB-FY23-0277.

and the 90th percentile of growth is consistently higher and growing faster over time.

Panels (c) and (d) reproduce panels (a) and (b) using AGI in IDDA and a similar income concept in the CPS. The takeaway is broadly similar, though the gaps between CPS and IDDA estimates of the 10th and 90th percentiles of growth are smaller in dollar terms when using AGI instead of wage and salary income. Aside from the change in income concept, the underlying samples also change from panels (a) and (b) to panels (c) and (d). In panels (a) and (b), each person must be observed and employed in consecutive years in order for income growth to be calculated. In panels (c) and (d), each person only has to be observed in a household in consecutive years. The

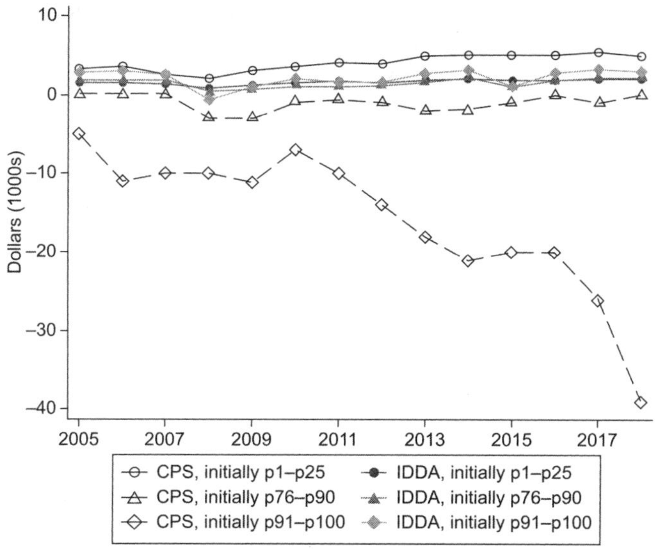

Fig. 11.6 Median annual wage and salary income growth by base year income
Source: CPS, IDDA and authors' calculations.
Note: Values are in nominal dollars. Growth measures are computed at the individual level. Release authorization CBDRB-FY23-0277.

broader sample, additional income sources included in AGI, and greater ability to capture extensive margin employment changes using a household income concept could all contribute to smaller gaps between IDDA and CPS in panels (c) and (d), although the impact of these differences on the relative magnitude is unclear a priori.

11.4.2 Granular Conditional Income Growth

Returning to wage and salary income, figure 11.6 illustrates how median growth differs between data sources for subgroups defined by initial earnings throughout the distribution, instead of how different percentiles of the growth distribution differ within a single initial earnings quartile. It shows median annual growth for people with base year incomes at higher and lower points in the income distribution, by data source. The CPS shows faster growth than IDDA for people with lower initial incomes, whose incomes are rising at the median. The CPS also shows sizable declines at the median for people with higher initial incomes, while IDDA shows modest increases at the median, a notable divergence across data sources.[30] Together with figure

30. The median decline in earnings in the top decile in the CPS in figure 11.6 is surprisingly large and grows over time. Much of this is driven by records with top coded or imputed income information. Removing those records maintains the tendency of the CPS to show declines among top earners but shows much smaller median declines in growth for people with base year income in the top decile, and a much less pronounced trend over time. See figure 11A.7.

11.5, this view of income growth across all percentiles of the distribution suggests a tendency of the CPS to spread out the distribution of income changes relative to that in IDDA, and produce larger magnitude estimates of both increases and decreases in income, rather than simply shifting the distribution by some fixed amount.

Consistent with both this tendency to measure larger gains and losses and the CPS's smaller sample sizes, CPS estimates are substantially more variable within states. Panel (a) of figure 11.7 shows the standard deviation within each state over time of median income growth estimates by base year income by average state population over the period considered. Within IDDA, variability is higher in the top quartile of initial income but generally low across income groups and consistent within income group over population levels. CPS standard deviations vary more substantially with population, with smaller states seeing higher standard deviations, especially for the top quartile of base year income.

Panel (b) of figure 11.7 plots these same standard deviation measures from the CPS (on the *y* axis) against those from IDDA (on the *x* axis), grouped by initial income quartile. In all states and across all income levels, the CPS standard deviation is greater than the IDDA standard deviation, often by a large margin. This is apparent from the different scales on the two axes; the 45-degree line is also plotted for comparison. Within the bottom three quartiles of base year income, the correlation between standard deviations from CPS and IDDA is positive. Within the top quartile of base year income, however, the sign flips, and states with lower standard deviations in IDDA tend to have higher standard deviations in the CPS. Similarities in standard deviations of income growth across the two sources are limited, but the pink cloud on the right shows that earnings variability is higher in both sources for the highest earners. In sum, variability in estimates of earnings dynamics measures is generally much higher in the CPS than in IDDA, and the sources often differ markedly on measures apart from median growth. We conclude that using the CPS to study earnings dynamics, as opposed to IDDA, can lead to meaningfully mischaracterized dynamics in many cases.

11.4.3 Income Growth by Race and Ethnicity from IDDA and the CPS

Having compared income growth over the initial earnings distribution in IDDA and the CPS, we next ask how income growth evolves for the race and ethnicity groups in section 11.3. Figure 11.8 shows median annual growth for prime-age workers by data source and race and ethnicity, revealing consistently faster growth in CPS estimates for White earners, but also noisier trends and larger differences across groups than those in IDDA. IDDA shows modest median growth for all groups that declined during the Great Recession before gradually recovering over the subsequent years. The CPS shows much larger gaps between groups in any given year as well as growth

(a) Standard deviation of state median wage and salary income growth by starting income and state population

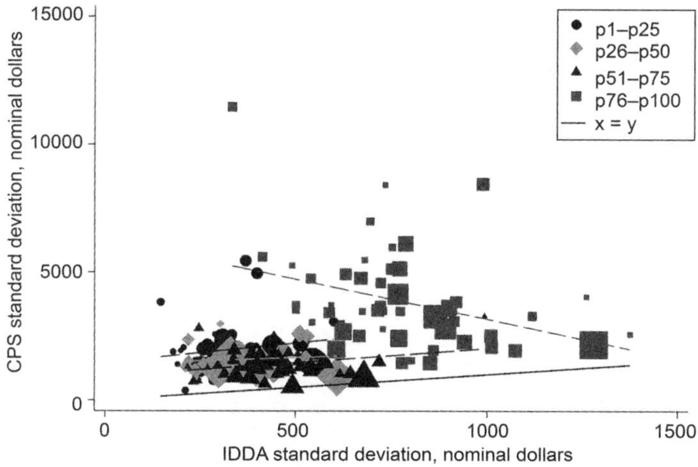

(b) Standard deviation of state median wage and salary income growth by starting income (markers weighted by state population)

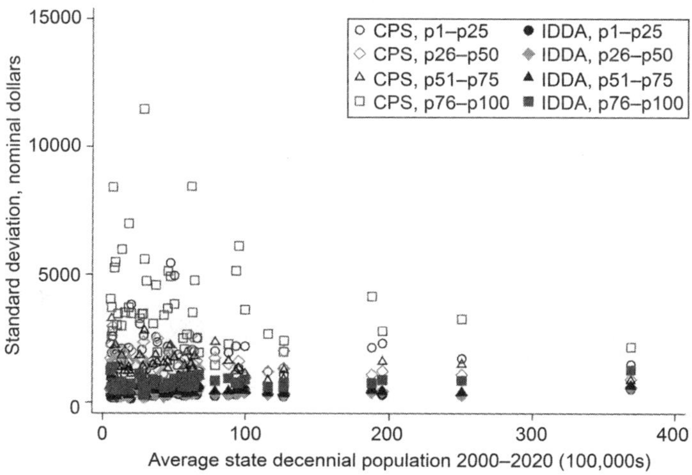

Fig. 11.7 Variation in income growth measures, CPS vs. IDDA

Source: CPS, decennial census, IDDA and authors' calculations.

Note: Panel (a) plots the IDDA and CPS standard deviation of the across-year distribution of median salary and income growth, grouped by income quantile and state, (n = 200). Panel (b) groups observations by source and graphs average state decennial population against standard deviation values (n = 400). Values are in nominal dollars. Underlying median growth measures are calculated at the individual level, using wage and salary income aggregated across employers within person. Release authorization CBDRB-FY23-0277.

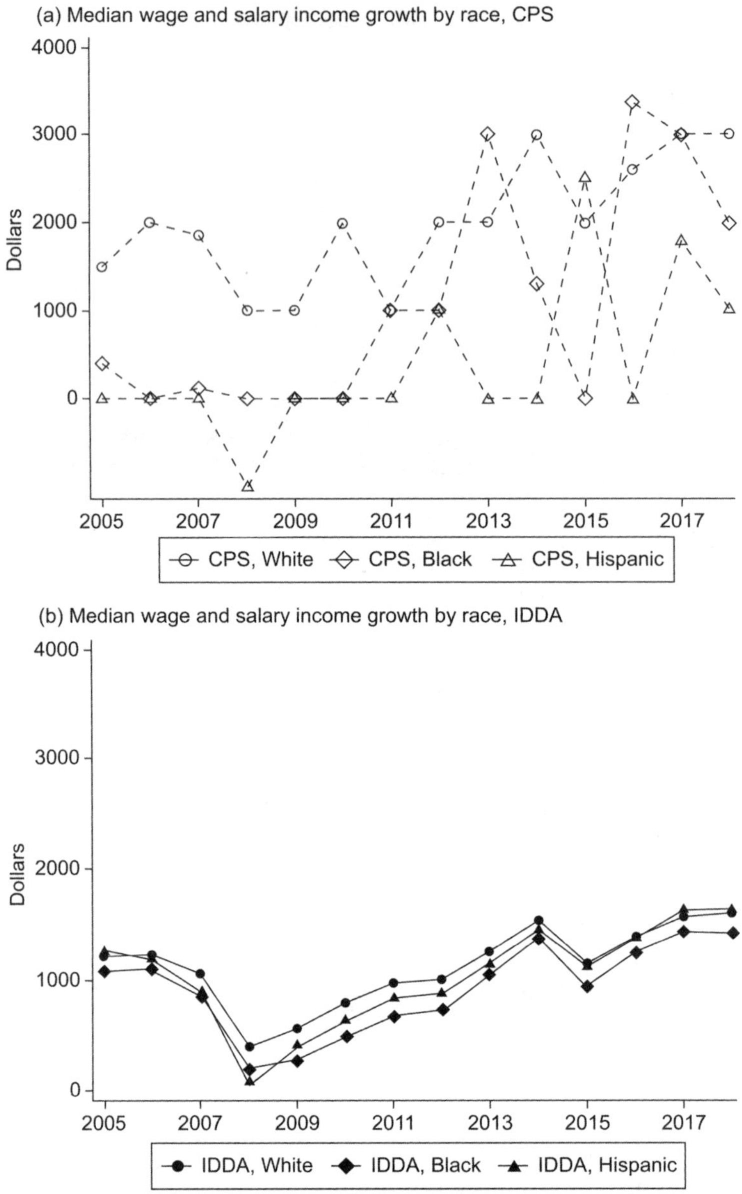

Fig. 11.8 Median annual wage and salary income growth by race/ethnicity, CPS vs. IDDA

Source: CPS, IDDA and authors' calculations.

Note: Values are in nominal dollars. Growth measures are computed at the individual level. Unless otherwise indicated, growth is calculated among prime-age workers with income in the 26th through 50th percentiles of base year income. Ethnicity is non-Hispanic unless otherwise specified. Release authorization CBDRB-FY23-0277.

trends that diverge much more substantially than those in IDDA, which are similar for all groups. Estimates for the smaller race/ethnicity groups in the CPS also see larger year-to-year fluctuations in growth than do the corresponding estimates from IDDA.

With the much larger sample sizes available in administrative data, IDDA allows for consideration of income growth in detail across a broader set of race/ethnicity and income groups than is feasible using the CPS. This could be especially helpful for understanding the changes in inequality discussed in section 11.3. In particular, non-Hispanic Black men have seen uniquely acute declines in earnings relative to non-Hispanic White men since the Great Recession. How did these compare to earnings dynamics for other non-White groups of men? Do the patterns differ across initial earnings quantiles?

Panel (a) of figure 11.9 plots one-year earnings growth in wage and salary income by race and ethnicity and by initial earnings percentile. It reveals that one-year earnings growth for Black earners over this period is on par with typical earnings growth, conditional on initial earnings below the 75th percentile. At higher percentiles, earnings growth for Black earners is comparable to that for AIAN earners and lags that for all other race and ethnicity groups. Panel (a) also shows relative declines in growth for Black earners that are most notable in 2010–2012 and among those with initial incomes in the top 10 percent. It also shows similar but smaller declines in growth among Black earners initially in the 76th through 90th percentiles and the 51st through 75th percentiles. Over a five-year horizon, shown in Panel (b) of figure 11.9, earnings growth for Black earners was again broadly in line with AIAN earners and consistently slower than growth for White and Asian earners across starting income groups, and any shifts in growth around the Great Recession are less stark. A second striking fact that emerges from this panel is that since 2005, five-year earnings growth has consistently been fastest for Asian earners at all income levels, with the largest relative gains in growth coming for the highest earners over this period.

The patterns in earnings growth reveal that Black earners experienced gaps in the level of growth, particularly over longer horizons, combined with a larger and more persistent slowdown in earnings growth after the Great Recession. While not definitive, this analysis suggests that earnings growth among higher-earning Black people may contribute to the decline in relative earnings identified for this group in section 11.3.

11.5 Distribution and Growth in Native Incomes in IDDA

IDDA is unique among publicly available data sources for allowing analysis of income distributions and their evolution for Native people and in Native land areas. As a final application, we extend the analysis of previous sections to these groups. In most cases, it is not possible to compare the pat-

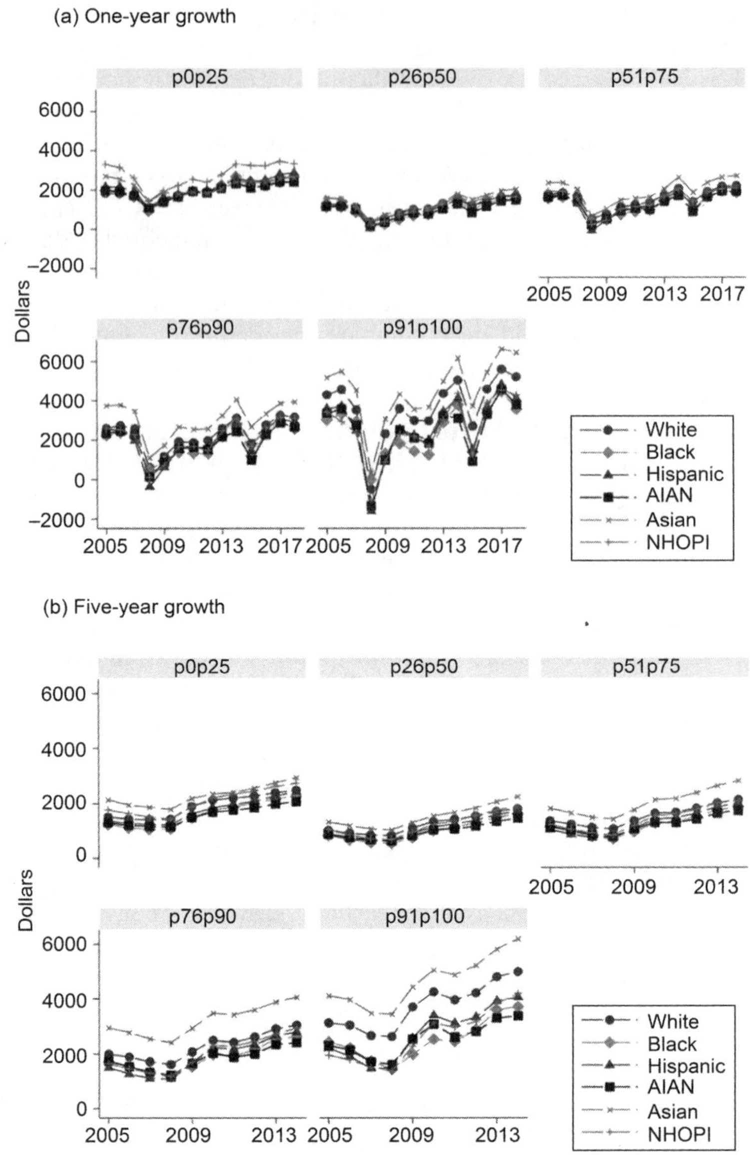

Fig. 11.9 Median wage and salary income growth by starting income and race/ethnicity, IDDA

Source: CPS, decennial census, IDDA and authors' calculations.

Note: Values are in nominal dollars. Underlying median growth measures are calculated at the individual level for prime-age workers using wage and salary income aggregated across employers within person. Ethnicity is non-Hispanic unless otherwise specified. AIAN abbreviates American Indian or Alaska Native. Release authorization CBDRB-FY23-0277.

terns we identify with other sources or earlier literature, so we present them independently, using only statistics from IDDA.

IDDA includes nearly 800,000 state- and US-level statistics describing income levels and mobility for non-Hispanic individuals who identify as American Indian or Alaska Native or as Native Hawaiian or other Pacific Islander. By providing these estimates at the subnational level, IDDA builds on the demographic granularity in Akee et al. (2019). Those authors used linked Census-IRS data to summarize national trends in income inequality and mobility for race and ethnicity groups, including AIAN and NHOPI individuals, and their paper is an important exception to the limited literature on the question of Native earnings distributions.

In addition, IDDA includes a supplement containing over 70,000 statistics describing incomes for both Native and non-Native populations living in Native areas. These include all American Indian and Alaska Native areas and Native Hawaiian Homelands as delineated by the Census Bureau in 2017, reported as one aggregate geography. To construct statistics for this supplement, we start with the 1040 and W-2 samples described in section 11.2 and identify individuals living in Native areas, using residential address information from the Master Address File-Auxiliary Reference File. Instead of the single race and ethnicity variable used at the state and US level, we use a broad definition of Native identity that includes individuals who identify any of their races as American Indian, Alaska Native, Native Hawaiian, or other Pacific Islander, regardless of Hispanic ethnicity. We prioritize sources that allow respondents to identify multiple races, using the most recent American Community Survey or decennial census (2010 or 2000) in which race/ethnicity is reported.[31] Aside from sample differences, construction of statistics in the supplement follows those for other geographies in IDDA.

Using statistics defined for Native areas, we reproduce our baseline analysis of cumulative changes in household income and individual earnings for individuals living in Native areas. Figure 11.10 presents the results. Comparing these to figures 11.1 and 11.2 shows that Native areas share some key features of income and earnings growth with the US-level IDDA data series. First, panel (a) shows that as in the United States broadly, household incomes in Native areas "fanned out" over the 1998–2018 period: incomes grew more at the top of the distribution than at the bottom. The ratio of the 90th to 10th percentile of household income rose from 8.4 to 11, mirroring the US-level increase (shown in figure 11A.1) almost exactly. The

31. Liebler et al. (2016) show that many individuals changed American Indian or Alaska Native response categories from the 2000 to the 2010 census, moving between single- and multi-racial categories or in and out of the AIAN label. IDDA takes the most recent race response observed for each PIK and uses that response for all data years. In 2010, about 15 percent of individuals in the Native areas 1040 sample and 20 percent of individuals in the Native areas W-2 sample identified as Native. The age and gender composition of the IDDA Native areas sample is reported in table 11A.5.

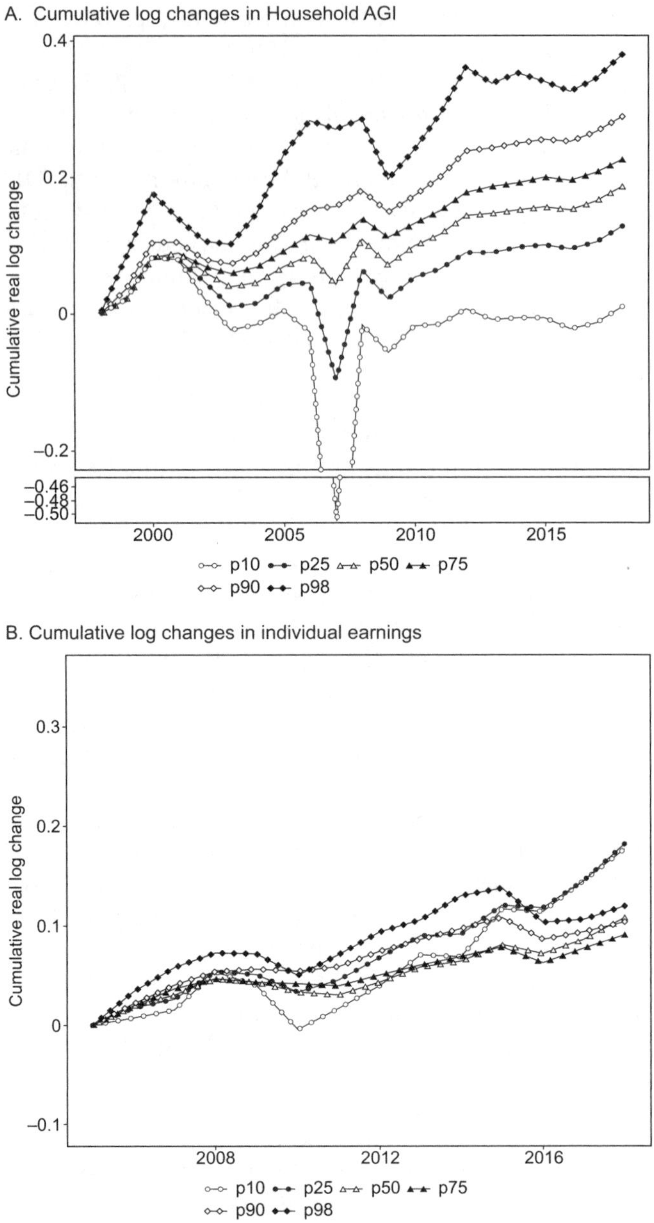

Fig. 11.10 Household income and earnings growth in Native areas

Source: IDDA and authors' calculations.

Note: The IDDA Native areas geography includes individuals living in American Indian and Alaska Native areas or Native Hawaiian Homelands as delineated by the Census Bureau. Data period is 2005–2018 for individual earnings and 1998–2018 for household income. We choose not to compare total income growth through 2019 due to changes in tax filing related to the COVID-19 pandemic. The large decline in household income in 2007 is similarly related to filing changes, as discussed in section 11.3. Release authorization CBDRB-FY23-0373.

98th/50th percentile ratio increased from 4.3 to 5.3. Second, across the distribution, the total percent change in household income from 1998 to 2018 was similar to the corresponding US-level change, within a few percentage points. However, the timing of this growth differs. In the United States overall, at the median and below, household incomes were flat or falling from 2001 through the Great Recession, but showed sustained growth in the subsequent recovery. In contrast, the 10th–50th percentiles in Native areas showed rapid growth before 2001 and had started to climb again in the run-up to the Great Recession—but increased more slowly through the recovery. Even at higher percentiles, relative to growth at the US level, income growth appears to have slowed in the late 2010s.

Panel (b) reports results on the same percentiles using the W-2 statistics on individual earnings. In the years leading up to the Great Recession, growth in individual earnings in Native areas also outpaced growth at the US level, particularly at the bottom of the distribution. The 10th and 25th percentiles of earnings never fell below their 2005 level, while still realizing relative growth after 2010. At the 10th percentile, individual earnings grew nearly 20 percent from 2010 to 2018, compared with 8 percent at the median. Meanwhile, top earners saw a decline in W-2 earnings after 2015. The result is a slight narrowing of the earnings distribution over time, similar to that observed in the United States broadly, but with some unique recession dynamics.

Understanding the big-picture evolution of incomes in Native areas is an important contribution of IDDA, given the limited availability of alternative data sources. But IDDA's demographic granularity allows us to go further and disentangle trends affecting tribal lands from those affecting Native earners. For instance, Akee et al. (2019) show that AIAN tax filers experience income gaps along the distribution and are more likely to experience downward income mobility than White earners. Do Native earners living in tribal areas experience a larger or smaller earnings gap than all AIAN earners? Within Native areas, do Native and non-Native individuals show similar patterns in income growth? IDDA provides the tools to answer these and similar questions at the intersection of place and identity.

Figure 11.11 shows how relative median earnings have changed over time for Native and non-Native earners in tribal areas, as well as for all AIAN and NHOPI earners. Each value is expressed as a percentage of the US population median. Large disparities in earnings levels immediately stand out. Earnings in Native areas are lower than those in the rest of the United States, and earnings for Native people in Native areas are lower than for AIAN and NHOPI earners elsewhere. In 2005, median earnings for Native workers living in Native areas were two-thirds of the US median, compared with 70 percent for all AIAN earners and over 90 percent for all NHOPI earners. Note that the group of all AIAN earners includes individuals living in tribal areas who identify as single-race American Indian or Alaska Native (i.e., the line with triangles contains some but not all of the population rep-

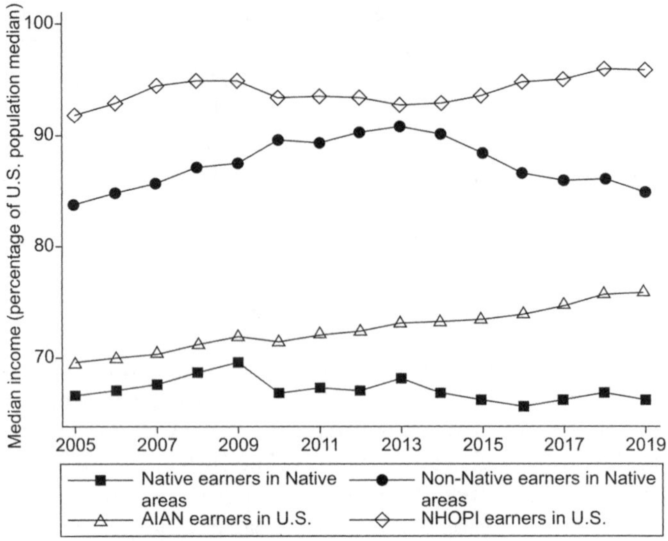

Fig. 11.11 Median earnings in Native areas and for Native groups, relative to US population

Source: IDDA and authors' calculations.

Note: Each point plots relative median earnings in the given race and ethnicity group, expressed as a percentage of the US population median. The groups of all American Indian or Alaska Native earners and all Native Hawaiian or other Pacific Islander earners include some individuals living in Native areas who identify only as single-race, non-Hispanic AIAN, or NHOPI. Release authorizations CBDRB-FY23-0373 and CBDRB-FY23-0277.

resented by the line with squares), and likewise with the group of NHOPI earners. The earnings differential between Native earners inside and outside of tribal areas may therefore be larger than the figure suggests.

Within Native areas, non-Native earners experienced a substantial earnings privilege, about 20 percentage points. It is also striking that these groups saw distinct earnings trajectories. Before the Great Recession, relative earnings for both Native and non-Native earners living in Native areas were increasing, consistent with figure 11.10. In 2010, relative earnings fell sharply for Native earners living in Native areas. Meanwhile, earnings for non-Native earners in tribal areas and for all AIAN earners continued to move toward the US median. By 2013, the gap in earnings between Native and non-Native earners had increased by 5 percentage points. After 2013, this period of widening inequality within Native areas appears to give way to a period of broad-based divergence between Native areas and the rest of the United States, as relative earnings declined for both Native and non-Native workers living in Native areas.

The trends shown in figure 11.11 are concerning and contrast with the long-run convergence of tribal incomes following the 1975 Indian Self-Determination and Education Assistance Act (Akee 2021). But Native

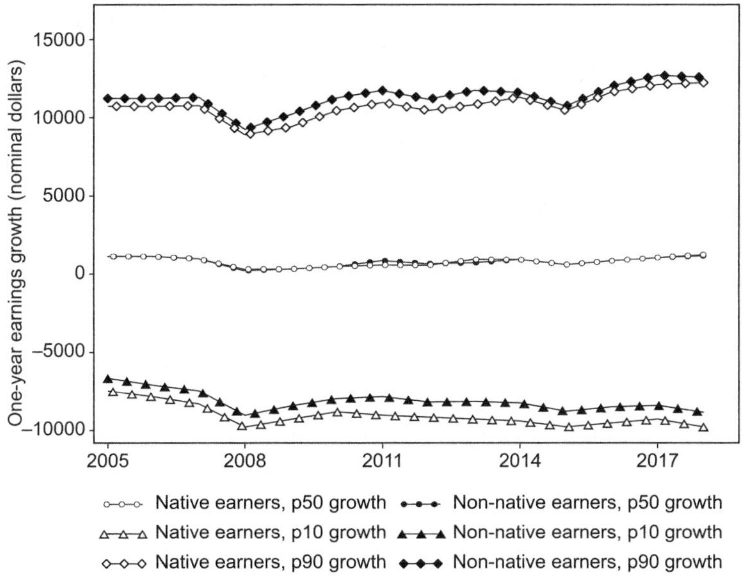

Fig. 11.12 Distribution of earnings growth for Native and non-Native earners in Native areas

Source: IDDA and authors' calculations.

Note: Each point shows the 10th, 50th, or 90th percentile of one-year earnings growth among Native and non-Native earners initially in the second quartile of the earnings distribution in Native areas. Initial year earnings quartiles are defined within a sample and geography but across demographic groups. Measures of earnings growth are computed among earners who remain in the W-2 sample and live in a Native area in both years. All values are in nominal dollars. Release authorization CBDRB-FY23-0373.

economies are unique, and economic activity outside of wage employment may play an important role.[32] Figure 11.11 also raises the question of whether Native and non-Native people living in Native areas experience different trends in migration, employment, or movement through the income distribution. Our final figure uses the one-year earnings growth measures highlighted in section 11.4 to explore one of these dimensions. However, the transition matrix module makes available information on conditional migration and employment flows for earners along the distribution.

Figure 11.12 shows the 10th, 50th, and 90th percentiles of earnings growth for Native and non-Native earners initially in the second quartile of the earnings distribution in Native areas. Median earnings growth in this group looks very similar for Native and non-Native earners, despite their different earnings levels and trajectories. However, looking at the full distribution of

32. For instance, median household income among Native tax filers in Native areas remained relatively stable until 2013, shown in figure 11A.8. Gubbay and Trostle (2023) discuss these trends in the context of the multifaceted economic landscape in Native areas. Self-employment, entrepreneurship, and subsistence economies are important and established parts of many tribal economies.

earnings growth shows that low growth is lower and high growth is slightly less high for Native earners than for non-Native earners in this quartile.[33] These differences are potentially large, particularly for those experiencing earnings losses: the loss at the 10th percentile of growth was 8 to 14 percent larger for Native earners than for non-Native earners. The gaps in earnings growth (or loss) also widened slightly from 2009 to 2013, the period of widening earnings inequality between Native and non-Native earners, but these trends are obscured by the much larger within-group differences between low and high earnings growth.

Together, these IDDA statistics add to the description of AIAN incomes provided in Akee et al. (2019), showing that median earnings are lower for Native earners living in Native areas than for AIAN earners throughout the United States and that this disparity has increased since the Great Recession. We identify distinct patterns in the distribution of earnings and earnings growth that are not explained by place or Native identity alone, but can be seen only at the intersection of these characteristics.

11.6 Conclusion

Considering income inequality and dynamics within granular demographic and geographic cells can reveal important facts about how inequality evolves in the United States. This approach also has the potential to enhance our understanding of the functioning of the broader economy, as economists turn to questions about potentially time-varying causes behind the changes we observe and to questions about the impacts these distributions and their dynamics have on other outcomes. To contribute to this agenda, we developed a set of statistics describing income distributions, income mobility, and conditional income growth for communities in the United States defined by place (US states) and demographics (race and ethnicity, sex, age, and birthplace). We used the universe of 1040 tax filings from 1998–2019 as well as the universe of W-2 filings for 2005–2019 to construct measures that reflect earnings distributions in these two populations. We label the resulting analytical dataset the Income Distributions and Dynamics in America data, or IDDA.

In this paper, we investigate what this approach reveals about patterns of evolving income inequality for groups defined by race and ethnicity, and we compare it with what can be observed in public sources. We find that gross features of US-level earnings distributions, like 75–25 percentile inequality, align well across the measures we construct from tax records and those that could be constructed using publicly available self-reports of earnings from survey data. But we find that public sources reproduce distributional pat-

33. Initial year earnings quartiles are defined across demographic groups. These patterns hold for earners initially in the third quartile of the distribution, capturing those just above and below the overall median.

terns for subnational groups with a low level of fidelity. Also, inequality in the earnings distribution is generally imprecisely captured using public data for the highest earnings percentiles. We also find that even standard measures of distributional features for race and ethnicity groups at the state level benefit from the large samples available in administrative data. Furthermore, the administrative data allow for construction of a longitudinal record of individual earnings. From these, we derive measures of earnings dynamics that cannot be constructed elsewhere. We show that earnings dynamics measured with the administrative panel data differ substantially from those inferred from changes in earnings at percentiles of the cross-section of earnings in survey data.

Finally, to demonstrate the breadth of potential future analysis, we present two applications of IDDA statistics. In the first application, we find that since the Great Recession, at most percentiles in the upper half of the distribution, labor earnings for Black men and Black women have declined relative to those for White men in contrast to relative gains for most other race, ethnicity, and sex groups. In the second application, we find that the earnings trajectories for Native people residing inside Native areas and the trajectories of those living outside them diverged after the Great Recession.

Much work remains to be done to provide a comprehensive view of how income and earnings distributions evolve for race, ethnicity, and other demographic groups in subnational communities across the United States. This paper has examined this topic from only a few angles. However, the wealth of information in IDDA provides several new insights in the space of even this single investigation. We encourage other researchers to use this and other newly available resources to begin addressing these questions more deeply.

Acknowledgments

The authors are grateful to Richard Liu and Zachary Swaziek for outstanding research assistance at different points in this project. Helpful comments from the following improved the paper: Andrew Goodman-Bacon, Amanda Eng, Adam Isen, Nick Pharris-Ciurej, Nathan Hendren, Jesse Rothstein, Michael Stepner, and seminar participants at the Federal Reserve Banks of Minneapolis and New York, the 2024 ASSA meetings, the 2024 NBER CRIW Spring conference, "Race, Ethnicity, and Economic Statistics for the 21st Century," and the 2024 Society of Labor Economists meeting. Kevin Rinz's work on this project was conducted primarily while he was a Census Bureau employee and a Visiting Scholar of the Opportunity & Inclusive Growth Institute. Disclaimer: The opinions and conclusions expressed here are those of the authors and should not be interpreted as reflecting the views of the Federal Reserve Board of Governors, the Federal Reserve Bank of Minneapolis, or any other person associated with the Federal Reserve System. Any opinions and conclusions expressed herein are those of the authors and do not represent the views of the US Census Bureau. The Census

Bureau has ensured appropriate access and use of confidential data and has reviewed these results for disclosure avoidance protection. (Project 7511151; Disclosure Authorization Numbers CBDRB-FY23-0277, CBDRB-FY23-0373, CBDRB-FY23-CES014-019, CBDRB-FY23-CES014-016, and CBDRB-FY24-0131.) For acknowledgments, sources of research support, and disclosure of the authors' material financial relationships, if any, please see https://www.nber.org/books-and-chapters/race-ethnicity-and-economic-statistics-21st-century/granular-income-inequality-and-mobility-using-idda-exploring-patterns-across-race-and-ethnicity.

Appendix

A Additional Figures and Tables

Table 11A.1 Educational attainment by demographic characteristics, ACS estimates

A. 4-year college attainment (2005)

Race/Ethnicity	Female	Male
Hispanic	15.0%	11.0%
NH AIAN	17.2%	14.7%
NH Asian	50.0%	54.2%
NH Black	20.7%	17.9%
NH NHOPI	16.6%	17.3%
NH Other	27.0%	24.3%
NH White	32.0%	31.7%

Data from the 2005 ACS. Table records the bachelor's degree attainment rate for the specified group. Sample is of members of the specified group between the ages of 25 and 54 whose annual earnings are at least equivalent to working half-time for 13 weeks at the federal minimum wage. Statistics are weighted.

B. Δ in 4-year college attainment (2005–2019)

Race/Ethnicity	Female	Male
Hispanic	48.7%	43.6%
NH AIAN	24.4%	3.4%
NH Asian	18.8%	11.6%
NH Black	41.1%	25.1%
NH NHOPI	28.3%	9.8%
NH Other	43%	32.9%
NH White	34.1%	18.9%

Note: Data from the 2005 and 2019 ACS. Table records the percentage change in bachelor's degree attainment rate for the specified group. Sample is of members of the specified group between the ages of 25 and 54 whose annual earnings are at least equivalent to working half-time for 13 weeks at the federal minimum wage. Statistics are weighted.

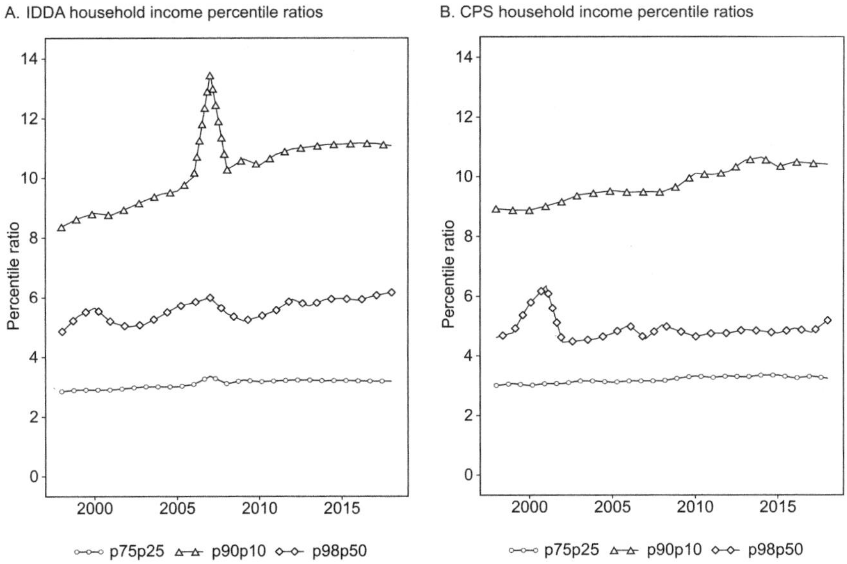

Fig. 11A.1 Household income percentile ratios in IDDA vs. CPS

Source: IDDA and IPUMS CPS.

Note: CPS statistics calculated by the authors following IDDA documentation and using the sample of all ASEC respondents aged 16 and over. Data period for both sources is 1998 to 2018. Release authorization CBDRB-FY23-0277.

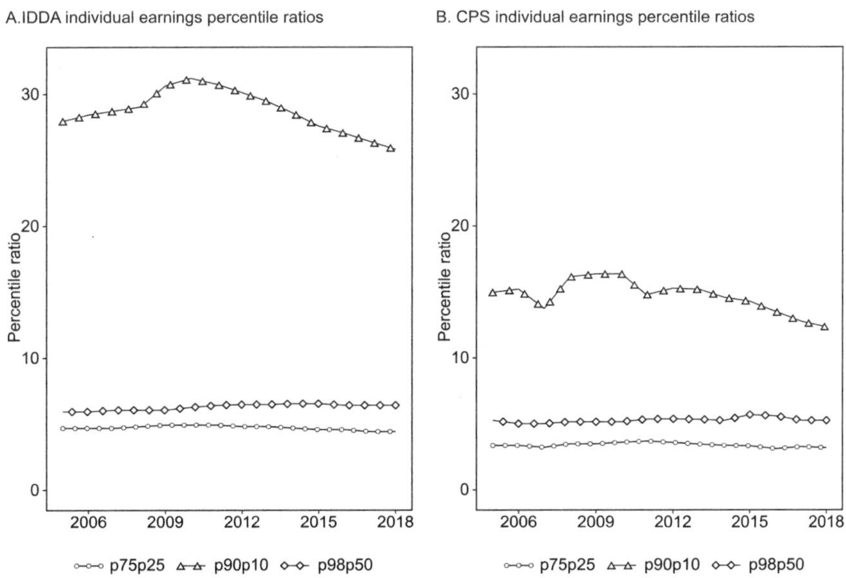

Fig. 11A.2 Individual earnings percentile ratios in IDDA vs. CPS

Source: IDDA and IPUMS CPS.

Note: CPS statistics calculated by the authors following IDDA documentation and using the sample of all ASEC respondents aged 16 and over who reported positive wage income. Data period for both sources is 2005 to 2018. Release authorization CBDRB-FY23-0277.

Table 11A.2 **Changes in state-level distributional statistics by race and ethnicity: ACS total household income vs. IDDA household AGI (2000–2018)**

		Estimated slope $\Delta(y)^{state}_{ACS} = \beta\Delta(y)^{state}_{IDDA} + \varepsilon^{state}$						
Group	N (1)	log(p10) (2)	log(p25) (3)	log(p50) (4)	log(p75) (5)	log(p90) (6)	p90p25 (7)	p98p50 (8)
All	51	0.359	1.075	1.107	1.099	1.064	0.744	1.948
		(0.159)	(0.080)	(0.039)	(0.026)	(0.031)	(0.056)	(0.174)
Hispanic	50	1.376	1.172	1.036	0.967	1.061	0.904	0.506
		(0.275)	(0.156)	(0.087)	(0.080)	(0.084)	(0.318)	(0.527)
AIAN	31	0.702	0.777	0.920	1.024	0.920	1.430	–0.314
		(0.403)	(0.284)	(0.227)	(0.192)	(0.175)	(0.618)	(1.184)
Asian	45	0.669	0.751	0.880	0.789	0.667	0.272	0.379
		(0.217)	(0.139)	(0.111)	(0.077)	(0.095)	(0.198)	(0.173)
Black	44	0.692	1.712	1.538	1.461	1.173	0.348	0.882
		(0.444)	(0.321)	(0.220)	(0.180)	(0.134)	(0.267)	(0.188)
NHOPI	3							
White	51	0.465	1.153	1.110	1.076	1.034	0.789	1.604
		(0.183)	(0.075)	(0.041)	(0.029)	(0.033)	(0.058)	(0.193)

Source: IDDA and authors' calculation using IPUMS ACS. Release authorization CBDRB-FY23-0277.

Note: Changes are computed from 2000 (the first year of ACS data) to 2018. For NHOPI and Asian earners, changes are computed from 2002–2018 to match data availability for these groups in the CPS comparison in table 11.6. We compute the 10th–90th percentiles of income for subnational populations with at least 50 observations in the ACS. We compute the 98th percentile of income for subnational populations with at least 250 observations in the ACS. Release authorization CBDRB-FY23-0277.

Table 11A.3 **Changes in state-level distributional statistics by race and ethnicity: ACS individual wage/salary income vs. IDDA W-2 earnings (2005–2018)**

		Estimated slope $\Delta(y)^{state}_{ACS} = \beta\Delta(y)^{state}_{IDDA} + \varepsilon^{state}$						
Group	N (1)	log(p10) (2)	log(p25) (3)	log(p50) (4)	log(p75) (5)	log(p90) (6)	p90p25 (7)	p98p50 (8)
All	51	1.018	0.857	0.793	0.977	0.895	0.571	1.120
		(0.067)	(0.046)	(0.039)	(0.035)	(0.030)	(0.104)	(0.136)
Hispanic	49	0.327	0.452	0.936	1.257	1.312	–0.137	1.128
		(0.214)	(0.106)	(0.108)	(0.100)	(0.120)	(0.210)	(0.458)
AIAN	36	1.436	0.679	0.794	0.712	0.618	0.895	0.759
		(0.242)	(0.185)	(0.165)	(0.162)	(0.229)	(0.374)	(1.244)
Asian	45	0.290	0.533	0.538	0.718	0.773	0.528	1.157
		(0.254)	(0.119)	(0.086)	(0.073)	(0.109)	(0.254)	(0.561)
Black	43	1.071	0.859	0.496	0.812	0.788	0.616	0.762
		(0.132)	(0.092)	(0.147)	(0.153)	(0.131)	(0.106)	(0.267)
NHOPI	8	0.792	0.688	0.457	0.656	0.517	0.140	
		(0.736)	(0.539)	(0.233)	(0.391)	(0.571)	(0.418)	
White	51	0.911	0.863	0.884	0.930	0.880	0.606	1.670
		(0.068)	(0.055)	(0.042)	(0.038)	(0.029)	(0.135)	(0.261)

Source: IDDA and authors' calculation using IPUMS CPS.

Note: Changes are computed from 2005–2018 for individual earnings. We compute the 10th–90th percentiles of income for subnational populations with at least 50 observations in the ACS. We compute the 98th percentile of income for subnational populations with at least 250 observations in the ACS. Release authorization CBDRB-FY23-0277.

Table 11A.4 IDDA prime-aged working sample composition (2010)

Demographic Composition	Prime-aged Working W-2	Prime-aged Working CPS
Female	49.0%	47.4%
Male	51.0%	52.6%
Hispanic	13.5%	16.3%
Non-Hispanic AIAN	0.9%	0.6%
Non-Hispanic Asian	5.2%	5.7%
Non-Hispanic Black	12.1%	11.2%
Non-Hispanic NHOPI	0.2%	0.3%
Non-Hispanic Other	1.4%	1.2%
Non-Hispanic White	66.6%	64.7%
Foreign born	15.2%	18.0%
Not Foreign born	84.8%	82.0%
25–34	33.0%	33.1%
35–44	32.1%	32.5%
45–54	34.9%	34.4%

Source: IDDA and IPUMS CPS.

Note: The IDDA Prime-aged working-W-2 sample includes individuals aged 25–54 with earnings at least equivalent to working 20 hours a week for 13 weeks at the federal minimum wage. In 2010, this was $1,885. Individuals in the 25–54 age bracket made up 63 percent of the overall W-2 sample in that year. The earnings threshold is much less restrictive: $1,885 fell substantially below the 10th percentile of individual earnings, which ranged from $4,174 for the 25–34-year-old group to $7,601 for the 45–54-year-old group. Earnings are measured using wage compensation reported on form W-2. Release authorization CBDRB-FY24-0131.

Table 11A.5 IDDA Native areas data source composition (2010)

Demographic composition	Household-1040	Individual-W-2
Female	51.9%	49.3%
Male	48.1%	50.7%
Native (AIAN or NHOPI)	14.6%	19.8%
Non-Native	85.4%	80.2%
16–24	10.3%	17.8%
25–34	19.1%	21.3%
35–44	17.6%	19.5%
45–54	20.1%	21.4%
55–64	17.3%	15.1%
65+	15.5%	5.0%

Source: IDDA.

Note: The Native areas data source includes individuals whose residential address falls within an American Indian or Alaska Native area or Native Hawaiian Homeland, using Census Bureau delineations from 2017. Individuals are coded as Native if they identify any of their races as American Indian, Alaska Native, Native Hawaiian, or other Pacific Islander, regardless of Hispanic ethnicity. Release authorization CBDRB-FY24-0131.

(a) Earnings difference between median Black and White men by state

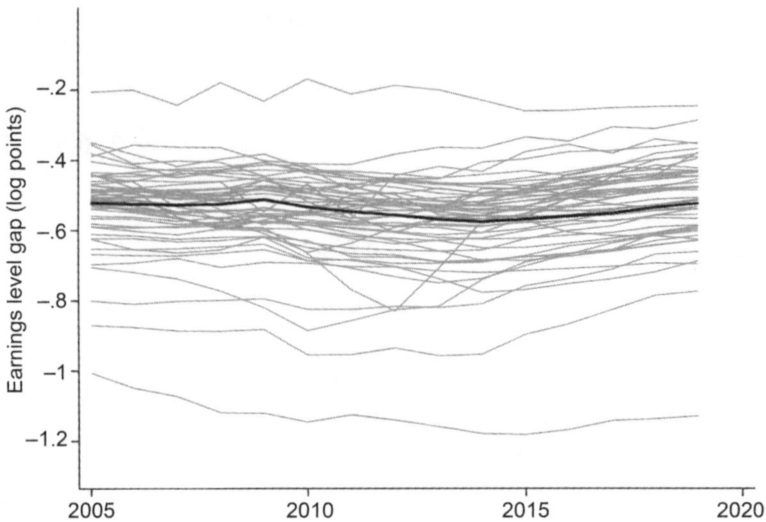

(b) Earnings difference between 90th percentile Black and White men by state

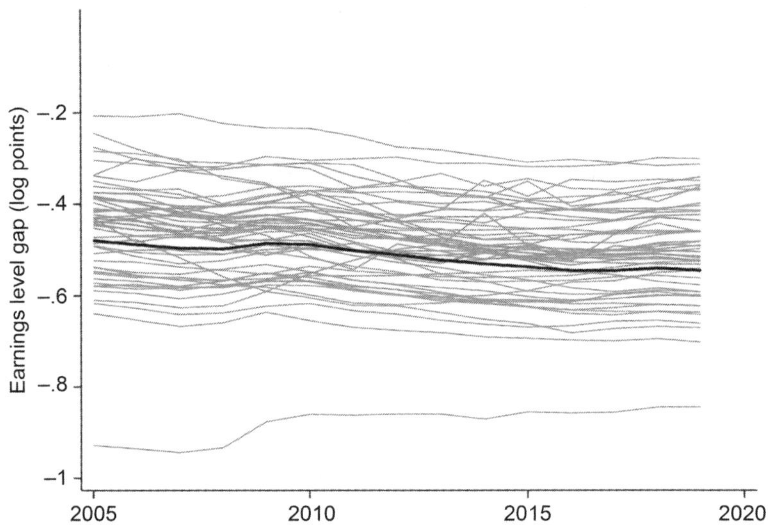

Fig. 11A.3 Level earnings differences between Black and White men by state

Source: IDDA and authors' calculations.

Note: In panel (a), lines plot the log point difference in median annual earnings between Black and White male earners in each state. In panel (b), lines plot the log point difference in the 90th percentile of annual earnings between Black and White male earners in each state. The black line is for the total United States. Ethnicity is non-Hispanic unless otherwise noted. Release authorization CBDRB-FY23-0277.

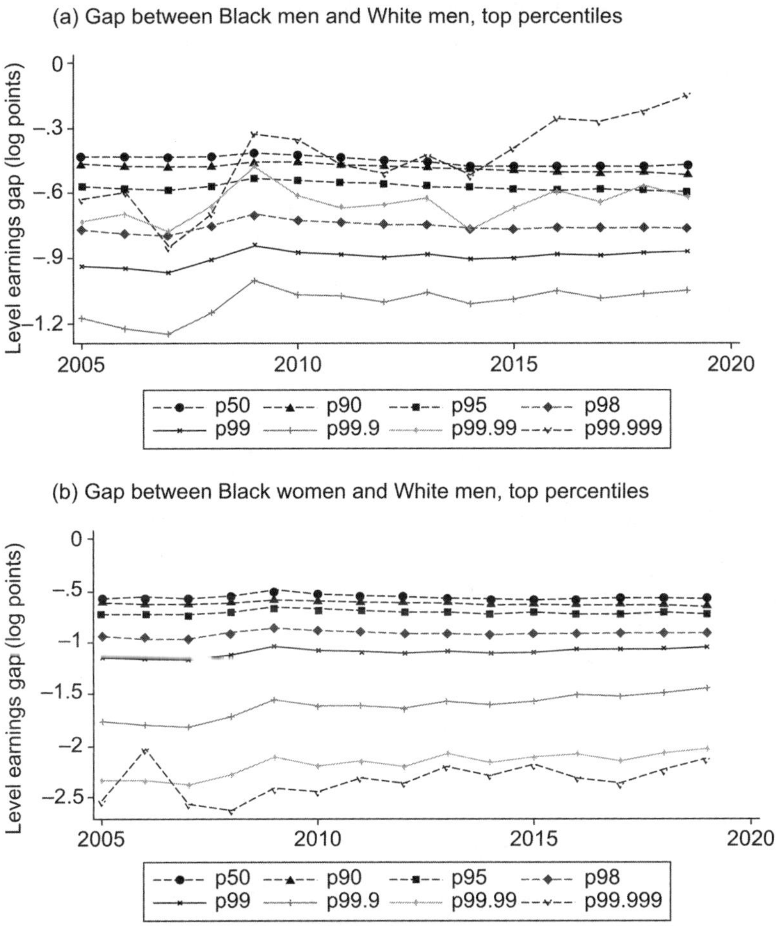

Fig. 11A.4 Gap between Black earners and White men, top percentiles

Source: IDDA and authors' calculations.

Note: Each panel plots the earnings gap between prime-age Black earners and White men, in log points. Includes workers aged 25–54 with earnings at least equivalent to working 20 hours a week for 13 weeks at the federal minimum wage. Ethnicity is non-Hispanic unless otherwise specified. Release authorization CBDRB-FY23-0277.

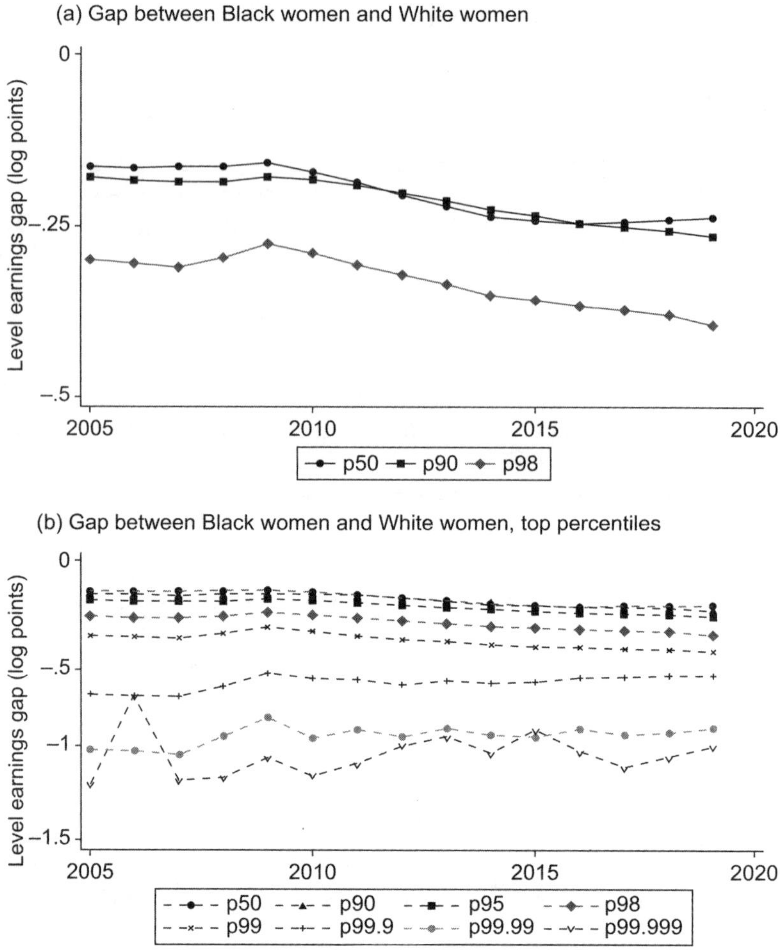

Fig. 11A.5 Gap between Black and White women

Source: IDDA and authors' calculations.

Note: Each panel plots the earnings gap between prime-age Black women and White women, in log points. Includes workers aged 25–54 with earnings at least equivalent to working 20 hours a week for 13 weeks at the federal minimum wage. Ethnicity is non-Hispanic unless otherwise specified. Release authorization CBDRB-FY23-0277.

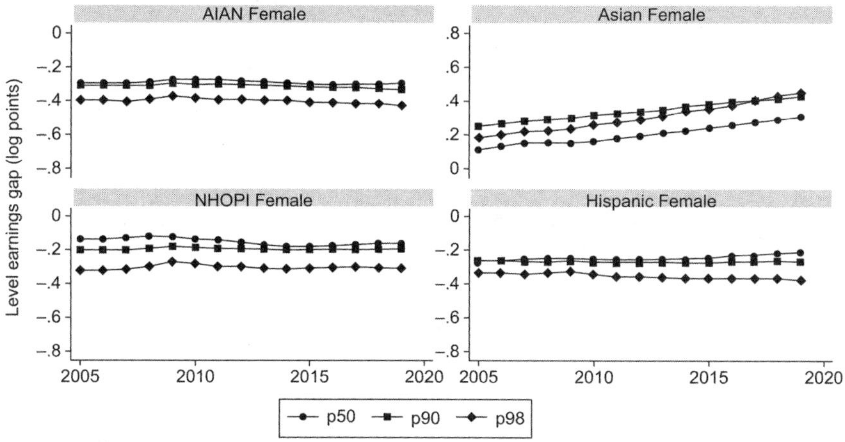

Fig. 11A.6 Gap between non-White and White women

Source: IDDA and authors' calculations.

Note: Each panel plots the earnings gap between prime-age non-White women and White women, in log points. Includes workers aged 25–54 with earnings at least equivalent to working 20 hours a week for 13 weeks at the federal minimum wage. Ethnicity is non-Hispanic unless otherwise specified. Release authorization CBDRB-FY23-0277.

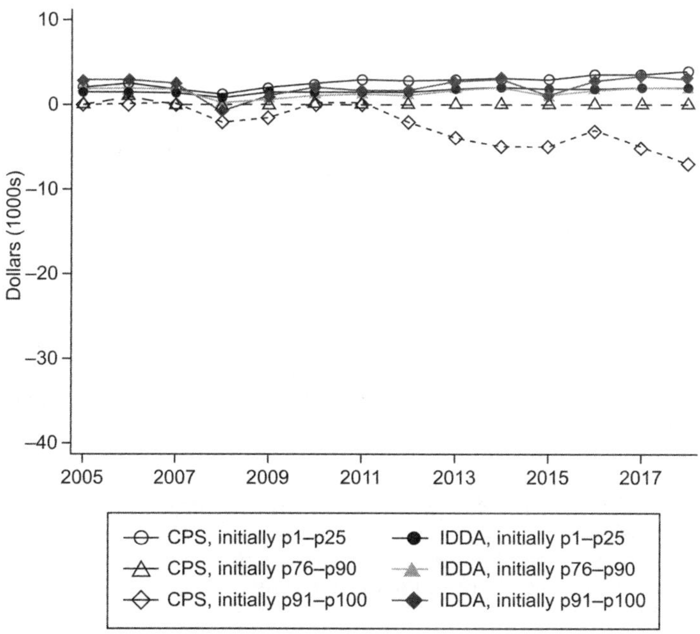

Fig. 11A.7 Median wage and salary income growth by base year income, excluding CPS top codes and imputed values

Source: CPS, IDDA and authors' calculations.

Note: Values are in nominal dollars. Growth measures are computed at the individual level. Release authorization CBDRB-FY23-0277.

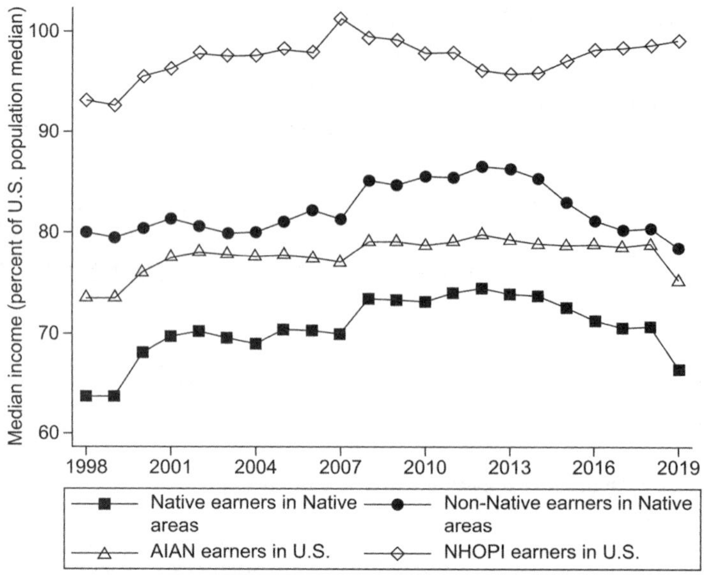

Fig. 11A.8 Median household income in Native Areas, relative to US population

Source: IDDA and authors' calculations.

Note: Each point plots relative median income in the given race and ethnicity group, expressed as a percentage of the US population median. Household income in IDDA is summed across all 1040 forms filed at a common address, and the household-level total is assigned to each adult resident. This provides a measure of resources available to individuals in different demographic groups. The groups of all American Indian or Alaska Native earners and all Native Hawaiian or other Pacific Islander earners include some individuals living in Native areas who identify only as single-race, non-Hispanic AIAN or NHOPI. Release authorizations CBDRB-FY23-0373 and CBDRB-FY23-0277.

References

Akee, Randall, Maggie R Jones, and Sonya R Porter. 2019. "Race Matters: Income Shares, Income Inequality, and Income Mobility for all US Races." *Demography* 56(3): 999–1021.

Akee, Randall. 2021. "Sovereignty and Improved Economic Outcomes for American Indians: Building on the Gains Made Since 1990." In *Boosting Wages for US Workers in the New Economy: Ten Essays on Worker Power, Worker Well-Being*, 147–64. Washington Center for Equitable Growth.

Auten, Gerald, and David Splinter. 2024. "Income Inequality in the United States: Using Tax Data to Measure Long-Term Trends." *Journal of Political Economy* 132(7): 2179–27.

Autor, David H., Lawrence F. Katz, and Melissa S. Kearney. 2008. "Trends in US Wage Inequality: Revising the Revisionists." *Review of Economics and Statistics* 90(2): 300–323.

Autor, David, Arindrajit Dube, and Annie McGrew. 2023. "The Unexpected Compression: Competition at Work in the Low Wage Labor Market." NBER Working Paper No. 31010. Cambridge, MA: National Bureau of Economic Research.

Bayer, Patrick, and Kerwin Kofi Charles. 2018. "Divergent Paths: A New Perspective on Earnings Differences between Black and White Men since 1940." *Quarterly Journal of Economics* 133(3): 1459–1501.

Bee, Adam, Joshua Mitchell, Nikolas Mittag, Johnathan Rothbaum, Carl Sanders, Lawrence Schmidt, and Matthew Unrath. 2023. "National Experimental Well-being Statistics Version 1." Center for Economic Studies Working Paper 23-04, United States Census Bureau.

Bee, Adam, and Joshua Mitchell. 2017. "Do Older Americans Have More Income Than We Think?" SEHSD Working Paper 2017-39, Social, Economic, and Housing Statistics Division, US Census Bureau.

Blanchet, Thomas, Emmanuel Saez, and Gabriel Zucman. 2022. "Real-Time Inequality." NBER Working Paper No. 30229. Cambridge, MA: National Bureau of Economic Research.

Bollinger, Christopher R., Barry T. Hirsch, Charles M. Hokayem, and James P. Ziliak. 2019. "Trouble in the Tails? What We Know about Earnings Nonresponse 30 Years after Lillard, Smith, and Welch." *Journal of Political Economy* 127(5): 2143–85.

Burkhauser, Richard V., Shuaizhang Feng, Stephen P. Jenkins, and Jeff Larrimore. 2011. "Estimating Trends in US Income Inequality Using the Current Population Survey: The Importance of Controlling for Censoring." *Journal of Economic Inequality* 9: 393–415.

Burkhauser, Richard V., Shuaizhang Feng, Stephen P. Jenkins, and Jeff Larrimore. 2012. "Recent Trends in Top Income Shares in the United States: Reconciling Estimates from March CPS and IRS Tax Return Data." *Review of Economics and Statistics* 94(2): 371–88.

Chetty, Raj, Nathaniel Hendren, John Friedman, Maggie R Jones, and Sonya R Porter. 2018. "The Opportunity Atlas: Mapping the Childhood Roots of Social Mobility." NBER Working Paper No. 25147. Cambridge, MA: National Bureau of Economic Research.

Chetty, Raj, Nathaniel Hendren, Patrick Kline, and Emmanuel Saez. 2014. "Where Is the Land of Opportunity? The Geography of Intergenerational Mobility in the United States." *Quarterly Journal of Economics* 129(4): 1553–1623.

Corinth, Kevin, Bruce Meyer, and Derek Wu. 2022. "The Change in Poverty from 1995 to 2016 among Single-Parent Families." *AEA Papers and Proceedings* 112: 345–50.

Erard, Brian, Patrick Langetieg, Mark Payne, and Alan Plumley. 2020. "Flying under the Radar: Ghosts and the Income Tax." *CESifo Economic Studies* 66(3): 185–97.

Flood, Sarah, Miriam King, Renae Rodgers, Steven Ruggles, J. Robert Warren, Daniel Backman, Annie Chen, Grace Cooper, Stephanie Richards, Megan Schouweiler, and Michael Westberry. 2023. Integrated Public Use Microdata Series, Current Population Survey: Version 11.0 [dataset]. Minneapolis, MN: IPUMS. https://doi.org/10.18128/D030.V11.0.

Frank, Mark. 2014. "A New State-Level Panel of Annual Inequality Measures over the Period 1916–2005." *Journal of Business Strategies* 31(1): 241–63.

Gubbay, Natalie, and H. Trostle. 2023. "The Geographic Divide in Native Incomes and Earnings." *For All*, Spring 2024: 20–24. Federal Reserve Bank of Minneapolis, November 13. https://www.minneapolisfed.org/article/2023/the-geographic-divide-in-native-incomes-and-earnings.

Guvenen, Fatih, Greg Kaplan, Jae Song, and Justin Weidner. 2022. "Lifetime Earnings in the United States over Six Decades." *American Economic Journal: Applied Economics* 14(4): 446–79.

Guvenen, Fatih, and Greg Kaplan. 2017. "Top Income Inequality in the 21st Century: Some Cautionary Notes." NBER Working Paper No. 23321. Cambridge, MA: National Bureau of Economic Research.

Hoffmann, Florian, David S. Lee, and Thomas Lemieux. 2020. "Growing Income Inequality in the United States and Other Advanced Economies." *Journal of Economic Perspectives* 34(4): 52–78.

Internal Revenue Service. 2009. Individual Income Tax Returns 2007. Statistics of Income Publication 1304. (Rev. 07-2009). Washington, DC: Internal Revenue Service, Department of the Treasury. https://www.irs.gov/pub/irs-soi/07inalcr.pdf.

IPUMS. 2020. Current Population Survey 2020 Annual Social and Economic (ASEC) Supplement. Codebook, Integrated Public Use Microdata Series, Minneapolis, MN. https://cps.ipums.org/cps/resources/codebooks/cpsmar20.pdf.

Kondo, Illenin O., Kevin Rinz, Natalie Gubbay, Brandon Hawkins, John Voorheis, and Abigail Wozniak. 2024. "Granular Income Inequality and Mobility Using IDDA: Exploring Patterns Across Race and Ethnicity." NBER Working Paper No. 32709. Cambridge, MA: National Bureau of Economic Research.

Kopczuk, Wojciech, Emmanuel Saez, and Jae Song. 2010. "Earnings Inequality and Mobility in the United States: Evidence from Social Security Data since 1937." *Quarterly Journal of Economics* 125(1): 91–128.

Layne, Mary, Deborah Wagner, and Cynthia Rothhaas. 2014. "Estimating Record Linkage False Match Rate for the Person Identification Validation System." CARRA Working Paper No. 2014–02. US Census Bureau, July.

Liebler, Carolyn A., Renuka Bhaskar, and Sonya R Porter. 2016. "Joining, Leaving, and Staying in the American Indian/Alaska Native Race Category between 2000 and 2010." *Demography* 53(2): 507–40.

McKinney, Kevin L., John M. Abowd, and Hubert P. Janicki. 2022. "US Long-Term Earnings Outcomes by Sex, Race, Ethnicity, and Place of Birth." *Quantitative Economics* 13(4): 1879–1945.

Meyer, Bruce, and Nikolas Mittag. 2019. "Combining Administrative and Survey Data to Improve Income Measurement." NBER Working Paper No. 25738. Cambridge, MA: National Bureau of Economic Research.

Morrill, Richard. 2000. "Geographic Variation in Change in Income Inequality among US States, 1970–1990." *Annals of Regional Science* 34: 109–30.

Mulrow, Edward, Ali Mushtaq, Santanu Pramanik, and Angela Fontes. 2011. "Assessment of the US Census Bureau's Person Identification Validation System." Report to the US Census Bureau, NORC at the University of Chicago.

Partridge, Mark D., Dan S. Rickman, and William Levernier. 1996. "Trends in US Income Inequality: Evidence from a Panel of States." *Quarterly Review of Economics and Finance* 36(1): 17–37.

Piketty, Thomas, Emmanuel Saez, and Gabriel Zucman. 2017. "Distributional National Accounts: Methods and Estimates for the United States." *Quarterly Journal of Economics* 133(2): 553–609.

Piketty, Thomas, and Emmanuel Saez. 2003. "Income Inequality in the United States, 1913–1998." *Quarterly Journal of Economics* 118(1): 1–41.

Rinz, Kevin, and John Voorheis. 2023. "Re-examining Regional Income Convergence: A Distributional Approach." Center for Economic Studies Working Paper 23-05, US Census Bureau.

Smith, Matthew, Danny Yagan, Owen Zidar, and Eric Zwick. 2019. "Capitalists in the Twenty-First Century." *Quarterly Journal of Economics* 134(4): 1675–1745.

Sommeiller, Estelle, and Mark Price. 2014. "The Increasingly Unequal States of

America: Income Inequality by State, 1917 to 2011." Economic Analysis and Research Network (EARN) report. Washington, DC: Economic Policy Institute.
US Census Bureau. Glossary: Household, 2024. Accessed June 15, 2024. https://www.census.gov/glossary/?term=Household.
Wagner, Deborah, and Mary Layne. 2014. "The Person Identification Validation System (PVS): Applying the Center for Administrative Records Research and Applications (CARRA) Record Linkage Software." CARRA Working Paper No. 2014-01, US Census Bureau, July.

12

Earnings Inequality and Immobility for Hispanics and Asians
An Examination of Variation Across Subgroups

Randall Akee, Sonya R. Porter, and Emilia Simeonova

12.1 Introduction

There is a reemergence of interest in understanding and ameliorating racial and ethnic socio-economic inequality. A vast literature explores and documents the substantial gaps in income, earnings, and wealth between the African American and White populations in the United States (Bloome 2014; Bloome and Western 2011; Chetty et al. 2020; Derenoncourt and Montialoux 2021; Reardon and Bischoff 2011). There is also a growing body of literature that demonstrates the evolution of income inequality for other racial and ethnic groups (Akee et al. 2019; Budiman and Neil 2021; Horowitz et al. 2020; Kochhar and Fry 2014; Snipp and Cheung 2016). Much less is known about the experiences of racial and ethnic subgroups within these larger groups primarily due to the fact that reliable analysis of subgroups requires a large amount of observations. Many nationally representative longitudinal datasets do not collect large enough samples needed to conduct reliable statistical analyses within Asian or Hispanic subgroups in the United States.

The most recent US Census data for 2020 indicates that the Asian and Hispanic groups have some of the largest gains in population growth over the past decade; both groups doubled their population shares (Bahrampour and Mellnik 2021). Asians and Hispanics, when they are included in analyses, are

Randall Akee is a professor in the Department of Public Policy and American Indian Studies and Chair of the America Indian Studies Interdepartmental Program at the University of California, Los Angeles, and a research associate of the National Bureau of Economic Research.

Sonya R. Porter is the Assistant Center Chief of Research in the Center for Administrative Records Research and Applications at the US Census Bureau.

Emilia Simeonova is a professor of economics at Johns Hopkins University and a research associate of the National Bureau of Economic Research.

often treated as monolithic or homogeneous groups. However, in contrast to the myth of the model minority, the experiences of Asian subgroups are varied. While Asian Indians have high levels of income (median household income in 2017–2019, $119,000) and low poverty rates (6 percent), Burmese experience low levels of income ($44,000) and high poverty rates (25 percent) (Budiman and Neil 2021). The experiences of Hispanic subgroups are similarly diverse. Argentinians had the highest median income among Hispanics in 2018 ($68,000), while Hondurans had the lowest median household income in 2018 ($41,000) (Noe-Bustamante 2019).

This study provides the first detailed analysis of earnings inequality and immobility within Asian and Hispanic subgroups in the United States. We focus on these two groups as they are often unreported in standard inequality analyses due to data limitations, yet they are also of interest due to the relatively large flows of immigrants in recent decades and because of their relatively young populations as compared to non-Hispanic Whites.

Our research explores two avenues of data disaggregation: along subgroups of race and ethnicity and between established workers and new immigrants and new labor market entrants. These two dimensions add nuance to our understanding of how earnings inequality and immobility progress. Using data from the American Community Survey (ACS), we identify Asian and Hispanic individuals and link them to their IRS earnings data (W-2s and 1099 forms). Newly arrived Asian and Hispanic individuals in the age group 18–45 are flagged based on responses to the year of immigration question contained in the ACS. We define persons as new entrants into the labor force as those who have no previous earnings records in the observation window. As a result, we can further disaggregate the Asian and Hispanic data into a long-term panel of workers and a dataset that also includes new immigrants and new labor market entrants.

Our analysis makes three contributions to the literature. First, we demonstrate that the share of earnings accruing to the top 10 percent of the earnings distribution is larger for certain Asian and Hispanic subgroups; the top 10 percent of the Asian Indian and Cuban earnings distribution tend to have a much larger share of earnings than other groups within their race or ethnic group. This type of variation is often obscured when data are either not reported for these groups or are aggregated up.

Second, we show that there are level differences in earnings inequality across the various Asian race subgroups and Hispanic ethnic subgroups. When we separate out new labor market entrants and immigrants, we find that the level of earnings inequality is flat or slightly downward trending over the period 2005–2015 for the long-term legal residents and native-born Asian and Hispanic population. This indicates that the inclusion of new labor market entrants and recent immigrants to the United States drives the upward trend in earnings inequality for these populations. These results are especially pronounced after the start of the Great Recession.

Finally, we find that earnings immobility has been increasing over the 2005–2015 period for all subgroups within the Asian racial group and the Hispanic ethnic group. While there is little to no change in earnings inequality for these groups, there is also very little movement within the earnings distribution. We do find evidence that the various Hispanic subgroups have slightly lower levels of earnings immobility, on average, as compared to non-Hispanic Whites. Asian subgroups have similar levels of earnings immobility to that of non-Hispanic Whites.

12.2 Data

In this analysis we link confidential-use individual records from the American Community Survey to the Internal Revenue Service W-2 and 1099 forms. We create a novel panel dataset that follows the evolution of earnings within disaggregated Hispanic ethnicity groups and the Asian race groups in the United States over the time period 2005–2015. We disaggregate the Hispanic category into individuals of Mexican, Central American, Puerto Rican, Cuban, Spanish, and South American descent; these are the largest sub-categories in the aggregated Hispanic ethnic group. We disaggregate the Asian race category into Asian Indians, Chinese, Filipino, Japanese, Korean, Vietnamese, and Other Asians.

Our process for linking administrative records starts with the 2005 American Community Survey. This representative survey is conducted annually for approximately 2–3 percent of the US population. Individual-level records are assigned a protected identification key (PIK) number which is unique across individuals and based on a person's name, birth date, address, and Social Security number (Wagner et al. 2014). The PIK is then used to identify an individual in the W-2 or 1099 data from the IRS. We use both survey weights and inverse probability weights of PIK assignment in the analyses that follow.

In table 12.1 we provide the total number of observations for the Hispanic and Non-Hispanic White samples from the 2005 ACS. There are approximately 1,319,000 observations in the 2005 ACS who are between the ages of 18 and 45 and we are able to assign PIKs to 91 percent of those observations.[1] In the next row, we show the number of observations that can be found in the IRS W-2 or 1099 data which is 1,196,000 or about 83 percent of the observations with a valid PIK. Similar results are provided in table 12.2 for the Asian and Non-Hispanic White samples from the 2005 ACS. There are approximately 1,295,000 observations in this data and we are able to assign PIKS to 92 percent of those observations. Finally, we are able to merge the IRS W-2 or 1099 data to about 83 percent of those observations.

1. Note that these sample sizes have been rounded according to US Census Disclosure Review Board rules to ensure confidentiality of the data.

Table 12.1 **Match rates for Hispanics and Non-Hispanic Whites, ages 18–45**

	Count	Percentage of Row Above
Total Observations in 2005 ACS	1,319,000	
Matched to PIKS	1,196,000	0.91
Merged to W-2 Data in 2005	988,000	0.83

Source: American Community Survey Data for 2005 linked to IRS W-2 or 1099 data for 2005–2015.

Table 12.2 **Match rates for Asians and Non-Hispanic Whites, ages 18–45**

	Count	Percentage of Row Above
Total Observations in 2005 ACS	1,295,000	
Matched to PIKS	1,193,000	0.92
Merged to W-2 Data in 2005	985,000	0.83

Source: American Community Survey Data for 2005 linked to IRS W-2 or 1099 data for 2005–2015.

We are interested in the evolution of earnings inequality and immobility, and thus our analysis will focus on individuals in the formal labor force and will not include those working in informal activities that do not result in recorded taxable earnings. We also cannot identify undocumented immigrants as they, by definition, will not have administrative records and will be less likely to have been assigned a PIK. Finally, we note that we do not have earnings or income data for individuals who are fully self-employed in this data and self-employment may be higher in these populations (Fernandez and Kim 1998; Robles and Cordero-Guzman 2007).

12.2.1 Panel Data of Individual Earnings

Using the annual earnings data, we create several different datasets that we use in the analysis. First, we construct an individual-level panel dataset of earnings across the disaggregated subgroups for Hispanics and Asians in the United States. This panel is fixed at 2005 for our purposes; the data follow the same individuals over time and examine their earnings inequality and trajectories. To be included in the panel data, an individual must have an IRS W-2 or 1099 record for at least two consecutive years starting in 2005. By design this allows individuals to leave the labor force and/or have no earnings for extended periods of time; this may add to observed earnings volatility and we believe this provides an accurate depiction of actual earnings inequality over time. Furthermore, we have restricted our analysis to individuals who were 18–45 years old in 2005. We focus on this relatively young population as they are the most likely to be affected by the inflow of new labor market entrants and/or new immigrant arrivals. We include individuals who are 18 years old and older to account for potential inflows into the labor market from post-secondary institutions either after degree completion or before.

12.2.2 Including Recent Immigrants and New Labor Market Entrants

While the main focus of this analysis follows a panel of individuals from 2005–2015, we can also conduct separate analyses that include new Hispanic and Asian workers over time, as they join the labor market after 2005. We call the first sample the panel data and we call the second the cross-section data. The second dataset is observationally equivalent to taking a repeated cross section of the Hispanic or Asian population in the United States annually where we include new labor market entrants or recent immigrants meeting the same age and ethnicity restrictions as in the panel data. These two types of flows, new labor market entrants and recent immigrants, are potentially important for these ethnic/race groups as they have younger age distributions relative to non-Hispanic Whites and high recent migration flows into the United States (Ong and Nakanishi 1996; Schaeffer 2019). As a result, earnings inequality estimates may differ for these groups depending on whether we include or exclude the new labor market entrants and recent immigrants.

In order to identify recent arrivals to the United States, we use information provided on date of arrival in the United States in the ACS data. We link those individuals to their W-2 and 1099 data for all years subsequent to their arrival. We include individuals in years after 2005 who report not working in the previous year. Finally, we restrict the sample to those within the same age and ethnic groups as the original base population in 2005 (properly adjusted by age group for each additional year, e.g., ages 19–46 for 2006, ages 20–47 for 2007 and so on).

In table 12.3 we provide a table of means for the characteristics of the analysis sample, the sample of individuals with a valid PIK, and all individuals identifying as Hispanic or non-Hispanic White in the 2005 ACS. The table contains three columns of means. We provide a similar table of means for Asians and non-Hispanic Whites in table 12.4. The final sample, in both cases, is positively selected with regard to earnings and income. We expect our sample, which consists of documented individuals working in the formal labor market, to have higher earnings and/or incomes than the broader samples contained in the ACS data; this is a result of focusing on the earnings of individuals in administrative data; we do not find a lot of evidence of selection on other characteristics. These results are shown directly in Panel A of tables 12.3 and 12.4.

In Panel B of both tables we show the proportions of each racial or ethnic subgroup in the respective analysis samples. We disaggregate the Asian race group into its largest subgroups: Asian Indian, Chinese, Filipino, Japanese,

Table 12.3 **Table of means for Hispanics and Non-Hispanic Whites, ages 18–45**

	ACS Means	PIK Matches	W-2 Matches
	A. Characteristics		
Ages 18–45	32.6	32.7	32.5
Wages/salary	27,900	29,100	33,300
Total Income	31,200	32,400	35,300
Married	0.55	0.55	0.54
HS or Less	0.41	0.38	0.36
Some College	0.32	0.34	0.33
College or More	0.26	0.29	0.29
In School	0.17	0.17	0.18
Male	0.49	0.49	0.51
Observations	1,319,000	1,196,000	988,000
	B. Racial and Ethnic Groups in Total Sample		
Total Hispanic	0.17	0.12	0.12
Mexican	0.59	0.6	0.6
Puerto Rican	0.16	0.1	0.1
Cuban	0.03	0.04	0.04
Central American	0.1	0.1	0.1
Latin American	0.06	0.07	0.07
Spanish	0.02	0.03	0.03
Other Hispanic	0.05	0.06	0.06
Non-Hispanic White	0.83	0.88	0.88
Observations	1,319,000	1,196,000	988,000

Note: Data for 2006 and 2014 are from the ACS Single Year Data. They represent new labor market entrants (individuals who did not work in the previous year) and new immigrants (individuals who indicate that they arrived in the United States in the previous year). In Panel B, Total Hispanic is comprised of Mexican, Puerto Rican, Cuban, Central American, Latin American, Spanish, and Other Hispanic. Those percentages should total the Total Hispanic category.

Korean, Vietnamese, and Other Asian groups. Similarly, for the Hispanic ethnic category we disaggregate the data into its largest subgroups: Mexican, Puerto Rican, Cuban, Central American, South American.[2]

Table 12A.1 provides the earnings data in 2006 for new labor market entrants and immigrants (and for 2014 as well) using the 2006 and 2014 ACS data for the three race and ethnic groups in this analysis. In all cases, the average earnings for the stock of the race or ethnic group is larger than that of newly arrived individuals from that same race or ethnic group. In later analysis, we will show how the addition of the new immigrants and new labor market entrants can serve to increase earnings volatility and inequality.

2. We do not report the category of Other Asian groups, Spanish or Other Hispanic in our main tables and figures, but they are available upon request.

Table 12.4 **Table of means for Asian and Non-Hispanic Whites, ages 18–45**

	ACS Means	PIK Matches	W-2 Matches
	A. Characteristics		
Ages 18–45	32.7	32.8	32.6
Wages/salary	28,900	29,800	34,200
Total Income	32,200	33,200	36,300
Married	0.55	0.56	0.55
HS or Less	0.38	0.37	0.34
Some College	0.33	0.33	0.34
College or More	0.29	0.3	0.32
In School	0.17	0.17	0.18
Male	0.48	0.49	0.51
Observations	1,295,000	1,193,000	985,000
	B. Racial and Ethnic Groups in Total Sample		
Asian Total	0.06	0.06	0.05
Asian Indian	0.21	0.21	0.21
Chinese	0.24	0.23	0.24
Filipino	0.18	0.19	0.21
Japanese	0.06	0.06	0.06
Korean	0.1	0.09	0.08
Vietnamese	0.11	0.11	0.1
Other Asian	0.11	0.11	0.11
Non-Hispanic White	0.94	0.94	0.95
Observations	1,295,000	1,193,000	985,000

Note: Data for 2006 and 2014 are from the ACS Single Year Data. They represent new labor market entrants (individuals who did not work in the previous year) and new immigrants (individuals who indicate that they arrived in the United States in the previous year). In Panel B, Total Asian is comprised of Asian Indian, Chinese, Filipino, Japanese, Korean, Vietnamese, and Other Asian. Those percentages should total the Total Asian category.

Differences in the size of relative immigration flows and relative fertility may explain a significant amount of earnings volatility in the Asian and Hispanic groups in the United States relative to non-Hispanic Whites.

The observations that satisfy these criteria are included in the Gini coefficient analyses and the analysis of log ratios of different quantiles of the earnings distribution. A comparison between the main panel data and this cross sectional data will highlight the effect that the new labor force entrants and recent immigrants have on overall group inequality for each of the Hispanic or Asian subgroups.

12.3 Analysis of Earnings Shares

We identify the proportion of total earnings by racial or ethnic group that accrue to the top and bottom 10 percent of the earnings distribution by each

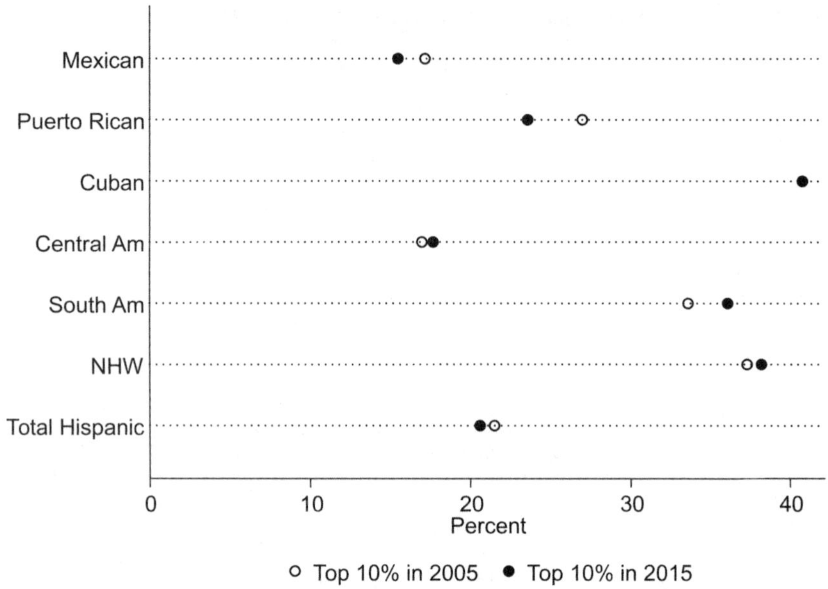

Fig. 12.1 Top 10 percent earnings shares panel for Hispanics in 2005 and 2015

Note: Income shares for the top 10 percent are calculated for all individuals within each of these ethnic group subpopulations for the year 2005 and 2015 and plotted accordingly. The category of non-Hispanic White is provided as a comparison; the Total Hispanic category indicates what would typically be shown with disaggregated data.

of the specified groups. We provide the bottom 10 percent, top 10 percent (90th percentile and greater of the earnings distribution), and the top 5 percent (95th percentile and greater) for both Hispanics and Asians in tables 12A.2 and 12A.3 for all years 2005–2015. These proportions are indicative of earnings inequality for this sample of employed individuals for the United States. In particular, they illustrate the proportion of total earnings for each racial or ethnic subgroup that is captured by either the top (or bottom) 10 percent of the respective populations. If earnings were completely equally distributed, then the top 10 percent and the bottom 10 percent (and all deciles in between) would all have 10 percent of earnings. Any deviation above or below 10 percent indicates increasing inequality in earnings shares.

Figure 12.1 provides a plot of the share of earnings that accrue to the top 10 percent of the Hispanic earnings distribution at the two end points in time—2005 and 2015 disaggregated by Hispanic subgroup.[3] There are several points to note from this figure. First, there is not a great amount of change in the decade between 2005 and 2015 in the earnings shares for most

3. Table 12A.2 provides the earnings shares for all years in the analysis for the bottom and top 10 percent as well as the top 5 percent.

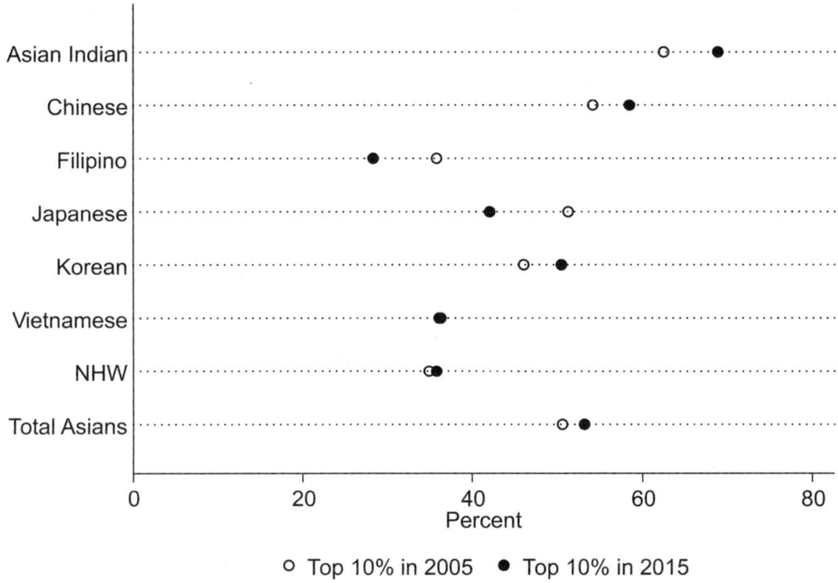

Fig. 12.2 Top 10 percent earnings shares panel for Asians in 2005 and 2015
Note: Income shares for the top 10 percent are calculated for all individuals within each of these race group subpopulations for the year 2005 and 2015 and plotted accordingly. The category of non-Hispanic White is provided as a comparison; the Total Asian category indicates what would typically be shown with disaggregated data.

of the Hispanic groups. Second, the top 10 percent of Cubans appear to be earning approximately 40 percent or more of the total earnings for their subgroup as a whole and this has remained constant between 2005 and 2015. The rest of the subgroups range between 15 percent (Mexican and Central American) and the high 30 percent range. In general, all of top 10 percent of each Hispanic subgroup earns more than their proportion if earnings were distributed equally.

Figure 12.2 provides similar descriptive data for the top 10 percent of the Asian earnings distribution at two points in time—2005 and 2015 disaggregated by Asian subgroup.[4] Unlike in the case of Hispanics, there do appear to be relatively large differences in the share of earnings that accrued to the top 10 percent of the Asian earnings distribution between 2005 and 2015. The richest Asian Indians increased their share from approximately 60 percent in 2005 to almost 70 percent in 2015. On the other hand, both the top 10 percent of the Japanese and Filipino earners realized a decrease in their share of earnings (as a group) by almost a full 10 percentage points.

4. Table 12A.3 provides the earnings shares for all years in the analysis for the bottom and top 10 percent as well as the top 5 percent.

The other subgroups do not have such dramatic changes. Another difference from that of the top 10 percent of the Hispanic earnings in the previous figure is that the magnitude of earnings share accruing to these subgroups is larger, with at least four Asian groups earning above the 40 percent threshold.

Figures 12A.1 and 12A.2 provide the share of earnings accruing to the bottom 10 percent of the earnings distribution for each group. We do not show those results in the main text, but note that none of the Asian groups at the very bottom earn above 1 percent of the total earnings. We find that Mexicans and Puerto Ricans at the bottom 10 percent of the earnings distribution earn slightly more than 1 percent of total earnings for their respective groups. Overall, this indicates that the very bottom of all of the groups are earning very small shares of total earnings.

12.4 Gini Coefficients

In this section we examine a more formal measure of earnings inequality by calculating the Gini coefficient for the Hispanic and Asian subgroups. In the first panel of figure 12.3 we plot the Gini coefficients by year for each of the Hispanic subgroups for the panel data.[5] The striking finding is that earnings inequality was unusually large in 2010 for Cubans. This marks the high-point of the Great Recession with respect to the level of unemployment in the country. This result suggests that the Great Recession resulted in a substantial reduction in the earnings of a large amount of the Cuban population, possibly due to either layoffs or reduced work hours. All other groups experience a slightly downward trend in inequality. Central Americans and Mexicans have the lowest level of earnings inequality for all years; both groups are below the Total Hispanics average for all years. On average, however, there appears to be a level or even slight downward trend in the Gini coefficient over time. This indicates that for the consistent panel of Hispanic earners, inequality remains constant or flat over time. Figures 12A.4 and 12A.5 show the log ratio of the 90th percentile of earnings to the 50th percentile and the log ratio of the 50th percentile of earnings to the 10th percentile, respectively, for Hispanics.

In the second panel of figure 12.3 we add the new Hispanic labor market entrants and recent Hispanic immigrants to the panel dataset as described above. We call this data the cross-section data as they replicate a standard cross-sectional sample that would be present in any publicly available dataset. Our main finding is that the Gini coefficients appear to increase for the majority of groups in the post–Great Recession years starting in 2010, which also affects the average for the Hispanic group. The cross-section data for

5. Figure 12A.3 provides the same set of figures with 2005 as the base year and subsequent years as deviations from this initial value normalized to one.

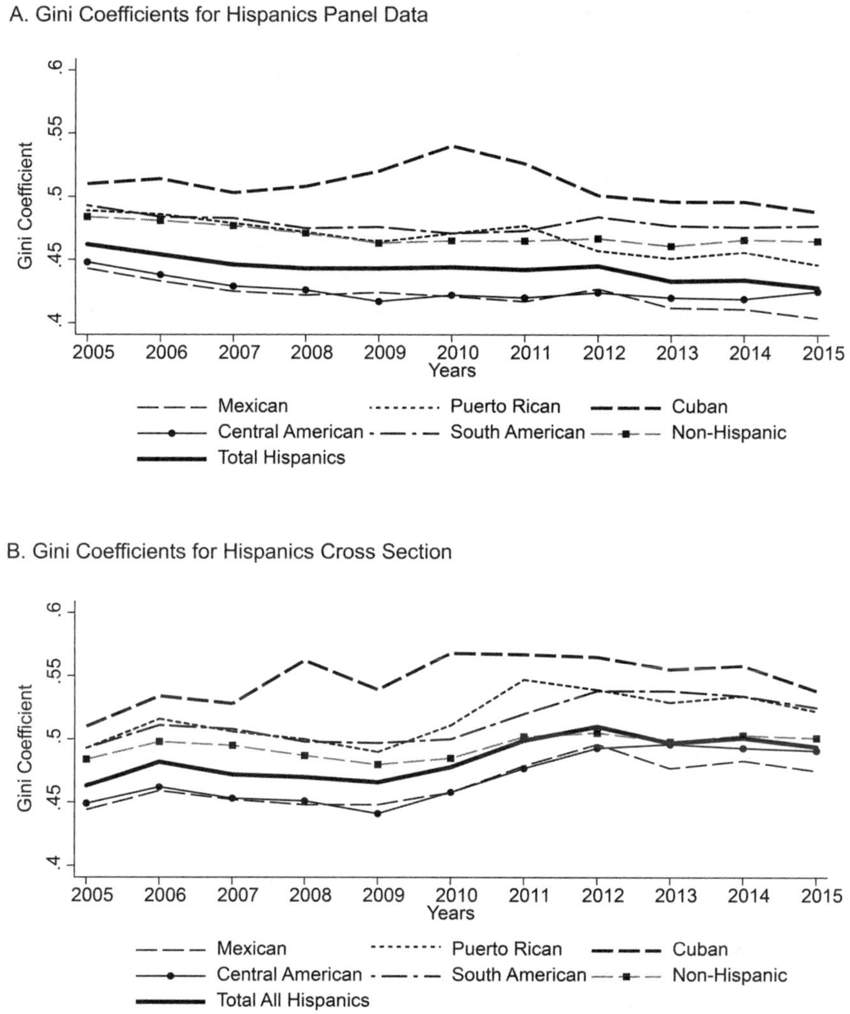

Fig. 12.3 Gini coefficients for Hispanics

Note: Gini coefficients are calculated within each year separately and plotted for each race or ethnic subgroup. The category of non-Hispanic White is provided as a comparison; the Total Hispanic category indicates what would typically be shown with disaggregated data. The first panel includes observations for individuals continually included in the data for all years 2005–2015; the second panel includes the observations from the prior panel plus new labor market entrants and any new immigrants as well.

Cubans appear to remain constant over most of the years in our data. The results suggest that new labor market entrants and new immigrant arrivals are responsible for the increase in earnings inequality observed in cross-sectional data for these groups. These new labor market entrants may be individuals who have recently graduated from high school or non-graduates.

Notably, this is not a large difference for the non-Hispanic Whites; this may be explained by the fact that both the proportion of new labor market entrants and the proportion of new immigrants for this race group are small relative to the overall population for non-Hispanic Whites in the United States and are not large enough to drive changes in earnings inequality. In figure 12A.6 we show the Gini coefficients for the new labor market entrants and new immigrant arrivals, respectively, for Hispanics. There is quite a lot of noise, however, it does appear that new labor market entrants tend to have higher average Gini coefficients than new immigrant arrivals. This may indicate that new immigrant arrivals have lower earnings on average and therefore less earnings inequality.

The first panel of figure 12.4 provides the Gini coefficients for Asians within the panel dataset.[6] On average, Filipinos tend to have much lower earnings inequality than all of the other Asian groups across all of the years in our data. Chinese and Asian Indians have higher earnings inequality than the other groups and there appears to be a slight increase for Asian Indians after 2010. Overall, there is a fairly constant level of earnings inequality for most of the other groups in this figure. Figures 12A.8 and 12A.9 show the log ratio of the 90th percentile of earnings to the 50th percentile and the log ratio of the 50th percentile of earnings to the 10th percentile, respectively, for Asians.

The second panel of figure 12.4 includes both the panel observations for the Asian group and the new labor market entrants and recent Asian immigrants. These cross-section data indicate that there is an increase in earnings inequality over time for Asian Indians, Chinese, and Koreans. There is little increase in earnings inequality for Japanese, Vietnamese, or Filipinos over this time period. Clearly, immigration plays a role in earnings inequality for certain race and ethnic groups. In figure 12A.10 we show the Gini coefficients for the new labor market entrants and new immigrant arrivals, respectively, for Asians.

12.5 Rank Mobility

In this section we calculate the rank mobility of individuals aggregated up to their race or ethnic categories. The individuals are aged 18–45 in 2005, and we follow them as they age. We treat missing income observations as missing, i.e., if a person does not have any reported income in a given year, their rank mobility for that year is not included in the aggregates. This analysis provides complementary insight to the previous results in that we are able to show the income mobility over time within individuals of the different race and ethnic subgroups. Conducting this type of analysis is data intensive and requires longitudinal data on the same individual over multiple time periods.

6. Figure 12A.7 provides the same set of figures with 2005 as the base year and subsequent years as deviations from this initial value normalized to one.

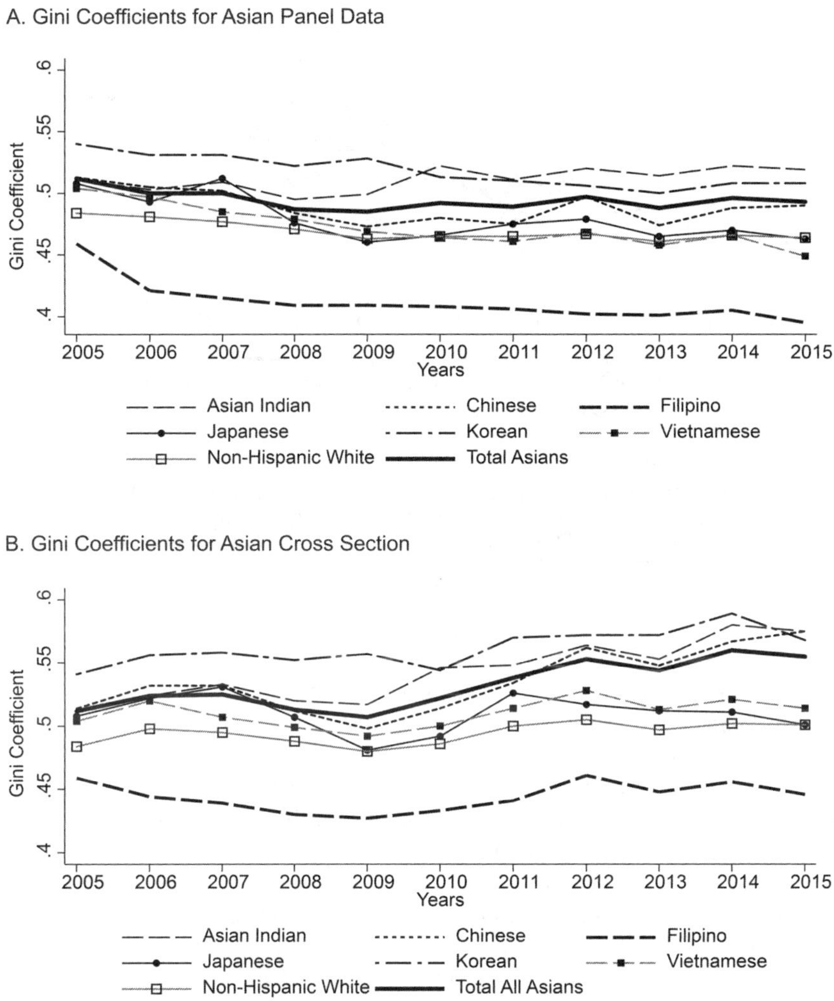

Fig.12.4 Gini coefficients for Asians

Note: Gini coefficients are calculated within each year separately and plotted for each race or ethnic subgroup. The category of non-Hispanic White is provided as a comparison; the Total Asian category indicates what would typically be shown with disaggregated data. The first panel includes observations for individuals continually included in the data for all years 2005–2015; the second panel includes the observations from the prior panel plus new labor market entrants and any new immigrants as well.

In figure 12.5 below, we show the estimated coefficients from a rank-rank correlation for individuals from various Hispanic subgroups. This measure simply calculates the correlation coefficient from a single individual's own rank in the earnings distribution in year *t* compared to year *t*+1 as is standard in the literature (see for example, Kopczuk et al. 2010). We then calculate the subgroup average for each year and report those in the figures

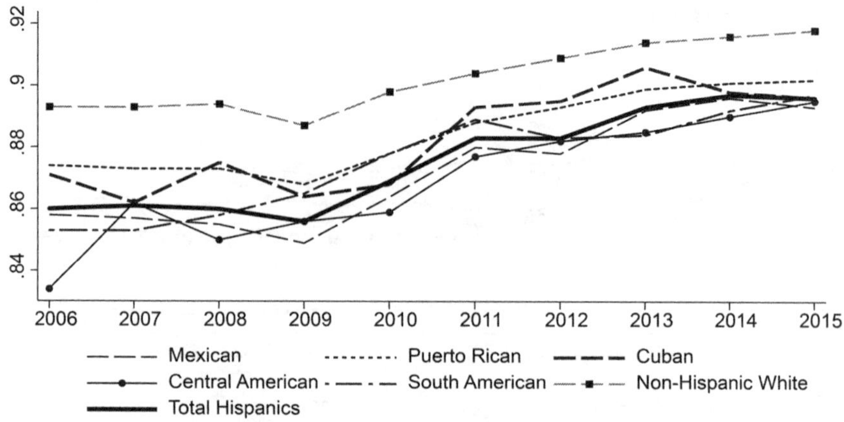

Fig. 12.5 Rank correlations for Hispanics panel

Note: Rank correlations of earnings are calculated for the same individual and then these are averaged among all observations within the same race or ethnic subgroup. These subgroup correlations are then plotted for each race or ethnic subgroup in the figure. The category of non-Hispanic White is provided as a comparison; the Total Hispanic category indicates what would typically be shown with disaggregated data.

shown.[7] A higher correlation indicates more immobility in the earnings distribution; values closer to one indicate more immobility while those closer to zero indicate more fluidity in the earnings distribution between time periods.

Over time the rank correlations for all groups move upward. There is more immobility for all of the Hispanic (and non-Hispanic White) subgroups between 2005 and 2015. In plain terms this implies that individuals are less likely to experience a change in their placement in the earnings distribution over time. Some of this reduction in mobility is likely moving into more stable employment, as individuals age. For all Hispanic subgroups, the level of mobility is higher than for non-Hispanic Whites at all years. As Hispanics are on average younger than non-Hispanic Whites, this correlation is partly due to age differences in income rank mobility. The rank correlations of the various Hispanic subgroups are relatively closely clustered with one another across all years with Puerto Ricans and Cubans experiencing the largest immobility in general.

Figure 12.6 provides a similar set of figures for Asians. There appears to be an overall increase in immobility for all Asian subgroups over time. The Chinese group has the highest persistent levels of earnings immobility across all years in our data. The range of rank correlations is more compact for Asians than it was for Hispanics; the values range from about 0.87 to 0.92

7. Our analysis is restricted to only the panel data for the rank correlation figure below as it is necessary to have an individual linked across time for these calculations. It is not possible to calculate a similar rank correlation for repeated cross-section data.

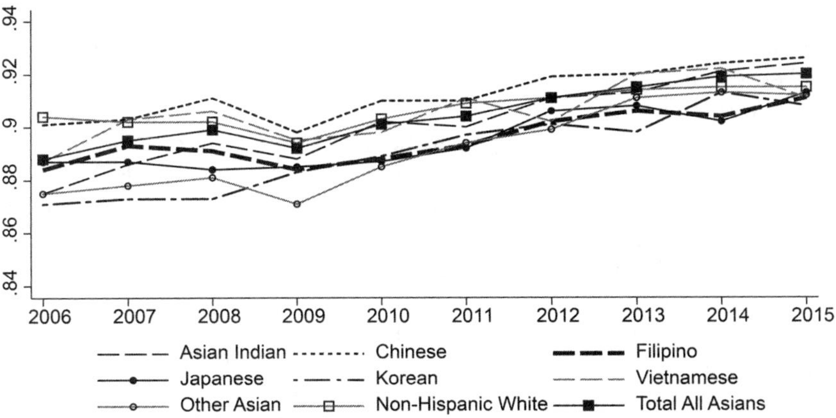

Fig. 12.6 Rank correlations for Asian panel

Note: Rank correlations of earnings are calculated for the same individual and then these are averaged among all observations within the same race or ethnic subgroup. These subgroup correlations are then plotted for each race or ethnic subgroup in the figure. The category of non-Hispanic White is provided as a comparison; the Total Asian category indicates what would typically be shown with disaggregated data.

while there was a larger range for Hispanics (0.83 to 0.92). Additionally, the various Asian subgroups tend to cluster around the non-Hispanic White rank correlations for almost all years.

12.6 Conclusion

Using a novel dataset that links detailed race and ethnicity information to individual IRS earnings information over the period 2005–2015, we document the difference in earnings inequality and immobility over the Asian and Hispanic groups. Our analysis focuses on disaggregated Asian and Hispanic earnings by their main subgroups for relatively young adults aged 18–45. To our knowledge, this is the first longitudinal study of earnings inequality and immobility for these two groups disaggregated into subgroups.

We find that for Hispanics and Asians there are significant differences in earnings inequality, as indicated by Gini coefficients. Filipinos tend to have much lower earnings inequality than all other groups—including non-Hispanic Whites. On the other hand, Asian Indians tend to have some of the highest levels of earnings inequality consistently over all of the sample years. In the data for Hispanic earnings inequality, Cubans have consistently higher inequality than all other groups with Central Americans and Mexicans having the lowest levels of earnings inequality.

Given the unique nature of our data and the available information on year of immigration to the United States (if at all) and prior earnings histories, we are able to observe new arrivals to the United States and new labor market entrants. In particular, this information allows us to compare earnings inequality by the established Asian and Hispanic earners and the new labor market entrants and/or recent immigrants. Our analysis shows that earnings inequality for most Asian and Hispanic groups remained fairly constant if not slightly downward trending over the time period in our analysis. However, including new arrivals and labor market entrants significantly increased earnings inequality for all of the groups examined. This suggests that for certain groups the increase in observed inequality may be a result of the influx of new individuals; earnings inequality may be increasing for different groups for different reasons. Our results indicate one potential explanation for the rise in observed earnings inequality among Asians and Hispanics in the United States.

Finally, we have examined the earnings mobility of these different race and ethnic subgroups. Using the individually linked earnings records over time, we find that all race and ethnic subgroups experience an upward trend in earnings immobility after the Great Recession. This indicates that there is less movement within the earnings distribution for all race and subgroups over time. On average, however, the Hispanic subgroups have lower absolute levels than non-Hispanic Whites for all years in our analysis; Cubans tend to have the highest levels of earnings immobility while Mexicans and South Americans tend to have the lowest levels of earnings immobility. Earnings immobility measures for the Asian subgroups tend to cluster around that of non-Hispanic Whites. In fact, several groups including Chinese have higher immobility than non-Hispanic Whites while Koreans and Filipinos have lower earnings immobility.

Our results show that group composition and data disaggregation can provide insight into the differences within race and ethnic groups. In the absence of disaggregated data, differential trends are obscured. We have also found that for certain groups, the impact of new entrants to the labor market or new immigrants can have a profound effect on aggregate measures of inequality. Future work should account for these compositional differences, especially for certain race and ethnic groups. If certain groups experience more or less earnings mobility due to the inflow of new workers, this may play a role in our estimates of cross-race and cross-ethnic intergenerational mobility as well.

Acknowledgments

Any opinions and conclusions expressed herein are those of the authors and do not reflect the views of the US Census Bureau. The Census Bureau has reviewed this data product for unauthorized disclosure of confidential information and has approved the disclosure avoidance practices applied to this release (Approval ID: CBDRB-FY19-170, CBDRB-FY19-370, CBDRB-FY19-CES005-015). Any errors are ours alone. Akee and Simeonova acknowledge funding from the Robert Wood Johnson Foundation. For acknowledgments, sources of research support, and disclosure of the authors' material financial relationships, if any, please see https://www.nber.org/books-and-chapters/race-ethnicity-and-economic-statistics-21st-century/earnings-inequality-and-immobility-hispanics-and-asians-examination-variation-across-subgroups.

Appendix

Table 12A.1 **Table of earnings for new labor market entrants and immigrants for 2006 and 2014, Hispanic and Asian populations**

	New Entrants 2006	New Entrants 2014	New Immigrants 2006	New Immigrants 2014
	A. Hispanic Labor Market Entrants and New Immigrants			
Ages 18–45	29.7	27.8	28.9	29
Wages/salary	15,600	15,000	25,300	19,800
Total Income	19,000	17,800	25,900	22,200
	B. Asian Labor Market Entrants and New Immigrants			
Ages 18–45	29.7	27.9	29.5	28.8
Wages/salary	16,180	15,500	23,500	19,900
Total Income	19,600	18,400	24,000	21,800

Table 12A.2 Earnings shares for Hispanics

Percentile		2005	2006	2007	2008	2009	2010	2011	2012	2013	2014	2015
10	NHW	0.004	0.004	0.005	0.005	0.005	0.005	0.005	0.005	0.006	0.006	0.006
10	Mexican	0.006	0.007	0.007	0.008	0.008	0.009	0.01	0.01	0.011	0.011	0.011
10	Puerto Rican	0.006	0.006	0.007	0.007	0.007	0.008	0.008	0.01	0.01	0.011	0.011
10	Cuban	0.003	0.004	0.005	0.004	0.005	0.005	0.005	0.005	0.005	0.006	0.005
10	Central Am	0.006	0.007	0.007	0.008	0.008	0.009	0.01	0.01	0.01	0.01	0.01
10	Latin Am	0.004	0.004	0.005	0.005	0.005	0.006	0.006	0.006	0.006	0.006	0.006
10	Total Hispanic	0.006	0.006	0.007	0.008	0.008	0.008	0.009	0.009	0.01	0.01	0.01
90	NHW	0.373	0.376	0.378	0.373	0.36	0.368	0.373	0.378	0.373	0.383	0.382
90	Mexican	0.172	0.169	0.166	0.164	0.157	0.154	0.153	0.172	0.155	0.159	0.155
90	Puerto Rican	0.27	0.279	0.277	0.279	0.268	0.268	0.276	0.257	0.246	0.249	0.236
90	Cuban	0.408	0.425	0.408	0.422	0.439	0.459	0.455	0.409	0.399	0.411	0.408
90	Central Am	0.17	0.167	0.17	0.176	0.16	0.16	0.159	0.17	0.166	0.167	0.177
90	Latin Am	0.336	0.339	0.338	0.336	0.333	0.33	0.335	0.356	0.35	0.359	0.361
90	Total Hispanic	0.215	0.217	0.214	0.213	0.207	0.207	0.209	0.217	0.204	0.209	0.206
95	NHW	0.261	0.267	0.27	0.265	0.251	0.26	0.266	0.272	0.266	0.276	0.276
95	Mexican	0.091	0.089	0.087	0.086	0.081	0.078	0.079	0.099	0.082	0.085	0.082
95	Puerto Rican	0.167	0.179	0.178	0.177	0.166	0.169	0.177	0.151	0.149	0.154	0.14
95	Cuban	0.292	0.309	0.29	0.315	0.324	0.349	0.351	0.304	0.299	0.301	0.308
95	Central Am	0.1	0.099	0.099	0.101	0.093	0.092	0.093	0.103	0.096	0.097	0.108
95	Latin Am	0.232	0.231	0.235	0.228	0.232	0.229	0.236	0.257	0.248	0.251	0.251
95	Total Hispanic	0.128	0.13	0.128	0.128	0.124	0.124	0.128	0.136	0.122	0.126	0.124

Source: American Community Survey Data for 2005 linked to IRS W-2 or 1099 data for 2005–2015. Note from May 2019 DRB.

Table 12A.3 **Earnings shares for Asians**

Percentile		2005	2006	2007	2008	2009	2010	2011	2012	2013	2014	2015
10	NHW	0.005	0.005	0.005	0.006	0.006	0.006	0.006	0.006	0.007	0.007	0.007
10	Asian Indian	0.002	0.002	0.002	0.002	0.002	0.002	0.002	0.002	0.002	0.002	0.002
10	Chinese	0.003	0.003	0.003	0.003	0.003	0.002	0.003	0.003	0.003	0.003	0.003
10	Filipino	0.003	0.003	0.004	0.003	0.004	0.004	0.004	0.004	0.004	0.005	0.004
10	Japanese	0.003	0.003	0.004	0.004	0.003	0.003	0.004	0.004	0.004	0.005	0.005
10	Korean	0.006	0.006	0.006	0.006	0.005	0.005	0.005	0.006	0.007	0.006	0.007
10	Vietnamese	0.005	0.006	0.006	0.006	0.006	0.006	0.007	0.006	0.007	0.008	0.007
10	Other Asian	0.006	0.006	0.006	0.007	0.007	0.006	0.007	0.006	0.007	0.008	0.008
10	Total Asians	0.003	0.003	0.003	0.003	0.003	0.003	0.003	0.003	0.004	0.004	0.004
90	NHW	0.349	0.353	0.354	0.349	0.338	0.345	0.35	0.356	0.349	0.359	0.358
90	Asian Indian	0.625	0.637	0.651	0.645	0.659	0.687	0.673	0.685	0.682	0.689	0.689
90	Chinese	0.542	0.552	0.559	0.552	0.551	0.565	0.564	0.591	0.572	0.586	0.585
90	Filipino	0.358	0.316	0.317	0.318	0.318	0.307	0.299	0.296	0.288	0.294	0.283
90	Japanese	0.513	0.484	0.481	0.443	0.424	0.439	0.435	0.44	0.429	0.435	0.421
90	Korean	0.461	0.467	0.478	0.488	0.502	0.483	0.486	0.497	0.497	0.514	0.505
90	Vietnamese	0.361	0.376	0.362	0.356	0.349	0.357	0.36	0.37	0.375	0.384	0.363
90	Other Asian	0.303	0.319	0.336	0.346	0.339	0.354	0.363	0.366	0.375	0.365	0.375
90	Total Asians	0.506	0.506	0.514	0.508	0.512	0.527	0.52	0.534	0.525	0.536	0.532
95	NHW	0.242	0.248	0.251	0.246	0.233	0.242	0.247	0.254	0.247	0.257	0.256
95	Asian Indian	0.446	0.453	0.472	0.468	0.478	0.517	0.504	0.512	0.509	0.523	0.524
95	Chinese	0.38	0.387	0.391	0.381	0.378	0.394	0.401	0.432	0.411	0.423	0.425
95	Filipino	0.212	0.155	0.162	0.158	0.165	0.156	0.148	0.147	0.149	0.158	0.143
95	Japanese	0.399	0.371	0.362	0.313	0.295	0.302	0.302	0.316	0.305	0.314	0.292
95	Korean	0.334	0.342	0.341	0.347	0.363	0.339	0.348	0.352	0.335	0.367	0.361
95	Vietnamese	0.225	0.242	0.239	0.227	0.225	0.226	0.224	0.248	0.24	0.255	0.232
95	Other Asian	0.206	0.215	0.223	0.236	0.236	0.246	0.262	0.258	0.275	0.263	0.271
95	Total Asians	0.351	0.346	0.355	0.345	0.349	0.367	0.363	0.379	0.369	0.384	0.379

Source: American Community Survey Data for 2005 linked to IRS W-2 or 1099 data for 2005–2015. Note from May 2019 DRB

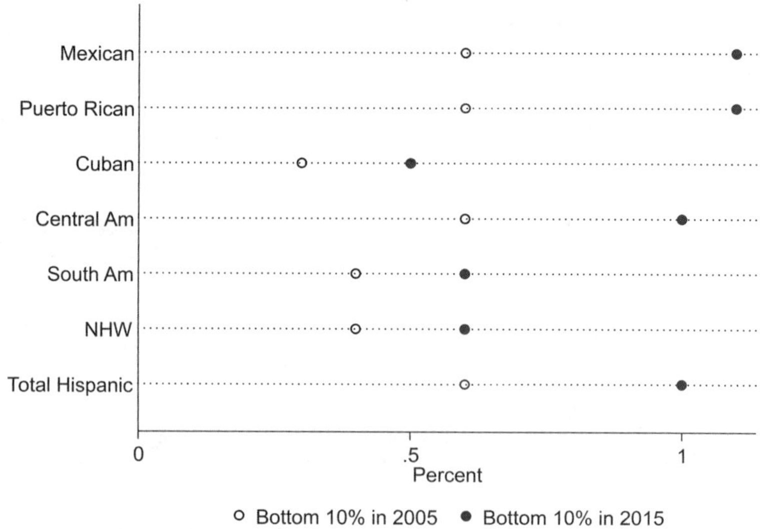

Fig. 12A.1 Bottom 10 percent earnings shares panel for Hispanics in 2005 and 2015

Note: Income shares for the bottom 10 percent are calculated for all individuals within each of these ethnic group subpopulations for the year 2005 and 2015 and plotted accordingly. The category of non-Hispanic White is provided as a comparison; the Total Hispanic category indicates what would typically be shown with disaggregated data.

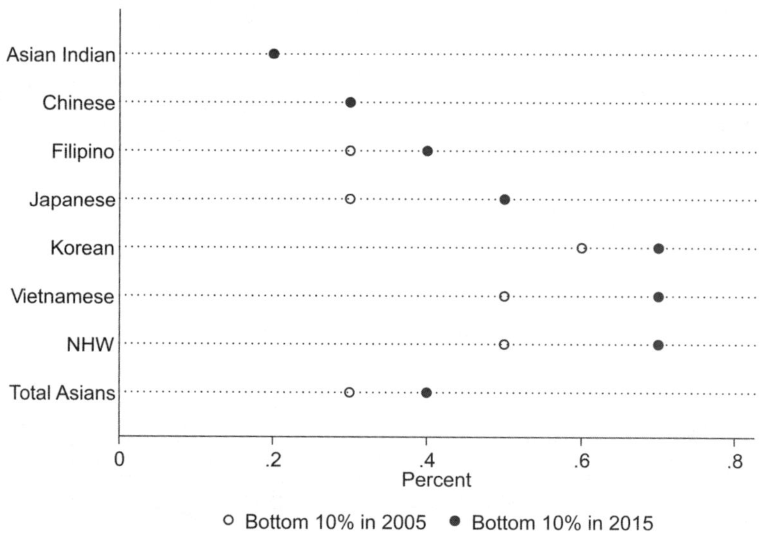

Fig. 12A.2 Bottom 10 percent earnings shares panel for Asians in 2005 and 2015

Note: Income shares for the bottom 10 percent are calculated for all individuals within each of these ethnic group subpopulations for the year 2005 and 2015 and plotted accordingly. The category of non-Hispanic White is provided as a comparison; the Total Hispanic category indicates what would typically be shown with disaggregated data.

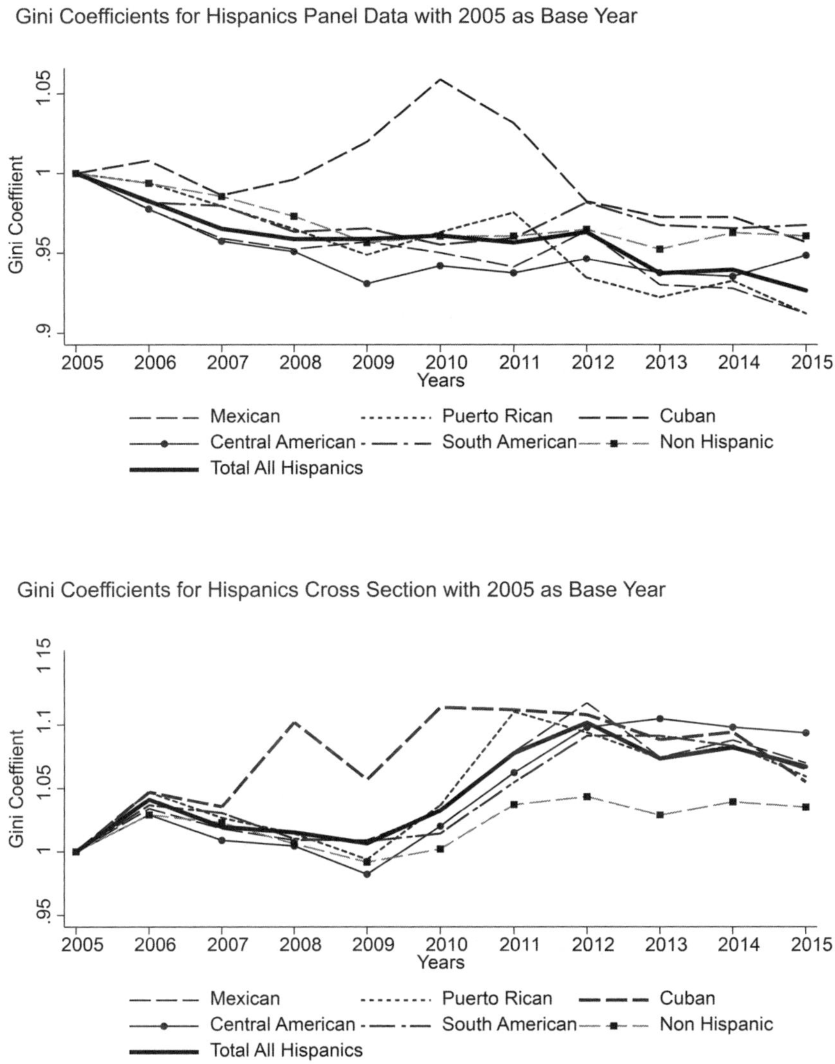

Fig. 12A.3 Gini coefficients for Hispanics with 2005 as base year

Note: These two figures take 2005 as the base year and normalize all subsequent Gini coefficients by that amount. Thus, these figures indicate a relative change for the Gini coefficients relative to 2005. As was done previously, the Gini coefficients are calculated within each year separately and plotted for each race or ethnic subgroup. The category of non-Hispanic White is provided as a comparison; the Total Hispanice category indicates what would typically be shown with disaggregated data. The first panel includes observations for individuals continually included in the data for all years 2005–2015; the second panel includes the observations from the prior panel plus new labor market entrants and any new immigrants as well.

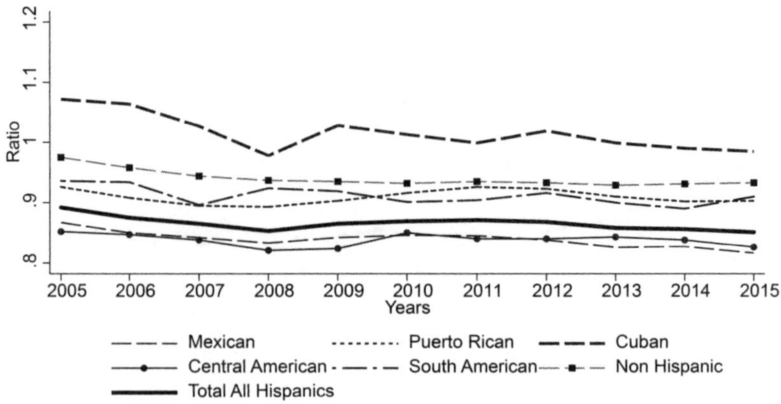

Fig. 12A.4 Log earnings ratios (90/50) for Hispanics panel

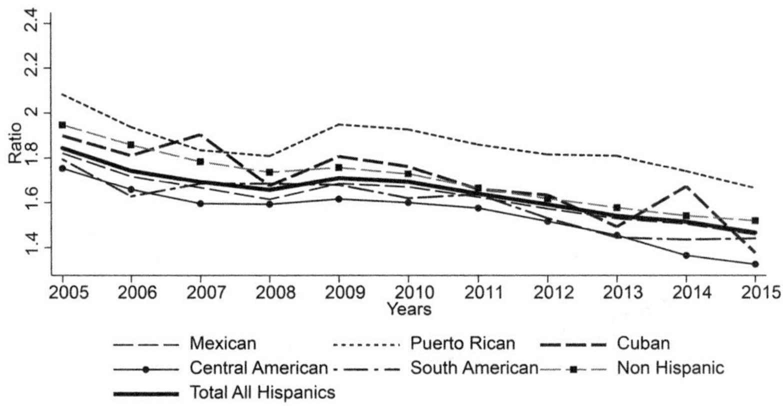

Fig. 12A.5 Log earnings ratios (50/10) for Hispanics panel

Gini Coefficients for Hispanics for New Labor Market Entrants

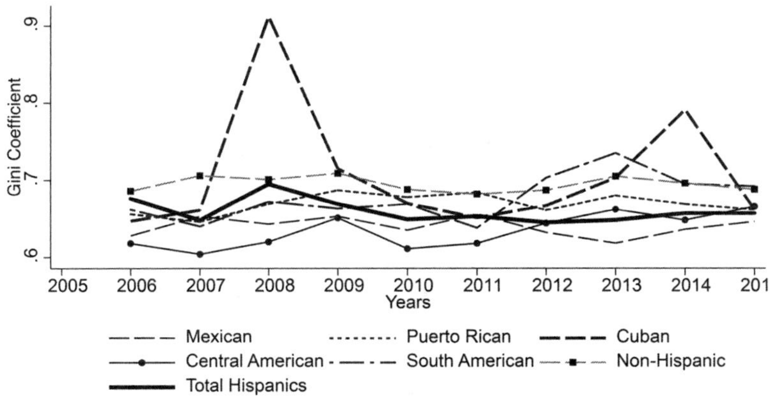

Gini Coefficients for Hispanics for New Immigrant Arrivals

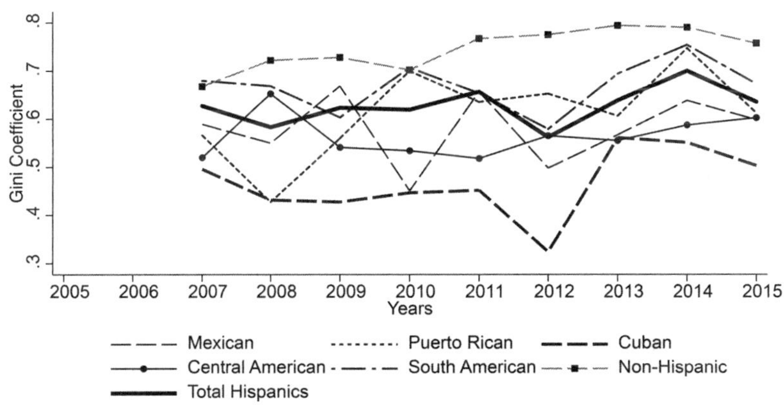

Fig. 12A.6 Gini coefficients for Hispanics for new labor market entrants and new immigrants only

Note: These two figures show the Gini coefficients for new labor market entrants and new immigrant arrivals, respectively. In the top figure, we start at the year 2006 since these individuals are new to the labor market; that is they were not working in 2005. In the bottom figure, we have individuals who arrived as new immigrants in 2005 but were not working in 2006 and, therefore, start the series in 2007. Both of these samples include the cumulative additions in each year of either new labor market entrants or new immigrant arrivals until the end of the series.

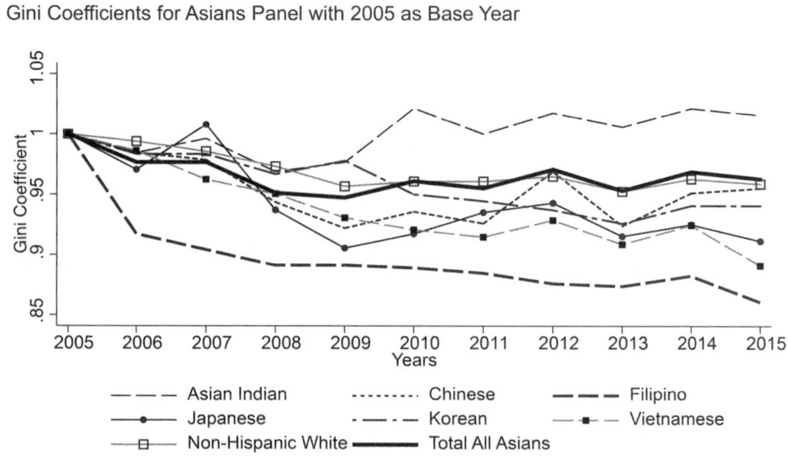

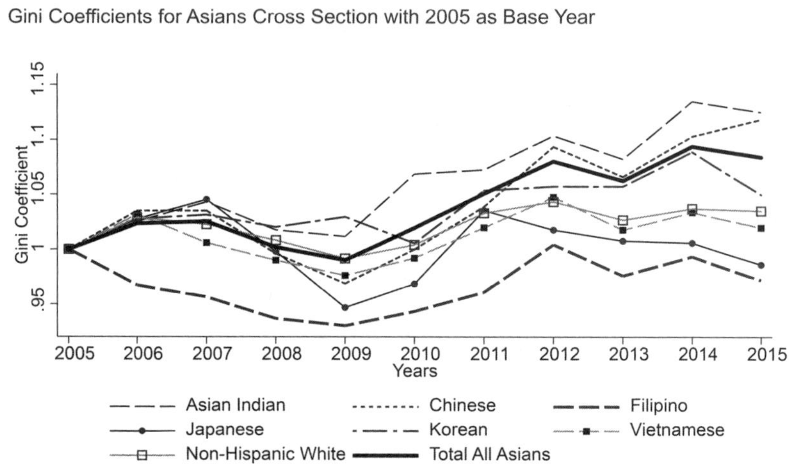

Fig. 12A.7 Gini coefficients for Asians with 2005 as base year

Note: These two figures take 2005 as the base year and normalize all subsequent Gini coefficients by that amount. Thus, these figures indicate a relative change for the Gini coefficients relative to 2005. As was done previously, the Gini coefficients are calculated within each year separately and plotted for each race or ethnic subgroup. The category of non-Hispanic White is provided as a comparison; the Total Asian category indicates what would typically be shown with disaggregated data. The first panel includes observations for individuals continually included in the data for all years 2005–2015; the second panel includes the observations from the prior panel plus new labor market entrants and any new immigrants as well.

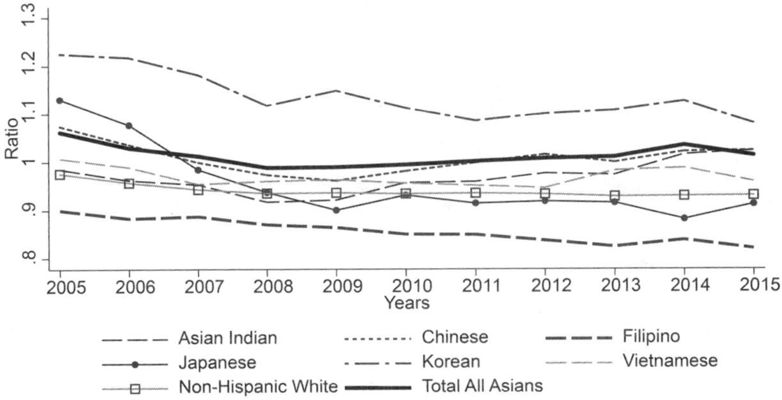

Fig. 12.A8 Log earnings ratios (90/50) for Asian panel

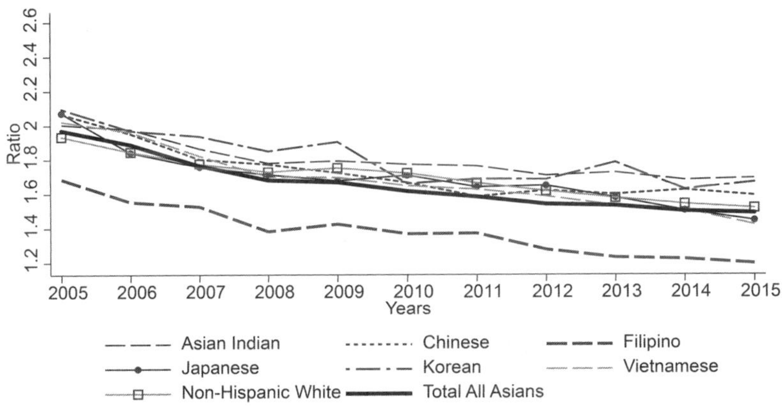

Fig. 12.A9 Log earnings ratios (50/10) for Asian panel

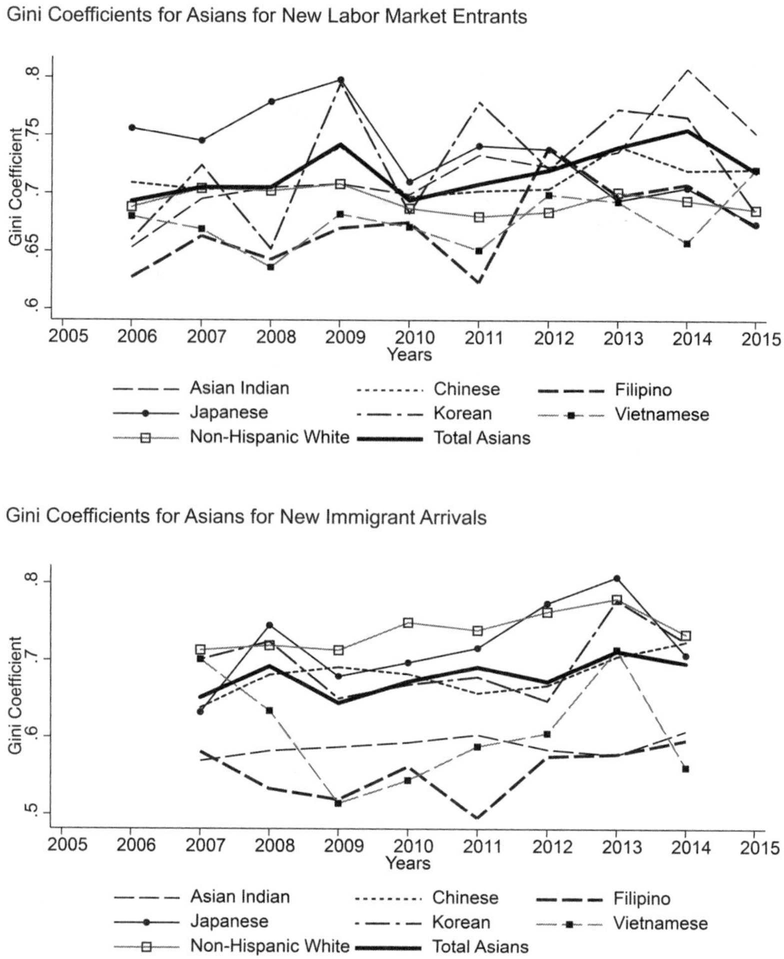

Fig. 12.A10 Gini coefficients for Asians for new labor market entrants and new immigrants only

Note: These two figures show the Gini Coefficients for new labor market entrants and new immigrant arrivals, respectively. In the top figure, we start at the year 2006 since these individuals are new to the labor market; that is they were not working in 2005. In the bottom figure, we have individuals who arrived as new immigrants in 2005 but were not working in 2006 and, therefore, start the series in 2007. Both of these samples include the cumulative additions in each year of either new labor market entrants or new immigrant arrivals until the end of the series.

References

Akee, Randall, Maggie R. Jones, and Sonya R. Porter. 2019. "Race Matters: Income Shares, Income Inequality, and Income Mobility for All US Races." *Demography* 56(3): 999–1021.

Bahrampour, Tara, and Ted Mellnik. 2021. "Census data shows widening diversity; number of White people falls for first time." *Washington Post*, August 12.

Bloome, Deirdre, and Bruce Western. 2011. "Cohort Change and Racial Differences in Educational and Income Mobility." *Social Forces* 90(2): 375–95.

Bloome, Deirdre. 2014. "Racial Inequality Trends and the Intergenerational Persistence of Income and Family Structure." *American Sociological Review* 79(6): 1196–225.

Abby, Budiman, and G. Ruiz Neil. 2021. "Key Facts about Asian Origin Groups in the US." Pew Research Center, April 29.

Chetty, Raj, Nathaniel Hendren, Maggie R. Jones, and Sonya R. Porter. 2020. "Race and Economic Opportunity in the United States: An Intergenerational Perspective." *Quarterly Journal of Economics* 135(2): 711–83.

Derenoncourt, Ellora, and Claire Montialoux. 2021. "Minimum Wages and Racial Inequality." *Quarterly Journal of Economics* 136(1): 169–228.

Fernandez, Marilyn, and Kwang Chung Kim. 1998. "Self-Employment Rates of Asian Immigrant Groups: An Analysis of Intragroup and Intergroup Differences." *International Migration Review* 32(3): 654–81.

Horowitz, Juliana Menasce, Ruth Igielnik, and Rakesh Kochhar. 2020. "Trends in Income and Wealth Inequality." *Pew Research Center,* January 9.

Kochhar, Rakesh, and Richard Fry. 2014. "Wealth Inequality Has Widened Along Racial, Ethnic Lines Since End of Great Recession." *Pew Research Center online report, December 12.*

Kopczuk, Wojciech, Emmanuel Saez, and Jae Song. 2010. "Earnings Inequality and Mobility in the United States: Evidence from Social Security Data Since 1937." *Quarterly Journal of Economics* 125(1): 91–128.

Noe-Bustamante, Luis. 2019. "Key Facts About US Hispanics and Their Diverse Heritage." *Pew Research Center*, September 16.

Ong, Paul, and Don T. Nakanishi. 1996. "Becoming Citizens, Becoming Voters: The Naturalization and Political Participation of Asian Pacific Immigrants." *In Reframing the Immigration Debate: A Public Policy Report*, edited by Bill Ong Hing and Ronald Lee. LEAP Asian Pacific American Public Policy Institute and UCLA Asian American Studies Center.

Reardon, Sean F., and Kendra Bischoff. 2011. "Income Inequality and Income Segregation." *American Journal of Sociology* 116(4): 1092–1153.

Robles, Barbara J., and Hector Cordero-Guzman. 2007. "Latino Self-Employment and Entrepreneurship in the United States: An Overview of the Literature and Data Sources." *ANNALS of the American Academy of Political and Social Science* 613(1): 18–31.

Schaeffer, Katherine. 2019. "The Most Common Age Among Whites in US Is 58—More Than Double That of Racial and Ethnic Minorities." *Pew Research Center*. July 30.

Snipp, C, Matthew, and Sin Yi Cheung. 2016. "Changes in Racial and Gender Inequality Since 1970." *ANNALS of the American Academy of Political and Social Science* 663(1): 80–98.

Wagner, Deborah, Mary Lane, et al. 2014. "The Person Identification Validation System (PVS): Applying the Center for Administrative Records Research and Applications'(CARRA) Record Linkage Software." Technical Report, Center for Economic Studies, US Census Bureau.

Author Index

Subject Index

Page numbers followed by "f" or "t" refer to figures and tables, respectively.